WEBSTER'S 21ST CENTURY
LARGE PRINT DICTIONARY

WEBSTER'S 21ST CENTURY LARGE PRINT DICTIONARY

Edited by The Princeton Language Institute

Barbara Ann Kipfer, Ph.D.,
Head Lexicographer

Produced by The Philip Lief Group, Inc.

Delta
Trade Paperbacks

A Delta Book
Published by
Dell Publishing
a division of
Bantam Doubleday Dell Publishing Group, Inc.
1540 Broadway
New York, New York 10036

Published by arrangement with
The Philip Lief Group, Inc.
6 West 20th Street
New York, New York 10011

Library of Congress Cataloging in Publication Data
Webster's 21st century large print dictionary / edited by the Princeton Language Institute: Barbara Ann Kipfer, head lexicographer; produced by the Philip Lief Group, Inc.
p.   cm.
"A Delta book."
ISBN 0-385-31643-7
1. English language—Dictionaries. 2. Large type books.
I. Kipfer, Barbara Ann. II. Princeton Language Institute.
III. Philip Lief Group.
[PE1628.W551656 1996]
423—dc20   96-14156
                                            CIP

Manufactured in the United States of America
Published simultaneously in Canada

August 1996

10 9 8 7 6 5 4 3 2 1

CWO

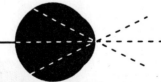

**This Large Print Book carries the
Seal of Approval of N.A.V.H.**

CONTENTS

INTRODUCTION

Webster's 21st Century Large Print Dictionary provides large print users with a legible, easy-to-use, concise, up-to-date, and thorough reference tool. Within its pages, readers will be able to find out what words mean, how to pronounce them, what their spellings and derivatives are, and much more. Readers will also be able to access lists, charts, and tables that may be needed on a regular basis.

Webster's 21st Century Large Print Dictionary has four sections: Introduction, Explanatory Notes, the A-Z dictionary, and appendices. This book conforms to the large print standards for reference books set by the National Association for the Visually Handicapped. The type is set in 16-points, while the guide words at the top of every page (running heads) are in 18-point type to help the reader locate the desired entries.

Readers may learn how to access dictionary information efficiently by reading the explanatory notes. There is a pronunciation key and table of abbreviations, also. The appendices consist of an assortment of information including style rules, signs and symbols used in proofreading and mathematics, affixes, forms of address, and geographical data.

Language and its meaning is complex. **Webster's 21st Century Large Print Dictionary** puts lexical information at the users' fingertips.

EXPLANATORY NOTES

Each entry consists of a headword (main entry word), variant forms, pronunciation, function label, and the definition(s). Additional features, where applicable, include: inflected forms, origin, and derivatives.

Headword

The headword, or main entry word, appears in boldface type and is lined up along the lefthand margin of the columns. The headword is the word or phrase to be defined. In this dictionary, single words, compounds, contractions, foreign terms, proper names, prefixes, suffixes, and abbreviations can be headwords. Headwords can be a set of solid letters, letters joined by a hyphen, or letters separated by a space.

The headwords offered are the most commonly used forms and will reflect whether the words are usually capitalized, hyphenated, or pluralized. If particular meanings are pluralized [Pl], capitalized [Cap], etc. the indication will be enclosed within brackets following the appropriate definition number. If a word is most often hyphenated, but also used without the hyphen, the forms will be given in that order.

The headwords appear in alphabetical order letter by letter. Main entries that are spelled alike, but have different uses or origins, are alphabetized by their function labels. The headword is repeated when a new part of speech is introduced.

Boldface guide words are printed at the top of each page—the first word matching the first headword on the page, the second being the last headword on the page.

Variant Forms

Variant forms are enclosed in parentheses, follow an italicized *also,* and appear in boldface type. The initial word variant is an alternate, commonly used spelling of the headword. If there is more than one initial word variant, the variants will be separated by "or."

Examples include:

afterward (<u>also</u> afterwards)
bogey (<u>also</u> bogy or bogie)
postmodern (<u>also</u> post-modern)
repellent (<u>also</u> repellant)

Variants are standard usage and may be used according to personal choice.

Pronunciation

Enclosed in brackets and immediately following the headword and variant forms is the pronunciation. Pronunciation will always be included unless the word or phrase has been previously pronounced, if the first part of the word precedes it (e.g., **air** for **airplane**), or if the word is pronounced as spelled (*a*).

The pronunciation field indicates three things to the user: 1) stress is noted by capital letters 2) syllable division is noted by hyphens and 3) the pronunciation is given in a respelled system.

The pronunciations given do not include any secondary, or weaker, stress that might be used. But these simplified respellings are much easier to understand. Educated speakers pronounce words acceptably in different ways and this dictionary does not attempt to include variant pronunciations.

Examples are:

accountable \uh-KOWN-tuh-bul\
depict \di-PIKT\
mutual \MYOO-choo-ul\
safety \SAYF-tee\

Pronunciation Key

a	add, map
ah	palm, father
ahr	ark, dark
air	care, fair
aw	all, order, paw
ay	ail, pay, same
b	bat, rub
ch	check, catch
d	dog, rod
e	end, pet
ee	easy, tree
eer	beer, ear
f	fit, half
g	go, log
h	hope, hate
i	it, give
ie	ice, write
j	joy, judge
k	cook, take
l	look, rule
m	move, seem
n	nice, tin
ng	ring, song
o	odd, hot

oh	open, so
oi	oil, boy
oo	pool, food
oor	poor, tour
ow	out, now
p	pit, stop
r	run, poor
s	see, pass
sh	sure, rush
t	talk, sit
th	thin, both, this, bathe
u	up, done
uh	schwa sound for the vowel in unstressed syllables
ur	urn, term
uu	took, full
v	vain, eve
w	win, away
y	yet, yearn
yoo	use, few
z	zest, muse
zh	vision, pleasure

In some words, such as button \BUT-n\ and sudden \SUD-n\, no vowel appears in the unstressed syllable; the "n" is the whole syllable.

Function Label

The italicized, bold element following the main entry, any variant forms, and the pronunciation is the function label or part of speech. This dictionary uses the following labels:

n.	noun
pl. n.	pluralized noun
adj.	adjective

adv.	adverb
v.	verb
pron.	pronoun
conj.	conjunction
interj.	interjection
prep.	preposition
def. art.	definite article
indef. art.	indefinite article
prefix	prefix
suffix	suffix
cont.	contraction

If there is more than one part of speech defined for a headword, the entries will follow the order of the above list of labels.

Inflected Forms

The inflected form(s) immediately follow the function label, appearing in **boldface** type and ending with a period. Nouns, verbs, adjectives, and adverbs may have inflected forms.

Since the plurals of most nouns are formed by adding -s, this dictionary shows plurals only when they are formed in a different or awkward manner. They are preceded by the function label *n. pl.* Variant plurals are separated by "or."

Examples include:

abacus [AB-uh-kus] *n. pl.* abaci.
echo [EK-oh] *n. pl.* echoes.
phenomenon [fi-NOM-uh-non] *n. pl.* phenomena or phenomenons.
wolf [wuulf] *n. pl.* wolves.

Nouns that are plural in form as headwords take the label *n. pl.* with no comma.

When a verb entry does not show the past tense or the participles, these forms are constructed regularly: by adding **-ed** to form the past tense and the past participle, and by adding **-ing** to form the present participle—as in bump, bumped, bumping. Parts of a verb not formed in a regular way are shown. Any variants are separated by "or."

Examples include:

bus *v.* bused; busing or bussed; bussing.
fry *v.* fried; frying.
oscillate *v.* oscillated; oscillating.
take *v.* took; taken; taking.

Regular comparative and superlative forms of adjectives and adverbs are made by adding **-er** or **-est.** For adverbs, they are made by adding the words **more** or **most** (cold, colder, coldest; slowly, more slowly, most slowly). The comparative is given, then a semicolon, then the superlative form.

Examples include:

bad *adj.* worse; worst
creamy *adj.* creamier; creamiest.
puny *adj.* punier; puniest
well *adv.* better; best

Origin

The origin code, enclosed in brackets, follows the function label and the inflected forms. The code indicates a word's etymology and appears for words that are either foreign, non-standard, or considered jargon in English language usage. The codes fall into three categories:

Foreign

[Ar]	Arabic
[Fo]	Other foreign language
[Fr]	French
[Gr]	German
[He]	Hebrew
[It]	Italian
[Lt]	Latin
[Sp]	Spanish
[Yd]	Yiddish

Jargon

[Bs]	Business
[Cm]	Computer
[Ja]	Other jargon
[Le]	Legal
[Md]	Medical
[Mu]	Music
[Po]	Political
[Sc]	Science

Non-Standard

[Cl]	Colloquial
[Id]	Idiomatic
[Sl]	Slang

Colloquial means informal or conversational. Idiomatic means an expression peculiar to a language and not readily understandable from the meaning of its parts. Slang refers to language that is vigorous, colorful, unconventional, or of a taboo nature.

If the origin code applies to particular definitions but not the entire entry, then the codes will appear after the relevant definition numbers instead of following the inflected forms.

Definition

The definition or definitions for a headword will follow the function label, inflected form(s), and origin code. Each definition begins with a capital letter and ends with a period. If there is only one definition, there will be no definition number preceding it.

Definitions are intended to explain the meaning of a headword in as many of its uses as space permits.

> **annual** \AN-yoo-ul\ *adj.* Occurring every year. annually *adv.*
>
> **annul** \uh-NUL\ *v.* annulled; annulling. To make legally invalid. annulment *n.*
>
> **anoint** \uh-NOINT\ *v.* anointed; anointing. To rub with oil, especially in religious rite. anointer *n.;* anointment *n.*
>
> **anomaly** \uh-NOM-uh-lee\ *n. pl.* anomalies. A departure from the common way. anomalous *adj.*

Derivatives

Entries may end with one or more derivatives of the headword. These are run-on entries that are not defined since their meanings are readily understood from the meaning of the root word.

Derivatives are presented in boldface, italic type, are followed by an italicized function label, and separated by semicolons. Derivatives are commonly used forms of the main entry word that are not inflected forms nor are they given separate entry in the dictionary.

A-Z Dictionary of the English Language

A

a \uh\ *indef. art.* An indicator used before nouns beginning with a consonant.

a \ay\ *n. pl.* a's or as. **1.** The first letter of the English alphabet. **2.** [Cap] The best letter grade.

AA *abbr.* **1.** Alcoholics Anonymous. **2.** Associate in Arts.

aardvark \AHRD-vahrk\ *n.* A burrowing mammal native to Africa.

aback \uh-BAK\ *adv.* By surprise.

abacterial \AY-back-teer-ee-uhl\ *adj.* (Md) Lacking bacteria.

abacus \AB-uh-kuhs\ *n. pl.* abaci. (Fo) A device that calculates through the manual movement of beads along rods.

abalone \ab-uh-LOH-nee\ *n.* A rock-clinging, edible mollusk.

abandon \uh-BAN-duhn\ *v.* abandoned; abandoning. **1.** To give up control. **2.** To withdraw. abandoner *n.*; abandonment *n.*

abandon \uh-BAN-duhn\ *n.* An overpowering loss of restraint.

abate \uh-BAYT\ *v.* abated; abating. **1.** To end. **2.** To reduce. abatement *n.*; abater *n.*

abbey \AB-ee\ *n. pl.* abbeys. A monastery or convent.

abbreviate \uh-BREE-vee-ayt\ *v.* abbreviated; abbreviating. To shorten. abbreviation *n.*; abbreviator *n.*

abdicate \AB-duh-kayt\ *v.* abdicated; abdicating. **1.** To give up a position of responsibility. **2.** To cast off. abdication *n.*; abdicator *n.*

abdomen \AB-duh-mun\ *n.* (Lt) **1.** The portion of a mammal's body between the chest and pelvis. **2.** The rear section abdominal *adj.*

abduct \ab-DUKT\ *v.* abducted; abducting. To carry off without consent. abductor *n.*

aberrant \AB-ur-unt\ *adj.* Not normal. aberration *n.*

abet \uh-BET\ *v.* abetted; abetting. To encourage. abettor *n.*

abeyance \uh-BAY-uns\ *n.* A suspended action.

abhor \ab-HOR\ *v.* abhorred; abhorring. To loathe. abhorrent *adj.*; abhorrence *n.*

abide \uh-BIED\ *v.* abode or abided; abiding. **1.** To wait for. **2.** To withstand. **3.** To stay in place.

abide by *v.* To adhere to.

ability \uh-BIL-uh-tee\ *n. pl.* abilities. **1.** A being able to perform. **2.** A natural or acquired talent.

abject \AB-jekt, ab JEKT\ *adj.* Existing in very low spirits. abjectly *adv.*; abjection *n.*

able \AY-buhl\ *adj.* abler; ablest. Being resourceful or skillful enough to accomplish an end.

able-bodied \AY-buhl-bah-deed\ *adj.* Being physically fit.

ablution \uh-BLOO-shun\ *n.* The cleansing of the body, especially in a religious rite.

abnormal \ab-NOR-muhl\ *adj.* Deviating from the normal. abnormally *adv.*; abnormality *n.*

aboard \uh-BORD\ *adv.* **1.** On or in a vehicle. **2.** [Sl] To join a group.

abode \uh-BOHD\ *n.* **1.** A dwelling place. **2.** A temporary journey.

abolish \uh-BOL-ish\ *v.* abolished; abolishing. To annul or destroy completely. abolishable *adj.*; abolishment *n.*

abolition \ab-uh-LISH-un\ *n.* **1.** An act of extinction or annulment. **2.** The ending of slavery. abolitionist *n.*

abominable \uh-BOM-in-uh-bul\ *adj.* Causing disgust. abominably *adv.*; abomination *n.*

aborigine \ab-uh-RIJ-uh-nee\ *n.* A native to a region.

abort \uh-BORT\ *v.* aborted; aborting. **1.** To end pregnancy before full term. **2.** To stop in early stages.

abortion \uh-BOR-shun\ *n.* An induced expulsion of a fetus.

abound \uh-BOWND\ *v.* abounded; abounding. To be present in great numbers or quantity.

about \uh-BOWT\ *adv.* **1.** Almost. **2.** In another direction.

about \uh-BOWT\ *prep.* **1.** Around. **2.** Near. **3.** On the brink of doing something.

above \uh-BUV\ *adv.* Overhead.

above \uh-BUV\ *prep.* **1.** In a higher place. **2.** Better than.

abrasion \uh-BRAY-zhun\ *n.* **1.** A scraping away by friction. **2.** A worn area.

abreast \uh-BREST\ *adj.* **1.** Being beside. **2.** Aware of new events. abreast *adv.*

abridge \uh-BRIJ\ *v.* abridged; abridging. **1.** To decrease. **2.** To condense. abridgment or abridgement *n.*

abrogate \AB-ruh-gayt\ *v.* abrogated; abrogating. To authoritatively abolish. abrogation *n.*

abrupt \uh-BRUPT\ *adj.* **1.** Unexpected. **2.** Sharply terminated. **3.** Suddenly rising or dropping. abruptly *adv.*; abruptness *n.*

abscess \AB-ses\ *n. pl.* abscesses. (Md) A localized collection of pus. abscessed *adj.*

abscond \ab-SKOND\ *v.* absconded; absconding. To flee and hide.

absent \AB-sunt\ *adj.* Not present. absence *n.*

absent-minded \AB-sunt-MINE-did\ *adj.* Unaware of one's surroundings due to preoccupation. absent-mindedly *adv.*; absent-mindedness *n.*

absolute \AB-suh-loot\ *adj.* **1.** Flawless. **2.** Unlimited. **3.** Fundamental. absolutely *adv.*; absolute *n.*

absolve \ab-ZOLV\ *v.* absolved; absolving. To remove from a duty or guilt.

absorb \ab-ZORB\ *v.* absorbed; absorbing. **1.** To take up through pores. **2.** To fascinate intensely. absorption *n.*

abstain \ab-STAYN\ *v.* abstained; abstaining. To hold back from doing something. abstention *n.*; abstinence *n.*

abstemious \ab-STEE-mee-uhs\ *adj.* Eating and drinking sparingly. abstemiously *adv.*

abstract \AB-strakt\ *n.* A summarized document.

abstract \ab-STRAKT\ *v.* abstracted; abstracting. To separate.

abstract \ab-STRAKT\ *adj.* Disassociated from specifics. abstraction *n.*

absurd \ab-SURD\ *adj.* **1.** Meaningless. **2.** Ridiculously unreasonable. absurdly *adv.* absurdity *n.*

abundance \uh-BUN-duhns\ *n.* A great quantity. abundant *adj.*

abuse \uh-BYOOS\ *n.* A mistreatment. abuse *v.*

abut \uh-BUT\ *v.* abutted; abutting. To touch against a side or end. abutment *n.*

abysmal \uh-BIZ-muhl\ *adj.* **1.** Extreme extension inward, downward, or backward. **2.** Profound. abysmally *adv.*

abyss \uh-BIS\ *n.* **1.** An immeasurable depth or void. **2.** A chaos.

academia \ak-uh-DEEM-ee-uh\ *n.* The academic realm.

academic *also* **academical** \ak-uh-DEM-ik\ *adj.* **1.** Associated with a school. **2.** Relating to liberal arts. **3.** Theoretical.

a cappella *also* **a capella** \ah-kuh-PEL-uh\ *adj.* [It] Lacking instruments. *adv.*

accede \ak-SEED\ *v.* acceded; acceding. **1.** To agree to. **2.** To enter into office.

accelerate \ak-SEL-uh-rayt\ *v.* accelerated; accelerating. To increase velocity or progress. acceleration *n.*

accent \AK-sent\ *n.* **1.** A mark placing stress on syllables words. **2.** Emphasis given speech, music.

accent \AK-sent\ *v.* accented; accenting. To stress.

accentuate \ak-SEN-choo-ayt\ *v.* accentuated; accentuating. To emphasize.

accept \ak-SEPT\ *v.* accepted; accepting. **1.** To receive willingly. **2.** To allow into a group. **3.** To agree to. acceptable *adj.*; acceptingly *adv.*

access \AK-ses\ *n.* A means of passage.

access \AK-ses\ *v.* accessed; accessing. To get at. accessible *adj.*; accessibility *n.*

accession \ak-SESH-uhn\ *n.* **1.** The attainment of a position of honor. **2.** An increase or acquisition.

accessory *also* **accessary** \ak-SES-ur-ee\ *n. pl.* accessories. **1.** A nonessential item. **2.** [Le] A contributor to a crime.

accident \ak-si-DEN-tuhl\ *n.* **1.** A chance happening. **2.** An unforeseen event that causes harm. **3.** A coincidence. accidental *adj.*; accidentally *adv.*

acclaim \uh-KLAYM\ *v.* acclaimed; acclaiming. To praise.

acclimate \AK-luh-mayt\ *v.* acclimated; acclimating. To get used to something, someone, or someplace new. acclimatization *n.*

accolade \AK-uh-layd\ *n.* **1.** A salute. **2.** The recognition for an accomplishment.

accommodate \uh-KOM-uh-dayt\ *v.* accommodated; accommodating. **1.** To adjust. **2.** To provide for. **3.** To make welcome. accomodating *adj.*; accommodatingly *adv.*; accommodation *n.*

accompaniment \uh-KUM-puh-ni-munt\ *n.* **1.** An addition for completeness. **2.** A melody's instrumental or vocal companion.

accompany \uh-KUM-puh-nee\ *v.* accompanied; accompanying. **1.** To associate with. **2.** To perform an accompaniment.

accomplice \uh-KOM-plis\ *n.* A partner, especially in crime.

accomplish \uh-KOM-plish\ *v.* accomplished; accomplishing. **1.** To finish. **2.** To achieve. accomplishment *n.*

accord \uh-KORD\ *n.* An agreement.

accord \uh-KORD\ *v.* accorded; according. **1.** To agree. **2.** To grant. accordant *adj.*; accordantly *adv.*

accordingly \uh-KOR-ding-lee\ *adv.* **1.** In an appropriate manner. **2.** Consequently.

accost \uh-KAWST\ *v.* accosted; accosting. To approach aggressively.

account \uh-KOWNT\ *n.* **1.** Explanation of events. **2.** Record of monetary transaction. **3.** Client, customer.

account \uh-KOWNT\ *v.* accounted; accounting. **1.** To explain. **2.** To take responsibility for. accountable *adj.*; accountably *adv.*; accountability *n.*

accounting \uh-KOWN-ting\ *n.* (Bs) The upkeep of the financial records of a business. accountant *n.*

accoutrement *also* **accouterment** \uh-KOO-treh-munt\ *n.* An accessory.

accredit \uh-KRED-it\ *v.* accredited; accrediting. **1.** To give approval or praise. **2.** To give credentials to. accreditation *n.*

accrue \uh-KROO\ *v.* accrued; accruing. To gain interest.

accumulate \uh-KYOOM-yuh-layt\ *v.* accumulated; accumulating. To collect. accumulation *n.*

accurate \AK-yur-it\ *adj.* **1.** Error free. **2.** Precise. accurately *adv.*; accurateness *n.*

accuse \uh-KYOOZ\ *v.* accused; accusing. To charge with blame. accusingly *adv.*; accusation *n.*; accused *n.*; accuser *n.*

accustom \uh-KUS-tum\ *v.* accustomed; accustoming. To become familiar with.

ace \AYS\ *n.* **1.** An expert. **2.** A die, playing card, or domino with one spot.

acerbate \AS-ur-bayt\ *v.* acerbated; acerbating. To annoy.

acetaminophen \uh-SEE-ti-min-oh-fen\ *n.* (Md) An aspirin substitute to relieve pain and fever.

acetate \AS-i-tayt\ *n.* (Sc) A fabric or plastic made from cellulose and the chief acid of vinegar.

ache \ayk\ *n.* A persistent pain.

ache \ayk\ *v.* ached; aching. **1.** To suffer from pain. **2.** To yearn.

achieve \uh-CHEEV\ *v.* achieved; achieving. To accomplish successfully. achievable *adj.*; achievement *n.*; achiever *n.*

acid \AS-id\ *n.* [Sc] A sour, water-soluble compound that can react with a base to form a salt. acidic *adj.*

acid rain \AS-id rayn\ *n.* (Sc) A liquid precipitation containing acid and causing environmental problems.

acid rock \AS-id rock\ *n.* (Mu) A music suggesting drug-induced experiences.

acknowledge \ak-NOL-ij\ *v.* acknowledged; acknowledging. **1.** To recognize the validity or authority of. **2.** To answer. **3.** To thank. acknowledged *adj.*; acknowledgment or acknowledgement *n.*

acne \AK-nee\ *n.* A skin disorder characterized by pimples.

ACOA *abbr.* Adult Children of Alcoholics.

acolyte \AK-uh-liet\ *n.* A religious assistant.

acoustics \uh-KOOS-tiks\ *n.* The science of sound.

acquaint \uh-KWAYNT\ *v.* acquainted; acquainting. To allow oneself or another person to learn about something new. acquaintance *n.*

acquiesce \ak-wee-ES\ *v.* acquiesced; acquiescing. To accept passively. acquiescent *adj.*; acquiescently *adv.*; acquiescence *n.*

acquire \uh-KWIRE\ *v.* acquired; acquiring. To obtain for personal possession. acquisition *n.*

acquit \uh-KWIT\ *v.* acquitted; acquitting. To clear of accused wrongdoing. acquittal *n.*

acre \AY-kur\ *n.* A unit of land or area.

acrid \AK-rid\ *adj.* **1.** Tasting or smelling bitter. **2.** Harsh words or behavior.

acrimony \AK-ruh-moh-nee\ *n. pl.* acrimonies. Nasty words or behavior. acrimonious *adj.*; acrimoniously *adv.*

acrobatics \AK-ruh-BAT-iks\ *n.* A gymnastic performance. acrobat *n.*

acronym \AK-ruh-nim\ *n.* A word formed by first letters of major words in a phrase.

acropolis \uh-KROP-uh-lis\ *n.* **1.** A capital. **2.** A fortified portion of ancient Greek city.

across \uh-KRAWS\ *adv.* From one side to the other.

across \uh-KRAWS\ *prep.* From one side to its opposite.

acrylic \uh-KRIL-ik\ *n.* A paint made of a polymer.

act \akt\ *n.* **1.** Something done. **2.** [Le] A law; edict. **3.** Division of a play, opera.

act \akt\ *v.* acted; acting. **1.** To represent or simulate. **2.** To behave. acting *n.*

action \AK-shun\ *n.* **1.** The condition of doing something. **2.** A court proceeding. **3.** [Le] A lawsuit.

active \AK-tiv\ *adj.* **1.** Characterized by movement. **2.** Participative.

actor \AK-tur\ *n.* **1.** A performer. **2.** A doer.

actress \AK-tris\ *n.* A female performer.

actual \AK-choo-uhl\ *adj.* Existing in reality. actually *adv.*; actuality *n.*

actuary \AK-choo-er-ee\ *n. pl.* actuaries. A person who figures out insurance premiums and risks.

acumen \uh-KYOO-mun\ *n.* An acute ability to understand reason.

acupressure \AK-yuu-presh-ur\ *n.* (Md) A healing method involving application of pressure on certain parts of the body.

acupuncture \AK-yuu-pungk-chur\ *n.* (Md) Chinese healing technique in which needles are inserted into the body. acupuncturist *n.*

acute \uh-KYOOT\ *adj.* acuter; acutest. **1.** Coming on quickly and severely and lasting a short time. **2.** Smart. **3.** Sharp. acupuncturist *n.*

adage \AD-ij\ *n.* A short saying that contains a common observation.

adamant \AD-uh-munt\ *adj.* Unyielding.

adapt \uh-DAPT\ *v.* adapted; adapting. To modify so as to fit. adaptable *adj.*; adaptation *n.*

add \ad\ *v.* added; adding. **1.** To unite for increase. **2.** To combine numbers. **3.** To further state.

addict \uh-DIKT\ *v.* addicted; addicting. To become psychologically or physically dependent, especially on a drug. addict *n.*; addiction *n.*

addition \uh-DISH-uhn\ *n.* **1.** The result of combining. **2.** The process of combining. additional *adj.*

additive \AD-i-tiv\ *n.* Something combined with another for improvement.

address \uh-DRES, AD-dres\ *n.* **1.** A formal lecture. **2.** An instruction for delivery. **3.** A place of residence.

address \uh-DRES\ *v.* addressed; addressing. **1.** To talk to.**2.** To focus the attention of. **3.** To write the directions for mailing.

adenoid \AD-n-oid\ *n.* (Md) An inflamed tissue mass at the back of the pharynx.

adept \AD-ept\ *n.* A highly skilled person.

adept \uh-DEPT\ *adj.* Having expertise.

adequate \AD-i-kwit\ *adj.* Meeting minimum requirements.

adhere \ad-HEER\ *v.* adhered; adhering. To stick to. adherence *n.*

adhesive \ad-HEE-siv\ *n.* A substance that allows fusion.

ad hoc \ad-HOK\ *adj.* [Lt] Formed for a specific end.

adjacent \uh-JAY-sunt\ *adj.* **1.** Near to. **2.** Having an end or side in common.

adjective \AJ-ik-tiv\ *n.* A part of speech used to add information to nouns.

adjoin \uh-JOIN\ *v.* adjoined; adjoining. To lie next to.

adjourn \uh-JURN\ *v.* adjourned; adjourning. **1.** To disband until a later stated time. **2.** To move location.

adjust \uh-JUST\ *v.* adjusted; adjusting. **1.** To make more com-fortable. **2.** To regulate. adjustable *adj.*; adjustment *n.*

ad-lib \ad-LIB\ *v.* [Lt] ad-libbed; ad-libbing. To deliver without contemplation.

administer \ad-MIN-is-tur\ *v.* administered; administering. **1.** To manage. **2.** To give out. administrator *n.*; administrate *v.*

administration \ad-min-is-TRAY-shun\ *n.* **1.** A group of managers. **2.** The performance of managerial duties. administrative *adj.*

admire \ad-MIRE\ *v.* admired; admiring. To regard highly. admiringly *adv.*; admiration *n.*; admirer *n.*

admission \ad-MISH-un\ *n.* **1.** Granting as valid. **2.** A fee for entrance. **3.** Anything conceded.

admit \ad-MIT\ *v.* admitted; admitting. **1.** To permit to enter. **2.** To confess. admittance *n.*

admonish \ad-MON-ish\ *v.* admonished; admonishing. To disapprove gently. admonitory *adj.*; admonishment *n.*; admonition *n.*

ad nauseum \ad-NAW-zee-um\ *adv.* (Lt) To a disgusting degree.

adobe \uh-DOE-bee\ *n.* (Sp) A building constructed of bricks of earth and straw.

adolescence \ad-uh-LES-uns\ *n.* **1.**

The process of maturing. **2.** Ages 12-19 approximately. adolescent *n.*

adopt \uh-DOPT\ *v.* adopted; adopting. **1.** To make one's own. **2.** To accept. adoption *n.*

adorable \uh-DOR-uh-bul\ *adj.* **1.** Worthy of worship. **2.** Very charming.

adore \uh-DOR\ *v.* adored; adoring. **1.** To worship as divine. **2.** To love greatly. adoration *n.*

adorn \uh-DORN\ *v.* adorned; adorning. To decorate.

adrenaline \uh-DREN-uh-lin\ *n.* (Md) A stimulating drug.

adrift \uh-DRIFT\ *adj.* Floating without power or guidance. adrift *adv.*

adroit \uh-DROIT\ *adj.* Being skillful or resourceful.

adulation \aj-uu-LAY-shun\ *n.* An excessive flattery. adulate *v.*

adult \uh-DULT\ *n.* One who has reached the legal age of consent.

adulterate \uh-DUL-tuh-rayt\ *v.* adulterated; adulterating. To make inferior by adding foreign ingredients. adulteration *n.*

adultery \uh-DUL-tur-ee\ *n. pl.* adulteries. Voluntary sexual intercourse outside of marriage. adulterer *n.*

advance \ad-VANS\ *v.* advanced; advancing. **1.** To go forward. **2.** To raise. **3.** To give money before it is due. advancement *n.*

advantage \ad-VAN-tij\ *n.* **1.** A better position or condition. **2.** A benefit. advantageous *adj.*; advantageously *adv.*

adventure \ad-VEN-chur\ *n.* An exciting experience or undertaking.

adventure \ad-VEN-chur\ *v.* adventured; adventuring. To risk. adventuresome *adj.*; adventurer *n.*

adverb \AD-vurb\ *n.* Part of speech that adds information to a verb, an adjective, or another adverb. adverbial *adj.*

adversary \AD-vur-sair-ee\ *n. pl.* adversaries. An opponent. adversarial *adj.*

adverse \ad-VURS\ *adj.* **1.** Opposing. **2.** Unfavorable.

advertise \AD-vur-tiez\ *v.* advertised; advertising. To announce to the public. advertisement *n.*; advertiser *n.*; advertising *n.*

advice \ad-VIES\ *n.* A counsel or recommendation.

advise \ad-VIEZ\ *v.* advised; advising. **1.** To give counsel. **2.** To inform. advisory *adj.*; advisement *n.*; adviser or advisor *n.*

advocate \AD-vuh-kit\ *n.* One that defends another's cause or proposal. advocacy *n.*

aegis \EE-jis\ *n.* Under the protection or sponsorship.

aerial \AIR-ee-uhl\ *adj.* **1.** Related to air. **2.** Existing above.

aerobic \air-OH-bik\ *adj.* Concerning the presence of oxygen.

aerodynamics \air-oh-die-NAM-iks\ *n. pl.* aerodynamics. (Sc) The study of the forces acting on the particles in atmospheric gases. aerodynamic *adj.*; aerodynamical *adj.*

aeronautics \air-uh-NAW-tiks\ *n. pl.* aeronautics. (Sc) The science of flight.

aerospace \AIR-oh-spays\ *adj.* (Sc) Relating to the Earth's atmosphere and beyond.

aesthetic *also* **aesthetical** \es-THET-ik\ *adj.* **1.** Relating to the beautiful. **2.** Aware of the beautiful. aesthetically *adv.*; aesthete *n.*

affable \AF-uh-bul\ *adj.* **1.** Likable. **2.** Pleasant in conversation.

affect \AF-ekt\ *n.* A conscious emotion.

affect \uh-FEKT\ *v.* affected; affecting. **1.** To influence. **2.** To display pretense.

affection \uh-FEK-shun\ *n.* Fond emotions toward someone or something. affectionate *adj.*; affectionately *adv.*

affidavit \af-uh-DAY-vit\ *n.* (Le) A written, sworn statement given to an authority.

affiliate \uh-FIL-ee-it\ *n.* A connected person or organization.

affiliate \uh-FIL-ee-ayt\ *v.* affiliated; affiliating. To interact with. affiliation *n.*

affinity \uh-FIN-uh-tee\ *n. pl.* affinities. **1.** A relationship. **2.** An attraction. **3.** A likeness.

affirm \uh-FURM\ *v.* affirmed; affirming. To assert as true. affirmative *adj.*; affirmation *n.*

affirmative action \uh-FUR-muh-tiv AK-shun\ *n.* (Le) Employment or educational improvement efforts for minorities.

affix \uh-FIKS\ *v.* affixed; affixing. To attach.

afflict \uh-FLIKT\ *v.* afflicted; afflicting. To harm or injure. affliction *n.*

affluent \AF-loo-unt\ *adj.* Possessing in abundance. affluence *n.*

afford \uh-FORD\ *v.* afforded; affording. To be able to purchase.

affront \uh-FRUNT\ *v.* affronted; affronting. To offend.

afghan \AF-gan\ *n.* **1.** Knitted or crocheted blanket. **2.** [Cap] A native of Afghanistan.

aficionado \uh-fish-uh-NAH-doh\ *n. pl.* aficionados. A fan.

afraid \uh-FRAYD\ *adj.* Fearful.

Africa \AF-ri-kuh\ *n.* A continent in the southern hemisphere. African *adj.*

African American \AF-ri-kun uh-MER-i-kun\ *n.* A person of African ancestry and American citizenship.

Afrikaner \af-ri-kahn-ur\ *n.* A South African native of European descent.

after \AF-tur\ *adv.* Behind.

after \AF-tur\ *prep.* **1.** Behind. **2.** Later in time than. **3.** In intense want of.

afterlife \AF-tur-life\ *n.* Existence after death.

aftermath \AF-tur-math\ *n.* **1.** The time following a disaster. **2.** A consequence.

afternoon \AF-tur-noon\ *n.* The portion of the day between noon and dusk.

afterthought \AF-tur-thawt\ *n.* A later idea.

afterwards *also* **afterward** \AF-tur-wurds\ *adv.* Occuring later.

again \uh-GEN\ *adv.* **1.** Repeatedly. **2.** In return. **3.** In addition to.

against \uh-GENST\ *prep.* **1.** In opposition to. **2.** In confrontation with.

agape \uh-GAYP\ *adv.* **1.** In wonder. **2.** Open wide. agape *adj.*

age \ayj\ *n.* **1.** A chronological tally of one's years. **2.** A method of surveying geological time via the number of years evident in rock strata.

aged \AY-jid\ *adj.* Having reached advanced age.

agency \AY-jun-see\ *n. pl.* agencies. **1.** A capability. **2.** A group with authority. **3.** A power exerting operation.

agenda \uh-JEN-duh\ *n.* A list of items for completion.

agent \AY-junt\ *n.* **1.** Something or someone with power to act. **2.** A person who represents another.

Agent Orange \AY-junt OR-inj\ *n.* A contaminant widely used in the Vietnam War.

aggrandize \uh-GRAN-dize\ *v.* aggrandized; aggrandizing. To enlarge or enhance. aggrandizement *n.*

aggravate \AG-ruh-vayt\ *v.* aggravated; aggravating. **1.** To worsen. **2.** To annoy. aggravation *n.*

aggravated assault \AG-ruh-vay-ted uh-SAWLT\ *n.* (Le) Assault plus intent.

aggregate \AG-ri-git\ *adj.* Formed by many parts.

aggression \uh-GRESH-un\ *n.* **1.** An assault. **2.** Hostile behavior.

aghast \uh-GAST\ *adj.* Shocked.

agile \AJ-ul\ *adj.* Physically or mentally quick.

agitate \AJ-i-tayt\ *v.* agitated; agitating. **1.** To excite. **2.** To disturb. agitation *n.*; agitator *n.*

agnosticism \ag-NOS-tuh-siz-um\ *n.* A system of belief that holds ultimate reality as unknown and unknowable.

ago \uh-GO\ *adv.* In the past. ago *adj.*

agony \AG-uh-nee\ *n. pl.* agonies. An extreme mental or physical pain.

agoraphobia \uh-GO-rah-FOE-bee-uh\ *n.* A fear of open or public places.

agrarian \uh-GRAIR-ee-un\ *adj.* (Sc) Concerning land.

agree \uh-GREE\ *v.* agreed; agreeing. **1.** To grant assent. **2.** To correspond.

agriculture \AG-ri-kul-chur\ *n.* The science of farming. agricultural *adj.*

aground \uh-GROWND\ *adv.* Upon the shore or land. aground *adj.*

ahead \uh-HED\ *adv.* In front of. ahead *adj.*

aid \ayd\ *n.* An assistance.

aid \ayd\ *v.* aided; aiding. To give assistance.

AIDS \ayds\ *n.* (Md) Acquired Immune Deficiency Syndrome.

ailing \ayl-ing\ *adj.* Not feeling well.

ailment \ayl-munt\ *n.* An illness.

aim \aym\ *v.* aimed; aiming. To direct towards someone or something.

aimless \AYM-lis\ *adj.* Without specific direction. aimlessly *adv.*; aimlessness *n.*

ain't \aynt\ *v.* (Sl) The contraction of are not.

air \air\ *n.* **1.** Gases surrounding earth. **2.** An empty space. **3.** A person's demeanor.

air bag *n.* A safety bag in the front of an automobile that inflate upon sudden impact.

airbus *n.* A short- or medium-range subsonic passenger airplane.

aircraft \AIR-kraft\ *n.* Any structure capable of air navigation.

airhead \AIR-hed\ *n.* **1.** Hostile territory secured by air troops. **2.** [Sl] One who lacks common sense.

airline \AIR-lien\ *n.* An air-based transportation company.

airplane \AIR-playn\ *n.* A heavier-than-air powered flying vehicle with wings.

airplay *n.* (Mu) The exposure of songs on the air by a radio station.

airport *n.* A ground location for air-transportation companies.

airs *n.* A false manner.

airtight \AIR-tite\ *adj.* **1.** Unable for air to penetrate. **2.** Having no weakness for attack.

airwave \AIR-wayv\ *n. pl.* airwaves. The medium for radio and television transmission.

airy \AIR-ee\ *adj.* airier; airiest **1.** Relating to atmosphere. **2.** Unreal or unsubstantial. **3.** Graceful. **4.** Light.

aisle \IEL\ *n.* A passageway.

ajar \uh-JAHR\ *adv.* Open slightly. ajar *adj.*

akin \uh-KIN\ *adj.* **1.** Associated by common ancestry. **2.** Alike.

a la \AH-lah\ *prep.* (Fr) In the way of.

a la carte \ah-luh-KAHRT\ *adj.* (Fr) Referring to a menu that prices items separately. a la carte *adv.*

Al-Anon *n.* A support group for friends and relatives of alcoholics.

alarm \uh-LAHRM\ *n.* **1.** A warning signal. **2.** A device that sounds. **3.** The fear caused by danger.

alarm \uh-LAHRM\ *v.* alarmed; alarming. **1.** To alert. **2.** To make afraid. alarmingly *adv.*; alarmist *n.*

alas \uh-LASS\ *interj.* Expresses disappointment, pity, or worry.

Alateen *n.* A support group for children of alcoholics.

albatross \AL-buh-traws\ *n. pl.* albatross or albatrosses. **1.** A large web-footed sea bird. **2.** Something causing anxiety. **3.** An encumbrance.

albeit \awl-BEE-it\ *conj.* Even though.

albino \al-BIE-noh\ *n. pl.* albinos. A person or animal that lacks coloration in the skin, hair, and eyes.

album \AL-bum\ *n.* **1.** A book for collecting objects. **2.** An anthology. **3.** A phonograph record.

alchemy \AL-kuh-mee\ *n.* (Sc) Medieval science that sought to transform common objects into precious material.

alcohol \AL-kuh-hawl\ *n.* **1.** Colorless, flammable liquid that is in liquor. **2.** Drinks containing alcohol.

alcoholic \al-kuh-HAW-lik\ *adj.* **1.** Containing alcohol. **2.** Excessively or compulsively drinking alcohol.

alcoholic \al-kuh-HAW-lik\ *n.* One who excessively or complusively drinks alcoholic beverages.

alcove \AL-kohv\ *n.* **1.** A small offset portion of a room. **2.** A secluded part-time residence.

al dente \al-DAHNT-ay\ *adj.* (It) Cooked only until firm.

ale \ayl\ *n.* A bitter alcoholic beverage brewed from malt and hops.

alert \uh-LURT\ *adj.* **1.** Watchful. **2.** Quick to respond.

al fredo \al-FRAY-doh\ *adj.* (It) With cream sauce.

alfresco \al-FRES-koh\ *adv.* (It) Outdoors. alfresco *adj.*

algae \al-JEE\ *n.* *sing.* alga. A group of primitive, chlorophyll-containing plants in fresh and salt water.

algebra \AL-juh-bruh\ *n.* A mathematical system using letters to figure out the relationship of numbers. algebraic *adj.*

alias \AY-lee-us\ *n.* A pretend name.

alibi \AL-uh-bie\ *n.* **1.** An excuse. **2.** [Le] The plea of having not been at the scene of a crime.

alien \AYL-yun or AY-lee-yun\ *adj.* Not familiar.

alien \AYL-yun or AY-lee-yun\ *n.* **1.** One born in another country. **2.** An extraterrestrial.

alienate \AYL-yu-nayt or AY-lee-uh-nayt\ *v.* alienated; alienating. To distance oneself from an attachment, especially through hostile actions. alienation *n.*

align *also* **aline** \uh-LINE\ *v.* aligned; aligning. **1.** To bring into correct position. **2.** To put oneself on one side of an issue.

alike \uh-LIKE\ *adj.* Similar.

alimentary \al-uh-MEN-tuh-ree\ *adj.* Nutrition related.

alimony \AL-uh-moh-nee\ *n. pl.* alimonies. Money paid to one's ex-spouse.

alive \uh-LIVE\ *adj.* **1.** Not dead. **2.** In activation. **3.** Characterized by much activity.

alkaline \AL-kuh-lin\ *adj.* (Sc) Having a pH greater than 7.0.

all \awl\ *adj.* **1.** The entire quantity. **2.** Every part of a group. **3.** The sum total.

Allah \AL-uh\ *n.* (Ar) The Islamic Supreme Being.

all-American \awl-uh-MER-i-kun\ *adj.* **1.** Consisting of American elements. **2.** Representing American ideals.

allay \uh-LAY\ *v.* allayed; allaying. **1.** To alleviate. **2.** To calm.

allege \uh-LEJ\ *v.* alleged; alleging. To set forth without proof.

allegiance \uh-LEE-juns\ *n.* The loyalty to a person, governing body, or cause.

allergy \AL-ur-jee\ *n. pl.* allergies. A bodily reaction to irritants.

alleviate \uh-LEE-vee-ayt\ *v.* alleviated; alleviating. To relieve. alleviation *n.*

alley \AL-ee\ *n. pl.* alleys. **1.** A

small passageway. **2.** A hardwood floor used for bowling.

alliance \uh-LIE-uns\ *n.* **1.** A close association. **2.** A treaty declaring a relationship.

alligator \AL-i-gay-tur\ *n.* A large reptile.

allocate \AL-uh-kayt\ *v.* allocated; allocating. **1.** To distribute. **2.** To set aside for a purpose. allocatable *adj.*; allocation *n.*

allot \uh-LOT\ *v.* allotted; allotting. To give in portions. allotment *n.*

allow \uh-LAOW\ *v.* allowed; allowing. **1.** To grant. **2.** To permit. **3.** To admit. allowable *adj.*; allowably *adv.*; allowance *n.*

alloy \AL-oi\ *n.* A mixture of metals.

all right \awl-RITE\ *adj.* **1.** Satisfactory. **2.** Not harmed. **3.** Nice.

all right \awl-RITE\ *adv.* **1.** Good enough. **2.** O.K. **3.** Beyond a doubt.

allude \uh-LOOD\ *v.* alluded; alluding. To indirectly refer to. allusive *adj.*

allure \uh-LUUR\ *n.* An attractiveness.

allure \uh-LUUR\ *v.* allured; alluring. To attract. allurement *n.*

allusion \uh-LOO-zhun\ *n.* A reference to something in literature.

ally \al-LY\ *v.* allied; allying. To come together in friendship.

alma mater \AL-muh-MAH-tur\ *n.* (Lt) **1.** The school from which one graduated. **2.** A school's song.

almanac \AWL-muh-nak\ *n.* A yearly publication of general information, especially astronomical and weather.

almighty \awl-MIE-tee\ *adj.* Possessing absolute power. Almighty *n.*

almond \AH-mund or AL-mund\ *n.* **1.** An edible nut. **2.** The tree that bears the edible nut.

almost \AWL-mohst\ *adv.* Very nearly.

alms \ahms\ *n. pl.* alms. Something donated to the poor.

aloe \AH-loe\ *n.* A plant, native to Africa, that yields a medicinal juice.

alone \uh-LOHN\ *adj.* **1.** Isolated. **2.** Unique.

along \uh-LAWNG\ *adv.* **1.** Ahead. **2.** With someone.

along \ah-LAWNG\ *prep.* **1.** In line with. **2.** At a point during.

aloof \uh-LOOF\ *adj.* Psychologically or physically distant.

aloud \uh-LOWD\ *adv.* So that others can hear.

alphabet \AL-fuh-bet\ *n.* A system of letters.

alphabetical \al-fuh-BET-i-kul\ *adj.* Following the order of the alphabet.

alpine \AL-pien\ *adj.* **1.** Relating to mountains, esp. the Alps. **2.** [Cap] Relating to a ski sport.

already \awl-RED-ee\ *adv.* Before now.

also \AWL-soh\ *adv.* In addition to.

altar \AWL-tur\ *n.* A table for worship.

alter \AWL-tur\ *v.* altered; altering. **1.** To change slightly. **2.** To spay. alteration *n.*

altercation \awl-tur-KAY-shun\ *n.* A noisy quarrel. altercate *v.*

alter ego \AWL-ter-EE-goh\ *n.* A counterpart.

alternate \AWL-tur-nit\ *n.* A replacement.

alternate \AWL-tur-nayt\ *v.* alternated; alternating. To perform by turns.

alternative \awl-TUR-nuh-tiv\ *adj.* Expressing an option. alternatively *adv.*

alternative \awl-TUR-nuh-tiv\ *n.* An option.

although *also* **altho** \awl-THOH\ *conj.* Despite the fact.

altitude \AL-tuh-tood\ *n.* An elevation above the Earth's surface.

alto \AL-toh\ *n. pl.* altos. (Mu) A person or instrument having a musical range below soprano.

altogether \awl-tuh-GETH-ur\ *adv.* Completely.

altruism \AL-troo-IZ-um\ *n.* An unselfish regard for others. altruistic *adj.*; altruistically *adv.*; altruist *n.*

aluminum \uh-LOO-muh-num\ *n.* A silver-white malleable metal.

alumna \uh-LUM-nuh\ *n. pl.* alumnae. (Lt) A female graduate.

alumnus \uh-LUM-nus\ *n. pl.* alumi. (Lt) A graduate.

always \AWL-wayz\ *adv.* Forever.

am *v.* Present first person singular of be.

amalgamate \uh-MAL-guh-mayt\ *v.* amalgamated; amalgamating. To unite. amalgam *n.*; amalgamation *n.*

amass \uh-MAS\ *v.* amassed; amassing. To gather.

amateur \AM-uh-chuur\ *n.* **1.** One who pursues something purely for pleasure. **2.** A nonprofessional. amateur *adj.*; amateurish *adj.*; amateurism *n.*

amaze \uh-MAY-zing\ *v.* amazed; amazing. To astound. amazingly *adv.*; amazement *n.*

ambassador \am-BAS-uh-dur\ *n.* **1.** An authorized messenger. **2.** A representative of a foreign land. ambassadorial *adj.*

ambidextrous \am-buh-DEK-strus\ *adj.* Able to use both hands. ambidextrously *adv.*

ambience *also* **ambiance** \ahm-BEE-ans\ *n.* (Fr) An atmosphere. **ambient** *adj.*

ambiguous \am-BIG-yoo-us\ *adj.* Capable of being interpreted in several ways. **ambiguously** *adv.*; **ambiguousness** *n.*

ambition \am-BISH-un\ *n.* A desire to achieve a goal. **ambitious** *adj.*

ambivalent \am-BIV-uh-lunt\ *adj.* Having feelings that change. **ambivalence** *n.*

amble \AM-bul\ *v.* ambled; ambling. To walk at a relaxing pace.

ambulance \AM-byuh-luns\ *n.* A vehicle to transport the sick or injured.

ambush \AM-buush\ *v.* ambushed; ambushing. To attack from a hidden location. **ambush** *n.*

amen \AY-MEN or AH-MEN\ *interj.* Expresses approval or faith.

amenable \uh-MEN-uh-bul\ *adj.* **1.** Responsible. **2.** Cooperative.

amend \uh-MEND\ *v.* amended; amending. **1.** To improve. **2.** To correct. **3.** To formally change a law.

amendment \uh-MEND-munt\ *n.* **1.** A correction. **2.** A formal change to the law.

amenity \un-MEN-i-tee\ *n. pl.* amenities. Something that brings comfort or convenience.

Amerasian \AM-ur-AY-zhun\ *n.* One of American and Asian descent.

Americanize \uh-MER-i-kuh-nize\ *v.* Americanized; Americanizing. To conform to American customs. **Americanization** *n.*

amiable \AY-mee-uh-bul\ *adj.* Friendly. **amiably** *adv.*

amicable \AM-ik-uh-bul\ *adj.* Agreeable. **amicably** *adv.*

amid *also* **amidst** \uh-MID\ *prep.* Among.

amiss \uh-MIS\ *adj.* **1.** Faulty. **2.** Out of order.

amiss \uh-MIS\ *adv.* **1.** Incorrectly. **2.** Imperfectly.

ammonia \uh-MOHN-yuh\ *n.* (Sc) A pungent gaseous compound.

ammunition \am-yuh-NISH-un\ *n.* **1.** Explosive weapons. **2.** Information that can be used to attack or defend.

amnesia \am-NEE-zhuh\ *n.* (Md) A memory loss. **amnesic** *adj.*; **amnesiac** *n.*

amnesty \AM-nus-tee\ *n. pl.* amnesties. An authoritative pardon.

amoeba \uh-MEE-buh\ *n. pl.* amoebas or amoebae. A protozoan that lives in water or moist environments.

among *also* **amongst** \uh-MUNG\

prep. **1.** In the middle of. **2.** In the company of. **3.** Through a grouping of.

amoral \ay-MOR-ul\ *adj.* Being outside of moral judgment. amorally *adv.*

amorous \AM-ur-us\ *adj.* Enamored. amorously *adv.*; amorousness *n.*

amortize \AM-ur-tize\ *v.* amortized; amortizing. (Bs) To end a debt through installments. amortization *n.*

amount \uh-MOWNT\ *n.* The complete quantity. amount *v.*

amp *n.* An electronic device that makes sound louder.

ampersand \AM-pur-sand\ *n.* A symbol for the word and.

amphetamine \am-FET-uh-meen\ *n.* (Md) A central nervous system stimulant.

amphibian \am-FIB-ee-un\ *n.* A cold-blooded vertebrate.

ample \AM-pul\ *adj.* ampler; amplest. Plentiful. amply *adv.*

amplify \AM-plu-fie\ *v.* amplifies; amplifying. **1.** To increase. **2.** To expand.

amputate \AM-pyuu-tayt\ *v.* amputated; amputating. To cut off. amputation *n.*; amputee *n.*

amuck *also* **amok** \uh-MUK\ *adv.* In a rage.

amulet \AM-yuh-lit\ *n.* A magic charm or symbol.

amuse \uh-MYOOZ\ *v.* amused; amusing. **1.** To entertain. **2.** To take one's mind off of. amusement *n.*

an *indef. art.* An indicator used before nouns beginning with a vowel.

anabolic steroid *n.* (Md) A synthetic hormone used to temporarily increase muscle strength.

anachronism \uh-NAK-ruh-niz-um\ *n.* Something out of its proper time. anachronic *adj.*; anachronistic *adj.*; anachronous *adj.*; anachronistically *adv.*

anal \AYN-l\ *adj.* [Md] Relating to the anus.

analogy \uh-NAL-uh-jee\ *n. pl.* analogies. A statement of similarity between two unlike things.

analyze \AN-l-iez\ *v.* analyzed; analyzing. To examine the parts of a whole. analytic *adj.*; analytical *adj.*; analyst *n.*

anarchy \AN-ur-kee\ *n.* **1.** Lacking governmental authority. **2.** Disorder. anarchic *adj.*; anarchist *n.*

anathema \uh-NATH-uh-muh\ *n.* **1.** A curse. **2.** One that is despised. anathematize *v.*

anatomy \un-NAT-uh-mee\ *n. pl.* anatomies. (Md) **1.** Structure of a plant or animal. **2.** Science of structure of plants and animals. anatomic *adj.*; anatomical *adj.*; anatomically *adv.*; anatomist *n.*

ancestor \AN-ses-tur\ *n.* A forerunner. ancestral *adj.*; ancestry *n.*

anchor \ANG-kur\ *n.* **1.** A metal object used to retain place. **2.** A chief broadcaster on a news show.

anchor \ANG-kur\ *v.* anchored; anchoring. To hold in place.

ancient \AYN-shunt\ *adj.* **1.** Antique. **2.** Relating to the time preceding the Middle Ages.

and *conj.* A word used to join two elements.

androgynous \an-DROJ-uh-nus\ *adj.* Having both male and female traits. androgyny *n.*

android \AN-droid\ *n.* A robot with human form.

anecdote \AN-ik-doht\ *n. pl.* anecdotes or anecdota. A short, fascinating story. anecdotal *adj.*; anecdotally *adv.*

anemia \uh-NEE-mee-uh\ *n.* (Md) A blood deficiency. anemic *adj.*; anemic *n.*

anesthesia \an-is-THEE-zhuh\ *n.* (Md) A loss of bodily feeling.

anesthetic \an-is-THET-ik\ *n.* (Md) A drug used to temporarily stop bodily feeling. anesthetize *v.*

aneurism *also* **aneurysm** \AN-yu-riz-um\ *n.* (Md) A swelling of a wall of a blood vessel.

anew \uh-NOO\ *adv.* Afresh.

angel \AYN-jul\ *n.* **1.** A being spiritually superior to man. **2.** A guardian spirit. **3.** A winged human. angelic *adj.*; angelical *adj.*; angelically *adv.*

anger \ANG-gur\ *n.* A strong negative emotion.

anger \ANG-gur\ *v.* angered; angering. To make upset.

angina \an-JIE-nuh\ *n.* (Md) A symptom of illness characterized by a suffocating, painful inflammation.

angle \ANG-gul\ *n.* **1.** A corner formed by joining two lines. **2.** An opponent's position.

angry \ANG-gree\ *adj.* angrier; angriest. Being upset.

angst *n.* An anxious feeling.

anguish \ANG-gwish\ *n.* An intense distress. anguished *adj.*

angular \ANG-gyuh-lur\ *adj.* **1.** Having angles. **2.** Being lean and bony. angularity *n.*

animal \AN-uh-mul\ *n.* **1.** A mammal. **2.** A nonrational person.

animate \AN-uh-mayt\ *v.* animated; animating. **1.** To give life to. **2.** To give movement to. animated *adj.*

animation \an-uh-MAY-shun\ *n.* **1.**

The act of giving movement to. **2.** Film that gives life to non-moving object.

animosity \an-uh-MOS-i-tee\ *n. pl.* animosities. An ill will.

ankle \ANG-kul\ *n.* A joint joining the foot with a leg.

annals \AN-ulz\ *n. pl.* annals. A historical record of events.

annex \ah-NEKS\ *n.* An addition.

annex \an-NEKS\ *v.* annexed; annexing. To add onto a larger thing.

annihilate \un-NIE-uh-layt\ *v.* annihilated; annihilating. To destroy. annihilation *n.*

anniversary \an-uh-VUR-sur-ee\ *n. pl.* anniversaries. An annual occurrence of a notable event.

annotate \AN-uh-tayt\ *v.* annotated; annotating. To provide explanations. annotation *n.*

announce \uh-NOWNS\ *v.* announced; announcing. To state publicly. announcement *n.*; announcer *n.*

annoy \un-NOI\ *v.* annoyed; annoying. To bother. annoyance *n.*

annual \AN-yoo-ul\ *adj.* Occurring every year. annually *adv.*

annul \uh-NUL\ *v.* annulled; annulling. To make legally invalid. annulment *n.*

anoint \uh-NOINT\ *v.* anointed; anointing. To rub with oil, especially in religious rite. anointer *n.*; anointment *n.*

anomaly \uh-NOM-uh-lee\ *n. pl.* anomalies. A departure from the common way. anomalous *adj.*

anonymous \uh-NON-uh-mus\ *adj.* Having no identity. anonymously *adv.*

anorexia \an-uh-REK-see-uh\ *n.* (Md) A prolonged loss of appetite. anorexic *adj.*

another \uh-NUTH-ur\ *adj.* **1.** In addition. **2.** Different from the first. another *pron.*

answer \AN-sur\ *n.* A reply. answerable *adj.*

answer \AN-sur\ *v.* answered; answering. **1.** To reply. **2.** To be accountable.

ant *n.* An insect that lives in communities in the earth or in wood.

antagonize \an-TAG-uh-nize\ *v.* antagonized; antagonizing. **1.** To provoke another's anger. **2.** To oppose. antagonistic *adj.*; antagonism *n.*; antagonist *n.*

Antarctica \ant-AHRK-ti-kuh\ *n.* The continent surrounding the South pole. antarctic *adj.*

antebellum \AN-tee-BEL-um\ *adj.* Existing before the American Civil War.

antecedent \an-tuh-SEED-nt\ *n.* **1.**

An earlier event or condition. **2.** A noun that a pronoun replaces.

antediluvian \an-ti-di-LOO-vee-un\ *adj.* **1.** Existing before the Biblical flood. **2.** Old.

antelope \AN-tl-ohp\ *n. pl.* antelope or antelopes. A fast-running, long-horned, hoofed animal.

antenna \an-TEN-uh\ *n. pl.* antennae or antennas. A sensory rod.

anterior \an-TEER-ee-ur\ *adj.* **1.** Being in front. **2.** Being earlier.

anthem \AN-thum\ *n.* A sacred song usually of joy or praise.

anthology \an-THOL-uh-jee\ *n. pl.* anthologies. A collection or literary passages. anthological *adj.*; anthologize *v.*

anthropology \an-thruh-POL-uh-jee\ *n.* The study of the development of human beings. anthropological *adj.*; anthropologist *n.*

antiabortion \an-tee-uh-BOR-shun\ *adj.* Being against abortion. antiabortionist *n.*

antibiotic \an-ti-bie-OT-ik\ *n.* (Md) A substance designed to kill microorganisms.

antic \AN-tik\ *n.* A playful act.

anticipate \an-TIS-uh-payt\ *v.* anticipated; anticipating. **1.** To predict. **2.** To look forward to. anticipation *n.*

anticlimactic \an-ti-KLIE-mak-tik\ *adj.* Relating to a finale that was unexciting in comparison to the earlier events. anticlimax *n.*

antidote \AN-ti-doht\ *n.* A remedy that counteracts a poison.

antiestablishment \an-tee-es-TAB-lush-munt\ *adj.* Being against societal norms.

anti-inflammatory \an-tee-in-FLAM-uh-toh-ree\ *n.* A substance that counteracts inflammation.

antinuclear \an-te-NYOO-clee-ur\ *adj.* Being against nuclear power.

antipathy \an-TIP-uh-thee\ *n. pl.* antipathies. A dislike. antipathetic *adj.*

antique \an-TEEK\ *n.* A very old object.

antiquity \an-TIK-wi-tee\ *n. pl.* antiquities. Existing before the Middle Ages.

anti-Semitic \an-tee-suh-MIT-ik\ *adj.* Relating to the discrimination against Jews. anti-Semitism *n.*

antiseptic \an-tuh-SEP-tik\ *adj.* **1.** Being very clean. **2.** Opposing the growth and spread of germs.

antisocial \an-tee-SOH-shul\ *adj.* Not wanting other people's company.

antiwar \AN-te-war\ *adj.* Being against war.

antonym \AN-tuh-nim\ *n.* A word that opposes another word's meaning.

anvil \AN-vil\ *n.* A heavy metal block used for metal working.

anxiety \ang-ZIE-uh-tee\ *n. pl.* anxieties. An apprehensive mental state.

anxious \ANGK-shus\ *adj.* **1.** Worried. **2.** Impatient. anxiously *adv.*; anxiousness *n.*

any \EN-ee\ *adj.* Chosen indiscriminately.

anybody \EN-ee-bod-ee\ *pron.* Any one person.

anymore \EN-ee-MOHR\ *adv.* **1.** Any longer. **2.** Now.

anyone \EN-ee-wun\ *pron.* Any single person.

anyplace \EN-ee-plays\ *adv.* Any one location.

anything \EN-ee-thing\ *pron.* Any single object.

anyway \EN-ee-way\ *adv.* In any case.

anywhere \EN-ee-hwair\ *adv.* To any place.

aorta \ay-OR-tuh\ *n. pl.* aortas or aortae. (Md) The artery that transports blood away from the heart. aortic *adj.*

apart \uh-PAHRT\ *adj.* Being disconnected.

apart \uh-PAHRT\ *adv.* **1.** Sepa-rated. **2.** In pieces. **3.** Separately for some reason. **4.** Aside.

apartheid \uh-PAHR-tayt\ *n.* **1.** Racial segregation. **2.** Political policy of forced segregation.

apartment \uh-PAHRT-munt\ *n.* One or more rooms designed for living.

apathy \AP-uh-thee\ *n.* An indifference. apathetic *adj.*; apathetically *adv.*

ape \ayp\ *n.* A large tailless primate.

aperitif \uh-per-uh-TEEF\ *n.* (Fr) An alcoholic drink before dinner.

aperture \AP-ur-chuur\ *n.* A hole especially in a photographic lens.

apex \AY-peks\ *n. pl.* apexes or apices. The tip.

aphasia \uh-FAY-zhuh\ *n.* (Md) A bodily defect that causes speech problems. aphasic *adj.*; aphasic *n.*

aphid \AY-fid\ *n.* A small sluggish insect.

aphrodisiac \af-ruh-DIZ-ee-ak\ *n.* A food or drug that arouses sexual desire.

apiece \uh-PEES\ *adv.* Individually.

apology \uh-POL-uh-jee\ *n. pl.* apologies. **1.** A defense. **2.** An admission of being sorry for wrongdoing. apologetic *adj.*

apoplexy \AP-uh-plek-see\ *n.* (Md) A stroke.

apostle \uh-POS-ul\ *n.* One of Christ's twelve disciples.

apostrophe \uh-POS-truh-fee\ *n.* A punctuation mark indicating omitted letters or possession.

apothecary \uh-POTH-uh-ker-ee\ *n. pl.* apothecaries. **1.** A pharmacist. **2.** A pharmacy.

appall *also* **appal** \uh-PAWL\ *v.* appalled; appalling. To fill with horror or dismay. appalling *adj.*

apparatus \ap-uh-RAT-us\ *n. pl.* apparatuses or apparatus. Equipment designed for a purpose.

apparel \uh-PAR-ul\ *n.* **1.** Clothing. **2.** Parts of a ship.

apparent \uh-PAR-unt\ *adj.* **1.** Obvious. **2.** In view.

apparition \ap-uh-RISH-un\ *n.* A ghost.

appeal \un-PEEL\ *v.* appealed; appealing. **1.** [Le] To carry a case to a higher court for review. **2.** To plead or request.

appear \uh-PEER\ *v.* appeared; appearing. **1.** To seem. **2.** To come into sight. appearance *n.*

appease \uh-PEEZ\ *v.* appeased; appeasing. To pacify. appeasement *n.*

append \uh-PEND\ *v.* appended; appending. To attach. appendage *n.*

appendectomy \ap-un-DEK-tuh-mee\ *n. pl.* appendectomies. (Md) The surgical removal of an appendix.

appendix \un-PEN-diks\ *n. pl.* appendixes or appendicies. **1.** An addition or supplement. **2.** [Md] A tube attached to the large intestine.

appetite \AP-uh-tiet\ *n.* **1.** The desire for food. **2.** A craving.

appetizer \AP-uh-tie-zer\ *n.* Food or drink served prior to a meal.

applaud \uh-PLAWD\ *v.* applauded; applauding. To praise especially by clapping the hands.

apple \AP-ul\ *n.* **1.** A fleshy fruit. **2.** Similar fruit of a related species, such as crab apple.

appliance \uh-PLIE-uns\ *n.* A device designed for a particular use.

applicable \AP-li-kuh-bul\ *adj.* Appropriate. applicability *n.*

applicant \AP-li-kunt\ *n.* A person who applies.

application \ap-li-KAY-shun\ *n.* **1.** A request. **2.** A form used to make a request.

apply \uh-PLIE\ *v.* applied; applying. **1.** To put into action. **2.** To make a request. **3.** To concentrate.

appoint \uh-POINT\ *v.* appointed; appointing. **1.** To name for a position. **2.** To fix a time. **3.** To furnish.

appointment \uh-POINT-munt\ *n.*
1. A prearranged meeting. 2. Furnishings. 3. A nonelective position.

appraise \uh-PRAYZ\ *v.* appraised; appraising. To determine the value of. appraisal *n.*; appraiser *n.*

appreciate \uh-PREE-shee-ayt\ *v.* appreciated; appreciating. 1. To cherish. 2. To be grateful for. 3. To increase in value. appreciative *adj.*; appreciation *n.*

apprehend \ap-ri-HEND\ *v.* apprehended; apprehending. 1. To arrest. 2. To perceive. 3. To anticipate with fear.

apprehension \ap-ri-HEN-shun\ *n.* 1. The power of understanding. 2. An arrest. 3. A prediction of evil. apprehensible *adj.*

apprentice \uh-PREN-tis\ *n.* A beginner learning from an experienced worker. apprenticeship *n.*

approach \uh-PROHCH\ *n.* 1. The act of nearing. 2. A manner of working. 3. An access way. approachable *adj.*

approach \uh-PROHCH\ *v.* approached; approaching. 1. To near. 2. To propose to.

appropriate \uh-PROH-pree-it\ *adj.* Fitting. appropriately *adv.*

appropriate \uh-PROH-pree-ayt\ *v.* appropriated; appropriating. 1. To take hold of. 2. To separate for a certain use.

approve \uh-PROOV\ *v.* approved; approving. 1. To ratify. 2. To endorse. approvingly *adv.*; approval *n.*

approximate \uh-PROK-suh-mayt\ *v.* approximated; approximating. To come close to. approximation *n.*

apricot \AP-ri-kot\ *n.* A small orange-colored fruit.

April \AY-prul\ *n.* The fourth month of the year.

apron \AY-prun\ *n.* A garment worn over clothes to protect them from dirt.

apropos \ap-ruh-POH\ *adv.* (Fr) Relevantly.

apropos \ap-ruh-POH\ *adj.* (Fr) Relevant and timely.

apt *adj.* 1. Being able. 2. Having an inclination. 3. Being suitable.

aptitude \AP-ti-tood\ *n.* 1. An ability to learn quickly. 2. An inclination.

aquarium \uh-KWAIR-ee-um\ *n. pl.* aquariums or aquaria. A glass container for fish and/or plants.

aquatic \uh-KWAT-ik\ *adj.* Relating to water.

aqueduct \AK-wi-dukt\ *n.* A pathway for flowing water.

arabesque \ar-uh-BESK\ *n.* 1. An

ornamental pattern. **2.** A ballet posture.

arachnid \uh-RAK-nid\ *n.* (Sc) Any of a class of eight-legged arthropods, including spiders.

arbiter \AHR-bi-tur\ *n.* A judge.

arbitrary \AHR-bi-trer-ee\ *adj.* **1.** Being subjective. **2.** Being chosen without reason. arbitrarily *adv.*; arbitrariness *n.*

arbitrate \AHR-bi-trayt\ *v.* arbitrated; arbitrating. **1.** To judge. **2.** To submit for judgment.

arboretum \ahr-buh-REE-tum\ *n. pl.* arboretums or arboreta. A place for plant life to grow for study purposes.

arc \ahrk\ *n.* A portion of a curved line.

arcade \ahr-KAYD\ *n.* An arched passageway, especially one lined with stores.

arcane \ahr-KAYN\ *adj.* Secret.

arch \ahrch\ *n.* The curved structure going over an opening.

archaic \ahr-KAY-ik\ *adj.* Belonging to the past.

archangel \AHRK-ayn-jul\ *n.* A chief angel.

archbishop \AHRCH-BISH-up\ *n.* The highest ranked bishop.

archdiocese \ahrch-DIE-uh-sees\ *n.* The area of an archbishop's jurisdiction.

archeology *also* **archaeology** \ahr-KEE-oowl-oh-jee\ *n.* The study of relics to learn about humankind's past. archaeological *adj.*; archaeologist *n.*

archery \AHR-chur-ee\ *n.* The game of shooting a bow and arrow.

archetype \AHR-kuh-tiep\ *n.* The original.

archipelago \ahr-kuh-PEL-uh-goh\ *n. pl.* archipelagoes or archipelagos. An area of water containing islands.

architecture \AHR-ki-tek-chur\ *n.* The art of planning and constructing buildings or landscapes. architectural *adj.*

archive \AHR-kiev\ *n.* A place for preservation of documents.

Arctic \AHRK-tik\ *adj.* Relating to the north pole and its surrounding area.

ardor \AHR-dur\ *n.* A passion.

are \ahr\ *v.* Present second and third person of be.

area \AIR-ee-uh\ *n.* A defined or bounded surface.

arena \uh-REE-nuh\ *n.* An enclosed space used for entertainment or competition.

argue \AHR-gyoo\ *v.* argued; arguing. **1.** To explain. **2.** To dispute. **3.** to debate.

aria \AHR-ee-uh\ *n.* (Mu) A solo vocal piece that is accompanied by music and is part of a larger work.

arid \AR-id\ *adj.* Being very dry. aridity *n.*; aridness *n.*

arise \uh-RIEZ\ *v.* arose; arisen; arising. **1.** To get up. **2.** To come into existence.

aristocrat \uh-RIS-tuh-krat\ *n.* **1.** One belonging to a noble family. **2.** One who has rich tastes. aristocratic *adj.*; aristocracy *n.*

arithmetic \uh-RITH-muh-tik\ *n.* A branch of mathematics dealing with numbers.

ark \ahrk\ *n.* **1.** In the Bible, the boat of Noah. **2.** The chest holding the Ten Commandments.

arm \ahrm\ *n.* **1.** An upper limb. **2.** Armlike part or appendage.

armada \ahr-MAH-duh\ *n.* A group of warships.

armadillo \ah-muh-DIL-oh\ *n. pl.* armadillos. A burrowing mammal protected on the head and body with bony plates.

Armageddon \ahr-muh-GED-n\ *n.* The final battle between good and evil.

armament \AHR-muh-munt\ *n.* **1.** Military equipment. **2.** The preparation for battle.

armistice \AHR-mi-stis\ *n.* A truce.

armor \AHR-mur\ *n.* A protective covering for the body. armored *adj.*

armory \AHR-muh-ree\ *n. pl.* armories. A storage place for military equipment.

army \AHR-mee\ *n. pl.* armies. A group of people trained for combat.

aroma \uh-ROH-muh\ *n.* A pleasant smell. aromatic *adj.*

around \uh-ROWND\ *adv.* **1.** On every side. **2.** In a circular way. **3.** In the opposite direction. **4.** Nearby.

around \uh-ROWND\ *prep.* **1.** On all sides. **2.** Encircling. **3.** Near.

arouse \uh-ROWZ\ *v.* aroused; arousing. **1.** To wake up. **2.** To excite. arousal *n.*

arraign \uh-RAYN\ *v.* arraigned; arraigning. **1.** To summon to a court. **2.** To blame. arraignment *n.*

arrange \uh-RAYNJ\ *v.* arranged; arranging. **1.** To organize. **2.** To reach an agreement. **3.** To change or adapt a musical piece. arrangement *n.*

array \uh-RAY\ *n.* **1.** An arrangement. **2.** Data arranged in rows and columns. **3.** Lavish atttire.

arrest \uh-REST\ *v.* arrested; arresting. **1.** To seize. **2.** To stop.

arrhythmia \uh-RITH-mee-uh\ *n.* (Md) An irregular heartbeat.

arrive \uh-RIEV\ *v.* arrived; arriving. **1.** To reach the end. **2.** To become successful. arrival *n.*

arrogant \AR-uh-gunt\ *adj.* Offensively proud.

arrow \AR-oh\ *n.* **1.** A slender missile shot from a bow. **2.** A mark used to show direction.

arsenal \AHR-suh-nl\ *n.* **1.** Government place for making and storing arms. **2.** A collection or store.

arsenic \AHR-suh-nik\ *n.* A poison.

arson \AHR-sun\ *n.* The illegal burning of property. arsonist *n.*

art \ahrt\ *n.* **1.** An acquired skill. **2.** The making of pleasing works. **3.** Literature, music, etc.

Art Deco \ahrt-DEK-oh\ *n.* An artistic style of the 1920s and 1930s. art deco *adj.*

arteriosclerosis \ahr-TEER-ee-oh-skluh-ROH-sis\ *n.* (Md) A hardening of the arteries.

artery \AHR-tuh-ree\ *n.* (Md) **1.** Any muscular vessels that take blood from the heart to other parts. **2.** Route.

arthritis \ahr-THRIE-tis\ *n. pl.* arthritides. (Md) A joint inflammation. arthritic *adj.*

artichoke \AHR-tuh-chohk\ *n.* A vegetable with an edible heart and leaves.

article \AHR-ti-kul\ *n.* **1.** A piece of writing. **2.** An element in a class. **3.** The words a, an, the.

articulate \ahr-TIK-yuh-late\ *v.* articulated; articulating. **1.** To state clearly. **2.** To connect. articulation *n.*

artificial \ahr-tuh-FISH-ul\ *adj.* **1.** Not real. **2.** Man-made. artificially *adv.*; artificiality *n.*; artificialness *n.*

artillery \ahr-TIL-uh-ree\ *n. pl.* artilleries. Military arms.

artist \AHR-tist\ *n.* **1.** One who is skilled. **2.** One who creates.

artistic \ahr-TIS-tik\ *adj.* **1.** Having skill. **2.** Having aesthetic qualities. artistically *adv.*

Art Nouveau \ahrt-NOO-voh\ *n.* (Fr) A late nineteenth century style.

arugula \ahr-OO-gyoo-luh\ *n.* A peppery salad green.

as \az\ *pron.* **1.** That. **2.** Who. **3.** Which.

as \az\ *conj.* **1.** Like. **2.** While. **3.** Since. **4.** Though.

ascent \uh-SENT\ *n.* **1.** A climb. **2.** A social advance. **3.** A degree of elevation.

ascertain \as-ur-TAYN\ *v.* ascertained; ascertaining. To discover through inquiry.

ascetic \uh-SET-ik\ *adj.* Denying

physical desires for spiritual development. asceticism *n.*

ascorbic acid \as-KOR-bik-AS-id\ *n.* (Sc) Vitamin C.

asexual \ay-SEK-shoo-ul\ *adj.* **1.** Lacking sexuality. **2.** Reproduced without sexual contact. asexually *adv.*

ash *n.* **1.** The remains of burned substances. **2.** A symbol of grief. **3.** A kind of tree.

ashamed \uh-SHAYMD\ *adj.* **1.** Feeling guilt. **2.** Experiencing unworthiness. **3.** Deterred by shame.

ashen \ASH-un\ *adj.* **1.** Relating to ashes. **2.** Being very pale.

ashore \uh-SHOR\ *adv.* On the shore.

Asia \AY-zhuh\ *n.* A large continent in the northern hemisphere.

Asian-American \AY-zhun-uh-MER-i-kun\ *n.* An American descended from Asian ancestors. Asian American *adj.*

aside \uh-SIDE\ *adv.* **1.** Away from a group. **2.** To one side.

ask *v.* asked; asking. **1.** To inquire. **2.** To request. **3.** To invite. **4.** To price.

askew \uh-SKYOO\ *adv.* Crookedly askew *adj.*

asleep \uh-SLEEP\ *adj.* Sleeping. asleep *adv.*

asparagus \uh-SPAR-uh-gus\ *n. pl.* asparagus. The edible green stalk of a cultivated perennial.

aspartame \as-PAR-tame\ *n.* (Sc) A low-calorie, artificial sweetener.

aspect \AS-pekt\ *n.* **1.** An angle. **2.** An appearance.

asphalt \AS-fawlt\ *n.* A dark material used in pavement, paint, and other products.

asphyxiate \as-FIK-see-ayt\ *v.* asphyxiated; asphyxiating. To prevent normal breathing. asphyxiation *n.*

aspiration \as-puh-RAY-shun\ *n.* **1.** A drawing in, especially of breath. **2.** An ambition.

aspire \uh-SPIER\ *v.* aspired; aspiring. **1.** To seek a goal. **2.** To ascend.

aspirin \AS-pur-in\ *n. pl.* aspirin or aspirins. A pain reliever.

ass *n.* **1.** A donkey. **2.** [Sl] A foolish person. **3.** [Sl] The buttocks.

assail \uh-SAYL\ *v.* assailed; assailing. To assault, especially with words.

assassin \uh-SAS-in\ *n.* A paid killer.

assassinate \uh-SAS-uh-nayt\ *v.* assassinated; assassinating. To kill an important person. assassination *n.*

assault \uh-SAWLT\ *v.* assaulted; assaulting. To attack. attack *n.*

assemble \uh-SEM-bul\ *v.* assembled; assembling. **1.** To congregate. **2.** To put together.

assembly \uh-SEM-blee\ *n.* **1.** A congregation. **2.** Manufacturing process. **3.** A fitting together.

assent \uh-SENT\ *v.* assented; assenting. To agree.

assert \uh-SURT\ *v.* asserted; asserting. To insist.

assertiveness training \uh-SUR-tiv-nus-TRAY-ning\ *n.* The learning of self-confident behavior.

assess \uh-SES\ *v.* assessed; assessing. **1.** To estimate the value of property. **2.** To judge.

asset \AS-et\ *n.* A resource.

assiduous \uh-SIJ-oo-us\ *adj.* Hard-working. assiduously *adv.*; assiduousness *n.*

assign \uh-SIEN\ *v.* assigned; assigning. **1.** To ask to complete. **2.** To differentiate. **3.** To appoint. **4.** To give property. assignment *n.*

assimilate \uh-SIM-uh-layt\ *v.* assimilated; assimilating. **1.** To become similar. **2.** To digest. assimilation *n.*

assist \uh-SIST\ *v.* assisted; assisting. To aid. assistance *n.*; assistant *n.*

associate \uh-SOH-shee-it\ *n.* **1.** A partner. **2.** [Cap] A two-year degree. association *n.*

associate \uh-SOH-shee-ayt\ *v.* associated; associating. **1.** To start a relationship. **2.** To make a connection.

assortment \uh-SORT-munt\ *n.* An array.

assume \uh-SOOM\ *v.* assumed; assuming. **1.** To take on or into. **2.** To fake. **3.** To take for granted. assumption *n.*

assure \uh-SHUUR\ *v.* assured; assuring. **1.** To convince. **2.** To guarantee. **3.** To promise. assurance *n.*

asterisk \AS-tuh-risk\ *n.* A symbol used as a reference mark.

astern \uh-STURN\ *adv.* **1.** Toward the back of a ship. **2.** Backward.

asteroid \AS-tu-roid\ *n.* **1.** A small planet. **2.** A starfish.

asthma \AZ-muh\ *n.* (Md) A condition marked by labored breathing. asthmatic *adj.*; asthmatic *n.*

astonish \uh-STON-ish\ *v.* astonished; astonishing. To greatly impress. astonishment *n.*

astray \uh-STRAY\ *adv.* **1.** Off the path. **2.** Into wrongdoing. astray *adj.*

astringent \uh-STRIN-junt\ *n.* A substance that shrinks body tissue. astringent *adj.*; astringency *n.*

astrolabe \AS-truh-layb\ *n.* A instrument for studying celestial bodies.

astrology \uh-STROL-uh-jee\ *n.* The forecasting of events based on the study of stars and planets. astrological *adj.*; astrologer *n.*

astronaut \AS-truh-nawt\ *n.* One trained to travel in and study space.

astronomy \uh-STRON-uh-mee\ *n.* The study of the solar system. astronomic *adj.*; astronomical *adj.*; astronomer *n.*

Astroturf \AS-troh-turf\ *n.* Artificial grass.

asylum \uh-SIE-lum\ *n.* **1.** A care institution for mentally ill. **2.** A place of refuge.

asymmetric *also* **asymmetrical** \ay-si-MEH-trik\ *adj.* Not balanced. assymetry *n.*

at *prep.* **1.** On. **2.** Near. **3.** In.

atheism \AY-thee-i-zum\ *n.* A belief that denies God. atheist *n.*

athlete \ATH-leet\ *n.* One trained for physical endurance, strength, or skill. athletic *adj.*; athletically *adv.*; athleticism *n.*

atlas \AT-lus\ *n.* A collection of maps.

atmosphere \AT-mus-feer\ *n.* **1.** The gaseous layer surrounding the Earth. **2.** A mood. atmospheric *adj.*

atoll \AT-ol\ *n.* A coral island that surrounds a lagoon.

atom \AT-um\ *n.* **1.** [Sc] The tiniest particle in a chemical element. **2.** A minute particle.

atomic \uh-TOM-ik\ *adj.* **1.** [Sc] Relating to the tiniest particle in a chemical element. **2.** Being small.

atone \uh-TOHN\ *v.* atoned; atoning. To make up for wrongdoing.

atrium \AY-tree-um\ *n. pl.* atria or atriums. **1.** A central area. **2.** [Md] One of the chambers of the heart. **3.** A court or hall.

atrocious \uh-TROH-shus\ *adj.* Offensive. atrocity *n.*

atrophy \A-truh-fee\ *n. pl.* atrophies. The wearing away of body tissues.

attach \uh-TACH\ *v.* attached; attaching. **1.** To connect. **2.** To attribute. **3.** To associate.

attaché \a-ta-SHAY\ *n.* (Fr) **1.** An expert serving an ambassador. **2.** A carrying case.

attack \uh-TAK\ *v.* attacked; attacking. **1.** To assault with force. **2.** To verbally put down. **3.** To begin work. attack *n.*

attain \uh-TAYN\ *v.* attained; attaining. To achieve. attainable *adj.*

attempt \uh-TEMPT\ *v.* attempted; attempting. To try.

attend \uh-TEND\ *v.* attended; attending. **1.** To care for. **2.** To be connected with. **3.** To be at. **4.** To pay attention to.

attendant \uh-TEN-dunt\ *n.* One who waits on another.

attention \uh-TEN-shun\ *n.* **1.** The application of one's conscious powers to. **2.** A taking notice of. attentive *adj.*; attentively *adv.*; attentiveness *n.*

attenuate \uh-TEN-yoo-ayt\ *v.* attenuated; attenuating. **1.** To make slender. **2.** To weaken.

attic \AT-ik\ *n.* The uppermost space in a house.

attire \uh-TIER\ *v.* attired; attiring. To dress.

attire \uh-TIER\ *n.* One's clothes.

attitude \AT-i-tood\ *n.* **1.** One's subjective state. **2.** A posture.

attorney \uh-TUR-nee\ *n. pl.* attorneys. A lawyer.

attract \uh-TRAKT\ *v.* attracted; attracting. To entice. attraction *n.*

attractive \uh-TRAK-tiv\ *adj.* Possessing enticing qualities. attractively *adv.*; attractiveness *n.*

attribute \A-trib-yoot\ *n.* A distinctive quality.

atypical \ay-TIP-i-kul\ *adj.* Not regular. atypically *adv.*

auburn \AW-burn\ *adj.* Reddish brown.

auction \AWK-shun\ *n.* The sale of items to the highest bidder. auctioneer *n.*; auction *v.*

audacity \aw-DAS-i-tee\ *n.* audacities. A boldness.

audible \AW-duh-bul\ *adj.* Able to be heard.

audience \AW-dee-uns\ *n.* **1.** A group of listeners. **2.** An interview.

audio \AW-dee-oh\ *adj.* (Sc) Relating to sound.

audiocassette \AW-dee-oh-kas-SET\ *n.* (Mu) A sound recording on a tape mounted in a frame.

audiotape \AW-dee-oh-TAPE\ *n.* (Mu) Sound recording.

audit \AW-dit\ *n.* (Bs) An official review of books.

audition \aw-DISH-un\ *n.* A trial for a performance part.

auditorium \aw-di-TOR-ee-um\ *n.* An area used for entertainment or public gatherings.

augment \awg-MENT\ *v.* augmented; augmenting. To supplement.

au gratin \oh-GRAW-tin\ *adj.* Covered with bread crumbs or cheese.

August \AW-gust\ *n.* The eighth month of the year.

au naturel \OH-nat-yoo-rel\ *adj.* (Fr) Naked.

aunt \ant\ *n.* One's father's or mother's sister.

au pair \oh-PAIR\ *n. pl.* au pairs. (Fr) A foreign person who does house keeping in exchange for room and board.

aura \OR-uh\ *n.* A particular atmosphere around an object.

aural \OR-ul\ *adj.* Related to the ear.

aureole *also* **aureola** \OR-ee-ohl\ *n.* **1.** A radiant light around a sacred person. **2.** A corona.

aurora borealis \aw-ROR-uh-bor-ee-AL-is\ *n.* (Sc) A natural light display in the Earth's northern hemisphere.

austere \aw-STEER\ *adj.* **1.** Severe. **2.** Strict. **3.** Unadorned. austerity *n.*

Australia \AW-stray-lee-uh\ *n.* A large continent in Southern hemisphere.

authentic \aw-THEN-tik\ *adj.* Being original. authentically *adv.*; authenticity *n.*

author \AW-thur\ *n.* One that originates a written work. authoritative *adj.*

authoritarian \uh-thor-i-TAIR-ee-un\ *adj.* **1.** Relating to concentrated power. **2.** Unquestionably in power. authoritative *adj.*

authority \uh-THOR-i-tee\ *n. pl.* authorities. **1.** An expert. **2.** A source of expert information. **3.** One in power.

authorize \AW-thuh-riez\ *v.* authorized; authorizing. **1.** To empower. **2.** To allow.

autism \AW-tiz-um\ *n.* A mental disorder marked by a withdrawal from reality. autistic *adj.*

auto \AW-toh\ *n. pl.* autos. A car.

autobiography \aw-tuh-bie-OG-ruh-fee\ *n.* A book about the writer's life. autobiographical *adj.*; autobiographer *n.*

autocracy \aw-TOK-ruh-see\ *n. pl.* autocracies. A government run by an absolute ruler. autocratic *adj.*; autocrat *n.*

autograph \AW-tuh-graf\ *n.* **1.** A handwritten signature. **2.** An original work.

autoimmune disorder \aw-TOH-im-MYOON-dis-OR-dur\ *n.* An illness in which the body's ability to fight irritants fails.

automate \AW-tuh-mayt\ *v.* automated; automating. **1.** To work mechanistically. **2.** To make something mechanical. automatic *adj.*; automatically *adv.*

automobile \aw-tuh-muh-BEEL\ *n.* A car.

autonomic \aw-tuh-NOM-ik\ *adj.* Acting involuntarily.

autonomous \aw-TON-uh-mus\ *adj.* **1.** Being self-contained. **2.** Being independent. autonomously *adv.*; autonomy *n.*

autopsy \AW-top-see\ *n. pl.* autopsies. The examination of a corpse.

autumn \AW-tum\ *n.* The season from the fall equinox to the winter solstice. autumnal *adj.*

auxiliary \awg-ZIL-yuh-ree\ *adj.* Being supplementary.

avail \uh-VAYL\ *v.* availed; availing. To be helpful. avail *n.*

available \uh-VAY-luh-bul\ *adj.* Being accessible.

avalanche \AV-uh-lanch\ *n.* A sudden collapse of snow, ice, rock, and earth.

avant-garde \uh-vahnt-GAHRD\ *n.* A group of thinkers who develop new ideas, especially in the arts. avant-garde *adj.*

avarice \AV-uh-ris\ *n.* Greediness. avaricious *adj.*

avenue \AV-uh-nyoo\ *n.* A passageway.

average \AV-ur-ij\ *adj.* **1.** Common. **2.** Coming near a mathematical average. **3.** Between two extremes. average *v.*

average \AV-ur-ij\ *n.* A mathematical mean.

averse \uh-VURS\ *adj.* Opposing.

avert \uh-VURT\ *v.* averted; averting. **1.** To look away. **2.** To avoid.

aviary \AY-vee-er-ee\ *n. pl.* aviaries. A place to house birds.

aviator \AY-vee-ay-tur\ *n.* One who operates an aircraft.

avid \AV-id\ *adj.* Eager. avidly *adv.*

avocado \av-uh-KAH-doh\ *n. pl.* avocados or avocadoes. A green, oily fruit.

avocation \av-uh-KAY-shun\ *n.* **1.** One's employment. **2.** One's hobby.

avoid \ah-VOID\ *v.* avoided; avoiding. **1.** To shun. **2.** To stop a future event. avoidable *adj.*; avoidance *n.*

await \uh-WAYT\ *v.* awaited; awaiting. To wait for.

awake \uh-WAYK\ *v.* awoke or awaked or awoken; awaking. To stop sleeping. awakening *n.*

award \uh-WORD\ *v.* awarded; awarding. **1.** To give in praise. **2.** To judge. award *n.*

aware \uh-WAIR\ *adj.* Having knowledge. awareness *n.*

away \uh-WAY\ *adj.* **1.** Being gone. **2.** Being at a distance.

away \uh-WAY\ *adv.* **1.** At a distance. **2.** To a new location.

awe \aw\ *n.* A wonder. awesome *adj.*; awe *v.*

awful \AW-ful\ *adj.* Very bad. awfully *adv.*

awhile \uh-HWILE\ *adv.* For a little time.

awkward \AWK-wurd\ *adj.* **1.** Being clumsy. **2.** Being hard to handle. **3.** Lacking comfort. **4.** Embarassing.

awning \AW-ning\ *n.* A covering.

awry \uh-RIE\ *adv.* Off the right course. awry *adj.*

ax *also* **axe** \aks\ *n.* **1.** A handheld chopping tool. **2.** Ax to grind [Id]: A personal problem to resolve.

axiom \AK-see-um\ *n.* A statement of an established truth. axiomatic *adj.*

axis \AK-sis\ *n. pl.* axes. **1.** A straight line bisecting a rotating body. **2.** A central line. **3.** Partnership.

axle \AK-sul\ *n.* A rod around which wheels rotate.

ayatollah \IE-uh-toh-luh\ *n.* (Ar) A Muslim religious leader.

aye *also* **ay** \IE\ *n. pl.* ayes. Yes.

azalea \uh-ZAYL-yuh\ *n.* A plant with funnel-shaped flowers.

B

b \bee\ *n. pl.* b's or bs. **1.** The second letter of the English alphabet. **2.** [Cap] Second in letter grades.

babble \BAB-ul\ *v.* babbled; babbling. **1.** To mutter trivially. **2.** To talk endlessly. babble *n.*; babbler *n.*

baboon \ba-BOON\ *n.* A large terrestrial monkey of Africa and Asia with a doglike muzzle.

babushka \buh-BUUSH-kuh\ *n.* (Fo) A head covering.

baby \BAY-bee\ *n. pl.* babies. **1.** An infant. **2.** [Sl] One who acts immaturely. babyish *adj.* babyhood *n.*

baby \BAY-bee\ *v.* babied; babying. To take excessive care of.

baby boom \BAY-bee-BOOM\ *n.* A period during which many babies are born.

baby-sit \BAY-bee-sit\ *v.* baby-sat; baby-sitting. To watch over children. baby-sitter *n.*

baccalaureate \bak-uh-LOR-ee-it\ *n.* **1.** A university degree. **2.** A speech for graduating students.

bacchanal \bah-kuh-NAHL\ *n.* **1.** A festive party. **2.** One who frequents festive parties.

bachelor \BACH-uh-lur\ *n.* **1.** An undergraduate degree or person holding one. **2.** An unmarried man. bachelorhood *n.*

bachelorette \BACH-uh-lur-et\ *n.* An unmarried female adult.

bacillus \buh-SIL-us\ *n. pl.* bacilli.

(Md) Any of a group of rod-shaped microorganisms.

back \bak\ *adv.* **1.** Away from the front. **2.** In return; reverse. **3.** In or toward former condition.

back \bak\ *n.* **1.** The part of the body nearest the spine. **2.** The backbone. **3.** The reverse side. back *adj.*

back \bak\ *v.* backed; backing. **1.** To go in an opposite way. **2.** To endorse. **3.** To make up the posterior side of.

backache \BAK-ayk\ *n.* A pain in one's back.

backbone \BAK-bohn\ *n.* **1.** The spine or vertebral column. **2.** Strength of character.

backer \BAK-ur\ *n.* One who endorses, especially through financial support.

backfire \BAK-fier\ *n.* A bang caused by the early ignition of fuel in the cylinder of an engine.

backfire \BAK-fier\ *v.* backfired; backfiring. **1.** To explode due to premature ignition of fuel. **2.** To have an unwelcome result.

back down \bak-DOWN\ *v.* To retreat from an assertion.

backgammon \BAK-gam-un\ *n.* A board game for two persons, with moves determined by dice throws.

backlash \BAK-lash\ *n.* **1.** A quick whipping movement in reaction to a motion. **2.** A negative reaction.

backlog \BAK-log\ *n.* A buildup of unfinished work.

backpack \BAK-pak\ *n.* A bag carried on one's back.

backpack \BAK-pak\ *v.* backpacked; backpacking. To hike while carrying one's camping equipment in a bag worn on the back. backpacker *n.*

backside \BAK-side\ *n.* The rear end.

backstage \BAK-stayg\ *adj.* **1.** Relating to the area behind a stage. **2.** Relating to action behind the scenes.

back-street *n.* A street not heavily traveled.

back talk \bak-TAWK\ *n.* A disrespectful reply.

back up *v.* **1.** To become congested. **2.** To support; accompany. **3.** [Cm] To copy computer data.

backup \BAK-up\ *n.* **1.** A substitute. **2.** A congested area. **3.** A musical accompaniment.

backward \BAK-wurd\ *adj.* **1.** Inverted. **2.** Timid. **3.** Underdeveloped.

backward *also* **backwards** \BAK-wurd\ *adv.* **1.** Toward the rear. **2.**

With the back facing ahead . **3.** In an opposite way. backwardness *n.*

backyard \BAK-YARD\ *n.* The area behind a house.

bacteriology \bak-teer-ee-OL-uh-jee\ *n.* (Md) The study of bacteria. bacteriologist *n.*

bacterium \bak-TEER-ee-um\ *n. pl.* bacteria. Any of many unicellular microorganisms, some harmless, some disease-causing. bacterial *adj.*

bad *adj.* worse; worst. **1.** Of poor quality. **2.** Dangerous. **3.** Corrupt. **4.** Disobedient. **5.** Full of decay. badly *adv.*

badge \baj\ *n.* **1.** Something worn to display rank. **2.** [Sl] A police officer.

badger \BAJ-ur\ *n.* A burrowing mammal.

badger \BAJ-ur\ *v.* badgered; badgering. To persistently bother.

badminton \BAD-min-tn\ *n.* A court game played by volleying a shuttlecock over a net with rackets.

bad-mouth \BAD-mowth\ *v.* bad-mouthed; bad-mouthing. To give unfair criticism.

baffle \BAF-ul\ *n.* Something used to direct the flow of something.

baffle \BAF-ul\ *v.* baffled; baffling. To confuse. bafflement *n.*; baffler *n.*

bag *n.* A flexible container used for storing or carrying purchases or possessions.

bag *v.* bagged; bagging. **1.** To trap. **2.** To kill. **3.** To drop loosely. baggy *adj.*; bagginess *n.*

bagel \BAY-gul\ *n.* A chewy doughnut-shaped roll.

baggage \BAG-ij\ *n.* **1.** Luggage. **2.** Something mental or physical that weighs down.

bagpipe \BAG-piep\ *n. pl.* bagpipes. (Mu) A reed instrument with several pipes through which air is forced via a bag. bagpiper *n.*

baguette \ba-GET\ *n.* (Fr) **1.** A slender loaf of bread. **2.** A rectangular gem.

bail \bayl\ *n.* [Le] Security given for a debt or default, esp. for a person under arrest.

bail \bayl\ *v.* bailed; bailing. **1.** To remove water from a boat. **2.** [Id] To abandon.

bailiff \BAY-lif\ *n.* (Le) An official employed to protect prisoners and keep the courtroom in order.

bailout \BAYL-owt\ *n.* A financial rescue.

bait \bayt\ *v.* baited; baiting. **1.** To put out food to catch prey. **2.** To tempt. **3.** To provoke.

bait \bayt\ *n.* **1.** A food used to attract prey. **2.** A lure.

bake \bayk\ *v.* baked; baking. To cook by exposing to dry heat.

baker \BAY-kur\ *n.* One who cooks goods.

bakery \BAY-kuh-ree\ *n. pl.* bakeries. A shop selling baked goods.

balance \BAL-uns\ *n.* **1.** A weighing instrument. **2.** Something that equalizes **3.** An even state.

balance \BAL-uns\ *v.* balanced; balancing. **1.** To weigh. **2.** To set 2 or more entities equal. **3.** To compare. **4.** To offset.

balance sheet \BAL-uns-sheet\ *n.* A financial statement.

balcony \BAL-kuh-nee\ *n. pl.* balconies. A porch built on an upper story that overlooks the area below.

bald \bawld\ *adj.* **1.** Having little to no hair on the head. **2.** Unadorned. balding *adj.*; baldness *n.*; bald *v.*

bale \bayl\ *n.* A large package of goods.

balk \bawk\ *v.* balked; balking. **1.** To stop short and refuse to continue. **2.** To obstruct. balky *adj.*; balk *n.*

Balkan \BAWL-kun\ *adj.* Relating to the countries of the Balkan Peninsula.

ball \bawl\ *n.* **1.** A spherical object.

2. Any such object used in a number of games.

ballad \BAL-ud\ *n.* (Mu) **1.** A narrative folk poem. **2.** A slow love song. balladeer *n.*

ballast \BAL-ust\ *n.* A heavy object used for balancing a ship or balloon. ballast *v.*

ballerina \bal-uh-REE-nuh\ *n.* A female ballet dancer.

ballet \ba-LAY\ *n.* A graceful, athletic dance set to music.

ballet dancer \ba-LAY-dans-ur\ *n.* A person who performs a ballet.

ballistic \buh-LIS-tiks\ *adj.* Relating to the study of moving projectiles. ballistics *n.*

balloon \buh-LOON\ *n.* A bag that inflates when a gaseous material is inserted.

balloon \buh-LOON\ *v.* ballooned; ballooning. **1.** To travel in a balloon. **2.** To billow out.

ballot \BAL-ut\ *n.* **1.** A paper on which a vote is cast. **2.** Act of voting. **3.** A list of candidates.

ballpark *adj.* Being approximate.

ballpark *n.* A place where ball games are played.

balm \bahm\ *n.* **1.** A healing salve. **2.** A type of plant.

balmy \BAH-mee\ *adj.* balmier; balmiest. **1.** Mild. **2.** Crazy.

baloney \bah-LOH-nee\ *n.* **1.** A type of lunch meat. **2.** Nonsense.

balsa \BAWL-suh\ *n.* A light, durable wood of a tree native to tropical America.

Baltic \BAWL-tik\ *adj.* Relating to the area around the Baltic Sea.

bamboo \bam-BOO\ *n. pl.* bamboos. A woody grass with hollow stems.

bamboozle \bam-BOO-zul\ *v.* bamboozled; bamboozling. To deceive.

ban *v.* banned; banning. To officially suppress. ban *n.*

banal \buh-NAL\ *adj.* Unoriginal. banality *n.*

banana \ba-NA-nuh\ *n.* A tropical plant with long, yellow tubular fruit.

band *n.* **1.** A group, especially of musicians. **2.** A flexible strip of material.

band *v.* banded; banding. To unite.

bandage \BAN-dij\ *n.* A strip of material used to bind a wound. bandage *v.*

bandanna *also* **bandana** \ban-DAN-uh\ *n.* A large kerchief.

bandit \BAN-dit\ *n.* A thief, especially one who commits crimes while on the run.

bane \bayn\ *n.* An origin of harm. baneful *adj.*

bang *n.* **1.** A sudden loud noise. **2.** A hard hit. **3.** An exciting event.

bang *v.* banged; banging. To bring together sharply.

bangle \BANG-gul\ *n.* A decorative bracelet.

banish \BAN-ish\ *v.* banished; banishing. **1.** To force one to leave a country. **2.** To expel. banishment *n.*

banister \BAN-uh-stur\ *n.* A guide rail, usually alongside stairs.

banjo \BAN-joh\ *n. pl.* banjos or banjoes. A stringed instrument with a hollow round body and a long neck.

bank \bangk\ *n.* **1.** A mound or ridge. **2.** A steep slope. **3.** An institution dealing with money.

bank \bangk\ *v.* banked; banking. **1.** To enclose or heap up. **2.** To do business with a financial institution.

bank on *v.* To rely on.

bankrupt \BANGK-rupt\ *adj.* **1.** Lacking finances. **2.** Without morals. bankruptcy *n.*

banquet \BANG-kwit\ *n.* A large formal dinner. banquet *v.*

banshee \BAN-shee\ *n.* **1.** A female spirit who warns of death. **2.** A wailing woman.

banter \BAN-tur\ *n.* A teasing speech. banter *v.*

banzai \bahn-ZIE\ *n.* (Fo) A Japanese war cry or cheer.

baptism \BAP-tiz-um\ *n.* A Christian rite using water to remove original sin. baptismal *adj.*; baptize *v.*

Baptist \BAP-tist\ *n.* A Protestant who advocates baptism.

baptistery *also* **baptistry** \BAP-tis-tree\ *n. pl.* baptisteries or baptistries. A church's area used for baptisms.

bar \bahr\ *n.* **1.** A straight length of material. **2.** A formed block of something. **3.** A barrier.

bar \bahr\ *v.* barred; barring. **1.** To prohibit. **2.** To fasten with a length of sturdy material.

bar code *n.* A series of lines and bars on an object that identifies it on a machine.

bar mitzvah \bahr-MITS-vuh\ *n.* A Jewish male who has reached the age of religious responsibility; the ceremony.

barbaric \bahr-BAR-ik\ *adj.* **1.** Concerning a people believed to be inferior to one's own group. **2.** Crude. barbarian *adj.*; barbarous *adj.*; barbarian *n.*; barbarism *n.*; barbarity *n.*

barbecue \BAHR-bi-kyoo\ *n.* **1.** A portable outdoor fireplace used for cooking. **2.** A cookout.

barbecue \BAHR-bi-kyoo\ *v.* barbecued; barbecuing. To roast over an open fire.

barbed wire *also* **barbwire** *n.* A bunch of wires with sharp points.

barbell *n.* An adjustable weight-lifting device.

barber \BAHR-bur\ *n.* A hairdresser, especially for men.

barbiturate \bahr-BICH-ur-it\ *n.* (Md) A drug that sedates.

bare \bair\ *adj.* barer; barest. **1.** Having no clothes on. **2.** Exposed. **3.** Plain. **4.** Just enough. barely *adv.*; bareness *n.*; bare *v.*

barefoot *also* **bare footed** \BAIR-fuut\ *adv.* Without foot coverings. barefoot *adj.*

bargain \BAHR-gun\ *n.* **1.** A 2-party agreement. **2.** A purchase where the buyer profits in some way. bargainer *n.*; bargain *v.*

bargaining chip \BAHR-guh-ning chip\ *n.* An item used for wagering.

barge \bahrj\ *n.* A flat-bottomed work boat.

barge \bahrj\ *v.* barged; barging. **1.** To transport on a flat-bottomed boat. **2.** To burst in thoughtlessly.

baritone \BAR-i-tohn\ *n.* (Mu) A range of notes between bass and tenor.

barium \BAR-ee-um\ *n.* A toxic silver-white metallic element.

bark \bahrk\ *n.* **1.** The exterior of a tree. **2.** The noise dogs make.

bark \bahrk\ *v.* barked; barking. **1.** To sound as a dog does. **2.** To speak suddenly and loudly.

barley \BAHR-lee\ *n.* A cereal grass whose seeds are edible and used in malt beverages.

bar mitzvah \bar-MITS-vuh\ *n.* A Jewish male who has reached 13 years of age and accepts religious duty; the ceremony.

barn \bahrn\ *n.* A farm building used to shelter harvested goods and animals.

barnstorm \BAHRN-storm\ *v.* barnstormed; barnstorming. **1.** To tour and/or perform in rural areas. **2.** To tour as a political candidate.

barometer \buh-ROM-i-tur\ *n.* An instrument used to determine atmospheric pressure. barometric *adj.*; barometrical *adj.*; barometry *n.*

baron \BAR-un\ *n.* A low-ranking member of English nobility.

baronness \BAR-uh-nis\ *n.* **1.** A baron's wife or widow. **2.** A low-ranking female member of English nobility.

baroque \buh-ROHK\ *adj.* Relating to the ornate artistic seventeenth century style.

barracks \BAR-uks\ *n. pl.* bar-racks. The buildings used to shelter soldiers.

barracuda \bar-uh-KOO-duh\ *n. pl.* barracuda or barracudas. **1.** A large vicious warm-water fish. **2.** [Sl] An unscrupulous person.

barrage \buh-RAHZH\ *n.* (Fr) **1.** An outpouring of artillery fire. **2.** A bombardment of something.

barrel \BAR-ul\ *n.* **1.** A cylindrical vessel. **2.** The amount contained in such a vessel.

barren \BAR-un\ *adj.* **1.** Unable to produce. **2.** Uninspiring. barrenness *n.*

barricade \BAR-i-kayd\ *n.* An obstacle.

barricade \BAR-i-kayd\ *v.* barricaded; barricading. To block off.

barrier \BAR-ee-ur\ *n.* Something that obstructs.

barter \BAHR-tur\ *v.* bartered; bartering. To exchange goods and/or services. barter *n.*; barterer *n.*

basal \BAY-sul\ *adj.* **1.** Relating to a base. **2.** Concerning something fundamental.

basalt \buh-SAWLT\ *n.* An igneous rock.

base \bays\ *adj.* baser; basest. Being disreputable. basely *adv.*; baseness *n.*

base \bays\ *n. pl.* bases. **1.** Bottom. **2.** Basic principle. **3.** Starting

point. **4.** A chemical compound.
basely *adv.*; baseness *n.*

baseline \BAYS-line\ *n.* **1.** A starting point. **2.** A field marking in baseball and other games.

basement \BAYS-munt\ *n.* The lowest floor of a building.

bashful \BASH-ful\ *adj.* Shy. bashfully *adv.*; bashfulness *n.*

BASIC \BAY-sik\ *abbr.* (Cm) Beginner's All-purpose Symbolic Instruction Code.

basic \BAY-sik\ *adj.* **1.** Elementary. **2.** Concerning a chemical compound that is a base. basically *adv.*

basil \BAZ-ul\ *n.* A sweet, peppery herb.

basilica \buh-SIL-i-kuh\ *n.* A place of worship built around a nave, aisles, clerestory, and apse.

basin \BAY-sun\ *n.* **1.** A container used for washing. **2.** A depressed area of land that holds water.

basis \BAY-sis\ *n. pl.* bases. **1.** The structural foundation of something. **2.** An underlying cause.

bask *v.* basked; basking. To expose oneself joyfully, especially to the sun.

basket \BAS-kit\ *n.* **1.** A woven carrying device. **2.** An open net used in games.

bas mitzvah \bahs-MITS-vuh\ *n.* A

Jewish female who has reached the age of religious duty; the ceremony.

bass *n. pl.* bass or basses. **1.** An edible fresh water fish. **2.** [Mu]: The lowest vocal range in a chorus. bass *adj.*

bassoon \ba-SOON\ *n.* (Mu) A double-reed low-pitched wind instrument. basoonist *n.*

bastard \BAS-turd\ *n.* **1.** A child born to unwed parents. **2.** [Sl]: A detestable person.

baste \bayst\ *v.* basted; basting. **1.** To sew with loose stitches. **2.** To pour liquid over.

bastion \BAS-chun\ *n.* A point or area considered a stronghold.

batch \bach\ *n.* A collection of elements produced or to be dealt with.

bath *n. pl.* baths. **1.** The act of cleaning one's body. **2.** A tub for washing. **3.** A room with a tub.

bathe \bayth\ *v.* bathed; bathing. **1.** To wash oneself in water. **2.** To go swimming. **3.** To cover with liquid. bather *n.*

bathing suit \BAYTH-ing-soot\ *n.* An article of clothing worn for swimming.

bathroom \BATH-room\ *n.* A room containing a sink, toilet, and tub or shower.

batik \buh-TEEK\ *n.* (Fo) A process for coloring fabrics using wax for uncolored parts; the fabric itself.

baton \buh-TON\ *n.* **1.** A type of club. **2.** A narrow rod, especially used to lead a band.

battalion \buh-TAL-yun\ *n.* A large army unit.

batter \BAT-ur\ *n.* **1.** A flour mixture for cooking. **2.** The hitter in baseball.

batter \BAT-ur\ *v.* battered; battering. To wear down by repeated blows.

battered child syndrome *n.* The mental attitude of abused children.

battery \BAT-uh-ree\ *n. pl.* batteries. **1.** [Le]: An illegal assault. **2.** A military grouping, especially of artillery.

battle \BAT-l\ *n.* A clash of opponents.

battle \BAT-l\ *v.* battled; battling. To fight.

battlefield \BAT-l-feeld\ *n.* An area of confrontation.

bauble \BAW-bul\ *n.* A trinket.

bauxite \BAWK-siet\ *n.* (Sc) An earthly mixture that is the source of aluminum.

bawdy \BAW-dee\ *adj.* Having a vulgar humor. bawdiness *n.*

bawl *v.* bawled; bawling. To cry loudly. bawler *n.*

bawl out *v.* To scold.

bay *n.* **1.** A rust-colored animal. **2.** A type of compartment. **3.** An offset window.

bay *v.* bayed; baying. To shout out with long deep cries.

bayonet \BAY-uh-net\ *n.* A blade attached to a rifle. bayonet *v.*

bayou \BIE-oo\ *n. pl.* bayous. A marsh ajoining a lake or river.

bazaar \buh-ZAHR\ *n.* **1.** [Fo] A shopping area. **2.** A charity fair.

be \bee\ *v.* **1.** To exist. **2.** To occupy a location. **3.** To relate equally. **4.** Auxiliary verb.

beach \beech\ *n.* An area of sand and rock leading to water.

beach \beech\ *v.* beached; beaching. To run ashore.

beacon \BEE-kun\ *n.* A guiding light.

bead \beed\ *n.* A small, usually round piece of material, pierced for stringing.

beagle \BEE-gul\ *n.* A small smooth-coated hound dog.

beak \beek\ *n.* A bird's bill. beaked *adj.*

beam \beem\ *n.* **1.** A piece of heavy timber used for support. **2.** A radio signal used to guide.

beam \beem\ *v.* **1.** To emit. **2.** To smile brightly. **3.** To broadcast.

beaming \BEE-ming\ *adj.* **1.** Smiling with joy. **2.** Glowing.

bean \been\ *n.* An edible seed of a leguminous plant.

bean sprout \BEEN-sprowt\ *n. pl.* bean sprouts. An edible baby seed of a leguminous plant.

bear \bair\ *n. pl.* bears. **1.** A large furry mammal. **2.** [Sl]: A big, clumsy person.

bear \bair\ *v.* bore; borne or born; bearing. **1.** To hold up. **2.** To carry. **3.** to give birth. **4.** To provide as testimony.

beard \beerd\ *n.* A male's unshaven facial hair. bearded *adj.*

bearing \BAIR-ing\ *n.* **1.** A manner of conduct. **2.** An orientation. **3.** An importance.

bearnaise \BAIR-nays\ *n.* (Fr) A sauce made with eggs, butter, herbs, and wine.

beast \beest\ *n.* **1.** A non-human mammal. **2.** [Sl] A vulgar person.

beat \beet\ *n.* **1.** A slap. **2.** A throbbing. **3.** A rhythmical unit. **4.** A patrol round. beater *n.*

beat \beet\ *v.* beat; beaten or beat; beating. **1.** To hit frequently. **2.** To whip together. **3.** To defeat. **4.** To pulsate. beater *n.*

beatify \bee-AT-i-FIE\ *v.* beatified; beatifying. **1.** To make very happy. **2.** To bestow religious honor. beatification *n.*

beatnik \BEET-nik\ *n.* An expressive, philosophical, nonconformist person.

beau \boh\ *n. pl.* beaux or beaus. (Fr) **1.** A boyfriend. **2.** A stylish man.

Beaufort scale \BOH-furt-skayl\ *n.* (Sc) A scale that measures the wind's force.

beautician \byoo-TISH-un\ *n.* A makeup artist.

beauty \BYOO-tee\ *n. pl.* beauties. **1.** A pleasing quality. **2.** A person or thing having a pleasing quality. beauteous *adj.*; beautiful *adj.*; beautifully *adv.*; beautify *v.*

beaver \BEE-vur\ *n. pl.* beavers. An aquatic, dam-building, furry rodent.

bebop *n.* (Mu) A 1940's style of jazz characterized by fast rhythms and nonsensical lyrics.

because \bi-KAWZ\ *conj.* **1.** On the grounds that. **2.** Due to. **3.** As a result of.

beckon \BEK-un\ *v.* beckoned; beckoning. To call nearer using a gesture.

become \bi-KUM\ *v.* became; become; becoming. **1.** To come into another form. **2.** To flatter. **3.** To show in the best way.

become of *v.* To happen to.

becoming \bi-KUM-ing\ *adj.* Flattering. becomingly *adv.*

bed *n.* **1.** A piece of furniture to sleep on. **2.** A ground area. **3.** A layer. **4.** A base. bed *v.*

bed-and-breakfast *n.* A lodge offering a sleeping room and a morning meal. bed-and-breakfast *adj.*

bedazzle \bi-DAZ-ul\ *v.* bedazzled; bedazzling. To bewilder, especially with a bright light.

bedding \BED-ing\ *n.* **1.** A base for plants. **2.** The materials used to cover a bed.

bedeck \bi-DEK\ *v.* bedecked; bedecking. To decorate.

bedlam \BED-lum\ *n.* **1.** A chaotic state. **2.** An insane asylum.

bedouin *also* **beduin** \BED-oo-in\ *n. pl.* bedouin or bedouins or beduin or beduins. A desert nomad.

bedraggled \bi-DRAG-uld\ *adj.* Muddied.

bedroom *n.* A room where one sleeps.

bedspread \BED-spred\ *n.* A bed covering.

bee *n.* A flying insect that colonizes hives and produces honey. **2.** A gathering.

beef *n. pl.* beefs or beeves. **1.** Steer, cow, or bull flesh. **2.** A person's strength. **3.** A grievance. beefy *adj.*; beef *v.*

beehive \BEE-hiev\ *n.* **1.** A bee home. **2.** A conically-shaped female hairdo.

beep *n.* A quick high-pitched sound. beep *v.*

beeper \BEE-pur\ *n.* A portable electronic paging device.

beer *n.* An alcoholic drink made from malt and hops.

beetle \BEET-l\ *n.* **1.** A small winged insect. **2.** [Sl] A car.

befall \bi-FAWL\ *v.* befell; befallen; befalling. To happen, especially by chance.

befit \bi-FIT\ *v.* befitted; befitting. To be appropriate.

before \bi-FOR\ *adv.* Formerly.

before \bi-FOR\ *conj.* **1.** Ahead of. **2.** More eagerly than.

before \bi-FOR\ *prep.* **1.** Previous to. **2.** In front of. **3.** Under the thought of.

beforehand \bi-FOR-hand\ *adj.* Advanced. beforehand *adv.*

befriend \bi-FREND\ *v.* befriended; befriending. To make friends with.

befuddle \bi-FUD-l\ *v.* befuddled; befuddling. To baffle. befuddlement *n.*

beg *v.* begged; begging. **1.** To request the charity of. **2.** To request earnestly.

beget \bi-GET\ *v.* begot; begotten or begot; begetting. **1.** To father. **2.** To start.

beggar \BEG-ur\ *n.* A person who requests charity.

beguile \bi-GIEL\ *v.* beguiled; beguiling. **1.** To deceive. **2.** To delight. beguilement *n.*; beguiler *n.*

behalf \bi-HAF\ *n.* An assistance.

behave \bi-HAYV\ *v.* behaved; behaving. **1.** To act according to the proper rules of conduct. **2.** To function. behavioral *adj.*; behavior *n.*

behead \bi-HED\ *v.* beheaded; beheading. To chop off the head. beheading *n.*

behind \bi-HIEND\ *adv.* **1.** Toward or in the back. **2.** Tardy. behind *adj.*

behind \bi-HIEND\ *n.* The buttocks.

behind \bi-HIEND\ *prep.* **1.** To the back of. **2.** In support of. **3.** In a following position.

behold \bi-HOHLD\ *v.* beheld; beholding. To observe. beholder *n.*

behoove *also* **behove** \bi-HOOV\ *v.* behooved; behooving or behoved; behoving. To suit.

beige \bayzh\ *n.* A very light brown color.

being \BEE-ing\ *n.* **1.** Any living thing. **2.** A vitality. **3.** An essence.

belch *v.* belched; belching. To burp. belch *n.*

beleaguer \bi-LEE-gur\ *v.* beleagured; beleaguring. **1.** To encircle with an army. **2.** To annoy.

belfry \BEL-free\ *n. pl.* belfries. The church bell tower.

belief \bi-LEEF\ *n.* **1.** A statement held as true. **2.** An opinion.

believe \bi-LEEV\ *v.* believed; believing. **1.** To hold as true. **2.** To think. believable *adj.*, believer *n.*

belittle \bi-LIT-l\ *v.* belittled; belittling. To render inferior.

bellhop \BEL-hop\ *n.* A hotel assistant.

belligerent \be-LIJ-ur-unt\ *adj.* **1.** Combative. **2.** Quarrelsome. belligerently *adv.*; belligerence *n.*; belligerency *n.*; belligerent *n.*

bellow \BEL-oh\ *v.* bellowed; bellowing. To shout in a deep voice. bellow *n.*

belong \bi-LAWNG\ *v.* belonged; belonging. **1.** To be a possession to. **2.** To be appropriately placed. **3.** To be a member of. belonging *n.*

beloved \bi-LUV-id\ *adj.* Dearly cherished. beloved *n.*

below \bi-LOH\ *prep.* Beneath in place or position. below *adv.*

belt *n.* **1.** A band of material worn around the waist. **2.** A distinctive geographic area.

belt *v.* belted; belting. **1.** To surround. **2.** To beat with a band of material.

beltway *n.* A highway that encircles a city.

bemoan \bi-MOHN\ *v.* bemoaned; bemoaning. To express regret.

bemuse \bi-MYOOZ\ *v.* bemused; bemusing. To confuse. bemusement *n.*

bench *n.* **1.** A long place to sit or work. **2.** A judge's seat. **3.** A group of judges.

bench *v.* benched; benching. **1.** To equip with long seat. **2.** To rest on such a seat. **3.** To take out of a game.

benchmark \BENCH-mahrk\ *n.* A point of reference or standard of comparison. benchmark *v.*

bench press *n.* A weight lifting machine for pressing up a weight while lying down. bench press *v.*

bend *n.* A curved section.

bend *v.* bent; bending. **1.** To cause to a curve. **2.** To influence. **3.** To succumb.

beneath \bi-NEETH\ *adv.* In a lower position.

beneath \bi-NEETH\ *prep.* **1.** Lower than. **2.** Not deserving of.

benediction \ben-i-DIK-shun\ *n.* A final prayer.

benefactor \BEN-uh-fak-tur\ *n.* **1.** A protector. **2.** One who donates to charity. beneficial *adj.*; beneficient *adj.*; beneficially *adv.*; benefaction *n.*; beneficence *n.*

benefit \BEN-uh-fit\ *n.* **1.** An instance of aid. **2.** An advantage. **3.** An event to raise money.

benefit \BEN-uh-fit\ *v.* benefited; benefiting or benefitted; benefitting. **1.** To be of assistance. **2.** To receive assistance.

benevolent \buh-NEV-uh-lunt\ *adj.* Possessing goodwill. benevolence *n.*

benign \bi-NIEN\ *adj.* **1.** Friendly. **2.** Harmless. **3.** Giving. **4.** Not causing cancer.

bent *adj.* **1.** Not straight. **2.** Being intent. **3.** [Sl] Very strange.

bent *n.* An ability.

benzene \BEN-zeen\ *n.* (Sc) A clear flammable liquid used as a solvent or a fuel.

bequeath \bi-KWEETH\ *v.* bequeathed; bequeathing. **1.** To legally bestow. **2.** To pass on.

bereft \bi-REFT\ *adj.* **1.** Deprived of. **2.** In mourning.

beret \buh-RAY\ *n.* (Fr) A head covering.

berry \BER-ee\ *n. pl.* berries. A pulpy, many-seeded fruit.

berserk \bur-SURK\ *adj.* Frantic. berserk *adv.*; berserker *n.*

berth \burth\ *n.* **1.** A ship's docking space. **2.** A bed on board a vehicle. **3.** A job. berth *v.*

beseech \bi-SEECH\ *v.* beseeched or besought; beseeching. To implore. beseecher *n.*

beside \bi-SIDE\ *prep.* **1.** Along side. **2.** (also besides) In addition to. **3.** Not important to.

besides \bi-SIDES\ *adv.* **1.** As well. **2.** Additionally.

besiege \bi-SEEJ\ *v.* besieged; besieging. **1.** To surround. **2.** To bother. besieger *n.*

best *adj.* Better than everything else. best *adv.*

best *n.* **1.** The one better than the others. **2.** The most outstanding effort.

best *v.* To triumph over.

bestow \bi-STOH\ *v.* bestowed; bestowing. To give as a gift. bestowal *n.*

bet *n.* A wager.

bet *v.* betted; betting. **1.** To place a wager on an outcome. **2.** To bet the farm [Id]: To risk all. bettor or better *n.*

beta-blocker \BAY-tuh-blok-ur\ *n.* (Md) A drug used to control blood pressure.

betray \bi-TRAY\ *v.* betrayed; betraying. **1.** To cheat. **2.** To give over to an enemy. **3.** To give out secrets. betrayal *n.*; betrayer *n.*

betroth \bi-TRAWTH\ *v.* betrothed; betrothing. To commit to marriage. betrothal *n.*; betrothed *n.*

better \BET-ur\ *adj.* **1.** Above average. **2.** More appropriate. **3.** Healthier. better *n.*; betterment *n.*

better \BET-ur\ *adv.* **1.** To a greater degree. **2.** In an improved way.

better \BET-ur\ *v.* **1.** To enhance. **2.** To outdo.

between \bi-TWEEN\ *prep.* **1.** In the moment or location dividing. **2.** Through the joint action of.

beverage \BEV-ur-ij\ *n.* A drink.

beware \bi-WAIR\ *v.* To be watchful of.

bewilder \bi-WIL-dur\ *v.* bewildered; bewildering. To confuse. bewilderment *n.*

bewitch \bi-WICH\ *v.* bewitched; bewitching. **1.** To put under a spell. **2.** To charm.

beyond \bee-OND\ *prep.* **1.** To a greater location than. **2.** After. **3.** Beyond the bounds of. beyond *adv.*

biannual \bie-AN-yoo-ul\ *adj.* Occurring twice a year. biannually *adv.*

bias \BIE-us\ *n.* **1.** A preference. **2.** A diagonal line for cutting fabric. bias *v.*

biathlon \BIE-ath-lon\ *n.* A competition involving cross-country skiing and rifle target-shooting. biathlete *n.*

bibliography \bib-lee-OG-ruh-fee\ *n. pl.* bibliographies. A list of relevant works. bibliographic *adj.*; bibliographical *adj.*; bibliographer *n.*

bibliophile \BIB-lee-uh-file\ *n.* One who loves books.

bicentennial \bi-sen-TEN-ee-ul\ *n.* A 200th anniversary. bicentenary *adj.*; bicentenary *n.*; bicentennial *n.*

bicker \BIK-ur\ *v.* bickered; bickering. To argue.

bicoastal \bie-cohs-tl\ *adj.* Relating to both US coasts.

bicycle \BIE-sie-kul\ *n.* A two-wheeled pedaled vehicle. bicyclist *n.*

bicycle \BIE-sie-kul\ *v.* bicycled; bicycling. To pedal a two-wheeled vehicle.

bid *n.* **1.** A financial or service-related offer. **2.** An invitation. **3.** An endeavor. bidder *n.*

bid *v.* bade or bid; bidden or bid-ding. **1.** To demand. **2.** To say. **3.** To offer money or services.

bidet \bi-DAY\ *n.* (Fr) A bathroom fixture used for washing the external genitals.

biennial \bie-EN-ee-ul\ *adj.* **1.** Happening once every two years. **2.** Lasting every two years.

big *adj.* bigger; biggest. **1.** Large. **2.** Mature. **3.** Influential. **4.** Considerate **5.** Conceited. biggish *adj.*; bigness *n.*

bigamy \BIG-uh-mee\ *n.* A crime where one is married to more than one person at once. bigamous *adj.*; bigamist *n.*

big bang theory *n.* (Sc) A theory that the universe began with a huge explosion and is contracting.

bigot \BIG-ut\ *n.* A prejudiced person. bigoted *adj.*; bigotry *n.*

biker \BIEK-ur\ *n.* Someone who often rides a bicycle or a motorcycle.

bikini \bi-KEE-nee\ *n.* **1.** A women's two-piece swimsuit. **2.** A type of underpants.

bilateral \bie-LAT-ur-ul\ *adj.* Relating to two sides. bilaterally *adv.*

bilge \bilj\ *n.* **1.** The rounded part of a ship's hull. **2.** Foul water.

bilingual \bie-LING-gwul\ *adj.* Relating to two languages. bilinguist *n.*

bill *n.* **1.** The mouthpart of a bird. **2.** A statement of money owed. **3.** A proposed law. bill *v.*

billiards \BIL-yurdz\ *n.* A table game played by using a cue to knock balls into pockets.

billion \BIL-yun\ *n.* The number 1,000,000,000. billion *adj.*; billionth *adj.*; billionth *n.*

billow \BIL-oh\ *n.* A surge of something.

billow \BIL-oh\ *v.* billowed; billowing. **1.** To roll forth. **2.** To balloon. billowy *adj.*

binary \BIE-nuh-ree\ *adj.* Relating to two parts. binarism *n.*; binary *n.*

bind \BYND\ *v.* bound; binding. **1.** To tie. **2.** To legally obligate. **3.** To dress a wound. **4.** To hold together.

binge \binj\ *n.* An unrestrained consumption. binger *n.*; binge *v.*

binomial \bie-NOH-mee-ul\ *n.* **1.** Two mathematical terms joined by a plus or minus sign. **2.** Scientific name. binomial *adj.*

biochip \BIE-oh-chip\ *n.* (Cm) A hypothetical computer logic pathway.

biodegradable \bie-oh-di-GRAY-duh-bul\ *adj.* (Sc) Capable of being broken down naturally.

biodegradability *n.*; biodegradation *n.*; biodegrade *v.*

bioengineering \bi-oh-en-jin-EER-ing\ *n.* (Sc) The use of engineering principles in biology or medicine. bioengineer *n.*

biofeedback \bi-oh-FEED-bak\ *n.* (Sc) The mental control of bodily processes.

biography \bi-OG-ruh-fee\ *n. pl.* biographies. A written account of someone's life. biographic *adj.*; biographical *adj.*; biographer *n.*

biological clock \bie-uh-LOJ-i-kul-klok\ *n.* A person's internal physical and mental timing device.

biology \bie-OL-uh-jee\ *n.* (Sc) The study of living things. biologic or biological *adj.*; biologist *n.*

bionic \bie-ON-iks\ *adj.* (Sc) Enhancing normal biological capacities through electronic means. bionics *n.*

biopsy \BIE-op-see\ *n. pl.* biopsies. (Md) The surgical removal and study of living tissues, cells, or fluids.

biorhythm \BIE-oh-rith-um\ *n.* (Md) An internal rhythm that seems to regulate biological processes.

biosphere \BIE-oh-sfeer\ *n.* (Sc) The area of the world that can support life.

biped \BIE-ped\ *n.* An animal with two feet. bipedal *adj.*

bipolar \bie-POH-lur\ *adj.* (Sc) Relating to opposite poles. bipolarity *n.*

biracial \bie-RAY-shul\ *adj.* Relating to two races.

bird \burd\ *n.* A warm-blooded, feathered, winged vertebrate that lays eggs.

birth \burth\ *n.* **1.** The act of being born or delivering. **2.** The origin.

birth control *n.* (Md) A method of preventing pregnancy.

birth defect \BURTH-dee-fect\ *n.* (Md) An inherited or environmentally-induced abnormality present since birth.

bisect \bie-SEKT\ *v.* bisected; bisecting. To cut into 2 parts. bisection *n.*; bisector *n.*

bison \BIE-sun\ *n. pl.* bison. A North American oxlike mammal with horns, a shaggy mane, and a muscular back.

bistro \BIS-troh\ *n. pl.* bistros. (Fr) **1.** A small European restaurant. **2.** A nightclub.

bit *n.* **1.** Cutting part of a tool. **2.** The mouthpiece of a bridle. **3.** A small quantity.

bite \biet\ *n.* **1.** Gripping with one's jaws. **2.** Injury by the penetration of teeth.

bite \biet\ *v.* bit; bitten; biting. **1.** To grip or wound with the teeth. **2.** To wear away. **3.** To grab bait.

bitter \BIT-ur\ *adj.* **1.** A sharp taste. **2.** Brutal. **3.** Hateful. bitterly *adv.*; bitterness *n.*

bivalence \bie-VAY-lens\ *n.* A degree of attractiveness equal to bivalent *adj.*

bivouac \BIV-oo-ak\ *n.* (Fr) A temporary camp. bivouac *v.*

bizarre \bi-ZAHR\ *adj.* Unusual. bizarrely *adv.*

blab *v.* blabbed; blabbing. To gossip. blabby *adj.*; blabber *n.*

black \blak\ *adj.* **1.** Lacking light. **2.** Depressive. **3.** Filthy. **4.** Wicked. **5.** Having dark skin. blackish *adj.*; blackly *adv.*; blackness *n.*

black \blak\ *n.* **1.** The darkest color. **2.** The near absence of light. **3.** A dark-skinned person.

black hole *n.* (Sc) A gravitational field theorized to exist in outer space.

black humor *n.* A funny situation based on horror.

blacklist \BLAK-list\ *v.* blacklisted; blacklisting. To put on a list of banned people. blacklist *n.*

blackmail \BLAK-mayl\ *v.* blackmailed; blackmailing. To be coerced into payment for maintenance of a secret. blackmail *n.*; blackmailer *n.*

blackout \BLAK-owt\ *n.* **1.** A power failure or extinguishing of lights. **2.** A ban. black out *v.*

Black Studies *n.* Academic discipline concerned with the history and culture of African Americans.

bladder \BLAD-ur\ *n.* A sac that holds liquid, especially urine.

blade \blayd\ *n.* **1.** A stem of grass. **2.** Something like a stem of grass. **3.** The cutting edge.

blah *adj.* Bored; boring.

blame \blaym\ *v.* blamed; blaming. **1.** To accuse. **2.** To censure. blamable *adj.*; blameless *adj.*; blamelessly *adv.*; blame *n.*

bland *adj.* **1.** Mild. **2.** Lacking distinction. blandly *adv.*; blandness *n.*

blank \blangk\ *adj.* **1.** Having no color or expression. **2.** Possessing no markings. blankly *adv.*

blank \blangk\ *n.* **1.** An empty space. **2.** A cartridge with no projectile. **3.** An area to be filled. blankness *n.*

blanket \BLANG-kit\ *n.* **1.** A bed covering. **2.** A thick coating. blanket *adj.*; blanket *v.*

blare \blair\ *v.* blared; blaring. To sound loudly. blare *n.*

blarney \BLAHR-nee\ *n.* Flattering, but nonsensical, talk.

blaspheme \blas-FEEM\ *v.* blasphemed; blaspheming. To curse. blasphemous *adj.*; blasphemy *n.*

blast *n.* **1.** Forceful gust of wind. **2.** A loud, sudden noise. **3.** An explosion.

blasé \blah-ZAY\ *adj.* (Fr) Bored from overindulgence.

blatant \BLAYT-nt\ *adj.* Outright. blatantly *adv.*

blaze \blayz\ *n.* **1.** A fire. **2.** A glaring light. **3.** A dazzling display.

blaze \blayz\ *v.* blazed; blazing. **1.** To burn brightly. **2.** To shine brightly. **3.** To mark a trail.

bleach \bleech\ *n.* A caustic solution for whitening.

bleach \bleech\ *v.* bleached; bleaching. To make white or bright.

bleak \bleek\ *adj.* Grim and depressing. bleakly *adv.*

bleat \bleet\ *n.* A cry of a sheep or goat. bleat *v.*

bleed *v.* bled; bleeding. **1.** To lose blood. **2.** To be wounded or in pain. **3.** To get money through coercion.

blemish \BLEM-ish\ *n.* An obvious imperfection. blemished *adj.*; blemish *v.*

blend *v.* blended; blending. To combine completely. blend *n.*; blender *n.*

bless \bles\ *v.* blessed or blest; blessing. **1.** To sanctify. **2.** To call God's care for. **3.** To make happy or fortunate. blessedness *n.*; blessing *n.*

blight \bliet\ *n.* **1.** A destructive plant infestation. **2.** A detrimental influence. blight *v.*

blind \bliend\ *adj.* **1.** Without vision. **2.** Not based on rationale. **3.** Concealed. **4.** Lacking an exit. blindly *adv.*; blindness *n.*

blind \bliend\ *n.* **1.** A shutter. **2.** A hiding place for hunters.

blink \blingk\ *v.* blinked; blinking. **1.** To open and close one's eyes. **2.** To flicker on and off. **3.** To neglect. blink *n.*

bliss \blis\ *n.* A feeling of complete peace. blissful *adj.*; blissfully *adv.*

blister \BLIS-tur\ *n.* **1.** A water-filled sac just under the skin. **2.** Something resembling such a sac. blister *v.*

blitz \blits\ *n.* A complete and sudden attack. blitz *v.*

blizzard \BLIZ-urd\ *n.* A snowstorm.

bloat \bloht\ *v.* bloated; bloating. To swell. bloated *adj.*

block \blok\ *n.* **1.** A solid mass of material. **2.** An obstacle. **3.** An auction stand. **4.** A casing.

block \blok\ *v.* blocked; blocking. **1.** To obstruct. **2.** To shape roughly. blockage *n.*

blockade \blo-KAYD\ *n.* An enforced isolation of an area. blockade *v.*

blond *also* **blonde** *n.* A person with light yellow hair. blond *adj.*

blood \blud\ *n.* **1.** [Md] The fluid that carries oxygen throughout the body. **2.** A kindred person.

blood-brain barrier *n.* (Md) A wall that protects the nervous system from harmful substances in the blood.

bloom *n.* **1.** A flower. **2.** A flourishing time. **3.** A healthy complexion.

bloom *v.* bloomed; blooming. **1.** To flower. **2.** To flourish. **3.** To glow.

blooper \BLOOP-ur\ *n.* An embarrassing mistake.

blossom \BLOS-um\ *n.* A flower. blossom *v.*

blot *n.* **1.** A discoloration. **2.** A flaw.

blot *v.* blotted; blotting. **1.** To discolor. **2.** To dry. **3.** To cancel.

blotch \bloch\ *n.* A stain. blotchy *adj.*; blotch *v.*

blouse *n. pl.* blouses. A loose shirt. blousy *adj.*; blouse *v.*

blow \bloh\ *n.* **1.** A rush of wind. **2.** The act of forcing air through something. **3.** A hit.

blow \bloh\ *v.* blew; blown; blowing. **1.** To move with the wind. **2.** To make a breeze. **3.** To sound an instrument.

blow away *v.* To astound.

blow off *v.* To ignore.

blowout *n.* **1.** The rupture of a tire. **2.** A burning out of a fuse. **3.** A huge party.

blowsy *also* **blowzy** \BLOW-zee\ *adj.* Having an unkept appearance.

blue \bloo\ *adj.* bluer; bluest. **1.** Having the color blue. **2.** Unhappy. bluish *adj.*

blue \bloo\ *n.* **1.** The color of the sea. **2.** [Pl] An unhappy state. **3.** [Pl] A jazz ballad.

blue-collar \BLOO-KOL-ur\ *adj.* **1.** Relating to manual, uniform-wearing laborers.

bluff \bluf\ *n.* **1.** The act of misleading. **2.** A steep hill. bluff *adj.*

bluff \bluf\ *v.* bluffed; bluffing. To deceive. bluffer *n.*

blunder \BLUN-dur\ *v.* blundered; blundering. **1.** To move clumsily. **2.** To make a careless error. blunder *n.*

blunt *adj.* **1.** Not sharp. **2.** Insensitive. bluntly *adv.*; bluntness *n.*; blunt *v.*

blur *n.* **1.** Anything out of focus. **2.** A smudge. blurry *adj.*

blur *v.* blurred; blurring. **1.** To make out of focus. **2.** To smudge.

blush *n.* **1.** A pink color. **2.** An expressive pink facial coloring. **3.** A colored powder. blush *v.*

blustery \BLUS-tur-ee\ *adj.* **1.** Having stormy winds. **2.** Intimidating speech or actions. bluster *n.*; bluster *v.*

board \bord\ *n.* **1.** A flat length of wood. **2.** A regular program of meals. **3.** A group.

board \bord\ *v.* boarded; boarding. **1.** To enter a vehicle, especially a ship. **2.** To give or receive regular meals. boarder *n.*

boast \bohst\ *v.* boasted; boasting. **1.** To brag. **2.** To happily possess. boastful *adj.*; boast *n.*; boaster *n.*

boat \boht\ *n.* A vehicle used for water transportation. boater *n.*

bob *n.* **1.** An up-and-down bouncing. **2.** A short haircut. **3.** A fishing float.

bob *v.* bobbed; bobbing. **1.** To bounce up and down. **2.** To cut short.

bodega \boh-DAY-guh\ *n.* (Sp) **1.** A cellar for storing groceries. **2.** A Hispanic grocery store.

body \BOD-ee\ *n. pl.* bodies. **1.** A mammal's physique. **2.** A cadaver. **3.** A person. **4.** The main portion.

body surf \BOD-ee-SURF\ *v.* body surfed; body surfing. To ride a wave without a surfboard.

bog *n.* A marshy area. boggy *adj.*; bog *v.*

bogey *also* **bogie or bogy** \BOH-gee\ *n. pl.* bogies or bogeys. **1.** A phantom. **2.** A golf score.

boggle \BOG-ul\ *v.* boggled; boggling. **1.** To frighten. **2.** To fascinate.

bogus \BOH-gus\ *adj.* Fraudulent.

boil *v.* boiled; boiling. **1.** To heat up a liquid by applying heat. **2.** To cook by applying heat. boiler *n.*

boil down *v.* To summarize.

boilerplate *n.* The material supplied to weekly newspaper.

boisterous \BOI-stur-us\ *adj.* Loud and unrestrained. boisterously *adv.*; boisterousness *n.*

bold \bohld\ *adj.* bolder; boldest. **1.** Lacking fear. **2.** Assertive. **3.** Distinct. boldly *adv.*; boldness *n.*

bolster \BOHL-stur\ *n.* A long pillow.

bolster \BOHT-stur\ *v.* bolstered; bolstering. **1.** To support. **2.** To reinforce.

bolt \bohlt\ *n.* **1.** Door fastener. **2.** Screw held in place with a nut. **3.** A streak of lightning.

bolt \bohlt\ *v.* bolted; bolting. **1.** To secure. **2.** To eat quickly. **3.** To run quickly. **4.** To break away.

bomb \bom\ *n.* **1.** An explosive device. **2.** A failure. bomb *v.*

bombard \bom-BAHRD\ *v.* bombarded; bombarding. To assault. bombardment *n.*

bombastic \bom-BAST-ik\ *adj.* Relating to pretentious communication. bombast *n.*

bona fide \BOH-nuh-FIED\ *adj.* (Lt) **1.** Authentic. **2.** Sincere.

bonanza \buh-NAN-za\ *n.* (Sp) **1.** A valuable mass of ore. **2.** A profitable discovery.

bonbon \BON-bon\ *n.* (Fr) A fondant-filled candy.

bond *n.* **1.** Fastener. **2.** A relationship. **3.** Bail money. **4.** Interest-producing certificate.

bond *v.* bonded; bonding. **1.** To guarantee payment. **2.** To secure together. **3.** [Sl] To form a close relationship. To become acquainted.

bondage \BON-dij\ *n.* A state of slavery.

bone \bohn\ *n.* [Md] **1.** The hard material forming the skeleton. **2.** One part of the skeleton. bony *adj.*; bone *v.*

bonkers \BON-kurs\ *adj.* Crazy.

bonsai \bon-SIE\ *n. pl.* bonsai. (Fo) A dwarfed plant.

bonus \BOH-nus\ *n.* An extra something.

bon vivant \BON-vee-VAHNT\ *n. pl.* bons vivants or bon vivants. (Fr) A person with refined tastes.

bon voyage \bon-voi-AHZH\ *n.* (Fr) A farewell statement or party.

book \buuk\ *n.* **1.** A bound manuscript. **2.** A piece of literature. **3.** A financial record. bookish *adj.*

book \buuk\ *v.* booked; booking. **1.** To reserve. **2.** [Le] To arrest. **3.** [Sl] To run fast.

boom *n.* **1.** An explosive noise. **2.** A rapid development. **3.** A long beam. boom *v.*

boomerang \BOO-muh-rang\ *v.* To backfire.

boomerang \BOO-muh-rang\ *n.* A bent missile that comes back to the thrower.

boonies \BOON-ees\ *n. pl.* boonies. A rural area.

boor \buur\ *n.* A rude person. boorish *adj.*; boorishness *n.*

boost *n.* **1.** An expansion. **2.** An assistance. **3.** A lift. booster *n.*

boost *v.* boosted; boosting. **1.** To increase. **2.** To raise. **3.** To promote.

boot *n.* **1.** A covering for the foot and lower leg. **2.** A kick. **3.** A dismissal.

boot *v.* booted; booting. **1.** To kick. **2.** To dismiss.

booth *n. pl.* booths. **1.** Small sales stand. **2.** An enclosed restaurant seat. **3.** A private voting area.

bootleg \BOOT-leg\ *v.* bootlegged; bootlegging. To produce, sell, or send illegally. bootleg *adj.*; bootleg *n.*; bootlegger *n.*

booze \booz\ *n.* An alcoholic beverage.

booze \booz\ *v.* boozed; boozing. To drink liquor excessively. boozy *adj.*; boozer *n.*

border \BOR-dur\ *n.* A boundary. border *v.*

borderline \BOR-dur-lien\ *adj.* **1.** Existing in a middle position. **2.** Not meeting expectations.

bore \bor\ *v.* bored; boring. **1.** To drill. **2.** To disinterest. bore *n.*

born *adj.* **1.** Carried into life through birth. **2.** Native. **3.** Having innate abilities.

born-again *adj.* Relating to a renewed faith.

borough \BUR-oh\ *n.* A political division of land.

borrow \BOR-oh\ *v.* borrowed; borrowing. **1.** To receive temporarily. **2.** To appropriate for one's own use. borrower *n.*

bosom \BUUZ-um\ *adj.* Intimate.

bosom \BUUZ-um\ *n.* **1.** A woman's breasts. **2.** The core.

boss \baws\ *n.* **1.** A person's overseer. **2.** A dictator.

boss \baws\ *v.* bossed; bossing. **1.** To oversee. **2.** To take charge. bossy *adj.*

botany \BOT-n-ee\ *n. pl.* botanies. (Sc) The biological study dealing with plant life. botanic *adj.*; botanical *adj.*; botanist *n.*

botch \boch\ *v.* botched; botching. To make a mistake.

both \bohth\ *adj.* Being one and the other. both *conj.*; both *pron*.

bother \BOTH-ur\ *n.* A fuss. bothersome *adj.*

bother \BOTH-ur\ *v.* bothered; bothering. **1.** To annoy. **2.** To take the trouble to.

bottle \BOT-l\ *n.* A container that can be sealed.

bottle \BOT-l\ *v.* bottled; bottling. To store in a container.

bottle up *v.* To suppress one's emotions.

bottom \BOT-um\ *n.* **1.** The lowest or deepest part. **2.** The side under another. **3.** The origin. bottom *adj.*; bottomless *adj.*

bottom-line \BOT-um-lien\ *n.* **1.** The financial net loss or gain. **2.** The ultimate result. **3.** The primary point.

boudoir \BOO-dwahr\ *n.* (Fr) A lady's private suite.

bouffant \boo-FAHNT\ *adj.* (Fr) Teased out.

bough \bow\ *n.* A main tree branch.

bouillabaisse \bool-yuh-BAYS\ *n.* (Fr) A spicy fish stew.

bouillon \BUUL-yon\ *n.* A clear meat broth.

boulder \BOHL-dur\ *n.* A large rock.

boulevard \BUUL-uh-vahrd\ *n.* A wide landscaped street.

bounce \bowns\ *v.* bounced; bouncing. **1.** To come back after collision. **2.** To go up and come back down.

bound \bownd\ *adj.* **1.** Obligated. **2.** Restrained. **3.** Determined. **4.** Enclosed in a cover. boundless *adj.*; boundlessness *n.*

bound \bownd\ *n.* **1.** A boundary. **2.** A leap. **3.** A bounce.

bound \bownd\ *v.* bounded; bounding. **1.** To leap. **2.** To restrain. **3.** To offset.

boundary \BOWN-duh-ree\ *n. pl.* boundaries. An outer limit.

bounty \BOWN-tee\ *n. pl.* bounties. **1.** Freedom in providing. **2.** A bonus. bountiful *adj.*; bountifully *adv.*

bouquet \boh-KAY\ *n.* (Fr) **1.** A flower arrangement. **2.** An aroma.

bouquet garni \bow-KAY-gar-NEE\ *n. pl.* bouquets garnis. (Fr) A collection of herbs used in cooking.

bourgeois \buur-ZHWAH\ *adj.* Belonging to the middle class. bourgeois *n.*

bourgeoisie \buur-zhwah-ZEE\ *n.* (Fr) A society ruled by the middle class.

bout \bowt\ *n.* **1.** A contest. **2.** A time of struggle, especially against an illness.

boutique \boo-TEEK\ *n.* A stylish specialty shop.

bow \boh\ *n.* **1.** Something arched. **2.** Bending over to express respect. **3.** An arrow shooter.

bow *v.* bowed; bowing. **1.** To lower one's head or upper body to express respect. **2.** To surrender.

bowel \BOW-ul\ *n. pl.* bowels. **1.** The intestine. **2.** The deepest part.

bowl \bohl\ *n.* **1.** A deepened dish. **2.** A hemispheric-shaped arena.

bowl \bohl\ *v.* bowled; bowling. **1.** To play bowling. **2.** To roll or throw, as a ball. **3.** To move swift and smooth. bowler *n.*; bowling *n.*

bowl over *v.* To amaze.

box \boks\ *n. pl.* boxes. **1.** A receptacle or case, usu. with a lid. **2.** The amount in such a container.

box \boks\ *v.* boxed; boxing. **1.** To punch. **2.** To enclose in a regular container.

boxing \BOK-sing\ *n.* A sport of attacking one's opponent using punches. boxer *n.*

boy \boi\ *n.* A male child. boyish *adv.*; boyishly *adv.*; boyhood *n.*

boycott \BOI-kot\ *v.* boycotted; boycotting. To protest any dealings with. boycott *n.*

boyfriend \BOI-frend\ *n.* A male friend or lover.

brace \brays\ *n. pl.* braces. **1.** A support, clasp, or clamp. **2.** A double curved line in punctuation.

brace \brays\ *v.* braced; bracing. **1.** To prepare for a negative event. **2.** To hold up. **3.** To energize.

bracelet \BRAYS-lit\ *n.* A decorative wrist band.

braid \brayd\ *n.* A length of woven fabric or hair.

braid \brayd\ *v.* braided; braiding. **1.** To weave strands of fabric or hair. **2.** To adorn with an ornamental edge.

Braille \brayl\ *n.* Raised dots that together form words able to be read by the blind.

brain \brayn\ *n.* **1.** The large organ of the nervous system. **2.** Mind; intellect. **3.** Control device. brainless *adj.*; brainy *adj.*

brain \brayn\ *v.* brained; braining. To kill by hitting on the skull.

brain-dead *adj.* In a condition in which brain waves are not detectable. brain death *n.*

brainwash \BRAYN-wosh\ *v.* brainwashed; brainwashing. To force to do or think.

braise \brayz\ *v.* braised; braising. To steam cook slowly in fat.

brake \brayk\ *n.* A motion-stopping device.

brake \brayk\ *v.* braked; braking. To stop.

branch *n.* **1.** A plant limb. **2.** A minor waterway. **3.** A subordinate, tributary, or division.

branch *v.* branched; branching. To expand and diverge from the main part.

brand *n.* **1.** A label. **2.** A company's product. **3.** An identifying mark on an animal. branded *adj.*

brand *v.* branded; branding. To mark.

brash *adj.* **1.** Hasty. **2.** Pushy.

brass *n.* **1.** A copper and zinc metal. **2.** A wind instrument made of such a metal.

brasserie \bra-SUR-ee\ *n.* (Fr) An informal restaurant.

brassiere \bru-ZEER\ *n.* A lady's undergarment made to support the breasts.

brat *n.* An ill-mannered child. bratty *adj.*

bravado \bruh-VAH-doh\ *n. pl.* bravadoes or bravados. A show of false bravery.

brave \brayv\ *adj.* braver; bravest. Having courage.

brave \brayv\ *n.* A Native American warrior.

brave \brayv\ *v.* braved; braving. To handle courageously. bravely *adv.*; bravery *n.*

bravo \BRAH-voh\ *n. pl.* bravos or bravoes. (It) A shout of praise.

brawl *n.* A loud fight. brawler *n.*; brawl *v.*

brazen \BRAY-zun\ *adj.* **1.** Constructed of brass. **2.** Loud. **3.** Pushy. brazenly *adv.*; brazenness *n.*

breach \breech\ *n.* **1.** A disobedience of the law, moral conduct, or a promise. **2.** A gap. breach *v.*

bread \bred\ *n.* **1.** A baked loaf. **2.** Nutrition. **3.** [Sl] Money.

breadth \bredth\ *n.* **1.** The width. **2.** The completeness.

break \brayk\ *n.* **1.** The act of fracturing. **2.** A hole or separation. **3.** A suspension of activity.

break \brayk\ *v.* broke; broken; breaking. **1.** To fracture. **2.** To disobey the law. **3.** To weaken. **4.** To suspend activity.

breakdown \BRAYK-down\ *n.* **1.**

Mechanical failure. **2.** Physical or mental collapse. **3.** An organized list.

break even *v.* broke even; broken even; breaking even. To emerge from a risky venture without taking a loss.

break in *v.* broke in; broken in; breaking in. **1.** To train. **2.** To intrude forcibly. **3.** To interrupt. break-in *n.*

break out *v.* broke out; broken out; breaking out. **1.** To erupt. **2.** to develop acne. **3.** To flee. breakout *n.*

breakthrough \BRAYK-throo\ *n.* A sudden development.

break up *v.* **1.** To interrupt a flow. **2.** To decompose. **3.** To smash. **4.** To end a romance. breakup *n.*

breast \brest\ *n.* **1.** A mammary gland. **2.** The chest.

breath \breth\ *n.* **1.** [Md] Air inhaled and expelled through mouth. **2.** An air stirring. **3.** Murmur.

breathe \breeth\ *v.* breathed; breathing. **1.** To inhale and exhale. **2.** To live. **3.** To pause. **4.** To speak. breathable *adj.*

breathless \BRETH-lis\ *adj.* Short of or without breath. breathlessly *adv.*; breathlessness *n.*

breathtaking \BRETH-tay-king\ *adj.* **1.** Exciting. **2.** Astonishing. breathtakingly *adv.*

breech *n. pl.* breeches. **1.** A pair of short pants. **2.** A fetus presented buttocks first.

breed *n.* **1.** A group related by descent. **2.** A type. breeder *n.*

breed *v.* bred; breeding. **1.** To reproduce. **2.** To bring about. **3.** To rear.

breeze \breez\ *n.* A light wind.

breeze \breez\ *v.* breezed; breezing. To progress quickly and effortlessly. breezy *adj.*

brew \broo\ *v.* brewed; brewing. **1.** To make using malt and hops. **2.** To make using liquid. **3.** [Sl] To plot.

brew \broo\ *n.* A drink. brewer *n.*; brewery *n.*

bribe \brieb\ *n.* A payment for dishonest behavior. briber *n.*

bribe \brieb\ *v.* bribed; bribing. To influence with money.

bric-a-brac \BRIK-uh-brak\ *n. pl.* bric-a-brac. A collection of small ornaments.

bridal \BRIED-l\ *adj.* Relating to a bride or wedding.

bride \bried\ *n.* A woman soon to be or recently married.

bridegroom *n.* A man soon to be or recently married.

bridesmaid \brieds-mayd\ *n.* A bride's attendant.

bridge \brij\ *n.* **1.** A structure erected over a waterway, road, etc. **2.** Transition. **3.** Control.

bridle \BRIED-l\ *n.* **1.** A horse's headgear. **2.** A type of restraint.

bridle \BRIED-l\ *v.* bridled; bridling. **1.** To put a bridle on a horse. **2.** Check or control.

brief \breef\ *adj.* Quick. briefly *adv.*; briefness *n.*

brief \breef\ *n.* **1.** [Le] A summary of a document. **2.** Snug-fitting underpants.

brief \breef\ *v.* briefed; briefing. To instruct.

briefcase \BREEF-kays\ *n.* A carrying case for papers.

brigade \bri-GAYD\ *n.* **1.** A military unit. **2.** An organized group.

bright \briet\ *adj.* brighter; brightest. **1.** Shining. **2.** Famous. **3.** Intelligent. **4.** Clear. **5.** Colorful. **6.** Happy. brightly *adv.*; brightness *n.*; brighten *v.*

brilliant \BRIL-yunt\ *adj.* **1.** Glittering. **2.** Having vivid color. **3.** Famous. **4.** Extremely intelligent. brilliancy *adv.*; brilliance *n.*; brilliancy *n.*

brim *n.* The edge of something, especially a cup or hat.

brine *n.* **1.** Saltwater. **2.** The sea. briny *adj.*; brininess *n.*

bring *v.* brought; bringing. **1.** To carry along with oneself. **2.** To influence. **3.** To draw a price.

bring about *v.* To make happen.

bring around *v.* To talk into.

bring in *v.* To profit.

bring off *v.* To succeed.

bring up *v.* **1.** To raise a child. **2.** To mention.

brink *n.* The edge.

brioche \BREE-ohsh\ *n.* (Fr) A light mildly-sweet bread.

brisk *adj.* **1.** Energetic. **2.** Keen. **3.** Chilly. briskly *adv.*; briskness *n.*

bristle \BRIS-ul\ *v.* bristled; bristling. **1.** To stand stiffly. **2.** To respond in anger. **3.** To be covered compactly. bristly *adj.*; bristle *n.*

broach \brohch\ *n.* **1.** A decorative pin. **2.** A piercing tool.

broach \brohch\ *v.* broached; broaching. **1.** To pierce. **2.** To mention a new conversation topic.

broad \brawd\ *adj.* **1.** Wide. **2.** Of great extent. **3.** Far-reaching. **4.** Liberal. **5.** Straightforward. broadly *adv.*; broadness *n.*; broaden *v.*

broadcast \BRAWD-kast\ *v.* broadcasted or broadcast; broadcasting.

1. To transmit. **2.** To make public. broadcast *adv.*; broadcast *n.*; broadcaster *n.*

broad-minded \BRAWD-MIEN-did\ *adj.* Accepting of various views. broad-mindedly *adv.*; broad-mindedness *n.*

broccoli \BROK-uh-lee\ *n.* A green vegetable with edible flower.

brochure \broh-SHUUR\ *n.* A pamphlet.

broil *v.* broiled; broiling. To cook under direct heat. broiling *adj.*; broil *n.*; broiler *n.*

broke \brohk\ *adj.* Without money.

brokenhearted \BROH-kun-HAHR-tid\ *adj.* Experiencing tremendous grief.

broker \BROH-kur\ *n.* An intermediary in transactions. brokerage *n.*; broker *v.*

bronco *also* **broncho** \BRONG-koh\ *n. pl.* broncos or bronchos. An untamed horse.

bronze \bronz\ *n.* **1.** A metal alloy of copper and tin. **2.** A reddish brown color. bronze *adj.*; bronze *v.*

brooch *also* **broach** \brohch\ *n.* A decorative pin.

brood *n.* A group of offspring. brood *adj.*

brood *v.* brooded; brooding. **1.** To incubate eggs. **2.** To dwell upon. brooder *n.*

brook \bruuk\ *n.* A freshwater creek.

broom *n.* **1.** A brush on a stick for sweeping. **2.** Any of various shrubs.

broth *n. pl.* broths. **1.** A thin soup. **2.** Water in which meat or vegetables were cooked.

brothel \BROTH-ul\ *n.* A house of prostitution.

brother \BRUTH-ur\ *n. pl.* brothers or brethren. **1.** A male born of one's parents. **2.** A close relation. brotherly *adj.*; brotherhood *n.*; brotherliness *n.*

brouhaha \BROO-hah-hah\ *n.* An uproar.

brow *n.* **1.** The forehead, eyebrow, or ridge over eyes. **2.** The top edge of a steep hill.

browbeat \BROW-beet\ *v.* browbeat; browbeaten; browbeating. To intimidate.

brown *n.* A color that is a mix between red, yellow, and black. brown *adj.*; brownish *adj.*

brown *v.* browned; browning. To make darker, especially in cooking.

browse \browz\ *n.* Vegetation fit for cattle food.

browse \browz\ *v.* browsed; browsing **1.** To glance through casually. **2.** To graze.

bruise \brooz\ *n.* (Md) A rupture of blood vessels under the skin.

bruise \brooz\ *v.* bruised; bruising. (Md) **1.** To rupture a blood vessel under the skin. **2.** To discolor by hitting.

brunette *also* **brunet** \broo-NET\ *n.* A person with brown hair. brunet or brunette *adj.*

brunt *n.* The primary impact.

brush *n.* **1.** Handheld tool with bristles for grooming, painting, sweeping. **2.** Brushwood.

brush *v.* brushed; brushing. To groom, paint, or sweep.

brush aside *v.* To ignore.

brush off *v.* To dismiss.

brush up *v.* To improve the state of.

brusque \brusk\ *adj.* Abrupt. brusquely *adv.*

brutal \BROOTl\ *adj.* Cruel. brutally *adv.*; brutality *n.*; brutalize *v.*

brute \broot\ *adj.* **1.** Relating to wild animals. **2.** Cruel. **3.** Senseless. brutish *adj.*

brute \broot\ *n.* **1.** A wild animal. **2.** A cruel person.

bubble \BUB-ul\ *n.* An air-filled sphere.

bubble \BUB-ul\ *v.* bubbled; bubbling. **1.** To form one or more air-filled spheres. **2.** To speak lively. bubbly *adj.*

bubblegum \BUB-ul-GUM\ *n.* A type of chewing gum.

buck \buk\ *n. pl.* bucks. **1.** A male animal. **2.** [Sl] A responsibility. **3.** [Sl] A dollar bill.

bucket \BUK-it\ *n.* A container with a handle for liquids. bucketful *n.*

buckle \BUK-ul\ *n.* A belt fastener.

buckle \BUK-ul\ *v.* buckled; buckling. **1.** To fasten a belt. **2.** To collapse or warp.

buckle down *v.* To focus on.

bud *n.* **1.** An undeveloped flower. **2.** An undeveloped state.

bud *v.* budded; budding. **1.** To produce undeveloped flowers. **2.** To sprout.

Buddhism \BOO-diz-um\ *n.* An Eastern religion. Buddhist *adj.*; Buddhist *n.*

buddy \BUD-ee\ *n. pl.* buddies. A friend.

budge \buj\ *v.* budged; budging. To yield slightly.

budget \BUJ-it\ *adj.* Cheap.

budget \BUJ-it\ *n.* A financial plan. budget *v.*

buff \buf\ *n.* **1.** A light, brown thick leather. **2.** A fan. **3.** A light brown color. buff *adj.*

buff \buf\ *v.* buffed; buffing. To polish.

buffer \BUF-ur\ *n.* A cushion.

buffet \buh-FAY\ *n.* **1.** A meal arranged on a counter of separate table. **2.** A sideboard table.

buffoon \buh-FOON\ *n.* A clownish person. buffoonery *n.*

bug *n.* **1.** An insect. **2.** A virus. **3.** Flaw. **4.** Enthusiast. **5.** Hidden listening device.

bug *v.* bugged; bugging. **1.** To bother. **2.** To hide a listening device.

bugle \BYOO-gul\ *n.* A brass trumpet lacking valves. bugler *n.*; bugle *v.*

build \bild\ *n.* The physical construction of something.

build \bild\ *v.* built; building. **1.** To construct. **2.** To establish. **3.** To increase. builder *n.*

building \BIL-ding\ *n.* **1.** An enclosed structure. **2.** Architecture.

buildup \BILD-up\ *n.* An accumulation of something. build up *v.*

built-in \BILT-in\ *adj.* **1.** Constructed as part of a whole. **2.** An inherent part of.

bulb *n.* **1.** Leaf bud of a plant. **2.** Plant growing from this. **3.** Rounded protuberance. bulbous *adj.*

bulge \bulj\ *n.* A swelling.

bulge \bulj\ *v.* bulged; bulging. To swell.

bulimia \boo-LEE-mee-uh\ *n.* (Md) An eating disorder characterized by binging and purging. bulimic *adj.*; bulimic *n.*

bulk *n.* **1.** The magnitude. **2.** A large mass, size, or volume. bulky *adj.*

bull \buul\ *n.* **1.** Adult male bovine animal. **2.** Something like a bull in power, strength. bulky *adj.*

bulldoze \BUUL-dohz\ *v.* bulldozed; bulldozing. **1.** To level with a tractor. **2.** To bully.

bullet \BUUL-it\ *n.* A missile shot from a gun. bulleted *adj.*

bulletin \BUUL-i-tn\ *n.* **1.** A short notice on a matter of public interest. **2.** A periodical.

bully \BUUL-ee\ *n. pl.* bullies. One who pushes weaker people around. bully *v.*

bulwark \BUUL-wurk\ *n.* **1.** A defensive barrier. **2.** Any means of defense.

bum *n.* **1.** A lazy person. **2.** [Sl] The buttocks. bum *adj.*

bum *v.* bummed; bumming. **1.** To beg. **2.** To be lazy.

bummer \BUM-ur\ *n.* (Sl) A disappointing experience.

bum out *v.* To be disappointed.

bump *n.* **1.** A collision. **2.** A surface swelling. bumpy *adj.*

bump *v.* bumped; bumping. To collide.

bun *n.* **1.** A sweet roll. **2.** A hair knot.

bunch *n.* A group. bunchy *adj.*

bunch *v.* bunched; bunching. To group.

bungle \BUNG-gul\ *v.* bungled; bungling. To mess up. bungle *n.*; bungler *n.*

bunk \bungk\ *n.* **1.** A tiered bed. **2.** Nonsense.

bunt *v.* bunted; bunting. To hit lightly. bunt *n.*

buoy \BOO-ee\ *n.* **1.** A warning float in water. **2.** A device for keeping someone afloat.

buoy \BOO-ee\ *v.* buoyed; buoying. **1.** To keep from sinking. **2.** To cheer.

buoyant \BOI-unt\ *adj.* **1.** Being light in water. **2.** Cheerful. buoyance *n.*; buoyancy *n.*

burden \BUR-dn\ *n.* An overbearing physical or mental load. burdensome *adj.*; burden *v.*

bureau \BYUUR-oh\ *n. pl.* bureaus or bureaux. **1.** A chest of drawers. **2.** Government department. **3.** Business center.

bureaucracy \byuu-ROK-ruh-see\ *n. pl.* bureaucracies. A complex, inflexible administrative system. bureaucratic *adj.*; bureaucrat *n.*

burglary \BUR-gluh-ree\ *n. pl.* burglaries. A break-in. burglar *n.*; burglarize *v.*; burgle *v.*

burial \BER-ee-ul\ *n.* The burying of a corpse.

burlesque \bur-LESK\ *n.* **1.** Entertainment involving music, dance, and skits. **2.** A mocking caricature. burlesque *adj.*; burlesque *v.*

burn *n.* A wound from exposure to heat.

burn *v.* burned or burnt; burning. **1.** To be on fire. **2.** To damage with fire. **3.** To sting. **4.** To feel heat.

burn out *v.* burned out or burnt out; flattening a tire. burn-out *n.*

burrito \bur-EE-toh\ *n. pl.* burritos. (Sp) A filled, wrapped flour tortilla.

burro \BUR-oh\ *n. pl.* burros. (Sp) A small donkey.

burrow \BUR-oh\ *n.* An underground shelter built by an animal. borrow *v.*

burst *v.* burst or bursted; bursting. **1.** To explode. **2.** To be filled to capacity. **3.** To appear suddenly. burst *n.*

bury \BER-ee\ *v.* buried; burying. **1.** To conceal underground. **2.** To hide.

bus *n. pl.* buses or busses. A motor vehicle for carrying several passengers.

bus *v.* bused; busing or bussed; bussing. **1.** To go or transport by bus. **2.** To clear tables in a restaurant.

bush \buush\ *n.* **1.** A shrub. **2.** A land area covered by shrubs.

bushy \BUUSH-ee\ *adj.* **1.** Thickly covered by shrubs. **2.** Full of hair.

business \BIZ-nis\ *n.* **1.** An occupation. **2.** A trade or commerce operation. **3.** Matter; affair.

bust *n.* **1.** Sculpture of a head and shoulders. **2.** A woman's bosom.

bust *v.* busted or bust; busting. **1.** To break. **2.** To make poor. **3.** To arrest.

bustle \BUS-ul\ *n.* **1.** A lot of activity. **2.** A woman's skirt support.

bustle \BUS-ul\ *v.* bustled; bustling. To move busily.

busy \BIZ-ee\ *adj.* busier; busiest. **1.** Active. **2.** Being used temporarily. **3.** Prying. busily *adv.*; busyness *n.*

busy \BIZ-ee\ *v.* busied; busying. To keep occupied.

busybody \BIZ-ee-bod-ee\ *n.* A prying person.

but *adv.* **1.** Merely. **2.** All but: Nearly.

but *conj.* **1.** Except for. **2.** On the contrary. **3.** That. **4.** However.

but *prep.* Except.

butcher \BUUCH-ur\ *n.* **1.** One who slaughters animals for market. **2.** One guilty of needless killing.

butcher \BUUCH-ur\ *v.* butchered; butchering. **1.** To slaughter an animal for market. **2.** To kill without regard. **3.** To bungle.

butcher block \BUUCH-ur-BLOK\ *n.* A slab of wood for cutting meat.

butte \byoot\ *n.* An isolated steep hill.

butterfly \BUT-ur-FLIE\ *n.* **1.** An insect with four colorful large wings. **2.** A swimming stroke.

butterfly \BUT-ur-FLIE\ *v.* butterflied; butterflying. To cut open and spread apart meat for cooking.

buttocks \BUT-uks\ *pl. n.* The fleshy back of the hips.

button-down \BUT-n-DOWN\ *adj.* Having buttons to secure.

buttress \BU-tris\ *n.* A structural support. buttress *v.*

buxom \BUK-sum\ *adj.* Having a shapely, full-blossomed figure.

buy \bie\ *v.* bought; buying. **1.** To purchase. **2.** To bribe. **3.** [Sl] To accept. **4.** Buy the farm [Id]: To die. buy *n.*; buyer *n.*

buzz \buz\ *n.* **1.** Droning sound of a bee. **2.** Talk or gossip. **3.** Hum or murmur. buzzer *n.*

buzz \buz\ *v.* buzzed; buzzing. **1.** To hum; vibrate. **2.** To talk; gossip. **3.** To bustle.

buzzword \BUZ-wurd\ *n.* A word that triggers a visual counterpart.

by \bie\ *adv.* **1.** In. **2.** Nearby. **3.** Past. **4.** Aside.

by \bie\ *prep.* **1.** Near to. **2.** With the use of. **3.** Past. **4.** Not after. **5.** To the extent of.

bye \bie\ *n.* **1.** A competitor who advances in an idle round. **2.** A farewell.

bygone \BIE-gawn\ *adj.* Relating to the past.

bypass \BIE-pas\ *n.* An alternative passageway. bypass *v.*

bystander \BIE-stan-dur\ *n.* A spectator.

byte \biet\ *n.* (Cm) A unit of computer information that contains eight bits.

C

c \see\ *n. pl.* c's or cs. **1.** The third letter of the English alphabet. **2.** Third in letter grade series.

cab \kab\ *n.* A hired vehicle.

caballero \kab-ul-YAIR-oh\ *n. pl.* caballeros. (Sp) A gentleman.

cabana \kuh-BAN-uh\ *n.* A small pool-side shelter.

cabaret \kab-uh-RAY\ *n.* A restaurant with entertainment; the entertainment provided.

cabbage \KA-baj\ *n.* An edible leafy green vegetable.

cabin \KAB-in\ *n.* **1.** A private compartment on a ship or aircraft. **2.** A tiny dwelling.

cabinet \KAB-uh-nit\ *n.* **1.** A display case. **2.** Executives serving a leader. **3.** A cupboard for storage.

cable \KAY-bul\ *n.* **1.** A thick, strong rope. **2.** Cable TV. **3.** A bunch of insulated wires. cable *v.*

cable TV \KAY-bul-tee-vee\ *n.* Television transmitted to paying subscribers. cable *v.*

caboodle \kuh-BOO-dul\ *n.* A collection.

caboose \kuh-BOOS\ *n.* The rear passenger car for a freight train.

cache \kash\ *n.* (Fr) A secure hiding place. cache *v.*

cackle \KAK-ul\ *v.* cackled; cackling. **1.** To laugh irritatingly. **2.** To utter an uneven cry of a hen. cackle *n.*; cackler *n.*

cacophony \kuh-KOF-uh-nee\ *n. pl.* cacophonies. A disharmonic sound. cacophonous *adj.*

cactus \KAK-tus\ *n. pl.* cacti or cactuses or cactus. A fleshy, water- retaining, prickly plant native to desert regions.

cad \kad\ *n.* An insensitive person. caddish *adj.*; caddishly *adv.*; caddishness *n.*

cadaver \kuh-DAV-ur\ *n.* A dead body. cadaverous *adj.*

caddy *also* **caddie** \KAD-ee\ *n. pl.* caddies. **1.** A golfer's helper. **2.** A storage container.

cadence \KAYD-ns\ *n.* A rhythmic sequence. cadenced *adj.*

cadet \kuh-DET\ *n.* A military trainee.

cadre \KAD-ree\ *n.* (Fr) **1.** A framework. **2.** A core group of trained personnel.

café \ka-FAY\ *n.* (Fr) A small restaurant.

café au lait \KAF-ay-oh-LAY\ *n.* (Fr) A drink consisting of equal amounts of coffee and hot milk.

café noir \KAF-ay-noh-woir\ *n.* (Fr) A black coffee.

cafeteria \kaf-i-TEER-ee-uh\ *n.* A self-serve restaurant.

caffeine \kaf-EEN\ *n.* A stimulant, such as the one found in coffee, tea, and chocolate.

caftan \kaf-TAN\ *n.* (Fo) An ankle-length, long-sleeved garb native to eastern Mediterranean countries.

cage \kayj\ *n.* A barred container, especially for securing an animal. cage *v.*

cagey *also* **cagy** \KAY-jee\ *adj.* cagier; cagiest. **1.** Fearful of entrapment. **2.** Shrewd. cagily *adv.*; caginess *n.*

caisson \KAY-sun\ *n.* **1.** A two-wheeled ammunition holder. **2.** Device to raise sunken ships.

cajole \kuh-JOHL\ *v.* cajoled; cajoling. To entice, especially through flattery. cajolement *n.*; cajolery *n.*

Cajun *also* **Cajan** \KAY-jun\ *n.* Descendant of Acadian French in Louisiana or their language.

cake \kayk\ *n.* **1.** A sweet baked good made from a batter. **2.** A mass of compressed matter.

cake \kayk\ *v.* caked; caking. **1.** To become crusty. **2.** To form into a solid bar.

calamari \KAL-uh-mah-ree\ *n.* (It) Squid.

calamity \kuh-LAM-i-tee\ *n. pl.* calamities. A distressing event. calamitous *adj.*; calamitously *adv.*; calamitousness *n.*

calash *also* **caleche** \kah-LASH\ *n.* (Fr) A lightweight horse-drawn carriage having a collapsible top.

calcium \KAL-see-um\ *n.* (Sc) A light silvery metallic element essential to bones amd shells.

calculate \KAL-kyuh-layt\ *v.* calculated; calculating. **1.** To figure out. **2.** To estimate the amount. **3.** To plan on. calculable *adj.*; calculation *n.*

calculated \KAL-kyuh-lay-tud\ *adj.* Proceeded with after judging the probability of success or failure.

calculating \KAL-kyuh-lay-ting\ *adj.* Scheming to manipulate. calculatingly *adv.*

calculator \KAL-kyuh-lay-tur\ *n.* An instrument used for mathematical figuring.

calculus \KAL-kyuh-lus\ *n. pl.* calculi or calculuses. **1.** An algebraic system of calculation. **2.** Stonelike mass.

caldron *also* **cauldron** \KALL-dron\ *n.* A large pot.

calendar \KAL-un-dur\ *n.* **1.** Various systems of keeping days, years. **2.** Schedule or list; agenda.

calf \kaf\ *n. pl.* calves. **1.** A young cow. **2.** The lower back part of a leg.

caliber *also* **calibre** \KAL-uh-bur\ *n.* **1.** The degree of quality. **2.** The interior diameter of a gun, bullet, or shell.

calibrate \KAL-uh-brayt\ *v.* calibrated; calibrating. **1.** Graduate or adjust a scale. **2.** To read a graded instrument.

calico \KAL-i-koh\ *n. pl.* calicoes or calicos. **1.** A printed fabric. **2.** An animal, such as a cat, having many colors of fur. calico *adj.*

caliph *also* **calif** \KAY-lif\ *n.* An Islamic leader. caliphate *n.*

calisthenics \kal-us-THEN-iks\ *pl. n.* Gymnastic exercises performed without equipment. calisthenic *adj.*

call \kawl\ *n.* **1.** A shout. **2.** An animal's cry. **3.** A demand. **4.** A summons to a meeting.

call \kawl\ *v.* called; calling. **1.** To shout. **2.** Arrange a meeting. **3.** To visit. **4.** To telephone. **5.** To address.

calligraphy \kuh-LIG-ruh-fee\ *n.* Elaborate handwriting. calligrapher *n.*

calling \KAW-ling\ *n.* A chosen profession.

calliope \kuh-LIE-uh-pee\ *n.* A musical instrument of steam whistles and a keyboard.

callous \KAL-us\ *adj.* **1.** Lacking emotional response. **2.** Thickened and insensitive. callously *adv.*; callousness *n.*

calm \kahm\ *adj.* **1.** At peace. **2.** Unexcitable. calmly *adv.*

calm \kahm\ *n.* **1.** The absence of wind. **2.** A state of peace or inactivity. calmness *n.*

calm \kahm\ *v.* calmed; calming. **1.** To put at peace. **2.** To make relaxed.

calorie \KAL-uh-ree\ *n. pl.* calories. **1.** A unit of measuring heat. **2.** A unit of measuring the energy of food.

calvary \KAL-vuh-ree\ *n. pl.* calvaries. A sculptured representation of Christ's crucifixion.

Calvinism \KAL-vuh-ni-zum\ *n.* A theological doctrine. Calvinist *adj.*; Calvinist *n.*

calypso \kuh-LIP-soh\ *n. pl.* calypsos. (Mu) A British West Indian music style.

camaraderie \kahm-RAH-duh-ree\ *n.* (Fr) A friendship.

camcorder \KAM-kor-dur\ *n.* A portable video recorder.

cameo \KAM-ee-oh\ *n. pl.* cameos. **1.** A gem or medallion carved in relief. **2.** A small part using a famous actor.

camera \KAM-ur-uh\ *n.* A photographic device.

camisole \KAM-i-sohl\ *n.* A woman's sleeveless undergarment.

camouflage \KAM-uh-flahzh\ *n.* (Fr) The covering up of something by making it appear like its surroundings. camouflage *v.*

camp \kamp\ *n.* **1.** Temporary settlement. **2.** Group rallying for a cause. **3.** Something tasteless. camp *adj.*; campy *adj.*; campily *adv.*; camper *n.*; campiness *n.*

camp \kamp\ *v.* camped; camping. **1.** To live in a temporary settlement. **2.** To do something silly. camp *adj.*; campy *adj.*; campily *adv.*; camper *n.*; campiness *n.*

campaign \kam-PAYN\ *n.* A series of steps taken in order to bring about a desired result. campaigner *n.*; campaign *v.*

campus \KAM-pus\ *n.* School grounds.

can \kan\ *n.* **1.** A cylindrical metal container. **2.** [Sl] A bathroom. **3.** [Sl] The buttocks.

can \kan\ *v.* canned; canning. **1.** To place in a cylindrical metallic container. **2.** [Sl] To fire from a job.

can \kan\ *v.* could. **1.** To be able to. **2.** To be allowed to.

canal \kuh-NAL\ *n.* **1.** An artificial waterway. **2.** [Md] A cylindrical passageway in the body.

canapé \KAN-uh-pé\ *n.* (Fr) A cracker, bread, or toast topped with food and served as an appetizer.

canary \kuh-NAIR-ee\ *n. pl.* canaries. **1.** A greenish-yellow finch. **2.** A bright yellow color.

canasta \kuh-NAS-tuh\ *n.* (Sp) A

card game involving two decks of cards and two to six players.

cancan \KAN-kan\ *n.* (Fr) A show dance in which women do high kicks.

cancel \KAN-sul\ *v.* canceled; canceling or cancelled; cancelling. **1.** To equal out. **2.** To delete. **3.** To render invalid. cancel *n.*; cancellation *n.*

cancer \KAN-sur\ *n.* **1.** [Md] An fatal growth that spreads. **2.** A growing evil.

candelabra \KAN-dl-LAH-bruh\ *n.* A multi-candle holder.

candescent \kan-DES-sent\ *adj.* Glowing. candescence *n.*

candid \KAN-did\ *adj.* **1.** Honest. **2.** Spontaneous. candidly *adv.*; candidness *n.*

candidate \KAN-di-dayt\ *n.* A person desiring a political office, position, membership, or award. candidacy *n.*

candle \KAN-dl\ *n.* A wax stick surrounding a wick and burned in order to provide light.

candlestick \KAN-dl-stik\ *n.* A candle holder.

candor \KAN-dur\ *n.* A complete honesty.

candy \KAN-dee\ *n. pl.* candies. A sweet confection.

candy \KAN-dee\ *v.* candied; can-

dying. To bake or encrust in sugar or syrup.

candy striper *n.* A hospital volunteer.

cane \kayn\ *n.* **1.** A woody hollow stem. **2.** A walking stick.

cane \kayn\ *v.* caned; caning. **1.** To whack with a stick. **2.** To weave cane. caner *n.*

canine \KAY-nien\ *n.* **1.** A sharp tooth. **2.** A dog. canine *adj.*

canister \KAN-uh-stur\ *n.* A container for storing dry goods.

cannabis \KAN-uh-bis\ *n.* The hemp plant.

cannelloni \KAN-uh-LOH-nee\ *pl. n.* (It) Tubular pasta filled with cheese and baked in a tomato sauce.

cannery \KAN-uh-ree\ *n. pl.* canneries. A factory for storing foods in cylindrical metal containers.

cannibal \KAN-uh-bul\ *n.* One that eats human flesh. cannibalistic *adj.*; cannabilism *n.*; cannibalize *v.*

cannon \KAN-un\ *n. pl.* cannon or cannons. A large, mounted gun.

canoe \kuh-NOO\ *n.* A lightweight boat with pointed ends and curved sides.

canon \KAN-un\ *n.* A religious code.

canonize \KAN-uh-nize\ *v.* canonized; canonizing. To confer sainthood. canonization *n.*

canopy \KAN-uh-pee\ *n. pl.* canopies. A covering.

can't \kant\ *cont.* The contraction of cannot.

cantalope *also* **canteloupe** \KAN-tuh-lope\ *n.* An orange melon enclosed by a rough skin.

cantankerous \kan-TANG-kur-us\ *adj.* Difficult to deal with. cantankerously *adv.*; cantankerousness *n.*

canteen \kan-TEEN\ *n.* **1.** A flask. **2.** A snack bar. **3.** A military recreational area.

canter \KAN-tur\ *n.* A horse's slow gallop. canter *v.*

cantor \KAN-tur\ *n.* A choir leader.

canvas *also* **canvass** \KAN-vus\ *n.* **1.** Heavy woven cloth of hemp, flat, or cotton. **2.** Painting on canvas.

canvass *also* **canvas** \KAN-vus\ *v.* To poll or solicit support. canvasser *n.*

canyon \KAN-yun\ *n.* A gulf in a mountain area.

cap \kap\ *n.* **1.** A hat. **2.** A cover.

cap \kap\ *v.* capped; capping. **1.** To cover. **2.** [Sl]To outdo a performance.

capable \KAY-puh-bul\ *adj.* Being able to. capably *adv.*; capability *n.*

capacity \kuh-PAS-i-tee\ *n. pl.* capacities. **1.** The limit of volume able to be held. **2.** Competency. **3.** A role.

cape \kayp\ *n.* **1.** An area of land projecting into a body of water. **2.** A sleeveless coat.

caper \KAY-pur\ *n.* **1.** A playful jump. **2.** An antic. **3.** A criminal act. **4.** A Mediterranean shrub.

capillary \KAP-uh-ler-ee\ *n. pl.* capillaries. (Md) A minute blood vessel that connects the arteries and veins.

capital \KAP-i-tl\ *adj.* **1.** Foremost. **2.** Superior. **3.** Written in the upper case. **4.** Punishable by death.

capital \KAP-i-tl\ *n.* **1.** A city that is the seat of government. **2.** A capital letter. **3.** Property owned

capitulate \kuh-PICH-uh-layt\ *v.* capitulated; capitulating. To yield. capitulation *n.*

cappuccino \kap-uu-CHEE-noh\ *n.* (It) A drink consisting of strong coffee mixed with steamed milk or cream.

caprice \kuh-PREES\ *n.* An impulsive action. capricious *adj.*

capsize \KAP-size\ *v.* capsized; capsizing. To turn over.

capsule \KAP-sul\ *adj.* Being shortened. capsular *adj.*; capsulize *v.*

capsule \KAP-sul\ *n.* **1.** A small sac, esp. enclosing medicine or vitamins. **2.** A pressurized aircraft. capsular *adj.*; capsulize *v.*

captain \KAP-tun\ *n.* **1.** A military officer. **2.** A team's leader. **3.** The person in charge of a ship. captainship *n.*; captain *v.*

caption \KAP-shun\ *n.* A brief explanatory note. caption *v.*

captivate \KAP-tuh-vayt\ *v.* captivated; captivating. To attract. captivation *n.*; captivator *n.*

captor \KAP-tur\ *n.* A kidnapper.

capture \KAP-chur\ *v.* captured; capturing. **1.** To seize. **2.** To win over. **3.** To always keep as is.

car \kahr\ *n.* A wheeled vehicle.

carafe \kuh-RAF\ *n.* A bottle having a wide flared opening that holds wine or water.

caramel \KAR-uh-mel or KAR-mul\ *n.* A brown, thick, sugary substance.

carapace \KAR-uh-pace\ *n.* A protective covering carried on the backs of some animals.

carat \KAR-ut\ *n.* A unit of weight for measuring precious stones.

caravan \KAR-uh-van\ *n.* A group traveling together.

caraway \KAR-uh-way\ *n.* A fragrant herb bearing seeds used in seasoning and healing.

carbohydrate \kahr-boh-HIE-drayt\ *n.* An organic compound composed of carbon, hydrogen, and oxygen.

carbon \KAHR-bun\ *n.* (Sc) A nonmetallic element.

carbon dating \KAR-bun-DAY-ting\ *n.* (Sc) An archaeological method of determining the age of an object or substance.

carburetor \KAHR-buh-ray-tur\ *n.* The part of an engine responsible for mixing fuel and air.

carcass \KAHR-kus\ *n.* A dead body.

carcinogen \kahr-SIN-uh-jun\ *n.* A cancer-causing substance. carcinogenic *adj.*; carcinogenicity *n.*

carcinoma \kahr-suh-NOH-muh\ *n. pl.* carcinomas or carcinomata (Md) A cancerous tumor.

card \kahrd\ *n.* **1.** A rectangular piece of paper, cardboard or plastic. **2.** One of a playing deck.

card \kahrd\ *v.* carded; carding. **1.** To ask for identification. **2.** To comb fibers before weaving.

cardamom \KAHR-duh-mum\ *n.* A fragrant fruit-bearing herb whose seeds are used in cooking.

cardboard \KAHRD-bord\ *n.* A thick, stiff paper.

cardiac \KAHR-dee-ak\ *adj.* (Md) Concerning the heart.

cardigan \KAHR-di-gun\ *n.* A button-down collarless sweater.

cardinal \KAHR-dn-l\ *adj.* Important.

cardinal \KAHR-dn-l\ *n.* **1.** [Cap] A Roman Catholic official. **2.** A deep bright red color. **3.** A bird.

cardinal number *n.* A counting unit.

cardiomyopathy \KAHR-dee-uh-MY-oh-path-ee\ *n. pl.* cardiomyopathies. (Md) Any disease of the heart muscle.

cardiovascular \KAHR-dee-oh-VAS-kyuu-lur\ *adj.* (Md) Concerning the heart and blood vessels.

care \kair\ *n.* **1.** Personal interest or concern. **2.** Attention to detail. **3.** Custody of something.

care \kair\ *v.* cared; caring. **1.** To be interested or concerned. **2.** To pay attention to detail. **3.** To tend to.

careen \kuh-REEN\ *v.* careened; careening. To lurch.

career \kuh-REER\ *n.* One's profession.

carefree \KAIR-free\ *adj.* Absent of worry.

careful \KAIR-ful\ *adj.* carefuller; carefullest. Cautious. carefully *adv.*; carefulness *n.*

careless \KAIR-lis\ *adj.* To act without attention. carelessly *adv.*; carelessness *n.*

caress \kuh-RES\ *v.* caressed; caressing. To stroke lightly. caress *n.*; caresser *n.*

caretaker \KAIR-tay-kur\ *n.* One who looks after. caretaking *n.* caress *n.*; caresser *n.*

cargo \KAHR-goh\ *n. pl.* cargoes or cargos. Freight transported by a vehicle.

caribou \KAR-uh-boo\ *n. pl.* caribou or caribous. A large reindeer native to North America and Siberia.

caricature \KAR-i-kuh-chur\ *n.* An exaggerated representation. caricaturist *n.*; caricature *v.*

carnage \KAHR-nij\ *n.* A mass slaughter.

carnal \KAHR-nl\ *adj.* Concerning physical desires. carnally *adv.*

carnation \KAHR-nay-shun\ *n.* A plant bearing aromatic many-petaled flowers.

carnival \KAHR-nuh-vul\ *n.* A outdoor festival.

carnivore \KAHR-nuh-vor\ *n.* A meat eater. carnivorous *adj.*; carnivorously *adv.*

carol \KAR-ul\ *n.* A joyful song. caroler *n.*; carol *v.*

carotene \KAR-oh-teen\ *n.* (Sc) A reddish pigment in animals and plants and is a source of Vitamin A.

carouse \kuh-ROWZ\ *v.* caroused; carousing. To partake in drunken revelry. carousal *n.*; carouser *n.*

carp \kahrp\ *n. pl.* carp or carps. An edible freshwater fish native to Europe and Asia.

carpal tunnel syndrome \KAHR-pul-TUN-nul-SIN-drohm\ *n.* (Md) A painful wrist condition caused by strenuously repeated hand motions.

carpenter \KAHR-punt-tur\ *n.* A woodworker. carpentry *n.*

carpet \KAHR-pit\ *n.* A floor or ground covering. carpet *v.*

car pool \KAR-puul\ *n.* Members of a group taking turns in providing transportation. carpool *v.*

carriage \KAR-ij\ *n.* **1.** One's posture. **2.** A vehicle. **3.** A moving portion of a machine.

carrier \KAR-ee-ur\ *n.* **1.** A messenger or transmitter. **2.** Container or vehicle used for transport.

carrion \KAR-ee-un\ *n.* Decaying flesh.

carrot \KAR-ut\ *n.* The edible orange vegetable root of a common garden plant.

carry \KAR-ee\ *v.* carried; carrying. **1.** To transport an object. **2.** To be victorious. **3.** To have or bear upon oneself.

carry-on \KAR-ee-on\ *n.* Baggage small enough to carried aboard an airplane by a passenger.

carry on *v.* **1.** To endure. **2.** To lose control emotionally. **3.** To manage operations.

carry out *v.* **1.** To complete an activity. **2.** To execute a plan.

cart \kahrt\ *n.* A wheeled vehicle, especially used for transporting a load. cart *v.*

carte blanche \KAHRT-BLAHNCH\ *n. pl.* cartes blanches. (Fr) Complete privilege.

cartilage \KAHR-tl-ij\ *n.* (Md) A connecting and supporting skeletal tissue. cartilaginous *adj.*

cartography \kahr-TOG-ruh-fee\ *n.* Map making. cartographer *n.*

carton \KAHR-tn\ *n.* A paper container.

cartoon \kahr-TOON\ *n.* **1.** A preliminary sketch. **2.** An amusing drawing. **3.** An animated film. **4.** A comic. cartoonist *n.*

cartridge \KAHR-trij\ *n.* A container or casing containing a firearm charge, projectile, or other material.

carve \kahrv\ *v.* carved; carving. To cut up. carver *n.*

cascade \kas-KAYD\ *n.* Something falling, especially water. cascade *v.*

case \kays\ *n.* **1.** A carrying container. **2.** A covering. **3.** An example. **4.** A convincing argument.

case \kays\ *v.* cased; casing. **1.** To enclose. **2.** To examine closely.

cash \kash\ *n.* Money.

cash \kash\ *v.* cashed; cashing. To exchange for money.

cash flow *n.* A person's available money.

cashew \KASH-oo\ *n.* An evergreen tree of tropical America that bears edible crescent-shaped nut.

cashier \ka-SHEER\ *n.* A money handler.

cashmere \KAZH-meer\ *n.* **1.** A fine, soft wool of a the Cashmere goat. **2.** A plush fabric made from it. cashmere *adj.*

casino \kuh-SEE-noh\ *n. pl.* casinos. A gambling establishment.

casserole \KAS-uh-rohl\ *n.* **1.** A covered baking dish. **2.** A dish of food, often a mixture, baked in this.

cassette *also* **casette** \kuh-SET\ *n.* A container of photographic film or magnetic tape wound on a spool.

cast \kast\ *n.* **1.** The actors in a performance. **2.** A throw outward. **3.** A shade of color.

cast \kast\ *v.* cast; casting. **1.** To choose the actors in a performance. **2.** To throw outward. **3.** To give off.

castanets \kas-tuh-NETS\ *n. pl.* (Sp) A percussion instrument of two small disks clapped together with the fingers.

castaway \KAST-uh-way\ *adj.* **1.** Something neglected. **2.** Shipwrecked. castaway *n.*

caste \kast\ *n.* **1.** A Hindu social class. **2.** Any rigid social class.

castle \KAS-ul\ *n.* An immense fortified structure.

castrate \KAS-trayt\ *v.* castrated; castrating. To remove the sexual organs of. castration *n.*

casual \KAZH-oo-ul\ *adj.* **1.** Relaxed in manner. **2.** Random. casually *adv.*; casualness *n.*

casualty \KAZH-oo-ul-tee\ *n. pl.* casualties. **1.** An accident. **2.** A victim of an accident.

cat \kat\ *n.* A feline.

cataclysm \KAT-uh-kliz-um\ *n.* A terrible, violent event. cataclysmal *adj.*; cataclysmic *adj.*

catacomb \KAT-uh-kohm\ *n.* Underground passageways, especially reserved for burial.

catalepsy \KAT-uh-lep-see\ *n. pl.*

catalepsies. (Md) Nervous condition characterized by a trancelike state and loss of muscle control. cataleptic *adj.*; cataleptic *n.*

catalog *also* **catalogue** \KAT-l-awg\ *n.* A list, especially one including details on the items within it. cataloger or cataloguer *n.*; catalog or catalogue *v.*

catalyst \KAT-l-ist\ *n.* Any substance or thing that causes a change without becoming changed itself. catalytic *adj.*; catalytically *adv.*; catalysis *n.*

catalytic converter \kat-l-IT-ik-kun-VER-tur\ *n.* Automobile exhaust part that transforms harmful gases into harmless byproducts.

catamaran \kat-uh-muh-RAN\ *n.* A boat having two parallel floats.

catapult \KAT-uh-pult\ *n.* A launching device. catapult *v.*

cataract \KAT-uh-rakt\ *n.* **1.** [Md] Opacity of the lens of the eye. **2.** A waterfall. **3.** A downpour.

catastrophe \kuh-TAS-truh-fee\ *n.* A disaster. catastrophic *adj.*; catastrophically *adv.*

catatonic \KAT-uh-tawn-ik\ *adj.* Having a nervous disorder in which muscles stiffen and movement is rigid. catatonic *n.*

catch \kach\ *n.* **1.** The act of taking hold of. **2.** A fastener. **3.** A hidden disadvantage.

catch \kach\ *v.* caught; catching. **1.** To take hold of. **2.** To overtake and capture. **3.** To discover. **4.** To contract.

Catch-22 *n.* Catch-22's or Catch-22s. An unsolvable or paradoxical situation.

catchy \KACH-ee\ *adj.* catchier; catchiest. **1.** Captivating. **2.** Addictive. **3.** Difficult to figure out.

catechism \KAT-uh-kiz-um\ *n.* A series of questions and answers designed to instruct. catechist *n.*; catechize *v.*

categorical \kat-i-GOR-i-kul\ *adj.* **1.** Without exception. **2.** Pertaining to a section of classification. categorically *adv.*

category \KAT-uh-gor-ee\ *n. pl.* categories. A section of a classification.

cater \KAY-tur\ *v.* catered; catering. **1.** To supply party food. **2.** To supply a need. caterer *n.*

caterpillar \KAT-uh-pil-ur\ *n.* The furry wormlike larva of a butterfly or moth.

catharsis \kuh-THAR-sis\ *n. pl.* catharses. A purification, especially of the emotions. cathartic *adj.*

cathedral \kuh-THEE-drul\ *n.* **1.** A large church. **2.** The central church under one bishop's control.

catheter \KATH-i-tur\ *n.* (Md) A flexible tube inserted into the body to remove or add fluid. catheterization *n.*; catheterize *v.*

cathode \KATH-ohd\ *n.* (Sc) **1.** The negative pole of an electric current. **2.** The positive end of a battery.

Catholicism \kuh-THOL-i-siz-um\ *n.* The religion, belief, institution, and practice of the Catholic church. catholic *adj.*; Catholic *n.*; catholicity *n.*

CAT scan *n.* (Md) A detailed image of the inner body produced by a machine.

catsup *also* **ketchup** \KAT-sup or KACH-up\ *n.* A sauce made of pureed tomatoes.

catty \KAT-ee\ *adj.* cattier; cattiest. (Sl) Ill-natured. cattily *adv.*; cattiness *n.*

catty-corner *also* **catty-cornered, kitty-cornered,** or **cater-cornered** *adj.* none \KAT-ee-kor-nur\ Resting on a diagonal line.

Caucasian \kaw-KAY-zhun\ *adj.* Pertaining to a race having light skin. Caucasian *n.*

caucus \KAW-kus\ *n. pl.* caucuses. A group gathered to make decisions.

cauliflower \KAW-luh-flow-ur\ *n.* A plant producing a white, edible head similar in appearance to broccoli.

caulk *also* **caulking** \kawk\ *n.* A white sealant. caulker *n.*; caulk *v.*

causal \KAW-zul\ *adj.* Relating to the initiator of an effect. causally *adv.*; causality *n.*

cause \kawz\ *n.* **1.** The initiator of an effect. **2.** A supported belief. **3.** Motive.

cause \kawz\ *v.* caused; causing. To initiate an effect.

cause celebre \KAWZ suh-LEB-ruh\ *n. pl.* causes celebres. (Fr) A well-noted event.

causeway \KAWZ-way\ *n.* A raised passageway.

caustic \KAW-stik\ *adj.* **1.** Sarcastic. **2.** Burning. caustically *adv.*; caustic *n.*

cauterize \KAW-tuh-riez\ *v.* cauterized; cauterizing. (Md) To burn or scar skin tissue in order to stop infection. cauterization *n.*

caution \KAW-shun\ *n.* **1.** A carefulness. **2.** A warning. cautionary. *adj.*; cautious *adj.*; cautiously *adv.*; cautiousness *n.*

cavalcade \kav-ul-KAYD\ *n.* A procession, especially of riders or vehicles.

cavalier \kav-uh-LEER\ *adj.* Arrogant.

cavalier \kav-uh-LEER\ *n.* **1.** A soldier atop a horse. **2.** An escort. **3.** A nobleman.

cavalry \KAV-ul-ree\ *n. pl.* cavalries. Soldiers on horseback or in motor vehicles.

cave \kayv\ *n.* An underground cavity.

caveat \KAV-ee-at\ *n.* A warning.

cave in *v.* **1.** To collapse. **2.** To yield.

cavern \KAV-urn\ *n.* A large underground cavity. cavernous *adj.*; cavernously *adv.*

caviar *also* **caviare** \KAV-ee-ahr\ *n.* Salted fish eggs served as an appetizer.

cavity \KAV-i-tee\ *n. pl.* cavities. **1.** An open space. **2.** [Md] A decayed area in a tooth.

cavort \kuh-VORT\ *v.* cavorted; cavorting. To play.

cayenne \KAY-en\ *n.* A spicy, red pepper.

CB radio *n.* A radio-frequency transmitter that sends and receives spoken signals.

CD \SEE-DEE\ *n. pl.* CD's. **1.** A compact disk. **2.** A certificate of deposit.

CD player *n.* An device that scans compact disks using a laser.

CD-ROM \SEE-DEE-ROM\ *n.* (Cm) Metal disk on which information is stored and accessed by a player on a computer.

cease \sees\ *v.* ceased; ceasing. To end.

cedar \SEE-dur\ *n.* A coniferous tree producing aromatic durable timber.

cede \seed\ *v.* ceded; ceding. To surrender.

cedilla \si-DIL-uh\ *n.* (Sp) A diacritical mark changing a c sound to an s sound.

ceiling \SEE-ling\ *n.* **1.** The maximum limit. **2.** The top of a room.

celebrate \SEL-uh-brayt\ *v.* celebrated; celebrating. **1.** To honor or mark. **2.** To observe with festivities. celebratory *adj.*; celebration *n.*; celebrator *n.*

celebrity \suh-LEB-ri-tee\ *n. pl.* celebrities. A famous person.

celery \SEL-uh-ree\ *n. pl.* celeries. A plant bearing crisp, ebible green stems.

celestial \suh-LES-chul\ *adj.* Relating to the sky or heavens.

celibate \SEL-uh-bit\ *adj.* Abstaining from sexual activity. celibacy *n.*

cell \sel\ *n.* **1.** A small room. **2.** [Sc] Smallest unit of living tissue. **3.** An electricical unit.

cellar \SEL-ur\ *n.* The underground story of a building.

cello violoncello \CHEL-oh\ *n. pl.* cellos. (Mu) A bass stringed instrument of the violin family.

Celsius \SEL-see-us\ *adj.* (Sc) On the temperature scale where freezing is zero and boiling is 100 degrees.

cement \si-MENT\ *n.* **1.** Binding mixture of limestone, clay, etc. **2.** Any adhesive or glue.

cemetery \SEM-i-ter-ee\ *n. pl.* cemeteries. A burial ground.

censor \SEN-sur\ *n.* One who has the power to ban material deemed offensive.

censor \SEN-sur\ *v.* censored; censoring. To selectively ban material deemed offensive. censorship *n.*

censure \SEN-shur\ *n.* Disapproval.

censure \SEN-shur\ *v.* censured; censuring. To criticize severely. censure *n.*

census \SEN-sus\ *n. pl.* censuses. A period tally of the population.

cent \sent\ *n.* A copper coin equal to 1/100th of the American dollar.

centaur \SEN-tor\ *n.* A Greek mythological creature that is half man and half horse.

center \SEN-tur\ *n.* **1.** The middle point. **2.** An area of concentrated attention. center *adj.*

center \SEN-tur\ *v.* centered; centering. **1.** To fix in the middle. **2.** To draw to a middle point. **3.** To concentrate. centered *adj.*

centerfold \SEN-tur-fohld\ *n.* A magazine's middle picture that is larger than surrounding pages.

centerpiece \SEN-tur-pees\ *n.* A decorative object placed in an area of focused attention.

central \SEN-trul\ *adj.* **1.** Pertaining to a middle area. **2.** Principal. centrally *adv.*

centrifugal \sen-TRIF-yuh-gul\ *adj.* Radiating from a central point.

cephalic \suh-FAL-ik\ *adj.* Concerning the head.

ceramics \suh-RAM-iks\ *pl. n.* **1.** Objects made by sculpting and firing clay. **2.** Art of creating such objects. ceramic *adj.*; ceramicist *n.*

cereal \SEER-ee-ul\ *n.* **1.** A grass with edible grains. **2.** Breakfast food made of these grains. cereal *adj.*

cerebellum \ser-uh-BEL-um\ *n. pl.* cerebellums or cerebella. (Md) The part of the brain where movement and equilibrium are coordinated. cerebellar *adj.*

cerebral \suh-REE-brul\ *adj.* **1.** Concerning the brain. **2.** Appealing to or needing the intellect.

cerebral palsy *n.* (Md) A paralysis affecting the control of movement caused by brain damage upon birth. cerebral palsied *adj.*

cerebrate \SER-uh-brayt\ *v.* cerebrated; cerebrating. To think.

cerebrum \suh-REE-brum\ *n. pl.* cerebrums or cerebra. The part of the brain where conscious processes take place.

ceremony \ser-uh-MOH-nee\ *n. pl.* ceremonies. **1.** A ritual act. **2.** Etiquette. ceremonial *adj.*; ceremonious *adj.*; ceremonially *adv.*; ceremoniously *adv.*

certain \SUR-tn\ *adj.* **1.** Sure. **2.** Inevitable. **3.** Fixed. **4.** Referring to a specifically known amount. certainly *adv.*; certainty *n.*

certificate \sur-TIF-i-kit\ *n.* An authorizing document.

certify \SUR-tuh-fie\ *v.* certified; certifying. To declare as true. certifiable *adj.*; certifiably *adv.*; certification *n.*; certifier *n.*

cervix \SUR-viks\ *n. pl.* cervices or cervixes. (Md) **1.** The narrow end of the uterus. **2.** The back section of the neck.

cetology \see-TOWL-oh-gee\ *n.* (Sc) The study of whales and related aquatic mammals. cetacean *adj.*; cetaceous *adj.*; cetacean *n.*; cetologist *n.*

chafe \chayf\ *v.* chafed; chafing. **1.** To rub to the point of irritation. **2.** To bother.

chagrin \shu-GRIN\ *v.* chagrined; chagrining. To disgrace. chagrin *n.*

chain \chayn\ *n.* **1.** Connected metal links. **2.** An interconnected series.

chain \chayn\ *v.* chained; chaining. To tie up using a length of connected metal links.

chair *n.* **1.** A seat with a back designed for holding one person. **2.** A position of authority.

chairperson \CHAIR-pur-sun\ *n.* A person in charge of proceedings.

chaise lounge *also* **chaise longue** \shayz-LAWNG\ *n. pl.* chaise lounges or chaise longues. (Fr) A long reclining chair.

chalet \sha-LAY\ *n.* A house or cottage in a Swiss style with gently sloping, projecting roof.

chalice \CHAL-is\ *n.* A drinking cup.

chalk \chawk\ *n.* A soft material used for marking up a blackboard. chalk *adj.*; chalky *adj.*; chalkiness *n.*; chalk *v.*

challah *also* **chalah or hallah** \CHA-lah\ *n.* (Yd) A braided loaf of sweet bread often consumed by Jews during holiday events.

challenge \CHAL-inj\ *n.* **1.** An invitation to compete. **2.** A demand for proof. **3.** A test or contest.

challenge \CHAL-inj\ *v.* challenged; challenging. **1.** To invite to compete. **2.** To demand proof. **3.** To push oneself to the limit.

challis \CHAL-is\ *n. pl.* challises. A lightweight textile of wool, cotton, or synthetic yarns.

chamber \CHAYM-bur\ *n.* **1.** A room, esp. a bedroom. **2.** A legislative assembly hall. **3.** [Pl] [Le] Judge's room.

chameleon \kuh-MEE-lee-un\ *n.* A lizard that hides by changing its body color to match its environment.

chamomile *also* **camomile** \KA-moh-meel\ *n.* A herb whose flower heads are used to produce an herbal tea, etc.

champagne \sham-PAYN\ *n.* A sparkling white wine.

champion \CHAM-pee-un\ *n.* **1.** A winner in a competition. **2.** One who fights for a cause.

champion \CHAM-pee-un\ *v.* championed; championing. **1.** To fight for. **2.** To protect.

championship \CHAM-pee-un-ship\ *n.* **1.** A competition to discover the winner. **2.** The winner's title or position.

chance \chans\ *n.* **1.** A random event. **2.** A predetermined course. **3.** A gamble. **4.** An opportunity. chance *adj.*; chancy *adj.*

chance \chans\ *v.* chanced; chancing. **1.** To happen randomly. **2.** To risk.

chancellery *also* **chancellory** \CHAN-suh-lur-ee\ *n. pl.* chancelleries or chancellories. A chancellor's court or office.

chancellor \CHAN-suh-lur\ *n.* **1.** A top-ranking state official. **2.** A university president. chancellorship *n.*

chandelier \shan-dl-EER\ *n.* An ornate suspended lighting device. chandeliered *adj.*

change \chaynj\ *n.* **1.** The act of transforming. **2.** A replacement. **3.** Smaller currency in exchange.

change \chaynj\ *v.* changed; changing. **1.** To transform. **2.** To replace. **3.** To give back for another. **4.** Become different.

channel \CHAN-l\ *n.* **1.** A water-way. **2.** A means of passage. **3.** A range of communication frequencies.

channel \CHAN-l\ *v.* channeled; chaneling or channelled; channelling. **1.** To cause to follow a course. **2.** To cut a groove in. **3.** To guide.

chant *n.* **1.** [Mu] A chorus of song. **2.** A way of singing or speaking that is monotone. chanter *n.*; chant *v.*

chaos \KAY-os\ *n.* Utter confusion. chaotic *adj.*; chaotically *adv.*

chaparral \shap-uh-RAL\ *n.* A dense thicket.

chapeau \sha-POH\ *n. pl.* chapeaux or chapeaus. (Fr) A hat.

chaperon *also* **chaperone** \SHAP-uh-rohn\ *n.* An escort. chaperon or chaperone *v.*

chaplain \CHAP-lin\ *n.* A minister chosen to lead religious exercises for a special group. chaplaincy *n.*

chapter \CHAP-tur\ *n.* **1.** A main section of a book. **2.** A local branch of a group.

char \chahr\ *v.* charred; charring. To scorch.

character \KAR-ik-tur\ *n.* **1.** A written symbol. **2.** Individual fea-

ture. **3.** An integrity. **4.** An odd person.

characteristic \kar-ik-tuh-RIS-tik\ *adj.* Pertaining to a distinctive mark or quality. characteristically *adv.*

charade \shuh-RAYD\ *n.* **1.** A pretense. **2.** A game.

charbroil \CHAR-broyl\ *v.* charbroiled; charbroiling. To cook over charcoals.

charcuterie \shar-KOO-tur-ee\ *n.* (Fr) Cooked or processed meats, such as sausages and pates.

chard *n.* The edible large leafy greens of a variety of beet.

charge \chahrj\ *n.* **1.** An accusation. **2.** An onslaught. **3.** A burden. **4.** A price asked for something.

charge \chahrj\ *v.* charged; charging. **1.** To accuse. **2.** To attack. **3.** To burden. **4.** To ask a price for something.

chariot \CHAR-ee-ut\ *n.* A two-wheeled, horse-drawn carriage, such as the one used in ancient times.

charisma *also* **charism** \kuh-RIZ-muh\ *n. pl.* charismata or charisms. A tremendous charm or appeal. charismatic *adj.*

charity \CHAR-i-tee\ *n. pl.* charities. **1.** Aid given to the needy. **2.** A group to aid the needy. **3.**

Brotherly love. charitable *adj.*; charitably *adv.*

charlatan \SHAHR-luh-tn\ *n.* A fraud. charlatanism *n.*

charm \chahrm\ *n.* **1.** Something believed to be magical. **2.** Something believed to bring good luck. charming *adj.*; charmingly *adv.*; charmer *n.*; charm *v.*

chart \chahrt\ *n.* **1.** A map. **2.** Information in graphs or tables. chart *v.*

charter \CHAHR-tur\ *n.* **1.** An agreement of rights and privileges. **2.** The act of hiring an aircraft. charter *v.*

chartreuse \shahr-TROOZ\ *n.* A bright green color.

chase \chays\ *n.* **1.** A pursuit. **2.** An area of land set aside for game hunting.

chase \chays\ *v.* chased; chasing. **1.** To pursue. **2.** To look for. **3.** To engrave a metal surface.

chasm \KAZ-um\ *n.* **1.** A deep cavity in the earth. **2.** A gap. **3.** A disagreement.

chassis \CHAS-ee\ *n. pl.* chassis. A supporting frame.

chaste \chayst\ *adj.* chaster; chastest. **1.** Not corrupted. **2.** Abstaining from sexual intercourse. **3.** Modest in design. chasteley *adv.*; chasteness *n.*

chastise \chas-TIEZ\ *v.* chastised; chastising. **1.** To discipline. **2.** To criticize harshly. chastisement *n.*

chat *v.* chatted; chatting. To talk informally. chat *n.*

chateau \sha-TOH\ *n. pl.* chateaus or chateaux. (Fr) **1.** A country mansion. **2.** A castle. **3.** A vineyard.

chatter \CHAT-ur\ *v.* chattered; chattering. **1.** To speak quickly and endlessly. **2.** To utter garbled sounds. chatter *n.*

chauffeur \SHOH-fur\ *n.* (Fr) A hired automobile driver. chauffeur *v.*

chauvinism \SHOH-vuh-niz-um\ *n.* (Fr) An unreasonable, fanatical pride in something. chauvinistic *adj.*; chauvinistically *adv.*; chauvinist *n.*

cheap \cheep\ *adj.* cheaper; cheapest. **1.** Costing little money. **2.** Inferior in quality. **3.** Vulgar. **4.** Miserly. cheaply *adv.*; cheapness *n.*; cheapen *v.*

cheap shot *n.* [Cl] A despicable and dishonest act.

cheat \cheet\ *n.* **1.** One who fools others. **2.** A trick.

cheat \cheet\ *v.* cheated; cheating. **1.** To fool another. **2.** To break the rules. **3.** To be sexually unfaithful. cheater *n.*

check \chek\ *n.* **1.** A hindrance. **2.** An inspection. **3.** A symbol of completion. **4.** A pattern.

check \chek\ *v.* checked; checking. **1.** To hinder. **2.** To inspect. **3.** To mark with a symbol to indicate completion.

cheddar \CHED-dur\ *n.* A smooth-textured, white or yellow, mild- to sharp-flavored cheese.

cheek *n.* **1.** The flesh of the face on either side of the nose. **2.** A boldness.

cheeky \CHEE-kee\ *adj.* cheekier; cheekiest. Brash. cheekily *adv.*; cheekiness *n.*

cheep *v.* To chirp, as a bird does. cheep *n.*

cheer *n.* **1.** Happiness. **2.** An approving or encouraging shout. **3.** Food and drink.

cheer *v.* cheered; cheering. **1.** To make happy. **2.** To support through approving or encouraging shouts. cheerful *adj.*; cheery *adj.*; cheerfully *adv.*; cheerily *adv.*; cheerfulness *n.*

cheese \cheez\ *n.* A food make from milk curd.

cheetah \CHEE-tuh\ *n. pl.* cheetahs or cheetah. A spotted, fast-moving cat native to Africa and Asia.

chef \shef\ *n.* A skilled cook, espe-

cially one who oversees a restaurant's kitchen.

chemical \KEM-i-kul\ *n.* A substance obtained by or used in a chemical process.

chemise \shu-MEEZ\ *n.* A woman's baggy undergarment.

chemistry \KEM-uh-stree\ *n. pl.* chemistries. **1.** The science of the composition of substances. **2.** Chemical processes.

chemotherapy \kee-moh-THER-uh-pee\ *n.* (Md) The treatment of disease using chemicals or drugs. chemotherapeutic *adj.*; chemotherapist *n.*

chenille \shu-NEEL\ *n.* **1.** A fluffy yarn. **2.** A deep, fluffy knit made of such a yarn.

cherish \CHER-ish\ *v.* cherished; cherishing. To treasure.

cherry \CHER-ee\ *n. pl.* cherries. **1.** Various trees with rounded fruit containing a pit. **2.** Bright red color.

cherub \CHER-ub\ *n. pl.* cherubim or cherubs. **1.** An angel depicted as a winged child. **2.** One resembling or acting as an angel.

chervil \CHER-vul\ *n.* An herb bearing fragrant leaves that are used as a seasoning.

chest *n.* **1.** A storage box. **2.** [Md]

The part of the body enclosed by the ribs.

chestnut \CHES-nut\ *n.* **1.** A tree of northern temperate regions with edible nuts. **2.** A reddish brown.

chevron \SHEV-run\ *n.* A V-shaped stripe or stripes worn on the sleeve to indicate symbol or rank.

chew \choo\ *v.* chewed; chewing. **1.** To grind with the teeth. **2.** Chew the fat [Id]: To talk for a long time. chewable *adj.*; chewy *adj.*

chew out *v.* To scold.

chic \sheek\ *n.* (Fr) A fashionableness. chic *adj.*; chicness *n.*

chicanery \shi-KAY-nur-ee\ *n. pl.* chicaneries. A deviousness.

Chicano \chi-KAH-noh\ *n. pl.* Chicanos. An American of Mexican descent.

chichi \SHEE-shee\ *adj.* (Fr) **1.** Very ornamental. **2.** Fashionable.

chick \chik\ *n.* A baby bird.

chicken \CHIK-un\ *n.* **1.** A common barnyard fowl or its edible meat. **2.** [Sl] A coward. chicken *adj.*

chicory \CHIK-uh-ree\ *n. pl.* chicories. An herb of North America that bears a root used as a salad green.

chide \chied\ *v.* chid or chided; chid or chided or chidden; chiding. To criticize.

chief \cheef\ *adj.* Having the highest office or influence.

chief \cheef\ *n.* **1.** The leader. **2.** The most important. chiefly *adv.*

chiffon \shif-FON\ *n.* A sheer fabric, often made of silk.

child \chield\ *n. pl.* children **1.** A young person. **2.** An immature person. childish *adj.*; childlike *adj.*; childishly *adv.*; childishness *n.*

childbirth \CHIELD-burth\ *n.* (Md) The act of bringing forth young.

childhood \CHIELD-huud\ *n.* The period of adolescence.

childproof \CHIELD-pruuf\ *adj.* Barring a child's access.

chili *also* **chile or chilli** \CHIL-ee\ *n. pl.* chilies or chiles or chillies. (Sp) **1.** A hot pepper. **2.** A powder made from hot pepper. **3.** A seasoned dish of beans.

chill \chil\ *v.* chilled; chilling. **1.** To cause to be cold. **2.** To cause to shiver.

chill out *v.* (Sl) To relax.

chilly \CHIL-ee\ *adj.* chillier; chilliest. **1.** Cold. **2.** Aloof. chilliness *n.*

chime \chiem\ *n.* A group of tuned bells or their ringing.

chime \chiem\ *v.* chimed; chiming.

1. To ring. **2.** To sound in harmony.

chimera *also* **chimaera** \ki-MEER-uh\ *n.* An imagined horror. chimeric *adj.*; chimerical *adj.*

chimney \CHIM-nee\ *n. pl.* chimneys. A smokestack.

china \CHIE-nuh\ *n.* Formal tableware, especially made of porcelain.

China syndrome *n.* (Sc) An accidental meltdown of a nuclear reactor core.

chip *n.* **1.** A fragment of wood. **2.** A thin slice of material. **3.** An electronics component.

chip *v.* chipped; chipping. To knock a piece out of.

chip in *v.* To contribute.

chiropractic \kie-ruh-PRAK-tik\ *n.* (Md) A method of healing involving the manipulation of the spinal column, etc. chiropractor *n.*

chirp \churp\ *v.* chirped; chirping. To utter a high-pitched noise, such as the one a bird or insect makes. chirp *n.*

chisel \CHIZ-ul\ *n.* A sharp-edged metal carving tool.

chisel \CHIS-zul\ *v.* chiseled; chiseling or chiselled; chiselling. **1.** To sculpture by chipping away at wood, stone, or metal. **2.** To trick. chiseler *n.*

chivalrous \SHIV-ul-rus\ *adj.* **1.** Gentlemanly. **2.** Courageous. chivalrously *adv.*; chivalrousness *n.*

chivalry \SHIV-ul-ree\ *n. pl.* chivalries. **1.** A group of knights. **2.** A politeness and courageousness. chivalrously *adv.*; chivalrousness *n.*

chlorine \KLOR-een\ *n.* (Sc) A pungent gaseous chemical element often used as a bleach and disinfectant.

chloroform \KLOR-uh-form\ *n.* (Sc) A colorless fluid often used as an anesthetic.

chlorophyll \KLOR-uh-fil\ *n.* (Sc) The green plant pigment responsible for photosynthesis.

choice \chois\ *adj.* choicer; choicest. **1.** Of superior quality. **2.** Worthy of selection. **3.** Selected carefully.

choice \chois\ *n.* **1.** The act of selecting. **2.** The power of selection. **3.** The thing selected.

choir \kwire\ *n.* **1.** A singing group. **2.** The part of a church where the singers sit.

choke \chohk\ *v.* choked; choking. **1.** To obstruct normal breathing. **2.** To suppress. **3.** To lessen air intake.

cholera \KOL-ur-uh\ *n.* (Md) An acute stomach illness characterized by vomiting and diarrhea.

cholesterol \kuh-LES-tuh-rohl\ *n.* (Md) A fatty substance in bile and distributed in animal fats and tissues.

choose \chooz\ *v.* chose; chosen; choosing. To make a thoughtful decision. choosy *adj.*; chooser *n.*

chop *n.* **1.** A quick blow. **2.** A portion of meat from the rib or shoulder.

chop *v.* chopped; chopping. **1.** To cut into pieces. **2.** To strike.

choppy \CHOP-ee\ *adj.* choppier; choppiest. **1.** Bouncy. **2.** Rough. choppily *adv.*; choppiness *n.*

choral \KOR-ul\ *adj.* Sung by a choir or chorus.

chord \kord\ *n.* **1.** [Mu] The simultaneous sounding of three or more musical notes. **2.** A rope.

choreography \kor-ee-OG-ruh-fee\ *n. pl.* choreographies. The step arrangements for a dance. choreographic *adj.*; choreographically *adv.*; choreographer *n.*; choreograph *v.*

chortle \CHOR-tl\ *v.* chortled; chortling. To giggle. chortle *n.*

chorus \KOR-us\ *n.* **1.** An singing group. **2.** A piece performed by a chorus. **3.** A refrain. chortle *n.*

chow *n.* **1.** Food. **2.** [Cl] An informal name for the Chow chow dog.

chow *v.* chowed; chowing. To eat.

christen \KRIS-un\ *v.* christened; christening. **1.** To baptize. **2.** To name through a religious rite or similar ceremony. christening *n.*

chronic \KRON-ik\ *adj.* Prolonged or recurring. chronically *adv.*

chronicle \KRON-i-kul\ *n.* A historical account. chronicler *n.*; chronicle *v.*

chronology \kruh-NOL-i-jee\ *n. pl.* chronologies. Something arranged in consecutive time order. chronological *adj.*; chronologically *adv.*

chubby \CHUB-ee\ *adj.* chubbier; chubbiest. Slightly overweight. chubbily *adv.*; chubbiness *n.*

chuckle \CHUK-ul\ *v.* chuckled; chuckling. To giggle. chuckle *n.*; chuckler *n.*

chum *n.* A good friend. chummy *adj.*; chummily *adv.*; chumminess *n.*; chum *v.*

chunk \chungk\ *n.* A slab of something.

chunky \CHUNG-kee\ *adj.* chunkier; chunkiest. **1.** Having slabs of something. **2.** Slightly overweight.

church *n.* **1.** A place of worship. **2.** A group of Christian believers.

churl *n.* A rude person. churlish *adj.*; churlishness *n.*

churn *n.* A holder in which milk or cream is whipped into butter.

churn *v.* churned; churning. **1.** To whip in a churn. **2.** To beat.

churn out *v.* To mechanistically produce large quantities of something.

chute \shoot\ *n.* **1.** A parachute. **2.** An inclined passageway.

chutzpah \KHUUT-spuh\ *n.* (Yd) An overwhelming self-confidence.

ciao \chow\ interj. (It) **1.** Hello! **2.** Goodbye!

cicada \si-KAY-duh\ *n. pl.* cicadas or cicadae. A chirping insect resembling a grasshopper.

cinder \SIN-dur\ *n.* A fragment of partially burnt coal or wood.

cinema \SIN-uh-muh\ *n.* **1.** A movie theater. **2.** Film as an art form. cinematic *adj.*

cipher \SIE-fur\ *n.* **1.** A zero. **2.** A system of secret code.

cipher \SIE-fur\ *v.* ciphered; ciphering. To calculate.

circa \SUR-kuh\ *prep.* About or around.

circle \SUR-kul\ *n.* **1.** A closed plane curve. **2.** A group with similar interests.

circle \SUR-kul\ *v.* circled; circling. To revolve around.

circuit \SUR-kit\ *n.* **1.** A circular route or course. **2.** An electrical current's path.

circuit breaker *n.* (Sc) An electric current interruption.

circular \SUR-kyuh-lur\ *adj.* Of or shaped like a circle.

circulate \SUR-kyuh-layt\ *v.* circulated; circulating. **1.** To flow in a circle. **2.** To move among many.

circulation \sur-kyuh-LAY-shun\ *n.* **1.** Flow. **2.** Transmission. **3.** Number of copies sold of a periodical.

circumference \sur-KUM-fur-uns\ *n.* **1.** The boundary of a circle. **2.** A circle's perimeter.

circumscribe \SUR-kum-skrieb\ *v.* circumscribed; circumscribing. **1.** To define limits. **2.** To surround.

circumspect \SUR-kum-spekt\ *adj.* Cautious. circumspection *n.*; circumspectly *adv.*

circumstance \SUR-kum-stans\ *n.* **1.** A particular instance. **2.** An eventuality.

circumstantial \sur-kum-STAN-shul\ *adj.* **1.** Dependent on circumstances. **2.** Incidental. **3.** Detailed. circumstantially *adv.*

circumvent \sur-kum-VENT\ *v.* circumvented; circumventing. To evade. circumvention *n.*

circus \SUR-kus\ *n. pl.* circuses. **1.** A traveling entertainment show. **2.** The arena for a circus performance.

cirrus \SIR-us\ *n. pl.* cirri. High wispy clouds.

citadel \SIT-u-dl\ *n.* A stronghold or fortress.

citation \sie-TAY-shun\ *n.* **1.** A specific mention. **2.** A quote.

cite \siet\ *v.* cited; citing. **1.** To call upon an authority. **2.** To quote or mention.

citizen \SIT-uh-zun\ *n.* An inhabitant of a governmental jurisdiction. citizenry *n.*, citizenship *n.*

city \SIT-ee\ *n. pl.* cities. A large town with a government.

civic \SIV-ik\ *adj.* Of or concerning a city and citizens.

civil \SIV-ul\ *adj.* **1.** Mannerly. **2.** Of or concerning citizens. civilly *adv.*

civilian \si-VIL-yun\ *n.* A person not in the armed services.

civilization \siv-uh-luh-ZAY-shun\ *n.* A stage of cultural development and society.

civilize \SIV-uh-liez\ *v.* civilized; civilizing. To increase cultural, social, or technological development.

claim \klaym\ *n.* **1.** A right or title to something. **2.** A demand or assertion.

claim \klaym\ *v.* claimed; claiming. To demand as one's right.

clairvoyance \klair-VOI-uns\ *n.* The ability to know without sensory data. clairvoyant *adj.*

clam \klam\ *n.* **1.** An edible mollusk. **2.** [Sl] A dollar.

clammy \KLAM-ee\ *adj.* clammier; clammiest Cold and damp. clamminess *n.*

clamor \KLAM-ur\ *n.* **1.** A loud confused noise. **2.** Insistent speech. clamorous *n.*

clamor \KLAM-ur\ *v.* clamored; clamoring. To make a loud confused noise.

clamp \klamp\ *n.* A device that holds something together.

clamp \klamp\ *v.* clamped; clamping. **1.** To hold together. **2.** To impose.

clan \klan\ *n.* A group of related people.

clandestine \klan-DES-tin\ *adj.* **1.** Secret. **2.** Surreptitious.

clang \klang\ *v.* clanged; clanging. To ring loudly with a metallic sound. clangor *n.*

clap \klap\ *n.* **1.** A loud striking noise. **2.** [Sl] Gonnorhea.

clap \klap\ *v.* clapped also clapt; clapping. To strike palms loudly together.

clarify \KLAR-uh-fie\ *v.* clarified; clarifying **1.** To explain or make clear. **2.** To make pure. clarification *n.*; clarifier *n.*

clarinet \klar-uh-NET\ *n.* A woodwind instrument. clarinetist or clarinettest *n.*

clash \klash\ *n.* **1.** A collision. **2.** A skirmish.

clash \klash\ *v.* clashed; clashing. To conflict.

clasp \klasp\ *n.* **1.** A fastener. **2.** An embrace.

clasp \klasp\ *v.* clashed; clashing **1.** To connect or fasten. **2.** To embrace.

class \klas\ *n.* **1.** A group of students. **2.** A set of people or things with something in common.

classic \KLAS-ik\ *adj.* **1.** Of high quality. **2.** Traditional and typical. **3.** Simple.

classical \KLAS-i-kul\ *adj.* **1.** Relating to ancient Greece. **2.** Concerning tradition. **3.** An academic branch.

classify \KLAS-uh-fie\ *v.* classified; classifying To arrange in categories. classification *n.*; classified *adj.*

clause \klawz\ *n.* **1.** A part of a sentence with its own verb. **2.** A specific section.

claustrophobia \klaw-struh-FOH-bee-uh\ *n.* A fear of enclosed spaces. claustrophobic *adj.*

claw \klaw\ *n.* **1.** A nail on an animal or bird foot. **2.** A pincer at the end of a limb. clawed *adj.*

claw \klaw\ *v.* clawed; clawing. To scratch at.

clay \klay\ *n.* Stiff sticky earth. clayey *adj.*

clean \kleen\ *adj.* **1.** Free from dirt. **2.** Morally upstanding. **3.** Skillful. **4.** Complete. cleanly *adv.*

clean \kleen\ *v.* cleaned; cleaning. **1.** To remove dirt. **2.** [Sl] To take away. cleaner *n.*

clean-cut \KLEEN-KUT\ *adj.* **1.** Cut smoothly. **2.** Wholesome.

cleanse \klenz\ *v.* cleansed; cleansing. To wash.

clear \kleer\ *adj.* clearer; clearest. **1.** Without dirt. **2.** Easily seen, heard, or understood. **3.** Free from difficulties. clearing *n.*

clear \kleer\ *v.* cleared; clearing. **1.** To remove obstacles. **2.** To explain. **3.** To authorize. **4.** To pass. clearer *n.*

clearance \KLEER-uns\ *n.* **1.** Authorization. **2.** Process of elimination. **3.** Space allowed for passage.

clear-cut \KLEER-KUT\ *adj.* Distinct.

clear-cut *v.* clear-cutting; clear cut. To remove all trees and shrubs.

clear out *v.* cleared out; clearing

out. **1.** To empty or remove. **2.** [Cl] To go away.

cleave \kleev\ **v.** cleaved also cleft or clove; cleft or cloven; cleaving **1.** To split apart. **2.** To hold closely.

cleft palate \kleft-PAH-lut\ **n.** (Md) Congenital mouth formation.

clemency \KLEM-un-see\ **n. pl.** clemencies. **1.** Mercy. **2.** Mildness.

clement \KLEM-unt\ **adj. 1.** Leniency. **2.** Mildness.

clench \klench\ **v.** clenched; clenching. **1.** To clutch. **2.** To hold together tightly.

clergy \KLUR-jee\ **pl. n.** Religious leaders.

cleric \KLER-ik\ **n.** A clergy member.

clever \KLEV-ur\ **adj.** cleverer; cleverest. **1.** Intelligent. **2.** Cunning. cleverly **adv.**; cleverness **n.**

cliche also **cliché** \klee-SHAY\ **n.** Trite phrase.

click \klik\ **n.** A quick sharp noise.

click \klik\ **v.** clicked; clicking. **1.** To make a sharp noise. **2.** [Cl] To function well together.

client \KLIE-unt\ **n.** A customer.

clientele \klie-un-TEL\ **n.** A group of customers.

cliff \klif\ **n.** A steep rock-face.

climate \KLIE-mit\ **n.** Average weather conditions of an area. climatic **adj.**

climax \KLIE-maks\ **n. 1.** The high point. **2.** Orgasm.

climax \KLIE-maks\ **v.** climaxed; climaxing To reach a high point.

climb \kliem\ **v.** climbed; climbing. To move upward. climber **n.**; climb **n.**

clinch \klinch\ **v.** clinched; clinching. **1.** To fasten. **2.** To settle. clincher **n.**

cling \kling\ **v.** clung; clinging. To stick to. clingy **adj.**

clinic \KLIN-ik\ **n. 1.** A place for medical treatment. **2.** A group meeting or discussion. clinical **adj.**

clip \klip\ **n. 1.** A clasping device. **2.** A newspaper article. **3.** A section of a video or movie.

clip \klip\ **v.** clipped; clipping. **1.** To cut off. **2.** To fasten. **3.** To block from behind in football. **4.** To cheat.

clique \kleek\ **n.** An exclusive group of people. cliquey or cliquy **adj.**; cliquish **adj.**

cloak \klohk\ **n. 1.** An outer garment. **2.** A disguise.

cloak \klohk\ **v.** cloaked; cloaking. To disguise.

clobber \KLOB-ur\ *v.* clobbered; clobbering. **1.** To hit. **2.** To defeat.

clock \klok\ *n.* **1.** A time-keeping instrument. **2.** An odometer.

clock \klok\ *v.* clocked; clocking. **1.** To keep time. **2.** To record on a timesheet.

clod \klod\ *n.* **1.** A lump of dirt and grass. **2.** A clumsy person.

clog \klog\ *n.* **1.** A blockage. **2.** A wooden-soled shoe.

clog \klog\ *v.* clogged; clogging. To block.

cloister \KLOI-stur\ *n.* A monastery or convent.

cloister \KLOI-stur\ *v.* cloistered; cloistering. To seclude.

clone \klohn\ *n.* A copy.

clone \klohn\ *v.* cloned; cloning. To copy.

close \klohs\ *adj.* closer; closest. **1.** Near to. **2.** Almost exact. closely *adv.*; closeness *n.*; closed *adj.*

close \klohz\ *v.* closed; closing. **1.** To block access to. **2.** To end. **3.** To draw near. close *n.*

closed-captioned \KLOHZ-cap-shund\ *adj.* Broadcast with words printed on the screen.

closet \KLOZ-it\ *n.* **1.** An enclosed private area. **2.** A storage room or area.

close-up \KLOHS-up\ *n.* A close-range film or movie shot.

closure \KLOH-zhur\ *n.* The process of ending.

clot \klot\ *n.* A coagulated mass.

clot \klot\ *v.* clotted; clotting. To coagulate.

cloth \klawth\ *n. pl.* cloths. **1.** A woven or knitted fabric. **2.** Religious dress.

clothes \klohz\ *n. pl.* clothes. Garments. clothing *n.*

cloud \klowd\ *n.* **1.** A mass of condensed vapor. **2.** Gloom.

cloud \klowd\ *v.* clouded; clouding. To obscure.

cloud nine \klowd nien\ *n.* Elation.

clout \klowt\ *n.* **1.** Influence. **2.** A blow.

club \klub\ *n.* **1.** A large stick. **2.** An exclusive group. **3.** A card suit. **4.** A meeting place.

club \klub\ *v.* clubbed; clubbing. To hit.

clue \cloo\ *n.* A piece of evidence.

clue \cloo\ *v.* clued; clueing or cluing. To provide a hint to.

clump \klump\ *n.* A condensed mass.

clumsy \KLUM-zee\ *adj.* clumsier; clumsiest. Awkward. clumsily *adv.*; clumsiness *n.*

clunker \KLUNK-ur\ *n.* An old, beatup car.

cluster \KLUS-tur\ *n.* A bunch of things in one area.

clutch \kluch\ *n.* **1.** Connecting and disconnecting mechanism. **2.** A tight grasp. **3.** A nest of eggs.

clutch \kluch\ *v.* clutched; clutching To hold tightly.

coach \kohch\ *n.* **1.** A horse-drawn carriage. **2.** A sports team instructor or manager.

coach \kohch\ *v.* coached; coaching. To instruct and manage.

coagulate \koh-AG-yuh-layt\ *v.* coagulated; coagulating. To thicken into a mass. coagulation *n.*

coalition \koh-uh-LISH-un\ *n.* A union or alliance.

coarse \kors\ *adj.* coarser; coarsest. **1.** Rough. **2.** Harsh. **3.** Vulgar.

coast \kohst\ *n.* The seashore and nearby land. coastal *adj.*

coast \kohst\ *v.* coasted; coasting. To move by gravity.

coat \koht\ *n.* **1.** An outerwear garment. **2.** A covering. coated *adj.*

coat \koht\ *v.* coated; coating. To cover.

coating \KOH-ting\ *n.* A covering.

coax \kohks\ *v.* coaxed; coaxing. To persuade gently.

cob \kob\ *n.* **1.** A male swan. **2.** A corncob.

COBOL \KOH-bawl\ *n.* (Cm) Common Business Oriented Language.

cobweb \KOB-web\ *n.* A spider web.

cocky \KOK-ee\ *adj.* cockier; cockiest. Arrogant. cockiness *n.*

cocoon \kuh-KOON\ *n.* **1.** A silk enclosure. **2.** A protective wrapping.

cod \kod\ *n. pl.* cod or cods. An edible bottom-dwelling fish.

co-dependent \KOH-dee-PEN-dunt\ *adj.* Mutually reliant.

coddle \KOD-l\ *v.* coddled; coddling. **1.** To cook slowly in hot liquid. **2.** To pamper.

code \kohd\ *n.* **1.** Set of instructions. **2.** Legal requirements. **3.** Symbols for obscuring meaning.

code \kohd\ *v.* coded; coding. To write in symbols.

coed \KOH-ED\ *n.* A female student. co-ed *adj.*; coeducation *n.*

coerce \koh-URS\ *v.* coerced; coercing. **1.** To force. **2.** To compel. coercive *adj.*

coexistence \koh-ig-ZIST-uns\ *n.* Living together in peace.

coffee \KAW-fee\ *n.* The seeds of a tropical shrub and the popular brewed beverage made from them.

coffin \KAW-fin\ *n.* A container for burying a corpse.

cognizant \KOG-nuh-zunt\ *adj.* Aware. cognizance *n.*

cohabit \koh-HAB-it\ *v.* cohabited; cohabiting. To live together. cohabitation *n.*

cohere \koh-HEER\ *v.* cohered; cohering. **1.** To stick together. **2.** To unite. coherence *n.*; coherent *adj.*

cohort \KOH-hort\ *n.* A companion.

coiffure \kwah-FYUUR\ *n.* (Fr) A hairstyle.

coin \koin\ *n.* A metal piece used as money.

coin \koin\ *v.* coined; coining. **1.** To mint. **2.** To invent.

coincide \koh-in-SIDE\ *v.* coincided; coinciding. To agree in space, time, or character.

coincidence \koh-IN-si-duns\ *n.* An accidental happening corresponding to another.

coin-op *n.* [Sl] A Laundromat.

coke \kohk\ *n.* **1.** Coal residue. **2.** [Sl] Cocaine. **3.** A cola beverage [Sl].

cola \KOH-luh\ *n.* A carbonated soft drink.

colander \KUL-un-dur\ *n.* A strainer.

cold \kohld\ *adj.* colder; coldest. **1.** Of or concerning a low temperature. **2.** Indifferent. **3.** Unconscious. coldly *adv.*; coldness *n.*

cold-blooded \KOHLD-BLUD-id\ *adj.* **1.** Without emotion. **2.** Having body temperature varying with the environment.

coleslaw \KOHL-slaw\ *n.* A chopped cabbage salad.

coliseum \kol-i-SEE-um\ *n.* A large building for public entertainment.

collaborate \kuh-LAB-uh-rayt\ *v.* collaborated; collaborating. To work together. collaboration *n.*; collaborative *adj.* or *n.*; collaborator *n.*

collage \kuh-LAHZH\ *n.* An artistic work of glued pieces.

collapse \kuh-LAPS\ *n.* A sudden breakdown.

collapse \kuh-LAPS\ *v.* collapsed; collapsing. **1.** To break down. **2.** To lose strength suddenly. collapsible *adj.*

collar \KOL-ur\ *n.* A neck band on a garment.

collar \KOL-ur\ *v.* collared; collaring. To seize.

collate \kuh-LAYT or koh-LAYT\ *v.* collated; collating. **1.** To compare. **2.** To put in order. collation *n.*

collateral \kuh-LAT-ur-ul\ *adj.* **1.** Parallel. **2.** Additional but subordinate.

collateral \kuh-LAT-ur-ul\ *n.* Money as security.

colleague \KOL-eeg\ *n.* A coworker.

collect \kuh-LEKT\ *v.* collected;

collecting. To gather together. collection *n.*

college \KOL-ij\ *n.* An institution of higher education.

collide \kuh-LIED\ *v.* collided; colliding. To crash.

collision \kuh-LIZH-un\ *n.* A crash.

colloquial \kuh-LOH-kwee-ul\ *adj.* Something used informally. colloquialism *n.*

collusion \kuh-LOO-zhun\ *n.* A secret agreement.

cologne \kuh-LOHN\ *n.* A fragrant liquid scent.

colon \KOH-lun\ *n.* colons or cola. **1.** Part of the large intestine. **2.** A punctuation mark.

colonel \KUR-nl\ *n.* A military rank.

colonial \kuh-LOH-nee-ul\ *adj.* **1.** Concerning the original 13 colonies. **2.** Forming a colony.

colony \KOL-uh-nee\ *n.* *pl.* colonies. **1.** Emigrants in a new land. **2.** A region with settlers. **3.** Group living together. colonize *v.*; colonization *n.*

color \KUL-ur\ *n.* **1.** The segments of visible light. **2.** Vividness. **3.** Pigment. colorize *v.*

color \KUL-ur\ *v.* colored; coloring. **1.** To put color on. **2.** To distort.

color-blind *adj.* **1.** Unable to differentiate between colors. **2.** Free from prejudice to race.

colossal \kuh-LOS-ul\ *adj.* Huge. colossally *adv.*

colt \kohlt\ *n.* **1.** A young horse. **2.** [Sl] An immature person.

coma \KOHM-uh\ *n.* An unconscious state.

comb \kohm\ *n.* **1.** A toothed hair implement. **2.** Decorative crest on a fowl's head.

comb \kohm\ *v.* combed; combing. **1.** To tidy or style the hair. **2.** [Cl] To search completely.

combat \KOM-bat\ *v.* combated or combatted; combating or combatting. **1.** To fight. **2.** To struggle to lose. combatant *n.*

combine \kum-BINE\ *v.* combined; combining. **1.** To merge. **2.** To harvest a crop. combination *n.*

combustion \kum-BUS-chun\ *n.* The process of burning. combustible *adj.*

come \kum\ *v.* came; come; coming. **1.** To approach. **2.** To occur to. **3.** To arrive. **4.** To occur in time; happen.

comeback \KUM-bak\ *n.* A witty retort. come back *v.*

comedy \KOM-i-dee\ *n.* *pl.* comedies. **1.** Light amusing drama. **2.** A funny event. comedic *adj.*

comet \KOM-it\ *n.* A celestial body with a luminous tail.

comfort \KUM-furt\ *v.* comforted; comforting **1.** To cheer. **2.** To console.

comfort \KUM-furt\ *n.* **1.** Ease. **2.** Solace.

comfortable \KUMF-tuhr-bul\ *adj.* **1.** Secure and having ease. **2.** Stress- free. comfortably *adv.*

comic \KOM-ik\ *adj.* Laughable.

comic \KOM-ik\ *n.* Comedian.

comma \KOM-uh\ *n.* A punctuation mark.

command \kuh-MAND\ *n.* **1.** An order. **2.** A goverened area. commander *n.*

command \kuh-MAND\ *v.* commanded; commanding **1.** To order. **2.** To govern.

commemorate \kuh-MEM-uh-rayt\ *v.* commemorated; commemorating. To celebrate by memorial. commemoration *n.*; commemorative *adj.*

commence \kuh-MENS\ *v.* commenced; commencing. To begin.

commend \kuh-MEND\ *v.* commended; commending. To praise. commendable *adj.*

commensurate \kuh-MEN-sur-it\ *adj.* Equal in extent. commensurable *adj.*

comment \KOM-ent\ *n.* A remark or opinion.

comment \KOM-ent\ *v.* commented; commenting. To remark or give an opinion.

commentary \KOM-un-ter-ee\ *n. pl.* commentaries. An explanatory statement, often opionionated.

commerce \KOM-urs\ *n.* Business and trade.

commercial \kuh-MUR-shul\ *adj.* Concerning business and trade.

commercial \kuh-MUR-shul\ *n.* An advertisement.

commissar \KOM-uh-sahr\ *n.* A communist official.

commission \kuh-MISH-un\ *n.* **1.** Military rank. **2.** A charge. **3.** A government agency. **4.** Payment.

commission \kuh-MISH-un\ *v.* commissioned; commissioning. **1.** To assign. **2.** To hire or place an order for.

commit \kuh-MIT\ *v.* committed; committing. **1.** To entrust. **2.** To obligate. commitment *n.*

committee \kuh-MIT-ee\ *n.* A group of people working toward an objective.

commode \kuh-MOHD\ *n.* **1.** Toilet. **2.** A chest of drawers.

commodity \kuh-MOD-i-tee\ *n.* A product.

common \KOM-un\ *adj.* commoner; commonest. **1.** Concerning the public. **2.** Second-rate. **3.** Familiar. commonly *adv.*; commonness *n.*

common market \KOM-un-MAR-kut\ *n.* An economic allegiance among nations.

commonplace \KOM-un-plays\ *adj.* Very ordinary.

common sense \KOM-un-SENS\ *n.* Sound unintellectual thinking. commonsense *adj.*

commonwealth \KOM-un-welth\ *n.* A republic.

commotion \kuh-MOH-shun\ *n.* A loud disturbance.

commune \kuh-MYOON\ *v.* communed; communing. To be in touch with.

communicate \kuh-MYOO-ni-kayt\ *v.* communicated; communicating. **1.** To make known. **2.** To pass news on. **3.** To connect. communicator *n.*; communication *n.*

communion \kuh-MYOON-yun\ *n.* **1.** A Christian rite. **2.** Sharing.

communique \kuh-myoo-ni-KAY\ *n.* (Fr) A message.

communism \KOM-yuh-niz-um\ *n.* A political and economic doctrine. communist *n.*

community \kuh-MYOO-ni-tee\ *n.* *pl.* communities. A unified people.

commute \kuh-MYOOT\ *v.* commuted; commuting. **1.** To travel regularly, esp. to work. **2.** To exchange. commuter *n.*

compact \kum-PAKT\ *adj.* Compressed into a small space. compactly *adv.*

compact \KOM-pakt\ *n.* **1.** A face powder case. **2.** A small car. compactor also compacter *n.*

compact disc compact disk \KOM-pakt-DISK\ *n.* (Ja) A small optical laser-made disk containing information.

companion \kum-PAN-yun\ *n.* One who accompanies. companionship *n.*

company \KUM-puh-nee\ *n.* *pl.* companies. **1.** Guests. **2.** A business.

compare \kum-PAIR\ *v.* compared; comparing. To look for similarities or differences.

comparison \kum-PAR-uh-sun\ *n.* A statement of similarity.

compartment \kum-PAHRT-munt\ *n.* A section. compartmentalize *v.*

compass \KUM-pus\ *n.* **1.** A direction indicating device. **2.** Range or scope.

compassion \kum-PASH-un\ *n.* Sympathy. compassionate *adj.*

compatible \kum-PAT-uh-bul\ *adj.* Able to exist together peacefully. compatibility *n.*; compatibly *adv.*

compel \kum-PEL\ *v.* compelled; compelling. To force.

compendium \kum-PEN-dee-um\ *n. pl.* compendiums or compendia. An abstract or summary.

compensate \KOM-pun-sayt\ *v.* compensated; compensating. **1.** To counterbalance. **2.** To pay. compensation *n.*

compete \kum-PEET\ *v.* competed; competing. To rival for something. competition *n.*

compile \kum-PIEL\ *v.* compiled; compiling. To collect and arrange. compiler *n.*; compilation *n.*

complacent \kum-PLAY-sunt\ *adj.* Unconcerned and self-satisfied. complacently *adv.*

complain \kum-PLAYN\ *v.* complained; complaining. To communicate discontent. complaint *n.*

complement \KOM-pluh-munt\ *n.* **1.** Matching. **2.** Completing part.

complete \kum-PLEET\ *adj.* completer; completest. **1.** Having all necessary elements. **2.** Absolute.

complete \kum-PLEET\ *v.* completed; completing. **1.** To end. **2.** To make perfect.

complex \kum-PLEKS\ *adj.* **1.** Composite. **2.** Intricate. complexness *n.*; complexly *adv.*

complex \KOM-pleks\ *n.* **1.** A whole. **2.** A set of feelings that make a behavior.

complexion \kum-PLEK-shun\ *n.* Skin's appearance.

compliance \kum-PLIE-uns\ *n.* **1.** Fulfilling requirements. **2.** Flexibility. compliant *adj.*

complicate \KOM-pli-kayt\ *v.* complicated; complicating. To make intricate. complication *n.*

compliment \KOM-pluh-munt\ *n.* **1.** Flattery. **2.** Praise. complimentary *adj.*

comply \kum-PLIE\ *v.* complied; complying. To conform.

component \kum-POH-nunt\ *n.* An element.

compose \kum-POHZ\ *v.* composed; composing. **1.** To put together. **2.** To create. composed *adj.*

composite \kum-POZ-it\ *adj.* A collection made into one.

composition \kom-puh-ZISH-un\ *n.* **1.** An arrangement. **2.** A created piece, as in the arts.

compost \KOM-pohst\ *n.* Decayed organic matter.

composure \kum-POH-zhur\ *n.* An air of self-assurance.

compound \KOM-pownd\ *n.* **1.** A

single thing formed by two or more parts. **2.** An enclosed area.

compound \KOM-pownd\ *v.* compounded; compounding. **1.** To combine. **2.** To add to.

comprehend \kom-pri-HEND\ *v.* comprehended; comprehending. To understand. comprehensible *adj.*; comprehension *n.*

compress \KOM-pres\ *n.* **1.** A folded cloth. **2.** A machine.

compress \kum-PRES\ *v.* compressed; compressing. To squeeze together.

comprise \kum-PRIZE\ *v.* comprised; comprising. **1.** To contain. **2.** To include.

compromise \KOM-pruh-mize\ *n.* An agreement reached by concession.

compromise \KOM-pruh-mize\ *v.* compromised; compromising. To agree to by concession.

compulsive \kum-PUL-siv\ *adj.* Compelled or obsessed. compulsion *n.*

compulsory \kum-PUL-suh-ree\ *adj.* Required.

compute \kum-PYOOT\ *v.* computed; computing. To calculate.

computer \kum-PYOO-tur\ *n.* (Cm) An electronic information processing device.

computer-literate *adj.* (Cm) Able to work with computers.

computer virus *n.* (Cm) An invasion and corruption of computer programs.

comrade \KOM-rad\ *n.* **1.** A friend. **2.** A communist.

con \kon\ *v.* conned; conning. To swindle.

con \kon\ *n.* **1.** A convict. **2.** A swindle.

concave \kon-KAYV\ *adj.* Rounded inward.

conceal \kun-SEEL\ *v.* concealed; concealing. To hide. concealer *n.*; concealment *n.*

concede \kun-SEED\ *v.* conceded; conceding. To yield.

conceit \kun-SEET\ *n.* Vanity. conceited *adj.*

conceive \kun-SEEV\ *v.* conceived; conceiving. **1.** To create. **2.** To imagine.

concentrate \KON-sun-trayt\ *v.* concentrated; concentrating. **1.** To focus. **2.** To gather.

concept \KON-sept\ *n.* An idea.

conception \kun-SEP-shun\ *n.* **1.** The beginning. **2.** A general idea.

concern \kun-SURN\ *n.* One's affair. concerned *adj.*

concern \kun-SURN\ *v.* concerned;

concerning. **1.** To be related or relevant to. **2.** To involve.

concert \KON-surt\ *n.* **1.** An agreement. **2.** A performance [Mu].

concert \kun-SURT\ *v.* concerted; concerting. To agree.

concerted \kun-SUR-tid\ *adj.* Done mutually.

concerto \kun-CHER-toh\ *n.* A symphonic piece.

concession \kun-SESH-un\ *n.* **1.** A granting. **2.** A leased area.

conch \konk\ *n. pl.* conchs or conches. A large spiral-shelled mollusk.

concierge \kon-see-AIRZH\ *n.* A building attendant.

conciliatory \kun-SIL-ee-uh-tor-ee\ *adj.* Concerning an appeasement. conciliate *v.*; conciliation *n.*

concise \kun-SISE\ *adj.* Brief. concisely *adv*; conciseness *n.*

conclude \kun-KLOOD\ *v.* concluded; concluding. To end.

conclusion \kun-KLOO-zhun\ *n.* **1.** The end. **2.** A logic proposition or opinion.

concoct \kon-KOKT\ *v.* concocted; concocting. To create. concoction *n.*

concord \KON-kord\ *n.* Agreement.

concourse \KON-kors\ *n.* **1.** A hallway. **2.** A spontaneous meeting.

concrete \KON-kreet\ *adj.* **1.** Existing in material form. **2.** Tangible.

concrete \KON-kreet\ *n.* Building material.

concur \kun-KUR\ *v.* concurred; concurring. To agree. concurrent *adj.*; concurrence *n.*

concussion \kun-KUSH-un\ *n.* A brain injury.

condemn \kun-DEM\ *v.* condemned; condemning. **1.** To convict. **2.** To criticize. condemnation *n.*

condensation \kon-den-SAY-shun\ *n.* Gas or vapor changed to a liquid.

condense \kun-DENS\ *v.* condensed; condensing. **1.** To compress or contract. **2.** To change from a gas or vapor to liquid.

condescend \kon-duh-SEND\ *v.* condescended; condescending *adv.* **1.** To lower. **2.** To look down on. condescending *adj.*

condition \kun-DISH-un\ *n.* **1.** A stipulation. **2.** A qualification. **3.** A physical or mental state. conditional *adj.*

condolence \kun-DOHL-ens\ *n.* An expression of sympathy.

condom \KON-dum\ *n.* A birth-control device.

condominium \kon-duh-MIN-ee-um\ *n. pl.* condominiums. Connected but individually owned housing.

condone \kun-DOHN\ *v.* condoned; condoning. To pardon.

condor \KON-dohr\ *n.* (Sp) A large bird.

conducive \kun-DOO-siv\ *adj.* **1.** Promoting. **2.** Assisting.

conduct \kun-DUKT\ *v.* conducted; conducting. **1.** To guide. **2.** To lead.

conduit \KON-dwit\ *n.* A passageway.

cone \kohn\ *n.* **1.** A pine tree seed. **2.** A geometric shape.

confection \kun-FEC-shun\ *n.* A sweet food.

confederacy \kun-FED-ur-uh-see\ *n. pl.* confederacies. A group for a common action.

confer \kun-FUR\ *v.* conferred; conferring. **1.** To give. **2.** To hold a discussion.

conference \KON-fur-ens\ *n.* A meeting for discussion. conferencing *n.*

confess \kun-FES\ *v.* confessed; confessing. To admit. confession *n.*; confessional *adj.*

confidant \KON-fi-dant\ *n.* A person told secrets. confidante *n.*

confide \kun-FIED\ *v.* confided; confiding. **1.** To tell confidentially. **2.** To entrust.

confidence \KON-fi-duns\ *n.* **1.** A feeling of assurance. **2.** A secret being held.

confident \KON-fi-dunt\ *adj.* Self-assured.

confidential \kon-fi-DEN-shul\ *adj.* Private.

confine \KON-fine\ *n.* An enclosed area.

confine \kun-FINE\ *v.* confined; confining. To keep within limits.

confirm \kun-FURM\ *v.* confirmed; confirming. To verify.

confirmation \kon-fur-MAY-shun\ *n.* **1.** A Christian rite. **2.** Verification.

confiscate \KON-fuh-skayt\ *v.* confiscated; confiscating. To take or seize by authority. confiscation *n.*

conflagration \kon-fluh-GRAY-shun\ *n.* **1.** A large fire. **2.** A conflict.

conflict \KON-flikt\ *n.* A fight or disagreement.

conflict \kun-FLIKT\ *v.* conflicted; conflicting. To disagree strongly or fight.

confluence \KON-floo-uns\ *n.* Place where two things flow together. confluent *adj.*

conform \kun-FORM\ *v.* conformed; conforming. **1.** To match. **2.** To adapt. conformist *n.*

confound \kon-FOWND\ *v.* coun-founded; confounding. To confuse. confounded *adj.*

confront \kun-FRUNT\ *v.* confronted; confronting. To face boldly. confrontation *n.*

Confucianism \kun-FYOO-shun-izm\ *n.* Chinese philosophical teachings. Confucian *adj.* or *n.*

confuse \kun-FYOOZ\ *v.* confused; confusing. To mix up. confused *adj.*; confusion *n.*

congeal \kun-JEEL\ *v.* congealed; congealing. To solidify.

congenial \kun-JEEN-yul\ *adj.* Pleasant. congeniality *n.*

congest \kun-JEST\ *v.* congested; congesting. To clog. congestion *n.*

conglomerate \kun-GLOM-ur-it\ *adj.* Concerning varied parts made into one.

congratulate \kun-GRACH-uh-layt\ *v.* congratulated; congratulating. To express happiness for another's accomplishment. congratulation *n.*

congregate \KONG-gri-gayt\ *v.* congregated; congregating. To gather. congregation *n.*

congress \KONG-gris\ *n.* A legislative body. congressional *adj.*

congruent \KONG-groo-unt\ *adj.* Corresponding. congruence *n.*

conical \KON-ik-ul\ *adj.* Cone shaped.

conifer \KON-uh-fur\ *n.* An evergreen tree or shrub.

conjecture \kun-JEK-chur\ *n.* A guess.

conjecture \kun-JEK-chur\ *v.* conjectured; conjecturing. To suppose.

conjugal \KON-juh-gul\ *adj.* Concerning a married couple. conjugally *adj.*; conjugate *v.*

conjunction \kun-JUNGK-shun\ *n.* 1. A union in time and space. 2. A combination.

conjure \KON-jur\ *v.* conjured; conjuring. 1. To contrive. 2. To summon. conjurer or conjuror *n.*

connect \kuh-NEKT\ *v.* connected; connecting. To join. connected *adj.*; connection *n.*

connive \kuh-NIVE\ *v.* connived; conniving. To conspire. conniver *n.*

connoisseur \kon-uh-SUR\ *n.* An expert.

connotation \kon-uh-TAY-shun\ *n.* An implication.

connote \kuh-NOHT\ *v.* connoted; connoting. To imply or suggest.

conquer \KONG-kur\ *v.* conquered; conquering. To overcome. conqueror *n.*

conquest \KON-kwest\ *n.* Something won by battle.

conquistador \kon-KWIS-tuh-dor\

n. pl. conquistadores or conquistadors. (Sp) A conqueror.

conscience \KON-shuns\ *n.* Awareness of moral right and wrong.

conscientious \kon-shee-EN-shus\ *adj.* **1.** Careful. **2.** Scrupulous.

conscious \KON-shus\ *adj.* **1.** Awake. **2.** Perceiving. consciousness *n.*; consciously *adv.*

consciousness-raising \KON-shus-nis-RAY-sing\ *n.* An issue of concern. consciousness *n.*; consciously *adv.*

consecrate \KON-si-krayt\ *v.* consecrated; consecrating. To declare sacred. consecration *n.*

consecutive \kun-SEK-yuh-tiv\ *adj.* Following in order.

consensus \kun-SEN-sus\ *n.* Complete agreement.

consent \kun-SENT\ *n.* Acquiescence.

consent \kun-SENT\ *v.* consented; consenting. To agree.

consequence \KON-si-kwens\ *n.* **1.** A result. **2.** Something important.

consequential \kon-si-KWEN-shul\ *adj.* Indirect.

conservation \kon-sur-VAY-shun\ *n.* Preservation.

conservative \kun-SUR-vuh-tiv\ *adj.* **1.** Traditional. **2.** Cautious. conservatively *adv.*

conservatory \kun-SUR-vuh-tor-ee\ *n. pl.* conservatories. **1.** A greenhouse. **2.** A school.

conserve \KON-surv\ *n.* Sweet fruit spread.

conserve \kun-SURV\ *v.* conserved; conserving. To keep safe.

consider \kun-SID-ur\ *v.* considered; considering. **1.** To contemplate. **2.** To suppose. consideration *n.*

considerable \kun-SID-ur-uh-bul\ *adj.* Significant.

considerate \kun-SID-ur-it\ *adj.* Thoughtful.

consignment \kun-SINE-munt\ *n.* **1.** Something entrusted to another. **2.** [Id] A process of selling.

consist \kun-SIST\ *v.* consisted; consisting. To be made up of.

consistency \kun-SIS-tun-see\ *n. pl.* consistencies. **1.** Thickness of a substance. **2.** Unchangeableness. **3.** Degree of harmony. consistently *adv.*

consolation \kon-suh-LAY-shun\ *n.* Comfort.

console \KON-sohl\ *n.* A storage case.

console \kun-SOHL\ *v.* consoled; consoling. To offer comfort.

consolidate \kun-SOL-i-dayt\ *v.* consolidated; consolidating. To unite. consolidation *n.*

consonant \KON-suh-nunt\ *adj.* Relating to harmony.

consonant \KON-suh-nunt\ *n.* Category of letters in English language.

consort \KON-sort\ *n.* **1.** A spouse. **2.** A group.

consort \kun-SORT\ *v.* consorted; consorting. To associate.

consortium \kun-SOR-shee-um\ *n.* *pl.* consortia *also* consortiums. An association.

conspicuous \kun-SPIK-yoo-us\ *adj.* Noticeable. conspicuously *adv.*

conspiracy \kun-SPIR-uh-see\ *n.* *pl.* conspiracies. Plot.

conspire \kun-SPIRE\ *v.* conspired; conspiring. **1.** To contrive. **2.** To scheme. conspiration *n.*

constant \KON-stunt\ *adj.* Unwavering. constantly *adv.*

consternation \kon-stur-NAY-shun\ *n.* Dismayed amazement.

constituent \kun-STICH-oo-unt\ *n.* A component.

constitute \KON-sti-toot\ *v.* contituted; constituting. **1.** To establish. **2.** To compose.

constitution \kon-sti-TOO-shun\ *n.* **1.** Legal document of rights. **2.** Something's makeup or condition.

constitutional \kon-sti-TOO-shunl\ *adj.* **1.** Concerning bodily and mental health. **2.** Concerning a constitution.

constrain \kun-STRAYN\ *v.* constrained; constraining. **1.** To confine. **2.** To impose.

constraint \kun-STRAYNT\ *n.* A constricting condition.

constrict \kun-STRIKT\ *v.* constricted; constricting. **1.** To compress. **2.** To inhibit.

construct \KON-strukt\ *n.* A working hypothesis.

construct \kun-STRUKT\ *v.* constructed; constructing. To build.

construction \kun-STRUK-shun\ *n.* A building or the process of building.

constructive \kun-STRUK-tiv\ *adj.* Helpful.

construe \kun-STROO\ *v.* construed; construing. **1.** To interpret. **2.** To explain.

consul \KON-sul\ *n.* Government official in a foreign country.

consulate \KON-suh-lit\ *n.* A consul's position or premises.

consult \kun-SULT\ *n.* A consultation.

consult \kun-SULT\ *v.* consulted; consulting. To seek information.

consultation \kon-sul-TAY-shun\ *n.* A information-seeking meeting. consultant *n.*

consume \kun-SOOM\ *v.* consumed; consuming. **1.** To eat or drink. **2.** To destroy. consumable *adj.*

consumer \kun-SOO-mur\ *n.* One who buys.

consummate \kon-SUM-it\ *adj.* Perfect.

consummate \KON-suh-mayt\ *v.* consummated; consummating. To complete. consummation *n.*

consumption \kun-SUMP-shun\ *n.* **1.** Use of economic goods. **2.** Tuberculosis. consumptive *adj.*

contact \KON-takt\ *n.* A connection.

contact \KON-takt\ *v.* contacted; contacting. **1.** To communicate with. **2.** To join.

contagion \kun-TAY-jun\ *n.* Disease transmission.

contain \kun-TAYN\ *v.* contained; containing. **1.** To hold within. **2.** To halt. contained *adj.*

container \kun-TAYN-ur\ *n.* A receptacle.

contaminate \kun-TAM-uh-nayt\ *v.* contaminated; contaminating. **1.** To infect. **2.** To pollute. contamination *n.*

contemplate \KON-tum-playt\ *v.* contemplated; contemplating. To consider. contemplation *n.*

contemporary \kun-TEM-puh-rer-ee\ *n. pl.* contemporaries. **1.** Current. **2.** Existing at the same time.

contempt \kun-TEMPT\ *n.* Disdain. contemptible *adj.*

contend \kun-TEND\ *v.* contended; contending. To struggle. contender *n.*

content *also* **contented** \kun-TENT\ *adj.* Satisfied.

content \KON-tent\ *n.* **1.** Substance. **2.** Capacity.

content \kun-TENT\ *v.* contented; contenting. To please.

contents \KON-tents\ *n.* Substance.

contest \KON-test\ *n.* Competition.

contest \kun-TEST\ *v.* contested; contesting. To strive for victory.

context \KON-tekst\ *n.* The setting. contextual *adj.*

contingent \kun-TIN-junt\ *adj.* **1.** Possible. **2.** Unpredictable. contingency *n.*

continue \kun-TIN-yoo\ *v.* continued; continuing. **1.** To move on. **2.** To maintain. continued *adj.*; continuing *adj.*

contort \kun-TORT\ *v.* contorted; contorting. To twist out of shape. contortion *n.*

contour \KON-tuur\ *n.* **1.** Outline. **2.** Shape.

contraband \KON-truh-band\ *n.* Illegal goods.

contraception \kon-truh-SEP-shun\ *n.* A pregnancy prevention method.

contract \KON-trakt\ *n.* **1.** A binding agreement. **2.** [Sl] An order to kill.

contract \kun-TRAKT\ *v.* contracted; contracting. **1.** To incur. **2.** [Sl] To restrict. **3.** To condense. **4.** To arrange work to be done. contractible *adj.*

contraction \kun-TRAK-shun\ *n.* A shortening. contractor *n.*

contradict \kon-truh-DIKT\ *v.* contradicted; contradicting. To go against. contradiction *n.*

contrary \KON-trer-ee\ *adj.* **1.** Unfavorable. **2.** Wayward.

contrary \KON-trer-ee\ *n. pl.* contraries. An opposite.

contrast \kun-TRAST\ *v.* contrasted; contrasting. To look for differences.

contravene \kon-truh-VEEN\ *v.* contravened; contravening. **1.** To violate. **2.** To contradict.

contribute \kun-TRIB-yoot\ *v.* contributed; contributing. **1.** To add to. **2.** To give. contributor *n.*

contribution \kon-truh-BYOO-shun\ *n.* Something given. contributory *adj.*

contrive \kun-TRIVE\ *v.* contrived; contriving. **1.** To devise. **2.** To plan.

control \kun-TROHL\ *n.* **1.** Restraint. **2.** Power. controlled *adj.*

control \kun-TROHL\ *v.* controlled; controlling. To regulate.

controversy \KON-truh-vur-see\ *n. pl.* controversies. A dispute. controversial *adj.*

contusion \kun-TOO-zhun\ *n.* A bruise.

convalescence \kon-vuh-LES-sens\ *n.* A recovery period. convalesce *v.*

convene \kun-VEEN\ *v.* convened; convening. To assemble or summon.

convenient \kun-VEEN-yunt\ *adj.* **1.** Handy. **2.** Suited. convenience *n.*

convent \KON-vent\ *n.* A religious community.

convention \kun-VEN-shun\ *n.* **1.** An assembly. **2.** Rules of conduct. **3.** Accepted custom.

conventional \kun-VEN-shun-ul\ *adj.* Commonplace.

converge \kun-VURJ\ *v.* converged; converging. To meet at a point. convergence *n.*

conversation \kon-vur-SAY-shun\ *n.* Verbal exchange. conversational *adj.*

conversion \kun-VUR-zhun\ *n.* **1.** A changeover. **2.** A mathematical operation.

convert \kun-VURT\ *v.* converted; converting. To transform.

convex \kon-VEKS\ *adj.* Curved outward.

convey \kun-VAY\ *v.* conveyed; conveying. To carry away or over.

convict \KON-vikt\ *n.* A criminal in prison.

convict \kun-VIKT\ *v.* convicted; convicting. To pronounce guilt.

conviction \kun-VIK-shun\ *n.* **1.** Statement of guilt. **2.** A strong belief.

convince \kun-VINS\ *v.* convinced; convincing. To persuade. convincing *adj.*

convoy \KON-voi\ *n.* **1.** An escort. **2.** A group.

convoy \KON-voi\ *v.* convoyed; convoying. To accompany.

convulsion \kun-VUL-shun\ *n.* Involuntary spasms. convulse *v.*

cook \kuuk\ *n.* One who prepares food.

cook \kuuk\ *v.* cooked; cooking. **1.** To prepare food. **2.** To concoct.

cookie *also* **cooky** \KUUK-ee\ *n. pl.* cookies. A sweet small cake.

cool \kool\ *adj.* **1.** Lacking warmth. **2.** [Sl] Excellent. coolly or cooly *adv.*

cool \kool\ *n.* Composure.

cool \kool\ *v.* cooled; cooling. **1.** To calm down. **2.** To remove heat.

coop \KOOP\ *n.* **1.** A building for chickens. **2.** Jail.

co-op \KOH-op\ *n.* A cooperative.

cooperate \koh-OP-uh-rayt\ *v.* cooperated; cooperating. To work with others. cooperation *n.*; cooperative *adj.*

coordinate \koh-OR-dn-it\ *n.* **1.** A set of numbers. **2.** An equal. **3.** Clothing that is part of a set.

coordinate \koh-OR-dn-ayt\ *v.* coordinated; coordinating. To harmonize.

cope \kohp\ *v.* coped; coping. To deal with.

cop out \kop-OWT\ *v.* copped out; copping out [Sl]. **1.** To back out. **2.** To avoid.

copulate \KOP-yuh-layt\ *v.* copulated; copulating. To have sexual relations. copulation *n.*

copy \KOP-ee\ *n. pl.* copies **1.** A duplicate. **2.** An imitation. **3.** A model.

copy \KOP-ee\ *v.* copied; copying. To imitate.

coquette *also* **coquet** \koh-KET\ *n.* A flirt.

coquette \koh-KET\ *v.* coquetted; coquetting. To trifle.

coral \KOR-ul\ *n.* Skeletal deposit left by sea creature.

cord \kord\ *n.* Flexible band or rope.

cordial \KOR-jul\ *adj.* Polite and friendly. cordially *adv.*

core \kor\ *n.* **1.** The innermost area. **2.** An essential part.

cornea \KOR-nee-uh\ *n.* (Md) Part of an eye.

corner \KOR-nur\ *n.* Intersection.

cornucopia \kor-nuh-KOH-pee-uh\ *n.* **1.** Horn of plenty. **2.** Abundance.

corny \KOR-nee\ *adj.* cornier; corniest **1.** Sentimental. **2.** Having corns.

corollary \KOR-uh-ler-ee\ *n. pl.* corollaries. **1.** A logical proposition. **2.** A result.

coroner \KOR-uh-nur\ *n.* One who investigates causes of death.

corporal \KOR-pur-ul\ *adj.* Concerning the body.

corporal \KOR-pur-ul\ *n.* A noncommissioned army officer.

corporate \KOR-pur-it\ *adj.* Concerning a legally unified body.

corporation \kor-puh-RAY-shun\ *n.* A legal company or business.

corporeal \kor-POR-ee-ul\ *adj.* **1.** Physical. **2.** Material. corporeally *adv.*

corps \kor\ *n. pl.* corps. **1.** A military subdivision. **2.** An organized group.

corpse \korps\ *n.* A dead body.

corral \kuh-RAL\ *n.* A livestock pen.

corral \kuh-RAL\ *v.* corralled; corralling. **1.** To enclose. **2.** To collect.

correct \kuh-REKT\ *v.* corrected; correcting. **1.** To amend or fix. **2.** To point out errors. correctly *adv.*; correctness *n.*

correction \kuh-REK-shun\ *n.* **1.** An amendment. **2.** Dealing with prisoners. corrective *adj.*

correlate \KOR-uh-layt\ *v.* correlated; correlating. To show relationship. correlation *n.*

correspond \kor-uh-SPOND\ *v.* corresponded; corresponding. **1.** To communicate. **2.** To match or go with.

correspondence \kor-uh-SPON-duns\ *n.* **1.** Letters exchanged. **2.** An agreement.

corridor \KOR-i-dur\ *n.* A passageway.

corroborate \kuh-ROB-uh-rayt\ *v.* corroborated; corroborating. **1.** To support. **2.** To confirm. corroboration *n.*

corrode \kuh-ROHD\ *v.* corroded; corroding. To eat away gradually. corrosion *n.*

corrugate \KOR-uh-gayt\ *v.* corrugated; corrugating. To furrow.

corrupt \kuh-RUPT\ *adj.* Depraved.

corrupt \kuh-RUPT\ *v.* corrupted; corrupting. **1.** To bribe. **2.** To taint.

corruption \kuh-RUP-shun\ *n.* An improper or illegal inducement.

corsage \kor-SAZH\ *n.* A flower accessory.

corset \KOR-sit\ *n.* A woman's undergarment.

cosmetic \koz-MET-ik\ *adj.* **1.** Relating to beauty makeup. **2.** Superficial. cosmetics *n.*

cosmic \KOZ-mik\ *also* **cosmical** *adj.* Concerning the universe.

cosmology \koz-MOL-uh-jee\ *n. pl.* cosmologies. Philosophical study of the universe's nature.

cosmonaut \KOZ-muh-nawt\ *n.* (Fo) A Russian astronaut.

cosmopolitan \koz-muh-POL-i-tn\ *adj.* Worldly. cosmopolitanism *n.*

cosmos \KOZ-mus\ *n.* (Sc) The universe.

cost \kawst\ *n.* **1.** Price. **2.** Loss. costless *adj.*

cost \kawst\ *v.* cost; costing. To require payment.

costume \KOS-toom\ *n.* A character dress.

cot \kot\ *n.* A small, foldable bed.

cotillion *also* **cotillon** \kuh-TIL-yun\ *n.* Ballroom dance.

cottage \KOT-ij\ *n.* A small house.

couch \kowch\ *n.* A sofa.

couch \kowch\ *v.* couched; couching. To phrase carefully.

cough \kawf\ *v.* coughed; coughing. To expel air forcefully.

could \kuud\ *v.* Past tense of can.

council \KOWN-sul\ *n.* An advisory group.

councilor \KOWN-suh-lur\ *n.* An advisory group member.

counsel \KOWN-sul\ *n.* **1.** Opionion. **2.** Advice.

counsel \KOWN-sul\ *v.* counseled; counseling. To advise.

counselor *also* **counsellor** \KOWN-suh-lur\ *n.* One who gives advice.

count \kownt\ *n.* **1.** A tally. **2.** An estimate.

count \kownt\ *v.* counted; counting. **1.** To add. **2.** To count on [Id]: To anticipate.

countenance \KOWN-tn-uns\ *n.* Facial expression.

countenance \KOWN-tn-uns\ *v.* countenanced; countenancing. To tolerate.

counter \KOWN-tur\ *n.* **1.** A level surface. **2.** Something that counts.

counter \KOWN-tur\ *v.* countered; countering. **1.** To oppose. **2.** To offset.

counteract \kown-tur-AKT\ *v.* counteracted; counteracting. To neutralize.

counterculture \KOWN-tur-kul-chur\ *n.* Anything running against established values.

counterfeit \KOWN-tur-fit\ *adj.* Forged or fake.

counterfeit \KOWN-tur-fit\ *v.* counterfeited; counterfeiting. To imitate or fake.

counterinsurgency \KOWN-tur-in-sur-jen-see\ *n.* Military action.

counterpart \KOWN-tur-pahrt\ *n.* A complement.

countless \KOWNT-lis\ *adj.* Too many to count. countlessly *adv.*

country \KUN-tree\ *n. pl.* countries. 1. A political area. 2. A rural area.

country rock *n.* (Mu) Popular music with western themes.

county \KOWN-tee\ *n. pl.* counties. A political division or a state or country.

coup \koo\ *n. pl.* coups. An overthrow of power.

coup d'état \koo-day-TAH\ *n. pl.* coups d'etat. (Fr) An overthrow of power.

couple \KUP-ul\ *n.* 1. A pair. 2. A small number.

couple \KUP-ul\ *v.* coupled; coupling. 1. To link. 2. Sexual relations.

couplet \KUP-lit\ *n.* Rhyming sequence.

coupon \KOO-pon\ *n.* A discount form.

courage \KUR-ij\ *n.* Mental or moral strength. courageous *adj.*

courier \KUUR-ee-ur\ *n.* A messenger.

course \kors\ *n.* A path.

course \kors\ *v.* coursed; coursing. To move quickly.

court \kort\ *n.* 1. Sovereign's residence. 2. Courtyard. 3. A game field. 4. Session with judge.

court \kort\ *v.* courted; courting. To tempt.

courteous \KUR-tee-us\ *adj.* Polite, respectful behavior.

courtesy \KUR-tuh-see\ *n. pl.* courtesies. Consideration.

courtship \KORT-ship\ *n.* A time of dating.

couscous \KOOS-koos\ *n.* [Fo] North African pasta.

cousin \KUZ-un\ *n.* A child of one's aunt or uncle.

couture \koo-TUUR\ *adj.* Relating to clothes design.

cove \kohv\ *n.* A small bay or sheltered area.

coven \KOH-vun\ *n.* A group of witches.

covenant \KUV-uh-nunt\ *n.* A formal agreement.

covenant \KUV-uh-nunt\ *v.*

covenanted; covenanting. To pledge.

cover \KUV-ur\ *n.* **1.** A coating, covering, or shelter. **2.** A top.

cover \KUV-ur\ *v.* covered; covering. **1.** To place or be over. **2.** To insure and protect. **3.** To have enough.

covert \KOH-vurt\ *adj.* Secret.

covert \KUV-urt\ *n.* Thick undergrowth.

cow \kow\ *n.* **1.** A female mammal. **2.** A domestic bovine.

coward \KOW-urd\ *n.* An overly fearful person. cowardly *adv.*; cowardice *n.*

cower \KOW-ur\ *v.* cowered; cowering. To shrink from.

coy \koi\ *adj.* Shy. coyness *n.*; coyly *adv.*

cozy \KOH-zee\ *adj.* cozier; coziest. **1.** Snug. **2.** Intimate.

cozy \KOH-zee\ *n. pl.* cozies. A padded cover.

crab \krab\ *n.* A ten-legged marine crustacean.

crab \krab\ *v.* crabbed; crabbing. To fish for crabs.

crabby \KRAB-ee\ *adj.* crabbier; crabbiest. Grumpy.

crack \krak\ *n.* **1.** A loud noise. **2.** An opening. **3.** An attempt. **4.** A drug.

crack \krak\ *v.* cracked; cracking. **1.** To break. **2.** To open. **3.** To wreck.

cracker \KRAK-ur\ *n.* **1.** A firecracker. **2.** Crispy bread.

cradle \KRAYD-l\ *n.* **1.** A baby's bed. **2.** Place of origin.

cradle \KRAYD-l\ *v.* cradled; cradling. **1.** To shelter. **2.** To support.

craft \kraft\ *n.* **1.** A creative art. **2.** A vehicle.

craft \kraft\ *v.* crafted; crafting. To make with care.

crafty \KRAF-tee\ *adj.* craftier; craftiest. Clever. craftiness *n.*

cram \kram\ *v.* crammed; cramming. **1.** To stuff. **2.** To study under pressure.

cramp \kramp\ *n.* A painful muscle spasm.

cramp \kramp\ *v.* cramped; cramping. **1.** To confine. **2.** To create a muscle spasm.

cramped \krampd\ *adj.* Confined.

cranberry \KRAN-bair-ee\ *n.* A small, red, tart berry.

cranky \KRANG-kee\ *adj.* crankier; crankiest. **1.** Fussy. **2.** Unpredictable. crankiness *n.*

crapshoot \KRAP-shuut\ *n.* An unpredictable circumstance.

crash \krash\ *n.* **1.** A loud noise. **2.** A sudden fall.

crash \krash\ *v.* crashed; crashing **1.** To smash. **2.** To fall suddenly. **3.** To fail. **4.** [Sl] To sleep.

crass \kras\ *adj.* **1.** Stupid. **2.** Gross.

crate \krayt\ *n.* A shipping box.

crate \krayt\ *v.* crated; crating. To pack in a shipping box.

crater \KRAY-tur\ *n.* A ground depression.

crave \krayv\ *v.* craved; craving. To desire.

crawl \krawl\ *n.* Slow movement.

crawl \krawl\ *v.* crawled; crawling. **1.** To move slowly. **2.** To advance on hands and knees. **3.** To spread.

crazy \KRAY-zee\ *adj.* crazier; craziest. **1.** Unsound. **2.** Unpredictable. **3.** Mad. **4.** Obsessed. craziness *n.*

creak \kreek\ *n.* A grating noise. creaky *adj.*

cream \kreem\ *n.* **1.** Milk product. **2.** The best part. **3.** Thick salve.

cream \kreem\ *v.* creamed; creaming. **1.** To beat until smooth. **2.** [Sl] To beat up or defeat.

crease \krees\ *n.* A line made by folding.

crease \krees\ *v.* creased; creasing. To wrinkle.

create \kree-AYT\ *v.* created; creating. **1.** To make. **2.** To design.

creation \kree-AY-shun\ *n.* The act of making.

creator \kree-AY-tur\ *n.* One who makes.

creature \KREE-chur\ *n.* **1.** Living being. **2.** A fearful, unknown animal.

crèche \kresh\ *n.* (Fr) A nativity representation.

credence \KREED-uns\ *n.* **1.** Credibility. **2.** Belief.

credential \kri-DEN-shul\ *n.* **1.** Testimonial. **2.** Authorization.

credible \KRED-uh-bul\ *adj.* Believable. credibly *adv.*

credit \KRED-it\ *n.* **1.** Loaned amount. **2.** Influence. **3.** Acknowledgement.

credit \KRED-it\ *v.* credited; crediting. **1.** To believe. **2.** To remove from amount owed.

credit card *n.* Charge card.

credo \KREE-doh\ *n. pl.* credos. Creed.

credulous \KREJ-uh-lus\ *adj.* Believing on little evidence. credulity *n.*

creed \kreed\ *n.* A set of beliefs.

creek \kreek\ *n.* **1.** A small river. **2.** Up the creek [Id]: In a difficult situation.

creep \kreep\ *n.* **1.** Moving slowly. **2.** [Sl] A rude person.

creep \kreep\ *v.* crept; creeping. To move slowly.

cremate \KREE-mayt\ *v.* cremated; cremating. To burn. cremation *n.*

crematorium \KREE-muh-tor-ee-um\ *n. pl.* crematoriums or crematoria. A place for burning, especially corpses.

crepe \krayp\ *n.* (Fr) A light fabric.

crescendo \kri-SHEN-doh\ *n. pl.* crescendos or crescendoes or crescendi. Increasing sound.

crescent \KRES-unt\ *n.* **1.** One of the moon's stages. **2.** A shape less than half a circle.

crest \krest\ *n.* **1.** An animal's plume. **2.** The high point. **3.** Climax.

crest \krest\ *v.* crested; cresting. To reach the top.

crestfallen \KREST-faw-lun\ *adj.* Dejected.

crevasse \kruh-VAS\ *n.* A deep fissure.

crevice \KREV-is\ *n.* **1.** A narrow opening. **2.** A crack.

crew \kroo\ *n.* A group of people engaged in one activity.

crib \krib\ *n.* A baby's bed.

crib death *n.* (Md) Sudden Infant Death Syndrome.

crick \krik\ *n.* A muscle spasm.

cricket \KRIK-it\ *n.* **1.** A winged insect resembling a grasshopper. **2.** An outdoor ball game.

crime \kriem\ *n.* Illegal activity.

criminal \KRIM-uh-nul\ *adj.* **1.** One who acts illegally. **2.** Disgraceful.

cringe \krinj\ *v.* cringed; cringing. To shrink away from.

crinkle \KRING-kul\ *v.* crinkled; crinkling. To wrinkle. crinkly *adj.*

cripple \KRIP-ul\ *n.* A lame or flawed person or animal.

cripple \KRIP-ul\ *v.* crippled; crippling. To weaken.

crisis \KRIE-sis\ *n. pl.* crises. **1.** A decisive moment. **2.** A juncture.

crisp \krisp\ *adj.* **1.** Brittle. **2.** Brisk. crispy *adv.*

criterion \krie-TEER-ee-un\ *n. pl.* criteria. A standard.

critic \KRIT-ik\ *n.* A judge.

criticize \KRIT-uh-siez\ *v.* criticized; criticizing. To evaluate harshly. critical *adj.*

critique \kri-TEEK\ *n.* An evaluation, sometimes harsh.

croak \krohk\ *n.* **1.** A guttural noise. **2.** [Sl] Something dead.

crochet \kroh-SHAY\ *n.* (Fr) A form of needlework.

crock \krok\ *n.* **1.** A pot or jar. **2.** [Sl] Nonsense.

croissant \kraw-SANT or kwaw-SANT\ *n. pl.* croissants. (Fr) A rich pastry roll.

crony \KROH-nee\ *n. pl.* cronies. A close friend or co-worker.

crook \kruuk\ *n.* **1.** Something hook-shaped. **2.** [Sl] A criminal.

crooked \KRUUK-id\ *adj.* Dishonest.

crop \krop\ *n.* **1.** Something green and harvested. **2.** A riding whip.

crop \krop\ *v.* cropped; cropping. To cut short.

croquet \kroh-KAY\ *n.* (Fr) A lawn game.

croquette \kroh-KET\ *n.* (Fr) Food.

cross \kraws\ *n.* **1.** The crucifixion. **2.** An intersection of two lines.

cross \kraws\ *v.* crossed; crossing. **1.** To go through. **2.** To oppose. **3.** To betray. **4.** To occur to.

cross-examine \KRAWS-ig-ZAM-in\ *v.* cross-examined; cross-examining. To question a witness.

crossing \KRAWS-ing\ *n.* **1.** A place for moving across. **2.** An act of opposition.

crossover \KRAWS-OH-vur\ *adj.* A critical point.

crossover \KRAWS-OH-vur\ *n.* Moving from one side to another.

crouch \krowch\ *v.* crouched; crouching. To lower.

crouton \KROO-ton\ *n.* (Fr) Toasted bread.

crow \kroh\ *n.* **1.** A black bird. **2.** [Cap] A native American tribe.

crow \kroh\ *v.* crowed; crowing. **1.** To make a shrill noise. **2.** To gloat.

crowd \krowd\ *n.* A large group of people.

crowd \krowd\ *v.* crowded; crowding. **1.** To press in on. **2.** To force.

crown \krown\ *n.* **1.** A headdress. **2.** The top. **3.** A monarch.

crown \krown\ *v.* crowned; crowning. **1.** To place on. **2.** To hit on the head.

crucial \KROO-shul\ *adj.* Vital. crucially *adv.*

crucify \KROO-suh-fie\ *v.* crucified; crucifying. **1.** To put to death. **2.** To torment.

crude \krood\ *adj.* cruder; crudest. **1.** Immature. **2.** Rude. crudely *adv.*; crudeness *n.*

cruel \KROO-ul\ *adj.* crueler or crueller; cruelest or cruellest. Causing pain and/or suffering. cruelly *adv.*

cruise \krooz\ *v.* cruised; cruising. **1.** To move smoothly. **2.** To move randomly.

cruise control *n.* An automotive electronic device.

cruise missile *n.* (Sc) A guided bomb.

crumb \krum\ *n.* A tiny morsel.

crumble \KRUM-bul\ *v.* crumbled; crumbling. **1.** To disintegrate. **2.** To collapse. crumbly *adj.*

crumple \KRUM-pul\ *v.* crumpled; crumpling. To rumple.

crunch \krunch\ *n.* **1.** A sound. **2.** A shortage.

crunch \krunch\ *v.* crunched; crunching. **1.** To chew. **2.** To process numbers.

crusade \kroo-SAYD\ *n.* **1.** Historical military action. **2.** Something done with enthusiasm.

crush \krush\ *n.* A crowd.

crush \krush\ *v.* crushed; crushing. **1.** To squeeze. **2.** To hug. **3.** To overwhelm.

crust \krust\ *n.* **1.** A hardened top layer. **2.** The outer surface.

crustacean \kru-STAY-shun\ *n.* (Sc) An aquatic animal.

crutch \kruch\ *n.* A brace.

crux \kruks\ *n. pl.* cruxes also cruces. An essential point or feature.

cry \krie\ *n. pl.* cries. A call.

cry \krie\ *v.* cried; crying. **1.** To shout. **2.** To beg. **3.** To weep. **4.** Cry wolf [Id]: To give a false alarm

cryogenic \krie-uh-JEN-ik\ *adj.* (Sc) Relating to very low temperatures. cryogenics *n.*

crypt \kript\ *n.* A hidden chamber.

cryptic \KRIP-tik\ *adj.* **1.** Obscure. **2.** Secret. cryptically *adv.*

crystal \KRIS-tl\ *n.* **1.** A quartz stone. **2.** Superior quality glassware. crystalline *adj.*

cube \kyoob\ *n.* **1.** A six-sided square block. **2.** A number taken three times itself.

cube \kyoob\ *v.* cubed; cubing. To cut into a six-sided square block.

cubicle \KYOO-bi-kul\ *n.* A small compartment.

cud \kud\ *n.* Regurgitated food.

cuddle \KUD-l\ *v.* cuddled; cuddling. To hold close. cuddly *adj.*; cuddler *n.*

cue \kyoo\ *n.* **1.** A hint. **2.** A rod in billiards and pool.

cuff \kuf\ *n.* **1.** Something that circles the wrist. **2.** A handcuff. **3.** A blood-pressure measure.

cuisine \kwi-ZEEN\ *n.* (Fr) A cooking style.

cul-de-sac \KUL-duh-SAK\ *n. pl.* culs-de-sac also cul-de-sacs. (Fr) A street with a closed- off end.

culinary \KYOO-luh-ner-ee\ *adj.* Concerning cooking.

cull \kul\ *v.* culled; culling. To select.

culminate \KUL-muh-nayt\ *v.* culminated; culminating. To reach the highest point. culmination *n.*

culpable \KUL-puh-bul\ *adj.* Deserving of blame. culpability *n.*; culpably *adv.*

cult \kult\ *n.* A group of people

completely devoted to a set of beliefs. cultist *n.*; cultism *n.*

cultivate \KUL-tuh-vayt\ *v.* cultivated; cultivating. **1.** To grow. **2.** To refine. cultivated *adj.*

culture \KUL-chur\ *n.* **1.** A group's beliefs and rituals. **2.** Living entities grown for experimentation. cultured *adj.*

culture shock *n.* Anxiety upon entrance into an unfamiliar culture.

cumbersome \KUM-bur-sum\ *adj.* **1.** Bulky. **2.** Heavy.

cummerbund \KUM-mur-bund\ *n.* A waistband.

cumulative \KYOO-myuh-luh-tiv\ *adj.* Increasing in amount or severity. cumulatively *adv.*

cuneiform \kyoo-NEE-uh-form\ *n..* Ancient writing system with wedge-shaped symbols.

cunning \KUN-ing\ *adj.* Clever. cunningly *adj.*; cunningness *n.*

cup \kup\ *n.* **1.** Handheld drinking container. **2.** Prize. **3.** Eight ounces. **4.** Cup-shaped object.

cup \kup\ *v.* cupped; cupping. To hold.

cupboard \KUB-urd\ *n.* An enclosed storage area.

cupola \KUP-oh-luh\ *n.* (It) Rounded vault.

curb \kurb\ *n.* A border.

curb \kurb\ *v.* curbed; curbing. To restrain.

curdle \KUR-dl\ *v.* curdled; curdling. To spoil.

cure \kyuur\ *n.* A remedy.

cure \kyuur\ *v.* cured; curing. **1.** To fix or mend. **2.** To prepare or preserve.

curious \KYUUR-ee-us\ *adj.* Inquisitive. curiously *adv.*

curl \kurl\ *n.* **1.** A ringlet. **2.** A coil.

curl \kurl\ *v.* curled; curling. To twist.

currant \KUR-unt\ *n.* A dried grape.

currency \KUR-un-see\ *n. pl.* currencies. Money in use.

current \KUR-unt\ *adj.* Concerning the moment.

current \KUR-unt\ *n.* A flow.

curriculum \kuh-RIK-yuh-lum\ *n. pl.* curricula or curriculums. A plan of learning.

curry *also* **currie** \KUR-ee\ *pl. n.* [Fo] An Indian food or spice.

curry \KUR-ee\ *v.* curried; currying, **1.** To brush a horse. **2.** To beat.

curse \kurs\ *n.* **1.** An evil prayer. **2.** A cause of misfortune.

curse \kurs\ *v.* cursed; cursing. **1.** To call on evil. **2.** To blaspheme.

cursor \KUR-sur\ *n.* A moveable cue or prompt.

cursory \KUR-suh-ree\ *adj.* Hasty.

curt \kurt\ *adj.* Rude. curtly *adv.*

curtail \kur-TAYL\ *v.* curtailed; curtailing. To shorten.

curtain \KUR-tn\ *n.* **1.** A fabric screen. **2.** A blocking device.

curtsy *also* **curtsey** \KURT-see\ *n. pl.* curtsies also curtseys. A bow with the whole body.

curtsy \KURT-see\ *v.* curtised also curtseyed; curtsying *also* curtseying. To bow the whole body.

curvature \KUR-vuh-chur\ *n.* The measured degree of a curve.

curve \kurv\ *n.* **1.** A bent line. **2.** A trick. **3.** A grade distribution.

curve \kurv\ *v.* curved; curving. To deviate from a straight path.

cushion \KUUSH-un\ *n.* **1.** A pillow. **2.** Something to lessen the effect of negative events.

cushion \KUUSH-un\ *v.* cushioned; cushioning. To protect against shock.

cusp \kusp\ *n.* **1.** A point. **2.** An edge. cusped *adj.*

custard \KUS-turd\ *n.* An egg pudding.

custodian \kuh-STOH-dee-un\ *n.* A caretaker.

custom \KUS-tum\ *n.* A tradition.

custom-made \KUS-tum-MAYD\ *adj.* Made-to-order.

customary \KUS-tuh-mer-ee\ *adj.* Traditional or usual.

cut \kut\ *n.* **1.** A wound. **2.** An absence.

cut \kut\ *v.* cut; cutting. **1.** To penetrate. **2.** To split. **3.** Make or shape by cutting. **4.** Mow or reap.

cutback \KUT-bak\ *n.* A reduction. cut back *v.*

cut-offs \KUT-awfs\ *n.* Shorts made from long pants.

cut short *v.* cut short; cutting short To stop before the end.

cutting \KUT-ing\ *adj.* **1.** Sharp. **2.** Intense.

cutting \KUT-ing\ *n.* **1.** A plant section. **2.** A recording.

cutting edge *n.* The front line or part.

cut up *v.* cut up; cutting up. **1.** To slash into pieces. **2.** To clown around.

cybernetics \sie-bur-NET-iks\ *n. pl.* cybernetics. (Sc) The study of mechanical communications systems.

cyborg \SIE-borg\ *n.* (Sc) A bionic human being.

cycle \SIE-kul\ *n.* **1.** The time period of a recurring event. **2.** An age. **3.** A bike.

cycle \SIE-kul\ *v.* cycled; cycling. To ride a bike.

cyclical *also* **cyclic** \SIE-klik-ul\ *n.* cyclically or cyclicly. *adv.* Concerning a cycle.

cylinder \SIL-in-dur\ *n.* A tube.

cynical \SIN-ik-ul\ *adj.* Pessimistic and distrustful.

cypress \SIE-prus\ *n.* A type of evergreen tree.

cyst \sist\ *n.* (Md) A fluid-filled closed sac.

czar \zahr\ *n.* [Fo] **1.** Russian emperor. **2.** One with great power.

D

d \dee\ *n. pl.* d's or ds. **1.** The fourth letter of the English alphabet. **2.** Fourth of the letter grades.

dab *n.* **1.** A small amount. **2.** A type of fish.

dab *v.* dabbed; dabbing. To pat.

dabble \DAB-ul\ *v.* dabbled; dabbling. To do superficially.

daffodil \daf-OH-dil\ *n.* A flower.

daft \daft\ *adj.* Foolish. daffy *adj.*

daguerreotype \duh-GAIR-uh-tipe\ *n.* An early photography method.

dahlia \DAL-yuh\ *n.* A flowering herb.

daily \DAY-lee\ *adj.* Happening or appearing every day.

daily \DAY-lee\ *n.* dailies. A newspaper published every weekday.

dainty \DAYN-tee\ *adj.* daintier; daintiest. Delicate. daintiness *n.*

daiquiri \DIE-kuh-ree or DAK-uh-ree\ *n.* A rum cocktail.

dairy \DAIR-ee\ *n. pl.* dairies. A farm devoted to milk production and products.

dalmation \dahl-MAY-shun\ *n.* A type of large white dog with spots.

dam *n.* A barrier built to hold back water.

dam *v.* dammed; damming. To block.

damage \DAM-ij\ *n.* **1.** An injury. **2.** Expense.

damage \DAM-ij\ *v.* damaged; damaging. To injure or spoil.

dame \daym\ *n.* A woman of authority.

damn \dam\ *v.* damned; damning. **1.** To condemn. **2.** To curse. damned *adj.*

damp *adj.* damper; dampest. **1.** Slightly wet. **2.** Depressed. dampness *n.*; dampen *v.*

damsel *also* **damosel or damozel** \DAM-zul\ *n.* A young woman.

dance \dans\ *n.* A rhythmic movement to music. dancer *n.*

dance \dans\ *v.* danced; dancing. To move to music.

dandelion \DAN-dl-IE-un or DAN-dee-LIE-un\ *n.* A yellow-flowered herb.

danger \DAYN-jer\ *n.* An exposure to harm.

dangerous \DAYN-jer-us\ *adj.* Likely to cause harm. dangerously *adv.*

dapper \DAP-ur\ *adj.* Stylish.

dare \dair\ *v.* dared; daring. **1.** To challenge. **2.** To defy.

daring \DAIR-ing\ *adj.* Adventurousness.

dark \dahrk\ *adj.* **1.** Without light. **2.** Gloomy. **3.** Swarthy. darkness *n.*

darken \DAHR-kun\ *v.* darkened; darkening. To remove light.

darling \DAHR-ling\ *n.* A favorite.

dart \dahrt\ *n.* **1.** A small arrow. **2.** A garment fold.

dart \dahrt\ *v.* darted; darting. **1.** To move suddenly. **2.** To thrust.

dash *n.* **1.** A punctuation mark. **2.** A little bit. **3.** A short race.

dash *v.* dashed; dashing. **1.** To break. **2.** To move suddenly.

data \DAY-tuh\ *n. pl.* data. Information.

data processing *n.* (Cm) The act of inputting information on computer.

database \DAY-tuh-BAIS\ *n.* (Cm) A large organized collection of computerized information.

date \dayt\ *n.* **1.** An edible fruit. **2.** A time within a calendar year. **3.** An appointment.

date \dayt\ *v.* dated; dating. **1.** To mark. **2.** To go out with socially.

daughter \DAW-tur\ *n.* One's female offspring.

dawdle \DAWD-l\ *v.* dawdled; dawdling. To delay.

day *n.* **1.** Period of light from dawn to dark. **2.** Twenty-four hours.

daybreak \DAY-brayk\ *n.* Dawn.

day-care \DAY-kair\ *n.* Care for children while parents work.

daydream \DAY-dreem\ *n.* A pleasant vision while awake.

Day-Glo \DAY-gloh\ *n.* A trademark for fluorescent materials.

daylight \DAY-liet\ *n.* **1.** Sunshine.

2. [Sl] One's wits. **3.** [Cl] Sudden comprehension.

daze \dayz\ *n.* Unfocused awareness.

daze \dayz\ *v.* dazed; dazing. To stun.

dazzle \DAZ-ul\ *v.* dazzled; dazzling. To overpower. dazzlingly *adv.*

deacon \DEE-kun\ *n.* A religious official.

deactivate \dee-AK-tuh-vayt\ *v.* deactivated; deactivating. To disarm.

dead \ded\ *adj.* **1.** Not alive. **2.** Exhausted. **3.** Inert. **4.** Absolute. **5.** Not functioning.

deadbeat \DED-beet\ *n.* A lazy non-working person.

deaden \DED-n\ *v.* deadened; deadened. **1.** To blunt. **2.** To remove the spirits.

dead-end *adj.* Able to go no further. dead end *n.*

deadlock \DED-lok\ *n.* A standstill.

deaf \def\ *adj.* **1.** Without hearing. **2.** Unwilling to listen.

deafening \DEF-un-ing\ *adj.* Very loud.

deal \deel\ *n.* **1.** An agreement. **2.** A card hand. **3.** A business transaction.

deal \deel\ *v.* dealt; dealing. **1.** To

administer. **2.** To sell. **3.** To handle or endure.

dean \deen\ *n.* A division head.

dear \deer\ *adj.* dearer; dearest. **1.** Heartfelt. **2.** Sweetheart. dearly *adv.*

death \deth\ *n.* **1.** The end of life. **2.** To death: [Id] excessively.

debacle \day-BAH-kul\ *n.* A violent collapse.

debase \di-BAYS\ *v.* debased; debasing. To reduce or lower in value. debaser *n.*

debate \di-BAYT\ *v.* debated; debating. To discuss or argue.

debauchery \di-BAW-chuh-ree\ *n. pl.* debaucheries. Excessive sexual activities.

debilitate \bi-BIL-i-tayt\ *v.* debilitated; debilitating. To weaken. debilitation *n.*

debonair \deb-uh-NAIR\ *adj.* **1.** Graceful. **2.** Charming.

debris \duh-BREE\ *n. pl.* debris. Waste material.

debt \det\ *n.* **1.** Something owed. **2.** A sin.

debut *also* **dibut** \day-BYOO\ *n.* A first appearance.

debutante \DEB-yuu-tahnt\ *n.* (Fr) One making a debut.

decade \DEK-ayd\ *n.* Ten years.

decadent \DEK-uh-dunt\ *adj.* Con-

cerning self-indulgence. deca-
dently *adv.*

decathlon \di-KATH-lon\ *n.* (Fr) A
track-and-field contest with 10
events.

decay \di-KAY\ *v.* decayed; decaying. To break down.

deceased \di-SEEST\ *n.* A dead
person. deceased *adj.*

deceit \di-SEET\ *n.* A trick. deceitful *adj.*

deceive \di-SEEV\ *v.* deceived; de-
ceiving. To mislead. deceiver *n.*

December \di-SEM-bur\ *n.* The
twelfth month of the year.

decent \DEE-sunt\ *adj.* 1. Proper. 2.
Good.

deception \di-SEP-shun\ *n.* A trick.

decibel \DES-uh-bel\ *n.* Sound
units.

decide \di-SIED\ *v.* decided; deciding. To arrive at an answer or solution. decided *adj.*

deciduous \di-SIJ-oo-us\ *adj.* Falling off or shedding, as a tree's
leaves.

decipher \di-SIE-fur\ *v.* deciphered;
deciphering. To decode or figure
out.

decision \di-SIZH-un\ *n.* A conclusion. decisive *adj.*

deck \dek\ *n.* 1. An outdoor platform. 2. A ship's floor. 3. A pack
of cards.

deck \dek\ *v.* decked; decking. 1. To
adorn. 2. To hit.

declaration \dek-luh-RAY-shun\ *n.*
An announcement.

declare \di-KLAIR\ *v.* declared; declaring. 1. To make known. 2. To
affirm.

declassify \dee-KLAS-i-fie\ *v.* de-
classified; declassifying. To remove a security restriction.

decline \di-KLIEN\ *n.* A change or
move to a lower state.

decline \di-KLIEN\ *v.* declined; de-
clining. 1. To descend. 2. To decrease or lose strength. 3. To
withhold. 4. To regret.

decompose \dee-kum-POHZ\ *v.* de-
composed; decomposing. To rot.
decomposition *n.*

decongestant \dee-kun-JES-tunt\
n. (Md) An agent that relieves
congestion.

decor *also* **dicor** \day-KOR\ *n.* (Fr)
1. The setting. 2. A style.

decorate \DEK-uh-rayt\ *v.* decorated; decorating. To adorn.

decoration \dek-uh-RAY-shun\ *n.*
1. An ornament. 2. A military
honor. decorative *adj.*

decorum \di-KOR-um\ *n.* 1. Polite
behavior. 2. Fitness.

decoupage *also* **dicoupage** \day-
KUU-pazh\ *n.* A surface decoration using paper cutouts.

decoy \DEE-koi\ *n.* A lure. decoy *v.*

decrease \DEE-krees\ *n.* A reduction.

decrease \di-KREES\ *v.* decreased; decreasing. To diminish or reduce.

decree \di-KREE\ *n.* An authoritative order.

decree \di-KREE\ *v.* decreed; decreeing. To demand.

decrepit \di-KREP-it\ *adj.* Weak.

dedicate \DED-i-kayt\ *v.* dedicated; dedicating. **1.** To devote. **2.** To address. dedicated *adj.*

dedication \ded-i-KAY-shun\ *n.* Intense devotion.

deduce \di-DOOS\ *v.* deduced; deducing. To figure by reason.

deduct \di-DUKT\ *v.* deducted; deducting. To subtract.

deduction \di-DUK-shun\ *n.* **1.** Something subtracted. **2.** A logical process.

deed *n.* **1.** A certificate of ownership. **2.** Something done.

deem *v.* deemed; deeming. To believe.

deep *adj.* **1.** Extending far down. **2.** Obscure. **3.** Wise. **4.** In deep water [Id]: In distress.

deer *n.* A ruminant fast-moving wild animal.

deface \di-FAYS\ *v.* defaced; defacing. To mar.

de facto \dee-FAK-toh\ *adj.* Actual, existing in fact.

defame \di-FAYM\ *v.* defamed; defaming. To malign. defamation *n.*

default \di-FAWLT\ *n.* **1.** Neglect. **2.** Failure to pay. default *v.*

defeat \di-FEET\ *v.* defeated; defeating. To win victory over.

defeat \di-FEET\ *n.* A contest loss.

defecate \DEF-i-kayt\ *v.* defecated; defecating. To discharge feces. defecation *n.*

defect \DEE-fekt\ *n.* **1.** An imperfection. **2.** A deficiency. defective *adj.*

defend \di-FEND\ *v.* defended; defending. **1.** To drive away danger. **2.** To protect or contest.

defense \di-FENS\ *n.* **1.** A supporting argument. **2.** A protecting move or series of moves. defensive *adj.*; defenseless *adj.*

defer \di-FUR\ *v.* deferred; deferring. **1.** To put off. **2.** To yield.

deferential \def-uh-REN-shul\ *adj.* Concerning respect. deference *n.*

deferred income \di-FURD-IN-cum\ *n.* Delayed payment.

defiance \di-FIE-uns\ *n.* **1.** Resistance. **2.** A challenge. **3.** In defiance of [Id]: despite. defiant *adj.*; defiantly *adv.*

defibrillation \di-FIB-ruh-lay-shun\ *n.* (Md) Application of a shock to restore heart rhythm.

deficit \DEF-uh-sit\ *n.* **1.** A lack. **2.** A disadvantage.

defile \di-FIEL\ *v.* defiled; defiling. **1.** To desecrate. **2.** To contaminate. defilement *n.*

define \di-FIEN\ *v.* defined; defining. **1.** To identify. **2.** To explain a meaning.

definite \DEF-uh-nit\ *adj.* Without doubt. definitely *adv.*

definition \def-uh-NISH-un\ *n.* **1.** A statement of meaning. **2.** Clear presentation.

deflate \di-FLAYT\ *v.* deflated; deflating. **1.** To let out air. **2.** To reduce.

deflect \di-FLEKT\ *v.* deflected; deflecting. To turn aside. deflector *n.*

deformed \di-FORMD\ *adj.* Misshapen.

defraud \di-FRAWD\ *v.* defrauded; defrauding. To cheat. defrauder *n.*

defunct \di-FUNGKT\ *adj.* Not functioning or no longer used.

defuse \dee-FYOOZ\ *v.* defused; defusing. To eliminate harm.

degenerate \di-JEN-ur-it\ *adj.* Declined from a former state.

degenerate \di-JEN-uh-rayt\ *v.* degenerated; degenerating. To decline.

degrade \di-GRAYD\ *v.* degraded;

degrading. **1.** To bring low. **2.** To corrupt. degradingly *adv.*

degree \di-GREE\ *n.* **1.** A rank. **2.** A step in a process. **3.** Academic title. **4.** A position on a scale.

dehydrate \dee-HIE-drayt\ *v.* dehydrated; dehydrating. To remove water. dehydration *n.*

deify \DEE-uh-fie\ *v.* deified; deifying. **1.** To glorify. **2.** To make a god.

deity \DEE-i-tee\ *n. pl.* deities. A god.

deja vu \DAY-zhuh-voo\ *n.* (Fr) The illusion that one is reliving an experience.

delay \di-LAY\ *n.* A waiting state.

delay \di-LAY\ *v.* delayed; delaying. To slow.

delectable \di-LEK-tuh-bul\ *adj.* Very pleasing. delectably *adv.*

delegate \DEL-i-git\ *n.* An elected representative.

delegate \DEL-i-gayt\ *v.* delegated; delegating. To entrust to another.

delegation \del-i-GAY-shun\ *n.* A group of representatives.

delete \di-LEET\ *v.* deleted; deleting. To eliminate. deletion *n.*

deliberate \di-LIB-uh-rut\ *adj.* **1.** Well thought out. **2.** Voluntary. deliberation *n.*

deliberate \di-LIB-uh-rayt\ *v.* deliberated; deliberating. To consider carefully. deliberation *n.*

delicate \DEL-i-kit\ *adj.* **1.** Fragile. **2.** Pleasing. **3.** Squeamish. delicately *adv.*

delicatessen *also* **deli** \del-i-kuh-TES-un\ *n.* An eatery.

delicious \di-LISH-us\ *adj.* Tasting or smelling great. deliciously *adv.*

delight \di-LIET\ *n.* **1.** Joy. **2.** Pleasure. delightful *adj.*

delight \di-LIET\ *v.* delighted; delighting. To make happy. delighted *adj.*

delinquent \duh-LING-kwunt\ *adj.* Overdue. delinquency *n.*

deliver \di-LIV-ur\ *v.* delivered; delivering. **1.** To take to. **2.** To speak or sing. **3.** To surrender. **4.** To rescue. deliverer *n.*; delivery *n.*

delude \di-LOOD\ *v.* deluded; deluding. To deceive.

deluge \DEL-yooj\ *n.* An overflowing or downpour.

deluge \DEL-yooj\ *v.* deluged; deluging. To inundate.

delusion \di-LOO-zhun\ *n.* A false belief. delusional *adj.*

deluxe \duh-LUKS\ *adj.* **1.** Very elegant. **2.** Expensive.

delve \delv\ *v.* delved; delving. To search deeply.

demand \di-MAND\ *n.* **1.** Need. **2.** Authoritative request. demanding *adj.*

demand \di-MAND\ *v.* demanded; demanding. **1.** To require. **2.** To request or command.

demean \di-MEEN\ *v.* demeaned; demeaning. **1.** To put down. **2.** To lower in status.

demeanor \di-MEEN-ur\ *n.* One's behavior and mental outlook.

dementia \di-MEN-shuh\ *n.* (Md) Madness. demented *adj.*

demise \di-MIZE\ *n.* **1.** An estate's transfer. **2.** A death.

demise \di-MIZE\ *v.* demised; demising. To die.

democracy \di-MOK-ruh-see\ *n. pl.* democracies. A government by the people through elected representation.

democratic \dem-uh-KRAT-ik\ *adj.* **1.** Concerning government by the people. **2.** Relating to one US political party.

demographics \dem-uh-GRAF-iks\ *n. pl.* demographics. Characteristics of a population.

demolish \di-MOL-ish\ *v.* demolished; demolishing. To destroy. demolition *n.*

demon *also* **daemon** \DEE-mun\ *n.* An evil spirit. demonic *also* demonical *adj.*

demonstrate \DEM-un-strayt\ *v.* demonstrated; demonstrating. **1.** To show clearly. **2.** To protest. demonstration *n.*

demoralize \di-MOR-uh-lize\ *v.* demoralized; demoralizing. **1.** To corrupt. **2.** To discourage. demoralization *n.*

demote \di-MOHT\ *v.* demoted; demoting. To reduce. demotion *n.*

demure \di-MUR\ *adj.* Shy.

den *n.* **1.** An animal's home. **2.** A boy scout troop. **3.** A study or private room.

denomination \di-nom-uh-NAY-shuh-nl\ *n.* **1.** A designation. **2.** A religious organization. denominational *adj.*

denote \di-NOHT\ *v.* denoted; denoting. To indicate. denontative *adj.*

denounce \di-NOWNS\ *v.* denounced; denouncing. **1.** To criticize publicly. **2.** To accuse.

dense \dens\ *adj.* denser; densest **1.** Compact. **2.** [Sl] Stupid. densely *adv.*

dent *n.* **1.** A depression. **2.** Beginning progress.

dental \DEN-tl\ *adj.* Concerning the teeth.

dentistry \DEN-tuh-stree\ *n.* (Md) The profession of caring for teeth. dentist *n.*

dentures \DEN-churs\ *n.* False teeth.

deny \di-NIE\ *v.* denied; denying. **1.** To disavow. **2.** To decline. denial *n.*

deodorant \dee-OH-dur-unt\ *n.* An odor-controlling substance.

deodorize \dee-OH-duh-rize\ *v.* deodorized; deodorizing. To eliminate odors. deodorizer *n.*

depart \di-PAHRT\ *v.* departed; departing. **1.** To leave. **2.** To deviate. departed *adj.*

department \di-PAHRT-munt\ *n.* **1.** A particular group. **2.** A category. **3.** A section of a business or store.

departure \di-PAHR-chur\ *n.* A leave-taking.

depend \di-PEND\ *v.* depended; depending. To rely on.

dependent \di-PEN-dunt\ *adj.* **1.** Being contingent or reliant upon. **2.** Subordinate. dependently *adj.*

dependent *also* **dependant** \di-PEN-dunt\ *n.* One who relies on another.

depict \di-PIKT\ *v.* depicted; depicting. To represent. depiction *n.*

deplete \di-PLEET\ *v.* depleted; depleting. To drain. depletion *n.*

deplore \di-PLOR\ *v.* deplored; deploring. To feel grief or regret. deplorable *adj.*

deploy \di-PLOY\ *v.* deployed; deploying. To send out. deployment *n.*

deport \di-PORT\ *v.* deported; deporting. To banish. deportation *n.*

depose \di-POHZ\ *v.* deposed; deposing. **1.** To remove from high position. **2.** To testify under oath.

deposit \di-POZ-it\ *n.* **1.** Money put in a bank. **2.** A natural accumulation.

deposit \di-POZ-it\ *v.* deposited; depositing. To place for safekeeping.

depot \DEE-poh\ *n.* **1.** A storage place. **2.** A train station.

deprave \di-PRAYV\ *v.* depraved; depraving. **1.** To corrupt. **2.** To pervert. depravation *n.*; depraved *adj.*

deprecate \DEP-ri-kayt\ *v.* deprecated; deprecating. To belittle.

depreciate \di-PREE-shee-ayt\ *v.* depreciated; depreciating. To make or become lower in value.

depressed \di-PREST\ *adj.* **1.** Sad. **2.** Underprivileged. **3.** Pressed down.

depression \di-PRESH-un\ *n.* **1.** Dejection or sadness. **2.** A hollow. **3.** Low economic time.

deprivation \dep-ruh-VAY-shun\ *n.* Hardship.

deprive \di-PRIEV\ *v.* deprived; depriving. To take away. deprived *adj.*

deprogram \dee-PROH-gram\ *v.* deprogrammed; deprogramming. To eliminate a belief.

depth *n. pl.* depths **1.** Deepness. **2.** An abyss. **3.** Intensity.

deputy \DEP-yuh-tee\ *n. pl.* deputies. A person who is second in command.

derange \di-RAYNJ\ *v.* deranged; deranging. To be or make crazy.

deregulate \dee-REG-yuu-layt\ *v.* deregulated; deregulating. To remove restrictions.

derelict \DER-uh-likt\ *adj.* **1.** Rundown. **2.** Negligent.

derivative \di-RIV-uh-tiv\ *n.* **1.** Something inferred. **2.** Something that came from something else.

derive \di-RIVE\ *v.* derived; deriving. **1.** To obtain. **2.** To infer.

dermabrasion \dur-muh-BRAY-zhun\ *n.* (Sc) Removal of skin imperfections.

dermatology \dur-muh-TOL-uh-jee\ *n.* (Sc) The study of skin. dermatologist *n.*

derogatory \di-ROG-uh-tor-ee\ *adj.* Disparaging. derogative *adj.*

descend \di-SEND\ *v.* descended; descending. To lower or go down.

descent \di-SENT\ *n.* **1.** A decline. **2.** Lineage or family origin.

describe \di-SKRIEB\ *v.* described;

describing. To explain with words. description **n.**

desecrate \DES-i-krayt\ **v.** desecrated; desecrating. To profane. desecration **n.**

desert \DEZ-urt\ **n.** A barren dry area.

desert \di-ZURT\ **v.** deserted; deserting. To leave.

deserve \di-ZURV\ **v.** deserved; deserving. To be worthy of. deserved **adj.**; deserving **n.**

desiccate \DES-i-kayt\ **v.** desicated; desiccating. To dry.

design \di-ZIEN\ **n.** **1.** A plot. **2.** A pattern or picture. **3.** An arrangement.

design \di-ZIEN\ **v.** designed; designing. **1.** To create. **2.** To intend.

designate \DEZ-ig-nayt\ **v.** designated; designating. To specify. designation **n.**

desire \di-ZIER\ **n.** A longing. desirous **adj.**

desire \di-ZIER\ **v.** desired; desiring. **1.** To crave. **2.** To request.

desist \di-SIST\ **v.** desisted; desisting. To stop.

desktop n. (Cm) A microcomputer.

desolate \DES-uh-lit\ **adj.** **1.** Without people. **2.** Gloomy. desolation **n.**

despair \di-SPAIR\ **n.** Hopelessness.

despair \di-SPAIR\ **v.** despaired; despairing. To lose hope.

desperate \DES-pur-it\ **adj.** **1.** Willing to use extreme means. **2.** Despondent. desperation **n.**

despicable \DES-pi-kuh-bul\ **adj.** Contemptible.

despise \di-SPIEZ\ **v.** despised; despising. To scorn.

despite \di-SPIET\ **n.** Contempt.

despite \di-SPIET\ **prep.** In spite of.

despondent \di-SPOND-unt\ **adj.** Discouraged.

despot \DES-put\ **n.** A tyrant. despotic **adj.**

dessert \di-ZURT\ **n.** A sweet food.

destabilize \dee-STAY-buh-liez\ **v.** destabilized; destabilizing. To make unstable.

destiny \DES-tuh-nee\ **n. pl.** destinies. A predetermined end.

destroy \di-STROI\ **v.** destroyed; destroying. To ruin or annihilate.

destruction \di-STRUK-shun\ **n.** Ruin.

detach \di-TACH\ **v.** detached; detaching. To separate. detachable **adj.**

detachment \di-TACH-munt\ **n.** **1.** Separation. **2.** Aloofness. **3.** A body of troops.

detail \di-TAYL\ **n.** **1.** A particular. **2.** A select group.

detail \DEE-tayl\ *v.* detailed; detailing. To specify.

detain \di-TAYN\ *v.* detained; detaining. **1.** To hold. **2.** To restrain.

detect \di-TEKT\ *v.* detected; detecting. To discover the presence of.

detective \di-TEK-tiv\ *n.* An investigator.

detente *also* **detente** \day-TAHNT\ *n.* Easing of strained relations.

deter \di-TUR\ *v.* deterred; deterring. To discourage.

deteriorate \di-TEER-ee-uh-rayt\ *v.* deteriorated; deteriorating. To disintegrate or become weakened. deterioration *n.*

determine \di-TUR-min\ *v.* determined; determining. **1.** To decide. **2.** To discover.

determined \di-TUR-mind\ *adj.* Resolved.

detest \di-TEST\ *v.* detested; detesting. To hate.

detonate \DET-n-ayt\ *v.* detonated; detonating. To set off.

detour \DEE-tuur\ *n.* A roundabout way.

detour \DEE-tuur\ *v.* detoured; detouring. To bypass.

detract \di-TRAKT\ *v.* detracted; detracting. To divert or lessen. detractor *n.*; detraction *n.*

deuce \doos\ *n.* **1.** The number two. **2.** A tie score in tennis.

devastate \DEV-uh-stayt\ *v.* devastated; devastating. To ravage. devastation *n.*

develop \di-VEL-up\ *v.* developed; developing. **1.** To clarify. **2.** To evolve. development *n.*

developmental \di-VEL-up-men-tul\ *adj.* **1.** Experimental. **2.** Part of or aiding growth.

deviant \DEE-vee-unt\ *adj.* Away from the norm. deviance *n.*

device \di-VIES\ *n.* **1.** A tool. **2.** A method.

devil \DEV-ul\ *n.* An evil spirit.

devious \DEE-vee-us\ *adj.* Deceptive. deviously *adv.*; deviousness *n.*

devise \di-VIEZ\ *v.* devised; devising. To plan.

devoid \di-VOID\ *adj.* Being without.

devote \di-VOHT\ *v.* devoted; devoting. To dedicate.

devoted \di-VOH-tid\ *adj.* Loyal.

devour \di-VOWR\ *v.* devoured; devouring. To consume.

devout \di-VOWT\ *adj.* **1.** Devoted. **2.** Earnest. devoutly *adv.*

dew \doo\ *n.* Moisture on a surface, esp. outside.

dextrous *also* **dexterous** \DEK-strus\ *adj.* Mental or physical skillfulness.

diabetes \die-uh-BEE-tis\ *n.* (Md) A disorder characterized by excessive urination. diabetic *adj.*

diabolic *also* **diabolical** \die-uh-BOL-ik\ *adj.* Concerning the devil. diabolical *adj.*

diagnose \DIE-ug-nohs\ *v.* diagnosed; diagnosing. To identify a specific disease.

diagnosis \die-ug-NOH-sis\ *n. pl.* diagnoses. (Md) An assessment or identification.

diagnostic \die-ug-NOS-tik\ *adj.* Concerning assessments.

diagonal \die-AG-uh-nl\ *adj.* An inclined line or plane.

diagram \DIE-uh-gram\ *n.* A drawing that shows the parts of a thing. diagrammatic *also* diagrammatical *adj.*

diagram \DIE-uh-gram\ *v.* diagramed or diagrammed; diagraming or diagramming. To draw the parts of a thing.

dial \DIE-ul\ *n.* A device with a moveable pointer on a machine.

dial \DIE-ul\ *v.* dialed or dialled; dialing or dialling. **1.** To call. **2.** To operate a dial.

dialect \DIE-uh-lekt\ *n.* A way of speaking in a district.

dialog *also* **dialogue** \die-uh-LAWG\ *n.* A conversation.

dialysis \die-AL-uh-sis\ *n. pl.* dialyses. (Md) Substance separation.

diameter \die-AM-uh-tur\ *n.* Distance across a shape going through its center. diametric or diametrical *adj.*

diamond \DIE-mund\ *n.* **1.** A crystalline stone. **2.** A geometric shape. **3.** A card suit.

diaper \DIE-u-pur\ *n.* An infant's undergarment.

diary \DIE-uh-ree\ *n. pl.* diaries. A journal.

dice \dies\ *n. pl.* dice. A marked gambling cube.

dice \dies\ *v.* diced; dicing. **1.** To chop finely. **2.** [Sl] To take a chance.

dichotomy \die-KOT-uh-mee\ *n. pl.* dichotomies. **1.** A division. **2.** A contradiction. dichotomize *v.*

dictate \DIK-tayt\ *n.* **1.** A rule. **2.** A command. dictation *n.*

dictate \DIK-tayt\ *v.* dictated; dictating. To direct.

dictator \DIK-tay-tur\ *n.* An absolute ruler.

diction \DIK-shun\ *n.* A manner of pronouncing words.

dictionary \DIK-shu-ner-ee\ *n. pl.* dictionaries. A book that explains words.

didactic \die-DAK-tik\ *adj.* Concerning teaching. **didactically** *adv.*

die \die\ *n. pl.* dice or dies. A single marked gambling cube.

die \die\ *v.* died; dying. **1.** To expire. **2.** To stop.

diehard \DIE-hahrd\ *n.* A determined person.

diesel \DEE-zul\ *n.* (Sc) A type of engine.

diet \DIE-it\ *n.* **1.** Nourishment. **2.** A weight loss plan. **dietary** *adj.*

different \DIF-ur-unt\ *adj.* Unlike.

differential \dif-uh-REN-shul\ *n.* **1.** A mathematical sum. **2.** A type of gear.

differentiate \dif-ur-EN-shee-ayt\ *v.* differentiated; differentiating. To discriminate.

difficult \DIF-i-kult\ *adj.* Hard. **difficultly** *adv.*

diffident \DIF-uh-dunt\ *adj.* Shy. **diffidently** *adv.*

diffuse \di-FYOOS\ *adj.* Wordy.

diffuse \di-FYOOZ\ *v.* diffused; diffusing. To scatter.

diffusion \di-FYOO-zhun\ *n.* (Sc) **1.** Particle intermingling. **2.** Light scattering.

dig *v.* dug; digging. **1.** To break up. **2.** To excavate. **3.** [Sl] To appreciate.

digestion \di-JES-chun\ *n.* (Md) The process of breaking down food. **digest** *v.*

digit \DIJ-it\ *n.* **1.** A number. **2.** A finger or toe.

digital \DIJ-i-tl\ *adj.* **1.** Performed with a finger. **2.** Concerning numbers. **digitally** *adv.*

dignitary \DIG-ni-ter-ee\ *n. pl.* dignitaries. An exalted person.

dignity \DIG-ni-tee\ *n. pl.* dignities. Pride. **dignify** *v.*; **dignified** *adj.*

digress \di-GRES\ *v.* digressed; digressing. To swerve off course. **digression** *n.*

dilapidated \di-LAP-i-day-tud\ *adj.* Run-down. **dilapidate** *v.*

dilate \die-LAYT\ *v.* dilated; dilating. To expand. **dilator** *n.*

dilemma \di-LEM-uh\ *n.* **1.** Predicament. **2.** An unpleasant choice.

dilettante \DIL-i-tahnt\ *n.* Amateur.

diligent \DIL-i-junt\ *adj.* Working with effort and care. **diligently** *adv.*

dilute \di-LOOT\ *v.* diluted; diluting. To weaken. **dilution** *n.*

dim *adj.* dimmer; dimmest. **1.** Dull. **2.** Faint. **dimly** *adv.*

diminish \di-MIN-ish\ *v.* diminished; diminishing. To make less. **diminished** *adj.*

dine \dien\ *v.* dined; dining. To eat dinner.

diner \DIE-nur\ *n.* **1.** One who dines. **2.** A type of restaurant.

dingy \DING-gee\ *adj.* dingier; dingiest. Discolored and shabby.

dinner \DIN-ur\ *n.* The evening meal.

dinosaur \DIE-nuh-sor\ *n.* Extinct lizard-like creature.

diocese \DIE-uh-sis\ *n. pl.* dioceses. A bishop's jurisdiction.

diode \DIE-ohd\ *n.* (Sc) An electronic device or semiconductor.

diorama \die-uh-RAM-uh\ *n.* A scenic representation.

dioxin \die-OK-sin\ *n.* (Sc) A toxic impurity.

dip *n.* **1.** A hollow. **2.** A food condiment. **3.** A brief swim.

dip *v.* dipped; dipping. **1.** To immerse. **2.** To ladle. **3.** To fall suddenly and briefly.

diphtheria \dif-THEER-ee-uh or dip-THEER-ee-uh\ *n.* [Md.] A contagious disease affecting the air passages and causing fever and weakness.

diploma \di-PLOH-muh\ *n. pl.* diplomas. A graduation certificate.

diplomacy \di-PLOH-muh-see\ *n.* **1.** Tact. **2.** Handling of international relations. diplomatic *adj.*

diplomat \DIP-luh-mat\ *n.* (Fr) One skilled in diplomacy.

diptych \DIP-tik\ *n.* A picture made of matching parts.

direct \di-REKT\ *v.* directed; directing. **1.** To point in the right direction. **2.** To supervise.

direct \do-REKT\ *adj.* **1.** Straight. **2.** Honest.

direction \di-REK-shun\ *n.* **1.** Management. **2.** Tendency. **3.** The proper route.

dirndl \DURN-dul\ *n.* A gathered-waist skirt.

dirt \durt\ *n.* **1.** Filth. **2.** Earth. **3.** [Sl] Gossip. dirty *adj.*

dirt bike \DURT-BIKE\ *n.* A lightweight motorcycle.

disability \di-uh-BIL-i-tee\ *n.* An impairment. disabled *adj.*

disadvantaged \dis-ud-VAN-tijd\ *adj.* Lacking the basics.

disagree \dis-uh-GREE\ *v.* disagreed; disagreeing. To differ in view.

disagreement \dis-uh-GREE-munt\ *n.* A quarrel.

disappear \dis-uh-PEER\ *v.* disappeared; disappearing. To leave from sight. disappearance *n.*

disappoint \dis-uh-POINT\ *v.* disappointed; disappointing. To let down. disappointed *adj.*; disappointment *n.*

disapprove \dis-uh-PROOV\ *v.* disapproved; disapproving. To reject. disapproval *n.*

disarm \dis-AHRM\ *v.* disarmed; disarming. **1.** To win over. **2.** To take away arms.

disarray \dis-uh-RAY\ *n.* Confusion.

disaster \di-ZAS-tur\ *n.* A sudden calamity. disastrous *adj.*

disbelief \dis-bi-LEEF\ *n.* Rejection as false.

discard \di-SKAHRD\ *v.* discarded; discarding. To throw away.

discern \di-SURN\ *v.* discerned; discerning. To figure out. discernible also discernable *adj.*

discharge \dis-CHAHRJ\ *n.* **1.** A release statement. **2.** An outpouring.

discharge \dis-CHAHRJ\ *v.* discharged; discharging. **1.** To shoot. **2.** To release from service. **3.** To perform. discharger *n.*

disciple \di-SIE-pul\ *n.* A follower.

discipline \DIS-uh-plin\ *n.* **1.** Punishment. **2.** Area of study. **3.** Self-control.

discipline \DIS-uh-plin\ *v.* disciplined; disciplining. **1.** To punish. **2.** To impose order. disciplinarian *n.*

disclose \di-SKLOHZ\ *v.* disclosed; disclosing. To reveal. disclosing *adj.*; disclosure *n.*

discomfort \dis-KUM-furt\ *n.* Mental or physical distress.

discontinue \dis-kun-TIN-yoo\ *v.* discontinued; discontinuing. To cease.

discord \DIS-kord\ *n.* Disagreement or quarreling. discordance *n.*

discotheque *also* **disco** \DIS-kuh-tek\ *n.* A nightclub for dancing.

discount \dis-KOWNT\ *n.* A price reduction.

discount \dis-KOWNT\ *v.* discounted; discounting **1.** To lower a price. **2.** To disregard.

discourage \di-SKUR-ij\ *v.* discouraged; discouraging. To remove one's confidence.

discourteous \dis-KUR-tee-us\ *adj.* Rude. discourteousness *n.*

discover \di-SKUV-ur\ *v.* discovered; discovering. **1.** To find. **2.** To learn. discoverer *n.*; discovery *n.*

discredit \dis-KRED-it\ *v.* discredited; discrediting. To deprive of a good reputation.

discreet \di-SKREET\ *adj.* **1.** Prudent. **2.** Unobtrusive. discreetly *adv.*

discrepancy \di-SKREP-un-see\ *n.* *pl.* discrepancies. A disagreement. discrepant *adj.*

discrete \di-SKREET\ *adj.* Distinct. discretely *adv.*

discretion \di-SKRESH-un\ *n.* **1.** Circumspection. **2.** Individual choice. discretionary *adj.*

discrimination \di-SKRIM-uh-nayt\ *n.* **1.** Discernment. **2.** Prejudice. discriminate *v.*

discuss \DIS-kus\ *v.* discussed; discussing. To talk about. discussion *n.*

disdain \dis-DAYN\ *n.* Contempt.

disease \di-ZEEZ\ *n.* An illness. diseased *adj.*

disembark \dis-em-BAHRK\ *v.* disembarked; disembarking. To exit a vehicle.

disengage \dis-en-GAYJ\ *v.* disengaged; disengaging. To release.

disfigure \dis-FIG-yur\ *v.* disfigured; disfiguring. To impair.

disgrace \dis-GRAYS\ *n.* The loss of reputation. disgraceful *adj.*

disgrace \dis-GRAYS\ *v.* disgraced; disgracing. **1.** To be a source of shame. **2.** To cause loss of reputation.

disguise \dis-GIZE\ *n.* **1.** A pretense. **2.** A mask.

disguise \dis-GIZE\ *v.* disguised; disguising. To conceal.

disgust \dis-GUST\ *n.* Strong dislike. disgusted. *adj.*; disgusting *adj.*

disgust \dis-GUST\ *v.* disgusted; disgusting. To be offensive to.

dish *n.* **1.** A plate. **2.** A type of food.

dish *v.* dished; dishing. To present.

disheveled *also* **dishevelled** \di-SHEV-uld\ *adj.* In disarray. dishevel *v.*

dishonest \dis-ON-ist\ *adj.* Deceptive. dishonesty *adv.*

dishonor \dis-ON-ur\ *n.* Disgrace.

dishonorable discharge *n.* Military release without honor.

disillusioned \dis-i-LOO-zhund\ *adj.* Disappointed. disillusion *v.*

disinfect \dis-in-FEKT\ *v.* disinfected; disinfecting. To kill germs. disinfectant *n.*

disinherit \dis-in-HAIR-it\ *v.* disinherited; disinheriting. To deliberately exclude from inheriting.

disintegrate \dis-IN-tuh-grayt\ *v.* disintegrated; disintegrating. To break down. disintegration *n.*

disinterest \dis-IN-tur-ist\ *n.* Indifference. disinterested *adj.*

disk *also* **disc** *n.* **1.** A flat circular body. **2.** A magnetic disk in or for a computer.

dislike \dis-LIKE\ *n.* Feeling of not liking something.

dislocate \DIS-loh-kayt\ *v.* dislocated; dislocating. To displace from normal position. dislocation *n.*

dismal \DIZ-mul\ *adj.* **1.** Gloomy. **2.** Without merit. dismally *adv.*

dismay \dis-MAY\ *n.* Feeling of surprise and disappointment.

dismay \dis-MAY\ *v.* dismayed; dismaying. **1.** To appall. **2.** To daunt.

dismember \dis-MEM-bur\ *v.* dismembered; dismembering. To take apart. dismemberment *n.*

dismiss \dis-MIS\ *v.* dismissed; dismissing. **1.** To let go. **2.** To reject. dismissed *n.*

disobey \dis-uh-BAY\ *v.* disobeyed; disobeying. To go against a request or order.

disorder \dis-OR-dur\ *n.* **1.** Chaos. **2.** An ailment. disordered *adj.*; disorder *v.*

disorganized \dir-OR-gun-izd\ *adj.* Lacking a system. disorganize *v.*

disown \dis-OHN\ *v.* disowned; disowning. To reject.

disparate \DIS-pur-it\ *adj.* Marked difference. disparately *adv.*

dispatch \di-SPACH\ *v.* dispatched; dispatching. **1.** To send off quickly. **2.** To kill.

dispense \di-SPENS\ *v.* dispensed; dispensing. **1.** To distribute. **2.** To prepare and give out. dispenser *n.*

disperse \di-SPURS\ *v.* dispersed; dispersing. To scatter. dispersion *n.*

display \di-SPLAY\ *n.* A presentation.

display \di-SPLAY\ *v.* displayed; displaying. To exhibit.

disposal \di-SPOH-zul\ *n.* **1.** The power to get rid of. **2.** A garbage grinder.

dispose \di-SPOHZ\ *v.* disposed; disposing. **1.** To arrange. **2.** To tend to. **3.** To get rid of. disposable *adj.*

disposition \dis-puh-ZISH-un\ *n.* **1.** A settlement. **2.** Temperament.

disprove \dis-PROOV\ *v.* disproved; disproving. To refute.

dispute \di-SPYOOT\ *v.* disputed; disputing. To debate.

disqualify \dis-KWOL-uh-fie\ *v.* disqualified; disqualifying. To make ineligibile. disqualification *n.*

disregard \dis-ri-GAHRD\ *v.* disregarded; disregarding. To neglect.

disrepair \dis-ree-PAIR\ *n.* Bad, broken-down condition.

disrespect \dis-ri-SPEKT\ *n.* Lack of respect. disprespectful *adj.*

disrobe \dis-ROHB\ *v.* disrobed; disrobing. To remove clothes.

disrupt \dis-RUPT\ *v.* disrupted; disrupting. To interrupt and throw off. disrupter *n.*; disruption *n.*

dissatisfied \di-SAT-is-fied\ *adj.* Not pleased.

dissect \di-SEKT\ *v.* dissected; dissecting. To separate into parts. dissection *n.*

dissent \di-SENT\ *v.* dissented; dissenting. To differ in opinion.

dissident \DIS-i-dunt\ *adj.* Disagreeing with established views. dissidence *n.*

dissipate \DIS-uh-payt\ *v.* dissipated; dissipating. To scatter. dissipated *adj.*; dissipation *n.*

dissolute \DIS-uh-loot\ *adj.* Indulgent.

dissolve \di-ZOLV\ *v.* dissolved; dissolving. **1.** To destroy. **2.** To liquefy. **3.** To fade away.

dissuade \di-SWAYD\ *v.* dissuaded; dissuading. To advise against.

distance \DIS-tans\ *n.* **1.** Length apart. **2.** Coldness. **3.** Go the distance [Id]: to complete.

distant \DIS-tunt\ *adj.* **1.** Far-off. **2.** Reserved. distantly *adv.*

distasteful \dis-TAYST-ful\ *adj.* Disliked or bad in some way. distastefully *adv.*

distinguish \di-STING-gwish\ *v.* distinguished; distinguishing. **1.** To detect a difference. **2.** To characterize.

distinguished \di-STING-gwisht\ *adj.* **1.** Famous. **2.** Refined.

distort \di-STORT\ *v.* distorted; distorting. **1.** To deform. **2.** To misrepresent. distortion *n.*

distract \di-STRAKT\ *v.* distracted; distracting. To divert. distracted *adj.*

distraction \di-STRAK-shun\ *n.* **1.** Mental disorder. **2.** Amusement.

distraught \di-STRAWT\ *adj.* Mentally disturbed.

distress \di-STRES\ *n.* **1.** Misfortune. **2.** Misery.

distress \di-STRES\ *v.* distressed; distressing. To cause to suffer.

distribute \di-STRIB-yoot\ *v.* distributed; distributing **1.** To dispense. **2.** To scatter. distribution *n.*

district \DIS-trikt\ *n.* A particular geographic area.

disturb \di-STURB\ *v.* disturbed; disturbing. **1.** To interrupt. **2.** To scare. disturbance *n.*; disturbed *adj.*

ditch \dich\ *n.* A long narrow ground depression.

ditto \DIT-oh\ *n. pl.* dittos. The same again.

diva \DEE-vuh\ *n. pl.* divas or dive. (It) A leading woman opera singer.

dive \diev\ *n.* A sharp descent.

dive \diev\ *v.* dove or dived; diving. To plunge downward.

diverge \di-VURJ\ *v.* diverged; diverging. **1.** To separate. **2.** To deviate. divergence *n.*

diverse \di-VURS\ *adj.* Different. diversely *adv.*; diversify *v.*

divert \di-VURT\ *v.* diverted; diverting. **1.** To move away from. **2.** To amuse. diversion *n.*

divest \di-VEST\ *v.* divested; divesting. **1.** To rid. **2.** To deprive. divestiture *n.*

divide \di-VIED\ *v.* divided; dividing. **1.** To separate. **2.** To distribute. divided *adj.*; division *n.*

dividend \DIV-i-dend\ *n.* A share.

divine \di-VIEN\ *adj.* diviner; divinest. Godlike. divinity *n.*

divorce \di-VORS\ *n.* **1.** Formal separation. **2.** Legal severance of marriage.

divorce \di-VORS\ *v.* divorced; divorcing. To separate or end a marriage.

divulge \di-VULJ\ *v.* divulged; divulging. To reveal.

dizzy \DIZ-ee\ *adj.* dizzier; dizziest. **1.** [Sl] Foolish. **2.** [Cl] Giddy. dizziness *n.*

DNA \DEE-EN-AY\ *n.* Deoxyribonucleic acid.

do \doh\ *v.* did; done; doing; does. **1.** To perform. **2.** To effect. **3.** To produce. **4.** To complete.

docile \DOS-ul\ *adj.* Obedient. docilely *adv.*

doctor \DOK-tur\ *n.* **1.** A physician. **2.** The highest academic degree.

doctorate \DOK-tur-it\ *n.* Highest academic degree.

doctrine \DOK-trin\ *n.* A set of beliefs.

docudrama \DOK-yuu-dra-muh\ *n.* An historically based play.

document \DOK-yuh-munt\ *n.* A written statement.

document \DOK-yuh-munt\ *v.* documented; documenting. To provide with written support.

doe \doh\ *n. pl.* does or doe. An adult female deer, hare, or rabbit.

dog \dawg\ *n.* **1.** A domestic carnivorous animal. **2.** [Sl] A worthless person.

doggy bag *also* **doggie bag** \DAW-gee-BAG\ *n.* A container for leftovers.

dogma \DAWG-muh\ *n. pl.* dogmas also dogmata. An authoritative doctrine.

dogmatic *also* **dogmatical** \dawg-MAT-ik\ *adj.* Dictatorial.

doldrums \DOHL-drumz\ *pl. n.* Sadness and inactivity.

dole \dohl\ *n.* Something distributed.

dole \dohl\ *v.* doled; doling. To give out.

doll \dol\ *n.* **1.** A small human-like toy. **2.** A pretty woman.

dollar \DOL-ur\ *n.* A monetary unit.

dollop \DOL-up\ *n.* A little bit.

domain \doh-MAYN\ *n.* **1.** A land

area. **2.** An area of influence or knowledge. **3.** A mathematical set.

dome \dohm\ *n.* A large hemispherical structure.

domestic \duh-MES-tik\ *adj.* **1.** Tame. **2.** Of or concerning the home. **3.** Of or concerning one's country.

domestic partner *n.* People sharing their lives without being married.

domesticate \duh-MES-ti-kayt\ *v.* domesticated; domesticating. **1.** To adopt. **2.** To familiarize or train.

domicile *also* **domicil** \DOM-uh-siel\ *n.* A residence.

dominate \DOM-uh-nayt\ *v.* dominated; dominating. To control completely. dominance *n.*; domination *n.*; dominant *adj.*

dominion \duh-MIN-yun\ *n.* Area of ownership or control.

domino \DOM-uh-noh\ *n. pl.* dominoes or dominos. **1.** A mask. **2.** A game played with marked black rectangles.

domino effect *n.* A succession of like events.

donate \doh-NAYT\ *v.* donated; donating. To give. donation *n.*

donkey \DONG-kee\ *n. pl.* don-

keys. **1.** A domestic mammal. **2.** [Sl] A foolish person.

donor \DOH-nur\ *n.* One who gives.

doom *n.* **1.** Death or ruin. **2.** A grim fate.

door \dor\ *n.* A way in and out of a room or building.

dope \dohp\ *n.* **1.** Drugs. **2.** A stupid person. **3.** Inside information.

dormant \DOR-munt\ *adj.* **1.** Asleep. **2.** Inactive.

dose \dohs\ *n.* A measured quantity. dosage *n.*

dossier \DOS-ee-ay\ *n.* A file of papers.

dot *n.* **1.** A speck. **2.** A small point.

dot-matrix *n.* (Cm) A method of printing.

double \DUB-ul\ *adj.* **1.** Dual. **2.** Deceitful.

double \DUB-ul\ *v.* doubled; doubling. To make twice as great.

double-entendre \DUB-ul-ahn-TAHN-druh\ *n. pl.* double-entendres. Ambigous meaning.

doubt \dowt\ *n.* Uncertainty. doubtfully *adv.*

doubt \dowt\ *v.* doubted; doubting. To distrust.

dough \doh\ *n.* **1.** A flour mixture. **2.** Money.

doughnut \DOH-nut\ *n.* A small, round cake.

douse \dows\ *v.* doused; dousing. **1.** To extinguish. **2.** To drench with water.

dowager \DOW-uh-jur\ *n.* A titled elderly woman.

down *adv.* **1.** Toward a lower position. **2.** Defeated.

down-and-out *adj.* Destitute.

downfall \DOWN-fawl\ *n.* Sudden ruin or decline.

downgrade \DOWN-grayd\ *n.* Movement to inferior state. downgrade *v.*

downpour \DOWN-por\ *n.* Very heavy rain.

downsize *v.* downsized; downsizing. To make smaller or less.

Down syndrome *n.* (Md) A congenital disorder causing mental retardation.

down-to-earth \DOWN-too-URTH\ *adj.* Practical.

dowry \DOW-ree\ *n. pl.* dowries. Gifts brought to a husband by his bride.

doyen \DOI-yun\ *n.* (Fr) Senior member of a staff.

doze \dohz\ *v.* dozed; dozing. To sleep lightly.

drab *adj.* drabber; drabbest. **1.** Dull. **2.** Without cheer.

drachma \DRAK-muh\ *n. pl.* drachmas or drachmai or drach-

mae. **1.** A Greek unit of weight. **2.** An ancient Greek silver coin.

draft *n.* **1.** Initial sketch or piece of writing. **2.** Military selection. **3.** Monetary check.

drag *n.* **1.** A device for pulling through water. **2.** A burden. **3.** A road. **4.** A race.

drag *v.* dragged; dragging. **1.** To pull. **2.** To draw on.

dragon \DRAG-un\ *n.* A mythical beast.

drain \drayn\ *n.* **1.** A device through which liquid flows. **2.** A burden. drainage *n.*

drain \drayn\ *v.* drained; draining. **1.** To exhaust. **2.** To empty.

drama \DRAH-muh\ *n.* **1.** A literary genre. **2.** An intense conflict.

dramatic \druh-MAT-ik\ *adj.* Theatrical.

drape \drayp\ *n.* A curtain.

drape \drayp\ *v.* draped; draping. To cover with cloth.

drastic \DRAS-tik\ *adj.* Extreme.

draw *v.* drew; drawn; drawing. **1.** To pull. **2.** To attract. **3.** To elicit. **4.** To match in a contest.

drawer \dror\ *n.* A storage unit in a chest or other container.

drawl *n.* A slow way of speaking.

drawn *adj.* Haggard.

dread \dred\ *n.* Great apprehension. dreadful *adj.*

dread \dred\ *v.* dreaded; dreading. To fear greatly.

dream \dreem\ *n.* **1.** An image in sleep. **2.** A goal. dreamy *adj.*

dream \dreem\ *v.* dreamed or dreamt; dreaming. **1.** To imagine or wish for. **2.** To be in a sleep fantasy.

dreary \DREER-ee\ *adj.* drearier; dreariest. Gloomy. dreariness *n.*

drench *v.* drenched; drenching. To soak.

dress \dres\ *n.* A woman's garment.

dress \dres\ *v.* dressed; dressing. **1.** To put on clothes. **2.** To embellish. **3.** To bandage. **4.** To fix.

dribble \DRIB-ul\ *v.* dribbled; dribbling. **1.** To trickle. **2.** To drool.

drift *n.* **1.** Flow. **2.** Mass of matter. **3.** Aimless path. **4.** A tendency. **5.** The general idea.

drift *v.* drifted; drifting. To move without resistance.

drill \dril\ *n.* **1.** A power tool. **2.** A repetitive exercise.

drill \dril\ *v.* drilled; drilling. **1.** To train by repetition. **2.** To make a hole.

drink \dringk\ *n.* A liquid safe for people.

drink \dringk\ *v.* drank; drunk; drinking. **1.** To swallow. **2.** To take in.

drip *n.* **1.** Water droplets. **2.** An unattractive person.

drip *v.* dripped; dripping. To leak slowly.

drive \driev\ *n.* **1.** A trip in a land vehicle. **2.** Cattle movement. **3.** A ball's flight.

drive \driev\ *v.* drove; driven; driving. **1.** To prod. **2.** To operate a land vehicle. **3.** To force on.

drive-in \DRIEV-in\ *n.* A service establishment where the customer stays in their vehicle.

drivel \DRIV-ul\ *n.* Nonsense.

driven \DRIV-un\ *adj.* Behaving compulsively.

drizzle \DRIZ-ul\ *v.* drizzled; drizzling. To sprinkle.

drone \drohn\ *n.* **1.** A male bee. **2.** A drudge.

drone \drohn\ *v.* droned; droning. To talk in a monotone.

drool *v.* drooled; drooling. **1.** To secrete saliva. **2.** To fawn over.

droop *v.* drooped; drooping. To hang down.

drop *n.* **1.** A small amount of liquid. **2.** A fall.

drop *v.* dropped; dropping. **1.** To let fall. **2.** To disappear.

drop-out \DROP-owt\ *n.* One who leaves school without graduating.

drought *also* **drouth** \drowt\ *n.* A dry spell.

drown *v.* drowned; drowning. **1.** To die by water inhalation. **2.** To overwhelm.

drowsy \DROW-zee\ *adj.* drowsier; drowsiest. Sleepy. drowsiness *n.*

drug *n.* A chemical substance.

drug *v.* drugged; drugging. To give a chemical substance to.

drum *n.* A percussion instrument.

drum *v.* drummed; drumming. **1.** To pound on or hit with drumsticks. **2.** To solicit.

drunk \drungk\ *adj.* **1.** [Cl] Consumed by emotion. **2.** Impaired by alcohol.

dry \drie\ *adj.* drier also dryer; driest also dryest. **1.** Without liquid. **2.** Stale.

dry \drie\ *v.* dried; drying. To eliminate water from.

dual \DOO-ul\ *adj.* Concerning two parts.

dubious \DOO-bee-us\ *adj.* Doubtful. dubiously *adv.*; dubiousness *n.*

dud *n.* Failure.

due \doo\ *adj.* **1.** Owed. **2.** Adequate. **3.** Scheduled. due *n.*

duet \doo-ET\ *n.* (Mu) A musical composition for two singers or players.

dull \dul\ *adj.* **1.** Stupid. **2.** Blunt. dullness or dulness *n.*

dumb \dum\ *adj.* **1.** Lacking speech. **2.** Unintelligent.

dummy \DUM-ee\ *n. pl.* dummies. **1.** Mannequin. **2.** One who is stupid. **3.** A mock-up publication.

dump *n.* A trash yard.

dump *v.* dumped; dumping. **1.** To let go of. **2.** To copy onto a disk. **3.** To sell cheaply.

dune \doon\ *n.* A large sand hill.

dune buggy \DOON-BUG-ee\ *n.* A vehicle designed to ride across sand.

dunk \dungk\ *v.* dunked; dunking. **1.** To submerge. **2.** To throw a ball into a basket.

duo \DOO-oh\ *n. pl.* duos. A pair.

duodenum \doo-uh-DEE-num or doo-uh-DEN-um\ *n. pl.* duodena or duodenums. (Md) The first part of the small intestine.

duplicate \DOO-pli-kit\ *n.* A reproduction.

duplicate \DOO-pli-kayt\ *v.* duplicated; duplicating. To copy.

durable \DUUR-uh-bul\ *adj.* Long-lasting. durability

duration \duu-RAY-shun\ *n.* Length in time.

duress \duu-RES\ *n.* **1.** Forcible restrain. **2.** Compulsion.

during \DUUR-ing\ *prep.* Throughout.

dusk *n.* Time of sunset and just after.

dust *n.* Fine particles of dirt. dusty *adj.*

duty \DOO-tee\ *n. pl.* duties. **1.** One's obligation. **2.** Work. **3.** Tax. dutiful *adj.*

duvet \doo-VAY\ *n.* Comforter.

dwarf \dworf\ *n. pl.* dwarfs *also* dwarves. **1.** A short person. **2.** A type of star.

dwell \dwel\ *v.* dwelled or dwelt; dwelling. **1.** To reside in. **2.** To think on.

dwelling \DWEL-ing\ *n.* A house.

dwindle \DWIN-dl\ *v.* dwindled; dwindling. To decrease.

dye \die\ *n.* A coloring substance.

dye \die\ *v.* dyed; dying. To color.

dynamic *also* **dynamical** \die-NAM-ik\ *adj.* **1.** Concerning energy. **2.** Forceful.

dynamite \DIE-nuh-mite\ *n.* **1.** A powerful explosive. **2.** A powerful effect.

dynasty \DIE-nuh-stee\ *n. pl.* dynasties. A powerful family.

dysentery \DIS-un-ter-ee\ *n. pl.* dysenteries. (Md) Diarrhea.

dysfunctional \DIS-fungk-shun-ul\ *adj.* Not normal.

dyslexia \dis-LEX-ee-uh\ *n.* (Md) A reading and spelling impairment. dyslexic *adj.* or *n.*

dystrophy \dis-TROH-fee\ *n. pl.* dystrophies. (Md) Progressive weakness of muscles.

E

e \ee\ *n. pl.* e's or es. The fifth letter of the English alphabet.

each \eech\ *pron.* Every one.

eager \EE-gur\ *adj.* Enthusiastic. eagerly *adv.*

ear \eer\ *n.* **1.** An organ that detects sound. **2.** A sensitivity to change in pitch or emphasis.

earache \EER-ayk\ *n.* A pain in one's ear.

earl \url\ *n.* A member of British nobility.

early \UR-lee\ *adv.* earlier; earliest. **1.** Near the beginning. **2.** Before the expected or usual time.

earn \urn\ *v.* earned; earning. To receive in return for work or effort. earnings *n.*

earnest \UR-nist\ *adj.* Serious in intention. earnestly *adv.*

Earth \urth\ *n.* The third planet from the Sun.

earth \urth\ *n.* Soil.

earthenware \UR-thun-wair\ *n.* Pottery made from baked clay.

earthly \UR-thee\ *adj.* **1.** Concerning earth. **2.** Mundane.

earthquake \URTH-kwayk\ *n.* **1.** A disturbance in the earth's crust. **2.** An upheaval.

earth tone *n.* Any brownish color.

earthy \UR-thee\ *adj.* earthier; earthiest. **1.** Concerning the earth. **2.** Practical. earthiness *n.*

ease \eez\ *n.* **1.** Comfort. **2.** Naturalness. **3.** At ease [Id]: free from pain.

ease \eez\ *v.* eased; easing. **1.** To alleviate. **2.** To moderate.

easel \EE-zul\ *n.* An artist's frame.

east \eest\ *n.* **1.** One of four compass points. **2.** The direction of sunrise. **3.** Asian culture. eastern *adj.*; easterly *adj.* or *adv.*

easy \EE-zee\ *adj.* easier; easiest. **1.** Concerning little difficulty. **2.** Lenient. **3.** Pleasant. easiness *n.*

easygoing \EE-zee-GOH-ing\ *n.* Relaxed.

eat \eet\ *v.* ate; eaten; eating. **1.** To consume as food. **2.** To corrode.

eating disorder *n.* A mental and physical problem.

eaves \eevz\ *pl. n.* A roof border.

eavesdrop \EEVZ-drop\ *v.* eavesdropped; eavesdropping. To listen to another's conversation.

ebb \eb\ *v.* ebbed; ebbing. To recede.

ebony \EB-uh-nee\ *adj.* Black.

ebony \EB-uh-nee\ *n.* A hardwood tree.

ebullient \i-BUUL-yunt\ *adj.* Agitated. ebullience *n.*

eccentric \ik-SEN-trik\ *adj.* Strange.

echelon \ESH-uh-lon\ *n.* A level within an arrangement of units.

echo \EK-oh\ *n. pl.* echoes. *also* echos. **1.** A reflected or repeated sound. **2.** An imitation.

echo \EK-oh\ *v.* echoed; echoing. To repeat or reflect a sound.

echocardiagram \EK-oh-KAR-dee-oh-gram\ *n.* (Md) A visual record of heart function. echocardiography *n.*

eclair \ay-KLAIR or ee-KLAIR\ *n.* (Fr) A cream-filled pastry.

eclat \ay-KLAH\ *n.* (Fr) **1.** Brilliance. **2.** Success.

eclectic \i-KLEK-tik\ *adj.* Selecting from various components.

eclipse \i-KLIPS\ *n.* **1.** A blocking of light of one heavenly body by another. **2.** A darkening.

ecology \i-KOL-uh-jee\ *n. pl.* ecologies. The study of the environment and its inhabitants. ecological also ecologic *adj.*

economical \ek-uh-NOM-i-kul\ *adj.* Concerning thrift.

economics \ek-uh-NOM-iks\ *n. pl.* economics. The study of the production and consumption of products.

economy \i-KON-uh-mee\ *n. pl.* economies. The science of production and consumption of products.

ecosystem \EK-oh-sis-tum\ *n.* (Sc) The interrelationship of organisms and their environment.

ecstasy \EK-stuh-see\ *n. pl.* ecstasies. State of rapture. ecstatic *adj.*

ecumenical \EK-yuu-men-i-kul\ *adj.* **1.** Of the whole Christian Church. **2.** Seeking Christian unity.

eczema \EG-zuh-muh\ *n.* A skin condition.

eddy \ED-ee\ *n. pl.* eddies. A swirling patch of water or air.

eddy \ED-ee\ *v.* eddied; eddying. To move in a circular current.

edelweiss \AY-dul-vise\ *n.* A perennial herb that grows in the Alps.

edema \i-DEE-muh\ *n.* An abnormal collection of fluid.

edge \ej\ *n.* **1.** The sharp side of a blade. **2.** A border. **3.** On edge [Id]: anxious.

edge \ej\ *v.* edged; edging. **1.** To border. **2.** To defeat by a little bit.

edible \ED-uh-bul\ *adj.* Able to be eaten.

edict \EE-dikt\ *n.* An order.

edifice \ED-uh-fis\ *n.* A large building.

edit \ED-it\ *v.* edited; editing. **1.** To correct. **2.** To alter. **3.** To prepare.

edition \i-DISH-un\ *n.* **1.** A version. **2.** Printing of a book.

editorial \ed-i-TOR-ee-ul\ *n.* An opinion statement.

educate \EJ-uu-kayt\ *v.* educated; educating. To teach. educated *adj.*

education \ej-uu-KAY-shun\ *n.* **1.** The learning process. **2.** formal training.

educational television *n.* Instruction on television.

eel *n.* A snakelike fish.

eerie *also* **eery** \EER-ee\ *adj.* eerier; eeriest. Very mysterious.

effect \i-FEKT\ *n.* A change produced by an action or cause.

effect \i-FEKT\ *v.* effected; effecting. To result in.

effective \i-FEK-tiv\ *adj.* **1.** Operative. **2.** Impressive.

effeminate \i-FEM-uh-nit\ *adj.* Marked by feminine qualities.

effervescent \ef-ur-VES-sunt\ *adj.* **1.** Marked by bubbles. **2.** Exhilarated. effervesce *v.*; effervescence *n.*

effete \i-FEET\ *adj.* **1.** Weak. **2.** Decadent.

efficient \i-FISH-unt\ *adj.* Effective and organized. efficiency *n.*

effluent \EF-loo-unt\ *n.* A stream.

effort \EF-urt\ *n.* **1.** Exertion. **2.** An attempt. **3.** Thing produced.

effortless \EF-urt-less\ *adj.* Easy. effortlessly *adv.*

egalitarian \i-gal-i-TAIR-ee-un\ *adj.* Believing in human equality.

egg \eg\ *n.* Reproductive substance.

eggplant \EG-plant\ *n.* An edible fruit-producing herb.

ego \EE-goh\ *n. pl.* egos. **1.** One's self-esteem. **2.** One of three psyche divisions. egotistical or egotistic *adj.*

egocentric \ee-goh-SEN-trik\ *adj.* Self-centered. egocentrism *n.*

ego trip *n.* Something that satisfies one's ego.

eight \ate\ *n.* A cardinal number one greater than seven.

either \EE-thur\ *pron.* One or the other.

eject \i-JEKT or ee-JEKT\ *v.* ejected; ejecting. To send out forcefully. ejection *n.*

elaborate \i-LAB-ur-it\ *adj.* Complex.

elaborate \ee-LAB-uh-rayt\ *v.* elaborated; elaborating. To develop. elaboration *n.*

elapse \i-LAPS\ *v.* elapsed; elapsing. To pass, as time.

elastic \i-LAS-tik\ *adj.* Flexible and stretchy.

elated \i-LAY-tud\ *adj.* Very happy.

elbow \EL-boh\ *n.* A joint connecting the upper and lower arm bones.

elder \EL-dur\ *n.* **1.** One of greater age. **2.** A religious officer.

elect \i-LEKT\ *adj.* Chosen by vote.

elect \i-LEKT\ *v.* elected; electing. To choose by voting.

election \i-LEK-shun\ *n.* The process of voting and choosing representation.

electorate \i-LEK-tur-it\ *n.* A group of voters.

electricity \i-lek-TRIS-i-tee\ *n. pl.* electricities. (Sc) A form of natu-rally occurring energy. electrical or electric *adj.*; electrician *n.*

electrocardiography \i-LEK-troh-KAHR-dee-uh-gra-fee\ *n.* (Md) An instrument that measures heartbeat. electrocardiogram *n.*

electrocution \i-LEK-truh-kyuu-shun\ *n.* Death by electric shock. electrocute *v.*

electroencephalogram \i-lek-troh-en-SEF-uh-luh-gram\ *n.* (Md) A machine tracing of brainwaves.

electronics \i-lek-TRON-iks\ *pl. n.* (Sc) **1.** Machines using electrons for energy. **2.** The study of electrons.

elegant \EL-i-gunt\ *adj.* Marked by grace. elegance *n.*

element \EL-uh-munt\ *n.* **1.** A basic unit. **2.** A part. **3.** One of about 100 basic chemical substances. elemental *adj.*

elevate \EL-uh-vayt\ *v.* elevated; elevating. To rise or raise above. elevated *adj.*; elevation *n.*

elf *n. pl.* elves. A fairy. elfish *adj.*; elfin *adj.*

elicit \i-LIS-it\ *v.* elicited; eliciting. To draw out.

eligible \EL-i-juh-bul\ *adj.* **1.** To fulfill requirements. **2.** To be worthy. eligibility *n.*

eliminate \i-LIM-uh-nayt\ *v.* eliminated; eliminating. To remove. elimination *n.*

elite \i-LEET\ *n.* (Fr) **1.** The best. **2.** A typeface. elitist *n.*

ellipsis \i-LIP-sis\ *n. pl.* ellipses. Punctuation mark indicating omission.

elocution \el-uh-KYOO-shun\ *n.* The art of public speaking. elocute *v.*

elongated \i-LAWNG-gay-tud\ *adj.* Stretched out. elongate *v.*

elope \i-LOHP\ *v.* eloped; eloping. To run away and get married. elopement *n.*

eloquent \EL-uh-kwunt\ *adj.* Expressive. eloquence *n.*

else \els\ *adv.* Otherwise.

elsewhere \ELS-hwair\ *adv.* Another place.

elude \i-LOOD\ *v.* eluded; eluding. To escape. elusive *adj.*

emaciate \i-MAY-shee-ayt\ *v.* emaciated; emaciating. To lose too much weight.

emanate \EM-uh-nayt\ *v.* emanated; emanating. To emit.

emancipate \i-MAN-suh-payt\ *v.* emancipated; emancipating To free. emancipation *n.*

emasculate \i-MAS-kyu-layt\ *v.* emasculated; emasculating. **1.** To weaken. **2.** To castrate.

embalm \em-BAHM\ *v.* embalmed; embalming. To preserve.

embankment \em-BANGK-munt\ *n.* A raised side.

embargo \em-BAHR-goh\ *n. pl.* embargoes. Prohibition on commerce.

embark \em-BAHRK\ *v.* embarked; embarking. To set out on a journey or undertaking.

embarrass \em-BAR-us\ *v.* embarrassed; embarrassing. To cause to feel awkward or ashamed.

embassy \EM-buh-see\ *n. pl.* embassies. A diplomat's residence and office.

embellish \em-BEL-ish\ *v.* embellished; embellishing. To enhance.

embezzle \em-BEZ-ul\ *v.* embezzled; embezzling. To take fraudulently.

emblem \EM-blum\ *n.* A symbol.

embody \em-BOD-ee\ *v.* embodied; embodying. **1.** To personify. **2.** To incorporate. embodiment *n.*

embolism \EM-buh-liz-um\ *n.* A clot or air bubble in a blood vessel.

embrace \em-BRAYS\ *v.* embraced; embracing. **1.** To hug. **2.** To include.

embroider \em-BROI-dur\ *v.* embroidered; embroidering. **1.** To do needlework. **2.** To embellish. embroidery **n.**

embroil \em-BROIL\ **v.** embroiled; embroiling. To surround with confusion or conflict.

emerge \i-MURJ\ **v.** emerged; emerging. To rise into view. emergence **n.**

emergency \i-MUR-jun-see\ **n. pl.** emergencies. A serious situation requiring attention.

emigrant \EM-i-grunt\ **n.** One who moves to another country.

emigrate \EM-i-grayt\ **v.** emigrated; emigrating. To leave one's country.

emigre \EM-i-gray\ **n.** A political emigrant.

eminence \EM-uh-nuns\ **n.** A superior position. eminent **adj.**

emir \i-MEER\ **n.** An Islamic leader. emirate **n.**

emissary \EM-uh-ser-ee\ **n. pl.** emissaries. An agent.

emission \uh-MISH-un\ **n.** Something that is sent forth.

emit \i-MIT\ **v.** emitted; emitting. **1.** To give off. **2.** To eject.

emote \i-MOHT\ **v.** emoted; emoting. To express emotion.

emotion \i-MOH-shun\ **n.** A mental feeling.

empathetic \em-puh-THET-ik\ **adj.** Involving an understanding of another's emotions. empathy **n.**

emphasis \EM-fuh-sis\ **n. pl.** emphases. **1.** Special importance. **2.** Stress. emphasize **v.**

emphatic \em-FAT-ik\ **adj.** Using or showing special importance.

empire \EM-pier\ **n.** A sovereign's territory.

employ \em-PLOI\ **v.** employed; employing. **1.** To use. **2.** To hire. employer **n.**; employment **n.**

employee \em-PLOI-ee\ **n.** One who exchanges labor for money.

emporium \em-POH-ree-um\ **n. pl.** emporiums or emporia. A place of trade.

empower \em-POW-ur\ **v.** empowered; empowering. To give authority to.

emulate \EM-yur-layt\ **v.** emulated; emulating. To imitate.

enable \en-AY-bul\ **v.** enabled; enabling. To make possible. enabler **n.**

enact \en-AKT\ **v.** enacted; enacting. To make into a law.

enamel \i-NAM-ul\ **n.** A glasslike protective covering.

enamel \i-NAM-ul\ **v.** enameled or enamelled; enameling or enamelling. To cover with a glasslike substance.

enamor \i-NAM-ur\ **v.** enamored; enamoring. To fall in love.

encephalitis \en-sef-uh-LIE-tis\ **n.**

pl. encephalitides (Md) Brain inflammation.

enchilada \en-CHIL-ah-duh\ *n.* (Sp) A filled tortilla.

encircle \en-SUR-kul\ *v.* encircled; encircling. To surround.

enclave \EN-klayv\ *n.* (Fr) An enclosed area within a territory.

enclose \en-KLOHZ\ *v.* enclosed; enclosing. **1.** To surround. **2.** To confine. enclosure *n.*

encompass \en-KUM-pus\ *v.* encompassed; encompassing. **1.** To include. **2.** To enclose.

encore \AHNG-kor\ *n.* (Fr) A demand for a reappearance or another performance.

encounter \en-KOWN-tur\ *v.* encountered; encountering. To come upon.

encounter group *n.* A therapy group.

encourage \en-KUR-ij\ *v.* encouraged; encouraging. **1.** To inspire. **2.** To hearten. encouragement *n.*

encroach \en-KROHCH\ *v.* encroached; encroaching. To tresspass. encroachment *n.*

encyclopedia *also* **encyclopaedia** \en-sie-kluh-PEE-dee-uh\ *n.* A reference work including many areas of knowledge.

end *n.* **1.** The conclusion. **2.** A result. **3.** Death. ending *n.*

endanger \en-DAYN-jur\ *v.* endangered; endangering. To bring into peril. endangered *adj.*

endeavor \en-DEV-ur\ *n.* An activity.

endeavor \en-DEV-ur\ *v.* endeavored; endeavoring. To attempt.

endemic \en-DEM-ik\ *adj.* Characteristic or commonly found.

endless \END-lis\ *adj.* Continual and without end. endlessly *adv.*

endocrinology \en-doh-kruh-NOL-uh-jee\ *n.* (Md) The study of glands.

endorse \en-DORS\ *v.* endorsed; endorsing. **1.** To support. **2.** To sign. **3.** To approve. endorsement *n.*

endure \en-DUUR\ *v.* endured; enduring. To bear. enduring *adj.*; endurance *n.*

enemy \EN-uh-mee\ *n. pl.* enemies. One hostile to another.

energy \EN-ur-jee\ *n. pl.* energies. **1.** Power. **2.** Usable natural resource. energetic *adj.*; energize *v.*

enervate \EN-ur-vayt\ *v.* enervated; enervating. To lessen the strength of.

enforce \en-FORS\ *v.* enforced; enforcing. **1.** To strengthen. **2.** To compel. enforcement *n.*

engage \en-GAYJ\ *v.* engaged; engaging. **1.** To bind. **2.** To agree to marry. **3.** To participate. engagement *n.*

engine \EN-jin\ *n.* **1.** A power-generating machine. **2.** An agent.

engineering \en-juh-NEER-ing\ *n.* (Sc) The application of science for the use of power and for human benefit.

engrave \en-GRAYV\ *v.* engraved; engraving. To cut a design into. engraving *n.*

engross \en-GROHS\ *v.* engrossed; engrossing. To be completely occupied. engrossing *adj.*

engulf \en-GULF\ *v.* engulfed; engulfing. To surround and overwhelm.

enhance \en-HANS\ *v.* enhanced; enhancing. To heighten or improve. enhancement *n.*

enigma \uh-NIG-muh\ *n.* A mystery. enigmatic also enigmatical *adj.*

enjoy \en-JOI\ *v.* enjoyed; enjoying. To take pleasure in. enjoyment *n.*; enjoyable *adj.*

enlarge \en-LAHRJ\ *v.* enlarged; enlarging. **1.** To make bigger. **2.** To elaborate. enlargement *n.*

enlighten \en-LITE-n\ *v.* enlightened; enlightening. To instruct and free from ignorance. enlightened *adj.*

enlist \en-LIST\ *v.* enlisted; enlisting. **1.** To join an armed service. **2.** To gain help. enlisted *adj.*

en masse \ahn-MAS\ *adv.* (Fr) As a whole.

enmesh \en-MESH\ *v.* enmeshed; enmeshing. To entangle in.

ennui \ahn-WEE\ *n.* (Fr) Boredom.

enormous \i-NOR-mus\ *adj.* Huge. enormously *adv.*

enough \i-NUF\ *adj.* Sufficient.

enrage \en-RAYJ\ *v.* enraged; enraging. To anger greatly.

enrich \en-RICH\ *v.* enriched; enriching. To make richer or improved.

enroll *also* **enrol** \en-ROHL\ *v.* enrolled; enrolling. To register for. enrollment *n.*

en route \ahn-ROOT\ *adv.* or *adj.* (Fr) Along the way.

ensemble \ahn-SAHM-bul\ *n.* (Fr) A group, especially of performers.

enshrine \en-SHRINE\ *v.* enshrined; enshrining. To cherish.

enshroud \en-SHROWD\ *v.* enshrouded; enshrouding. To cover with a burial cloth.

ensign \EN-sin\ *n.* **1.** A symbol. **2.** A military or naval officer.

ensue \en-SOO\ *v.* ensued; ensuing. To follow.

entail \en-TAYL\ *v.* entailed; entailing. **1.** To involve as necessary. **2.** To restrict.

entangle \en-TANG-gul\ *v.* entangled; entangling. To interweave. entanglement *n.*

enter \EN-tur\ *v.* entered; entering. **1.** To go in. **2.** To insert. **3.** To report or register.

enterprise \EN-tur-priez\ *n.* **1.** A project. **2.** Initiative.

entertain \en-tur-TAYN\ *v.* entertained; entertaining. To amuse or perform. entertainment *n.*

enthrall *also* **enthral** \en-THRAWL\ *v.* enthralled; enthralling. To spellbind.

enthusiastic \en-THOO-zee-as-tik\ *adj.* Filled with excitement. enthusiasm *n.*; enthuse *v.*

entice \en-TIES\ *v.* enticed; enticing. To lure. enticingly *adv.*

entire \en-TIER\ *adj.* Complete. entirely *adv.*

entitle \en-TIET-l\ *v.* entitled; entitling. **1.** To designate. **2.** To deserve. entitlement *n.*

entomology \en-tuh-MOL-uh-jee\ *n.* (Sc) The study of insects.

entourage \ahn-tuu-RAHZH\ *n.* One's attendants.

entrance \EN-truns\ *n.* **1.** Means of entry. **2.** Permission to enter.

entrap \en-TRAP\ *v.* entrapped; entrapping. To catch. entrapment *n.*

entreaty \en-TREE-tee\ *n. pl.* entreaties. A plea.

entrée *also* **entree** \AHN-tray\ *n.* (Fr) The main course.

entrepreneur   \ahn-truh-pruh-NUUR\ *n.* (Bs) A person who organizes a risky commercial undertaking. entrepreneurial *adj.*

entrust \en-TRUST\ *v.* entrused; entrusting. To give over with confidence.

entry \EN-tree\ *n. pl.* entries **1.** An opening. **2.** A door.

entry-level *adj.* Beginning.

enunciate \i-NUN-see-ayt\ *v.* enunciated; enunciating. **1.** To pronounce clearly. **2.** To announce.

envelope \EN-vuh-lohp\ *n.* A paper wrapper for mail, etc.

environment \en-VIE-run-munt\ *n.* **1.** Surroundings. **2.** Natural world. environ *v.*; environs *n.*

envoy \EN-voi\ *n.* A messenger.

envy \EN-vee\ *v.* envied; envying. To feel resentment. envious *adj.*

epaulet *also* **epaulette** \EP-uh-let\ *n.* (Fr) Uniform shoulder decoration.

ephemeral \i-FEM-ur-ul\ *adj.* Lasting only a short time.

epic \EP-ik\ *n.* **1.** A long narrative poem. **2.** A story broken into segments.

epicure \EP-i-kyuur\ *n.* One who enjoys food and music.

epidemic \ep-i-DEM-ik\ *adj.* Affecting many people.

epidermis \ep-i-DUR-mis\ *n.* (Sc) Outer layer of skin.

epilepsy \EP-uh-lep-see\ *n. pl.* epilepsies (Md) A central nervous system disorder. epileptic *adj.*

epilogue *also* **epilog** \EP-uh-lawg\ *n.* Concluding section.

epiphany \uh-PIF-uh-nee\ *n. pl.* epiphanies **1.** A Christian festival. **2.** A sudden understanding.

episode \EP-uh-sohd\ *n.* A segment in a drama. episodic also episodical *adj.*

epitaph \EP-i-taf\ *n.* **1.** Inscription on a gravestone. **2.** A brief mention of something past.

epithet \EP-uh-thet\ *n.* An identifying word or phrase.

epitome \i-PIT-uh-mee\ *n.* **1.** A typical example. **2.** An embodiment.

epoch \EP-uk\ *n.* A particular time period.

epoxy \i-POX-see\ *v.* epoxied; epoxying. To glue together with resin.

Epstein-Barr virus *n.* (Md) A virus that causes infectious mononucleosis.

equal \EE-kwul\ *adj.* Same in size, amount, or value. equalize *v.*

equality \i-KWOL-i-tee\ *n. pl.* equalities. Being the same in some way.

equal opportunity employer *n.* An employer who doesn't discriminate.

equanimity \ee-kwuh-NIM-i-tee\ *n. pl.* equanimities **1.** Composure. **2.** Balance.

equate \i-KWAYT\ *v.* equated; equating. To consider to be equal or equivalent.

equation \i-KWAY-zhun\ *n.* A statement expressing balance.

equestrian \i-KWES-tree-un\ *adj.* Concerning horseback riding.

equidistant \EE-kwu-dis-tunt\ *adj.* At an equal distance.

equilibrium \ee-kwuh-LIB-ree-um\ *n. pl.* equilibriums or equilibria. A state of balance.

equip \i-KWIP\ *v.* equipped; equipping. To furnish.

equipment \i-KWIP-munt\ *n.* Things needed.

equity \EK-wi-tee\ *n. pl.* equities. **1.** [Le] Justice. **2.** Property value.

equivalent \i-KWIV-uh-lunt\ *adj.* Being equal in amount, value, etc. equivalence *n.*

equivocate \i-KWIV-uh-kayt\ *v.* equivocated; equivocating. To mislead or be ambiguous. equivocation *n.*

era \EER-uh\ *n.* A time period in history.

eradicate \i-RAD-i-kayt\ *v.* eradicated; eradicating. To eliminate.

erase \i-RAYS\ *v.* erased; erasing. To remove. erasable *adj.*

ere \air\ *prep.* Before.

erect \i-REKT\ *adj.* Upright.

erect \i-REKT\ *v.* erected; erecting. To build.

ergonomics \ER-goh-nom-iks\ *n. pl.* ergonimics. The study of safe, efficient work and its environment.

ermine \UR-min\ *n. pl.* ermines. A weasel.

erosion \i-ROH-zhun\ *n.* The process of wearing away. erode *v.*

erotic *also* **erotical** \i-ROT-ik\ *adj.* Concerning strong sexual desire. erotica *n.*; erotically *adv.*

err \er\ *v.* erred; erring. To make a mistake.

errand \ER-und\ *n.* A short journey and its purpose.

erratic \i-RAT-ik\ *adj.* Wandering.

erroneous \i-ROH-nee-us\ *adj.* Mistaken. erroneously *adv.*

error \ER-ur\ *n.* **1.** A mistake. **2.** The difference or inaccuracy in measurement.

erstwhile \URST-hwile\ *adj.* Former.

erudite \ER-yuu-dite\ *adj.* Learned.

erupt \i-RUPT\ *v.* erupted; erupting. To emerge suddenly and violently. eruption *n.*

escalate \ES-kuh-layt\ *v.* escalated; escalating. To expand or increase in intensity. escalation *n.*

escalator \ES-kuh-lay-tur\ *n.* Moving stairs.

escapade \ES-kuh-payd\ *n.* An adventure.

escape \i-SKAYP\ *n.* **1.** A way out. **2.** A breakout.

escape \i-SKAYP\ *v.* escaped; escaping. **1.** To get free. **2.** To avoid.

escargot \es-KAR-goh\ *n. pl.* escargots. (Fr) Edible snails.

escort \ES-kort\ *n.* A person who accompanies, esp. socially.

escrow \ES-kroh\ *n.* Something of value held in trust.

esophagus \i-SOF-uh-gus\ *n. pl.* esophagi. (Md) A tube running from the trachea to the stomach. esophageal *adj.*

esoteric \es-uh-TER-ik\ *adj.* Limited to a small circle.

esplanade \ES-pluh-nahd\ *n.* A stretch of ground.

espresso \es-PRES-soh\ *n. pl.* espressos. Strong coffee.

essay \ES-ay\ *n.* A composition.

essence \ES-uns\ *n.* **1.** The nature of something. **2.** A quality or element. **3.** An odor.

essential \i-SEN-shul\ *adj.* **1.** Vital. **2.** Inherent. essentially *adv.*

establish \i-STAB-lish\ *v.* established; establishing. **1.** To set up. **2.** To prove.

establishment \i-STAB-lish-munt\ *n.* **1.** Something in place. **2.** A controlling group.

estate \i-STAYT\ *n.* One's property.

esteem \i-STEEM\ *n.* One's perceived value.

esthete \ES-theet\ *n.* Variation of aesthete.

estimate \ES-tuh-mayt\ *v.* estimated; estimating. To assess value. estimation *n.*

estrange \i-STRAYNJ\ *v.* estranged; estranging. To alienate.

estrogen \ES-truh-jun\ *n.* (Md) A female hormone.

estuary \ES-choo-er-ee\ *n. pl.* estuaries. A waterway.

et cetera \et-SET-ur-uh\ *n.* (Lt) And so forth.

eternal \i-TUR-nl\ *adj.* Forever.

eternity \i-TUR-ni-tee\ *n. pl.* eternities. **1.** Infinite time. **2.** Endless period.

ethereal \i-THEER-ee-ul\ *adj.* **1.** Concerning the heavens. **2.** Spiritual.

ethical *also* **ethic** \ETH-i-kul\ *adj.* Concerning moral behavior.

ethics \ETH-iks\ *n.* The study of moral issues.

ethnic \ETH-nik\ *adj.* Concerning a particular culture.

ethnocentric \eth-NOH-sen-trik\ *adj.* Belief in one's cultural superiority.

ethnology \eth-NOL-uh-jee\ *n.* The study of cultural divisions.

etiquette \ET-i-kit\ *n.* (Fr) Proper manners.

etymology \et-uh-MOL-uh-jee\ *n.* The study of word origins.

eucalyptus \YOO-kuh-lip-tus\ *n. pl.* eucalypti or eucalyptuses. A fragrant evergreen or shrub.

eulogy \YOO-luh-jee\ *n. pl.* eulogies. Statement of praise.

eunuch \YOO-nuk\ *n.* A castrated male.

euphemism \YOO-fuh-miz-um\ *n.* Mild substitute expression.

euphoria \yoo-FOR-ee-uh\ *n.* Elation. euphoric *adj.*

eureka \yuu-REE-kuh\ *interj.* An expression of triumph or discovery.

Eurodollar \YUUR-oh-DOL-ur\ *n.* American money used in European markets.

Europe \YUUR-up\ *n.* A continent in the Northern hemisphere, by Asia.

eurythmic *also* **eurhythmic** \yuu-RITH-mik\ *adj.* In harmony.

euthanasia \yoo-thuh-NAY-zhuh\ *n.* Mercy killing.

evacuate \i-VAK-yoo-ayt\ *v.* evacuated; evacuating. **1.** To empty. **2.** To leave. evacuation *n.*

evade \i-VAYD\ *v.* evaded; evading. To elude.

evaluate \i-VAL-yuu-ayt\ *v.* evaluated; evaluating. To assess. evaluation *n.*

evangelism \i-VAN-juh-liz-um\ *n.* Crusading for Christianity.

evaporate \i-VAP-uh-rayt\ *v.* evaporated; evaporating. **1.** To change into vapor. **2.** To disappear. evaporation *n.*

eve \eev\ *n.* **1.** Evening. **2.** The time prior to.

even \EE-vun\ *adj.* **1.** Flat. **2.** Fair. **3.** Calm. evenly *adv.*

even \EE-vun\ *adv.* Precise.

evening \EEV-ning\ *n.* The close of a day.

event \i-VENT\ *n.* An occurrence. eventful *adj.*

eventual \i-VEN-choo-ul\ *adj.* At some future point. eventually *adv.*

ever \EV-ur\ *adv.* **1.** Always. **2.** At any time.

every \EV-ree\ *adj.* Each one.

evict \i-VIKT\ *v.* evicted; evicting. To throw out. eviction *n.*

evidence \EV-i-duns\ *n.* Proof.

evident \EV-i-dunt\ *adj.* Obvious. evidently *adv.*

evil \EE-vul\ *adj.* eviler or eviller; evilest or evillest. Wicked. evilly *adv.*

evolution \ev-uh-LOO-shun\ *n.* (Sc) **1.** A gradual change. **2.** A process of developing into a different form. evolve *v.*; evolutionary *n.*

ewe \yoo\ *n.* A female sheep.

exacerbate \ig-ZAS-ur-bayt\ *v.* exacerbated; exacerbating. To make worse. exacerbation *n.*

exact \ig-ZAKT\ *adj.* Correct or precise.

exact \ig-ZAKT\ *v.* exacted; exacting. To demand.

exactly \ig-ZAKT-lee\ *adv.* **1.** In an exact manner. **2.** Strictly.

exaggerate \ig-ZAJ-uh-rayt\ *v.* exaggerated; exaggerating. To overstate. exaggeration *n.*

exalt \ig-ZAWLT\ *v.* exalted; exalting. **1.** To elevate. **2.** To glorify. exaltation *n.*

examination \ig-zam-uh-NAY-shun\ *n.* A test.

examine \ig-ZAM-in\ *v.* examined; examining. To look at closely.

example \ig-ZAM-pul\ *n*. **1.** A model. **2.** A punishment used as warning.

exasperate \ig-ZAS-puh-rayt\ *v*. exasperated; exasperating. To inflame. exasperation *n*.

excavate \EKS-kuh-vayt\ *v*. excavated; excavating. To uncover or dig up. excavation *n*.

exceed \ik-SEED\ *v*. exceeded; exceeding. To surpass.

excel \ik-SEL\ *v*. excelled; excelling. To be superior to.

excellence \EK-suh-luns\ *n*. **1.** Superior quality. **2.** Virtue. excellent *adj*.

except \ik-SEPT\ *conj*., *prep*. Not including.

except \ik-SEPT\ *v*. excepted; excepting. To leave out. exception *n*.

excerpt \EK-surpt\ *v*. excerpted; excerpting. To take out.

excess \ik-SES\ *n*. **1.** Amount exceeded. **2.** Immoderation in drinking or eating. excessive *adj*.

exchange \iks-CHAYNJ\ *v*. exchanged; exchanging. **1.** To substitute. **2.** To give and receive.

excise \EK-size\ *n*. A tax.

excite \ik-SITE\ *v*. excited; exciting. **1.** To provoke. **2.** To energize. excitement *n*.

exclamation \ek-skluh-MAY-shun\ *n*. A sudden outcry. exclaim *v*.

exclude \ik-SKLOOD\ *v*. excluded; excluding. To leave out.

exclusive \ik-SKLOO-siv\ *adj*. **1.** Restricted. **2.** Undivided.

excommunicate \eks-kuh-MYOO-ni-kayt\ *adj*. To exclude from church membership. excommunication *n*.

excursion \ik-SKUR-zhun\ *n*. **1.** An outing. **2.** A digression.

excuse \ik-SKYOOS\ *n*. A reason.

excuse \ik-SKYOOZ\ *v*. excused; excusing. **1.** To release. **2.** To forgive.

execute \EK-si-kyoot\ *v*. executed; executing. **1.** To perform or carry out. **2.** To put to death.

executive \ig-ZEG-yuh-tiv\ *adj*. **1.** Concerning a governmental branch. **2.** Concerning management or supervision. executive *n*.

exempt \ig-ZEMPT\ *adj*. Free from requirements. exemption *n*.

exercise \EK-sur-size\ *n*. **1.** Training or preparation. **2.** Physical exertion for good health.

exercise \EK-sur-size\ *v*. exercised; exercising. **1.** To train or prepare. **2.** To exert physically.

exert \ig-ZURT\ *v*. exerted; exerting. To put forth. exertion *n*.

exhaust \ig-ZAWST\ *v*. exhausted; exhausting. **1.** To use up. **2.** To empty. exhaustion *n*.

exhibit \ig-ZIB-it\ *n.* **1.** A document or object put on display. **2.** A showing. exhibition *n.*

exhibit \ig-ZIB-it\ *v.* exhibited; exhibiting. To show.

exile \EG-zile\ *n.* Forced absence from one's home.

exile \EG-zile\ *v.* exiled; exiling. To banish.

exist \ig-ZIST\ *v.* existed; existing. To be. existence *n.*

existential \eg-zi-STEN-shul\ *adj.* Concerning existence.

existentialism \eg-zi-STEN-shuh-liz-um\ *n.* A philosophical movement. existentialist *n.*

exit \EG-zit\ *n.* A doorway.

exit \EG-zit\ *v.* exited; exiting. **1.** To leave. **2.** [SI] To die.

exodus \EK-suh-dus\ *n.* A large group's departure.

exonerate \ig-ZON-uh-rayt\ *v.* exonerated; exonerating. To clear of blame.

exorbitant \ig-ZOR-bi-tunt\ *adj.* Excessive.

exotic \ig-ZOT-ik\ *adj.* **1.** Not native. **2.** Mysterious.

expand \ik-SPAND\ *v.* expanded; expanding. **1.** To enlarge. **2.** To spread out. expansion *n.*

expatriate \eks-PAY-tree-ayt\ *v.* expatriated; expatriating. To exile oneself.

expect \ik-SPEKT\ *v.* expected; expecting. **1.** To wait for. **2.** To wish for and think about. expectation *n.*

expedite \EK-spi-dite\ *v.* expedited; expediting. To help or hurry progress.

expedition \ek-spi-DISH-un\ *n.* A journey.

expel \ik-SPEL\ *v.* expelled; expelling. To eject.

expensive \ik-SPEN-siv\ *adj.* Having a high price.

experience \ik-SPEER-ee-uns\ *n.* Practical learning from participation.

experience \ik-SPEER-ee-uns\ *v.* experienced; experiencing. To participate in.

experiment \ik-SPER-uh-munt\ *n.* A test. experimentation *n.*; experimental *adj.*

expert \EK-spurt\ *n.* One who has great knowledge or skill. expertise *n.*

expire \ik-SPIER\ *v.* expired; expiring. To die.

explain \ik-SPLAYN\ *v.* explained; explaining. **1.** To give reasons for. **2.** To interpret or describe. explanation *n.*

expletive \EK-spli-tiv\ *n.* **1.** An exclamation. **2.** A curse word.

explicit \ik-SPLIS-it\ *adj.* Specific. explicitly *adv.*

explode \ik-SPLOHD\ *v.* exploded; exploding. To burst forth suddenly and violently. exploded *adj.*

exploit \EK-sploit\ *n.* A feat.

explore \ik-SPLOR\ *v.* explored; exploring. To investigate by travel. exploration *n.*

export \ik-SPORT\ *v.* exported; exporting. To send something for sale abroad.

expose *also* **expose** \ik-SPOHZ\ *n.* (Fr) A statement of exposure.

expose \ik-SPOHZ\ *v.* exposed; exposing. To deprive of protection.

express \ik-SPRES\ *v.* expressed; expressing. **1.** To make known. **2.** To symbolize. **3.** To press or squeeze out. **4.** To send fast.

expressionism \ik-SPRESH-uh-niz-um\ *n.* A style of painting, drama, or music.

expulsion \ik-SPUL-shun\ *n.* The state of being ejected.

exquisite \ek-SKWI-zit\ *adj.* **1.** Perfected or best. **2.** Beautiful. exquisitely *adv.*

extend \ik-STEND\ *v.* extended; extending. **1.** To spread out. **2.** To prolong. extended *adj.*; extension *n.*; extensive *adj.*

extent \ik-STENT\ *n.* **1.** The area. **2.** The scope.

exterior \ik-STEER-ee-ur\ *adj.* On the outside. exterior *n.*

exterminate \ik-STUR-muh-nayt\ *v.* exterminated; exterminating. To kill. extermination *n.*

external \ik-STUR-nl\ *adj.* Concerning the outside.

extinct \ik-STINGKT\ *adj.* No longer alive. extinction *n.*

extinguish \ik-STING-gwish\ *v.* extinguished; extinguishing. **1.** To put out. **2.** To nullify.

extortion \ik-STOR-shun\ *n.* Gaining by illegal means. extort *v.*

extra \EK-struh\ *adj.* Additional.

extract \ik-STRAKT\ *v.* extracted; extracting. **1.** To draw out. **2.** To separate. extraction *n.*

extraordinary \ik-STROR-dn-er-ee\ *adj.* Exceptional.

extraterrestrial \ek-struh-tuh-RES-tree-ul\ *adj.* Beyond earth.

extravagant \ik-STRAV-uh-gunt\ *adj.* **1.** Lavish. **2.** Excessive. extravagance *n.*

extreme \ik-STREEM\ *adj.* To the greatest degree. extremist *n.*; extremely *adv.*

extremity \ik-STREM-i-tee\ *n. pl.* extremities **1.** A body's limb. **2.** The farthest point.

extrovert *also* **extravert** \EK-struh-vurt\ *n.* One who is open, friendly, and outgoing. extroverted *adj.*

exuberant \ig-ZOO-bur-unt\ *adj.* **1.** Profuse. **2.** Joyous. exuberance *n.*

exude \ig-ZOOD\ *v.* exuded; exuding. **1.** To ooze. **2.** To spread.

exult \ig-ZULT\ *v.* exulted; exulting. To rejoice. exultation *n.*

eye \ie\ *n.* **1.** [Md] The sight organ. **2.** An ability to appreciate.

eyeglasses \IE-glas-suhs\ *pl. n.* Corrective lenses.

eyesore \IE-sor\ *n.* Ugly object.

eyewitness \ie-WIT-nis\ *n.* One who saw something happen.

F

f \ef\ **n. pl.** f's or fs. **1.** The sixth letter of the English alphabet. **2.** The worst letter grade.

fable \FAY-bul\ **n. 1.** A legend. **2.** A lie. fabled *adj.*

fabric \FAB-rik\ **n. 1.** Cloth. **2.** Framework. **3.** Texture.

fabricate \FAB-ri-kayt\ **v.** fabricated; fabricating. **1.** To construct. **2.** To invent or lie.

fabulous \FAB-yuh-lus\ **adj. 1.** Wonderful. **2.** Fictitious.

facade \fuh-SAHD\ **n.** (Fr) A building's front.

face \fays\ **n. 1.** The front of one's head. **2.** A grimace. **3.** The surface. **4.** Front side.

face-lift \FAYS-lift\ **n.** Plastic surgery lifting the skin of the face.

facet \FAS-it\ **n. 1.** Small flat surface. **2.** One aspect.

facetious \fuh-SEE-shus\ **adj.** Intended to be amusing.

facial \FAY-shul\ **adj.** Concerning the face.

facility \fuh-SIL-i-tee\ **n. pl.** facilities. **1.** Aptitude. **2.** Something that makes action easier. **3.** A building.

facsimile *also* **fax** \fak-SIM-uh-lee\ **n.** A reproduction.

fact \fakt\ **n.** Something believed to be real or true.

fact-finding \FAKT-fyn-ding\ **n.** or *adj.* Investigative mission.

faction \FAK-shun\ *n.* A specific group within another.

factor \FAK-tur\ *n.* **1.** An ingredient. **2.** A number which can be divided exactly.

factor \FAK-tur\ *v.* factored; factoring. To include.

factory \FAK-tuh-ree\ *n. pl.* factories. A building used for manufacturing.

factual \FAK-choo-ul\ *adj.* Concerning facts. factualness *n.*

fad *n.* Something followed temporarily.

fade \fayd\ *v.* faded; fading. **1.** To wither. **2.** To vanish.

fail \fayl\ *v.* failed; failing. **1.** To stop. **2.** To neglect. failure *n.*; failing *n.*

fail-safe \FAYL-sayf\ *adj.* Assured of success.

fain \fayn\ *adj.* Gladly.

faint \faynt\ *adj.* **1.** Weak. **2.** Dim. **3.** Cowardly. faintly *adv.*

faint \faynt\ *v.* fainted; fainting. To lose consciousness.

fair *adj.* **1.** Light in color. **2.** Unbiased. Pleasing. **2.** Just. **3.** Not stormy. fairness *n.*

fair *n.* A festive gathering.

fair market value *n.* A price that buyer and seller agree on.

fairy \FAIR-ee\ *n. pl.* fairies A small, mythical being.

faith \fayth\ *n. pl.* faiths. **1.** Belief, esp. religious. **2.** Trust. **3.** Loyalty. faithful *adj.*

fake \fayk\ *n.* Not real.

fake \fayk\ *v.* faked; faking. **1.** To manipulate. **2.** To pretend or forge.

falafel \fuh-LAH-ful\ *n. pl.* falafel [Ar]. A spicy food made with vegetables.

fall \fawl\ *n.* **1.** Autumn. **2.** Collapse or decrease.

fall \fawl\ *v.* fell; fallen; falling. **1.** To come or go down. **2.** To decrease. **3.** To act immorally. **4.** To happen upon.

fallacy \FAL-uh-see\ *n. pl.* fallacies. **1.** A logic error. **2.** A mistaken idea.

fallible \FAL-uh-bul\ *adj.* Liable to be wrong.

fallopian tube \fuh-LOH-pee-un-TOOB\ *n.* Canals leading from the ovaries to the uterus.

fallout \FAWL-owt\ *n.* Radioactive pollution. fall out *v.*

fallow \FAL-oh\ *adj.* Inactive.

fallow \FAL-oh\ *n.* Tilled land.

false \fawls\ *adj.* falser; falsest **1.** Wrong. **2.** Disloyal. falsify *v.*

falsehood \FAWLS-huud\ *n.* A lie.

falsetto \fawl-SET-oh\ *n. pl.* falsettos. Artificially high voice.

fame \faym\ *n.* Renown or good reputation. famous *adj.*

familiar \fuh-MIL-yur\ *adj.* **1.** Common. **2.** Too informal.

familiar \fuh-MIL-yur\ *n.* A companion. familiarize *v.*; familiarity *n.*

family \FAM-uh-lee\ *n. pl.* families. **1.** Parents and their children. **2.** A group of related animals or plants.

famine \FAM-in\ *n.* Severe food shortage.

fan *n.* **1.** A device that blows air for cooling. **2.** A devoted follower.

fan *v.* fanned; fanning. **1.** To move the air. **2.** To spread out.

fanatic *also* **fanatical** \fuh-NAT-ik\ *adj.* Excessively enthusiastic. fanatic *n.*

fancy \FAN-see\ *adj.* fancier; fanciest. **1.** Elaborate. **2.** Extravagant. fanciness *n.*

fancy \FAN-see\ *v.* fancied; fancying. **1.** To like. **2.** To think.

fanfare \FAN-fair\ *n.* (Fr) A short trumpet introduction.

fantail \FAN-tayl\ *n.* **1.** A pigeon. **2.** A ship's part.

fantastic *also* **fantastical** \fan-TAS-tik\ *adj.* **1.** Relating to fantasy. **2.** Wonderful. **3.** Bizarre.

fantasy \FAN-tuh-see\ *n. pl.* fantasies. An imagined story.

far \fahr\ *adv.* farther or further; farthest or furthest. At a great distance.

far-fetched \FAHR-FECHT\ *adj.* Improbable.

far-out \FAH-OWT\ *adj.* Very nontraditional.

faraway \FAHR-uh-way\ *adj.* Remote.

far-sighted \FAHR-SIE-tid\ *adj.* **1.** Able to see a long way. **2.** Using good judgement.

farce \fahrs\ *n.* **1.** A light comedy. **2.** Pretense.

fare \fair\ *v.* fared; faring. To get along.

fare \fair\ *n.* **1.** Food. **2.** Price.

farewell \fair-WELL\ *n.* A good-bye.

farm \fahrm\ *n.* A piece of land or business for raising animals or crops. farming *n.*; farm *v.*

farmhand \FAHRM-hand\ *n.* A hired farm worker.

farther \FAHR-thur\ *adv.* At a greater distance.

fascinate \FAS-uh-nayt\ *v.* fascinated; fascinating. To attract and hold the interest of. fascinating *adj.*; fascination *n.*

fascism \FASH-iz-um\ *n.* (It). Philosophy exalting race or nation and dictatorship. fascist *n.*

fashion \FASH-un\ *n.* Prevailing style. fashionable *adj.*

fashion \FASH-un\ *v.* fashioned; fashioning. **1.** To mold. **2.** To adapt.

fast *adj.* **1.** Quickly. **2.** Fixed. **3.** Immoral and wild.

fasten \FAS-un\ *v.* fastened; fastening. To fix securely.

fast-food *n.* Prepared food served quickly and for quick consumption.

fastidious \fa-STID-ee-us\ *adj.* Having high standards.

fast-track *adj.* Concerning a sped-up process.

fat *n.* Animal matter.

fat *adj.* fatter; fattest. **1.** Overweight. **2.** [Sl] Wealthy.

fatal \FAYT-l\ *adj.* Deadly. fatalist *n.*

fate \fayt\ *n.* **1.** Destiny. **2.** Disaster. fated *adj.*

father \FAH-thur\ *v.* fathered; fathering. To originate or beget.

father \FAH-thur\ *n.* **1.** One's male parent. **2.** A priest. fatherhood *n.*

fathom \FATH-um\ *n.* **1.** A measuring unit for water. **2.** Comprehension.

fathom \FATH-um\ *v.* fathomed; fathoming. **1.** To measure the depth of water. **2.** To understand.

fatigue \fuh-TEEG\ *n.* **1.** Exhaustion. **2.** Military uniform.

fatten \FAT-n\ *v.* fattened; fattening. To make fat.

faucet \FAW-sit\ *n.* A fixture to regulate water flow.

fault \fawlt\ *n.* **1.** A weakness. **2.** A mistake. **3.** At fault [Id]: responsible.

faux \foh\ *adj.* (Fr) Imitation.

faux pas \foh-PAH\ *n. pl.* faux pas. A blunder.

favor \FAY-vur\ *v.* favored; favoring. To show preference. favorable *adj.*; favorite *n.*; favoritism *n.*

favor \FAY-vur\ *n.* **1.** A help. **2.** Sexual privileges. **3.** Out of favor [Id]: unpopular.

favorite son *n.* A favored politician.

fawn *n.* A young deer.

fawn *v.* fawned; fawning. To show great affection.

fax \faks\ *n.* An electronic machine that sends reproductions. fax *v.*; facsimile *n.*

faze \fayz\ *v.* fazed; fazing. To disrupt composure.

fear \feer\ *n.* Dread. fearful *adj.*

fear \feer\ *v.* feared; fearing. To approach with dread.

feasible \FEE-zuh-bul\ *adj.* **1.** Possible. **2.** Suitable. feasibly *adv.*

feast \feest\ *n.* A banquet.

feat \feet\ *n.* **1.** An exploit. **2.** An act of courage.

feather \FETH-ur\ *n.* Bird coverings. feathered *adj.*

feather \FETH-ur\ *v.* feathered; feathering. To make in the shape of a feather.

featherweight \FETH-ur-wayt\ *n.* A weight class in boxing.

feature \FEE-chur\ *n.* **1.** A prominent part. **2.** A special attraction. **3.** Characteristic.

feature \FEE-chur\ *v.* featured; featuring. To give importance to. featured *adj.*

February \FEB-roo-er-ee\ *n.* The month after January and before March.

feces \FEE-seez\ *n. pl.* feces. Body waste.

fecund \FEE-kund\ *adj.* **1.** Fruitful. **2.** Fertile.

fed *n.* A federal agent.

fed *v.* Past tense of feed.

federal \FED-ur-ul\ *adj.* **1.** Concerning a distribution of power. **2.** Concerning the US government.

federalism \FED-ur-uh-liz-um\ *n.* A distribution of power between a central agency and its divisions.

federation \fed-uh-RAY-shun\ *n.* **1.** A union. **2.** A group of states.

fed up *adj.* Very tired.

fee *n.* Money paid for access.

feeble \FEE-bul\ *adj.* feebler; feeblest. **1.** Weak. **2.** Inadequate.

feed *v.* fed; feeding. **1.** To give food to. **2.** To support. **3.** To route.

feed *n.* Livestock food.

feedback \FEED-bak\ *n.* Corrective or evaluative information.

feel *v.* felt; feeling. **1.** To touch. **2.** To believe. feeling *n.*

feline \FEE-line\ *n.* A cat.

fell \fel\ *n.* A field or moor.

fell \fel\ *v.* Past tense of fall.

fellow \FEL-oh\ *n.* **1.** An associate. **2.** A student.

fellowship \FEL-oh-ship\ *n.* **1.** Company. **2.** An association.

felony \FEL-uh-nee\ *n. pl.* felonies. A serious crime. felon *n.*

female \FEE-mayl\ *n.* The gender that bears young.

feminine \FEM-uh-nin\ *adj.* Concerning women.

femur \FEE-mur\ *n. pl.* femurs or femora. (Md) The thigh bone.

fence \fens\ *v.* fenced; fencing. **1.** To enclose or protect. **2.** To sell stolen goods.

fence \fens\ *n.* **1.** A barrier or enclosing structure. **2.** [Sl] One who receives stolen goods.

fence-mending *n.* A restored relationship.

fennel \FEN-nul\ *n.* A perennial, edible herb.

feral \FER-ul\ *adj.* Wild.

ferment \FUR-ment\ *v.* fermented; fermenting. To change chemically with an organic substance.

ferocious \fuh-ROH-shus\ *adj.* Fierce. ferociousness *n.*

ferry \FER-ee\ *v.* ferried; ferrying. **1.** To transport. **2.** To convey across water.

fertile \FUR-tl\ *adj.* Productive.

fervent \FUR-vunt\ *adj.* Impassioned. fervor *n.*

festival \FES-tuh-vul\ *n.* A celebration. festive *adj.*

festoon \fuh-STOON\ *n.* A decorative chain.

fetal \FEET-l\ *adj.* Concerning a fetus.

fetal position *n.* Curled up position.

fête \fet or fayt\ *n.* A festival or outdoor entertainment.

fetid \FET-id\ *adj.* Having an offensive smell.

fetish *also* **fetich** \FET-ish\ *n.* **1.** An object endowed with magical power. **2.** A fixation. fetishism or fetichism *n.*

fettuccine *also* **fettucine or fettucinin.** \FET-uu-chee-nee\ *n.* Ribbon-like pasta.

fetus \FEE-tus\ *n.* An unborn child.

feud \fyood\ *n.* A lasting fight.

feudal \FYOOD-l\ *adj.* Of or relating to a economic, political, and social system of medieval Europe. feudalism *n.*

fever \FEE-vur\ *n.* **1.** A high temperature. **2.** A craze. feverish *adj.*

few \fyoo\ *pron.* Not many.

fiancé \fee-ahn-SAY\ *n.* (Fr) An engaged man.

fiancée \FEE-ahn-SAY\ *n.* (Fr) An engaged woman.

fiasco \fee-AS-koh\ *n. pl.* fiascos. A total failure.

fib *n.* A lie.

fiber *also* **fibre** \FIE-bur\ *n.* **1.** A slender thread. **2.** Roughage.

fiber optics *n. pl.* fiber optics. Thin glass strands used in telecommunications.

fickle \FIK-ul\ *adj.* Unstable and changing. fickleness *n.*

fiction \FIK-shun\ *n.* **1.** An invented story. **2.** An assumed fact. fictional *adj.*; fictitious *adj.*

fidelity \fi-DEL-i-tee\ *n. pl.* fidelities. Loyalty.

fidget \FIJ-it\ *n.* Restless movement.

fiduciary \fi-DOO-shee-er-ee\ *adj.* Held in trust.

fief \fyf\ *n.* An area in one's control, as in the feudal system. fiefdom *n.*

field \feeld\ *n.* **1.** An area of open land. **2.** Area of information. **3.** A profession. **4.** A surface.

fiend \feend\ *n.* Demon. fiendish *adj.*

fierce \feers\ *adj.* fiercer; fiercest Savage.

fiery \FIE-uh-ree\ *adj.* fierier; fieriest. **1.** Blazing. **2.** Irritable.

fiesta \fee-ES-tuh\ *n.* (Sp) Festival.

fight \fiet\ *n.* **1.** Combat. **2.** An argument.

fight \fiet\ *v.* fought; fighting. To do battle.

figment \FIG-munt\ *n.* Something that exists in the imagination.

figure \FIG-yur\ *n.* **1.** A number. **2.** A shape or being. **3.** A figure of speech. **4.** A famous person.

figure \FIG-yur\ *v.* figured; figuring. **1.** To calculate. **2.** To consider.

figurehead \FIG-yur-hed\ *n.* An ornamental figure.

file \fiel\ *n.* **1.** An instrument for smoothing surfaces. **2.** A collection of papers.

file \fiel\ *v.* filed; filing. **1.** To rub smooth. **2.** To arrange. **3.** To march.

filibuster \FIL-uh-bus-tur\ *n.* A long speech designed to delay action.

fill \fil\ *v.* filled; filling. **1.** To put in as much as possible. **2.** To satiate. **3.** To hold a place.

fillet *also* **filet** \FIL-it or FIL-ay\ *n.* A thin strip of material.

fillet \FIL-it or FIL-ay\ *v.* filleted; filleting. To cut into strips.

film *n.* **1.** A thin covering. **2.** A radiation-sensitive sheet. **3.** A movie.

filmscript *n.* An explanatory, directional piece of writing.

filmstrip \FILM-strip\ *n.* A series of pictures on film.

filter \FIL-tur\ *n.* **1.** A device for sifting out particles. **2.** A screen for absorbing something. filter *v.*

filth *n.* **1.** Dirt. **2.** Moral corruption. filthy *adj.*

finagle \fi-NAY-gul\ *v.* finagled; finagling. To swindle or manipulate.

final \FIEN-l\ *adj.* **1.** Last. **2.** Conclusive. finale *n.*; finally *adv.*; finalize *v.*

finance \fi-NANS or fie-NANS\ *n.* The management and study of money. financial *adj.*

find \fiend\ *v.* found; finding. **1.** To come upon by accident. **2.** To experience. finding *n.*

find out *v.* found out; finding out. To discover.

fine \fien\ *adj.* finer; finest. **1.** Of a very thin texture. **2.** Superior. **3.** All right.

fine \fien\ *n.* **1.** A financial penalty. **2.** An end [Mu].

finesse \fi-NES\ *n.* **1.** Delicate craftsmanship. **2.** Skillful handling.

fine-tune *v.* fine-tuned; fine-tuning. To adjust to perfection.

finger \FING-gur\ *n.* A digit.

finger \FING-gur\ *v.* fingered; fingering. **1.** To touch or play with fingers. **2.** To identify.

finish \FIN-ish\ *v.* finished; finishing. **1.** To end. **2.** To put a final coat on.

finish \FIN-ish\ *n.* The final stage or ending.

finite \FIE-nite\ *adj.* Possessing a definable limit.

fiord *also* **fjord** \fyord\ *n.* A narrow sea inlet.

fir \fur\ *n.* A pinetree.

fire \fier\ *n.* **1.** Combustion or burning. **2.** Ardor. **3.** Brilliancy.

fire \fier\ *v.* fired; firing. **1.** To ignite. **2.** To release or discharge. **3.** [Cl] To dismiss from a job. **4.** To begin.

fireplace \FIER-plays\ *n.* A fire-containing area.

fireproof \FIER-proof\ *adj.* Resistant to fire.

fireworks \FIRE-wuurks\ *n.* Combustible materials producing a brilliant display.

firm \furm\ *adj.* **1.** Steadfast. **2.** Secure and stable.

firm \furm\ *n.* A company.

firmament \FUR-muh-munt\ *n.* The vault of the heavens.

first \furst\ *adj.* Earliest.

first \furst\ *n.* The beginning one.

first-class \FURST-KLAS\ *adj.* Best in quality.

First World *n.* Industrialized nations.

fiscal \FIS-kul\ *adj.* Concerning finances. fiscally *adv.*

fish *n. pl.* fish or fishes. A cold-blooded vertebrate animal living in water.

fish *v.* fished; fishing. **1.** To catch fish. **2.** To seek in a roundabout way.

fishery \FISH-uh-ree\ *n. pl.* fisheries. An area where fish are raised and fishing is done.

fission \FISH-un\ *n.* Splitting of an atom's nucleus.

fissure \FISH-ur\ *n.* A crack.

fit *adj.* fitter; fittest. **1.** Adapted. **2.** Healthy. **3.** Suitable.

fit *n.* **1.** A sudden attack. **2.** An explanation of closeness.

fit *v.* fitted or fit; fitting. **1.** To conform. **2.** To accommodate. **3.** To supply. **4.** To adjust or match up.

fitness \FIT-nis\ *n.* **1.** The ability to survive. **2.** The physical condition of the body.

fix \fiks\ *n.* **1.** A predicament. **2.** A dose or shot.

fix \fiks\ *v.* fixed; fixing. **1.** To make fast. **2.** To repair. fixed *adj.*

fixate \FIKS-ayt\ *v.* fixated; fixating. To focus one's gaze on. fixated *adj.*

fixture \FIKS-chur\ *n.* A permanent attachment.

fizz \fiz\ *n.* A hissing sound. fizzy *adj.*

flab *n.* Soft body tissue.

flabbergast \FLAB-ur-gast\ *v.* flabbergasted; flabbergasting. To surprise.

flaccid \FLAK-sid\ *adj.* Hanging loose or wrinkled.

flack *also* **flak** \flak\ *n.* **1.** Criticism. **2.** Back talk.

flag *n.* A fabric symbol or sign.

flag *v.* flagged; flagging. **1.** To signal. **2.** To penalize.

flagellant \FLAJ-uh-lunt\ *n.* One who beats himself. flagellate *v.*

flagrant \FLAY-grunt\ *adj.* Deliberate.

flail \flayl\ *v.* flailed; flailing. To strike out widely.

flair *n.* A talent for doing something.

flake \flayk\ *n.* **1.** A small piece. **2.** [Sl] A strange person.

flambé \flahm-BAY\ *adj.* (Fr) Covered with flaming liquor.

flamboyant \flam-BOI-unt\ *adj.* Marked by colorful display or behavior.

flame \flaym\ *n.* **1.** A blaze of a fire. **2.** [Sl] A love.

flamenco \flah-MENG-koh\ *n. pl.* flamencos. (Sp) A gypsy singing and dancing style.

flap *n.* **1.** A cover. **2.** Wing motion. **3.** A hinged piece. **4.** An uproar.

flap *v.* flapped; flapping. **1.** To move loosely. **2.** To beat as if with wings.

flare \flair\ *n.* **1.** A signal. **2.** A sudden outburst.

flare \flair\ *v.* flared; flaring. **1.** To burn brightly and quickly. **2.** To become angry.

flash *n.* **1.** A sudden light burst. **2.** A quick look.

flash *v.* flashed; flashing. **1.** To suddenly appear. **2.** To sparkle.

flashback \FLASH-bak\ *n.* A past event examined in the present.

flask *n.* A small container.

flat *adj.* flatter; flattest. **1.** Having a smooth surface. **2.** Existing horizontally. **3.** Deflated. flatten *v.*

flatiron *n.* An iron.

flatter \FLAT-ur\ *v.* flattered; flattering. To give excessive praise.

flatulence \FLACH-uh-luns\ *n.* Intestinal gas.

flaunt \flawnt\ *v.* flaunted; flaunting. To show off.

flavor \FLAY-vur\ *n.* **1.** Taste. **2.**

Variety. flavored *adj.*; flavorful *adj.*

flaw *n.* An imperfection. flawed *adj.*

flea \flee\ *n.* A tiny bloodsucking insect.

fledgling \FLEJ-ling\ *n.* **1.** A young bird. **2.** An inexperienced person.

flee *v.* fled; fleeing. To run from.

fleet *adj.* Swift.

fleet *n.* A group of ships or planes.

flesh *n.* **1.** Skin. **2.** Human nature. **3.** In the flesh [Id]: in person.

flex \fleks\ *v.* flexed; flexing. To bend.

flexible \FLEK-suh-bul\ *adj.* **1.** Elastic and bendable. **2.** Adaptable. flexibility *n.*

flick \flik\ *n.* A movie.

flick \flik\ *v.* flicked; flicking. **1.** To turn on or off. **2.** To strike lightly.

flicker \FLIK-ur\ *v.* flickered; flickering. To burn unsteadily.

flight \fliet\ *n.* **1.** Passing through the air. **2.** Traveling via aircraft. **3.** A set of stairs.

flight attendant *n.* One who works for an airline.

flimsy \FLIM-zee\ *adj.* flimsier; flimsiest. **1.** Weak. **2.** Unstable. **3.** Unsound.

fling *n.* A brief romantic involvement.

fling *v.* flung; flinging. To cast away.

flip *n.* A somersault in the air.

flip *v.* flipped; flipping. To toss in the air.

flip-flop *n.* **1.** A sudden move to the other side. **2.** A plastic or rubber sandal. flip-flop *v.*

flip out *v.* flipped out; flipping out. To go crazy.

flippant \FLIP-punt\ *adj.* Lacking proper respect.

flip side *n.* The back or opposite side.

flirt \flurt\ *v.* flirted; flirting. To trifle with. flirtation *n.*; flirtatious *adj.*

float \floht\ *n.* **1.** Device for laying on water. **2.** A tool. **3.** A parade unit. **4.** Government grant.

float \floht\ *v.* floated; floating. **1.** To rest on a fluid's surface. **2.** To give money to.

flock \flok\ *n.* A group of birds or people.

flock \flok\ *v.* flocked; flocking. To gather and move together.

flood \flud\ *n.* A liquid overflow.

flood \flud\ *v.* flooded; flooding. To inundate with liquid.

floor \flor\ *n.* **1.** A room's base. **2.** The ocean surface. **3.** A building's levels.

floor \flor\ *v.* floored; flooring. To dumbfound.

flop *v.* flopped; flopping. **1.** To hang or fall heavily or loosely. **2.** To fail.

floppy disk \FLOP-ee-DISK\ *n.* (Cm) A disk for storing computer data.

flora \FLOR-uh\ *n. pl.* floras. also florae An area's plants.

floret \FLOR-ay\ *n.* **1.** A cluster of buds. **2.** A small flower.

florid \FLOR-id\ *adj.* **1.** Very ornate. **2.** Fully developed.

flounder \FLOWN-dur\ *n. pl.* flounder or flounders. A fish.

flounder \FLOWN-dur\ *v.* floundered; floundering. To struggle ineffectually.

flour \flowr\ *n.* Finely ground grain.

flourish \FLUR-ish\ *n.* **1.** A fanfare. **2.** Sudden activity.

flourish \FLUR-ish\ *v.* flourished; flourishing. **1.** To thrive. **2.** To brandish.

flow \floh\ *n.* **1.** A stream. **2.** Movement.

flow \floh\ *v.* flowed; flowing. **1.** To move. **2.** To abound.

flower \FLOW-ur\ *n.* A blossom.

flower \FLOW-ur\ *v.* flowered; flowering. To flourish.

flower child *n.* A hippie.

flu \floo\ *n.* Influenza.

fluctuate \FLUK-choo-ayt\ *v.* fluctuated; fluctuating. To swing back and forth between extremes.

fluent \FLOO-unt\ *adj.* Speaking or spoken easily.

fluid \FLOO-id\ *n.* A substance that flows.

fluke \flook\ *n.* **1.** A fish. **2.** Anchor part. **3.** Part of a whale's tail. **4.** Instance of good luck.

fluorescent \fluu-RES-unt\ *adj.* Concerning a time of flower growth.

flurry \FLUR-ee\ *n. pl.* flurries. **1.** A sudden snowfall. **2.** Commotion.

flush *n.* **1.** A card hand. **2.** Sudden rush of water. **3.** Emotional surge. **4.** Sudden reddening

flush *v.* flushed; flushing. **1.** To blush. **2.** To wash out.

fluster \FLUS-tur\ *v.* flustered; flustering. To agitate.

flute \floot\ *n.* **1.** A wind instrument. **2.** A grooved pattern.

fly \flie\ *n.* **1.** An insect. **2.** A fishhook.

fly \flie\ *v.* flew; flying; flown. **1.** To pass through the air. **2.** To move swiftly.

foal \fohl\ *n.* A young horse.

foam \fohm\ *v.* foamed; foaming. **1.** To produce froth. **2.** To become angry.

foam \fohm\ *n.* **1.** Froth. **2.** Lightweight cellular material.

focal \FOH-kus\ *adj.* Of or at a convergence point. focus *n.*

foe \foh\ *n.* An enemy.

fog *n.* Condensed vapor or thick mist.

fog *v.* fogged; fogging. To obscure.

foible \FOI-bul\ *n.* Fault.

foil \foyl\ *n.* **1.** Very thin metal. **2.** Saber.

fold \fohld\ *n.* **1.** A pleat or folded part. **2.** An enclosure for sheep. **3.** A group of people.

fold \fohld\ *v.* folded; folding. **1.** To bend or overlap. **2.** To collapse.

foliage \FOH-lee-ij\ *n.* Leaves.

folk \fohk\ *adj.* Concerning common or rural people.

folk \fohk\ *n. pl.* folk or folks. A group of like or related people.

folklore \FOHK-lor\ *n.* Traditional cultural stories and dances.

follicle \FOL-i-kul\ *n.* A small cavity with hairlike root.

follow \FOL-oh\ *v.* followed; following. **1.** To pursue. **2.** To imitate. following *n.*; follower *n.*

follow-through \FOL-oh-throo\ *n.* To continue.

follow up \FOL-oh-up\ *v.* followed up; following up. To maintain contact.

folly \FOL-ee\ *n. pl.* follies. Foolish behavior.

foment \foh-MENT\ *v.* fomented; fomenting. To start trouble.

fond *adj.* **1.** Liking. **2.** Silly.

fondle \FON-dl\ *v.* fondled; fondling. To caress.

fondue *also* **fondu** \fon-DOO\ *n.* Food dipped in hot liquid, as cheese.

food *n.* Substances that sustain life.

food processor *n.* An electric food chopper.

food stamp *n.* Government coupon used to buy food.

fool *n.* One lacking good judgement. foolish *adj.*

fool *v.* fooled; fooling. To deceive.

foot \fuut\ *n. pl.* feet. **1.** The appendage at the end of a leg. **2.** A unit of length measurement.

footage \FUUT-ij\ *n.* Length expressed in feet.

football \FUUT-bawl\ *n.* An outdoor ball game played by two teams.

footloose \FUUT-loos\ *adj.* Carefree.

footnote \FUUT-noht\ *n.* A reference or commentary placed at the page's bottom.

fop *n.* A vain man.

for *prep.* **1.** In place of. **2.** Concerning. **3.** After.

forage \FOR-ij\ *v.* foraged; foraging. **1.** To raid. **2.** To rummage.

foray \FOR-ay\ *v.* forayed; foraying. To go searching or rummaging.

forbear *also* **forebear** \for-BAIR\ *v.* forbore; forborne; forbearing. **1.** To refrain. **2.** To be patient.

forbid \fur-BID\ *v.* forbade also forbad; forbidden; forbidding. To prohibit.

force \fors\ *n.* **1.** Physical power. **2.** Mental strength.

force \fors\ *v.* forced; forcing. **1.** To rape. **2.** To coerce. forced *adj.*

forceps \FOR-seps\ *n. pl.* forceps. A grasping tong-like instrument.

forearm \FOR-ahrm\ *n.* The arm between wrist and elbow.

forecast \FOR-kast\ *n.* A prediction.

forecast \FOR-kast\ *v.* forecast also forecasted; forecasting. To foretell.

foreclose \for-KLOHZ\ *v.* foreclosed; foreclosing. To take possession of property when a loan is not repaid.

foreign \FOR-in\ *adj.* **1.** Concerning a country that is not one's own. **2.** Not belonging naturally. foreigner *n.*

forensic \fuh-REN-sik\ *adj.* **1.** Argumentative. **2.** Concerning science applied to the law.

foresee \for-SEE\ *v.* foresaw; foreseen. To be aware of beforehand.

foreshadow \for-SHAD-oh\ *v.* foreshadowed; foreshadowing. To indicate beforehand.

foresight \FOR-site\ *n.* Ability to foresee and prepare for the future.

forest \FOR-ist\ *n.* Dense wooded land. forestry *n.*

foretell \for-TEL\ *v.* foretold; foretelling. To predict.

forever \for-EV-ur\ *adv.* **1.** Without end. **2.** Continually.

forfeit \FOR-fit\ *n.* forfeited; forfeiting. To lose or give up.

forge \forj\ *n.* A metalworking shop.

forge \forj\ *v.* forged; forging. **1.** To form. **2.** To counterfeit. **3.** To move.

forget \fur-GET\ *v.* forget; forgotten; forgetting. **1.** To lose memory of. **2.** To neglect.

forgive \fur-GIV\ *v.* forgave; forgiven; forgiving. **1.** To excuse. **2.** To pardon.

fork *n.* **1.** A pronged eating instrument. **2.** A division into two or more branches.

form *n.* **1.** A shape. **2.** A frame. **3.** A document with blank spaces requiring information.

form *v.* formed; forming. **1.** To arrange. **2.** To shape. **3.** To develop.

formal \FOR-mul\ *adj.* **1.** Concerning or conforming to rules or custom. **2.** Methodical.

formal \FOR-mul\ *n.* **1.** A dance. **2.** Formal wear.

formaldehyde \for-MAL-duh-hide\ *n.* (Sc) Gas used as a preservative.

format \FOR-mat\ *n.* General organizational arrangement.

format \FOR-mat\ *v.* formatted; formatting. To arrange in a pattern or style.

formation \for-MAY-shun\ *n.* **1.** Development. **2.** Structure.

formidable \FOR-mi-duh-bul\ *adj.* Inspiring fear or wonder.

formula \FOR-myuh-luh\ *n. pl.* formulas or formulae. **1.** A symbolic representation. **2.** A recipe. **3.** Special milk for babies.

forsake \for-SAYK\ *v.* forsook; forsaken; forsaking. To abandon.

fort *n.* An enclosed area used for defense.

forte \FOR-tay\ *n.* (Fr) One's strong point.

forth *adv.* Forward.

fortify \FOR-tuh-fie\ *v.* fortified; fortifying. **1.** To strengthen. **2.** To encourage.

fortunate \FOR-chuh-nit\ *adj.* Lucky. fortunately *adv.*

fortune \FOR-chun\ *n.* **1.** Money. **2.** Luck.

fortune-teller \FOR-chun-tel-ur\ *n.* A predictor.

forum \FOR-um\ *n. pl.* forums or fora. **1.** A public meeting place. **2.** A public discussion.

forward \FOR-wurd\ *adj.* **1.** Near the front. **2.** Brash. **3.** Extreme.

fossil \FOS-ul\ *n.* Preserved remains of an animal or plant from past ages.

foul \fowl\ *adj.* **1.** Dirty. **2.** Obscene. **3.** Dishonorable. **4.** Stinking.

foul \fowl\ *n.* A move that breaks a rule, esp. in sports.

foul \fowl\ *v.* fouled; fouling. **1.** To rot. **2.** To pollute. **3.** To violate.

found \fownd\ *v.* Past tense of find.

foundation \fown-DAY-shun\ *n.* **1.** A support. **2.** A basis. **3.** An organization.

foundry \FOWN-dree\ *n. pl.* foundries. A metal-working place.

fountain \FOWN-tn\ *n.* **1.** A source. **2.** A water jet.

four \for\ *n.* One greater than three.

foursome \FOR-sum\ *n.* A group of four.

fourth \forth\ *n. pl.* fourths. **1.** The next after the third. **2.** A quarter of a whole. **3.** [Mu] An interval.

Fourth World *n.* A group of nations with very low per capita income.

fowl *n. pl.* fowl also fowls. A game bird.

fox \foks\ *n. pl.* foxes also fox. **1.** A small wild mammal of the dog family. **2.** [Sl] An attractive woman.

foxy \FOK-see\ *adj.* foxier; foxiest **1.** Cunning. **2.** Attractive.

foyer \FOI-ur\ *n.* (Fr) An entrance-way.

fraction \FRAK-shun\ *n.* **1.** A fragment. **2.** A mathematical unit that is not a whole number.

fracture \FRAK-chur\ *v.* fractured; fracturing. To break.

fragile \FRAJ-ul\ *adj.* Delicate.

fragment \FRAG-munt\ *n.* A portion. fragment *v.*; fragmentation *n.*

fragrant \FRAY-grunt\ *adj.* Having a pleasant smell. fragrance *n.*

frail \frayl\ *adj.* **1.** Slight. **2.** Weak.

frame \fraym\ *n.* **1.** Rigid structure. **2.** A plan. **3.** Physique. **4.** Single film exposure or picture.

frame \fraym\ *v.* framed; framing. **1.** To construct. **2.** To enclose. **3.** To set up.

franchise \FRAN-chize\ *n.* **1.** Special privilege. **2.** Authorization to have a business branch.

Francophile *also* **Francophil** \FRANK-koh-file\ *adj.* Concerning the French culture.

frankfurter *also* **frankfurt** \FRANK-fur-tur\ *n.* A hot dog.

frantic \FRAN-tik\ *adj.* Highly anxious.

frappé \FRAP-pay\ *adj.* (Fr) Almost frozen.

fraternal \fruh-TUR-nl\ *adj.* **1.** Brotherly. **2.** Concerning twins.

fraternity \fruh-TUR-ni-tee\ *n. pl.* fraternities. **1.** A university social organization. **2.** Brotherhood. fraternize *v.*

fraud \frawd\ *n.* Criminal deception.

fray *n.* **1.** A struggle. **2.** An unraveled thing.

frazzle \FRAZ-ul\ *v.* frazzled; frazzling. To upset.

freak \freek\ *n.* Something or someone odd.

freak out *v.* freaked out; freaking out. To make or go crazy. freakout *n.*

freckle \FREK-ul\ *n.* A small brownish spot on the skin.

free *adj.* freer; freest. **1.** Without constraint. **2.** Able to move. **3.** Outspoken. **4.** Separate, independent.

free *v.* freed; freeing. To release.

free agent *n.* A professional not bound by a contract.

freedom \FREE-dum\ *n.* Independence.

freestyle \FREE-stile\ *n.* A competition with few required moves.

freeze \freez\ *v.* froze; frozen; freezing. **1.** To solidify from coldness. **2.** To stop motion.

freight \frayt\ *n.* **1.** Cargo. **2.** Payment for transport.

French fry *n.* Potato strip or chunk fried in fat.

frenzy \FREN-zee\ *n. pl.* frenzies. Violent agitation or excitement. frenzied *adj.*; frenetic *adj.*

frequency \FREE-kwun-see\ *n. pl.* frequencies. **1.** Number of times something happens, appears. **2.** Measure of alternating current

frequent \FREE-kwunt\ *adj.* **1.** Happening or appearing often. **2.** Persistent.

frequent \FREE-kwunt\ *v.* frequented; frequenting. To go to often.

fresco \FRES-koh\ *n. pl.* frescos. (It) Painting style.

fresh *adj.* **1.** Pure. **2.** Original. **3.** Impudent. **4.** Clean. **5.** New. freshen *v.*

fret *v.* fretted; fretting. **1.** To fray. **2.** To worry or agitate. **3.** To emboss.

Freudian \FROI-dee-un\ *adj.* Concerning Freud's theories.

friar \FRIE-ur\ *n.* A member of a religious order.

friction \FRIK-shun\ *n.* **1.** Opposing force. **2.** Disagreement.

Friday \FRIE-day\ *n.* The day after Thursday and before Saturday.

friend \frend\ *n.* One of a pair that feels mutual affection. friendly *adj.*; friendship *n.*

frieze \freez\ *n.* **1.** Coarse wool. **2.** A band of sculpture.

frigate \FRIG-ut\ *n.* A small ship.

fright \frite\ *n.* Fear. frighten *v.*

frigid \FRIJ-id\ *adj.* **1.** Extremely cold. **2.** Lacking sexual warmth.

frill \fril\ *n.* **1.** A garment edging. **2.** A luxury.

fringe \frinj\ *n.* **1.** An ornamental edge. **2.** The periphery.

frisk *v.* frisked; frisking. **1.** To dance or play. **2.** To search.

frivolous \FRIV-uh-lus\ *adj.* Lacking credibility or importance.

frock \frok\ *n.* An outer garment.

frog *n.* A small amphibian with long legs.

frolic \FROL-ik\ *v.* frolicked; frolicking. To romp and play.

from \frum\ *prep.* **1.** Indicates the source. **2.** Indicates removal.

front \frunt\ *n.* **1.** Area prior. **2.** Area between air masses. **3.** Area of action. **4.** Appearance. frontal *adj.*

frontier \frun-TEER\ *n.* **1.** An unexplored wild land area. **2.** The limit of knowledge about a subject.

frontispiece \FRUN-tis-pees\ *n.* **1.** A decorative cover. **2.** An illustration prior to text.

frost \frawst\ *n.* **1.** Small ice crystals. **2.** Cold manner.

frost \frawst\ *v.* frosted; frosting. **1.** To cover or coat. **2.** To make angry.

frostbite \FRAWST-bite\ *n.* The partial or total freezing of a body part.

frostbite \FRAWST-bite\ *v.* frostbit; frostbitten; frostbiting. To be injured by freezing.

frothy \FRAWTH-ee\ *adj.* frothier; frothiest. Foamy.

frown *n.* An expression of displeasure.

frozen \FROH-zun\ *adj.* **1.** Solid due to cold. **2.** Fixed.

frozen \FROH-zun\ *v.* Past tense of freeze.

fruit \froot\ *n.* **1.** Edible product of plant growth. **2.** Offspring. **3.** Result.

fruitful \FROOT-ful\ *adj.* Abundant.

frustrate \FRUS-trayt\ *v.* frustrated; frustrating. **1.** To obstruct. **2.** To thwart. frustration *n.*

fry \frie\ *v.* fried; frying. To cook in heated fat.

fuchsia \FYOO-shuh\ *n.* A reddish purple color.

fudge \fuj\ *n.* A soft rich chocolate candy.

fudge \fuj\ *v.* fudged; fudging. To falsify.

fuel \FYOO-ul\ *n.* **1.** Combustable material. **2.** Reinforcement.

fuel \FYOO-ul\ *v.* fueled or fuelled; fueling or fuelling. **1.** To stimulate. **2.** To put fuel in a machine.

fugitive \FYOO-ji-tiv\ *n.* One trying to escape the law.

fulfill *also* **fulfil** \fuul-FIL\ *v.* fulfilled; fulfilling. **1.** To perform. **2.** To satisfy.

full \fuul\ *adj.* **1.** Complete. **2.** Containing as much as possible.

full-scale \FUUL-SKAYL\ *adj.* **1.** Complete. **2.** All-out.

fumble \FUM-bul\ *v.* fumbled; fumbling. **1.** To blunder. **2.** To drop, as a ball.

fume \fyoom\ *n.* Irritating gas or vapor.

fume \fyoom\ *v.* fumed; fuming. To rant and rave.

fun *adj.* sometimes funner; sometimes funnest. Enjoyable.

fun *n.* **1.** Play. **2.** Sport.

function \FUNGK-shun\ *v.* functioned; functioning. To work or be in action.

function \FUNGK-shun\ *n.* **1.** A special activity or purpose. **2.** A mathematical relationship. functional *adj.*

fund *n.* A monetary source.

fund *v.* funded; funding. To provide money to.

fundamental \fun-duh-MEN-tl\ *adj.* **1.** Primary and basic. **2.** Deep- rooted.

funeral \FYOO-nur-ul\ *n.* Burial ceremony. funereal *adj.*

fungus \FUNG-gus\ *n. pl.* fungi or funguses (Sc) Spore-producing organisms.

funicular \fyoo-NIK-yuh-lur\ *n.* A cable-car going up a mountain.

funk \fungk\ *n.* Depression.

funnel \FUN-l\ *n.* A tube that narrows at one end.

funny \FUN-ee\ *adj.* funnier; funniest **1.** Amusing. **2.** Peculiar.

funny farm *n.* A psychiatric hospital.

fur *n.* Animal hair or pelt. furry *adj.*

furious \FYUUR-ee-us\ *adj.* Extremely angry. furiously *adv.*

furlough \FUR-loh\ *n.* A leave of absence.

furnish \FUR-nish\ *v.* furnished; furnishing. To equip.

furniture \FUR-ni-chur\ *n.* Household or room objects.

furor \FYUUR-or\ *n.* **1.** Rage. **2.** An uproar.

furrier \FUR-ee-ur\ *n.* One who deals with or sells animal pelts.

further \FUR-thur\ *adv.* **1.** To a greater degree. **2.** Moreover.

fury \FYUUR-ee\ *n. pl.* furies. **1.** A mythical avenging spirit. **2.** A frenzy.

fuse \fyooz\ *n.* An electrical device.

fuse \fyooz\ *v.* fused; fusing. To join together.

fuselage \FYOO-suh-lahzh\ *n.* An airplane's main section.

fusion \FYOO-zhun\ *n.* **1.** [Sc] The union of atomic nuclei. **2.** Merging of separate elements or groups.

fuss \fus\ *n.* **1.** A commotion. **2.** A protest. fussy *adj.*

fuss \fus\ *v.* fussed; fussing. **1.** To go to much trouble. **2.** To complain.

futile \FYOOT-l\ *adj.* Without purpose. futility *n.*

future \FYOO-chur\ *n.* Time yet to come. futuristic *adj.*

future shock *n.* Stress from change.

fuzz \fuz\ *n.* **1.** Fluff. **2.** [Sl] Police officer.

fuzzy \FUZ-ee\ *adj.* fuzzier; fuzziest **1.** Furry. **2.** Blurry or unclear. fuzziness *n.*

G

g \jee\ ***n. pl.*** g's or gs. The seventh letter of the English alphabet.

gab *v.* gabbed; gabbing. To talk.

gabardine \GAB-ur-deen\ ***n.*** Strong twilled fabric.

gable \GAY-bul\ ***n.*** A triangular portion of a structure.

gadget \GAJ-it\ *n.* A small mechanical device. gadgetry *n.*

gag *n.* **1.** A mouth cover. **2.** A trick.

gag *v.* gagged; gagging. **1.** To restrict speech. **2.** To retch.

gag-order *n.* An order not to give out information.

gain \gayn\ ***n.*** **1.** Profit. **2.** An increase. **3.** Gain ground [Id]: to make progress.

gain \gayn\ *v.* gained; gaining. **1.** To add to. **2.** To attain or acquire. **3.** To catch up with.

gait \gayt\ *n.* A manner of walking.

gala \GAY-luh\ *n.* A festival or ball.

galaxy \GAL-uk-see\ *n. pl.* galaxies. (Sc) A system of stars. galactic *adj.*

gale \gayl\ *n.* **1.** A very strong wind. **2.** An emotional outburst.

gall \gawl\ *n.* **1.** Bile. **2.** Impudence.

gallant \GAL-unt\ *adj.* **1.** Brave. **2.** Chivalrous or courteous. gallantry *n.*

gallbladder \GAWL-blad-ur\ ***n.*** (Md) Sac in which bile is stored.

galleon \GAL-ee-un\ *n.* An old Spanish war ship.

gallery \GAL-uh-ree\ *n. pl.* galleries. **1.** A balcony. **2.** An art display place.

gallivant \GAL-uh-vant\ *v.* gallivanted; gallivanting. To travel for pleasure.

gallop \GAL-up\ *n.* A rapid gait.

galore \guh-LOR\ *adj.* Many.

galoshes \guh-LOSH-uz\ *n. pl.* galoshes. Protective shoe coverings.

galvanize \GAL-vuh-nize\ *v.* galvanized; galvanizing. **1.** To stimulate or shock. **2.** To coat with zinc.

gamble \GAM-bul\ *v.* gambled; gambling. To risk money.

game \gaym\ *adj.* Brave and willing.

game \gaym\ *n.* **1.** A fun activity. **2.** A sport or recreation **3.** A tactic. **4.** Animals.

game plan *n.* A strategy.

gamma ray \GAM-uh-RAY\ *n.* (Sc) A photon from a radioactive substance.

gamut \GAM-ut\ *n.* The entire range.

gangrene \GANG-green\ *n.* (Md) Tissue death.

gangster \GANG-stur\ *n.* A criminal in a gang.

gap *n.* **1.** An opening. **2.** Hiatus. gaping *adj.*

gape \gayp\ *v.* gaped; gaping. **1.** To open wide. **2.** To stare in wonder.

garage \guh-RAHZH\ *n.* A building to house or repair cars.

garbage \GAHR-bij\ *n.* Trash.

garbanzo \gahr-BAHN-zoh\ *n.* Chick pea.

garden \GAHR-dn\ *n.* A place for plants to grow. gardener *n.*

garden \GAHR-dn\ *v.* gardened; gardening. To cultivate plants.

gardenia \gahr-DEE-nyuh\ *n.* A fragrant white or yellow flower.

gargantuan \gahr-GAN-choo-un\ *adj.* Colossal.

gargle \GAHR-gul\ *v.* gargled; gargling. To force air through a liquid held in one's throat.

gargoyle \GAHR-goil\ *n.* A grotesque animal or human statue.

garish \GAIR-ish\ *adj.* Flashy.

garland \GAHR-lund\ *n.* Wreath.

garlic \GAHR-lik\ *n.* A cultivated edible herb.

garment \GAHR-munt\ *n.* Clothing.

garnish \GAHR-nish\ *n.* An embellishment.

garnish \GAHR-nish\ *v.* garnished; garnishing. To adorn.

gas *n. pl.* gases also gasses. **1.** A fluid with neither shape nor volume. **2.** Gasoline. gaseous *adj.*; gassy *adj.*

gas-guzzler *n.* A large car that gets poor mileage.

gash *n.* A long deep cut.

gasket \GAS-kit\ *n.* A seal or ring of rubber.

gasohol \GAS-uh-hawl\ *n.* (Sc) A fuel blend of gasoline and alcohol.

gasp *v.* gasped; gasping. A sharp intake of breath.

gastrointestinal \gas-troh-in-TES-tuh-nl\ *adj.* (Md) Concerning the stomach and intestines.

gastronomic *also* **gastronomical** \gas-truh-NOM-ik\ *adj.* Concerning good eating.

gate \gayt\ *n.* A fence or wall opening.

gather \GATH-ur\ *v.* gathered; gathering. **1.** To collect. **2.** To harvest. **3.** To assemble. gathering *n.*

gauche \gohsh\ *adj.* sometimes gaucher; sometimes gauchest. **1.** Awkward. **2.** Crude.

gaudy \GAW-dee\ *adj.* gaudier; gaudiest. **1.** Flashy. **2.** Tawdry.

gauge \gayj\ *n.* **1.** A measuring device. **2.** A standard.

gauge \gayj\ *v.* gauged; gauging. To estimate.

gaunt \gawnt\ *adj.* Lean.

gauze \gawz\ *n.* Thin fabric for wrapping or covering.

gawk *v.* gawked; gawking. To stare at.

gay *adj.* **1.** Happy. **2.** Lively. **3.** Concerning homosexual activity.

gaze \gayz\ *v.* gazed; gazing. To look at steadily.

gazebo \guh-ZAY-boh\ *n. pl.* gazebos also gazeboes. An outside open, roofed structure.

gazelle \guh-ZEL\ *n. pl.* gazelles also gazelle. A small antelope.

gazette \guh-ZET\ *n.* A newspaper.

gazpacho \gaz-PACH-oh\ *n. pl.* gazpachos. (Sp) Cold vegetable soup.

gear \geer\ *n.* **1.** Clothing. **2.** Equipment. **3.** A set of toothed wheels in a machine.

geese \gees\ *n.* Plural of goose.

Geiger counter \GIE-gur\ *n.* A radiation detector.

geisha \GAY-shuh\ *n. pl.* geisha or geishas. A Japanese female entertainer.

gelatin *also* **gelatine** \JEL-uh-tn\ *n.* A binding substance. gelatinous *adj.*

geld *v.* gelded; gelding. To castrate.

gem \jem\ *n.* **1.** A jewel. **2.** Something precious.

gender \JEN-dur\ *n.* One's sex.

gene \jeen\ *n.* (Md) A factor controlling heredity. genetic also genetical *adj.*; geneticist *n.*

genealogy \jee-nee-AL-uh-jee\ *n. pl.* genealogies. List of ancestors.

gene pool *n.* A collection of genes.

general \JEN-ur-ul\ *adj.* **1.** Concerning a whole. **2.** Not specific.

general \JEN-ur-ul\ *n.* An army officer or commander.

generalize \JEN-ur-uh-lize\ *v.* generalized; generalizing. To draw a general conclusion. generalized *adj.*; generally *n.*

generate \JEN-uh-rayt\ *v.* generated; generating. To produce.

generation \jen-uh-RAY-shun\ *n.* **1.** People of about the same age. **2.** Production.

generation gap *n.* The cultural differences between age groups.

generator \JEN-uh-ray-tur\ *n.* A machine that generates energy.

generic \juh-NER-ik\ *adj.* Concerning the whole.

generous \JEN-ur-us\ *adj.* Liberal. generosity *n.*

genesis \JEN-uh-sis\ *n. pl.* geneses. The beginning.

gene-splicing *n.* (Sc) Technique that produces recombinant DNA.

genetic engineering \juh-NET-ik\ *n.* (Sc) Manipulation of genetic material.

genial \JEEN-yul\ *adj.* Gracious. geniality *n.*

genie \JEE-nee\ *n. pl.* genies also genii. A magic spirit.

genitalia *also* **genitals** \jen-i-TAY-lee-uh\ *pl. n.* External reproductive organs.

genius \JEEN-yus\ *n. pl.* geniuses or genii. A very smart person.

genocide \JEN-uh-side\ *n.* The destruction of an entire group.

genre \ZHAHN-ruh\ *n.* A kind of art or literature.

genteel \jen-TEEL\ *adj.* **1.** Polite. **2.** Elegant. **3.** Polite.

gentile \JEN-tile\ *n.* A non-Jewish person.

gentle \JEN-tl\ *adj.* gentler; gentlest. **1.** Kind. **2.** Mild and moderate. **3.** Delicate.

gentrify \JEN-tri-fie\ *v.* gentrified; gentrifying. To renew an old neighborhood by the entry of middle-class people. gentrification *n.*

genuflect \JEN-yuu-flekt\ *v.* genuflected; genuflecting. To bend at the knee.

genuine \JEN-yoo-in\ *adj.* **1.** Authentic. **2.** Sincere. genuinely *adv.*

genus \JEE-nus\ *n. pl.* genera or genuses. **1.** A category. **2.** Common kind.

geography \jee-OG-ruh-fee\ *n. pl.* geographies. (Sc) **1.** Study of the earth's surface and its features. **2.** A description of a landform geographical or geographic *adj.*; geographer *n.*

geology \jee-OL-uh-jee\ *n. pl.* geologies. (Sc) The study of the earth's crust. geologist *n.*

geopolitical \jee-oh-puh-LIT-i-kul\ *adj.* Concerning world politics and land division.

geranium \juh-RAY-nee-um\ *n.* A flowering garden plant.

geriatric \jer-ee-A-trik\ *adj.* Concerning the elderly.

germ \jurm\ *n.* A microorganism that causes disease.

germ warfare *n.* The use of bacteria in war.

germane \jer-MAYN\ *adj.* Relevant.

germicide \JUR-muh-side\ *n.* (Sc) Something that kills germs.

germinate \JUR-muh-nayt\ *v.* germinated; germinating. To sprout. germination *n.*

gerontology \jer-un-TOL-uh-jee\ *n.* (Sc) The study of aging. gerontologist *n.*

gestate \JES-tayt\ *v.* gestated; gestating. To conceive and develop. gestation *n.*

gesticulate \je-STIK-yuh-layt\ *v.* gesticulated; gesticulating. To make hand movements.

gesture \JES-chur\ *n.* **1.** A body movement. **2.** Something said or done.

get *v.* got; gotten; getting. **1.** To re-ceive. **2.** To retrieve. **3.** To understand. **4.** Get cracking [Id]: to start.

getaway \GET-uh-way\ *n.* A vacation place.

get down *v.* got down; getting down. To focus on.

geyser \GIE-zur\ *n.* A natural spring that spouts hot water or steam.

ghastly \GAST-lee\ *adj.* ghastlier; ghastliest. Frightening.

ghetto \GET-oh\ *n. pl.* ghettos also ghettoes. An area of a city where minorities live.

ghost \gohst\ *n.* **1.** A spirit. **2.** One's soul. **3.** A shadowy image. ghostly *adj.*

giant \JIE-unt\ *n.* A mythical large being.

gibberish \JIB-ur-ish\ *n.* Nonsensical language.

giblet \JIB-lit\ *pl. n.* Fowl viscera.

giddy \GID-ee\ *adj.* giddier; giddiest. **1.** Lightheaded. **2.** Euphoric.

gift *n.* **1.** Talent. **2.** Something given.

gifted \GIF-tid\ *adj.* Talented.

gigabyte \GI-guh-bite\ *n.* (Cm) One billion bits or bytes.

gigantic \jie-GAN-tik\ *adj.* Huge.

giggle \GIG-ul\ *v.* giggled; giggling. To laugh in small bursts.

GIGO. *abbr.* (Cm) Garbage in, garbage out.

gigolo \JIG-uh-loh\ *n. pl.* gigolos. A paid male escort.

gill \gil\ *n.* A fish respiratory organ.

gimmick \GIM-ik\ *n.* **1.** A gadget. **2.** A scheme.

ginger \JIN-jur\ *n.* A tropical plant and the spice it yields.

gingivitis \jin-juh-VIE-tis\ *n.* (Md) Gum inflammation.

ginseng \JIN-seng\ *n.* A fragrant Chinese herb.

giraffe \juh-RAF\ *pl. n.* A long-necked African mammal.

girl \gurl\ *n.* A female. girlish *adj.*

girlfriend \GURL-frend\ *n.* A female friend.

gist \jist\ *n.* The essence or general meaning.

give \giv\ *v.* gave; given; giving. **1.** To grant. **2.** To bestow. **3.** To produce. **4.** Give way [Id]: To retreat.

gizzard \GIZ-urd\ *n.* Bird's second stomach.

glacier \GLAY-shur\ *n.* A large body of slowly moving ice. glacial *adv.*

glad *adj.* gladder; gladdest. Happy. gladly *adv.*; gladness *n.*

glamour *also* **glamor** \GLAM-ur\ *n.* Attractiveness or beauty. glamorous also glamourous *adj.*

glance \glans\ *v.* glanced; glancing. **1.** To look at briefly. **2.** To bounce off at an angle. **3.** To deal with briefly.

gland *n.* An animal organ that extracts substances from the blood. glandular *adj.*

glare \glair\ *v.* glared; glaring. **1.** To stare at in anger. **2.** To shine harshly. glaring *adj.*

glasnost \GLAS-nohst\ *n.* A Soviet policy of free discussion.

glass \glas\ *n.* **1.** A transparent solid. **2.** A mirror. **3.** A drinking vessel. glassy *adj.*

glasses *also* **eyeglasses** \GLAS-sus\ *n.* Corrective lenses.

glaucoma \glow-KOH-muh\ *n.* (Md) An eye disease caused by fluid pressure.

glaze \glayz\ *n.* A thin coating.

gleam \gleem\ *v.* gleamed; gleaming. To shine with a constant light.

glee *n.* High spirits. gleeful *adj.*

glen *n.* A secluded land area.

glide \glied\ *v.* glided; gliding. To move over slowly and smoothly.

glimmer \GLIM-ur\ *n.* An inkling.

glimmer \GLIM-ur\ *v.* glimmered; glimmering. To shine with a faint light.

glimpse \glimps\ *n.* A quick look.

glimpse \glimps\ *v.* glimpsed; glimpsing. To look quickly.

glisten \GLIS-un\ *v.* glistened; glistening. To shine from being wet.

glitch *n.* A small problem.

glitter \GLIT-ur\ *v.* glittered; glittering. To sparkle.

glitterati \GLIT-tur-rah-tee\ *pl. n.* Celebrities.

glitz \glits\ *n.* Extravagant showiness. glitzy *adj.*

gloat \gloht\ *v.* gloated; gloating. To brag.

glob *n.* A rounded mass. globular *adj.*

globe \glohb\ *n.* A ball-shaped object, as the earth. global *adj.*

gloom *n.* **1.** Darkness. **2.** Depression. gloomy *adj.*

glory \GLOR-ee\ *n. pl.* glories. **1.** Renown. **2.** An exalted state. **3.** Magnificence. glorify *v.*

gloss \glos\ *n.* A shiny surface layer. glossy *adj.*

gloss \glos\ *v.* glossed; glossing. **1.** To mask. **2.** To review briefly. **3.** To interpret. **4.** To make shiny.

glossary \GLOS-uh-ree\ *n. pl.* glossaries. A list of meanings.

glove \glov\ *n.* A hand covering with fingers.

glow \gloh\ *n.* **1.** Redness. **2.** Light.

glow \gloh\ *v.* glowed; glowing. To shine with heat or color.

glue \gloo\ *v.* glued; gluing. also glueing. To stick together.

glue \gloo\ *n.* A sticky adhesive that hardens to hold fast.

gluten \GLOOT-un\ *n.* A wheat protein.

gluteus maximus \GLOO-tee-us-MAKS-i-mus\ *n. pl.* glutei maximi. (Md) The outer large muscle of the buttocks.

glutton \GLUT-n\ *n.* One who eats or desires too much. gluttonous *adj.*

glycerin *also* **glycerine** \GLIS-ur-in\ *n.* (Sc) A thick liquid used in medicines and as a solvent.

gnarled \nahlrd\ *adj.* Knotty.

gnaw \naw\ *v.* gnawed; gnawing. To chew on.

gnu \noo\ *n. pl.* gnu also gnus. A large African antelope.

go \goh\ *v.* went; gone; going. **1.** To leave. **2.** To break. **3.** To complement. **4.** Go fly a kite [Id]: stop annoying

goad \gohd\ *v.* goaded; goading. To incite.

go-ahead \GOH-uh-hed\ *n.* Authority to proceed.

goat \goht\ *n. pl.* goats. A small horned mammal.

go-between *n.* An intermediary.

gobble \GOB-ul\ *v.* gobbled; gobbling. To consume with greed.

God *n.* The creator and deity.

god *n.* A supreme being. godless *adj.*; godly *adj.*; godlike *adj.*; godliness *n.*

gofer \GOH-fur\ *n.* One who runs errands.

goiter \GOI-tur\ *n.* (Md) A thyroid gland enlargement.

gold \gohld\ *n.* **1.** A precious metal. **2.** A dark yellow color. **3.** Something prized. golden *adj.*

gold-digger *n.* One who uses charm to gain money or favors.

golden parachute \GOHL-dun\ *n.* Generous severance pay.

golf *n.* A outdoor game played with clubs and a small ball. golfer *n.*

gonad \GOH-nad\ *n.* (Md) A male reproductive gland.

gondola \GON-dl-uh\ *n.* (It) A long flat-bottomed boat. gondolier *n.*

gone \gawn\ *adj.* **1.** Dead. **2.** Ruined. **3.** Infatuated. **4.** Past.

good \guud\ *adj.* better; best. **1.** Favorable. **2.** Amusing. **3.** Virtuous.

good-bye *also* **good-by** \guud-BIE\ *n.* Expression when leaving.

good-natured \GUUD-NAY-churd\ *adj.* Amiable.

goodness \GUUD-nus\ *n.* The positive part of something or someone.

goods \guudz\ *n.* Products.

goodwill \GUUD-WIL\ *n.* Kindness and support.

gooey \GOO-ee\ *adj.* Sticky.

goose \goos\ *n. pl.* geese **1.** Large web-footed waterfowl. **2.** A simpleton.

gopher \GOH-fur\ *n.* Burrowing rodent.

gorge \gorj\ *n.* A narrow steep land passage.

gorge \gorj\ *v.* gorged; gorging. To fill fully.

gorgeous \GOR-jus\ *adj.* Extremely brilliant or beautiful.

gorilla \GOH-ri-luh\ *n.* **1.** A large African ape. **2.** A thug.

gory \GOH-ree\ *adj.* gorier; goriest. Bloody.

gosling \GOZ-ling\ *n.* A young goose.

gospel \GOS-pul\ *n.* **1.** Christ's message. **2.** First four books of the New Testament.

gossamer \GOS-uh-mur\ *n.* Something light or insubstantial.

gossip \GOS-up\ *n.* **1.** A rumor. **2.** Casual talk.

Gothic \GOTH-ik\ *adj.* Concerning a Germanic people and style of the third–fifth centuries.

gouache \gwahsh\ *n.* (Fr) A method of watercolor painting.

goulash \GOO-lahsh\ *n.* Beef and vegetable stew.

gourd \guurd\ *n.* Ornamental fruit.

gourmet \guur-MAY\ *n.* A food connoisseur.

gout \gowt\ *n.* (Md) A metabolic disease with joint inflammation.

govern \GUV-urn\ *v.* governed; governing. To rule with authority.

government \GUV-urn-munt\ *n.* Authoritative political control.

governor \GUV-ur-nur\ *n.* One that governs, especially the head of a state.

gown *n.* A long dress.

grab *v.* grabbed; grabbing. To take suddenly.

grace \grays\ *n.* **1.** God's virtue. **2.** Pardon. **3.** Charm and beauty. **4.** A title. graceful *adj.*

gracious \GRAY-shus\ *adj.* **1.** Courteous. **2.** Compassionate.

grade \grayd\ *n.* **1.** Assessment measure. **2.** A level in school. **3.** A group of similar things.

grade \grayd\ *v.* graded; grading. **1.** To assess. **2.** To level off a slope.

gradual \GRAJ-oo-ul\ *adj.* Proceeding slowly.

graduate \GRAJ-oo-ayt\ *v.* graduated; graduating. **1.** To take a degree or diploma. **2.** To separate into intervals.

graft *v.* grafted; grafting. **1.** To unite. **2.** To implant.

grain \grayn\ *n.* **1.** A small seed. **2.** Wood fiber pattern. **3.** Temper.

grammar \GRAM-ur\ *n.* The study of the usage of words of a language. grammarian *n.*; grammatical *adj.*

granary \GRAY-nuh-ree\ *n. pl.* granaries. A warehouse for grain.

grand *adj.* **1.** Magnificent. **2.** Definitive. **3.** Lavish. grandeur *n.*; grandiose *adj.*

grandfather \GRAND-fah-thur or GRAN-fah-thur\ *n.* One's father's or mother's father. grandpa *n.*

grandfather clause *n.* A statement of possible exemption.

grandmother \GRAND-muth-ur or GRAN-muth-ur\ *n.* One's father's or mother's mother. grandma *n.*; granny *n.*

granola \gruh-NOH-luh\ *n.* A cereal of grains.

grant *n.* A monetary gift.

grant *v.* granted; granting. **1.** To allow. **2.** To bestow.

granular \GRAN-yuh-lur\ *adj.* Like grains.

grape \grayp\ *n.* A small clustered berry fruit.

grapefruit \GRAYP-froot\ *n.* A large yellow citrus fruit.

graphic *also* **graphical** \GRAF-ik\ *adj.* **1.** Relating to writing and/or drawing. **2.** Realistic.

graphic *also* **graphics** \GRAF-ik\

n. A diagram or pictorial representation.

grapple \GRAP-ul\ *v.* grappled; grappling. To wrestle with.

grasp *n.* **1.** An embrace. **2.** Comprehension. grasping *adj.*

grasp *v.* grasped; grasping. To clutch.

grass \gras\ *n.* **1.** A low-growing herbaceous plant. **2.** Marijuana.

grasshopper \GRAS-hop-ur\ *n.* A jumping insect that chirps.

grate \grayt\ *v.* grated; grating. **1.** To shred. **2.** To irritate.

grateful \GRAYT-ful\ *adj.* Appreciative. gratify *v.*; gratitude *n.*

gratuitous \gruh-TOO-i-tus\ *adj.* Unearned.

gratuity \gruh-TOO-i-tee\ *n. pl.* gratuities. A monetary tip for service.

grave \grayv\ *adj.* graver; gravest. **1.** Important. **2.** Somber and serious.

grave \grayv\ *n.* **1.** A burial place. **2.** An accent mark.

gravel \GRAV-ul\ *n.* Small rocks.

graveyard \GRAYV-yahrd\ *n.* Cemetery.

gravity \GRAV-i-tee\ *n. pl.* gravities. **1.** Attractive force [Sc]. **2.** Seriousness and solemnity. gravitate *v.*; gravitation *n.*; gravitational *adj.*

gray *also* **grey** *adj.* **1.** A color lighter than black. **2.** Gloomy. **3.** Having vague definition.

graze \grayz\ *v.* grazed; grazing. **1.** To feed slowly. **2.** To touch lightly.

grease \grees\ *n.* Animal fat. greasy *adj.*

grease \grees\ *v.* greased; greasing. To lubricate.

great \grayt\ *adj.* **1.** Huge. **2.** Predominant. **3.** Primary. **4.** Noble.

greed *n.* Avarice. greedy *adj.*

green *adj.* **1.** The color of grass. **2.** New and fresh. **3.** Young and inexperienced.

green *n.* **1.** [Pl] Leafy vegetables. **2.** Putting area on a golf hole. **3.** Money.

greenery \GREE-nuh-ree\ *n. pl.* greeneries Plants.

greenhouse \GREEN-hows\ *n.* A place where plants can grow year round.

greenhouse effect *n.* (Sc) Warming effect caused by solar radiation.

green revolution *n.* An increase in the production of grains.

greet *v.* greeted; greeting. **1.** To address politely on arrival or meeting. **2.** To react to. **3.** To hail. greeting *n.*

gregarious \gri-GAIR-ee-us\ *adj.* Sociable.

grid \grid\ *n.* **1.** A metal plate used as a conductor. **2.** A network of lines.

gridlock \GRID-lok\ *n.* A traffic jam.

grief \greef\ *n.* **1.** Sorrow. **2.** Disaster.

grill \gril\ *v.* grilled; grilling. **1.** To cook on a hot metal grid. **2.** To question.

grim *adj.* grimmer; grimmest **1.** Stern. **2.** Gloomy. **3.** Unyielding. grimly *adv.*

grimace \GRIM-us\ *n.* An expression of pain or disgust.

grimy \GRIEM-ee\ *adj.* grimier; grimiest. Dirty. grime *n.*

grin *v.* grinned; grinning. To smile broadly.

grind \griend\ *v.* ground; grinding. **1.** To wear down. **2.** To rub into fragments. **3.** To crank.

grip \grip\ *n.* **1.** A strong grasp. **2.** A handle.

grip *v.* gripped; gripping. To hold firmly.

gripe \griep\ *v.* griped; griping. **1.** To complain. **2.** To vex.

grippe \grip\ *n.* (Fr) Influenza.

grisly \GRIZ-lee\ *adj.* grislier; grisliest. Ghastly or horrible.

grit *n.* **1.** Gravel. **2.** Mental resolve.

grizzly bear \GRIZ-lee-BAIR\ *n.* A large brown or gray bear.

groan \grohn\ *v.* groaned; groaning. To moan.

groggy \GROG-ee\ *adj.* groggier; groggiest. Feeling unsteady and weak.

groin *n.* The juncture of the lower abdomen and legs.

groom *n.* **1.** A man about to be married. **2.** A servant. **3.** A person who cares for horses.

groom *v.* groomed; grooming. **1.** To clean. **2.** To prepare.

groove \groov\ *n.* **1.** A narrow depression. **2.** A rut. **3.** An enjoyable rhythm.

groovy \GROO-vee\ *adj.* groovier; grooviest. Wonderful.

grope \grohp\ *v.* groped; groping. To feel for blindly.

grotesque \groh-TESK\ *adj.* **1.** Bizarre. **2.** Horrific. gross *adj.*

grotto \GROT-oh\ *n. pl.* grottoes also grottos. Picturesque caves.

grouch \growch\ *n.* A grumpy person. grouchy *adj.*

ground \grownd\ *n.* **1.** Surface of the earth. **2.** A foundation. **3.** Reason for an action. **4.** Sediment.

ground \grownd\ *v.* grounded;

grounding. **1.** To punish. **2.** To run into the ground. **3.** To give basic training.

groundless \GROWND-lis\ *adj.* Without reason.

groundwork \GROWND-wurk\ *n.* Preparatory or basic work.

group \groop\ *n.* A collection or class.

groupie \GROO-pee\ *n.* A rock fan.

group therapy *n.* A discussion with a number of patients and a therapist.

grovel \GRUV-ul\ *v.* groveled or grovelled; groveling or grovelling. **1.** To crawl face-down. **2.** To wallow.

grow \groh\ *v.* grew; grown; growing. **1.** To increase. **2.** To become or develop. growth *n.*

growl *v.* growled; growling. **1.** To rumble. **2.** To speak in anger. **3.** To utter a guttural noise.

grown-up \GROHN-UP\ *n.* An adult.

grub *n.* **1.** Food. **2.** A drudge. **3.** An insect.

grub *v.* grubbed; grubbing. To dig for.

grudge \gruj\ *n.* A feeling of ill-will.

grueling *also* **gruelling** \GROO-uh-ling\ *adj.* Exhausting.

gruff \gruf\ *adj.* **1.** Brusque. **2.** Hoarse.

grumpy \GRUM-pee\ *adj.* grumpier; grumpiest Surly. grump *n.*

grungy \GRUN-jee\ *adj.* grungier; grungiest. **1.** Shabby. **2.** Dirty.

grunt *n.* **1.** A deep short sound. **2.** A type of fish. **3.** A dessert.

guarantee *also* **guaranty** \gar-un-TEE\ *n.* Something given as security.

guard \gahrd\ *n.* **1.** Protector, protecting device. **2.** Football position. **3.** State of watchfulness.

guard \gahrd\ *v.* guarded; guarding. **1.** To protect. **2.** To defend.

guarded \GAHR-did\ *adj.* Cautious.

guardian \GAHR-dee-un\ *n.* A caretaker.

guava \goo-AH-vah\ *n.* A sweet fruit.

gubernatorial \goo-bur-nuh-TOR-ee-ul\ *adj.* Concerning the governor.

guerrilla *also* **guerilla** \guh-RIL-uh\ *n.* An independent soldier.

guess \ges\ *n.* **1.** An assumption. **2.** An opinion or belief.

guesstimate \GES-ti-mut\ *n.* An assumed estimate.

guest \gest\ *n.* A visitor or person entertained.

guide \gied\ *n.* One who leads.

guide \gied\ *v.* guided; guiding. To direct. guidance *n.*

guild \gild\ *n.* An association of craftspeople.

guile \giel\ *n.* **1.** Deceitful. **2.** Cunning.

guillotine \GIL-uh-teen\ *n.* (Fr) An instrument for beheading.

guilt \gilt\ *n.* **1.** Self-reproach. **2.** Feeling of self-blame. guilty *adj.*

guise \giez\ *n.* **1.** Costume or false appearance. **2.** Pretence.

guitar \GI-tar\ *n.* A stringed musical instrument.

gulag \GOO-lahg\ *n.* USSR labor camp.

gulf *n.* **1.** A large area of sea partly surrounded by land. **2.** An abyss.

gullet \GUL-it\ *n.* The throat.

gullible *also* **gullable** \GUL-uh-bul\ *adj.* Easily fooled. gullibility *n.*

gully *also* **gulley** \GUL-ee\ *n. pl.* gullies. A narrow channel or valley.

gulp *v.* gulped; gulping. To swallow quickly and loudly.

gum *n.* **1.** Tissue surrounding the teeth. **2.** Chewing substance.

gum *v.* gummed; gumming. To clog.

gumption \GUM-shun\ *n.* **1.** Shrewdness. **2.** Initiative.

gun *n.* A firearm.

gun *v.* gunned; gunning. To shoot with a gun.

guppy \GUP-ee\ *n. pl.* guppies. A small tropical fish.

gurgle \GUR-gul\ *v.* gurgled; gurgling. To move irregularly.

guru \GUUR-oo\ *n. pl.* gurus. **1.** A religious guide. **2.** An expert.

gush *v.* gushed; gushing. To flow freely and copiously.

gust *n.* A surge or rush.

gusto \GUS-toh\ *n. pl.* gustoes. Enthusiasm.

gut *n.* **1.** Abdomen. **2.** [Pl] Courage.

gut *v.* gutted; gutting. To remove or destroy everything inside.

gutter \GUT-ur\ *n.* **1.** A trough. **2.** Vulgar conditions.

guttural \GUT-ur-ul\ *adj.* Throaty or unpleasant sounding.

guy \gie\ *n.* A man.

guzzle \GUZ-ul\ *v.* guzzled; guzzling. To drink quickly and greedily.

gymnasium \gim-NAY-zee-um\ *n. pl.* gymnasiums or gymnasia. A large room used for physical activities.

gymnastic *also* **gymnastics** \jim-

NAS-tik\ *n.* A physical exercise. gymnast *n.*

gynecology \gie-ni-KOL-uh-jee\ *n.* (Md) The study and care of the female reproductive system. gynecologist *n.*

gypsy \JIP-see\ *n. pl.* gypsies. **1.** A cultural group. **2.** A wanderer.

gypsy cab *n.* A passenger cab.

gypsy moth *n.* A destructive moth.

gyrate \JIE-rayt\ *v.* gyrated; gyrating. To revolve.

gyroscope \JIE-roh-skohp\ *n.* A spinning device used in navigation instruments.

H

h \aych\ ***n. pl.*** h's or hs. The eighth letter of the English alphabet.

habeas corpus \HAY-bee-us-KOR-pus\ ***n.*** (Le) An order to bring someone before a judge.

habit \HAB-it\ ***n.*** **1.** A settled way of behaving. **2.** A usual practice. habitual ***adj.***

habitat \HAB-i-tat\ ***n.*** An animal's or plant's natural environment.

habituate \huh-BICH-oo-ayt\ ***v.*** habituated; habituating. To frequent.

hacienda \hah-see-EN-duh\ ***n.*** (Sp) A large home or estate in South America.

hacker \HAK-ur\ ***n.*** A computer programming expert.

haddock \HAD-dock\ ***n.*** A white food fish.

hadji *also* **hajji** \HAJ-ee\ ***n.*** A Muslim traveler to Mecca.

haggard \HAG-urd\ ***adj.*** Ugly from exhaustion.

haiku \HIE-koo\ ***n. pl.*** haiku. (Fo) Japanese poem form.

hail \hayl\ ***n.*** Frozen precipitation.

hail \hayl\ ***v.*** hailed; hailing. **1.** To rain frozen precipitation. **2.** To greet.

hair ***n.*** Threadlike growth from the skin, esp. the head.

hairspray \HAIR-spray\ ***n.*** A sticky substance for holding hair in place.

hairstyle \HAIR-stiel\ ***n.*** A way of wearing hair.

halcyon \HAL-see-un\ ***adj.*** **1.** Calm and peaceful. **2.** Prosperous.

halcyon \HAL-see-un\ *n.* A legendary bird.

half \haf\ *n. pl.* halves. One of two equal parts.

half-breed \HAF-breed\ *n.* Disparaging term for offspring of racially different parents.

half-way \HAF-WAY\ *adj.* Midpoint.

halibut \hal-i-BUT\ *n. pl.* halibut *also* halibuts. A large flat food fish.

halitosis \hal-i-TOH-sis\ *n.* Bad breath.

hall \hawl\ *n.* **1.** A passageway. **2.** An entranceway. **3.** A large structure or room.

hallelujah \hal-uh-LOO-yuh\ *interj.* An expression of joy and praise.

hallmark \HAWL-mahrk\ *n.* An official stamp.

hallowed \HAL-ohd\ *adj.* Sacred.

hallucinate \huh-LOO-suh-nayt\ *v.* hallucinated; hallucinating. To see visions. hallucination *n.*; hallucinogen *n.*

hallway \HAWL-way\ *n.* A corridor.

halo \HAY-loh\ *n. pl.* halos or haloes. A circle of light.

halogen \hal-OH-jen\ *n.* (Sc) A category of non-metallic chemical elements.

halt \hawlt\ *v.* halted; halting. To stop.

halve \hav\ *v.* halved; halving. To divide into two equal parts.

ham *n.* **1.** A cut of meat from a hog. **2.** An exaggerating performer.

hamburger *also* **hamburg** \HAM-bur-gur\ *n.* **1.** Ground beef. **2.** A sandwich of ground beef.

hamlet \HAM-lit\ *n.* A small town.

hammer \HAM-ur\ *n.* A pounding tool.

hammer \HAM-ur\ *v.* hammered; hammering. To strike repeatedly.

hammock \HAM-uk\ *n.* A swinging bed.

hamper \HAM-pur\ *n.* A large basket with a lid.

hamper \HAM-pur\ *v.* hampered; hampering. To hinder.

hamster \HAM-stur\ *n.* A small rodent with cheek pouches.

hand *n.* **1.** An appendage at the arm's end. **2.** Direction. **3.** Help. **4.** Unit of measurement.

hand out *v.* handed out; handing out. To give.

handbag \HAND-bag\ *n.* A purse for personal items.

handbook \HAND-buuk\ *n.* A reference book.

handful \HAND-fuul\ *n. pl.* handfuls. A few.

handicap \HAN-di-kap or HAN-dee-kap\ *n.* **1.** A disability. **2.** An artificial advantage. handicapped *adj.*

handicraft \HAN-dee-kraft or HAN-di-kraft\ *n.* Artwork or work needing skill with the hands.

handkerchief \HANG-kur-chif\ *n.* A small square of cloth for personal needs.

handle \HAN-dl\ *n.* **1.** A carrying, controlling, or opening device. **2.** A nickname.

handle \HAN-dl\ *v.* handled; handling. **1.** To manage. **2.** To touch. **3.** To buy or sell something.

handsome \HAN-sum\ *adj.* **1.** Appropriate. **2.** Pleasing appearance.

hands-on \HANDZ-on\ *adj.* Concerning practical experience.

handwriting \HAND-rie-ting\ *n.* Writing by hand with an implement.

handy \HAN-dee\ *adj.* handier; handiest. **1.** Convenient. **2.** Good with one's hands.

hang *v.* hung or hanged; hanging. **1.** To suspend. **2.** To rest or support upon a wall. **3.** To cling. **4.** [Sl] To be loose.

hang-glider *n.* A large kite-like craft for one person.

hang-up \HANG-up\ *n.* A problem.

hangar \HANG-ur\ *n.* Aircraft shelter.

hanky-panky \HANG-kee-PANG-kee\ *n.* Questionable behavior.

haphazard \hap-HAZ-urd\ *adj.* Random.

happen \HAP-un\ *v.* happened; happening. To occur, sometimes by chance.

happening \HAP-uh-ning\ *n.* **1.** An event. **2.** Something significant.

happy \HAP-ee\ *adj.* happier; happiest. **1.** Glad. **2.** Fortunate. happiness *n.*; happily *adv.*

hara-kiri \HAH-ruh-KEER-ee\ *n.* (Fo) Ritual suicide.

harass \huh-RAS\ *v.* harassed; harassing. **1.** To worry. **2.** To bother. harassment *n.*

harbor \HAHR-bur\ *n.* **1.** A water port. **2.** A refuge or shelter.

harbor \HAHR-bur\ *v.* harbored; harboring. To give shelter to.

hard \hahrd\ *adj.* harder; hardest. **1.** Not soft. **2.** Difficult. **3.** Definite. **4.** Unfeeling. **5.** Extreme. harden *v.*

hard-core \HAHRD-KOR\ *adj.* **1.** Concerning confirmed participation or belief. **2.** Explicit.

hard drive *n.* (Cm) Internal computer magnetic storage disk.

hard-line \HAHRD-lien\ *adj.* Uncompromising.

hardly \HAHRD-lee\ *adv.* **1.** Harshly. **2.** Minimally.

hardship \HAHRD-ship\ *n.* Something causing suffering.

hardware \HAHRD-wair\ *n.* **1.** Tools and implements. **2.** Machinery. **3.** A computer other than the programs.

hardy \HAHR-dee\ *adj.* hardier; hardiest. **1.** Strong. **2.** Brave.

hare \hair\ *n.* A field animal like a large rabbit.

harebrained \HAIR-braynd\ *adj.* Foolish.

Hare Krishna \HAHR-ee-krish-nuh\ *n. pl.* Hare Krishna or Hare Krishnas. A religious group.

harem \HAIR-um\ *n.* A group of women serving one Muslim male.

harlequin \HAHR-luh-kwin\ *n.* **1.** A buffoon. **2.** A varicolored pattern.

harm \hahrm\ *v.* harmed; harming. To injure or damage. harmful *adj.*; harmless *adj.*

harmonica \hahr-MON-i-kuh\ *n.* (Mu) A small wind instrument or mouth organ.

harmony \HAHR-muh-nee\ *n. pl.* harmonies. **1.** Combination of compatible notes [Mu]. **2.** Peace. harmonize *v.*

harness \HAHR-nis\ *n.* An animal's yoke.

harp \hahrp\ *n.* **1.** A stringed instrument. **2.** A harmonica.

harp \hahrp\ *v.* harped; harping. To dwell on.

harsh \hahrsh\ *adj.* **1.** Rough. **2.** Painful. **3.** Severe.

harvest \HAHR-vist\ *n.* A crop yield.

harvest \HAHR-vist\ *v.* harvested; harvesting. To gather a crop.

hassle \HAS-ul\ *n.* An argument.

hassle \HAS-ul\ *v.* hassled; hassling. **1.** To fight. **2.** To harass or bother.

haste \hayst\ *n.* Swiftness. hasten *v.*; hasty *adj.*

hat *n.* A head covering.

hatch \hach\ *n.* A small opening.

hatch \hach\ *v.* hatched; hatching. To emerge from an egg.

hatchback \HACH-bak\ *n.* A hinged rear opening for some vehicles.

hate \hayt\ *n.* Intense dislike. hateful *adj.*; hatred *n.*

hate \hayt\ *v.* hated; hating. To feel intense dislike.

haughty \HAW-tee\ *adj.* haughtier; haughtiest. Overly proud.

haul \hawl\ *v.* hauled; hauling. **1.** To transport. **2.** Haul ass [Id]: To move quickly.

haunt \hawnt\ *v.* haunted; haunting. **1.** To reappear frequently. **2.** To linger. **3.** To frighten and bother.

haute couture \oht-koo-TUUR\ *n.*

(Fr) High-fashion women's clothing.

have \hav\ *v.* had; having; has. **1.** To possess. **2.** To contain. **3.** To experience. **4.** To undergo. **5.** To give birth.

haven \HAY-vun\ *n.* A safe place.

havoc \HAV-uk\ *n.* Destruction.

hay *n.* Dried grass for fodder.

hazard \HAZ-urd\ *n.* **1.** A risk. **2.** A danger. hazardous *adj.*

haze \hayz\ *n.* Cloudy atmosphere. hazy *adj.*

haze \hayz\ *v.* hazed; hazing. **1.** To harass. **2.** To initiate roughly.

head \hed\ *n.* **1.** The top of the body. **2.** One's mind. **3.** A superior. **4.** A leader.

headhunter \HED-hun-tur\ *n.* One searching for people to be employed.

headlong \HED-lawng\ *adv.* **1.** Headfirst. **2.** Recklessly.

headstrong \HED-strawng\ *adj.* **1.** Stubborn. **2.** Unruly.

headway \HED-way\ *n.* Progress.

heal \heel\ *v.* healed; healing. **1.** To form health flesh again. **2.** To restore health. healer *n.*

health \helth\ *n.* Physical and mental well-being. healthy *adj.*

health-care *also* **health care** *n.* Medical services for human well-being.

health food *n.* Food conducive to well-being.

health spa *n.* An establishment focusing on well-being.

heap \heep\ *v.* heaped; heaping. **1.** To pile high. **2.** To give lavishly.

hear \heer\ *v.* heard; hearing. **1.** To perceive with one's ear. **2.** To comprehend. hearing *n.*

hearken \HAHR-kun\ *v.* hearkened; hearkening. To listen.

hearsay \HEER-say\ *n.* A rumor.

hearse \hurs\ *n.* A vehicle for transporting a coffin.

heart \hahrt\ *n.* **1.** Muscular organ that pumps the blood. **2.** A card suit. **3.** Love and emotion.

heartbreak \HAHRT-brayk\ *n.* Overwhelming grief.

heartless \HAHRT-lis\ *adj.* Cruel.

hearty \HAHR-tee\ *adj.* heartier; heartiest. **1.** Sincere. **2.** Very healthy.

heat \heet\ *n.* **1.** Warmth. **2.** Intense feeling. **3.** Stressful persuasion. heater *n.*

heated \HEE-tid\ *adj.* Angry.

heathen \HEE-then\ *n. pl.* heathens or heathen. A person who is regarded as uncivilized or unenlightened

heather \HETH-ur\ *n.* Flowering evergreen plant.

heave \heev\ *v.* heaved; heaving. **1.** To throw. **2.** To retch.

heaven \HEV-un\ *n.* **1.** The place where God lives **2.** The sky. heavenly *adj.*

heavy \HEV-ee\ *adj.* heavier; heaviest. **1.** Weighing much. **2.** Serious. **3.** Intense. **4.** Dull.

heavy-duty \HEV-ee-DOO-tee\ *adj.* **1.** Intense. **2.** Strong.

heavy metal *n.* (Mu) A type of loud rock music.

hectic \HEK-tik\ *adj.* Confused and busy.

hedge \hej\ *n.* **1.** A barrier of shrubs. **2.** A means of protection.

hedonism \HEED-n-iz-um\ *n.* A belief in happiness or pleasure as life's only good. hedonistic *adj.*; hedonist *n.*

heed *v.* heeded; heeding. To pay attention to.

heel *n.* Back part of a human foot.

hefty \HEF-tee\ *adj.* heftier; heftiest. **1.** Powerful. **2.** Large and heavy.

heifer \HEF-ur\ *n.* A young cow.

height \hite\ *n.* **1.** Altitude. **2.** Measurement to top. heighten *v.*

heinous \HAY-nus\ *adj.* Very evil.

heir \air\ *n.* One who inherits property.

heirloom \AIR-loom\ *n.* Something handed down through generations.

helicopter \HEL-i-kop-tur\ *n.* An aircraft with one large propeller.

Hell \hel\ *n.* Christian place of damnation. hellish *adj.*; hellion *n.*

helm *n.* **1.** Position of control. **2.** A helmet.

helmet \HEL-mit\ *n.* A protective head covering.

help *n.* **1.** Aid. **2.** Relief.

help *v.* helped; helping. **1.** To assist. **2.** To relieve. **3.** To prevent.

helpful \HELP-ful\ *adj.* Useful.

helping \HEL-ping\ *n.* A serving of food.

hem *n.* A cloth border.

hem *v.* hemmed; hemming. **1.** To confine. **2.** To edge.

hematology \hee-muh-TOL-uh-jee\ *n.* (Md) The study of blood. hemolotogist *n.*; hemotological or hemotologic *adj.*

hemisphere \HIM-i-sfeer\ *n.* One half of a celestial sphere, as divided by the equator.

hemodialysis \HEE-muh-die-al-i-sus\ *n.* (Md) A blood purification process.

hemoglobin \HEE-muh-gloh-bin\ *n.* (Md) A substance in the blood. hemophiliac *adj.*

hemorrhage \HEM-ur-ij\ *v.* hemorrhaged; hemorrhaging. (Md) To bleed uncontrollably.

hemorrhoid \HEM-uh-roid\ *n.* (Md) Veins in swollen tissue near the anus.

hence \hens\ *adv.* **1.** From this time on. **2.** Therefore.

hepatitis \hep-uh-TIE-tis\ *n. pl.* hepatitides. (Md) An inflammatory liver disease.

her \hur\ *pron.* Concerning a woman as object or possessor.

herald \HER-uld\ *v.* heralded; heralding. **1.** To announce. **2.** To foreshadow. heraldry *n.*

herb \urb\ *n.* A plant used for seasoning or medicine. herbaceous *adj.*

herculean \hur-kyuh-LEE-un\ *adj.* Extremely powerful, intense or difficult.

herd \hurd\ *n.* A group of animals staying together.

herd \hurd\ *v.* herded; herding. To gather or lead a group of animals.

here \heer\ *adv.* In this place.

hereafter \heer-AF-tur\ *n.* **1.** In the future. **2.** An otherworldly place.

hereditary \huh-RED-i-ter-ee\ *adj.* **1.** Handed down from parents by birth. **2.** Innate or inherited. heredity *n.*

heresy \HER-uh-see\ *n. pl.* heresies. Denial of religious truth. heretic *n.*

heritage \HER-i-tij\ *n.* **1.** Tradition. **2.** Birthright or things inherited.

hermaphrodite \hur-MAF-ruh-dite\ *n.* Possessing male and female reproductive organs.

hermit \HUR-mit\ *n.* One who lives in solitude.

hernia \HUR-nee-uh\ *n. pl.* hernias or herniae. (Md) An organ's abnormal protrusion.

hero \HEER-oh\ *n. pl.* heroes. **1.** A great man. **2.** The primary male character in literature. heroic *adj.* or *n.*; heroism *n.*

heroine \HER-oh-in\ *n.* **1.** A great woman. **2.** The primary female character in literature.

heron \HER-un\ *n.* A long-legged wading bird.

herpes \HUR-peez\ *n.* (Md) A virus causing blisters.

herpetology \hur-puh-TOL-uh-jee\ *n.* (Sc) The study of reptiles and amphibians. herpetologist *n.*

herring \HER-ing\ *n. pl.* herring or herrings. A North Atlantic food fish.

herstory \HER-stor-ee\ *n. pl.* herstories. A feminist view of history.

hesitate \HEZ-i-tayt\ *v.* hesitated; hesitating. To pause. hesitant *adj.*; hesitation *n.*

heterogeneous \het-ur-uh-JEE-nee-us\ *adj.* Mixed and made up of various sorts.

heterosexual \het-ur-uh-SEK-shoo-ul\ *adj.* Concerning attraction to the opposite gender. heterosexuality *n.*

hex \heks\ *v.* hexed; hexing. An evil spell.

hexagon \HEK-suh-gon\ *n.* A six-sided polygon. hexagonal *adj.*

hey \hay\ *interj.* Exclamation of surprise.

heyday \HAY-day\ *n.* One's best or most prosperous time.

hiatus \hie-AY-tus\ *n.* A break or gap in events.

hiccup *also* **hiccough** \HIK-up\ *n.* A spasmodic intake of breath.

hickory \HIK-oh-ree\ *n. pl.* hickories. A hardwood tree related to the walnut.

hide \hied\ *v.* hid; hidden; hiding. **1.** To put out of view. **2.** To keep secret.

hideous \HID-ee-us\ *adj.* Very ugly.

hierarchy \HIE-uh-rahr-kee\ *n. pl.* hierarchies. A division of a whole into grades or ranks. hierarchical or hierarchic *adj.*

high \hie\ *adj.* higher; highest. **1.** Distance upwards, esp. above ground. **2.** Extreme. **3.** Greater than normal.

highlight \HIE-LIET\ *n.* **1.** Some-thing of major interest. **2.** Best or most outstanding feature.

highlight \HIE-LIET\ *v.* high-lighted; highlighting. To focus on.

high-strung \HIE-STRUNG\ *adj.* Very nervous or sensitive.

highway \HIE-way\ *n.* A public road or main route.

hike \hiek\ *n.* A long walk.

hike \hiek\ *v.* hiked; hiking. **1.** To walk. **2.** To pull something up.

hilarious \hi-LAIR-ee-us\ *adj.* Extremely funny. hilarity *n.*

hill \hil\ *n.* Elevated land area.

him *pron.* Concerning a man as object or possessor.

hinder \HIN-dur\ *v.* hindered; hindering. To delay progress of. hindrance *n.*

Hinduism \HIN-doo-iz-um\ *n.* An East Indian religion and philosophy.

hinge \hinj\ *n.* A flexible joint.

hinge \hinj\ *v.* hinged; hinging. To be contingent upon.

hint *n.* A clue.

hint *v.* hinted; hinting. To suggest.

hip *n.* The juncture of pelvis and thigh.

hip-hop *n.* An inner-city subculture.

hippie *also* **hippy** \HIP-ee\ *n. pl.* hippies. A person who rejects the establishment and is unconventional.

Hippocratic \HIP-oh-krat-ik\ *adj.* Concerning Hippocrates or the Hippocratic school of medicine.

hippopotamus \hip-uh-POT-uh-mus\ *n. pl.* hippopotamuses or hippopotami. A large African river mammal.

hire \hier\ *v.* hired; hiring. To employ.

Hispanic \hi-SPAN-ik\ *adj.* Of or concerning Spain or a Spanish-speaking country.

hiss \his\ *v.* hissed; hissing. **1.** To make a hissing sound. **2.** To threaten or disapprove.

histamine \HIS-tuh-meen\ *n.* (Md) A compound that causes allergic reactions.

history \HIS-tuh-ree\ *n. pl.* histories. **1.** Past events. **2.** An account of the past. historian *n.*; historical *adj.*

hit *v.* hit; hitting. **1.** To strike. **2.** To attain. **3.** Hit the sack [Id]: go to bed.

hitch \hich\ *n.* **1.** A limp. **2.** A connecting part. **3.** A knot.

hitch \hich\ *v.* hitched; hitching. **1.** To connect. **2.** [Cl] To hitchhike. **3.** [Sl] To marry.

hitchhiker \HICH-hiek-ur\ *n.* One who travels by getting free rides.

hither \HITH-ur\ *adv.* To this place.

HMO \aych-em-oh\ *abbrv.* Health Maintenance Organization.

hoagie *also* **hoagy** \HOH-gee\ *n. pl.* hoagies. A submarine sandwich.

hoard \hord\ *n.* **1.** A group. **2.** A hidden supply.

hoarse \hors\ *adj.* hoarser; hoarsest. Having a rough sound.

hoax \hohks\ *n.* An instance of trickery or deceit.

hoax \hohks\ *v.* hoaxed; hoaxing. To trick or deceive.

hobby \HOB-ee\ *n. pl.* hobbies. A thing done for pleasure in one's spare time.

hobo \HOH-boh\ *n. pl.* hoboes also hobos. A wanderer.

hockey \HOK-ee\ *n.* A team game played on grass or ice.

hocus-pocus \HOH-kus-POH-kus\ *n.* **1.** A trick. **2.** Nonsense.

hodgepodge \HOJ-poj\ *n.* A jumble.

hogwash \HAWG-wosh\ *n.* Nonsense.

hoist *v.* hoisted; hoisting. To raise into position.

hold \hohld\ *v.* held; holding. **1.** To possess. **2.** To hang onto. **3.** To restrain. **4.** To contain. **5.** To conduct.

hold \hohld\ *n.* **1.** A prison. **2.** A grip. **3.** Cargo compartment.

holding pattern *n.* A plane's path while waiting to land.

holdup *also* **hold-up** \HOHLD-up\ *n.* **1.** A delay. **2.** A robbery.

hole \hohl\ *n.* **1.** An opening. **2.** Bad or awkward situation.

holiday \HOL-i-day\ *n.* **1.** A special event. **2.** A holy day. **3.** A vacation day.

holistic \HOH-lis-tik\ *adj.* Relating to mind, body, etc as a whole, esp. for treatment.

hollandaise \HOL-un-dayz\ *n.* (Fr) A rich cream sauce.

hollow \HOL-oh\ *adj.* hollower; hollowest **1.** Possessing a cavity. **2.** False or meaningless.

holly \HOH-lee\ *n. pl.* hollies. An evergreen bush with red berries and green leaves.

Holocaust \HOL-uh-kawst\ *n.* **1.** The WWII mass slaughter of Jews and other minorities by Nazis. **2.** Large-scale destruction (holocaust).

hologram \HOL-uh-gram\ *n.* (Sc) A three-dimensional image. holography *n.*

holster \HOHL-stur\ *n.* A gun holder on a belt.

holy \HOH-lee\ *adj.* holier; holiest. **1.** Sacred. **2.** Religious. holiness *n.*

homage \HOM-ij\ *n.* Tribute.

home \hohm\ *n.* **1.** One's residence. **2.** A caregiving place for certain people.

homebody \HOHM-buh-dee\ *n. pl.* homebodies A person whose life focuses on the home.

homeboy \HOHM-boy\ *n.* A neighbor.

homeland \HOHM-land\ *n.* One's native land.

homeless \HOHM-lis\ *adj.* Without a residence.

homeless \HOHM-lis\ *n.* One without a home.

homely \HOHM-lee\ *adj.* homelier; homeliest. **1.** Concerning a home. **2.** Plain.

homeopathy \hoh-mee-OP-uh-thee\ *n.* (Sc) A medical treatment method.

Homeric \hoh-MAIR-ik\ *adj.* Concerning Homer's style.

homestead \HOHM-sted\ *n.* **1.** A house and the surrounding land. **2.** Land acquired by living on it.

homicide \HOM-uh-side\ *n.* Murder. homicidal *adj.*

homily \HOM-uh-lee\ *n. pl.* homilies. A moralizing sermon.

homoerotic \HOHM-oh-er-ot-ik\ *adj.* Concerning homosexuality.

homogeneous *also* **homogenous** \hoh-muh-JEE-nee-us\ *adj.* Of the same kind.

homogenize \huh-MOJ-uh-niez\ *v.* homogenized; homogenizing. To treat milk so that the cream blends in and does not rise.

homophobia \HOHM-uh-FOH-bee-uh\ *n.* Fear or hatred of homosexuals.

Homo sapiens \HOH-moh-SAY-pee-unz\ *n.* Man.

homosexual \hoh-muh-SEK-shoo-ul\ *adj.* Concerning attraction to the same gender. homosexuality *n.*

homunculus \huh-MUNG-kyuh-lus\ *n. pl.* homunculi. Theory of miniature adult in cells.

honcho \HON-choh\ *n. pl.* honchos. The boss.

honest \ON-ist\ *adj.* **1.** Truthful **2.** Real. **3.** Trustworthy. honesty *n.*

honk *n.* A noise like the cry of a wild goose.

honor \ON-ur\ *n.* **1.** Great respect, regard. **2.** A good reputation. **3.** A privilege. **4.** A title. honorable *adj.*

honorarium \on-uh-RAIR-ee-um\ *n. pl.* honoraria. Small payment for unpriced services.

hood \huud\ *n.* **1.** A head covering attached to a garment. **2.** An academic scarf. **3.** A hoodlum.

hoodwink \HUUD-wingk\ *v.* hoodwinked; hoodwinking. To deceive.

hoof \huuf\ *n. pl.* hooves also hoofs. The nail or horny part of a quadruped's foot.

hook \huuk\ *n.* **1.** Something curved. **2.** A ball's flight. **3.** A short curved blow in boxing.

hooker \HUUK-ur\ *n.* A prostitute.

hookworm \HUUK-wurm\ *n.* A parasite that lives in one's intestines.

hooligan \HOO-li-gun\ *n.* A ruffian.

hoop *n.* **1.** A ringlike object. **2.** A basketball rim.

hoot *n.* **1.** An owl's cry. **2.** Something amusing.

hop *v.* hopped; hopping. To leap on one foot.

hope \hohp\ *n.* A desire or expectation. hopeless *adj.*; hopeful *n.*

hope \hohp\ *v.* hoped; hoping. **1.** To wish and desire. **2.** To expect.

horde \hord\ *n.* A swarm.

horizon \huh-RIE-zun\ *n.* **1.** A line where earth meets sky. **2.** Soil lines.

horizontal \hor-uh-ZON-tl\ *adj.* Running parallel to.

hormone \HOR-mohn\ *n.* A substance that stimulates cells.

horrendous \haw-REN-dus\ *adj.* Dreadful.

horrible \HOR-uh-bul\ *adj.* Extremely unpleasant. horror *n.*; horrid *adj.*; horrific *adj.*; horrify *v.*

hors d'oeuvres *also* **hors d'oeuvre** \or-DURVZ\ *pl. n.* (Fr) An appetizer.

horse \hors\ *n. pl.* horses also horse. A strong quadruped with long mane and tail.

horticulture \HOR-ti-kul-chur\ *n.* (Sc) The practice and study of gardening. horticulturist *n.*

hose \hohz\ *n. pl.* hose or hoses. **1.** Nylon leg coverings. **2.** A tube of plastic or other flexible material.

hospice \HOS-pis\ *n.* (Fr) **1.** A lodge for travelers. **2.** Home and care for terminally ill.

hospitable \HOS-pi-tuh-bul\ *adj.* Welcoming.

hospital \HOS-pi-tl\ *n.* A medical institution. hospitalize *v.*

hospitality \hos-pi-TAL-i-tee\ *n. pl.* hospitalities. Friendly entertainment for guests.

host \hohst\ *n.* **1.** A large number. **2.** One who receives guests. **3.** A support animal.

hostage \HOS-tij\ *n.* One held captive.

hostel \HOS-tl\ *n.* An inn.

hostess \HOH-stis\ *n.* A woman who entertains guests.

hostile \HOS-tl\ *adj.* **1.** Concerning an enemy. **2.** Unfriendly.

hot *adj.* hotter; hottest. **1.** Possessing a high temperature. **2.** Violent. **3.** Spicy. **4.** Sexually desirable.

hotel \hoh-TEL\ *n.* Temporary lodging. hotelier *n.*

hot line *n.* A direct telephone connection for emergencies.

hot pants *n.* Women's short shorts.

hot tub *n.* A large tub for soaking.

hot-wire *v.* hot-wired; hot-wiring. To start up a car without keys in the ignition.

hound \hownd\ *n.* A hunting dog.

hound \hownd\ *v.* hounded; hounding. **1.** To harass. **2.** To pursue.

hour \owr\ *n.* A unit of time equal to sixty minutes.

hourglass \OWR-glas\ *n.* A measuring device for time.

house \hows\ *n. pl.* houses. **1.** A building that people live in. **2.** A legislative body. **3.** A business firm.

household \HOWS-hohld\ *n.* A group of people living together.

housemate \HOWS-mayt\ *n.* One who lives with another.

housework \HOWS-wurk\ *n.* Cleaning a house.

housing \HOW-zing\ *n.* **1.** Lodging. **2.** A cover.

hovel \HUV-ul\ *n.* An open, small dirty shelter.

hover \HUV-ur\ *v.* hovered; hovering. To hang suspended.

hovercraft \HUV-ur-KRAFT\ *n.* A vehicle supported by downward air thrust.

how *adv.* In what manner.

how *conj.* The condition in which.

however \how-EV-ur\ *adv.* On the other hand.

however \how-EV-ur\ *conj.* Although.

howl *v.* howled; howling. To cry out loudly.

HTLV-III *n.* (Md) A virus.

hub *n.* **1.** The center point. **2.** A focal point.

hubris \HYOO-bris\ *n.* Arrogant pride.

huckleberry \HUK-ul-bair-ee\ *n. pl.* huckleberries. An edible dark blue-to-black berry.

huddle \HUD-l\ *n.* A group meeting.

huddle \HUD-l\ *v.* huddled; huddling. To crowd together.

hue \hyoo\ *n.* Color.

huff \huf\ *v.* huffed; huffing. **1.** To bluster. **2.** To blow out. huffy *adj.*

hug *v.* hugged; hugging. To clasp someone or something with both arms.

huge \hyooj\ *adj.* huger; hugest. Enormous.

hulk *n.* Large clumsy thing.

hull \hul\ *n.* **1.** The outer covering. **2.** A ship's frame.

hum *v.* hummed; humming. To make a droning sound.

human \HYOO-mun\ *adj.* Concerning a person.

human \HYOO-mun\ *n.* A human being, man or woman.

humane \hyoo-MAYN\ *adj.* **1.** Kind. **2.** Compassionate.

humanitarian \hyoo-man-i-TAIR-ee-un\ *n.* One who promotes social good.

humanities \hyoo-MAN-i-teez\ *n. pl.* humanities. Academic disciplines devoted to human concerns, esp. the arts.

humankind \HYOO-mun-kind\ *n.* People.

humble \HUM-bul\ *adj.* humbler; humblest. Modest.

humdrum \HUM-drum\ *adj.* Dull.

humid \HYOO-mid\ *adj.* Very moist.

humiliate \hyoo-MIL-ee-ayt\ *v.* humiliated; humiliating. To completely embarrass.

humility \hyoo-MIL-i-tee\ *n.* State of being humble.

humongous *also* **humungous** \hyoo-MUNG-gus\ *adj.* Huge.

humor \HYOO-mur\ *n.* Funniness or wit. humorous *adj.*

hump *n.* A rounded mass.

hunch *n.* An instinct.

hunch *v.* hunched; hunching. To curl up.

hundred \HUN-drid\ *n. pl.* hundreds or hundred. Ten times ten. hundredth *n.* or *adj.*

hungry \HUNG-gree\ *adj.* hungrier; hungriest. **1.** Craving food or drink. **2.** Desirous or eager. hunger *n.*

hunk \hungk\ *n.* **1.** A large mass. **2.** An attractive man.

hunt *v.* hunted; hunting. To pursue for food or sport. hunter *n.*

hurdle \HUR-dl\ *n.* A barrier or difficulty.

hurl *v.* hurled; hurling. To throw.

hurrah \huh-RAH\ *n.* A cheer.

hurricane \HUR-uh-kayn\ *n.* A violent wind storm.

hurry \HUR-ee\ *v.* hurried; hurrying. To move quickly.

hurt *v.* hurt; hurting. To damage or injure.

hurtle \HUR-tl\ *v.* hurtled; hurtling. To move or throw rapidly.

husband \HUZ-bund\ *n.* A married man.

hush *v.* hushed; hushing. To quiet.

husk *n.* A shell.

husky \HUS-kee\ *adj.* huskier; huskiest. Hoarse.

husky \HUS-kee\ *n. pl.* huskies. A northern dog breed.

hustle \HUS-ul\ *v.* hustled; hustling. **1.** To shove. **2.** To hurry. hustler *n.*

hut *n.* A shack.

hyacinth \HIE-ah-sinth\ *n.* A fragrant plant with bell-shaped flowers.

hybrid \HIE-brid\ *n.* Offspring of two different species or varieties.

Hydra \HIE-druh\ *n.* A many-headed serpent in Greek mythology.

hydrate \HIE-drayt\ *v.* hydrated; hydrating. (Sc) To put in water. hydration *n.*

hydraulic \hie-DRAW-lik\ *adj.* (Sc) Concerning liquids conveyed through pipes or channels, for water power.

hydrochloride \hie-droh-KLOH-ride\ *n.* (Sc) A chemical complex.

hydroelectric \hie-droh-i-LEK-trik\ *adj.* (Sc) Producing electricity using waterpower.

hydrogen \HIE-druh-jen\ *n.* (Sc) The lightest chemical element, an odorless gas.

hydroplane \HIE-druh-playn\ *v.* hydroplaned; hydroplaning. (Sc) To skim the surface of water.

hyena \hie-EE-nuh\ *n. pl.* hyenas also hyena. A large carnivorous wolflike mammal.

hygiene \HIE-jeen\ *n.* Cleanliness for health maintenance. hygienist *n.*

hymn \him\ *n.* A sacred song. hymnal *n.*

hype \hiep\ *n.* **1.** Deception. **2.** Promotion.

hyperbola \hie-PUR-buh-luh\ *n. pl.* hyperbolas or hyperbolae. A geometric figure.

hyperbole \hie-PUR-buh-lee\ *n.* Exaggerated writing.

hyperinflation \hie-pur-IN-flay-shun\ *n.* Fast growing inflation.

hyperthyroid \hie-pur-THIE-roid\ *adj.* (Md) Concerning excessive functioning of the thyroid.

hyperventilate \hie-pur-VEN-tuh-layt\ *v.* hyperventilated; hyperventilating. To breathe quickly.

hypnosis \hip-NOH-sis\ *n. pl.* hypnoses. A state resembling sleep. hypnotize *v.*; hypnotist *n.*; hypnotic *adj.*

hypnotherapy \hip-NOH-thair-uh-pee\ *n.* (Md) Psychotherapy using hypnosis.

hypoallergenic \HIE-poh-al-ur-JEN-ik\ *adj.* (Md) Not likely to cause allergic reactions.

hypochondria \hie-puh-KON-dree-uh\ *n.* (Md) Having imaginary health problems. hypochondriac *n.*

hypocritical \HI-puh-KRI-tik-ul\ *adj.* Concerning falsely pretending to be virtuous. hypocrit *n.*

hypodermic \hie-puh-DUR-mik\ *adj.* (Md) Injected beneath the skin.

hypoglycemia \hie-poh-glie-SEE-mee-uh\ *n.* (Md) Low blood sugar.

hypotenuse *also* **hypothenuse** \hie-POT-n-oos\ *n.* A right-triangle side.

hypothermia \hie-puh-ther-mee-uh\ *n.* A lowered body temperature.

hypothesis \hie-POTH-uh-sis\ *n. pl.* hypotheses. A supposition or theory. hypothesize *v.*; hypothetical *adj.*

hysterectomy \his-tuh-REK-tuh-mee\ *n. pl.* hysterectomies. (Md) Removal of the uterus.

hysterical *also* **hysteric** \hi-STER-i-kul\ *adj.* Concerning uncontrollable emotions. hysteria *n.*

I

I \ie\ *pron.* First person personal pronoun.

i \ie\ *n. pl.* i's or is. The ninth letter of the alphabet.

ibuprofen \ie-BYOO-pro-fen\ *n.* [Md] An anti-inflammatory drug.

ice \ise\ *n.* **1.** Frozen water. **2.** Diamonds.

ice \ise\ *v.* iced; icing. **1.** To chill with frozen water. **2.** To put frosting on a confection. **3.** [Sl] To kill. icy *adj.*

iceberg \ISE-burg\ *n.* A floating ice mass from a glacier.

ice cream *n.* Frozen creamy dairy food.

icicle \IE-si-kul\ *n.* A long strip of frozen water.

icky \IK-ee\ *adj.* ickier; ickiest. Distasteful.

icon \IE-kon\ *n.* **1.** A graphic symbol. **2.** A sacred painting in the Eastern Church.

iconoclasm \ie-KON-uh-klazm\ *adj.* Concerning the destruction or attack of religious images. iconoclast *n.*

idea \ie-DEE-uh\ *n.* **1.** A thought. **2.** A design.

ideal \ie-DEE-ul\ *n.* **1.** A mental image of perfection. **2.** A model or standard.

idealism \ie-DEE-uh-liz-um\ *n.* Theory of high ideals. idealist *n.*; idealize *v.*

identical \ie-DEN-ti-kul\ *adj.* The same.

identify \ie-DEN-tuh-fie\ *v.* identified; identifying. **1.** To recognize.

2. To consider to be identical. **3.** To associate with. identification *n.*

identity \ie-DEN-ti-tee\ *n. pl.* identities. One's distinguishing characteristics.

ideology *also* **idealogy** \ied-ee-OL-uh-jee\ *n. pl.* ideologies. Beliefs that form a theory. ideological *also* ideologic *adj.*; ideologue *n.*

idiom \ID-ee-um\ *n.* Phrase or usage particular to a language. idiomatic *adj.*

idiosyncrasy \id-ee-uh-SING-kruh-see\ *n. pl.* idiosyncrasies. Peculiarity of habit or behavior.

idiot \ID-ee-ut\ *n.* A stupid or foolish person. idiotic also idiotical *adj.*; idiocy *n.*

idle \IED-l\ *adj.* Doing no work or being inactive.

idle \IED-l\ *v.* idled; idling. To pass time.

idol \IED-l\ *n.* An object of worship. idolize *v.*

idyllic \ie-DIL-ik\ *adj.* Peaceful or romantic. idyll or idyl *n.*

igloo \IG-loo\ *n. pl.* igloos. An Eskimo snow house.

ignite \ig-NIET\ *v.* ignited; igniting. To cause to burn. ignition *n.*

ignorant \IG-nur-unt\ *adj.* **1.** Lacking knowledge. **2.** Uninformed. ignorance *n.*; ignoramus *n.*

ignore \ig-NOR\ *v.* ignored; ignoring. To neglect and take no notice of.

iguana \i-GWAH-nuh\ *n.* A tree-climbing lizard.

ileum \IL-ee-um\ *n. pl.* ilea. (Md) Small intestine part.

ilium \IL-ee-um\ *n. pl.* ilia. (Md) Hipbone part.

I'll \ile\ *cont.* I will.

ill \il\ *adj.* worse; worst **1.** Sick. **2.** Bad or harmful. **3.** Unkind.

ill \il\ *n.* **1.** Sickness. **2.** Misfortune.

ill-advised \IL-ud-VIZD\ *adj.* Unwise.

ill at ease *adj.* Uncomfortable.

ill-bred \IL-BRED\ *adj.* Impolite.

illegal \i-LEE-gul\ *adj.* Unlawful.

illegible \i-LEJ-uh-bul\ *adj.* Undecipherable.

illegitimate \il-i-JIT-uh-mit\ *n.* **1.** Born of unwed parents. **2.** Not logical.

illicit \i-LIS-it\ *adj.* Unlawful.

illiterate \i-LIT-ur-it\ *adj.* **1.** Unable to read or write. **2.** Uneducated.

ill-mannered \IL-MAN-urd\ *adj.* Rude.

illness \IL-nis\ *n.* A sickness.

illogical \i-LOJ-i-kul\ *adj.* Senseless.

illuminate \i-LOO-muh-nayt\ *v.* illuminated; illuminating. **1.** To brighten or light up. **2.** To throw light on a subject. illumination *n.*

illusion \i-LOO-zhun\ *n.* False impression or belief.

illustrate \IL-uh-strayt\ *v.* illustrated; illustrating. **1.** To clarify. **2.** To draw pictures. illustration *n.*; illustrator *n.*

illustrious \i-LUS-tree-us\ *adj.* Famous.

ill-will *n.* Hostility.

image \IM-ij\ *n.* **1.** A reproduction or picture. **2.** An incarnation **3.** An ideal. imagery *n.*

imagine \i-MAJ-in\ *v.* imagined; imagining. **1.** To form a mental image of. **2.** To think or suppose. **3.** To guess. imaginable *adj.*; imagination *n.*; imaginative *adj.*

imbalanced \im-BAL-unsd\ *adj.* Out of equilibrium.

imbecile \IM-buh-sul\ *n.* A mentally deficient person.

imitate \IM-i-tayt\ *v.* imitated; imitating. To copy. imitation *n.*

immaculate \i-MAK-yuh-lit\ *adj.* **1.** Pure. **2.** Clean.

immature \IM-uh-CHUUR\ *adj.* Childish.

immediate \i-MEE-dee-it\ *adj.* **1.** Without hesitation. **2.** Direct.

immense \i-MENS\ *adj.* Huge.

immerse \i-MURS\ *v.* immersed; immersing. **1.** To plunge into. **2.** To absorb.

immigrant \IM-i-grunt\ *n.* One who goes to live in another country.

immigrate \IM-i-grayt\ *v.* immigrated; immigrating. To come to another country to live. immigration *n.*

imminent \IM-uh-nunt\ *adj.* About to occur.

immobile \i-MOH-bul\ *adj.* Motionless or unable to be moved. immobilize *v.*

immoral \i-MOR-ul\ *adj.* Lacking ethics.

immortal \i-MOR-tl\ *adj.* Free from death. immortalize *v.*

immune \i-MYOON\ *adj.* **1.** Exempt. **2.** [Md] Not susceptible. immunity *n.*

immune system \i-MYOON-SIS-tum\ *n.* [Md] The body's defense system against disease.

immunize \IM-yuh-niez\ *v.* (Md) immunized; immunizing. To make unsusceptible to a disease.

immunodeficiency \IM-yuh-noh-duh-FISH-un-see\ *n.* (Md) Unable to produce protective antibodies to fight disease.

immunology \im-yuh-NOL-uh-jee\ *n.* (Md) The study of the immune system. immunological *adj.*

immunosuppression \IM-myoo-noh-soo-PRESH-un\ *n.* (Md) Suppression of immune system.

imp *n.* A mischievous person.

impact \IM-pakt\ *v.* impacted; impacting. To press or wedge firmly.

impair \im-PAIR\ *v.* impaired; impairing. To damage or weaken.

impale \im-PAYL\ *v.* impaled; impaling. To pierce.

impartial \im-PAHR-shul\ *adj.* Not favoring one over another. impartiality *n.*

impasse \IM-pas\ *n.* **1.** A stalemate. **2.** A passage with no exit.

impatient \im-PAY-shunt\ *adj.* Restless and intolerant. impatience *n.*

impeach \im-PEECH\ *v.* impeached; impeaching. **1.** To charge with a crime. **2.** To remove from elected office. impeachment *n.*

impend \im-PEND\ *v.* impended; impending. **1.** To be imminent. **2.** To menace.

impenetrable \im-PEN-i-truh-bul\ *adj.* Unable to be penetrated.

imperative \im-PER-uh-tiv\ *n.* **1.** A grammatical form. **2.** A command.

imperative \im-PER-uh-tiv\ *adj.* Necessary.

imperfect \im-PUR-fekt\ *adj.* Flawed.

imperialism \im-PEER-ee-uh-liz-um\ *n.* The practice of extending political power beyond a country. imperialist *n.*

impersonal \im-PUR-suh-nl\ *adj.* Not influenced by feeling or a person.

impersonate \im-PUR-suh-nayt\ *v.* impersonated; impersonating. To act like someone else. impersonator *n.*; impersonation *n.*

impertinent \im-PUR-tn-unt\ *adj.* Not showing respect.

impetigo \im-pi-TIE-goh\ *n.* (Md) Contagious skin disease.

impetuous \im-PECH-oo-us\ *n.* Acting or done on impulse.

impetus \IM-pi-tus\ *n.* A moving force.

implant \im-PLANT\ *v.* implanted; implanting. To instill or insert.

implausible \im-PLAW-zuh-bul\ *adj.* Unbelievable.

implement \IM-pluh-munt\ *n.* A tool.

implement \IM-plu-ment\ *v.* implemented; implementing. To put into effect.

implicate \IM-pli-kayt\ *v.* implicated; implicating. To involve or connect to a crime.

implore \im-PLOR\ *v.* implored; imploring. To beg.

imply \im-PLIE\ *v.* implied; implying. To suggest.

impolite \im-puh-LITE\ *adj.* Rude.

import \im-PORT\ *v.* imported; importing. To bring in saleable goods from abroad.

important \im-POR-tnt\ *adj.* Having a great effect, authority, or influence. importance *n.*

impose \im-POHZ\ *v.* imposed; imposing. **1.** To establish by authority. **2.** To force. imposing *adj.*

impossible \im-POS-uh-bul\ *adj.* Unable to be done. impossibility *n.*

impostor *also* **imposter** \im-POS-tur\ *n.* A fake or fraud.

impotent \IM-puh-tunt\ *adj.* **1.** Helpless. **2.** Unable to perform sexually. impotency *n.*

impoverished \im-POV-ur-ishd\ *adj.* Poor.

impractical *also* **impracticable** \im-PRAK-ti-kul\ *adj.* **1.** Unrealistic. **2.** Idealistic.

impregnable \im-PREG-nuh-bul\ *adj.* Safe from attack.

impregnate \im-PREG-nayt\ *v.* impregnated; impregnating. **1.** To fertilize. **2.** To fill.

impress \im-PRES\ *v.* impressed; impressing. **1.** To influence favorably. **2.** To affix. **3.** To force into.

impression \im-PRESH-un\ *n.* **1.** An effect on the mind. **2.** An uncertain idea. **3.** Imitation for entertainment.

impressionism \im-PRESH-uh-niz-um\ *n.* A style of painting without detail. impressionist *n.*

impressive \im-PRES-iv\ *adj.* Memorable.

imprint \im-PRINT\ *v.* imprinted; imprinting. To press into.

imprison \im-PRIZ-un\ *v.* imprisoned; imprisoning. To put into prison.

improbable \im-PROB-uh-bul\ *adj.* Unlikely.

impromptu \im-PROMP-too\ *adj.* Without preparation.

improper \im-PROP-ur\ *adj.* **1.** Incorrect or unsuitable. **2.** Indecent. impropriety *n.*

improve \im-PROOV\ *v.* improved; improving. To make better. improvement *n.*

improvisation \im-prov-uh-ZAY-shun\ *n.* Dramatic work performed without preparation.

improvise \IM-pruh-viez\ *v.* improvised; improvising. To perform without preparation.

impulse \IM-puls\ *n.* **1.** An impetus. **2.** A motive. impulsive *adj.*

impunity \im-PYOO-ni-tee\ *n.* Freedom from punishment or injury.

impurity \im-PYUUR-i-tee\ *n. pl.* impurities. Something that makes something else dirty. impure *adj.*

in absentia \IN-ab-SEN-shee-uh\ *adv.* (Lt) In absense.

inability \in-uh-BIL-i-tee\ *n. pl.* inabilities. State of being unable.

inaccessible \in-ak-SES-uh-bul\ *adj.* Not able to get to.

inaccurate \in-AK-yur-it\ *adj.* Not correct. inaccurately *adv.*; innaccuracy *n.*

inactive \in-AK-tiv\ *adj.* Idle. inactivity *n.*

inadequate \in-AD-i-kwit\ *adj.* Insufficient. inadequately *adv.*; inadequacy *n.*

inadmissible \in-ud-MIS-uh-bul\ *adj.* Not permitted. inadmissibly *adv.*

inane \i-NAYN\ *adj.* inaner; inanest. **1.** Insubstantial. **2.** Silly.

inanimate \in-AN-uh-mit\ *adj.* Lacking life.

inaugural \in-AW-gyur-ul\ *adj.* Concerning a beginning, esp. in public office. inauguration *n.*

inbred \IN-BRED\ *adj.* Inborn or produced by breeding closely related individuals.

incapable \in-KAY-puh-bul\ *adj.* Not able. incapability *n.*

incapacitate \in-kuh-PAS-i-tayt\ *v.* incapacitated; incapacitating. To disable. incapacity *n.*

incense \IN-sens\ *n.* A fragrant scent.

incense \in-SENS\ *v.* incensed; incensing. To anger.

incentive \in-SEN-tiv\ *n.* A motive.

incessant \in-SES-unt\ *adj.* Constant. incessantly *adv.*

incest \IN-sest\ *n.* Sexual relations with a close relative. incestuous *adv.*

inch *n.* A unit of length measurement.

inch *v.* inched; inching. To move slowly and in small steps.

incident \IN-si-dunt\ *n.* An event or occurrence. incidence *n.*

incidental \in-si-DEN-tl\ *n.* A small item.

incision \in-SIZH-un\ *n.* A cut.

incite \in-SIET\ *v.* incited; inciting. To urge to action. incitement *n.*

inclement \in-KLEM-unt\ *adj.* Cold, wet, or stormy.

inclination \in-kluh-NAY-shun\ *n.* **1.** A nod. **2.** A slant. **3.** A tendency. incline *v.*; inclined *adj.*

include \in-KLOOD\ *v.* included; including. **1.** To treat as part of a whole. **2.** To put in a category. inclusion *n.*; inclusive *adj.*

incognito \in-kog-NEE-toh\ *adv.* or *adj.* (It) Concerning a concealed identity.

incoherent \in-koh-HEER-unt\ *adj.* Rambling in speech or reasoning. incoherence *n.*

income \IN-kum\ *n.* Amount of wages.

incommunicado \in-kuh-myoo-ni-KAH-doh\ *adv.* or *adj.* (Sp) Without a way of communicating.

incompatible \in-kum-PAT-uh-bul\ *adj.* Unable to associate.

incompetent \in-KOM-pi-tunt\ *adj.* Unable to function adequately. incompetence *n.*

incomplete \in-kum-PLEET\ *adj.* Not finished.

incomprehensible \in-kom-pri-HEN-suh-bul\ *adj.* Unintelligible. incomprehension *n.*

inconceivable \in-kun-SEE-vuh-bul\ *adj.* Unbelievable. inconceivably *adv.*

inconclusive \in-kun-KLOO-siv\ *adj.* Without a definite result.

inconsequential \in-kon-si-KWEN-shul\ *adj.* 1. Irrelevant. 2. Unimportant.

inconsiderate \in-kun-SID-ur-it\ *adj.* Thoughtless.

inconspicuous \in-kun-SPIK-yoo-us\ *adj.* Not easily noticed.

incontinent \in-KON-tn-unt\ *adj.* Lacking restraint.

inconvenient \in-kun-VEEN-yunt\ *adj.* Troublesome and not convenient. inconvenience *n.*

incorporate \in-KOR-puh-rayt\ *v.* incorporated; incorporating. 1. To include as part. 2. To form a corporation. incorporation *n.*

incorrect \in-kuh-REKT\ *adj.* Wrong.

incorrigible \in-KOR-i-juh-bul\ *adj.* Unruly.

increase \in-KREES\ *v.* increased; increasing. To make or become greater.

incredible \in-KRED-uh-bul\ *adj.* Difficult to believe. incredibly *adv.*

increment \IN-kruh-munt\ *n.* 1. A unit of change. 2. An increase.

incriminate \in-KRIM-uh-nayt\ *v.* incriminated; incriminating. To involve or indicate involvement in a crime. incrimination *n.*

incubate \IN-kyuh-bayt\ *v.* incubated; incubating. To give warmth to eggs for hatching. incubation *n.*

incumbent \in-KUM-bunt\ *n.* Someone holding public office. incumbency *n.*

incur \in-KUR\ *v.* incurred; incurring. To bring upon oneself.

incurable \in-KYUUR-uh-bul\ *adj.* Unable to heal or fix.

indebted \in-DET-id\ *adj.* Owing a debt. indebtedness *n.*

indecent \in-DEE-sunt\ *adj.* Offensive.

indecisive \in-di-SIE-siv\ *adj.* Not decisive.

indeed \in-DEED\ *adv.* **1.** Of course. **2.** Undeniable.

indefinite \in-DEF-uh-nit\ *adj.* Vague or not fixed. indefinitely *adv.*

indent \in-DENT\ *v.* indented; indenting. **1.** To set in from margin. **2.** To force inward.

independent \in-di-PEN-dunt\ *adj.* **1.** Self-governing or self-controlled. **2.** Free. independence *n.*

indescribable \in-di-SKRIE-buh-bul\ *adj.* Beyond description.

indestructible \in-di-STRUK-tuh-bul\ *adj.* Unable to be destroyed.

indeterminate \in-di-TUR-muh-nit\ *adj.* Vague or not fixed.

index \IN-deks\ *n. pl.* indexes or indices. A reference list to a larger body of work.

indicate \IN-di-kayt\ *v.* indicated; indicating. To point out. indication *n.*; indicative *adj.*

indict \in-DITE\ *v.* indicted; indicting. **1.** To accuse. **2.** To charge. indictment *n.*

indifferent \in-DIF-runt\ *adj.* **1.** Showing no interest. **2.** Neutral. indifference *n.*

indigenous \in-DIJ-uh-nus\ *adj.* Native.

indigent \IN-di-junt\ *adj.* Impoverished.

indignant \in-DIG-nunt\ *adj.* Concerning anger arroused by injustice. indignation *n.*

indigo \IN-di-goh\ *n. pl.* indigos or indigoes. Blue dye.

indirect \in-duh-REKT\ *adj.* Roundabout.

indiscreet \in-di-SKREET\ *adj.* Not cautious. indiscretion *n.*

indiscriminate \in-di-SKRIM-uh-nit\ *adj.* **1.** Random. **2.** Unrestrained.

individual \in-duh-VIJ-oo-ul\ *adj.* **1.** Single or separate. **2.** Special.

individual \in-duh-VIJ-oo-ul\ *n.* A particular person or thing. individuality *n.*; individualism *n.*

indoctrinate \in-DOK-truh-nayt\ *v.* indoctrinated; indoctrinating. To teach.

induct \in-DUKT\ *v.* inducted; inducting. To initiate.

induction \in-DUK-shun\ *n.* **1.** Initiation. **2.** A logic process. **3.** Electrical process.

indulge \in-DULJ\ *v.* indulged; indulging. **1.** To humor. **2.** To pamper. indulgence *n.*; indulgent *adj.*

industrious \in-DUS-tree-us\ *adj.* Hard-working. industriousness *n.*

industry \IN-duh-stree\ *n. pl.* industries. **1.** Manufacture of goods. **2.** Business. industrial *adj.*; industrialization *n.*

inebriated \in-EE-bree-aytd\ *adj.* Intoxicated. inebriate *v.*

ineffective *also* **ineffectual** \in-i-FEK-tiv\ *adj.* Incapable.

inefficient \in-i-FISH-unt\ *adj.* Wasteful. inefficiency *n.*

ineligible \in-EL-i-guh-bul\ *adj.* Not eligible.

inept \in-EPT\ *adj.* Awkward or unskillful. ineptitude *n.*

inequality \in-i-KWOL-i-tee\ *n.* Lack of equality.

inert \in-URT\ *adj.* **1.** Inactive. **2.** Lacking.

inertia \in-UR-shuh\ *n.* (Sc) Matter's resistence to motion.

inevitable \in-EV-i-tuh-bul\ *adj.* Unavoidable. inevitability *n.*

inexcusable \in-ik-SKYOO-zuh-bul\ *adj.* Lacking justification.

inexpensive \in-ik-SPEN-siv\ *adj.* Cheap.

inexperienced \in-ik-SPEER-ee-ensd\ *adj.* Lacking knowledge.

inexplicable \in-EK-spli-kuh-bul\ *adj.* Lacking explanation.

infamous \IN-fuh-mus\ *adj.* Having a bad reputation.

infamy \IN-fuh-mee\ *n. pl.* infamies. Disgrace.

infant \IN-funt\ *n.* A very young baby.

infatuate \in-FACH-oo-ayt\ *v.* infatuated; infatuating. To love foolishly or extravagantly. infatuation *n.*

infection \in-FEK-shun\ *n.* A disease. infect *v.*; infectious *adj.*

infer \in-FUR\ *v.* inferred; inferring. To reach an opinion from facts or reasoning. inference *n.*

inferior \in-FEER-ee-ur\ *adj.* Of lower or lesser quality.

infernal \in-FUR-nl\ *adj.* Concerning hell.

inferno \in-FUR-noh\ *n. pl.* infernos. **1.** A roaring fire or intense heat. **2.** Hell.

infertile \in-FUR-til\ *adj.* Unproductive.

infest \in-FEST\ *v.* infested; infesting. To swarm over. infestation *n.*

infidelity \in-fi-DEL-i-tee\ *n. pl.* infidelities. Disloyalty.

infiltrate \in-FIL-trayt\ *v.* infiltrated; infiltrating. **1.** To enter. **2.** To pass through. infiltration *n.*

infinity \in-FIN-i-tee\ *n. pl.* infinities. Boundlessness. infinite *adj.* or *n.*

infirmary \in-FUR-muh-ree\ *n. pl.* infirmaries. Hospital. infirm *adj.*

inflammatory \in-FLAM-uh-tor-ee\ *adj.* Tending to excite or swell. inflame *v.*

inflate \in-FLAYT\ *v.* inflated; inflating. **1.** To fill with air or gas. **2.** To expand.

inflation \in-FLAY-shun\ *n.* General increase in prices and fall in money's worth.

inflexible \in-FLEK-suh-bul\ *adj.* Unyielding.

inflict \in-FLIKT\ *v.* inflicted; inflicting. To cause something to be suffered. infliction *n.*

influence \IN-floo-uns\ *n.* 1. Authority. 2. Power. 3. Under the influence [Id]: Drunk. influential *adj.*

influence \IN-floo-uns\ *v.* influenced; influencing. To produce an effect.

influx \IN-fluks\ *n.* Many coming in.

infomercial \IN-fo-mur-shul\ *n.* A long paid commercial that offers information and advice.

informal \in-FOR-mul\ *adj.* Casual.

information \in-fur-MAY-shun\ *n.* Knowledge or facts. inform *v.*; informant *n.*; informative *adj.*

infraction \in-FRAK-shun\ *n.* A violation.

infrequent \in-FREE-kwunt\ *adj.* Not often. infrequency *n.*

infringe \in-FRINJ\ *v.* infringed; infringing. To intrude on.

infuriate \in-FYUUR-ee-ayt\ *v.* infuriated; infuriating. To make very angry.

ingenious \in-JEEN-yus\ *adj.* Clever.

ingenue *also* **ingénue** \AN-zhuh-noo\ *n.* A naive young woman.

ingrained \in-GRAYND\ *adj.* Deep-seated.

ingrate \IN-grayt\ *n.* Someone who is ungrateful.

ingratiate \in-GRAY-shee-ayt\ *v.* ingratiated; ingratiating. To attempt to gain favor.

ingredient \in-GREE-dee-unt\ *n.* A component.

inhabit \in-HAB-it\ *v.* inhabited; inhabiting. To live in. inhabitable *adj.*; inhabitant *n.*

inhale \in-HAYL\ *v.* inhaled; inhaling. To breathe in. inhalant *n.*

inherent \ih-HER-it\ *adj.* Existing as a permanent quality.

inherit \in-HER-it\ *v.* inherited; inheriting. To receive from a predecessor or a former owner. inheritance *n.*

inhibition \in-i-BISH-un\ *n.* 1. Something that impedes. 2. Resistance. inhibit *v.*

inhuman \ih-HYOO-mun\ *adj.* Lacking warmth and kindness.

iniquity \i-NIK-wi-tee\ *n. pl.* iniquities. Great injustice.

initial \i-NISH-ul\ *adj.* Concerning the first.

initiate \i-NISH-ee-ayt\ *v.* initiated;

initiating. **1.** To begin. **2.** To introduce. initiation *n.*

initiative \i-NISH-uh-tiv\ *n.* **1.** A first step. **2.** An independent action.

inject \in-JEKT\ *v.* injected; injecting. **1.** To force or drive into. **2.** To introduce. injection *n.*

injunction \in-JUNGK-shun\ *n.* (Le) An order.

injure \IN-jur\ *v.* injured; injuring. **1.** To harm. **2.** To wrong. injurious *adj.*

injustice \in-JUS-tis\ *n.* Unfair action or treatment.

ink \ingk\ *n.* A colored liquid used for writing and printing.

inkling \INGK-ling\ *n.* A little knowledge.

inlet \IN-let\ *n.* A water passage.

inmate \IN-mayt\ *n.* A confined person.

inn \in\ *n.* A hotel, often in the country.

innate \i-NAYT\ *adj.* Inborn.

inner \IN-ur\ *adj.* Existing within or toward the center.

innocent \IN-uh-sunt\ *adj.* **1.** Blameless. **2.** Unaware. innocence *n.*

innovate \IN-uh-vayt\ *v.* innovated; innovating. To do something in a new way. innovation *n.*; innovative *adj.*

innuendo \in-yoo-EN-doh\ *n. pl.* innuendos or innuendoes. (Lt) A veiled suggestion.

inoculate \i-NOK-yuh-layt\ *v.* inoculated; inoculating. To infuse.

inopportune \in-op-ur-TOON\ *adj.* Inconvenient or unsuitable.

inquest \IN-kwest\ *adj.* (Le) An investigation.

inquiry \in-KWIRE-ee\ *n. pl.* inquiries. **1.** A search. **2.** A question. inquire *v.*; inquisitive *adj.*

insane \in-SAYN\ *adj.* Crazy or very foolish.

insecure \in-si-KYUUR\ *adj.* Not secure. insecurity *n.*

insensitive \in-SEN-si-tiv\ *adj.* Without tact.

insert \in-SURT\ *v.* inserted; inserting. To put into, between, or among.

inside \IN-SIED\ *n.* **1.** Central part. **2.** Power position. insider *n.*

insider trading *n.* (Bs) Illegal use of information in financial transactions.

insidious \in-SID-ee-us\ *adj.* Treacherous.

insight \IN-site\ *n.* Perception and understanding. insightful

insignia *also* **insigne** \in-SIG-nee-uh\ *n. pl.* insignia or insignias. An honor symbol.

insignificant \in-sig-NIF-i-kunt\ *adj.* **1.** Unimportant. **2.** Small.

insincere \in-sin-SEER\ *adj.* Hypocritical.

insinuate \in-SIN-yoo-ayt\ *v.* insinuated; insinuating. To suggest subtly. insinuation *n.*; insinuating *adj.*

insipid \in-SIP-id\ *adj.* Lacking flavor or liveliness.

insist \in-SIST\ *v.* insisted; insisting. To declare or demand emphatically. insistent *adj.*; insistence *n.*

insomnia \in-SOM-nee-uh\ *n.* Sleeplessness.

inspect \in-SPEKT\ *v.* inspected; inspecting. To scrutinize. inspection *n.*

inspire \in-SPIER\ *v.* inspired; inspiring. **1.** To motivate. **2.** To bring about. inspired *adj.*; inspiration *n.*

instability \in-stuh-BIL-i-tee\ *n.* Lack of stability.

install *also* **instal** \in-STAWL\ *v.* installed; installing. **1.** To put in place. **2.** To set up and make ready for use. installation *n.*

instance \IN-stuns\ *n.* An example.

instant \IN-stunt\ *adj.* **1.** Immediate. **2.** Pre-cooked.

instant \IN-stunt\ *n.* A point in time or moment. instantaneous *adj.*; instantly *adv.*

instead \in-STED\ *adv.* Rather.

instigate \IN-sti-GAYT\ *v.* instigated; instigating. To provoke.

instill *also* **instil** \in-STIL\ *v.* instilled; instilling. To implant. instillation *n.*

instinct \IN-stingkt\ *n.* An inborn sense or behavior. instinctive *adj.*

institute \IN-sti-toot\ *n.* A research or educational organization.

institute \IN-sti-toot\ *v.* instituted; instituting. To establish.

institution \in-sti-TOO-shun\ *n.* **1.** An establishment. **2.** An established rule or custom. institutional *adj.*; institionalize *v.*

instruct \in-STRUKT\ *v.* instructed; instructing. To teach. instruction *n.*; instructive *adj.*

instrument \IN-struh-munt\ *n.* **1.** (Mu) A musical device. **2.** A tool or implement. **3.** A measuring device.

instrumental \in-struh-MEN-tl\ *adj.* **1.** Important. **2.** Performed on musical instruments.

insubordinate \in-suh-BOR-dn-it\ *adj.* Disobedient.

insufferable \in-SUF-ur-uh-bul\ *adj.* Unbearable.

insufficient \in-suh-FISH-unt\ *adj.* Not enough.

insulate \IN-se-layt\ *v.* insulated; insulating. **1.** To detach. **2.** To erect a barrier or padding. insulation *n.*; insular *adj.*

insulin \IN-suh-lin\ *n.* A protein used to metabolize carbohydrates.

insult \in-SULT\ *v.* insulted; insulting. To offend.

insure \in-SHUUR\ *v.* insured; insuring. To provide financial security against loss. insurance *n.*

insurrection \in-suh-REK-shun\ *n.* Rebellion.

intact \in-TAKT\ *adj.* **1.** Uninjured. **2.** Perfect.

integer \IN-ti-jur\ *n.* A number.

integral \in-TEG-rul\ *adj.* Essential.

integrate \IN-tuh-grayt\ *v.* integrated; integrating. To incorporate into. integration *n.*; integrated *adj.*

integrity \in-TEG-ri-tee\ *n.* Honesty.

intellect \IN-tl-ekt\ *n.* The capacity for thought. intellectual *adj.*

intelligent \in-TEL-i-juns\ *adj.* Possessing a high level of reason and knowledge. intelligence *n.*

intelligentsia \in-tel-i-JENT-see-uh\ *n.* Intellectual group.

intend \in-TEND\ *v.* intended; intending. **1.** To mean. **2.** To have in mind or plan to. intended *adj.*

intense \in-TENS\ *adj.* Having a high degree. intensity *n.*; intensify *v.*; intensive *adj.*

intensive care \in-TEN-siv-KAIR\ *n.* (Md) Special medical care for serious cases.

interact \in-tur-AKT\ *v.* interacted; interacting. To have an effect upon each other.

intercept \in-tur-SEPT\ *v.* intercepted; intercepting. To stop or catch before the end. interception *n.*

interest \IN-tur-ist\ *n.* **1.** Feeling of curiosity. **2.** One's concern. **3.** Legal share or financial stake.

interest \IN-tur-ist\ *v.* interested; interesting. To engage or arouse. interested *adj.*

interfere \in-tur-FEER\ *v.* interfered; interfering. **1.** To step in. **2.** To hinder. interference *n.*

interferon \in-tur-FEE-ron\ *n.* (Md) Protein produced by the cells to fight a virus.

interim \IN-tur-um\ *n.* An interval.

interior \in-TEER-ee-ur\ *n.* On the inside.

interject \in-tur-JEKT\ *v.* interjected; interjecting. To put between, esp. in speech. interjection *n.*

interleukin \in-tur-LOO-kin\ *n.* (Md) Substance that helps regulate the immune system.

interlude \IN-tur-lood\ *n.* A short interval.

intermediary \in-tur-MEE-dee-er-ee\ *adj.* A go-between or messenger.

intermediate \in-tur-MEE-dee-it\ *n.* **1.** An in-between step. **2.** Mediator.

intermingle \in-tur-MING-gul\ *v.* intermingled; intermingling. Intermix.

intermittent \in-tur-MIT-nt\ *adj.* Occurring at intervals.

intern *also* **interne** \IN-turn\ *n.* One gaining practical experience.

internal \in-TUR-nl\ *adj.* Of or on the inside. internalize *v.*

international \in-tur-NASH-uh-nl\ *adj.* Between countries.

internment \in-TURN-munt\ *n.* Confinement.

interpret \in-TUR-prit\ *v.* interpreted; interpreting. To explain. interpretation *n.*

interracial \in-tur-RAY-shul\ *adj.* Concerning different races.

intersect \in-tur-SEKT\ *v.* intersected; intersecting. **1.** To cross. **2.** To overlap. intersection *n.*

interval \IN-tur-vul\ *n.* A length of time between two events.

intervene \in-tur-VEEN\ *v.* intervened; intervening. **1.** To come between two events. **2.** To hinder.

interview \IN-tur-vyoo\ *n.* A meeting involving questions.

interview \IN-tur-vyoo\ *v.* inter-

viewed; interviewing. To question.

intestine \in-TES-tin\ *n.* Part of the alimentary canal. intestinal *adj.*

intimidate \in-TIM-i-dayt\ *v.* intimidated; intimidating. **1.** To bully. **2.** To frighten. intimidation *n.*

intolerable \in-TOL-ur-uh-bul\ *adj.* Unbearable. intolerant *adj.*

intoxicated \in-TOK-si-kay-tud\ *adj.* Drunk. intoxicate *v.*; intoxication *n.*

intravenous \in-truh-VEE-nus\ *adj.* (Md) Entering through the veins. intravenously *adv.*

intricate \IN-tri-kit\ *adj.* Complex.

intrigue \in-TREEG\ *v.* intrigued; intriguing. **1.** To plot. **2.** To arouse interest. intriguing *adj.*

intrinsic \in-TRIN-sik\ *adj.* Belonging to the basic nature of something. intrinsically *adv.*

introduce \in-truh-DOOS\ *v.* introduced; introducing. **1.** To make known. **2.** To institute. introduction *n.*

introspective \in-truh-SPEK-tiv\ *adj.* Looking inward. introspection *n.*

introvert \IN-truh-vurt\ *n.* A reserved person.

introvert \IN-truh-vurt\ *v.* introverted; introverting. To focus on oneself.

intrude \in-TROOD\ *v.* intruded; intruding. To invade without being invited or wanted. intrusion *n.*

intuition \in-too-ISH-un\ *n.* Power of knowing without reasoning. intuitive *adj.*

inundate \IN-un-dayt\ *v.* inundated; inundating. To flood with.

in utero \IN-YOO-tur-oh\ *adv.* or *adj.* (Lt) In the uterus.

invade \in-VAYD\ *v.* invaded; invading. To trespass or penetrate hostilely. invasion *n.*

invalid \in-VAL-id\ *adj.* Without foundation. invalidate *v.*

invaluable \in-VAL-yoo-uh-bul\ *adj.* Priceless.

invariable \in-VAIR-ee-uh-bul\ *adj.* Constant.

invasion \in-VAY-zhun\ *n.* Trespassing or penetrating hostilely. invasive *adj.*

invent \in-VENT\ *v.* invented; inventing. **1.** To create. **2.** To fabricate. invention *n.*; inventive *adj.*

inventory \IN-vun-tor-ee\ *n. pl.* inventories. Stock of goods.

invest \in-VEST\ *v.* invested; investing. **1.** To buy shares or property. **2.** To give rank or power. **3.** To give a quality. investment *n.*

investigate \in-VES-ti-gayt\ *v.* investigated; investigating. To study carefully. investigation *n.*; investigative *adj.*

invigorate \in-VIG-uh-rayt\ *v.* invigorated; invigorating. To stimulate.

invincible \in-VIN-suh-bul\ *adj.* Unconquerable.

invisible \in-VIZ-uh-bul\ *adj.* Not able to be seen.

invite \in-VIET\ *v.* invited; inviting. **1.** To entice or tempt. **2.** To ask for or welcome. invitation *n.*

invoke \in-VOHK\ *v.* invoked; invoking. **1.** To call for help or protection. **2.** To summon.

involuntary \in-VOL-un-ter-ee\ *adj.* **1.** Reflex. **2.** Without choice.

involve \in-VOLV\ *v.* involved; involving. **1.** To have as a consequence. **2.** To include. involved *adj.*; involvement *n.*

inward \IN-wurd\ *adj.* Concerning the inside.

iodine \IE-uh-dine\ *n.* (Sc) A chemical substance.

ion \IE-un\ *n.* (Sc) An electrically subatomic particle. ionize *v.*

ionosphere \ie-ON-uh-sfeer\ *n.* (Sc) Ionized part of earth's atmosphere.

iota \ie-OH-tuh\ *n.* A very small amount.

IRA \ie-ar-ay\ *abbr.* **1.** Individual

Retirement Account. **2.** Irish Republican Army.

irate \ie-RAYT\ *adj.* Angry.

iridescent \ir-i-DES-unt\ *adj.* Colored like a rainbow.

iridology \ir-i-DOL-oh-gee\ *n. pl.* iridologies. Study of the eye for body's health state.

iris \IE-ris\ *n. pl.* irises or irides. **1.** Colored portion of the eye. **2.** A lilylike perennial flower.

irk \urk\ *v.* irked; irking. To annoy.

iron \IE-urn\ *n.* **1.** Elemental metal. **2.** A device used to remove wrinkles.

Iron Curtain *n.* A symbolic and military barrier for the former Soviet Union.

irony \IE-ruh-nee\ *n. pl.* ironies. **1.** Perversity of fate. **2.** Difference between actual and expected consequences. ironic *adj.*

irrational \i-RASH-uh-nl\ *adj.* Lacking reason.

irreconcilable \i-REK-un-sie-luh-bul\ *adj.* Impossible to come together.

irregardless \ir-REE-gard-lus\ *adv.* Regardless.

irregular \i-REG-yuh-lur\ *adj.* **1.** Not normal. **2.** Unnatural.

irrelevant \i-REL-uh-vunt\ *adj.* Not applicable. irrelevance *n.*

irreparable \i-REP-ur-uh-bul\ *adj.* Beyond fixing.

irreproachable \ir-i-PROH-chuh-bul\ *adj.* Blameless.

irresponsible \ir-i-SPON-suh-bul\ *adj.* Cannot be counted on.

irreverent \i-REV-ur-unt\ *adj.* Disrespectful.

irritate \IR-i-tayt\ *v.* irritated; irritating. To annoy. irritation *n.*

Islam \is-LAHM\ *n.* Muslim religion. Islamic *adj.*

island \IE-lund\ *n.* A body of land surrounded by water.

isle *also* **islet** \iel\ *n.* A small island.

isn't \IZ-unt\ *cont.* Is not.

isolation \IE-suh-lay-shun\ *n.* Solitude. isolated *adj.*; isolate *n.*

isometric \ie-suh-ME-trik\ *adj.* Equality of measure.

isosceles \ie-SOS-uh-leez\ *adj.* (Sc) Concerning two equal sides.

issue \ISH-oo\ *n.* **1.** An exit. **2.** An offspring. **3.** A dispute. **4.** An edition.

issue \ISH-oo\ *v.* issued; issuing. **1.** To come or flow out. **2.** To supply or publish. **3.** To send out. **4.** To result.

isthmus \IS-mus\ *n.* A narrow land area connecting two large masses.

italics \i-TAL-iks\ *adj.* A slanted type style. italic *n.*; italicize *v.*

itch \ich\ *n.* **1.** A tickling sensation. **2.** A restless desire. itchy *adj.*

item \IE-tum\ *n.* **1.** A single thing in a collection. **2.** A piece of news.

itemize \IE-tuh-mize\ *v.* itemized; itemizing. To break down into units.

itinerary \ie-TIN-uh-rer-ee\ *n. pl.* itineraries. A traveler's agenda.

IUD \ie-yoo-dee\ *abbr.* [Med] Intrauterine birth control device.

ivory \IE-vuh-ree\ *n. pl.* ivories. **1.** Material of animal tusks. **2.** Piano keys.

ivy \IE-vee\ *n. pl.* ivies. A climbing evergreen shrub.

Ivy League *adj.* Concerning older eastern U.S. colleges.

J

j \jay\ *n. pl.* j's or js. The tenth letter of the English alphabet.

jab *v.* jabbed; jabbing. **1.** To thrust at. **2.** To pierce.

jacket \JAK-it\ *n.* **1.** A short coat. **2.** An outer covering.

Jacuzzi \juh-KOO-zee\ *n.* A trademark for a whirlpool hot tub.

jade \jayd\ *n.* A green jemstone.

jaded \JAY-did\ *adj.* Exhausted.

jagged \JAG-id\ *adj.* Uneven.

jaguar \JAG-gwar\ *n.* A large cat.

jail \jayl\ *n.* Prison.

jalopy \juh-LOP-ee\ *n. pl.* jalopies. A run-down car.

jam *n.* **1.** A sweet fruit spread. **2.** A predictament.

jam *v.* jammed; jamming. **1.** To block. **2.** To fit into a tight space. **3.** [Sl] To make music.

jambalaya \jam-BAY-yuh\ *n.* A seasoned rice dish.

janitor \JAN-i-tur\ *n.* One who takes care of a building.

January \JAN-yoo-er-ee\ *n.* The first month, before February.

jar \jahr\ *n.* **1.** A glass container. **2.** An unexpected movement.

jar \jahr\ *v.* jarred; jarring. **1.** To make a grating sound. **2.** To shake.

jargon \JAHR-gun\ *n.* Language developed for use by a particular group.

jaundice \JAWN-dis\ *n.* (Md) Bile disease.

jaunt \jawnt\ *n.* A short pleasure trip.

javelin \JAV-lin\ *n.* A light spear.

jaw *n.* **1.** Skull part that forms the mouth. **2.** [Sl] A friendly exchange.

Jaws of Life *n.* Device for removing crash victims from vehicles.

jazz \jaz\ *n.* (Mu) Type of music with strong rhythm and syncopation.

jazzy \JAZ-ee\ *adj.* Flashy.

jealous \JEL-us\ *adj.* Resentful toward a supposed rival. jealousy *n.*

jeer *v.* jeered; jeering. To taunt.

jell \jel\ *v.* jelled; jelling. To become solidified.

jelly \JEL-ee\ *n. pl.* jellies. A sweet fruit spread.

jeopardy \JEP-ur-dee\ *n.* Danger.

jerk \jurk\ *n.* **1.** A sudden jolt. **2.** A foolish person.

jerk \jurk\ *v.* jerked; jerking. To change direction suddenly.

jest *n.* A prank or joke.

jester \JES-tur\ *n.* A fool.

Jesuit \JEZH-oo-it\ *n.* A member of the Society of Jesus, a Catholic order.

Jesus \JEE-zus\ *n.* The Christian savior.

jet *n.* **1.** A stream of fluid. **2.** An engine using jet propulsion.

jet lag *n.* Delayed tiredness from crossing time zones quickly.

jet set *n.* International social elite.

jettison \JET-uh-sun\ *v.* jettisoned; jettisoning. To eject or throw overboard.

jewelry *also* **jewels** \JOO-ul-ree\ *n.* Body ornaments made from metals, gems, etc.

Jewish *also* **Jews** \JOO-ish\ *adj.* Concerning the culture and religion of Judaism.

jiffy \JIF-ee\ *n. pl.* jiffies. An instant.

jiggle \JIG-ul\ *v.* jiggled; jiggling. To move with quick, little movements.

jilt *v.* jilted; jilting. To abandon without feeling.

jinni *also* **jinn** \jin\ *n. pl.* [Ar] jinn or jinns. A Muslim demon.

jinx \jingks\ *v.* jinxed; jinxing. To bring bad luck.

jitters \JIT-urs\ *n. pl.* jitters. Extremely nervous energy.

job *n.* **1.** A piece of work. **2.** A paid position of employment.

job market *n.* Employment possibilities.

jocular \JOK-yuh-lur\ *adj.* Playful.

jog *v.* jogged; jogging. **1.** To nudge. **2.** To run slowly.

join *v.* joined; joining. To connect.

joint *adj.* Combined or shared.

joint *n.* **1.** Connection point. **2.** Crummy establishment. **3.** Prison. **4.** Marijuana cigarette.

joke \johk\ *n.* Something said or done to get a laugh. joker *n.*

jolly \JOL-ee\ *adj.* jollier; jolliest. Merry.

jolt \johlt\ *n.* **1.** An abrupt movement. **2.** A small bit.

jostle \JOS-ul\ *v.* jostled; jostling. To bump into.

journal \JUR-nl\ *n.* A written daily record.

journalism \JUR-nl-iz-um\ *n.* The newspaper and periodical business. journalist *n.*

journey \JUR-nee\ *n. pl.* journeys. A long trip.

journey \JUR-nee\ *v.* journeyed; journeying. To travel.

joust \jowst\ *v.* jousted; jousting. To fight from horseback.

jovial \JOH-vee-ul\ *adj.* Happy.

joy \joi\ *n.* Delight.

jubilation \joo-buh-LAY-shun\ *n.* Great joy. jubilant *adj.*

Judaism \JOO-dee-iz-um\ *n.* Hebrew religion of the Jewish people based on the Old Testament and Talmud. Judaic also Judaical *adj.*

judge \juj\ *n.* One who makes de-cisions, esp. about law. judgment *n.*

judge \juj\ *v.* judged; judging. **1.** To decide based on evidence. **2.** To decide a law case. **3.** To estimate.

judicial \joo-DISH-ul\ *adj.* **1.** Concerning the justice department of government. **2.** Critical. judiciary *n.*

judo \JOO-doh\ *n.* (Fo) Japanese unarmed combat sport.

jug *n.* A device for carrying fluids.

juggle \JUG-ul\ *v.* juggled; juggling. **1.** To toss and catch objects. **2.** To manipulate many things or events. juggler *n.*

jugular \JUG-yuh-lur\ *n.* (Md) Primary veins of the neck.

juice \joos\ *n.* **1.** Natural fluid from fruits or vegetables. **2.** Strength. **3.** [Sl] Influence.

juicer \JOOS-ur\ *n.* (Sl) A heavy drinker.

juicy \JOO-see\ *adj.* juicier; juiciest **1.** Succulent. **2.** Colorful. **3.** Lusty.

jujitsu *also* **jujutsu** \joo-JIT-soo\ *n.* (Fo) Japanese unarmed combat sport.

julep \JOO-lip\ *n.* A sweetened mint spirit drink.

July \juu-LIE\ *n.* The seventh month of the year, after June and before August.

jumble \JUM-bul\ *n.* Confusion.

jumbo \JUM-boh\ *n. pl.* jumbos. Very large thing.

jumbo jet *n.* Very large jet plane.

jump *v.* jumped; jumping. **1.** To leap up and off. **2.** To start. **3.** To shift suddenly. **4.** To rise suddenly.

jumper \JUM-pur\ *n.* **1.** One who jumps. **2.** A jumping device. **3.** A sleeveless dresslike garment.

jumping jack *n.* **1.** A toy. **2.** A jumping exercise.

jumpsuit *n.* A one-piece garment.

jumpy \JUM-pee\ *adj.* jumpier; jumpiest. Nervous.

junction \JUNGK-shun\ *n.* An intersection.

June \joon\ *n.* The sixth month of the year, after May and before July.

jungle \JUNG-gul\ *n.* **1.** Tangled, overgrown forest. **2.** A maze.

junior \JOON-yur\ *adj.* **1.** Younger in age. **2.** Lower in rank or authority.

junior \JOON-yur\ *n.* **1.** A son. **2.** A third year student in high school or college.

juniper \JOON-i-pur\ *n.* An evergreen tree.

junk \jungk\ *n.* **1.** Trash. **2.** A Chinese ship. **3.** [Sl] Heroin.

junk bond *n.* A high-risk bond.

junk food *n.* Food with little nutritional value.

junky \JUNG-kee\ *adj.* Worthless.

Jupiter \JOO-pi-tur\ *n.* **1.** Roman god. **2.** The fifth planet from the Sun.

jurisdiction \juur-is-DIK-shun\ *n.* Area of authority or power.

jury \JUUR-ee\ *n. pl.* juries. A judging group. juror *n.*

just *adj.* **1.** Reasonable. **2.** Fair. justly *adv.*

just *adv.* **1.** Exactly. **2.** Barely. **3.** Perhaps.

justice \JUS-tis\ *n.* Impartial and fair treatment.

justify \JUS-tuh-fie\ *v.* justified; justifying. **1.** To explain. **2.** To space lines. justification *n.*

jut *v.* jutted; jutting. To project.

juvenile \JOO-vuh-niel\ *adj.* **1.** Young. **2.** Childish.

juvenile \JOO-vuh-niel\ *n.* A young person.

juvenile deliquent *n.* A young person doing illegal or antisocial actions.

K

k \kay\ *n. pl.* k's or ks. The 11th letter of the English alphabet.

kaiser \KIE-zur\ *n.* A former title for German and Austrian emperors.

kangaroo \kang-guh-ROO\ *n. pl.* kangaroos. A leaping Australian marsupial.

kangaroo court *n.* A farcical legal proceding.

karaoke \kah-ROH-kee\ *n.* A machine which allows people to sing along with recorded music.

karat \KAR-ut\ *n.* Gold standard.

karma \KAHR-muh\ *n.* Belief that one's actions affect their own future and reincarnation.

kayak \KIE-ak\ *n.* An Eskimo canoe.

keel *n.* Structure along the base of a ship.

keel over *v.* keeled over; keeling over. To faint.

keen *adj.* **1.** Sharp. **2.** Intense. **3.** Shrewd. **4.** Wonderful.

keep *v.* kept; keeping. **1.** To retain or have. **2.** To fulfill. **3.** To maintain. **4.** To save. **5.** To manage.

keepsake \KEEP-sayk\ *n.* A memento.

keg *n.* A liquid container.

Keogh plan \KEE-oh-PLAN\ *n.* Self-employment retirement plan.

keratine *also* **keratin** \KAIR-uh-tin\ *n.* (Md) Tissue protein.

kernel \KUR-nl\ *n.* A whole seed.

key \kee\ *n.* **1.** A tool that opens a

lock. **2.** A clue to a solution. **3.** [Mu] A tone.

keyboard \KEE-bord\ *n.* **1.** A set of keys for making music. **2.** A set of typewriter or computer keys.

keypad \KEE-pad\ *n.* A small keyboard.

khaki \KAK-ee\ *n.* **1.** Light brownish-yellow color. **2.** A type of material.

kibbutz \ki-BUUTS\ *n. pl.* kibbutzim. A communal settlement in Israel.

kick \kik\ *n.* **1.** A sudden blow. **2.** A fun activity or thrill.

kick \kik\ *v.* kicked; kicking. **1.** To strike or propel with the foot. **2.** To stop a habit.

kickback \KIK-bak\ *n.* **1.** A sudden reaction. **2.** A return.

kid *n.* **1.** A child. **2.** A young goat.

kid *v.* kidded; kidding. **1.** To deceive. **2.** To joke with.

kidnap \KID-nap\ *v.* kidnapped or kidnaped; kidnapping or kidnaping. To carry off a person by force. kidnaper *n.*

kidney \KID-nee\ *n. pl.* kidneys. An bodily organ important for eliminating wastes.

kielbasa \kil-BAH-suh\ *n. pl.* kielbasas or kielbasy. Polish sausage.

kill \kil\ *v.* killed; killing. **1.** To murder. **2.** To defeat. killer *n.*

kiln *n.* An oven.

kilometer \ki-LOM-i-tur\ *n.* A unit of distance measurement.

kin *n.* One's relatives.

kind \kiend\ *adj.* Affectionate and considerate.

kind \kiend\ *n.* A class of similar things. kindness *n.*

kindhearted \KIEND-hAHR-tid\ *adj.* Sympathetic.

kindle \KIN-dl\ *v.* kindled; kindling. **1.** To light. **2.** To arouse. kindling *n.*

kindly \KIEND-lee\ *adj.* kindlier; kindliest. **1.** Pleasant. **2.** Generous.

kindred \KIN-drid\ *adj.* Like.

kinesiology \kin-EE-see-OL-oh-gee\ *n.* (Md) The study of bodily movement. kinesiologist *n.*

king *n.* **1.** Supreme ruler of a country. **2.** Chess piece. kingdom *n.*

kink \kingk\ *n.* **1.** A short bend. **2.** A quirk.

kinky \KING-kee\ *adj.* kinkier; kinkiest. **1.** Concerning sexual deviancy. **2.** Strange. **3.** Closely twisted.

kismet \KIZ-mit\ *n.* Fate.

kiss \kis\ *v.* kissed; kissing. To touch with one's lips.

kiss \kis\ *n.* **1.** A touch with the lips. **2.** A small chocolate candy.

kit *n.* A collection of things in one container.

kitchen \KICH-un\ *n.* A room for cooking and eating.

kitsch \kich\ *n.* A popular item.

kitten \KIT-n\ *n.* A baby cat.

kiwi \KEE-wee\ *n.* **1.** A wingless bird. **2.** A fruit.

kiwifruit \KEE-wee-FRUUT\ *n.* A Chinese fruit.

kleptomania \klep-tuh-MAY-nee-uh\ *n.* An impulse for theft. kleptomaniac *n.*

klutz \kluts\ *n.* (Yd) A clumsy person.

knack \nak\ *n.* Ability to do something skillfully.

knave \nayv\ *n.* A tricky person.

knead \need\ *v.* kneaded; kneading. To work hard with the hands.

kneel \neel\ *v.* knelt or kneeled; kneeling. To bend one's knees.

knew \noo\ *v.* Past tense of know.

knickers \NIK-urs\ *n. pl.* knickers. Pants that end under the knees.

knife \nief\ *n. pl.* knives. A cutting implement.

knife \nief\ *v.* knifed; knifing. To stab.

knight \niet\ *n.* **1.** A mounted warrior. **2.** A chess piece. knighthood *n.*

knit \nit\ *v.* knit or knitted; knitting. **1.** To form a garment with yarn. **2.** To bring together.

knob \nob\ *n.* A round handle.

knock \nok\ *v.* knocked; knocking. **1.** To strike. **2.** [Id] To knock one's socks off: To amaze.

knockout \NOK-owt\ *n.* To knock down and end a boxing match.

knoll \nohl\ *n.* A hill.

knot \not\ *n.* **1.** An intertwining of one or more pieces of rope. **2.** A problem. **3.** Marriage.

knot \not\ *v.* knotted; knotting. **1.** To tie. **2.** To unite.

know \noh\ *v.* knew; known; knowing. **1.** To have in one's mind or memory. **2.** To understand. **3.** To recognize. knowable *adj.*

know-how \NOH-how\ *n.* Expertise.

knowledge \NOL-ij\ *n.* Body of information. knowledgeable *adj.*

known \nohn\ *adj.* Familiar.

kook *n.* A strange person. kooky *adj.*

Koran \kuh-RAN\ (Ar) *n.* Sacred Muslim text.

kowtow \KOW-TOW\ *v.* kowtowed; kowtowing. To fawn over.

kudos \KOO-dohz\ *n.* **1.** Praise. **2.** Fame.

kung fu \KUUNG-FOO\ *n.* (Fo) Chinese unarmed combat sport.

kvetch \kvech\ *v.* (Yd). To complain.

kyack \KIE-ak\ *n.* A packsack.

L

l \el\ *n. pl.* l's or ls. The 12th letter of the English Language.

label \LAY-bul\ *n.* A note naming or describing something.

label \LAY-bul\ *v.* labeled or labelled; labeling or labelling. **1.** To describe or name. **2.** To distinguish.

labor \LAY-bur\ *n.* **1.** Physical or mental work. **2.** An economic class.

labor \LAY-bur\ *v.* labored; laboring. To work or exert oneself.

laboratory *also* lab \LAB-ruh-tor-ee\ *n. pl.* laboratories. A room or building equipped for scientific work.

labor-intensive *adj.* Requiring a lot of work.

labyrinth \LAB-uh-rinth\ *n.* A maze. labyrinthine *adj.*

lace \lays\ *n.* **1.** A string. **2.** An ornamental openwork fabric covering.

lacerate \LAS-uh-rayt\ *v.* lacerated; lacerating. To injure by tearing. laceration *n.*

lacework \LAYS-wurk\ *n.* Patterns resembling lace.

lachrymose \LAK-ruh-mohs\ *adj.* Tearful.

lack \lak\ *v.* lacked; lacking. To be without.

lackadaisical \lak-uh-DAY-zi-kul\ *adj.* Without spirit.

lackluster \LAK-lus-tur\ *adj.* Dull.

laconic \luh-KON-ik\ *adj.* Terse.

lacquer \LAK-ur\ *n.* A varnish.

lactate \LAK-tayt\ *v.* lactated; lactating. To secrete milk.

lactose \LAK-tohs\ *n.* A milk sugar.

lactose-intolerant *adj.* Unable to digest lactose.

lad *n.* A young boy.

ladder \LAD-ur\ *n.* A device for climbing.

laden \LAYD-n\ *adj.* Carrying a lot.

ladle \LAYD-l\ *n.* A long-handled spoon.

Laetrile \LAY-uh-tril\ *n.* (Md) A cancer drug.

lag *n.* An interval.

lag *v.* lagged; lagging. To fall behind.

lager \LAH-gur\ *n.* A light beer.

lagoon \luh-GOON\ *n.* **1.** A saltwater lake beside a sea. **2.** A freshwater lake beside a lake or river.

laid \layd\ *v.* Past tense of lay.

laid-back \LAYD-BAK\ *adj.* Relaxed.

lair *n.* A den or hiding place.

laissez-faire \les-ay-FAIR\ *n.* (Fr) A doctrine of non-interference by government.

lake \layk\ *n.* An inland body of water.

Lamaze \LAH-mahz\ *adj.* Concerning a method of childbirth.

lamb \lam\ *n.* **1.** A young sheep. **2.** A weak person.

lambaste *also* **lambast** \lam-BAYST\ *v.* lambasted; lambasting. To assault physically or verbally.

lame \laym\ *adj.* lamer; lamest. **1.** Unable to walk normally. **2.** Weak.

lamé \lah-MAY\ *n.* (Fr) A type of shiny cloth.

lament \luh-MENT\ *v.* lamented; lamenting. **1.** To mourn. **2.** To wail. lamented *adj.*; lamentable *adj.*; lamentation *n.*

laminate \LAM-uh-nayt\ *v.* laminated; laminating. **1.** To make from layers. **2.** To unite.

lamp *n.* A device for giving light.

lampoon \lam-POON\ *n.* A harsh satire.

lampoon \lam-POON\ *v.* lampooned; lampooning. To ridicule.

lamppost \LAMP-pohst\ *n.* A lamp support.

land *n.* **1.** That portion of the earth not covered by water. **2.** One's country.

land *v.* landed; landing. To touch or bring down onto land or water.

landlocked \LAND-lokt\ *adj.* Surrounded by land.

landlord \LAND-lord\ *n.* A keeper of a premises.

landmark \LAND-mahrk\ *n.* **1.** A recognizable point. **2.** A historic event marking a major stage or change.

landowner \LAND-oh-nur\ *n.* One who owns land.

landscape \LAND-skayp\ *n.* **1.** Scenery. **2.** A picture of a scenic place.

lane \layn\ *n.* A narrow road, track, or passage.

language \LANG-gwij\ *n.* A system for communicating by a group or country.

languid \LANG-gwid\ *adj.* Listless.

languish \LANG-gwish\ *v.* languished; languishing. To lose or lack vitality.

lanky \LANG-kee\ *adj.* lankier; lankiest. Tall and lean.

lap *n.* **1.** The thighs when seated. **2.** Distance around a course. **3.** Control; care.

lap *v.* lapped; lapping. **1.** To fold over. **2.** To take in with the tongue. **3.** To pass.

laparoscopy \LAP-uh-ruh-skah-pee\ [Md] *n. pl.* laparoscopies. Visual investigation of the abdomen.

lapel \luh-PEL\ *n.* A collar part on a jacket.

lapis lazuli \LAP-is-LAZ-yuu-lee\ *n.* A semi-precious blue stone.

lapse \laps\ *v.* lapsed; lapsing. **1.** To subside. **2.** To cease. **3.** To forfeit.

laptop \LAP-TOP\ *adj.* Portable.

larceny \LAHR-suh-nee\ *n. pl.* larcenies. Theft of personal goods.

large \lahrj\ *adj.* larger; largest. Of great size or extent.

largesse *also* **largess** \lahr-JES\ *n.* Generosity.

lariat \LAR-ee-ut\ *n.* A long light rope.

larva \LAHR-vuh\ *n. pl.* larvae or larvas. Immature worms or insects. larval *adj.*

laryngitis \lar-un-JIE-tis\ *n.* (Md) Larynx inflammation.

larynx \LAR-ingks\ *n. pl.* larynges or larynxes. The upper part of the trachea, known as the vocal cords.

lasagna \luh-ZAHN-yuh\ *n.* (It) **1.** Ribboned pasta. **2.** A baked dish made with this pasta.

lascivious \luh-SIV-ee-us\ *adj.* Lewd.

laser \LAY-zur\ *n.* A device emitting an intense beam of light.

lash *n.* **1.** A whip. **2.** A caustic remark. **3.** An eyelash.

lash *v.* lashed; lashing. **1.** To move in a whiplike manner. **2.** To beat or strike violently. **3.** To attack.

last *adj.* **1.** Final. **2.** Most recent.

last *adv.* In conclusion.

last *v.* lasted; lasting. To endure or continue.

latch \lach\ *n.* A fastener.

latch \lach\ *v.* latched; latching. To seize.

late \layt\ *adj.* later; latest. **1.** After the usual or proper time. **2.** Recent. **3.** Dead.

lately \LAYT-lee\ *adv.* Recently.

latent \LAYT-nt\ *adj.* Inactive.

later \LAY-tur\ *adv.* At sometime afterward.

lateral \LAT-ur-ul\ *adj.* Concerning the side.

lathe \layth\ *n.* A machine for holding and rotating a work.

lather \LATH-ur\ *n.* **1.** Foam. **2.** A state of upset.

Latin \LAT-n\ *n.* Language of ancient Rome.

Latin America *n.* Parts of Central and South America where Spanish or Portuguese are spoken.

Latino \la-TEE-noh\ *n. pl.* Latinos. A native of Latin America.

latitude \LAT-i-tood\ *n.* **1.** Distance of a place from the equator. **2.** Freedom.

latter \LAT-ur\ *adj.* **1.** Concerning the second of two. **2.** Nearer to the end.

lattice \LAT-is\ *n.* A framework of crossed strips.

laud \lawd\ *v.* lauded; lauding. To praise. laudable *adj.*

laugh \laf\ *v.* laughed; laughing. To express happiness with sound and movement of the face. laughter *n.*; laughable *adj.*

launch \lawnch\ *v.* launched; launching. **1.** To send forth. **2.** To put into action.

laundry \LAWN-dree\ *n. pl.* laundries. **1.** Dirty clothes. **2.** A place with washers and driers.

laurels \LOR-uls\ *n. pl.* laurels. Victories or honors.

lava \LAH-vuh\ *n.* Volcanic rock.

lavatory \LAV-uh-tor-ee\ *n. pl.* lavatories. A bathroom.

lavish \LAV-ish\ *adj.* Profuse. lavishly *adv.*

law *n.* **1.** [Le] Rule or regulation. **2.** A statement of principle. **3.** Legal profession.

lawful \LAW-ful\ *adj.* Legal.

lawless \LAW-lis\ *adj.* Disregarding the law.

lawn *n.* The grounds and grass around a home.

lawn mower *n.* A grass cutting machine.

lawsuit \LAW-soot\ *n.* (Le) A court case.

lawyer \LOI-yur\ *n.* One who practices law.

lax \laks\ *adj.* **1.** Loose. **2.** Negligent.

lay *v.* laid; laying. **1.** To put down. **2.** To calm. **3.** To prepare.

layer \LAY-ur\ *n.* One thickness of material.

layer \LAY-ur\ *v.* layered; layering.

To set one covering on top of another.

layoff \LAY-awf\ *n.* A period of shutdown. lay off *v.*

layperson \LAY-pur-sun\ *n.* **1.** A non-professional person. **2.** A member of a religious faith.

lazy \LAY-zee\ *adj.* lazier; laziest. **1.** Unwilling to work or make an effort. **2.** Sluggish. laziness *n.*

leach \leech\ *v.* leached; leaching. To draw out.

lead \leed\ *v.* led; leading. **1.** To guide. **2.** To direct. leader *n.*; leadership *n.*

leading edge *n.* The front part of something moving.

leaf \leef\ *n. pl.* leaves. **1.** Foliage. **2.** A single thickness, as a thin sheet.

leaflet \LEEF-lit\ *n.* A printed information paper for distribution.

league \leeg\ *n.* **1.** A distance unit. **2.** A union or association.

leak \leek\ *n.* An opening. leaky *adj.*

leak \leek\ *v.* leaked; leaking. **1.** To escape. **2.** To disclose.

lean \leen\ *adj.* leaner; leanest. Spare.

lean \leen\ *v.* leaned; leaning. **1.** To tilt or slope against for support. **2.** To rely on.

leaning \LEE-ning\ *n.* A preference.

lean-to \LEEN-too\ *n. pl.* lean-tos. A shed.

learn \lurn\ *v.* learned; learning. **1.** To discover. **2.** To acquire knowledge.

learned \LUR-nid\ *adj.* Having great learning.

lease \lees\ *n.* A rental contract.

lease \lees\ *v.* leased; leasing. To allow or hold by rental contract.

least \leest\ *adj.* **1.** Lowest. **2.** [Id] Least of all: especially not.

leather \LETH-ur\ *n.* Material made from treated animal skins.

leave \leev\ *v.* left; leaving. **1.** To part from or go away. **2.** To let remain. **3.** To deposit or entrust.

lecher *also* **lech** \LECH-ur\ *n.* One who shows no restraint in sexual lust. lecherous *adj.*

lecture \LEK-chur\ *n.* **1.** A speech given about a subject. **2.** A warning.

led *v.* Past tense of lead.

lederhosen \LED-ur-hoh-sun\ *n. pl.* lederhosen. Leather shorts.

ledge \lej\ *n.* An outward projection.

leech *n.* **1.** A bloodsucking worm. **2.** A sail's edge.

leek *n.* An edible herb related to the onion.

leer *v.* leered; leering. To gaze at suggestively.

leeward \LOO-urd or LEE-wurd\ *adj.* On the side away from the wind.

leeway \LEE-way\ *n.* A margin of tolerance.

left *adj.* **1.** Pertaining the body side containing the heart. **2.** Liberal, socialistic view.

left *n.* An extreme political position.

left field *n.* **1.** Part of a ballfield. **2.** Away from the mainstream.

leftover \LEFT-oh-vur\ *n.* Things remaining, after a meal etc.

leg *n.* **1.** A body limb. **2.** Something like or covering a leg. **3.** One part of a race.

legacy \LEG-uh-see\ *n. pl.* legacies. Something left to someone in a will.

legal \LEE-gul\ *adj.* Lawful. legalize *v.*

legend \LEJ-und\ *n.* **1.** A story passed down through many generations. **2.** A caption. legendary *adj.*

legible \LEJ-uh-bul\ *adj.* Readable. legibility *n.*

legion \LEE-jun\ *adj.* Numerous.

legion \LEE-jun\ *n.* An army or organized group.

Legionnaire's disease *also* **Legionnaires' disease** *n.* (Md) Bacterial pneumonia.

legislation \LEJ-is-LAY-shun\ *n.* Making rules and laws.

legislature \LEJ-is-lay-chur\ *n.* Law-making body. legislator *n.*; legislative *adj.*

legitimate \li-JIT-uh-mit\ *adj.* **1.** Lawful. **2.** Acceptable. legitimize *v.*

legume \LEG-yoom\ *n.* Any of a family of plants bearing seeds in pods.

lei \lay\ *n.* A flower necklace.

leisure \LEE-zhur\ *n.* Relaxation or free time. leisurely *adv.*

leisure suit *n.* Informal, outdated jacket and pants.

lemming \LEM-ing\ *n.* A mouse-like rodent.

lemon \LEM-un\ *n.* **1.** A small yellow citrus fruit. **2.** A defective machine.

lend *v.* lent; lending. To loan.

length \lengkth\ *n. pl.* lengths. Measurement from end to end.

lenient \LEEN-yunt\ *adj.* Indulgent.

Lent *n.* Christian time of fasting, 40 weekdays before Easter.

lentil \LEN-til\ *n.* A plant with edible beans.

leopard \LEP-urd\ *n.* A large flesh-eating dark-spotted cat.

leotard \LEE-uh-tahrd\ *n.* A close-fitting dance and gymnastic garment.

leprechaun \LEP-ruh-kawn\ *n.* A mischievous Irish elf.

leprosy \LEP-ruh-see\ *n.* (Md) A degenerative disease of the skin and nerves. leper *n.*

lesbian \LEZ-bee-un\ *n.* A female homosexual. lesbianism *n.*

lesion \LEE-zhun\ *n.* (Md) A harmful change in body tissue.

less \les\ *adj.* **1.** Not so much of. **2.** Smaller in amount or degree. lesser *adj.*; lessen *v.*

lesson \LES-un\ *n.* **1.** Something taught. **2.** A helpful experience.

let *v.* letted; letting. **1.** To lease or hire. **2.** To free. **3.** To permit.

letdown \LET-down\ *n.* Disappointment.

lethal \LEE-thul\ *adj.* Deadly.

lethargic \luh-THAHR-jik\ *adj.* Sluggish. lethargy *n.*

letter \LET-ur\ *n.* **1.** A piece of written correspondence. **2.** A writing symbol.

letter bomb *n.* A bomb contained in a letter.

lettuce \LET-is\ *n.* A plant with leaves used for salad.

leukemia \loo-KEE-mee-uh\ *n.* (Md) A disease in which white blood cells grow uncontrollably.

levee \LEV-ee\ *n.* (Fr) A buildup to prevent flooding.

level \LEV-ul\ *n.* **1.** A measuring device. **2.** On the level [Id]: Honest.

level \LEV-ul\ *v.* leveled or levelled; leveling or levelling. **1.** To make flat. **2.** To destroy or knock down.

level \LEV-ul\ *adj.* **1.** Horizontal. **2.** Reasonable.

levelheaded \LEV-uh-HED-id\ *adj.* Sensible.

lever \LEV-ur\ *n.* A tool and simple machine.

leverage \LEV-ur-ij\ *n.* Power or influence.

leveraged \LEV-ur-ijd\ *adj.* Having borrowed large funds for investment purposes.

levity \LEV-i-tee\ *n.* **1.** Frivolity. **2.** Lightness.

levy \LEV-ee\ *n.* A tax.

lewd \lood\ *adj.* Obscene.

lexicon \LEK-si-kon\ *n. pl.* lexicons or lexica. **1.** Dictionary. **2.** The vocabulary of a language.

liable \LIE-uh-bul\ *adj.* **1.** Responsible. **2.** Likely. liability *n.*

liaison \LEE-uh-zon or LEE-ay-zon\ *n.* **1.** Communication and cooperation. **2.** An affair.

liar \LIE-ur\ *n.* One who doesn't speak the truth. lie *n.*

libation \lie-BAY-shun\ *n.* A beverage.

libber \LIB-ur\ *n.* [Sl] One who supports liberation.

libel \LIE-bul\ *n.* Published false statement. libelous *adj.*

liberal \LIB-ur-ul\ *adj.* **1.** Generous. **2.** Broad-minded.

liberate \LIB-uh-rayt\ *v.* liberated; liberating. To set free. liberation *n.*

libertarian \lib-ur-TAIR-ee-un\ *n.* One who advocates free will.

liberty \LIB-ur-tee\ *n. pl.* liberties. Freedom.

libido \li-BEE-doh\ *n.* Sexual drive. libidinous *adj.*

library \LIE-brer-ee\ *n. pl.* libraries. **1.** Collection of books, etc. for reference. **2.** Building or room for this. librarian *n.*

Librium \LIB-ree-um\ *n.* (Sc) A trademark drug compound.

license *also* **licence** \LIE-suns\ *n.* **1.** Freedom of action. **2.** Official permit.

licentious \lie-SEN-shus\ *adj.* Sexually immoral.

lichen \LIE-kun\ *n.* Complex plants growing on rocks.

lick \lik\ *v.* licked; licking. **1.** To pass tongue over. **2.** To defeat.

licorice \LIK-ur-ish\ *n.* **1.** A candy flavor. **2.** A plant root.

lie *n.* **1.** A falsehood. **2.** A position or way a thing lies.

lie *v.* lay; lain; lying. **1.** To recline or rest in a position. **2.** To exist. **3.** To extend.

lief \leef\ *adv.* Willingly.

liege \leej\ *adj.* Subject or feudal lord.

lien \leen\ *n.* **1.** Right to hold another's property until a debt is paid. **2.** Security.

lieu \loo\ *n.* In place of.

lieutenant \loo-TEN-unt\ *n.* **1.** An assistant. **2.** A military officer.

life \lief\ *n. pl.* lives. The ability to function and grow, for both animals and plants.

lifeless \LIEF-lus\ *adj.* Dead.

lifelong \LIEF-lawng\ *adj.* Throughout life.

lifestyle *also* **life-style or life style** \LIEF-styl\ *n.* Way of living.

life-support system *n.* (Md) Machinery for maintaining life.

lifetime \LIEF-time\ *n.* Life's duration.

lift *v.* lifted; lifting. **1.** To raise or rise. **2.** To steal or plagiarize.

ligature \LIG-uh-chur\ *n.* **1.** Binding material. **2.** Letters joined in writing.

light \liet\ *adj.* **1.** Having little weight. **2.** Bright. **3.** Trivial. **4.** Gentle. **5.** Cheerful.

light \liet\ *n.* **1.** A type of radiation that stimulates sight. **2.** Spiritual awareness.

light \liet\ *v.* lit or lighted; lighting. **1.** To start burning or brighten. **2.** To enlighten.

light-headed \LIET-HED-id\ *adj.* Dizzy.

lighthearted \LIET-HAHR-tid\ *adj.* Easygoing and cheerful.

lightning \LIET--ning\ *adj.* Sudden.

lightning \LIET-ning\ *n.* A flash of light from a cloud due to natural electricity.

lightweight \LIET-wayt\ *n.* Boxing class.

lightweight \LIET-wayt\ *adj.* Inconsequential.

light-year \LIET-yeer\ *n.* Distance light travels in one year.

like \liek\ *adj.* Almost the same.

like \liek\ *n.* Something similar.

like \liek\ *prep.* Similar to.

like \liek\ *v.* liked; liking. **1.** To enjoy. **2.** To regard.

likelihood \LIEK-lee-huud\ *n.* Probability.

likely \LIEK-lee\ *adv.* Probably.

liken \LIE-kun\ *v.* likened; likening. To compare.

likeness \LIEK-nis\ *n.* A resemblance.

likewise \LIEK-wiez\ *adv.* Similarly.

lilliputian \lil-i-PYOO-shun\ *adj.* Miniature.

limb \lim\ *n.* **1.** An extension. **2.** An appendage.

limber \LIM-bur\ *adj.* Flexible.

limbo \LIM-boh\ *n. pl.* limbos. **1.** An intermediate state. **2.** A West Indian dance.

lime *n.* **1.** A small green citrus fruit. **2.** A calcium-based solid.

limelight \LIME-lite\ *n.* The center of attention.

limerick \LIM-ur-ik\ *n.* A humorous verse.

limey \LIEM-ee\ *n.* (Sl) An Englishman.

limit \LIM-it\ *n.* A boundary.

limit \LIM-it\ *v.* limited; limiting. To restrict.

limitation \LIM-i-tay-shun\ *n.* Something that restrains.

limited \LIM-i-tid\ *adj.* Confined.

limitless \LIM-it-lus\ *adj.* Without boundary.

limousine \LIM-uh-zeen\ *n.* A long car with a hired driver.

limp *adj.* Weary. limply *adv.*

limp *v.* limped; limping. To walk unsteadily.

line \lien\ *n.* **1.** Long narrow mark. **2.** Thread. **3.** Row of text. **4.** Route. **5.** A row of something.

lineage *also* **linage** \LIN-ee-ij\ *n.* (It) Ancestry.

lineament \LIN-ee-uh-munt\ *n.* Facial features.

linebacker \LINE-bak-ur\ *n.* A defensive football player.

linen \LIN-un\ *n.* A cloth made of flax.

lineup \LINE-up\ *n.* People arranged for identification purposes.

linger \LING-gur\ *v.* lingered; lingering. To dawdle.

lingo \LING-goh\ *n.* Language.

linguine *also* **linguini** \lin-GWEE-nee\ *n.* (It) Flat pasta.

linguistics \ling-GWIS-tiks\ *n. pl.* linguistics. The study of languages and their structure. **linguist** *n.*

liniment \LIN-uh-munt\ *n.* Liquid balm.

link \lingk\ *n.* **1.** A ring of a chain. **2.** A connection.

link \lingk\ *v.* linked; linking. To join.

linkage \LING-kij\ *n.* A type of bond or connection.

lint *n.* Fuzz.

lintel \LIN-tl\ *n.* An architectual support.

lion \LIE-un\ *n.* A large flesh-eating animal of the cat family.

lip *n.* **1.** The fleshy edges of the mouth. **2.** [Sl] Back talk.

lipid *also* **lipide** \LIP-id\ *n.* A soluable organic substance.

lip service *n.* Insincere support.

lip-synch *also* **lip-sync** \LIP-SINGK\ *v.* lip-sinched; lip-synching. To mouth lyrics to a song.

liqueur \li-KUR\ *n.* Strong flavored alcholic drink.

liquid \LIK-wid\ *adj.* **1.** Fluid-like. **2.** Clear and smooth. **3.** Convertible to cash.

liquid \LIK-wid\ *n.* A fluid with volume not shape.

liquidate \LIK-wi-dayt\ *v.* liquidated; liquidating. To settle with payment.

liquor \LIK-ur\ *n.* Alcoholic drink.

list *n.* A written or printed series of items.

list *v.* listed; listing. **1.** To write a series of things down. **2.** To lean to one side.

listen \LIS-un\ *v.* listened; listening. **1.** To hear. **2.** To pay attention.

listless \LIST-lis\ *adj.* Without energy or enthusiasm.

lit *v.* Past tense of light.

litany \LIT-n-ee\ *n. pl.* litanies. **1.** A chant. **2.** A prayer.

literal \LIT-ur-ul\ *adj.* **1.** Actual. **2.** Exact.

literally \LIT-ur-uh-lee\ *adv.* Virtually.

literary \LIT-uh-rer-ee\ *adj.* Concerning writers and their professions.

literate \LIT-ur-it\ *adj.* Able to read and write. literacy *n.*

literature \LIT-ur-uh-chur\ *n.* Written works.

lithe \lieth\ *adj.* Flexible.

litigate \LIT-i-gayt\ *v.* litigated; litigating. (Le). To contest in law. litigant *n.*

litmus paper \LIT-mus-PAY-pur\ *n.* (Sc) A test paper for acids and alkalis.

litmus test \LIT-mus-TEST\ [Sc] *n.* (Sc) A test with one deciding factor.

litter \LIT-ur\ *n.* **1.** A carriage. **2.** Trash. **3.** Off-spring.

litter \LIT-ur\ *v.* littered; littering. To throw trash about.

little \LIT-l\ *adj.* littler or less or lesser; littlest or least. **1.** Small. **2.** Young. **3.** Trivial.

little \LIT-l\ *adv.* less; least. **1.** Slightly. **2.** Rarely.

liturgy \LIT-ur-jee\ *n. pl.* liturgies. Form of worship service or ritual. liturgical *adj.*

live \liev\ *adj.* **1.** Being alive, conscious. **2.** Full of life. **3.** Alert. **4.** Full of curiosity. living *adj.*; livable *adj.*

live \liv\ *v.* lived; living. **1.** To have life. **2.** To endure. **3.** To sustain life. **4.** To support oneself.

livelihood \LIEV-lee-huud\ *n.* **1.** One's means of earning a living. **2.** A job. **3.** An avocation.

lively \LIEV-lee\ *adj.* **1.** Full of energy. **2.** Spirited. **3.** Exciting.

liven \LIEV-un\ *v.* **1.** To give life. **2.** To grow more lively.

liver \LIV-ur\ *n.* A large organ in the abdomen that performs various metabolic functions.

liver spots *n.* Collections of pigment on the hands and face.

liverwurst \LIV-ur-wurst\ *n.* (Gr) Sausage made with liver.

livid \LIV-id\ *adj.* **1.** Extremely angry. **2.** Bluish-gray or bluish-purple.

llama \LAH-muh\ *n.* A large South American mammal related to the camel.

load \lohd\ *n.* **1.** Thing or quantity carried. **2.** A burden. **3.** The charge of a firearm.

load \lohd\ *v.* loaded, loading. **1.** To put a quantity or thing in or on. **2.** To supply abundantly. **3.** To fill.

loaf \lohf\ *n. pl.* loaves. **1.** A quantity of cake or bread. **2.** A shaped mass of food.

loaf \lohf\ *v.* **1.** To delay or be lazy. **2.** To waste time.

loafer \LOH-fur\ *n.* **1.** [Cl] One who is lazy. **2.** A slip-on shoe.

loan \lohn\ *n.* **1.** Lending. **2.** The thing lent.

loath \lohth\ *adj.* Unwilling.

loathe \lohth\ *v.* **1.** To hate. **2.** To be disgusted with.

loathsome \LOHTH-sum\ *adj.* Something hated or disgusting.

lobby \LOB-ee\ *n. pl.* lobbies. **1.** An entrance hall. **2.** Body of people seeking to influence legislation.

lobby \LOB-ee\ *v.* lobbied; lobbying. To seek to influence legislation. lobbyist *n.*

lo-cal *also* **low-cal** \LOH-KAL\ *adj.* **1.** Low calorie.

local \LOH-kul\ *adj.* **1.** Pertaining to a particular place. **2.** Stopping at all stations.

local \LOH-kul\ *n.* **1.** A train or bus that makes all stops. **2.** An inhabitant of a particular area.

locale \loh-KAL\ *n. pl.* locales; localities. A place or area.

locate \loh-KAYT\ *v.* located; locating. **1.** To find. **2.** To fix or establish in time or place.

location \loh-KAY-shun\ *n.* **1.** A place of residence or settlement. **2.** A tract of land. **3.** A movie set.

loch \lok\ *n.* (Fo) **1.** A lake. **2.** An arm of a sea.

lock \lok\ *n.* **1.** A device to secure something. **2.** A part of a canal for water control.

lock \lok\ *v.* locked; locking. **1.** To fasten with a lock. **2.** To hold or keep from moving. **3.** To enclose within.

loco \LOH-KOH\ *n.* (Sl) Crazy.

locomotion \loh-kuh-MOH-shun\ *n.* Movement.

locomotive \loh-kuh-MOH-tiv\ *adj.* **1.** Moving under self-power. **2.** Concerning to movement.

locomotive \loh-kuh-MOH-tiv\ *n.* **1.** A train. **2.** Anything that moves under its own power.

locust \LOH-kust\ *n.* A kind of grasshopper.

lode \lohd\ *n.* A vein of metal ore.

lodge \loj\ *n.* **1.** A small shelter or temporary dwelling. **2.** A meeting place for an organization. lodging *n.*

lodge \loj\ *v.* lodged; lodging. **1.** To live in a temporary dwelling. **2.** To fix in place or implant.

loft \lawft\ *n.* **1.** An attic. **2.** A space elevated from another floor.

loft \lawft\ *v.* lofted; lofting. To lift or suspend an object.

lofty \LAWF-tee\ *adj.* loftier; loftiest. **1.** High in the air. **2.** Well regarded. **3.** Stylish. loftiness *n.*

log \lawg\ *n.* **1.** A large part cut off a tree. **2.** Thing shaped like a log. **3.** A record or list.

log \lawg\ *v.* logged; logging. **1.** To

cut trees in quantity. **2.** To enter in a journal or record.

logarithm \LAW-guh-rith-um\ *n.* One of a series of numbers in tables used to simplify calculations.

logger \LAW-gur\ *n.* A person who cuts trees. logging *n.*

logic \LOJ-ik\ *n.* **1.** The science or method of reasoning. **2.** Correct reasoning.

logical \LOJ-ik-ul\ *adj.* Reasonable or reasoning correctly. logically *adv.*

logistics \loh-JIS-tiks\ *n.* Organization or plan.

loin *n.* The side and back of the body between ribs and hipbone. [Cl,Pl]: Genitals. loins *n.*

loincloth \LOIN-klawth\ *n.* A piece of cloth that covers the loins.

loiter \LOI-tur\ *v.* loiter; loitering. To linger. loiterer *n.*; loiteringly *adv.*

lone \lohn\ *adj.* Solitary. loner *n.*

lonely \LOHN-lee\ *adj.* lonelier; loneliest. **1.** Solitary. **2.** Lacking benefit of companionship. **3.** Not frequented. lonesome *adj.*

long \lawng\ *adj.* longer; longest. Of great or specified length.

long \lawng\ *adv.* For a long or specified time.

long \lawng\ *v.* longed; longing. To desire or yearn.

longevity \lon-JEV-i-tee\ *n.* longevities. **1.** The duration of a life. **2.** Long life.

longhorn \LAWNG-horn\ *n.* A breed of cattle with long horns.

longing \LAWNG-ing\ *n.* Intense wish.

longitude \LON-ji-tood\ *n.* The distance east or west from the Greenwich meridian. longitudinal *adj.*

long-lived \LAWNG-LIVD\ *adj.* longer-lived; longest-lived. Having longevity. long-living *adj.*

long-term \LAWNG-turm\ *adj.* Of an extended duration.

loo *n.* [Sl] Toilet or bathroom.

look \luuk\ *n.* (Id) A style or fashion.

look \luuk\ *v.* looked; looking. **1.** To fix the eyes upon. **2.** To see. **3.** To search. **4.** To face. **5.** To examine.

lookout \LUUK-owt\ *n.* **1.** A watch or vigil. **2.** An observation post.

loom *n.* A machine used to weave fabric.

loom *v.* loomed; looming. **1.** To weave on a loom. **2.** To appear threateningly.

looming \LOOM-ing\ *adj.* Appearing threateningly.

loop *n.* **1.** A curve that is U-shaped or crosses itself. **2.** A thing shaped like this.

loop *v.* looped; looping. **1.** To form a loop. **2.** To fasten or enclose with a loop. **3.** looped [Cl]: Drunk.

loose \loos\ *adj.* looser; loosest. **1.** Free from restraint. **2.** Unattached. **3.** Unpackaged. **4.** Not tight. **5.** Slack.

loose \loos\ *v.* loosed. **1.** To set free. **2.** Untie or unbind. loosely *adv.*; looseness *n.*

loosen \LOO-sun\ *n.* loosened; loosening. **1.** To make or become loose or looser **2.** loosen up [Cl]: Relax. loosener *n.*

loot *n.* Stolen goods.

loot *v.* looted; looting. To steal without caution. looter *n.*

lopsided \LOP-SIE-did\ *adj.* Tilted.

lore \lor\ *n.* A body or history of related stories.

lose \looz\ *v.* lost; losing. **1.** To cease to have or maintain. **2.** To be unable to find or follow. **3.** To fail.

loss \laws\ *n. pl.* losses. **1.** Losing or amount lost. **2.** Disadvantage.

lost \lawst\ *adj.* Separated from its owner.

lot *n.* **1.** A plot of land. **2.** Something determined by chance. **3.** One's fate or share.

lotion \LOH-shun\ *n.* A liquid skin ointment.

lottery \LOT-uh-ree\ *n.* A drawing for prizes for which tickets are sold.

loud \lowd\ *adj.* **1.** Producing much noise. **2.** Gaudy. loudness *n.*

Lou Gehrig's Disease \loo-gair-igz\ *n.* (Md) A terminal disease that affects nerve and muscular function.

lounge \lownj\ *n. pl.* loungers. **1.** A sitting or waiting room. **2.** A bar.

lounge \lownj\ *v.* lounged; lounging. To loll or be idle. lounger *n.*

louse \lows\ *n. pl.* lice. **1.** A small parasitical insect. **2.** [Sl] A distasteful person.

lousy \LOW-zee\ *adj.* lousier; lousiest. **1.** [Sl] Very bad. **2.** Full of lice.

lovable *also* **loveable** \LUV-uh-bul\ *adj.* Easy to love.

love \luv\ *n.* **1.** Warm liking or affection. **2.** A loved person. **3.** No score, in tennis. lover *n.*

love \luv\ *v.* loved; loving. To feel warm liking or affection for.

lovely \LUV-lee\ *adj.* lovelier; loveliest. Beautiful and attractive.

loving \LUV-ing\ *adj.* Feeling or showing love.

low \loh\ *adj., adv.* lower; lowest. **1.** Not high. **2.** Ranking below. **3.** Vulgar. **4.** Less than normal. **5.** Not loud.

low \loh\ *n.* **1.** Low level. **2.** Area of low pressure.

low \loh\ *v.* lowed; lowing. The deep vocal sound of cattle.

lowball \LOW-bawl\ *v.* lowballed; lowballing. (Sl). To underestimate a value.

lower \LOH-ur\ *v.* lowered; lowering. **1.** To let down. **2.** To make lower.

low-key \LOH-KEE\ *adj.* Restrained.

lowly \LOH-lee\ *adj.* lowlier; lowliest. Of humble rank or condition.

lox \loks\ *n.* Salmon cured in salt or sugar.

loyal \LOI-ul\ *adj.* loyalties Faithful and responsible. loyalty *n.* loyally *adv.* loyalness *n.*

loyalist \LOI-uh-list\ *n.* A person who is faithful during a revolt. Loyalist *n.*

lozenge \LOZ-inj\ *n.* A small medicinal tablet.

luau \loo-OW\ *n. pl.* luaus. (Fo) A Hawaiian party held outdoors.

lubricate \LOO-bri-kayt\ *v.* lubricated; lubricating. To oil or grease. **2.** [Sl]. To bribe. lubricant *n.*

lucid \LOO-sid\ *adj.* **1.** Clearly expressed. **2.** Rational. lucidity *n.*; lucidness *n.*

luck \luk\ *n.* **1.** Good or bad fortune. **2.** Chance.

luck \luk\ *v.* lucked; lucking. To happen into good fortune.

lucky \LUK-ee\ *adj.* luckier; luckiest. Having or bringing good luck. luckily *adv.*

lucrative \LOO-kruh-tiv\ *adj.* Profitable.

ludicrous \LOO-di-krus\ *adj.* Ridiculous.

lug *n.* **1.** Dragging or carrying. **2.** An earlike projection **3.** [Sl] A big, clumsy man.

lug *v.* lugged; lugging. To drag or carry a heavy burden.

luge \loozh\ *n.* A sled, its course, and the sport.

luggage \LUG-ij\ *n.* Baggage or suitcases.

lukewarm \LOOK-WORM\ *adj.* **1.** Only slightly warm. **2.** Not enthusiastic.

lull \lul\ *n.* Period of quiet or inactivity.

lull \lul\ *v.* lulled; lulling. **1.** To soothe or put to sleep. **2.** To become quiet. **3.** To make falsely secure.

lumbar \LUM-bar\ *n.* (Md) A vertebra of the lower back. lumbar *adj.*

lumber \LUM-bur\ *n.* Wood sawn into boards. lumber *v.*

luminary \LOO-muh-ner-ee\ *n. pl.* luminaries. **1.** A light-giving body. **2.** An important person. lu-minary *adj.*

luminescent \loo-muh-NES-unt\ *adj.* Giving light. luminescence *n.*

lump *n.* **1.** A hard mass. **2.** A swelling or swelling. lump *adj.*

lump *v.* lumped; lumping. To put or consider together.

lumpectomy \lump-EK-toh-mee\ *n. pl.* lumpectomies. (Md) The surgical removal of a lump.

lunacy \LOO-nuh-see\ *n. pl.* luna-cies. Insanity.

lunar \LOO-nur\ *adj.* Concerning to the moon.

lunatic \LOO-nuh-tik\ *n.* A crazy person. lunatic *adj.*

lunch *n. pl.* lunches. **1.** The meal eaten at midday. **2.** A morning snack.

lunch *v.* lunched; lunching. **1.** To eat a midday meal or snack. **2.** Out to lunch [Sl]: confused or dis-oriented.

luncheon \LUN-chun\ *n.* A meal eaten at midday.

luncheonette \lun-chuh-NET\ *n.* A small diner. lunch counter *n.*; lunch room *n.*

lung *n.* Either of the pair of breath-ing organs in the chest of most vertebrates.

lunge \lunj\ *v.* lunged; lunging. A sudden forward movement or thrust. lunger *n.*

lupus \LOO-pus\ *n.* (Md) An auto-immune disease that sometimes causes blotchy skin. lupus erythe-matosus *n.*; lupus vulgaris *n.*

lurch *v.* lurched; lurching. **1.** To stagger or lunge. **2.** To leave in the lurch [Id]: to abandon.

lure \luur\ *n.* **1.** An enticement. **2.** Bait or decoy to attract fish or an-imals.

lure \luur\ *v.* lured; luring. To en-tice.

lurid \LUUR-id\ *adj.* **1.** Sensational and shocking. **2.** In glaring colors.

lurk *v.* lurked; lurking. To lie hid-den and in wait.

luscious \LUSH-us\ *adj.* **1.** Deli-cious. **2.** Sexually appealing. lus-ciously *adj.*; lusciousness *n.*

lush *adj.* **1.** Growing thickly and strongly. **2.** Luxuriant.

lust *n.* **1.** A strong sexual desire. **2.** Any strong desire. lusty *adj.*

lust *v.* lusted; lusting. To have a great desire for.

luster *also* [Br.] **lustre** \LUS-tur\ *n.* **1.** A shine or glow. **2.** Glory. luster *v.*; lusterless *adj.*

lustrous \LUS-trus\ *adj.* **1.** Shiny or glowing. **2.** Glorious.

luxurious \lug-ZHUUR-ee-us\ *adj.*

Supplied with luxuries and very comfortable. luxuriate *v.*; luxuri-ant *adj.*; luxurious *adj.*

Lyme disease \LIEM-DI-zeez\ *n.* (Md) A chronic, tick-borne dis-ease that causes neurological damage.

lymph \limf\ *n.* (Md) Colorless fluid of body tissue or organs.

lymph nodes *n.* (Md) Any of the glands that secrete lymphocytes.

lymphoma \lim-FOH-muh\ *n. pl.* lymphomas; lymphomata. (Md) A tumor found in lymphomatic tissue.

lynch \linch\ *v.* lynched; lynching. To execute or punish violently without trial. lyncher *v.*

M

m \em\ **n. pl.** m's or ms. **1.** The 13th letter of the alphabet. **2.** [Cap] Roman numeral for 1000.

macabre \muh-KAHB\ **adj.** Gruesome.

macadam \muh-KAD-um\ **n.** Asphalt.

Mace \mays\ **n.** A chemical used to repel attackers. Maced **v.**

machine \muh-SHEEN\ **n. 1.** A mechanism that uses mechanical power. **2.** (Sl) or (Cl) A controlling organization. machine **v.** machined **v.** machining **v.**

machinery \muh-SHEE-nuh-ree\ **n. 1.** Machines. **2.** A mechanism.

macho also **machismo** \MAH-choh\ **adj.** (Sp) Excessively masculine. [Cl]: macho man.

macrobiotics \mak-roh-bie-OT-iks\ **n.** A natural diet meant to prolong life. macrobiotic **adj.**

macroeconomics \MAK-roh-EK-oh-NOM-iks\ **n.** The study of large economic systems. macroeconomist **n.**

mad **adj.** madder; maddest. **1.** Angry. **2.** Insane. **3.** Infected with rabies. **4.** Extremely enthused. madly **adv.**

madcap \MAD-kap\ **adj.** Recklessly rash or impulsive.

made \mayd\ **adj.** Produced or manufactured. made **v.**

made-up \MAYD-UP\ **adj. 1.** Imaginary or fabricated. **2.** Wearing facial cosmetics. **3.** Built.

madhouse \MAD-hows\ **n. 1.** A

hospital for the mentally ill. **2.** [Cl]: Any disorganized place.

madness \MAD-nus\ *n.* **1.** Insanity. **2.** Extreme anger.

Mafia \MAH-fee-uh\ *n.* (Fo) A secret organization that conducts organized crime. Mafioso *n.*

magazine \mag-uh-ZEEN\ *n.* **1.** Illustrated periodical. **2.** Storage for firearms, explosives. **3.** Gun chamber.

magic \MAJ-ik\ *n.* **1.** Practice and art of illusion. **2.** Supernatural control or influence. magic *adj.* magical *adj.*

magician \muh-JISH-un\ *n.* One who practices the arts of illusion.

magma \MAG-muh\ *n.* Molten rock found beneath the earth's surface.

magna cum laude \MAG-nuh-kum-LOW-day\ *adv.* **1.** [Lt]: With great praise. **2.** Graduating with the next to highest honors.

magnanimous \mag-NAN-uh-mus\ *adj.* Noble and generous. magnanimously *adj.*

magnate \MAG-nayt\ *n.* A person of great importance or wealth.

magnet \MAG-nit\ *n.* **1.** Metal that attracts other metals. **2.** A person or thing that attracts. magnetic *adj.* magnetize *v.*

magnificent \mag-NIF-uh-sunt\ *adj.*

1. Splendid. **2.** Excellent. magnificently *adv.*

magnify \MAG-nuh-fie\ *v.* magnified; magnifying. **1.** To make an object appear larger by using a lens. **2.** To exaggerate. magnification *n.* magnifier *n.* magnifiable *adj.*

magnitude \MAG-ni-tood\ *n.* **1.** Size or dimension. **2.** Importance. **3.** The brightness of a star.

magnolia \mag-NOH-lee-uh\ *n. pl.* magnolias. A tree with large white or pink flowers.

magnum \MAG-num\ *n.* A bottle holding two quarts of wine or spirits.

maharaja \mah-huh-RAH-juh\ *n.* (Fo) A ruling prince of a province in India.

maharanee \mah-huh-RAH-nee\ *n.* (Fo) **1.** A ruling princess of a province in India. **2.** The wife of a maharaja.

mahatma \muh-HAHT-muh\ *n.* (Fo) A title of a man regarded with reverence in India or Tibet.

mahjong \muh-ZHAWNG\ *n.* (Fo) A domino game invented in China.

maid \mayd\ *n. pl.* maids, maidens. **1.** A woman hired to perform domestic work. **2.** An unmarried woman.

maiden \MAYD-n\ *n.* **1.** An unmarried woman. **2.** A virgin. maiden *adj.*

mail \mayl\ *n.* **1.** Materials delivered by a postal system. **2.** Armor made of loops of steel. mail *v.*; mailed *v.*; mailing *v., n.*; mails *n.*

mail carrier *also* **mail man** *n.* A person who delivers the mail.

maim \maym\ *v.* To seriously wound or injure, making useless.

main \mayn\ *adj.* **1.** Most important. **2.** Greatest in size or extent.

main \mayn\ *n.* Main pipe, channel, or part.

mainframe \MAYN-FRAYM\ *n.* A large computer to which terminals are connected to use its data and power.

mainstay \MAYN-stay\ *n.* **1.** A primary support. **2.** A strong rope the mast of a ship.

mainstream \MAYN-streem\ *n.* Dominant course or trend. mainstream. *adj., v.* mainstreamed *v.* mainstreaming *v.*

maintain \mayn-TAYN\ *v.* maintained; maintaining. **1.** To cause to continue. **2.** To keep in good shape. **3.** To assert. maintainability *n.*; maintainer *n.*

maître d' *also* **maitre d'** \may-tur-DEE\ *n.* The host in a restaurant.

maize \mayz\ *n.* **1.** Corn. **2.** A pale yellow color.

majestic \muh-JES-tik\ *adj.* Stately and dignified.

majesty \MAJ-uh-stee\ *n. pl.* majesties. **1.** Stateliness or dignity. **2.** Sovereign power. **3.** Title of a king or queen. majesterial *adj.*

major \MAY-jur\ *adj.* **1.** Greater. **2.** Very important. **3.** [Mu] Denoting a diatonic scale or key on it.

major \MAY-jur\ *n.* **1.** High-up military officer. **2.** Band director. **3.** Study course in college. major *v.*

majority \muh-JOR-i-tee\ *n. pl.* majorities. **1.** The greater part of a set of things. **2.** More than half of a group.

make \mayk\ *v.* made; making. **1.** To form or produce. **2.** To cause to exist. **3.** To achieve or acquire.

make believe \MAYK-bi-leev\ *n.* (Id) Pretending. make believe *v.*

makeshift \MAYK-shift\ *n.* Temporary. makeshift *adj.*

make up \MAYK-up\ *v.* **1.** To form. **2.** To invent. **3.** To compensate. **4.** To reconcile. **5.** To complete.

makeup *also* **make-up** \MAYK-up\ *n.* **1.** Cosmetics for the face. **2.** The way a thing is made. **3.** Person's character.

maladroit \mal-uh-DROIT\ *adj.* Clumsy.

malaise \ma-LAYZ\ *n.* Feeling of illness or weakness.

malamute \MA-luh-myoot\ *n.* **1.** A native tribe of western Alaska. **2.** A long haired dog from Alaska.

male \mayl\ *n.* **1.** A boy or man. **2.** A plant with a stamen. maleness *n.*

malevolent \muh-LEV-uh-lunt\ *adj.* Wishing harm to others. malevolence *adj.*

malfeasance \mal-FEE-zuns\ *n.* Misconduct.

malformed \mal-FORMD\ *adj.* Misshapen or improperly constructed.

malfunction \mal-FUNGK-shun\ *v.* To function faultily.

malice \MAL-is\ *n.* Desire to harm others. malicous *adj.*

malign \muh-LIEN\ *v.* maligned; maligning. To say unpleasant and untrue things about another. malign *adj.*

malignant \muh-LIG-nunt\ *adj.* **1.** Harmful. **2.** Growing harmfully and cancerous. malignancy *n.* malignancies *n.*

mall \mawl\ *n.* **1.** An enclosed shopping center. **2.** A sheltered walkway.

mallard \MAL-urd\ *n.* A wild common duck.

malleable \MAL-ee-uh-bul\ *adj.* **1.** Capable of being easily shaped and formed. **2.** Easily influenced.

mallet \MAL-it\ *n.* A hammer or similarly shaped instrument.

malnutrition \mal-noo-TRISH-un\ *n.* Lack of proper nutrition.

malpractice \mal-PRAK-tis\ *n.* **1.** Wrongdoing. **2.** Negligent or improper medical treatment or legal advice.

malt \mawlt\ *n.* Barley or other grain prepared for distilling and brewing. malt *v.*

malted \MAWL-tid\ *n.* Malted milk.

maltreat \mal-TREET\ *v.* maltreated; maltreating. To handle roughly and inconsiderately.

mam *also* **ma'am** *n.* (Cl) Madam.

mambo \MAHM-boh\ *n. pl.* mambos. (Fo) A Caribbean ballroom dance. mambo *v.*

mammal \MAM-ul\ *n.* Any animal that suckles its young.

mammary \MAM-uh-ree\ *adj.* Pertaining to glands secreting milk.

mammogram \MAM-uh-gram\ *n.* (Md) An X-ray of the mammary glands. mamography *n.*

mammoth \MAM-uth\ *n.* A large extinct elephant. mammoth *adj.*

man *n. pl.* men. **1.** An adult male person. **2.** Human being or mankind. **3.** Male servant. manliness *n.*; manhood *n.*; manly *adv.*

man *v.* manned; manning. To supply with people for an operation.

manage \MAN-ij\ *v.* managed; managing. **1.** To have control of. **2.** To operate effectively. **3.** To deal with tactfully. manage *n.*

management \MAN-ij-munt\ *n.* **1.** Managing. **2.** People managing a business. managerial *adj.* manager *n.*

manana \mah-NYAH-nuh\ *n.* (Sp) Tomorrow.

manatee \MAN-uh-tee\ *n. pl.* manatees. A large tropical aquatic mammal.

mandala \mahn-DAHL-uh\ *n. pl.* mandalas. A Hindu or Buddhist artistic representation of the cosmos.

mandarin \MAN-duh-rin\ *n.* **1.** [Ch] A spoken form of Chinese. **2.** A senior official. **3.** A kind of orange. mandarin *adj.*

mandate \MAN-dayt\ *n.* Authority to perform certain tasks. mandate *v.*

mandatory \MAN-duh-tor-ee\ *adj.* Compulsory.

mandolin \MAN-dl-in\ *n.* A small guitar-like instrument with a short neck.

mandrel \MAN-drul\ *n.* A shaft holding work in a lathe.

mane \mayn\ *n.* The long hair on a horse's or lion's neck.

maneuver \muh-NOO-vur\ *n.* **1.** A planned movement. **2.** A skillful proceeding.

maneuver \muh-NOO-vur\ *v., n.* manuevered; manuevering. **1.** To perform a planned movement. **2.** To guide skillfully.

mangle \MANG-gul\ *v.* mangled; mangling. To damage or mutilate.

mango \MANG-goh\ *n.* (Fo) A juicy pear-like tropical fruit.

mangy \MAYN-jee\ *adj.* **1.** Having mange, a skin disease of hairy animals. **2.** Shabby and bare.

manhood \MAN-huud\ *n.* **1.** State of being a man. **2.** Manly qualities.

mania \MAY-nee-uh\ *n.* **1.** Extreme enthusiasm. **2.** Insanity.

maniac \MAY-nee-ak\ *n.* **1.** An insane person. **2.** A very enthusiastic person.

manic \MAN-ik\ *adj.* Concerning to mania.

manic-depression \MAN-ik-di-PRES-shun\ *n.* (Md) A psychosis with periods of mania and depression. manic-depressive *n.*

manicotti \man-i-KOT-ee\ *n.* [It.] An baked Italian pasta dish.

manicure \MAN-uh-kyuur\ *n.* To trim and care for the fingernails. manicurist *n.*

manifest \MAN-uh-fest\ *adj.* Obvious.

manifest \MAN-uh-fest\ *n.* A ship's record.

manifest \MAN-uh-fest\ *v.* manifested; manifesting. To prove or show clearly.

Manifest Destiny *n.* An event believed to be inevitable or God-willed.

manifesto \man-uh-FES-toh\ *n.* Public declaration of policies and principles.

manifold \MAN-uh-fohld\ *adj.* Of many kinds.

manifold \MAN-uh-fohld\ *n.* A pipe or chamber with many openings.

manipulate \muh-NIP-yuh-layt\ *v.* manipulated; manipulating. To handle or manage skillfully. manipulation *n.*; manipulator *n.*

mannequin \MAN-i-kin\ *n.* **1.** An model of the human body. **2.** A live human model.

manner \MAN-ur\ *n.* **1.** Way a thing is done or happens. **2.** A person's behavior. **3.** Style of speech. mannerly *adv.*

mannerism \MAN-uh-riz-um\ *n.* Distinctive habit or way of doing something.

mansion \MAN-shun\ *n.* A grand and beautiful house.

manslaughter \MAN-slaw-tur\ *n.* The unpremeditated killing of another.

mantle *also* **mantel** \MAN-tl\ *n.* **1.** A cloak. **2.** A covering.

mantle \MAN-tl\ *v.* mantled; mantling. To cover or become covered.

mantra \MAHN-truh\ *n.* (Fo) A simple audible prayer that is repeated.

manual \MAN-yoo-ul\ *n.* **1.** A handbook. **2.** An organ keyboard.

manufacture \man-yuh-FAK-chur\ *v.* manufactured; manufacturing. **1.** To make or produce goods with machines. **2.** To invent manufacturer *n.*; manufacturing *n., v.*

manure \muh-NYUUR\ *n.* Dung or other material used to fertilize. manure *v.*

many \MEN-ee\ *adj.* more; most Numerous.

map *n.* A two dimensional representation of a surface or space. map *v.*

mar \mahr\ *v.* marred; marring. To damage or spoil.

maraud \muh-RAWD\ *v.* marauded; maruading. To plunder. marauder *n.*

March \mahrch\ *n.* The third month of the year, after February and before April.

march \mahrch\ *v.* marched; marching. **1.** To walk in regular rhythm. **2.** To walk purposefully. **3.** To progress steadily. marcher *n.*; marchers *n.*

mare \mair\ *n.* A female horse, mule, or donkey.

margarine \MAHR-jur-in\ *n.* A butter substitute made of corn or vegetable oils.

margarita \mar-guh-REE-tuh\ *n.* (Sp) A cocktail made with tequila and lime juice.

margin \MAIR-jin\ *n.* **1.** Edge, border. **2.** Blank space around printed, written matter. **3.** Amount extra.

marginal \MAHR-jn-ul\ *adj.* **1.** Of or in a margin. **2.** Near a limit. **3.** Very slight. marginality *n.*; marginally *adv.*

marigold \MAR-i-gohld\ *n.* A garden plant with small daisy-like flowers.

marijuana *also* **marihuana** \mair-uh-WAH-nuh\ *n.* Dried hemp, smoked as a hallucinogenic drug.

marina \muh-REE-nuh\ *n.* A dock and harbor for boats.

marinara \mair-i-NAIR-uh\ *adj.* A plain tomato sauce.

marine \muh-REEN\ *adj.* Concerning the sea and shipping.

mariner \MAR-uh-nur\ *n.* A sailor or seaman.

marionette \mar-ee-uh-NET\ *n.* A puppet worked by strings.

marital \MAR-uh-tl\ *adj.* Concerning marriage. maritally *adv.*

mark \mahrk\ *n.* **1.** A trace left on an object. **2.** Distinguishing feature. **3.** A sign or symbol. marker *n.*

mark \mahrk\ *v.* marked; marking. **1.** To make a mark on. **2.** To characterize. **3.** To assign merit by marking.

marked \mahrkt\ *adj.* Clearly noticeable.

market \MAHR-kit\ *n.* **1.** A place for selling goods. **2.** Demand for goods. market *v.*; marketed *v.*; marketing *n.*

marketable \MAHR-ki-tuh-bul\ *adj.* Able to be sold.

marketing \MAHR-ki-ting\ *n.* **1.** Buying and selling. **2.** The study of selling goods.

maroon \muh-ROON\ *n.* A deep red color.

maroon \muh-ROON\ *v.* marooned; marooning. To leave stranded.

marquee \mahr-KEE\ *n.* **1.** A large open-sided tent. **2.** A large sign.

marquis \MAHR-kwis\ *n. pl.* marquises. (Fo) A rank of nobility in some European countries.

marriage \MAR-ij\ *n.* **1.** The legal union of two people. **2.** The ceremony that unites two people.

marrow \MAR-oh\ *n.* **1.** The soft tissue within bones. **2.** A core. marrowed *v.*

marry \MAR-ee\ *v.* married; marrying. **1.** To be legally wed. **2.** To perform a wedding ceremony. **3.** To put together. marriageable *adj.*

Mars \mahrz\ *n.* **1.** The fourth planet from the Sun. **2.** The ancient Roman god of war.

marsh \mahrsh\ *n.* **1.** A low-lying area of wet land. **2.** A bog or swamp.

marshal \MAHR-shul\ *n.* **1.** High-ranking police or military officer. **2.** A parade leader.

marshal \MAHR-shul\ *v.* marshalled; marshalling. **1.** To perform the duties of a marshal. **2.** To arrange in order. **3.** To usher.

marsupial \mahr-SOO-pee-ul\ *n.* A mammal that usually carries its young in a pouch.

martial \MAHR-shul\ *adj.* Warlike.

martial arts *n.* Various oriental combat and self-defensive sports.

martyr \MAHR-tur\ *n. pl.* martyrs. A person who chooses to suffer for his or her beliefs. martyrdom *n.*

marvel \MAHR-vul\ *n.* A wonderful thing. marvel *v.*

marvelous \MAHR-vuh-lus\ *adj.* Wonderful.

Marxism \MAHRK-siz-um\ *n.* An economic philosophy developed by Karl Marx upon which Communism is based. Marxist *n.*

mascara \ma-SKAIR-uh\ *n.* Makeup applied to the eye lashes.

masculine \MAS-kyuh-lin\ *adj.* **1.** Of or concerning a man. **2.** Of a grammatical form suitable for males. masculinity *n.*

mash *n.* A soft mixture of grain or bran.

mash *v.* mashed; mashing. To beat or crush into a soft mixture. masher *n.*

mask *n.* **1.** Covering on the face for disguise or protection. **2.** A replica of the face.

mask *v.* masked; masking. **1.** To cover with a mask. **2.** To disguise or conceal. masker *n.*

masonry \MAY-sun-ree\ *n. pl.* masonries. Mason's stone work. mason *n.*

masquerade \mas-kuh-RAYD\ *n.* **1.** A false show. **2.** A costume ball. masquerade *v.*

mass \mas\ *n. pl.* masses. **1.** A unit of matter. **2.** Large quantity of something. **3.** A Catholic celebration.

massacre \MAS-uh-kur\ *v.* massacred; massacring. To kill in large numbers. massacre *n.*

massage \muh-SAHZH\ *v.* massaged; massaging. To rub or knead the body. massage *n.*

masseur *also* **masseuse** \muh-SUR\ *n.* (Fr) A person who gives a massage.

massive \MAS-iv\ *adj.* **1.** Huge. **2.** Large and heavy. massively *adv.*; massiveness *n.*

mass-produce *also* **mass produce** \MAS-pruh-DOOS\ *v.* mass-produced; mass-producing. To make in large numbers.

mastectomy \ma-STEK-tuh-mee\ *n. pl.* mastectomies. Surgical removal of the breast.

master \MAS-tur\ *n.* **1.** A person in control. **2.** Owner of a slave or animal. **3.** Expert player.

master \MAS-tur\ *v.* mastered; mastering. **1.** To show expertise at a task or job. **2.** To control. **3.** To defeat. masterdom *n.*; mastery *n.*

masterful \MAS-tur-ful\ *adj.* Having skill or expertise. masterfully *adv.*

masterpiece \MAS-tur-pees\ *n.* An outstanding piece of work.

masturbate \MAS-tur-bayt\ *v.* masturbated; masturbating. Sexual self-stimulation.

mat *n.* **1.** Piece of material for the floor. **2.** Small piece of material. **3.** Dense mass.

mat *v.* matted; matting. **1.** To cover with a mat. **2.** To form a mat. **3.** To tangle.

matador \MAT-uh-dor\ *n.* (Sp) A bullfighter.

match \mach\ *n. pl.* matches. **1.** A contest or game. **2.** Something exactly like or corresponding to another. matchable *adj.*; matcher *n.*

match \mach\ *v.* matched; matching. **1.** To contest. **2.** To equal or be alike. **3.** To find similar thing. matchable *adj.*; matcher *n.*

mate \mayt\ *n.* **1.** A spouse. **2.** One of a pair. **3.** A friend or associate. **4.** An assistant.

mate \mayt\ *v.* mated; mating. **1.** To combine or match. **2.** To copulate or breed. mateless *adj.*

material \muh-TEER-ee-ul\ *n.* **1.** That from which somehting is made. **2.** Cloth or fabric. materials *n.*

materialistic \muh-TEER-ee-uh-

LIS-tik\ *adj.* Preoccupied with possessions. materialism *n.*

materialize \muh-TEER-ee-uh-lize\ *v.* materialized; materializing. **1.** To appear. **2.** To happen.

matériel *also* **materiel** \muh-teer-ee-EL\ *n.* (Fr) Military supplies.

maternal \muh-TUR-nl\ *adj.* Of or concerning a mother. maternalism *n.*; maternalistic *adj.*

maternity \muh-TUR-ni-tee\ *n.* Motherhood. maternity *adj.*

math *n.* Mathematics, the science of numbers, quantities, and measurements. mathemetician *n.*; mathematical *adj.*; mathematics *n.*

matinee \mat-n-AY\ *n. pl.* matinees. Afternoon performance.

matriarch \MAY-tree-ahrk\ *n.* The female leader of a family, group, or culture.

matriarchy \MAY-tree-ahr-kee\ *n.* A family or society lead by women.

matricide \MA-tri-side\ *n.* The murder of one's mother.

matriculate \muh-TRIK-yuh-layt\ *v.* matriculated; matriculating. To enroll at a college or university.

matrimony \MA-truh-moh-nee\ *n. pl.* matrimonies. Marriage.

matrix \MAY-triks\ *n. pl.* matrixes.

1. A mold in which something is shaped. **2.** A mass of rock with gems inside.

matron \MAY-trun\ *n.* **1.** A married woman. **2.** The female head of a household or institution. matronly *adj.*

matte *also* **mat or matt** \mat\ *n.* A dull surface. matte *adj.*

matter \MAT-ur\ *n.* **1.** That which takes up space. **2.** A substance or material. **3.** Business dealing.

matter-of-fact *also* **matter of fact** \MAT-ur-uv-FAKT\ *n.* (Id) Strictly factual.

mattress \MA-tris\ *n. pl.* mattresses. Case filled with paddding and springs for a bed.

mature \muh-CHUUR\ *adj.* maturer; maturest. **1.** Fully grown or developed. **2.** Due for payment. maturely *adv.*; maturity *n.*; matureness *n.*; maturate *v.*; maturation *n.*

mature \muh-CHUUR\ *v.* matured; maturing. To make or become mature.

matzoh *also* **matzoh** \MAHT-zuh\ *n. pl.* matzos or matzohs. Unleavened bread wafers eaten by Jews at Passover.

maudlin \MAWD-lin\ *adj.* Embarassingly sentimental.

maul \mawl\ *n.* A heavy, long handled axe or hammer used to hit and split wood.

maul \mawl\ *v.* mauled; mauling. To treat roughly and injure.

mausoleum \maw-suh-LEE-um\ *n. pl.* mausoleums or mausolea. A grand tomb.

mauve \mohv or mawv\ *n.* A pale bluish purple color.

maven \MAY-vun\ *n.* An expert or connoisseur.

maverick \MAV-ur-ik\ *n.* An unorthodox or undisciplined person.

maxi \MAK-see\ *prefix* **1.** Maximum. **2.** Large when compared to others.

maxilofacial \MAK-suh-loh-FAY-shul\ *adj.* Pertaining to the face and jaw.

maxim \MAK-sim\ *n.* A statement of general truth or conduct.

maximum \MAK-suh-mum\ *n.* Greatest amount possible. maximum *adj.*

May *n.* The fifth month of the year, after April and before June.

may *v.* **1.** To be possible. **2.** To be allowed or permitted. might *v.*

maybe \MAY-bee\ *adv.* Possibly. maybe *n.*

mayhem \MAY-hem\ *n.* Chaos and confusion.

mayonnaise \MAY-uh-NAYZ\ *n.* A creamy condiment made of eggs and vegetable oil.

mayor \MAY-ur\ *n.* The head of a city or borough government. mayoral *adj.*

maze \mayz\ *n.* A complex and confusing network or system of paths, lines, etc.

mea culpa \may-uh-KUL-puh\ *n.* (Lt.) It is my fault.

meadow \MED-oh\ *n.* An open grassy field.

meager \MEE-gur\ *adj.* Scant in amount. meagerness *n.*

meal \meel\ *n.* **1.** Food served and eaten. **2.** The occasion of eating. **3.** Coarsely ground grain. mealless *adj.*

mealtime \MEEL-time\ *n.* The given time of a meal.

mean \meen\ *adj.* meaner; meanest. **1.** Unkind. **2.** Selfish and miserly. **3.** Poor in quality. **4.** Low in rank.

mean \meen\ *v.* meant; meaning. **1.** To intend. **2.** To have as a sense. **3.** To involve.

meander \mee-AN-dur\ *v.* meandered; meandering. **1.** To follow a winding course. **2.** To wander leisurely.

meaning \MEE-ning\ *n.* **1.** What is meant. **2.** Significance. meaningful *adj.*; meaningfully *adv.*; meaningly *adv.*

meaningless \MEE-ning-lis\ *adj.* Having no use or intention.

means \meens\ *n.* Resources.

meantime \MEEN-time\ *adv.* Meanwhile.

meanwhile \MEEN-hwile\ *adv.* **1.** In the interval. **2.** At the same time. meanwhile *n.*

measles \MEE-zulz\ *pl. n.* An acute infectious viral disease producing small red skin spots.

measly \MEE-zlee\ *adj.* measlier; measliest. Small and inconsequential.

measurable \MEZH-ur-uh-bul\ *adj.* Capable of being measured.

measure \MEZH-ur\ *n.* **1.** Size or quantity figured. **2.** Extent. **3.** A standard or system used to estimate.

measure \MEZH-ur\ *v.* measured; measuring. **1.** To find a size or quantity within a system. **2.** To set apart. **3.** Estimate.

meat \MEET\ *n.* **1.** The flesh of animals as food. **2.** The edible part of anything. meatless *adj.*

meaty \MEE-tee\ *adj.* meatier; meatiest **1.** Like or full of meat. **2.** Full of substance. meatiness *n.*

mechanical \muh-KAN-i-kul\ *adj.* **1.** Concerning machinery. **2.** Done without conscious thought. mechanize *v.*

mechanism \MEK-uh-niz-um\ *n.* **1.** A machine. **2.** The way a machine operates. **3.** A machine's parts.

medal \MED-l\ *n.* A flat piece of metal with a design.

meddle \MED-l\ *v.* meddled; meddling. To interfere in other's affairs. meddlesome *adj.*

media \MEE-dee-uh\ *n.* Periodicals and broadcasting as a way of conveying information.

media event *n.* An occasion staged to make news.

median \MEE-dee-un\ *adj.* In or passing through the middle.

median \MEE-dee-un\ *n.* A middle point or line.

mediate \MEE-dee-ayt\ *v.* mediated; mediating. To act as a peacemaker and work on a settlement. mediation *n.*; mediator *n.*

Medicaid \MED-i-kayd\ *n.* A federal program offering financial health assistance.

Medicare \MED-i-kair\ *n.* A federal program that provides health insurance to the elderly and disabled.

medicate \MED-i-kayt\ *v.* medicated; medicating. To treat with medicine. medication *n.*

medicine \MED-uh-sin\ *n.* **1.** A substance used to treat an illness, disease. **2.** Health care profession. medicine *v.*; medicinal *adj.*

medieval *also* **mediaeval** \mid-EE-vul\ *adj.* Pertaining to the Middle Ages, 500-1500 A.D. medievalist *n.*; medievally *adv.*

mediocre \mee-dee-OH-kur\ *adj.* Second-rate.

meditate \MED-i-tayt\ *v.* meditated; meditating. **1.** To think deeply or quietly. **2.** To sit in complete quiet. **3.** To plan. meditation *n.*

medium \MEE-dee-um\ *n.* **1.** Singular form of media. **2.** A middle size, quality, etc. **3.** Means or agency.

medley \MED-lee\ *n. pl.* medleys. **1.** An assortment. **2.** Excerpts from various musical sources. medley *adj.*

meek *adj.* meeker; meekest. Quiet and obedient. meekly *adv.*

meet *n.* An athletic contest between two or more teams.

meet *v.* met; meeting. **1.** Come face to face with. **2.** Be present for arrival. **3.** To make an acquaintance. meeting *n.*

megabyte \MEG-uh-bite\ *n. pl.* megabytes. One million bytes, in computer storage.

megadose \MEG-uh-dohs\ *n.* A large quantity of a drug or vitamin.

megalomania \meg-uh-loh-MAY-nee-uh\ *n.* Exaggerated self-esteem.

megalopolis *also* **megapolis** \meg-uh-LOP-oh-lis\ *n.* A large city and the adjoining area.

megaton \MEG-uh-tun\ *n.* One million tons.

megavitamin \MEG-uh-vie-tuh-mun\ *n.* Very large vitamin dose.

meiosis \my-OH-sis\ *n.* Gamete and chromosomal formation in newly formed cells. meitotic *adj.*

melancholy *also* **melancholia** \MEL-un-kol-ee\ *n. pl.* melancholies. Mental depression. melancholic *n.*

melange *also* **mélange** \may-LAHNZH\ *n. pl.* melanges. (Fr) A mixture.

melanin \MEL-uh-nin\ *n.* A dark pigment found in humans and animals.

melanoma \mel-uh-NOH-muh\ *n. pl.* melanomas, melanomata. (Md) A type of malignant skin cancer.

melee *also* **mêlée** \MAY-lay\ *n.* **1.** A confused fight. **2.** A chaotic state.

mellow \MEL-oh\ *adj.* mellower; mellowest. **1.** Ripe and sweet. **2.**

Soft and rich. **3.** Becoming kindly and calm. mellow *v.*

melodrama \MEL-uh-drah-muh\ *n.* Sensational or emotional drama. melodramatic *adj.*

melody \MEL-uh-dee\ *n.* *pl.* melodies. **1.** Sounds in patterned succession. **2.** Song. melodius. *adj.*

melon \MEL-un\ *n.* A large sweet fruit of the gourd family.

melt *v.* melted; melting. **1.** To make into or become liquid. **2.** To soften in emotions. **3.** To fade. meltable. *adj.*; meltability *n.*; meltingly *adv.*

meltdown *also* **melt down** \MELT-down\ *n.* **1.** Accidental disintegration of the core of a nuclear reactor. **2.** Rapid decline.

member \MEM-bur\ *n.* A person or things belonging to a particular group.

membership \MEM-bur-ship\ *n.* **1.** State of belonging to a particular group. **2.** A population of members.

membrane \MEM-brayn\ *n.* Thin flexible skinlike tissue.

memento \muh-MEN-toh\ *n.* *pl.* mementos, mementoes. Souvenir or reminder of an experience.

memoir \MEM-wahr\ *n.* A written account of remembered events.

memorabilia \mem-ur-uh-BIL-ee-uh\ *n.* A collection of souvenirs.

memorable \MEM-ur-uh-bul\ *adj.* Worth remembering and easily remembered.

memorandum *also* **memo** \mem-uh-RAN-dum\ *n.* *pl.* memorandums, memorandi. **1.** A note written as a reminder. **2.** An informative message.

memorial \muh-MOR-ee-ul\ *n.* Something preserving the memory of a person or event. memorial *adj.*

memory \MEM-uh-ree\ *n.* *pl.* memories. **1.** Ability to remember. **2.** Things remembered. **3.** Computer storage for data. memorize *v.*

memory lane *n.* (Id) The recalled events of one's own life.

menace \MEN-is\ *n.* **1.** A threat. **2.** Annoying or threatening person or thing. menace *v.*

menagerie \muh-NAJ-uh-ree\ *n.* A collection of wild animals.

mend *v.* mended; mending. **1.** To repair. **2.** To stitch fabric. **3.** To make or become better.

menial \MEE-nee-ul\ *adj.* Lowly. menial *n.*

meningitis \men-in-JIE-tis\ *n.* (Md) Inflammation of the membranes covering the brain and spinal cord.

menopause \MEN-uh-pawz\ *n.* The period that marks the end of menstruation.

Mensa \MEN-suh\ *n.* **1.** A constellation. **2.** Organization of intelligent people.

menstruate \MEN-stroo-ayt\ *v.* To discharge blood and dead cell debris from the uterus each month. menstruation *n.*

mental \MEN-tl\ *adj.* Of, in, or performed by the mind. mentally *adj.*

mentality \men-TAL-i-tee\ *n.* *pl.* mentalities. A person's mental ability or general attitude.

mental retardation *n.* A developmental disorder that is characterized by difficulty in learning. mentally retarded *adj.*

mention \MEN-shun\ *v.* mentioned; mentioning. To refer to something.

mentor \MEN-tur\ *n.* A trusted teacher.

menu \MEN-yoo\ *n.* **1.** Food list for a meal. **2.** Food served at a meal. **3.** Computer list of options.

mercenary \MUR-suh-nair-ee\ *adj.* **1.** Working solely for monetary reward. **2.** Hired to serve a foreign country. mercenary *n.*

merchandise \MUR-chun-dize\ *n.* Goods to be bought or sold.

merchandise \MUR-chun-dize\ *v.* merchandised; merchandising. **1.** To buy or sell. **2.** To promote or advertise goods for sale. merchandiser *n.*

merchant \MUR-chunt\ *n.* **1.** One who buys and sells goods for a profit. **2.** A storekeeper.

merciless \MUR-si-lis\ *adj.* Showing no mercy. mercilessly *adv.*

Mercury \MUR-kyuh-ree\ *n.* **1.** The Roman god of commerce and travel. **2.** The planet closest to the Sun.

mercury \MUR-kyuh-ree\ *n.* (Sc) A highly poisonous silver metallic element used in thermometers.

mercy \MUR-see\ *n.* *pl.* mercies. Kindness shown to an offender or enemy. merciful *adj.*

mercy killing *n.* The act of taking of a life for compassionate reasons; euthanasia. mercy killer *n.*

mere \meer\ *adj.* merest. **1.** Small or trifling. **2.** Not important. **3.** Pure.

merge \murj\ *v.* merged; merging. To combine or blend.

merger \MUR-jur\ *n.* (Bs) A combining of commercial companies.

meridian \muh-RID-ee-un\ *n.* A great semicircle on the earth's surface passing through the poles.

meringue \muh-RANG\ *n.* A pastry topping made with beaten baked egg whites.

merit \MAIR-it\ *n.* **1.** Feature deserving praise. **2.** Excellence. meritorious *adj.*

merit \MAIR-it\ *v.* merited; meriting. To deserve.

merry \MAIR-ee\ *adj.* merrier; merriest. Cheerful and joyous. merrily *adv.*; merriness *n.*

mesa \MAY-suh\ *n.* A flat-topped elevation with cliff-like sides.

mesh *n. pl.* meshes. The open spaces in a woven object or fabric.

mesh *v.* meshed; meshing. To engage with another and fit harmoniously. meshy *adv.*

mesmerize \MEZ-muh-rize\ *v.* mesmerized; mesmerizing. To hypnotize or capture the attention of. mesmerizer *n.*

Mesozoic \MEZ-oh-zoh-ik\ *adj.* (Sc) The third era of geologic time, 65 to 240 million years ago.

mesquite \muh-SKEET\ *n.* The wood of a shrub or small tree often used to barbeque food.

mess \mes\ *n. pl.* messes. **1.** Disorder. **2.** A chaotic arrangement. **3.** A confusing condition. **4.** A group.

mess \mes\ *v.* messed; messing. **1.** To make chaotic or unclean. **2.** To mismanage. **3.** To interfere.

message \MES-ij\ *n.* **1.** Written or spoken communication. **2.** A teaching.

messenger \MES-n-jur\ *n.* One who delivers a message.

met *v.* Part participle and past tense of meet.

metabolic \met-uh-BOL-ik\ *adj.* Pertaining to the processes involved in the maintenance of life. metabolism *n.*

metal \MET-l\ *n.* (Sc) **1.** Elements such as gold, silver and platinum. **2.** An alloy. metallic *adj.*

metallurgy \MET-l-ur-jee\ *n.* The science of metal and metal making. metallurgical *adj.*

metamorphosis \met-uh-MOR-fuh-sis\ *n. pl.* metamorphoses. A change in form or character. metamorphose *v.*

metaphor \MET-uh-for\ *n.* The transferred use of a word or phrase suggesting comparison.

metaphysical \met-uh-FIZ-i-kul\ *adj.* Concerning the nature of existence.

metaphysics \met-uh-FIZ-iks\ *n.* A branch of philosophy that deals with the nature of existence.

metastasis \muh-TAS-tuh-sis\ *n.* [Md] Movement of a disease from one part of the body to another. metastasize *v.*

meteor \MEE-tee-ur\ *n.* (Sc) A small mass of matter from outer space.

meteoric \mee-tee-OR-ik\ *adj.* **1.** [Sc] Concerning meteors and meteorites. **2.** Swift and successful.

meteorite \MEE-tee-uh-rite\ *n.* (Sc) A meteor fallen to earth.

meteorology \mee-tee-uh-ROL-uh-jee\ *n.* The study of the weather. meteorologist *n.*

meter \MEE-tur\ *n.* **1.** A length or distance equal to 39.4 inches. **2.** A rhythm or cadence. meter *v.*

method \METH-ud\ *n.* A procedure or way of doing something.

methodical *also* **methodic** \muh-THOD-i-kul\ *adj.* Orderly and systematic. methodology *n.*

meticulous \muh-TIK-yuh-lus\ *adj.* Careful and exact. meticulously *adv.*

metric \ME-trik\ *adj.* Concerning a system of measure based on a unit of length about 39.4 inches.

metropolis \mi-TROP-uh-lis\ *n.* A city or area considered the center of activity or commerce.

mezuza *also* **mezuzah** \me-ZOO-zuh\ *n.* (He) A small parchment inscribed with Biblical passage.

miasma \mie-AZ-muh\ *n. pl.* miasmas; miasmata. Unhealthy air.

micro \MIE-kroh\ *prefix* Small.

microbe \MIE-krohb\ *n.* (Sc) A tiny life form. microbial *adj.*; microbic *adj.*

microchip \MIE-kroh-chip\ *n.* (Cm) A small computer chip.

microcomputer \MIE-kroh-kom-pyoo-tur\ *n.* (Cm) A small computer.

microeconomics \mie-kroh-EK-oh-NOM-iks\ *n.* The study of the aspects of economic exchange.

microscope \MIE-kruh-skohp\ *n.* An optical instrument used to magnify objects undetectable with the naked eye.

microscopic \mie-kruh-SKOP-ik\ *adj.* **1.** Extremely small. **2.** Too small to be seen without a microscope.

microsurgery \mie-kroh-SUR-jur-ee\ *n. pl.* microsurgeries. (Md) Surgery performed on a minute scale. microsurgeon *n.*; microsurgical *adj.*

microwave \MIE-kruh-wayv\ *n.* **1.** A short electromagnetic wave. **2.** An oven using these waves to cook.

mid *prefix* Middle.

midday \MID-DAY\ *n.* The middle of daytime.

middle \MID-l\ *n.* Occurring at an equal distance from extremes or limits. middle *adj.*

middleman *also* **middle man** \MID-l-man\ *n. pl.* middlemen; middle men. A trader between producer and consumer.

midget \MIJ-it\ *n.* An extremely small person or thing.

midi \MID-ee\ *n.* A skirt or dress reaching the middle of the calf.

mid-life crisis *n. pl.* mid-life crises. A period of disorder and confusion that may occur in middle age.

midst *n.* In the middle of or among.

might \miet\ *n.* Great strength or power.

might \miet\ *v.* may **1.** Expressing a request for permission. **2.** Expressing possibility.

mighty \MIE-tee\ *adj.* mightiest; mightier. Very strong or powerful.

migraine \MIE-grayn\ *n.* (Md) A severe and chronic headache.

migrant \MIE-grunt\ *n.* Person or animal that moves for employment or settlement.

migrate \MIE-grayt\ *v.* migrated; migrating. To go from one place to another, for employment, settlement, or due to seasons. migration *n.*

mild \mield\ *adj.* milder; mildest **1.** Moderate. **2.** Not harsh. **3.** Gentle. **4.** Not strong.

mile \miel\ *n.* A unit of length measurement equalling 5280 feet or 1760 yards.

mileage \MIE-lij\ *n.* **1.** Distance in miles. **2.** Advantage to be gained.

milestone \MIEL-stohn\ *n.* **1.** A significant event or stage. **2.** A stone marker showing distance in miles.

milieu \mil-YUU\ *n. pl.* milieus. (Fr) One's surroundings or environment.

militant \MIL-i-tunt\ *adj.* Prepared for aggressive action.

military \MIL-i-ter-ee\ *n. pl.* militaries. **1.** Armed forces. **3.** Army personnel. military *adj.*; militarization *n.*

militia \mi-LISH-uh\ *n.* Military force made up of civilians.

milk *n.* **1.** White fluid secreted by female mammals. **2.** Prepared milk as food.

milk *v.* milked; milking. **1.** To obtain milk from a mammal. **2.** To exploit. milker *n.*

milky \MIL-kee\ *adj.* milkier; milkiest. Of or like milk.

mill \mil\ *n.* **1.** A factory where things are ground. **2.** Machinery for grinding.

mill \mil\ *v.* milled; milling. **1.** To grind or produce in a mill. **2.** To move without aim. miller *n.*

millennium \mi-LEN-ee-um\ *n. pl.* millenniums; millennia. A period of one thousand years.

millet \MIL-it\ *n.* A type of cereal grass.

milliliter \MIL-uh-lee-tur\ *n.* One one-thousandth of a liter.

millimeter \MIL-uh-mee-tur\ *n.* One one-thousandth of a meter or one-tenth of a centimeter.

million \MIL-yun\ *n. pl.* millions. A number equal to 1000 times 1000.

millionaire *also* **millionairess** \mil-yuh-NAIR\ *n.* A person who has at least one million dollars or its equivalent.

mime *n.* A person who communicates with gestures but no words.

mime *v.* mimed; miming. To communicate with gestures but no words. mimer *n.*

mimetics \mi-ME-tiks\ *n.* The study or practice of mime. mimetic *adj.*; mimesis *n.*

mimic \MIM-ik\ *v.* mimicked, mimicking. To imitate. mimic *n.*; mimic *adj.*

mimosa \mi-MOH-suh\ *n. pl.* mimosas. **1.** A plant with small ball-shaped flowers. **2.** Champagne and orange juice.

minaret \min-uh-RET\ *n.* A high slender tower attached to a mosque.

mince \mins\ *v.* minced; mincing. **1.** To chop finely. **2.** To talk or walk with refinement. mincer *n.*

mind \miend\ *n.* **1.** Ability to think, reason. **2.** Attention, remembrance, or opinion. **3.** Sanity.

mind \miend\ *v.* minded; minding. **1.** To have charge of. **2.** To object to. **3.** To bear in mind. **4.** To feel concern.

mindblowing \MIEND-bloh-ing\ *adj.* (Sl) Very surprising.

mind-expanding *adj.* (Id) Intellectually illuminating.

mindful \MIEND-ful\ *adj.* Aware or attentive. mindfulness *n.*; mindfully *adv.*

mindless \MIEND-lis\ *adj.* Heedless or uncaring. mindlessly adv; mindlessness *n.*

mine \MIEN\ *n.* **1.** Excavation for natural resources. **2.** Deposit of ore, etc. **3.** Abundant source.

mine \MIEN\ *see* my *pron.* That which belongs to me.

mine \MIEN\ *v.* mined; mining. **1.** To excavate to obtain natural resources. **2.** To lay explosive mines.

minestrone \min-uh-STROH-nee\ *n.* (It) A thick soup of vegetables, beans and pasta.

mingle \MING-gul\ *v.* mingled; mingling. **1.** To mix or blend. **2.** To socialize.

mini \MI-nee\ prefix Miniature.

miniature \MIN-ee-uh-chur\ *n.* A small-scale model, copy, or painting. miniature *adj.*

minicab \MI-nee-kab\ *n.* A small car used as a taxi.

minicam \MI-nee-kam\ *n.* A small video camera.

minicar \MI-nee-kar\ *n.* A very small car.

minimal \MIN-uh-mul\ *adj.* **1.** Very small. **2.** Least possible. minimally *adv.*

minimalism \MIN-uh-mul-iz-um\ *n.* An art style in which content and material are minimal. minimalist *n.*

minimize \MIN-uh-miez\ *v.* minimized; minimizing. **1.** To reduce to a minimum. **2.** To consider small and unimportant. minimizer *n.*

minimum \MIN-uh-mum\ *n. pl.* minimums; minima. Smallest amount possible.

miniseries \MI-nee-SEER-eez\ *n.* A television movie shown in a few episodes.

miniskirt \MI-nee-skurt\ *n.* A skirt that ends above the knees.

minister \MIN-uh-stur\ *n.* **1.** Government department head. **2.** Member of the clergy. **3.** A senior diplomat. minister *v.*

minor \MIE-nur\ *adj.* **1.** Lesser. **2.** Not very important. **3.** [Mu] With a semitone above the second note. minor *n.*

minstrel \MIN-strul\ *n.* A medieval singer and musician.

mint *n.* **1.** A place where coins and money are made. **2.** A large amount of money.

minuet \min-yoo-ET\ *n.* A slow stately dance conducted in 3/4 time and its music.

minuscule \MIN-uh-skyool\ *adj.* Extremely small.

minute \MIN-it\ *n.* **1.** Sixty seconds. **2.** A brief amount of time. **3.** A moment. minute *v.*

minutia \mi-NOO-shee-uh\ *n. pl.* minutiae. Precise details.

minx \mingks\ *n.* (Sl) A flirtatious woman.

miosis \MIE-oh-sis\ *n.* (Md) Excessive contraction of the pupil.

miracle \MIR-uh-kul\ *n.* A remarkable occurrence or event. miraculous *adj.*

mirage \mi-RAHZH\ *n.* An optical illusion caused by atmospheric conditions.

mirror \MIR-ur\ *n.* A piece of glass coated with reflecting material. mirror *v.*

mirror-image *also* **mirror image** *n.* A duplicate or corresponding image.

mirth \murth\ *n.* Happiness or glee. mirthful *adj.*; mirthfully *adv.*

misanthrope \MIS-un-throhp\ *n.* One who hates humankind. misanthropic *adj.*

misbegotten *also* **misbegot** \MIS-bee-got-n\ *adj.* Contemptible.

misbehave \mis-bi-HAYV\ *v.* misbehaved; misbehaving. To act improperly.

miscarriage \mis-KAIR-ij\ *n.* A naturally occurring abortion of a fetus. miscarry *v.*

miscellaneous \mis-uh-LAY-nee-us\ *adj.* Assorted. miscellaneously *adv.*; miscellaneousness *n.*

mischief \MIS-chif\ *n.* Annoying behavior. mischievous *adj.*

misdemeanor \mis-duh-MEE-nur\ *n.* (Le) A crime less serious than a felony.

mise-en-scene \meez-ahn-SEN\ *n. pl.* mise-en-scenes. (Fr) Stage settings or surroundings.

miser \MIE-zur\ *n.* One who hoards money, spending as little as possible. miserly *adv.*

miserable \MIZ-ur-uh-bul\ *adj.* **1.** Full of misery. **2.** Very poor. miserably *adv.*; misery *n.*

misfortune \mis-FOR-chun\ *n.* **1.** Bad luck. **2.** Unfortunate event.

misgiving \mis-GIV-ing\ *n.* Doubt or apprehension. misgivingly *adv.*

mishap \MIS-hap\ *n.* **1.** A mistake. **2.** An accident.

mislead \mis-LEED\ *v.* misled; misleading. To cause to form a wrong impression. misleader *n.*

misplace \mis-PLAYS\ *v.* misplaced; misplacing. **1.** To put in a wrong place. **2.** To accredit mistakenly.

miss \mis\ *n. pl.* misses. A young unmarried woman.

miss \mis\ *v.* missed; missing. **1.** To fail to hit. **2.** To fail to meet. **3.** To fail to be present or notice.

misshapen \mis-SHAY-pun\ *adj.* Deformed or shaped poorly. misshape *v.*; misshapen *v.*; misshaper *n.*

missile \MIS-ul\ *n.* A weapon that is propelled toward a target.

missing \MIS-ing\ *adj.* Not present.

mission \MISH-un\ *n.* **1.** People sent to another country to perform a job. **2.** A task to be performed.

missionary \MISH-uh-ner-ee\ *n. pl.* missionaries. A person sent by a religious organization to conduct humanitarian work. missionary *adj.*

mist *n.* Fine particles of water suspended in air. misty *adj.*; mist *v.*

mistake \mi-STAYK\ *n.* **1.** An error. **2.** A misconception.

mistake \mi-STAYK\ *v.* mistook; mistaken; mistaken. **1.** To make an error. **2.** To misidentify. **3.** To misunderstand. mistaken *adj.*; mistakenly *adv.*

mistreat \mis-TREET\ *v.* mistreated; mistreating. To treat poorly or abusively. mistreatment *n.*

misunderstand \mis-un-dur-STAND\ *v.* misunderstood; misunderstanding. To interpret incorrectly.

misuse \mis-YOOS\ *v.* misused; misusing. To use improperly. misuse *n.*

mitosis \mie-TOH-sis\ *n. pl.* mitoses. [Sc]: The duplication of chromosomes within cells preceeding division.

mix \miks\ *n. pl.* mixes. **1.** The act of mixing. **2.** A combination. **3.** A recorded selection of music. mixable *adj.*

mix \miks\ *v.* mixed; mixing. **1.** To combine. **2.** To join elements. **3.** To socialize. **4.** To cross-breed. mixer *n.*

mixed media *n.* The use of sound, pictures, text or other media in a product.

mixture \MIKS-chur\ *n.* **1.** Something made by mixing. **2.** Something made of diverse elements.

mix-up \MIKS-up\ *n.* (Cl) **1.** A confused state. **2.** A fight or melee.

mnemonic \ni-MON-ik\ *adj.* Related to memory. mnemonic *n.*

moan \mohn\ *v.* moaned; moaning. **1.** To make a low mournful sound. **2.** To complain. **3.** To lament. moan *n.*; moaner *n.*

moat \moht\ *n.* A water-filled ditch dug around a structure. moat *v.*

mob *n.* **1.** A large unruly crowd. **2.** Organized crime group. mob *v.*; mobbed *v.*

mobile \MOH-bul\ *adj.* **1.** Able to be moved. **2.** Moving quickly or often. **3.** Flowing. mobile *n.*

moccasin \MOK-uh-sin\ *n.* **1.** A leather slipper. **2.** A snake.

mock \mok\ *v.* mocked; mocking. **1.** To ridicule. **2.** To mimic. **3.** To frustrate hope. mock *n.*; mockery *n.*

mod *adj.* Modern fashion.

modal \MOH-dul\ *adj.* **1.** Pertaining to a mode. **2.** Pertaining verb mood. modality *n.*

mode \mohd\ *n.* **1.** A way of doing something. **2.** The current style. **3.** A type.

model \MOD-l\ *n.* **1.** A small scale replica. **2.** A preliminary plan. **3.** A design. **4.** An example.

model \MOD-l\ *v.* modelled, mod-elling. **1.** To make a copy. **2.** To conform to a standard. **3.** To pose.

modem \MOH-dum\ *n.* (Cm) A de-vice that moves data between computers via telephone lines.

moderate \MOD-ur-it\ *adj.* **1.** Rea-sonable. **2.** Mild. **3.** Not exces-sive. moderate *v.*; moderation *n.*

modern \MOD-urn\ *adj.* **1.** Up-to-date. **2.** Of advanced style. mod-ern *n.*; modernize *v.*; modernity *n.*

modest \MOD-ist\ *adj.* Humble and unpretentious. modesty *n.*

modicum \MOD-i-kum\ *n. pl.* modicums; modica. (Lt) A small amount.

modify \MOD-uh-fie\ *v.* modified; modifying. **1.** To change. **2.** To make less extreme. modification *n.*

module \MOJ-ool\ *n.* **1.** Unit of measurement. **2.** Architectural model. **3.** Self-contained compo-nent.

modus operandi \MOH-dus-op-uh-RAN-dee\ *n.* (Lt) Method of operation.

mogul \MOH-gul\ *n.* **1.** A powerful person. **2.** A bump on a ski slope.

moist *adj.* moister; moistest. **1.** Damp. **2.** Filled with wetness. **3.** Tearful. moisten *v.*; moisture *n.*; moisturize *v.*

molar \MOH-lur\ *adj.* (Sc) **1.** Per-taining to a body of matter. **2.** Con-taining one mole of a substance.

molar \MOH-lur\ *n.* A broad crowned tooth used for grinding food. molar *adj.*

mold \mohld\ *n.* **1.** A hollow cast. **2.** A model around which something is shaped. **3.** A fungus. mold *v.*; moldy *adj.*; moldable *adj.*

mole \mohl\ *n.* **1.** A small pig-mented growth on the skin. **2.** A small burrowing animal.

molecule \MOL-uh-kyool\ *n.* A sta-ble arrangement of atoms. molec-ular *adj.*

molest \muh-LEST\ *v.* molested; molesting. **1.** To assault. **2.** To in-terfere with. molester *n.*

moll \mol\ *n.* (Sl) **1.** A ganster's girlfriend. **2.** A prostitute.

moment \MOH-munt\ *n.* **1.** A brief interval of time. **2.** An important event. momentous *adj.*

momentary \MOH-mun-ter-ee\ *adj.* **1.** Lasting a brief time. **2.** Temorary. momentariness *n.*

momentum \moh-MEN-tum\ *n. pl.* momenta. **1.** Impetus or contin-ued movement. **2.** [Sc] The prod-uct of mass and movement.

monarchy \MON-ur-kee\ *n. pl.* monarchies. A state ruled by one with absolute power. monarch *n.*

monastery \MON-uh-ster-ee\ *n. pl.* monasteries. Residence of a community of monks. monasterial *adj.*; monastic *adj.; n.*

Monday \MUN-day\ *n.* The day of the week after Sunday and before Tuesday.

monetary \MON-i-ter-ee\ *adj.* Pertaining to money. monetarily *adv.*

money \MUN-ee\ *n. pl.* monies. **1.** Coin and paper currency of a government. **2.** Property of monetary value. monetarily *adv.*

mongrel \MUNG-grul\ *n.* An interbred animal or plant. mongrel *adj.*

monitor \MON-i-tur\ *n.* **1.** One who admonishes or chides. **2.** A device used for control or surveillance.

monitor \MON-i-tur\ *v.* monitored; monitoring. **1.** To watch over. **2.** To keep track of. **3.** To check on.

monk \mungk\ *n.* A member of a religious group who lives in a monastery. monkish *adj.*; monkishness *n.*

monkey \MUNG-kee\ *n. pl.* monkies. A primate with long tail and closely related to man.

monkey \MUNG-kee\ *v.* monkeyed; monkeying. (Cl) **1.** To fool around. **2.** To act like a monkey.

monogamy \muh-NOG-uh-mee\ *n.* Having one mate for at a time. monogamist *n.*; monogamous *adj.*; monogamously *adv.*

monolith \MON-uh-lith\ *n.* A huge block of stone. monolithic *adj.*

monologue *also* **monolog** \MON-uh-lawg\ *n.* A speech made by one person.

monopoly \muh-NOP-uh-lee\ *n. pl.* monopolies. Total control of production and distribution of a product. monopolize *v.*

monotony \muh-NOT-uh-nee\ *n.* **1.** Uniform pitch or tone. **2.** Dullness. monotonous *adj.*

monsoon \mon-SOON\ *n.* The storm-bringing wind of the Indian Ocean and its rainy season.

monster \MON-stur\ *n.* **1.** A grotesque being. **2.** A person who horrifies or frightens. monster *adj.*

monstrous \MON-strus\ *adj.* **1.** Shocking or horrible. **2.** Very large. monstrosity *n.*; monstrously *adv.*; monstrousness *n.*

montage \mon-TAZH\ *n. pl.* montages. (Fr) A rapid sequence of images. montage *v.*

monument \MON-yuh-munt\ *n.* A structure built as a memorial.

monumental \mon-yuh-MEN-tl\ *adj.* **1.** Large and imposing. **2.** Significant. monumentally *adv.*; monumentality *n.*

mood *n.* **1.** A temporary attitude. **2.** Perception or intuition. **3.** A disposition. moody *adj.*

moolah \MOO-lah\ *n.* (Sl) money.

moon *n.* **1.** The Earth's satellite. **2.** Any planetary satellite.

moon *v.* mooned; mooning. To behave dreamily.

moor \muur\ *n.* A large open tract of boggy land.

moor \muur\ *v.* moored; mooring. To fasten or tie down.

moose \moos\ *n. pl.* moose. A large hoofed, broad-antlered forest animal.

moot *adj.* **1.** Subject to debate. **2.** [Le] Not significant.

mop *n.* A long-handled tool used to dust or wash floors. mop *v.*

mope \mohp\ *v.* moped; moping. To sulk. mope *n.*

moped \MOH-ped\ *n.* A motorized bicycle.

moral \MOR-ul\ *adj.* **1.** Concerned with right or wrong conduct. **2.** Virtuous. morality *n.*; morals *n.*

moral \MOR-ul\ *n.* **1.** Moral lesson or principle. **2.** Sexual conduct. morally *adv.*

morale \muh-RAL\ *n.* The attitude of an organized group.

moratorium \mor-uh-TOR-ee-um\ *n. pl.* moratoriums; moratoria.

1. (Lt) A suspension of all action. **2.** (Le) A suspension of payments.

moray \MOH-ray\ *n.* A type of tropical marine eel.

morbid \MOR-bid\ *adj.* Preoccupied with gloomy or gross things. morbidity *n.*; morbidly *adv.*; morbidness *n.*

mordant \MOR-dnt\ *adj.* **1.** Accurately sarcastic. **2.** Painfully trenchant and inciting. mordantly *adv.*

more \mor\ *adj.* **1.** Greater in quality or quantity. **2.** Extra or additional. more *n.*

morel \mor-EL\ *n.* A type of edible mushroom.

moreover \mor-OH-vur\ *adv.* In addition to what already has been said.

morgue \morg\ *n.* Mortuary.

moribund \MOR-uh-bund\ *adj.* Approaching death.

morn *n.* Morning.

morning \MOR-ning\ *n.* **1.** The early part of the day. **2.** The dawn.

morning-after pill *n.* [Sl] An oral contraceptive taken after intercourse.

moron \MOR-on\ *n.* A stupid person. moronic *adj.*

morose \muh-ROHS\ *adj.* Sullen and gloomy. morosely *adv.*; moroseness *n.*

morphology \mor-FOL-uh-jee\ *n.* (Sc) The study of the forms of animals, plants, or words. morphological *adj.*; morphologically *adv.*; morphologic *adj.*; morphologist *n.*

Morse Code *n.* A system of coded communication.

morsel \MOR-sul\ *n.* A small amount, esp. of food.

mortal \MOR-tl\ *adj.* 1. Subject to death. 2. Deadly.

mortality \mor-TAL-i-tee\ *n. pl.* mortalities. 1. The state of being mortal. 2. Large loss of life. 3. Death rate.

mortar \MOR-tur\ *n.* 1. Bowl for grinding substances with a pestle. 2. A muzzle loading cannon.

mortgage \MOR-gij\ *n.* (Le) Loan for the purchase of property. mortgage *v.*

mortify \MOR-tuh-fie\ *v.* mortified; mortifying. 1. To humiliate greatly. 2. To become gangrenous.

mortuary \MOR-choo-er-ee\ *n. pl.* mortuaries. A place where dead bodies are kept before funerals. mortician *n.*

mosaic \moh-ZAY-ik\ *n.* 1. A picture made of pieces of stone or tile. 2. Overlapping images. mosaic *v.*

Moslem \MOZ-lum\ *n.* A believer in the Islamic religion. Moslem *adj.*

mosque \mosk\ *n.* A place of worship for Moslems.

most \mohst\ *adj.* 1. The greatest in quantity or number. 2. The biggest part. 3. Very. 4. Almost.

motel \moh-TEL\ *n.* A roadside tourist hotel.

mother \MUTH-ur\ *n.* 1. A female parent. 2. A female in a position of authority. mom *n.*; mama *n.*; ma *n.*

mother \MUTH-ur\ *v.* mothered; mothering. 1. To give birth to. 2. To create. 3. To take care of. motherless *adj.*; motherlessness *n.*

motherhood \MUTH-ur-huud\ *n.* The condition of being a mother.

motif \moh-TEEF\ *n.* 1. A repeated element. 2. A short musical phrase.

motion \MOH-shun\ *n.* 1. The act of changing position. 2. A gesture. 3. The power to move.

motivate \MOH-tuh-vayt\ *v.* motivated; motivating. To give incentive. motivation *n.*

motive \MOH-tiv\ *n.* An impulse that incites to action.

motley \MOT-lee\ *adj.* 1. Assorted. 2. Multicolored. motley *n.*

motto \MOT-oh\ *n. pl.* mottoes. A catchy phrase or brief principle.

mound \mownd\ *n.* **1.** A pile of earth or debris. **2.** A natural land elevation. mound *v.*

mount \mownt\ *v.* mounted; mounting. To climb upon.

mountain \MOWN-tn\ *n.* A massive natural land elevation. mountainy *adj.*

mourn \morn\ *v.* mourned; mourning. To grieve. mourner *n.*; mourning *n.*

mouse \mows\ *n. pl.* mice. **1.** Small rodent with hairless tail. **2.** [Cm] A computer pointing device. mouse *v.*

moussaka \moo-SAH-kuh\ *n.* (Fo) A Greek dish made with meat, eggplant, and cheese.

mousse \moos\ *n.* **1.** A whipped dessert made with cream. **2.** A hairstyling product.

mouth \mowth\ *n. pl.* mouths. **1.** An animal's respiratory and digestive body opening. **2.** A similar opening. mouth *v.*

movable *also* **moveable** \MOO-vuh-bul\ *adj.* **1.** Able to be moved. **2.** Varying in date or time. movability *adj.*; movableness *n.*; movably *adj.*

move \moov\ *v.* moved; moving. **1.** To change position or location. **2.** To progress. **3.** To follow a course.

movement \MOOV-munt\ *n.* **1.** Change of position, location. **2.** Group working for social, political change.

movie \MOO-vee\ *n.* An extended film narrative.

movie star *n.* (Cl) A famous film actor or actress.

moving \MOO-ving\ *adj.* **1.** Changing position or location. **2.** Emotionally touching.

mow \moh\ *v.* mowed; mowing. To cut hay or grass by machine.

much *adj.* more; most. **1.** Great in number or quantity. **2.** Something important.

mucous *also* **mucose** \MYOO-kus\ *adj.* Concerning mucus.

mucus \MYOO-kus\ *n.* The slimy substance coating the inside of some body organs.

mud *n.* Soft, wet earth. mud *v.*; muddy *adj.*

muffle \MUF-ul\ *v.* muffled; muffling. **1.** To repress sound. **2.** To deaden. **3.** To suppress. muffle *n.*

mug *n.* **1.** A cup with a handle. **2.** [Sl] A photograph of a face. **3.** A criminal. mug *v.*

mug *v.* mugged; mugging. **1.** To assault. **2.** To exaggerate facial expressions. mugger *n.*

muggy \MUG-ee\ *adj.* (Cl) Hot and humid weather. mugginess *n.*

mulatto \muh-LAT-oh\ *n. pl.* mullatoes. A person of Caucasian and African descent. mulatto *adj.*

mule \myool\ *n.* The sterile offspring of a horse and donkey. mulish *adj.*; mulishness *n.*

mull \mul\ *v.* mulled; mulling. **1.** To consider carefully. **2.** To ponder. **3.** To sweeten with spices and heat. mulled *adj.*

multicolored \mul-ti-KUL-urd\ *adj.* Made of several colors.

multicultural \mul-ti-KUL-churul\ *adj.* Combining the viewpoints of several cultures.

multifarious \mul-tuh-FAIR-ee-us\ *adj.* **1.** Made of many parts. **2.** Varied and numerous. multifariously *adv.*; multifariousness *n.*

multimedia \mul-ti-MEE-dee-uh\ *adj.* Using several media elements. multimedia *n.*

multinational \mul-tee-NASH-uhnul\ *n.* (Bs) A corporation with holdings in several countries. multinational *adj.*

multiple \MUL-tuh-pul\ *adj.* Having many parts or elements.

multiple \MUL-tuh-pul\ *n.* A number that contains an evenly divisible number.

multiplication \mul-tuh-pli-KAY-shun\ *n.* **1.** The act of multiplying. **2.** Math operation of numerous additions.

multiply \MUL-tuh-plie\ *v.* multiplied; multiplying. **1.** Increase in number, amount. **2.** Find the sum of a repeated number. multiply *adv.*

multitude \MUL-ti-tood\ *n.* Great number of things or people. multitudinous *adj.*; multitudinousness *n.*

mumble \MUM-bul\ *v.* mumbled; mumbling. **1.** To speak unclearly. **2.** To chew with toothless gums. mumbler *n., adj.*

munch *v.* munched; munching. **1.** To chew quickly and carelessly. **2.** [Sl] To eat. **3.** [Sl] Munchies. Junk food. muncher *n.*

mundane \mun-DAYN\ *adj.* **1.** Routine and dull. **2.** Pertaining to this world. mundanity *n.*; mundanely *adv.*

municipal \myoo-NIS-uh-pul\ *adj.* Pertaining to the government of a city or borough. municipality *n.*

munitions \myoo-NISH-uns\ *n.* Military weapons and supplies.

mural \MYUUR-ul\ *n.* A painting or drawing made on a wall. muralist *n.*; mural *adj.*

murder \MUR-dur\ *v.* murdered; murdering. To kill another. murder *n.*; murderer *n.*; murderous *adj.*

murky \MUR-kee\ *adj.* murkier; murkiest. Dark and gloomy. murkiness *n.*; murkily *adv.*

murmur \MUR-mur\ *v.* murmured; murmuring. To make a low continuous sound. murmurer *n.*; murmuringly *adv.*; murmurous *adj.*

muscle \MUS-ul\ *n.* **1.** Fibrous tissue that makes the body move. **2.** Muscular strength. muscle *v.*

muse \myooz\ *n.* **1.** Spirit or power. **2.** One of nine Greek goddesses of the arts and sciences.

muse \myooz\ *v.* mused; musing. To ponder. muser *n.*; musingly *adv.*

mush *n.* **1.** Soft pulpy material. **2.** Weak sentimentality. **3.** Dog-sledding command. musher *n.*

mushroom \MUSH-room\ *n.* A fungus with a stem and a domed cap. mushroom *v.*

music \MYOO-zik\ *n.* **1.** Art of combined sounds. **2.** The sounds so produced. **3.** Musical composition. musician *n.*

musical \MYOO-zi-kul\ *adj.* **1.** Pertaining to music. **2.** Melodious or harmonious. **3.** Skilled in music. musician *n.*

muslin \MUZ-lin\ *n.* **1.** A finely woven cotton fabric. **2.** Plain weave cotton. muslined *adj.*

mussel \MUS-sul\ *n.* A bivalve mollusk eaten for food.

must *n.* Moldiness. mustiness *n.*; musty *adj.*

must *v.* **1.** To be forced to. **2.** To be certain to.

mustard \MUS-turd\ *n.* A spicy condiment made of the seeds of a plants.

muster \MUS-tur\ *v.* mustered; mustering. To gather troops for inspection. muster *n.*

musty \MUS-tee\ *adj.* mustier; mustiest. Moldy or stale.

mutant \MYOOT-nt\ *n.* The product of a mutation.

mutate \MYOO-tayt\ *v.* mutated; mutating. To change in form. mutation *n.*

mute \myoot\ *adj.* **1.** Silent. **2.** Unable to talk.

mutilate \MYOOT-l-ayt\ *v.* mutilated; mutilating. To injure or disfigure, usu. by cutting. mutilator *n.*; mutilation *n.*

mutiny \MYOOT-n-ee\ *n. pl.* mutinies. A revolt against established authority. mutiny *v.*; mutinous *adj.*; mutineer *n.*

mutter \MUT-ur\ *v.* muttered; muttering. To speak in a low unclear voice. mutterer *n.*

mutual \MYOO-choo-ul\ *adj.* Felt or done by two or more. mutuality *n.*

muzzle \MUZ-ul\ *n.* 1. Nose, jaws of some animals. 2. Open end of a firearm. 3. Animal nose cover. muzzle *v.*

myelitis \mie-uh-LIE-tis\ *n.* (Md) Inflammation of the spinal cord. myelitic *adj.*

myopathy \mie-OP-uh-thee\ *n. pl.* myopathies. (Md) Any disease affecting the muscles. myopathic *adj.*

myriad \MIR-ee-ud\ *n.* A vast number. myriad *adj.*

myrrh \mur\ *n.* A gum resin used for perfume. myrrhy *adj.*

mystery \MIS-tuh-ree\ *n. pl.* mysteries. 1. Unexplained or secret quality or matter. 2. A suspenseful story, movie, etc. mysterious *adj.*

mysticism \MIS-tuh-siz-um\ *n.* Hidden or symbolic meaning in religion. mystic *n.*

mystify \MIS-tuh-fie\ *v.* mystified; mystifying. To cause to feel puzzled.

mystique \mi-STEEK\ *n.* An aura of mystery.

myth \mith\ *n.* 1. A traditional tale of beliefs. 2. Imaginary person or thing. mythological *adj.*; mythically *adv.*

mythical \MITH-uh-kul\ *adj.* Concerning a myth.

mythology \mi-THOL-uh-jee\ *n. pl.* mythologies. 1. Myths. 2. The study of myths. mythological *adj.*

N

n \en\ *n. pl.* n's or ns. **1.** The 14th letter of the alphabet. **2.** In math, an indefinite number.

nab *v.* nabbed; nabbing. **1.** Grab or seize. **2.** Catch or arrest.

nag *v.* nagged; nagging. **1.** To annoy by persistent fault-finding. **2.** A persistent ache. **3.** To worry.

nail \nayl\ *n.* **1.** Thin metal used to hold or fasten. **2.** Plate at ends of fingers and toes.

nail \nayl\ *v.* nailed; nailing. **1.** To fasten with a nail. **2.** To fix in place. **3.** To understand, accomplish. nailer *n.*

naive *also* **naive** \nah-EEV\ *adj.* **1.** Innocent and unaffected. **2.** Simple and gullible.

naked \NAY-kid\ *adj.* **1.** Unclothed. **2.** Plain or undisguised. **3.** Unprotected from wind or sun.

name \naym\ *n.* **1.** Word(s) by which something is known. **2.** A person's given title.

name \naym\ *v.* named; naming. **1.** To give a name to a person or thing. **2.** To call by name. **3.** To mention.

nameless \NAYM-lis\ *adj.* **1.** Without title or name. **2.** Inexpressible. **3.** Anonymous or obscure. namelessly *adv.*

namely \NAYM-lee\ *adv.* In other words.

nan *also* **nana, nanna** *n.* (Cl) Grandmother.

nanny \NAN-ee\ *n. pl.* nannies. **1.** A person hired to nurse and supervise a child. **2.** A female goat. nanny *v.*

nanosecond \NAN-oh-sek-und\ *n.* (Sc) One billionth of a second.

nap *n.* **1.** A short sleep. **2.** The raised texture of textiles and rugs. **3.** A soft surface.

nape \nayp\ *n.* The back of the neck.

narc \nark\ *n.* (Cl) **1.** A narcotics policeman. **2.** Narcotics. narc *v.*

narcissism \NAHR-suh-siz-um\ *n.* Excessive self love. narcissist *n.*

narcolepsy \nahr-koh-LEP-see\ *n.* (Md) A disease characterized by the sudden onset of sleep. narcoleptic *n.*

narcotic \nahr-KOT-ik\ *n.* **1.** A substance that causes sleep or drowsiness. **2.** A drug affecting the mind. narcotic *adj.*; narcotics *n.*

narrate \NAR-ayt\ *v.* narrated; narrating. **1.** To tell a story. **2.** To provide a spoken commentary. narration *n.*

narrative \NAR-uh-tiv\ *n.* **1.** A written or spoken story. **2.** The art of story telling. narration *n.*

narrow \NAR-oh\ *adj.* narrower; narrowest. **1.** Of small width. **2.** Of limited scope or vision. **3.** With little space. narrow *n.*; narrow *v.*

narrow-minded \NAR-oh-MIEN-did\ *adj.* Rigid or intolerant in one's beliefs. narrow-mindedly *adv.*; narrow-mindedness *n.*

narrowly \NAR-oh-lee\ *adv.* By the smallest margin.

narwhal \NAHR-wahl\ *n.* An artic whale with a long spiral tusk.

nasturtium \nas-TUR-zhum\ *n.* A trail-growing plant with bright yellow, red, or orange flowers.

nasty \NAS-tee\ *adj.* nastier; nastiest. **1.** Highly unpleasant or annoying. **2.** Mean-spiritied. **3.** Difficult to do.

nation \NAY-shun\ *n.* **1.** A people sharing common culture, language, borders, and identity. **2.** A tribe.

national \NASH-uh-nul\ *adj.* **1.** Pertaining to a nation or nations. **2.** Characteristic of a particular country.

nationalism \NASH-uh-nl-iz-um\ *n.* **1.** Patriotic feelings and beliefs. **2.** Policy of being independent as a country. nationality *n.*

native \NAY-tiv\ *n.* **1.** A person born in a specific place. **2.** An indigenous person, animal, or plant. native *adj.*; natively *adv.*

Native American *n.* A person of indigenous ancestry preceeding colonization.

natural \NACH-ur-ul\ *adj.* **1.** Pertaining to or caused by nature. **2.** Not surprising. **3.** Spontaneous. natural *n.*; naturalness *n.*

natural food *n.* Food that is grown and processed without use of man-made chemicals.

natural gas *n. pl.* natural gases An energy source found in sedimentary rock and used as fuel.

naturalist \NACH-ur-uh-list\ *n.* **1.** One who studies nature. **2.** A person who believes in naturalism. naturalist *adj.*

naturally \NACH-ur-uh-lee\ *adv.* **1.** Achieved in a natural manner. **2.** As a natural result. **3.** To be expected.

nature \NAY-chur\ *n.* **1.** The living world. **2.** Inherent character. **3.** Universe and its phenomena.

naught *also* **naught** \nawt\ *n.* **1.** Zero. **2.** Nothing.

naughty \NAW-tee\ *adj.* naughtier; naughtiest. **1.** Disobedient and badly behaved. **2.** Indecent or wicked. naughtiness *n.*; naughtily *adv.*

nausea \NAW-zee-uh\ *n.* **1.** Stomach sickness with an inclination to vomit. **2.** Revulsion and loating. nauseous *adj.*

nautical \NAW-ti-kul\ *adj.* Pertaining to navigation by sea. nautically *adv.*

naval \NAY-vul\ *adj.* **1.** Pertaining to the navy. **2.** Concerning ships.

nave \nayv\ *n.* **1.** The central room of a church. **2.** The hub of a wheel.

navel \NAY-vul\ *n.* The depression on the abdomen where the umbilical cord was attached.

navigate \NAV-i-gayt\ *v.* navigated; navigating. **1.** To direct the course of a vehicle. **2.** To plot a course. navigation *n.*

Nazi \NAHT-see\ *n. pl.* Nazis. (Gr) **1.** A fascist. **2.** A member of the German National Socialist Party. Nazism *n.*

near \neer\ *adj.* nearer; nearest. **1.** Close in distance, space or time. **2.** Proximate to. **3.** Intimate with. near *adv.*; near *n.*; near *prep.*

nearby \NEER-BIE\ *adj.* Positioned next to or close by. nearby *adv.*

nearly \NEER-lee\ *adv.* **1.** Almost. **2.** Closely.

neat \neet\ *adj.* neater; neatest. **1.** Clean and tidy. **2.** Simple in form. **3.** Brief and pointed language. **4.** Clever. neatly *adv.*; neatness *n.*

nebbish \NEB-ish\ *n.* (Yd) A timid or submissive person. nebbish *adj.*

nebula \NEB-yuh-luh\ *n. pl.* nebulae (Sc) A glowing cloud of dust or gas found in outer space. nebular *adj.*

nebulous \NEB-yuh-lus\ *adj.* **1.** Like a cloud. **2.** Formless and indistinct. **3.** Like a nebula. nebulously *adv.*; nebulousness *n.*

necessary \NES-uh-ser-ee\ *adj.* **1.** Having to be accomplished. **2.** Determined by natural laws; inevitable. necessary *n.*; necessarily *adv.*

neck \nek\ *n.* **1.** The body part connecting head with trunk. **2.** The narrowed part of an object.

neck \nek\ *v.* necked; necking. (Sl). To kiss passionately for an extended period of time. necker *n.*

necklace \NEK-lis\ *n.* Jewelry worn around the neck.

necromancy \NEK-ruh-man-see\ *n.* Divining the future through supposed communication with the dead. necromania *n.*

necrophilia \NEK-ruh-FIL-ee-uh\ *n.* An erotic attraction to corpses. necrophiliac *n.*

nectar \NEK-tur\ *n.* **1.** The thick sugary juice of fruit. **2.** The blessed beverage of Greek gods. nectarous *adj.*

nectarine \NEK-tur-een\ *n.* **1.** A type of peach with smooth skin. **2.** The tree that bears this fruit.

nee \nay\ *adj.* Preceeding mention of a married woman's maiden name.

need *n.* **1.** Requirement or desire. **2.** Circumstance that requires action. **3.** Obligation. needful *adj.*

need *v.* needed; needing. **1.** To want or require. **2.** To be under an obligation. needy *adj.*

needle \NEED-l\ *n.* **1.** An extremely thin piece of metal, etc. **2.** A pointer on a dial.

needle \NEED-l\ *v.* needled; needling. **1.** To sew or pierce with a needle. **2.** [Cl]: To tease or bother.

needless \NEED-lis\ *adj.* **1.** Unnecessary. **2.** Gratuitous and uncalled for. needlessly *adv.*; needlessness *n.*

negative \NEG-uh-tiv\ *adj.* **1.** Expressing refusal or prohibition. **2.** Lacking positive characteristics. negative *v.*; negative *n.*; negate *v.*

neglect \ni-GLEKT\ *v.* neglected; neglecting. **1.** To ignore. **2.** To leave unattended. **3.** To allow to come to ruin. neglectful *adj.*

negligee or negligé \neg-li-ZHAY\ *n.* **1.** A thin undergarment or dressing gown. **2.** Informal attire.

negligent \NEG-li-junt\ *adj.* Using improper care or attention. negligence *n.*; negligibly *adv.*

negotiate \ni-GOH-shee-ayt\ *v.* negotiated; negotiating. **1.** Discuss to reach an agreement. **2.** To arrange by discussion. negotiation *n.*; negotiable *adj.*

neighbor \NAY-bur\ *n.* **1.** One who lives nearby. **2.** A friendly and generous person. neighborly *adj.*

neighborhood \NAY-bur-huud\ *n.* **1.** A residential district. **2.** The people of a residential district.

neither \NEE-thur\ *pron.* **1.** Not one nor the other. **2.** None.

nemesis \NEM-uh-sis\ *n. pl.* nemeses. **1.** Just retribution. **2.** A downfall caused by retribution or its agent.

neoclassical \nee-oh-KLAS-ik-ul\ *adj.* Relating to a revival of classical style. neoclassicism *n.*; neoclassic *adj.*; neoclassically *adv.*; neoclassicist *n.*

neon \NEE-on\ *n.* (Sc) Gaseous element in the atmosphere in very small amounts.

neonatology \nee-oh-nay-TOL-oh-jee\ *n.* (Md) Medical speciality concerned with newborn children. neonatologist *n.*; neonate *n.*

neophyte \NEE-uh-fite\ *n.* **1.** A new convert. **2.** A beginner or novice.

nephew \NEF-yoo\ *n.* The son of one's brother or sister or brother-in-law or sister-in-law.

nephritis \nuh-FRIE-tis\ *n.* (Md) Disease of the kidney, character-

ized by inflammation, etc. nephritic *adj.*

nephrology \NEF-rol-oh-jee\ *n.* (Md) The study of kidneys and their disorders. nephrologist *n.*

nepotism \NEP-uh-tiz-um\ *n.* Privileges and favors granted to family members. nepotist *n.*; nepotistic *adj.*

Neptune \NEP-toon\ *n.* The fourth largest planet and eighth in distance from the Sun.

nerd \nurd\ *n.* (Sl) An awkward person who is often dull and preoccupied in asocial pursuits.

nerve \nurv\ *n.* **1.** Body fiber that transmits impulses or sensations. **2.** Audacity or impudence.

nerves \nurvz\ *n.* **1.** A group of nerve fibers. **2.** Nervousness.

nervous \NUR-vus\ *adj.* **1.** Pertaining to the body's nerve system. **2.** Restless and anxious.

nervy \NUR-vee\ *adj.* **1.** Easily disturbed or excited. **2.** Bold and impudent.

nest *n.* **1.** Bird dwelling. **2.** Fish or reptile dwelling. **3.** Haunt or home.

nest *v.* nested; nesting. **1.** To build and use a nest. **2.** To fit one inside another.

nest egg *n.* (Cl) Money saved for future use.

nestle \NES-ul\ *v.* nestled; nestling.

1. To settle oneself comfortably. **2.** To press against in affection.

net *n.* **1.** An open mesh fabric. **2.** A fabric snare for catching fish, etc.

net *v.* netted; netting. **1.** To catch or cover with a net. **2.** In sports, to put into a net or goal.

nettle \NET-l\ *n.* Any plant with jagged leaves and stinging hairs.

nettle \NET-l\ *v.* nettled; nettling. **1.** To irritate or provoke. **2.** To sting with nettles. nettlesome *adj.*

network \NET-wurk\ *n.* **1.** System of connected components. **2.** Communications or transportation system.

networking \NET-wur-king\ *n.* **1.** The informal sharing of information and services. **2.** Communications.

neuron \NUUR-on\ *n.* (Md) A single nerve cell.

neurosis \nuu-ROH-sis\ *n. pl.* neuroses. (Md) A mental disturbance of anxiety and depression. neurotic *n.*

neutral \NOO-trul\ *adj.* **1.** Neither helping nor hindering. **2.** Uninvolved. **3.** Indistinct. **4.** In the middle. neutral *n.*; neutralize *v.*

neutron \NOO-tron\ *n.* (Sc) An atomic particle without electrical charge.

neutron bomb \NOO-tron-BOM\ *n.* (Sc) A nuclear weapon producing radiation but limited property damage.

never \NEV-ur\ *adv.* **1.** At no time. **2.** An emphatic negative. **3.** Not at all.

never-ending \nev-ur-EN-ding\ *adj.* **1.** Perpetual. **2.** Not ceasing.

nevertheless \nev-ur-thuh-LES\ *adv.* In spite of that.

new \noo\ *adj.* **1.** Recently made or arrived. **2.** In original condition. **3.** Reformed or renewed.

New Age *n.* A philosophy of previously discounted ideas.

new wave *n.* A movement that breaks with tradition.

newcomer \NOO-kum-ur\ *n.* **1.** A person who has just arrived. **2.** A novice.

newfangled \NOO-FANG-guld\ *adj.* (Sl) Different from what is expected and desired.

newly \NOO-lee\ *adv.* **1.** Freshly. **2.** Just arrived. **3.** In a different way.

news \nooz\ *n.* **1.** Information about recent event. **2.** A journalistic account of recent events.

newsmagazine \NOOZ-mag-uh-zeen\ *n.* A periodical that specializes in the publication of news.

newspaper \NOOZ-pay-pur\ *n.* A printed publication containing news, ads, etc.

next \nekst\ *adj.* **1.** Being nearest. **2.** The nearest in time. next *adv.*; next *n.*; next *prep.*

niacin \NIE-uh-sin\ *n.* (Md) Nicotinic acid used as a vitamin.

nice \nise\ *adj.* nicer; nicest **1.** Pleasant and agreeable. **2.** Kind and good-natured. **3.** Extremely sensitive. nicely *adv.*; niceness *n.*; nicety *n.*

niche \nich\ *n.* **1.** A shallow recess. **2.** A comfortable position. **3.** Someone's calling. niche *v.*

nick \nik\ *n.* A small notch or cut. nick *v.*

nickel \NIK-ul\ *n.* **1.** A malleable silver-white metal. **2.** A five cent coin.

nickname \NIK-naym\ *n.* An informal name given to a person or thing.

nicotine \NIK-uh-teen\ *n.* A colorless and poisonous substance found in tobacco.

niece \nees\ *n.* The daughter of one's sister or brother or sister-in-law or brother-in-law.

night \niet\ *n.* **1.** Darkness between one day and the next. **2.** The onset of darkness.

nightclub \NIET-klub\ *n.* A late-night lounge or bar often featuring dancing and live music.

nightfall \NIET-fawl\ *n.* The onset of darkness.

nightgown \NIET-gown\ *n.* A loose fitting garment worn at night or to bed.

nightingale \niet-IN-gayl\ *n.* A small reddish brown bird that sings at night.

nightly \NIET-lee\ *adj.* **1.** Occurring every night. **2.** Occurring at night.

nightmare \NIET-mair\ *n.* **1.** A frightening dream. **2.** [Cl]: A terrifying experience. nightmarish *adj.*; nightmarishly *adv.*

nightshade \NIET-shayd\ *n.* A type of poisonous plant.

nighttime or night time \NIET-time\ *n.* The interval between evening and morning.

nihilism \NIE-uh-liz-um\ *n.* (Lt) **1.** Rejection of all moral and religious beliefs. **2.** Destruction of institutions.

nil *n.* (Lt) **1.** Nothing. **2.** No amount or number.

nimble \NIM-bul\ *adj.* nimbler; nimblest **1.** Quick and agile in movement. **2.** Quick to understand. nimbleness *n.*; nimbly *adv.*

nimbus \NIM-bus\ *n. pl.* nimbi; nimbuses. **1.** A bright halo. **2.** A saint's halo. **3.** A type of rain cloud.

nip *v.* nipped; nipping. **1.** To pinch or bite sharply. **2.** To remove by pinching. **3.** To check or arrest. nip *n.*; nipping *adj.*

nirvana \nir-VAH-nuh\ *n.* (Fo) Bliss achieved by the extinction of individuality.

nitpick \NIT-pik\ *v.* nitpicked; nitpicking. To find fault with inconsequential details. nitpicker *n.*

nitric \NIE-trik\ *adj.* (Sc) **1.** Containing nitrogen. **2.** nitric acid: A colorless poisonous liquid.

nitroglycerin \nie-truh-GLIS-ur-un\ *n.* (Sc) An explosive liquid made with glycerol and sulphuric and nitric acids.

nitrous \NIE-trus\ *adj.* (Sc) Pertaining to or infused with nitrogen. none.

nitty-gritty \NIT-ee-GRIT-ee\ *n.* (Sl) The core of a matter.

no \noh\ *adv.* **1.** The answer is negative. **2.** By no amount.

no \noh\ *adj.* **1.** Not any. **2.** Not a. **3.** Very little. **4.** An emphatic negative slogan.

No or **Noh** \noh\ *n.* (Fo) Classical drama of Japan with music and dancing.

noble \NOH-bul\ *adj.* nobler; noblest. **1.** Aristocratic. **2.** Of superior character. **3.** Of stately appearance.

nobody \NOH-bod-ee\ *n. pl.* nobodies. A person of no importance or authority.

nobody \NOH-bod-ee\ *pron.* No person.

nocturnal \nok-TUR-nl\ *adj.* **1.** Pertaining to the night. **2.** Active in the night.

nod *v.* nodded; nodding. **1.** To tip one's head in greeting. **2.** To let one's head tip forward in weariness.

nodule \NOJ-ool\ *n.* **1.** A small lump of something. **2.** A small swelling of cells. nodular *adj.*; nodulated *adj.*; nodulation *n.*; nodulose *adj.*; nodulous *adj.*

no-frills *adj.* (Sl) The lack of luxuries or extras.

noise \noiz\ *n.* **1.** Loud and unpleasant sound. **2.** Electronic disturbance. noisy *adj.*

noise pollution *n.* The disturbing and predominate presence of loud sounds in an area.

nomad \NOH-mad\ *n.* **1.** A member of a migratory tribe. **2.** One who travels a great deal. nomad *adj.*; nomadic *adj.*; nomadism *n.*

nomenclature \NOH-mun-klay-chur\ *n.* **1.** A system of names. **2.** The terminology of an art or science. **3.** A register. nomenclatural *adj.*

nominal \NOM-uh-nul\ *adj.* **1.** Not actual. **2.** Of virtually no value. **3.** Pertaining to names. nominally *adv.*

nominate \NOM-uh-nayt\ *v.* nominated; nominating. **1.** To propose for election. **2.** To appoint. nomination *n.*

nominative \NOM-uh-nuh-tiv\ *n.* The case of a noun, pronoun or adjective that expresses the subject of the verb. nominative *adj.*

nominee \nom-uh-NEE\ *n. pl.* nominees. **1.** One who is nominated. **2.** [Bs] A person who is named on a stock register.

nonaligned \non-uh-LYND\ *adj.* Not associated with any other political power.

nonchalant \non-shu-LAHNT\ *adj.* **1.** Calm and relaxed. **2.** Apparently unaffected. nonchalantly *adv.*; nonchalance *n.*

noncommittal \non-kuh-MIT-l\ *adj.* Avoiding decision or opinion. noncomittally *adv.*

nonconformity \non-kun-FOR-mi-tee\ *n. pl.* nonconformities. **1.** Failure or unwillingness to accept a rule. **2.** A lack of correspondence. noncomformist *n.*

nondairy \non-DAIR-ee\ *adj.* Sub-

stituting for milk or milk products without containing milk or milk products.

nondescript \non-di-SKRIPT\ *adj.* Lacking recogizable characteristics. nondescriptically *adv.*

none \nun\ *adv.*; *adj.* **1.** Having not any. **2.** Neither. **3.** No persons or things.

nonexistent \non-ek-ZIST-unt\ *adj.* Not present or in fact or material.

non grata \non-GRAH-tuh\ *adj.* (Lt) Not welcome.

nonpareil \non-puh-REL\ *adj.* (Fr) Unique and not to be matched. nonpareil *n.*

nonplus \non-PLUS\ *v.* nonplussed; nonplussing. To completely mystify. nonplus *n.*

nonprofit \non-PROF-it\ *adj.* Not making a profit.

nonreturnable \non-ree-TURN-uh-bul\ *adj.* Not needing to be returned.

nonsense \NON-sens\ *n.* **1.** Meaningless words, conduct. **2.** A disapproved plan. **3.** Absurdity. nonsensical *adj.*

non sequitur \non-SEK-qwi-tur\ *n.* (Lt) A statement that does not logically follow from its precedent.

nonstop \NON-stop\ *adj.* (Cl) Unending.

noodle \NOOD-l\ *n.* **1.** A piece of

pasta. **2.** (Sl) A stupid person. **3.** The head.

nook \nuuk\ *n.* **1.** A recess or corner. **2.** A small place.

noon *n.* **1.** Twelve o'clock p.m. **2.** Midday. **3.** A culmination.

norm *n.* **1.** Standard or model. **2.** A rule that governs behavior. **3.** A typical behavior.

normal \NOR-mul\ *adj.* **1.** Conforming to rules and standards. **2.** Free from disorder. normal *n.*; normalcy *n.*; normality *n.*

normalization \nor-mul-iz-AY-shun\ *n.* **1.** The state of conformity to standards. **2.** The condition of normalcy.

north *n.* The point on the compass 90 degrees between west and east, respectively. north *adj.*; north *adv.*; northern *adj.*; northerly *adj.*, *adv.*

North America *n.* Western Hemisphere continent that lies between the Arctic Ocean and Mexico. North American *n.*

nose \nohz\ *n. pl.* noses. **1.** Organ of smell on the face. **2.** Sense of smell. **3.** [Cl] or [Sl] Perception.

nose \nohz\ *v.* nosed; nosing. **1.** To discover by smell. **2.** To touch the nose on. **3.** To pry.

nosh *v.* noshed; noshing. (Yd). To eat or drink. nosh *n.*

nostalgia \no-STAL-juh\ *n.* **1.** Yearning for the past. **2.** Memory of the past. **3.** Extreme homesickness. nostalgic *adj.*; nostalgically *adv.*

nosy \NOH-zee\ *adj.* nosier; nosiest. (Cl) Prying and intrusive behavior.

not *adv.* A grammatical expression of negation.

notable \NOH-tuh-bul\ *adj.* Worthy of recognition and praise. notable *n.*

notary \NOH-tuh-ree\ *n. pl.* notaries. [Le] A person licensed to process legal documents.

notation \noh-TAY-shun\ *n.* **1.** Musical representation by symbols. **2.** Symbols used to represent dance steps. notational *adj.*

notch \noch\ *n. pl.* notches. **1.** A cut made on a surface. **2.** A degree of advancement. **3.** A swale or gorge. notch *v.*

note \noht\ *n.* **1.** Brief written record. **2.** An observation. **3.** A short letter or memo. note *v.*; noted *v.*

noteworthy \NOHT-wur-thee\ *adj.* Worth mention or attention. noteworthiness *n.*

nothing \NUTH-ing\ *n.* **1.** Not anything. **2.** Absence of. **3.** A person of no importance. **4.** Zero. nothing *adv.*

nothingness \NUTH-ing-ness\ *n.* **1.** The absence of existence. **2.** Triviality or worthlessness.

notice \NOH-tis\ *n.* **1.** Attention or observation. **2.** A displayed written announcement. **3.** A warning.

notice \NOH-tis\ *v.* noticed; noticing. **1.** To be attentive to or observe. **2.** To speak of.

noticeable \NOH-ti-suh-bul\ *adj.* **1.** Easily perceptible. **2.** Worthy of being watched. noticeably *adv.*

notify \NOH-tuh-fie\ *v.* notified; notifying. **1.** To inform. **2.** To make known or announce. notifies *v.*

notion \NOH-shun\ *n.* **1.** Idea or conception. **2.** Intention or inclination. **3.** A small useful object. notional *adj.*

notoriety \noh-tuh-RIE-uh-tee\ *n.* **1.** An unfavorable fame. **2.** State of being well known. notoriously *adv.*

notorious \noh-TOR-ee-us\ *adj.* **1.** Having unfavorable fame. **2.** Being well known.

notwithstanding \not-with-STAN-ding\ *prep.* In spite of. notwithstanding *adv.*; notwithstanding *conj.*

nourish \NUR-ish\ *v.* nourished; nourishing. **1.** To supply with food. **2.** To enrich. nourishment *n.*; nourishing *adj.*

nouveau \NOO-voh\ *adj.* (Fr) New.

nouveau riche \NOO-voh-REESH\ *n. pl.* nouveau riches. (Fr) One who has recently acquired extreme wealth.

nouvelle cuisine \NOO-vel-kwee-zeen\ *n.* (Fr) Contemporary cooking style of light fare and aesthetic presentation.

novel \NOV-ul\ *adj.* New and unusual.

novel \NOV-ul\ *n.* **1.** An extended prose narrative. **2.** Literature of this type. novelist *n.*

novelette \nov-uh-LET\ *n.* (Fr) A short novel.

novella \noh-VEL-uh\ *n.* (It) A short novel.

November \noh-VEM-bur\ *n.* The eleventh month of the year.

novena \noh-VEE-nuh\ *n.* A cycle of prayers made on nine successive days.

novice \NOV-is\ *n.* **1.** An inexperienced beginner. **2.** An initiate into a religious order.

novitiate *also* **noviciate** \nov-i-TEE-ayt\ *n.* **1.** A religious initiate. **2.** The period of being a novice. **3.** Novices' quarters.

now *adv.* **1.** At the present time. **2.**

Immediately. **3.** By this time. now *conj.*; now *n.*

nowhere \NOH-hwair\ *adv.* In no place. nowhere *pron.*

no-win *adj.* (Cl) A situation in which a favorable outcome is prohibited to all parties.

noxious \NOK-shus\ *adj.* Harmful. noxiousness *n.*; noxiously *adv.*

nozzle \NOZ-ul\ *n.* The spout on a hose or tube.

nuance \NOO-ahns\ *n.* A subtle difference in tone or meaning. nuanced *adj.*

nubile \NOO-bile\ *adj.* **1.** An attractive woman. **2.** A marriageable woman.

nubs *n.* **1.** Knobs or protuberances. **2.** Lumps of something. nubbin *n.*; nub *n.*

nuclear \NOO-klee-ur\ *adj.* (Sc) **1.** Pertaining to having a nucleus. **2.** Using nuclear energy or weapons.

nuclear energy *n.* (Sc) Energy derived from the splitting of atoms in a controlled environment.

nuclear weapon *n.* (Sc) A highly destructive device whose force derives from the splitting of atoms. nuclear weaponry *n.*

nucleic acid \noo-KLEE-ik\ *n.* (Sc) **1.** One of two complex molecules that exist in DNA and RNA.

nucleon \NOO-klee-on\ *n.* (Sc) A neutron or proton.

nucleus \NOO-klee-us\ *n. pl.* nuclei. (Sc) **1.** Core of an atom. **2.** The center of things or ideas. **3.** A central part. nuclear *adj.*

nude \nood\ *n.* **1.** A representation of a naked figure. **2.** A naked figure. **3.** An unclothed state. nude *adj.*; nudity *n.*

nudge \nuj\ *v.* nudged; nudging. **1.** To prod with the elbow. **2.** To push gently. **3.** To kindly remind. nudge *n.*

nudnick \NOOD-nik\ *n.* (Sl) **1.** A boorish pest. **2.** A stupid and supercilious person.

nugget \NUG-it\ *n.* **1.** Lump of gold or ore. **2.** Something compared to this. **3.** Something valuable.

nuisance \NOO-suns\ *n.* Something causing trouble or annoyance.

nuke \nook\ *n.* (Sl) A nuclear weapon.

null \nul\ *adj.* **1.** Invalid and non-binding. **2.** Nonexistent. **3.** Having the value of zero. null *n.*; nullity *n.*; nullify *v.*

numb \num\ *adj.* Having no sensation or feeling. numb *v.*; numbly *adv.*, numbness *n.*

number \NUM-bur\ *n.* **1.** A quantity or place in a sequence. **2.** Symbol or word for such; numeral.

numeral \NOO-mur-ul\ *n.* **1.** A number. **2.** A figure denoting a number. numeral *adj.*

numerical \noo-MER-i-kul\ *adj.* Pertaining to a number or numbers. numerically *adv.*

numero uno \NOO-mur-oh-OO-noh\ *n.* (It) **1.** Number one. **2.** [Sl] The most important thing or person.

numerous \NOO-mur-us\ *adj.* **1.** Large in number. **2.** Many.

nun *n.* A woman who has taken religious vows. nunnish *adj.*; nunhood *n.*; nunlike *adj.*

nuptial \NUP-shul\ *adj.* Pertaining to matrimony or weddings.

nuptial \NUP-shul\ *n.* A wedding. nuptials *n.*

nurse \nurs\ *n.* **1.** A person trained to care for the sick. **2.** A graduate of nursing school. nursing *n.*

nurse \nurs\ *v.* nursed; nursing. **1.** To care for the sick. **2.** To coddle or support. **3.** [Sl] To drink slowly.

nursery \NUR-suh-ree\ *n. pl.* nurseries. **1.** A room set up for a young child. **2.** A place where trees, etc. are raised.

nurture \NUR-chur\ *v.* nurtured; nurturing. **1.** To raise or train. **2.** To provide nourishment. nurture *n.*; nurturing *n.*

nut *n.* **1.** Fruit of a walnut, etc. **2.** Block of metal into which a bolt, screw, etc. goes. nutlike *adj.*

nutrient \NOO-tree-unt\ *n.* A substance that provides nourishment. nutrient *adj.*

nutrition \noo-TRISH-un\ *n.* **1.** Providing or obtaining nourishment. **2.** Food. **3.** The study of eating habits. nutritionist *n.*; nutritious *adj.*

nuts *adj.* (Sl) Crazy or insane. nut *n.*; nutty *adj.*

nuzzle \NUZ-ul\ *v.* nuzzled; nuzzling. **1.** To rub or press with the nose. **2.** To lie snuggly against. nuzzler *n.*

nymph \nimf\ *n.* **1.** A legendary female spirit. **2.** A beautiful young woman. **3.** Immature insect. nymphal *adj.*; nymphean *adj.*; nymphlike *adj.*

nymphomania \nim-fuh-MAY-nee-uh\ *n.* Extreme sexual desire in women. nymphomaniac *n.*

O

o \oh\ *n. pl.* o's or os. **1.** The 15th letter of the alphabet. **2.** Zero.

oaf \ohf\ *n. pl.* oafs. A large awkward person. oafish *adj.*; oafishly *adv.*; oafishness *n.*

oar \or\ *n.* **1.** A bladed pole used to propel a boat or canoe. **2.** One who rows. oared *adj.*; oarless *adj.*

oasis \OH-ay-sis or OH-uh-sis\ *n. pl.* oases. An area in a desert which has groundwater or some irrigation.

oat often oats \oht\ *n.* A cereal grain eaten by humans and animals.

oater \OH-tur\ *n.* (Cl) A western.

oath \ohth\ or *n. pl.* oaths. **1.** A declaration of commitment. **2.** A vow. **3.** A profane or obscene utterance.

obeisance \oh-BAY-suns\ *n.* **1.** A submissive or respective gesture. **2.** Deference and homage. obeisant *adj.*; obeisantly *adv.*

obelisk \OB-uh-lisk\ *n.* **1.** A thin and pointed stone pillar. **2.** A monument in this shape.

obese \oh-BEES\ *adj.* Very fat. obesity *n.*

obey \oh-BAY\ *v.* obeyed; obeying. **1.** To follow the orders of another. **2.** To do what one is told. obeyer *n.*; obedience *n.*; obedient *adj.*

Obie \OH-bee\ *n.* An annual award given each year for excellence in off-Broadway theatre.

obituary often obit \oh-BICH-oo-er-ee\ *n. pl.* obituaries. **1.** A death notice, usu. in a newspaper. **2.** An account of a dead person's life.

object \OB-jikt\ *n.* **1.** Something that can be seen or touched. **2.** Recipient of an action.

object \ub-JEKT\ *v.* objected; objecting. **1.** To feel or express opposition. **2.** To state opposition. objection *n.*; objector *n.*

objective \ub-JEK-tiv\ *adj.* **1.** External to mind or spirit. **2.** Existing materially. **3.** Unbiased. objection *n.*; objector *n.*

objective \ub-JEK-tiv\ *n.* A goal or aim.

objet d'art \OB-jay-dart\ *n. pl.* objets d'art. (Fr) A small curio or decorative object.

oblige \uh-BLIEJ\ *v.* obliged; obliging. **1.** To compel to perform or react. **2.** To be made indebted to. obliger *n.*; obligated *v.*

oblique \uh-BLEEK or oh-BLEEK\ *adj.* **1.** At an angle. **2.** Not being direct or open. obliquely *adv.*; oblique *n.*

obliterate \uh-BLIT-uh-rayt\ *v.* obliterated; obliterating. **1.** To destroy totally and leave no trace. **2.** To ruin and prevent use. obliteration *n.*; obliterative *adj.*; obliterator *n.*

oblivion \uh-BLIV-ee-un\ *n.* **1.** Total obscurity. **2.** An unnoticed, forgotten state.

oblivious \uh-BLIV-ee-us\ *adj.* **1.** Forgetful and unaware. **2.** Unconscious of. obliviously *adv.*; obliviousness *n.*

oblong \OB-lawng\ *adj.* **1.** Greater in breadth than height. **2.** Oval. **3.** Deviating from an axial symmetry. oblong *n.*

obnoxious \ob-NOK-shus\ *adj.* Annoying to the point of distatefulness. obnoxiously *adv.*; obnoxiousness *n.*

oboe \OH-boh\ *n. pl.* oboes. A woodwind instrument with a thin double reed, having a penetrating tone. oboist *n.*

obscene \ub-SEEN\ *adj.* **1.** Repulsive and indecent. **2.** [Le]: That which offends accepted sexual morals. obscenity *n.*; obscenely *adv.*; obsceneness *n.*

obscure \ub-SKYUUR\ *adj.* **1.** Not clear; hard to understand. **2.** Unexplained and dubious. **3.** Hidden. obscure *v.*; obscure *n.*

obsequious \ub-SEE-kwee-us\ *adj.* Overly obedient or servile. obsequiously *adv.*; obsequiousness *n.*

observe \ub-ZURV\ *v.* observed; observing. **1.** To watch closely or systematically. **2.** To notice. **3.** To adhere to or follow. observant *adv.*; observation *n.*

obsess \ub-SES\ *v.* obsessed; obsessing. To have a persistent idea that dominates one's mind. obsession *n.*

obsolete \ob-suh-LEET\ *adj.* **1.** No longer of value. **2.** Discarded and antiquated. obsoletely *adv.*; obsolescent *adj.*; obsolescence *n.*

obstacle \OB-stuh-kul\ *n.* Anything that prevents progress.

obstinate \OB-stuh-nit\ *adj.* **1.** Stubborn. **2.** Determined to remain on a course. **3.** Strong-willed. obstinancy *n.*; obstinately *adv.*

obstruct \ub-STRUKT\ *v.* obstructed; obstructing. **1.** To block or forbid movement. **2.** To slow progress. obstruction *n.*

obtain \ub-TAYN\ *v.* obtained; obtaining. **1.** To secure or acquire. **2.** To be prevalent or established. obtainable *adj.*; obtainability *n.*; obtainer *n.*

obtrusive \ub-TROO-siv\ *adj.* **1.** Unpleasantly noticeable. **2.** To thrust oneself forward. obtrusively *adv.*; obtrusiveness *n.*

obtuse \ub-TOOS\ *adj.* **1.** Slow to understand. **2.** An angle less than ninety degrees. **3.** Dully painful. obtusively *adv.*; obtuseness *n.*

obvious \OB-vee-us\ *adj.* **1.** Easily understood or perceived. **2.** Undeniable. obviousness *n.*; obviously *adv.*

occasion \uh-KAY-zhun\ *n.* **1.** A special event. **2.** The time of occurence. **3.** A reason or justification. occasional *adj.*; occasionally *adv.*

occult \uh-KULT\ *adj.* **1.** Mysterious and supernatural. **2.** Kept secret. **3.** Beyond human understanding. occult *n.*

occupation \ok-yuh-PAY-shun\ *n.* **1.** One's business or job. **2.** The state or act of occupying. **3.** Taking by force.

occupy \OK-yuh-pie\ *v.* occupies; occupied. **1.** To live in. **2.** To fill or take up. **3.** To take military possession of.

occur \uh-KUR\ *v.* occurred; occurring. **1.** To happen. **2.** To exist in a place. **3.** To come to mind. occurrence *n.*

ocean \OH-shun\ *n.* **1.** A large expanse of sea. **2.** The body of water surrounds continents. oceanic *adj.*

oceanography \oh-shuh-NOG-ruh-fee\ *n.* (Sc) The study of the physical properties of oceans. oceanographer *n.*

ocher or **ochre** \OH-kur\ *n.* **1.** A light brownish yellow color. **2.** A mineral of clay and ferrous oxide. ocherous *adj.*

octagon \OK-tuh-gon\ *n.* An eight sided figure. octagonal *adj.*

octane \OK-tayn\ *n.* (Sc) A chemical additive in gasoline that enhances combustion and performance.

octave \OK-tiv\ *n.* (Mu) **1.** Musical interval between a tone and another. **2.** Any group or series of eight.

October \ok-TOH-bur\ *n.* The tenth month of the year.

odd \od\ *adj.* odder; oddest. **1.** Strange and extraordinary. **2.** Occasional and casual. **3.** Abnormal.

oddball \OD-bawl\ *n.* (Cl) **1.** A strange and eccentric person. **2.** Something bizarre and unordinary.

odds and ends \odz-and-endz\ *n.* (Cl) Miscellaneous items.

ode \ohd\ *n.* Lyric poem of celebration or address.

odor \OH-dur\ *n.* **1.** Any smell. **2.** An unpleasant smell. **3.** A lasting smell. **4.** [Sl] A poor reputation. odorous *adj;* odorless *adj.*

Oedipus Complex \ED-uh-pus\ *n.* Freud's theory of children's attraction to the parent of opposite sex.

of \uv\ *prep.* **1.** Coming from. **2.** Characterized by. **3.** Belonging or connected to.

off \awf\ *adv.* **1.** At a distance. **2.** Loose and not not in position. **3.** To interrupt continuity.

off \awf\ *prep.* **1.** Away from. **2.** Not on. **3.** Not acting or involved. off *adj.*; off *n.*

off Broadway *adj.* Theatre not presented in the major Broadway theaters.

offbeat \AWF-beet\ *adj.* (Sl) Not typical.

off-camera *adj.* (Id) **1.** Not within view of a video or movie camera. **2.** Not meant to be recorded.

off-color \AWF-KUL-ur\ *adj.* (Id) **1.** Prurient and obscene. **2.** Potentially offensive.

offend \uh-FEND\ *v.* **1.** offended; offending. To hurt another's feelings. **2.** To anger and displease. **3.** To do wrong. offensive *adj.*

offer \AW-fur\ *v.* offered; offering [Sl]. **1.** To present for judgment or consideration. **2.** To express willingness.

offering \AW-fur-ing\ *n.* **1.** Gift of money. **2.** Religious sacrifice. **3.** Contribution. offertory *n.*

office \AW-fis\ *n.* **1.** Place of business. **2.** A business room or building. **3.** Position of authority.

officer \AW-fuh-sur\ *n.* **1.** Person in authority. **2.** Law enforcement person. **3.** Armed forces authority.

official \uh-FISH-ul\ *adj.* **1.** Pertaining to an office. **2.** Bureaucratic. **3.** Formal. **4.** In or of authority.

off off Broadway *adj.* Obscure, unconventional theatre.

offset \AWF-set\ *n.* **1.** A balance or compensation. **2.** Printing by impression. **3.** Bend in pipe, etc.

offshore \AWF-SHOR\ *adj.* **1.** Located at sea. **2.** Wind blowing toward the sea. **3.** Beyond boundaries.

offspring \AWF-spring\ *n.* **1.** An person or animal's children and descendants. **2.** A result of something.

off-the-wall \AWF-thuh-WAHL\ *adj.* (Sl) Bizzare and unconventional.

often \AW-fun\ *adv.* oftener; oftenest **1.** Occuring frequently. **2.** Occuring at short intervals.

oftentimes \AW-fun-tymz\ *adv.* (Id) Often.

ogle \OH-gul\ *v.* ogled; ogling. **1.** To watch with lecherous intent. **2.** To look at amorously. ogler *n.*

ogre \OH-gur\ *n.* **1.** A man eating monster. **2.** A large and terrifying person. ogreish *adj.*

oil *n.* **1.** Thick and viscous liquid. **2.** Petroleum. **3.** Painting with oil-based paint. oil *v.*

oily \OI-lee\ *adj.* oilier; oiliest. **1.** Containing oil. **2.** Slimey. **3.** Suave in behavior. oiliness *n.*

ointment \OINT-munt\ *n.* A greasy substance applied to the skin.

okay or OK \OH-KAY\ *adj.* **1.** Yes. **2.** An expression of consent or agreement. okay *n.*; okay *prep.*; okay *adv.*; okay *v.*

okra \OH-kruh\ *n.* A vegetable plant that grows in long ridged seed pods.

old \ohld\ *adj.* older; oldest. **1.** Advanced in age or time. **2.** Made long ago. **3.** Used for a long time. **4.** Worn.

old age *n.* The latter part of normal life.

old money *n.* Money that is inherited.

oleander \OH-lee-an-dur\ *n.* An evergreen shrub that bears clusters of red, pink and white flowers.

olfactory \ol-FAK-tuh-ree\ *adj.*

(Md) Pertaining to the sense of smell.

oligarchy \OL-i-gahr-kee\ *n. pl.* oligarchies. **1.** Government by a small group. **2.** The members of such a government. oligarchic *adj.*; oligarchical *adj.*; oligarchically *adv.*

oligopoly \OL-i-gop-uh-lee\ *n. pl.* oligopolies. The state of economic competition limited between a few parties. oligopolistic *adj.*; oligopolist *n.*

ombudsman/ombudswoman \OM-budz-mun\ *n.* Government official investigating employee or citizen grievances.

omega \oh-MAY-guh\ *n.* (Fo) **1.** The last letter of the Greek alphabet. **2.** The last of a kind or series.

omen \OH-men or OH-mun\ *n.* **1.** Event portending good or evil. **2.** Something of prophetic significance. omen *v.*

ominous \OM-uh-nus\ *adj.* **1.** Indicating a threat or disaster. **2.** Of evil omen. **3.** Pertaining to omens. ominously *adv.*; ominousness *n.*

omit \oh-MIT\ *v.* omitted; omitting. **1.** To not include. **2.** To leave unfinished. **3.** To fail or neglect. omission *n;* omissible *adj.*

omnibus \OM-nuh-bus\ *adj.* **1.** Serving several purposes. **2.** Comprised of several things.

omnibus \OM-nuh-bus\ *n.* **1.** A bus. **2.** A volume containing several novels published elsewhere.

omnipotent \om-NIP-uh-tunt\ *adj.* **1.** All powerful. **2.** Having the influence of God. omnipotence *n.*

on *prep.* **1.** Enclosing or covering. **2.** Carried with. **3.** The exact time. **4.** As a result of. omnipotence *n.*

once \wuns\ *adv.* **1.** For one time only. **2.** At some point in time. once *conj.*; once *n.*

oncogene \ON-cuh-jeen\ *n.* (Md) A gene that transforms a cell into a tumorous cell. oncogenic *adj.*

oncology \ON-col-uh-jee\ *n.* (Md) The study of tumorous growth. oncologist *n.*; oncological *adj.*

oncoming \ON-kum-ing\ *n.* **1.** Imminent. **2.** Approaching from the front.

one \wun\ *adj.* **1.** Single in number. **2.** Exemplary. **3.** Designating a specified thing or person.

one \wun\ *n.* **1.** The lowest whole number. **2.** A unity or unity. **3.** A single person or object. one *pron.*

one-liner \wun-LIEN-ur\ *n.* (Id) A joke or witticism told in a single sentence.

one-on-one *adj.* (Id) Occurring between two individuals.

onerous \ON-ur-us\ *adj.* **1.** Difficult or burdensome. **2.** [Le] Involving heavy obligations. onerously adv; onerousness *n.*

ongoing \ON-goh-ing\ *adj.* **1.** Continuing to exist. **2.** In progress.

onion \UN-yun\ *n.* Edible bulb of an herb of the lily family. oniony *adj.*

onlooker \ON-luuk-ur\ *n.* **1.** A witness. **2.** A spectator. onlooking *adj.*

only \OHN-lee\ *adj.* **1.** Alone; sole. **2.** The best. only *conj.*

only \OHN-lee\ *adv.* **1.** Merely and exclusively. **2.** Not until. **3.** No longer ago than. **4.** Solely.

onset \ON-set\ *n.* **1.** The beginning. **2.** An attack.

onus \OH-nus\ *n. pl.* onuses. A responsibility or burden.

onward *also* **onwards** \ON-wurd\ *adv.* **1.** Further. **2.** Advancing motion. **3.** Toward the front. onward *adj.*

opaque \oh-PAYK\ *adj.* **1.** Not transmitting light. **2.** Not allowing light to pass through. **3.** Not clear. opaque *n.*

op-ed page \OP-ed\ *n.* The page in a newspaper where independent editorials and colums are printed.

open \OH-pun\ *adj.* **1.** Not closed. **2.** Having an access. **3.** Unsealed. **4.** Bare or uncovered.

open \OH-pun\ *v.* opened; opening. **1.** To allow entry or access. **2.** To remove a seal or cover. **3.** To start.

open enrollment *n.* Policy of colleges and universities that admits any applying students.

opening \OH-puh-ning\ *n.* **1.** A gap or hole that allows access. **2.** A start or beginning. opening *adj.*

operate \OP-uh-rayt\ *v.* operated; operating. **1.** To work or manage. **2.** To be in action. **3.** To perform surgery. opening *adj.*

operation \op-uh-RAY-shun\ *n.* **1.** Mode of action or working. **2.** Active process. **3.** Surgery. **4.** Military action. operational *adj.*; operationally *adv.*

operative \OP-ur-uh-tiv\ *adj.* **1.** In process. **2.** Moving. **3.** Effective. **4.** Surgical. **4.** Concerning work. operative *n.*; operatively *adv.*; operativeness *n.*

opinion \uh-PIN-yun\ *n.* **1.** A belief expressed without citation of proof. **2.** A view believed to be true. opinionated *adj.*

opponent \uh-POH-nunt\ *n.* One who stands in opposition to another. opponent *adj.*

opportune \op-ur-TOON\ *adj.* **1.** Well chosen. **2.** Well and usefully timed. opportunely *adv.*

opportunity \op-ur-TOO-ni-tee\ *n. pl.* opportunities. **1.** A good chance. **2.** A chance afforded by circumstance. **3.** Good luck.

oppose \uh-POHZ\ *v.* opposed; opposing. **1.** To stand against and idea or person. **2.** To be hostile to or in conflict with. opposer *n.*

opposition \op-uh-ZISH-un\ *n.* **1.** Resistance. **2.** Conflict or disagreement. **3.** Group that opposes something.

oppress \uh-PRES\ *v.* oppressed; oppressing. **1.** To keep in subservience. **2.** To treat cruelly or harshly. **3.** To weigh down. oppression *n.*; oppressive *adj.*; oppressor *n.*

optical \OP-ti-kul\ *adj.* Pertaining to optics, eyesight, and the improvement of vision. optician *n.*

optical illusion *n.* An inaccurate or false perception of phyical phenomenon.

optics \OP-tiks\ *n.* (Sc) The study of light and its perception.

optimism \OP-tuh-miz-um\ *n.* **1.**

Confidence and hopefulness. **2.** Doctrine that things are improving. optimist *n.*; optimistic *adj.*; optimistically *adv.*

option \OP-shun\ *n.* **1.** The act of choosing. **2.** A choice. **3.** [Bs] The right to trade in stocks. optional *adj.*

optometry \op-TOM-i-tree\ *n.* (Md) The practise of examining and treating eye disorders. optometrist *n.*

oracle \OR-uh-kul\ *n.* **1.** Person who gives prophecies. **2.** Wise person. **3.** Wise, knowledgeable saying.

oral \OR-ul\ *adj.* **1.** Spoken. **2.** Pertaining to the mouth or voice. oral *n.*; orally *adv.*

orange \OR-inj\ *n.* **1.** A juicy citrus fruit with red-yellow skin and fruit. **2.** Red-yellow color. orange *adj.*

orate \aw-RAYT\ *v.* orated; orating. **1.** To speak. **2.** To make a speech. orator *n.*; oration *n.*

orb *n.* **1.** A globe or sphere. **2.** A heavenly body. **3.** An eyeball or eye. orb *v.*

orbit \OR-bit\ *n.* (Sc) **1.** Path in space of a planet or satellite. **2.** Range of influence or action. orbit *v.*; orbiter *n.*

orchestra \OR-kuh-struh\ *n.* **1.** A group of musicians. **2.** Musical performance section of a theatre. orchestral *adj.*; orchestrally *adv.*

orchestrate \OR-kuh-strayt\ *v.* orchestrated; orchestrating. (Mu) **1.** To arrange or compose music. **2.** Organize for desired continuity. orchestration *n.*; orchestrator *n.*

ordain \or-DAYN\ *v.* ordained; ordaining. **1.** To invest another with the powers of a priest or minister. **2.** To decree. ordination *n.*; ordainer *n.*

order \OR-dur\ *v.* ordered; ordering. **1.** To command. **2.** To place in sequence. **3.** To ask that something be done or sent. orderer *n.*

order \OR-dur\ *n.* **1.** Methodical arrangement. **2.** Command or direction. **3.** Instruction. **4.** Group. orderer *n.*

orderly \OR-dur-lee\ *adj.* **1.** Arranged in sequence. **2.** Observant of law. **3.** Pertaining to orders. orderly *adv.*

orderly \OR-dur-lee\ *n. pl.* orderlies. **1.** A hospital attendant. **2.** A soldier who performs duties for an officer.

ordinal \OR-dn-ul\ *n.* A number or word that defines an object's sequence: first, second, third, etc. ordinal *adj.*; ordinally *adv.*

ordinance \OR-dn-uns\ *n.* **1.** A cod-ified rule or law. **2.** A local code. **3.** A religious service.

ordinarily \or-dn-ER-uh-lee\ *adv.* **1.** Generally. **2.** Most of the time. **3.** In an unusual manner.

ordinary \OR-dn-er-ee\ *adj.* **1.** Regular and usual. **2.** Common or boring. ordinariness *n.*

ordination \or-dn-AY-shun\ *n.* **1.** Investment with holy orders. **2.** State of regulation.

organ \OR-gun\ *n.* **1.** A body or plant part with a specific function. **2.** Pipe, reed instrument.

organdy \OR-gun-dee\ *n. pl.* organdies. A translucent and stiffened cotton material.

organic \or-GAN-ik\ *adj.* **1.** Pertaining to plants and animals. **2.** Pertaining to a living organ.

organization \or-guh-nuh-ZAY-shun\ *n.* **1.** Making order. **2.** A business or government. **3.** Group united for work or cause. organizational *adj.*; organizationally *adv.*

organize \OR-guh-niez\ *v.* organized; organizing. **1.** To place in order or a system. **2.** To clean or make tidy. **3.** Enlist. organizational *adj.*; organizationally *adv.*

orgy \OR-jee\ *n. pl.* orgies. **1.** A wild festivity. **2.** An act of group sex. **3.** Indulgent behavior. orgiastic *adj.*

orient \OR-ee-unt\ *v.* oriented; orienting. **1.** To face or turn east. **2.** To adjust to a situation or within a place. orientation *n.*

Oriental \or-ee-EN-tl\ *adj.* Pertaining to Asian countries and customs.

origami \or-i-GAH-mee\ *n.* (Fo) The Japanese art of paper sculpture.

origin \OR-i-jin\ *n.* **1.** A starting point or beginning. **2.** A source. **3.** Ancestry. originality *adj.*

originally \uh-RIJ-uh-nuh-lee\ *adv.* **1.** Initially. **2.** First to occur or exist. originality *n* or original *adj.*

oriole \OH-ree-ohl\ *n.* A bird of bright yellow and orange and black coloration.

ornament \OR-nuh-munt\ *n.* **1.** Decoration. **2.** Embellishments or additions. ornamentation *n.*; ornamental *adj.*; ornamentally *adv.*

ornate \or-NAYT\ *adj.* **1.** Elaborately decorated. **2.** Flowery and complex in structure and detail. ornately *adv.*; ornateness *n.*

ornery \OR-nuh-ree\ *adj.* (Cl) **1.** Unpleasant and grouchy. **2.** Poorly made. orneriness

ornithology \or-nuh-THOL-uh-jee\ *n.* (Sc) The study of birds. ornithologist *n.*; ornithological *adj.*; ornithologically *adv.*

orphan \OR-fun\ *n.* **1.** A child whose parents have died. **2.** A child with one surviving parent. orphanage *n.*; orphaned *v.*

orthodox \OR-thu-doks\ *adj.* **1.** Widely accepted. **2.** Not of an independent mind. orthodoxy *n.*

orthotics \or-THOT-iks\ *n.* (Md) The study and use of devices used to relieve or correct foot problems. orthotic *adj.*

oscillate \OS-uh-layt\ *v.* oscillated; oscillating. **1.** To swing back and forth. **2.** To vary between extremes. **3.** To move periodically oscillator *n.*; oscillation *n.*; oscillatory *adj.*

osculate \OS-kyuh-layt\ *v.* osculated; osculating. (Sc) **1.** To kiss. **2.** To come into close contact. osculator *n.*; osculation *n.*

osprey \OS-pree\ *n.* A fish eating bird of prey characterized by light markings.

ossify \OS-i-fie\ *v.* ossified; ossifying. **1.** To turn to bone. **2.** To harden or become rigid. ossific *adj.*; ossification *n.*

ostentatious \os-tun-TAY-shus\ *adj.* **1.** Exhibiting a vulgar display of wealth. **2.** Attempting to attract attention. ostentatiously *adv.*; ostentation *n.*

osteopath \OS-tee-uh-path\ *n.* (Md) One who studies and treats diseases through the manipulation of bones. osteopathic *adj.*; osteopathically *adv.*

ostracize \OS-truh-size\ *v.* ostracized; ostracizing. **1.** To exclude from society or favor. **2.** To banish or condemn. ostracizer *n.*; ostracism *n.*

other \UTH-ur\ *adj.* **1.** Different; defined or distinct. **2.** Additional to. **3.** Remaining. other *n.*; other *pron.*; other *adv.*

otherwise \UTH-ur-wiez\ *adv.* **1.** Or else. **2.** In another sense. **3.** In a different manner. **4.** Alternatively. otherwise *adj.*

otherwordly \UTH-ur-WURLD-lee\ *adj.* Pertaining to ideas and things outside common realities. otherworldliness *n.*

ought \awt\ *v.* Expressing duty, shortcoming, or probability.

ounce \owns\ *n.* **1.** One sixteenth of a pound. **2.** One sixteenth of a pint. **3.** A small quantity.

our \OW-ur\ *pron.* Belonging to us. ours *pron.*

out \owt\ *adv.* **1.** Away from. **2.** Not in. **3.** At an end. **4.** Not burning or lit. **5.** In error. out *prep.*; out *interj.*

out \owt\ *v.* **1.** To extinquish. **2.** To come or go from. out *n.*; out *adj.*

outage \OW-tij\ *n.* The time during which electricity is not operating.

outbreak \OWT-brayk\ *n.* **1.** A sudden occurrence of war or disease. **2.** An outcrop in rock.

outburst \OWT-burst\ *n.* **1.** A sudden spoken display of emotion. **2.** An eruption.

outcast \OWT-kast\ *n.* **1.** One banished from society or a country. **2.** A tramp or bum. outcast *adj.*

outcome \OWT-kum\ *n.* The result.

outdo \owt-DOO\ *v.* outdid; outdone. To surpass in performance or achievement. outdoes *v.*

outdoors \owt-DORZ\ *adj.* outdoor. **1.** In the open air. **2.** the great outdoors [Id]: the remote countryside.

outer \OW-tur\ *adj.* external; further from the center.

outfit \OWT-fit\ *n.* **1.** The clothes a person wears. **2.** A specialized uniform.

outfit \OWT-fit\ *v.* To equip with specialized tools.

outgoing \OWT-goh-ing\ *adj.* **1.** Departing. **2.** Friendly, responsive.

outing \OW-ting\ *n.* A brief outdoor trip.

outlandish \owt-LAN-dish\ *adj.* Stikingly unusual or bizarre.

outlast \OWT-last\ *v.* outlasted; outlasting. To be around longer than others of the same type.

outlaw \OWT-law\ *n.* One who habitually breaks the law; criminal. outlaw *v.*

outlet \OWT-let\ *n.* **1.** Passage for escape, discharge. **2.** Market for commodity. **3.** Electical device.

outline \OWT-line\ *n.* **1.** Sketch or plan of something. **2.** Statement of structure. **3.** Bordering line. outline *v.*

outlook \OWT-luuk\ *n.* **1.** A point of view. **2.** Prospects for something. **3.** Place or expanse for viewing.

output \OWT-puut\ *n.* **1.** Amount produced. **2.** Work done by a machine. **3.** Electrical energy generated.

outrage \OWT-rayh\ *n.* **1.** Shocking act. **2.** Insult or injury. **3.** Anger over an outrageous act. outrageous *adj.*; outrage *v.*

outrageous \owt-RAY-jus\ *adj.* **1.** Awful or insulting. **2.** Heedless of authority or decency. outrageously *adv.*; outrageousness *n.*

outreach \owt-REECH\ *v.* To reach beyond; extend or surpass. outreach *n.*

outside \OWT-SIED\ *n.* **1.** The outer side; exterior. **2.** The part seen. **3.** Outward display. outside *adj.*

outsider \owt-SIED-ur\ *n.* A person who is not accepted by a group.

outskirts \OWT-skurts\ *pl. n.* A place remote from a central town or area.

outspoken \OWT-SPOH-kun\ *adj.* Very honest.

outstanding \owt-STAN-ding\ *adj.* **1.** Conspicuous. **2.** Very good. **3.** Not yet paid or settled. outstandingly *adv.*

outtake \OWT-tayk\ *n.* A segment of a TV show or film that is edited out of the final version.

ouzo \OO-zoh\ *n.* [Fo] A Greek anise seed-flavored spirit.

oval \OH-vul\ *adj.* Egg-shaped. oval *n.*

Oval Office *n.* The office of the president of the United States.

ovary \OH-vuh-ree\ *n. pl.* ovaries. An organ producing egg cells. ovarian *adj.*

ovation \oh-VAY-shun\ *n.* Enthusiastic applause.

oven \UV-un\ *n.* A cooking stove or

part of one in which food is baked, broiled, or roasted.

over \OH-vur\ *prep.*, *adv.* **1.** On, above, covering. **2.** To or on the other side. **3.** From one side to another.

overabundant \OH-vur-uh-BUN-dunt\ *adj.* Having too much. overabundance *n.*

overachiever \OH-vur-uh-CHEE-vur\ *n.* A person who is judged to work too hard.

overall \OH-vur-awl\ *adj.* Covering or including everything.

overall *also* **overalls** \OH-vur-awl\ *n.* A loose-fitting garment worn over other clothes.

overbearing \oh-vur-BAIR-ing\ *adj.* Pushy and domineering.

overcast \OH-vur-KAST\ *adj.* Covered with clouds.

overcome \oh-vur-KUM\ *v.* overcame; overcome; overcoming. **1.** To win or succeed in subduing. **2.** To make someone helpless or weak.

overconfident \OH-vur-KON-fuh-dunt\ *adj.* Having too much or false confidence. overconfidence *n.*

overdo \oh-vur-DOO\ *v.* overdid; overdone; overdoing. To do something too much.

overflow \oh-vur-FLOH\ *v.* overflowed; overflowing. To flood or spill over. overflow *n.*

overhang \oh-vur-HANG\ *v.* overhung; overhanging. To jut out over something. overhang *n.*

overhaul \oh-vur-HAWL\ *v.* overhauled; overhauling. **1.** To examine and repair. **2.** To revise and refurbish. **3.** To overtake. overhaul *n.*

overhead \OH-vur-hed\ *adj.* **1.** Above the head; in the sky. **2.** Concerning the fixed costs of a business. overhead *n.*

overindulge \OH-vur-IN-dulj\ *v.* overindulged; overindulging. To use and enjoy too much. overindulgence *n.*

overjoyed \oh-vur-JOID\ *adj.* Extremely happy.

overkill \OH-vur-kil\ *n.* More than is necessary to destroy or defeat.

overlap \oh-vur-LAP\ *v.* overlapped; overlapping. To extend beyond the edge of another thing. overlap *n.*

overlook \oh-vur-LUUK\ *v.* overlooked; overlooking. **1.** To have a view of from above. **2.** To fail to notice. **3.** To ignore.

overpower \oh-vur-POW-ur\ *v.*

overpowered; overpowering. To overcome or defeat soundly.

overreact \oh-vur-REE-akt\ *v.* overreacted; overreacting. To react more strongly than appropriate. **overreaction** *n.*

overrun \oh-vur-RUN\ *v.* overran; overrun; overrunning. **1.** To spread over and occupy. **2.** To use more time or money than expected.

overseas \oh-vur-SEEZ\ *adj., adv.* Beyond or across the sea.

overseer \OH-vur-seer\ *n.* A supervisor or superintendent.

oversight \OH-vur-siet\ *n.* **1.** An unintentional mistake or omission. **2.** Supervision.

overt \oh-VURT\ *adj.* Done or shown openly. **overtly** *adv.*

overtake \oh-vur-TAYK\ *v.* overtook; overtaken; overtaking. **1.** To pass a moving vehicle and go in front of it. **2.** To come upon suddenly.

overthrow \oh-vur-THROH\ *v.* overthrew; overthrown; overthrowing. To defeat and take over.

overtone \OH-vur-tohn\ *n.* An additional implicit meaning or quality.

overture \OH-vur-chur\ *n.* A piece of music performed at the beginning of a concert or opera.

overview \OH-vur-vyoo\ *n.* A general survey.

overweight \oh-vur-WAYT\ *adj.* Heavier than is reasonable or normal.

overwhelm \oh-vur-HWELM\ *v.* overwhelmed; overwhelming. **1.** To overcome completely. **2.** To bury or submerge.

overwrought \OH-vur-RAWT\ *adj.* Nervously agitated or overly excited.

ovulate \OV-yuh-layt\ *v.* ovulated; ovulating. To produce or release an egg cell from the ovary. **ovulation** *n.*

ovum \OH-vum\ *n. pl.* ova. The reproductive egg cell made by a female.

owe \oh\ *v.* owed; owing. **1.** To have a duty to pay money for something. **2.** To feel a debt of gratitude towards someone.

owl *n.* A bird of prey active at night.

own \ohn\ *adj.* Belonging to oneself or itself.

own \ohn\ *v.* owned; owning. **1.** To have as one's own. **2.** To admit or confess. **3.** To acknowledge. **owner** *n.*; **ownership** *n.*

ox \oks\ *n. pl.* oxen. A male animal of the cow family.

oxide \OK-sied\ *n.* A compound of

oxygen and one other element. oxidize *v.*; oxidation *n.*

oxygen \OK-si-jun\ *n.* A colorless gas existing in the air and needed for all life.

oxymoron \ok-si-MOR-on\ *n.* Putting together of words which seem to contradict each other.

oyster \OI-stur\ *n.* A type of shell-fish eaten as food. oysterer *n.*

ozone \OH-zohn\ *n.* A form of oxygen that forms a protective layer of the stratosphere.

P

p \pee\ **n. pl.** p's or ps. The 16th letter of the English alphabet.

pablum \PAB-lum\ **n.** An easily di-
gested food.

pace \pays\ **n. 1.** A footstep. **2.** The
speed of progress. **3.** Gait of a
horse.

pace \pays\ **v.** paced; pacing. **1.** To
measure by footsteps. **2.** To walk
back and forth. **3.** To set a speed
for. pacer **n.**

pacifism \PAS-uh-fiz-um\ **n.** An opposition to settling disputes
through war or violence. pacifist
adj.; pacifistic **adj.**; pacifist **n.**

pacify \PAS-uh-fie\ **v. 1.** To lessen
anger in. **2.** To make peaceful.
pacification **n.**; pacifier **n.**

pack \pak\ **n. 1.** A soft container. **2.**
A bunch of. **3.** A deck of playing
cards. package **n.**; packet **n.**;
package **v.**

pack \pak\ **v.** packed; packing. **1.** To
place items in a container for
transport. **2.** To stuff. **3.** To carry.
packer **n.**

pact \pakt\ **n. 1.** An agreement. **2.** A
treaty.

pad **n. 1.** Soft cushion. **2.** Sheets of
paper fastened together. **3.** Foot-
print of an animal. padding **n.**;
pad **v.**

paddle \PAD-l\ **n.** An oar used by a
single rower. paddle **v.**

padre \PAH-dray\ **n.** (Sp) A priest.

paella \pie-AY-yuh\ **n.** A saffron-
flavored recipe consisting of rice,
meat, seafood, and vegetables.

paganism \PAY-gun-iz-um\ *n.* The worship of a pre-Christian nature religion. pagan *n.*

page \payj\ *n.* **1.** One side of a leaf of a book. **2.** Male attendant. **3.** Legislative attendant.

page \payj\ *v.* paged; paging. **1.** To mark pages of a book. **2.** To flip through a book. **3.** To summon someone.

pageant \PAJ-unt\ *n.* A pompous show. pageantry *n.*

paginate \PAJ-uh-nayt\ *v.* paginated; paginating. To number the pages of. pagination *n.*

pagoda \puh-GOH-duh\ *n.* (Fo) A Far Eastern tower or temple containing an idol.

pail \payl\ *n.* A vessel for holding liquids.

pain \payn\ *n.* **1.** An uneasy sensation of the body or mind. **2.** Care or great effort. painful *adj.*; painless *adj.*; painfully *adv.*; painlessly *adv.*

paint \paynt\ *n.* **1.** Coloring substance of pigment. **2.** A cosmetic. **3.** Coat of pigment applied.

paint \paynt\ *v.* painted; painting. **1.** To lay color upon a surface. **2.** To lay colors on the face. **3.** To represent.

pair *n.* Two things suited to each other. pair *v.*

paisley \PAY-zlee\ *adj.* Ornamented with colorful teardrop-shaped figures.

pajamas \puh-JAH-muz\ *pl. n.* Sleepwear consisting of loose trousers and a jacket.

pal *n.* An intimate friend.

palace \PAL-is\ *n.* A royal or splendid house. palatial *adj.*

palate \PAL-it\ *n.* **1.** The roof of the mouth. **2.** A sense of taste. palatable *adj.*; palatal *adj.*

palaver \puh-LAV-ur\ *n.* **1.** Idle chatter. **2.** A conference. palaver *v.*

palazzo \puh-LAH-zoh\ *n. pl.* palazzi. (It) A spacious house.

pale \payl\ *adj.* **1.** Lacking color. **2.** Appearing sickly. pale *v.*

pale \payl\ *n.* **1.** A stake. **2.** An enclosure. **3.** [Pl] A fence.

paleontology \pay-lee-un-TOL-uh-jee\ *n.* (Sc) The study of fossil remains. paleontologist *n.*

palette \PAL-it\ *n.* **1.** A flat board upon which an artist mixes colors. **2.** A range of colors.

palimony \PAH-li-moh-nee\ *n.* An allowance for support paid to a former cohabitant.

pall \pawl\ *n.* A covering for the dead.

pall \pawl\ *v.* palled; palling. **1.** To cover the dead. **2.** To become tasteless.

palladium \puh-LAY-dee-um\ *n.* *pl.* palladia. **1.** A safeguard. **2.** A ductile and malleable whitish metal.

palm \pahm\ *n.* **1.** The flat of the hand. **2.** A tropical tree **3.** A palm leaf as a victory symbol.

palmistry \PAH-muh-stree\ *n.* A fortune telling using the lines on the palm of the hand. palm reader *n.*

palomino \pal-uh-MEE-noh\ *n. pl.* palominos. (Sp) A horse having slender legs, a buff-colored coat, and a flaxen and white mane.

palpable \PAL-puh-bul\ *adj.* That may be felt. palpably *adv.*

palpitate \PAL-pi-tayt\ *v.* palpitated; palpitating. To beat, as the heart. palpitation *n.*

palsy \PAWL-zee\ *n.* A paralysis of motion. palsied *adj.*; palsy *v.*

paltry \PAWL-tree\ *adj.* **1.** Worthless. **2.** Despicable. paltriness *n.*

pamper \PAM-pur\ *v.* pampered; pampering. To treat luxuriously.

pamphlet \PAM-flit\ *n.* A paper bounded booklet.

pan *n.* A broad and shallow vessel for cooking.

pan *v.* panned; panning. **1.** To sort through earth for precious metals. **2.** To harshly criticize.

panacea \pan-uh-SEE-uh\ *n.* A remedy for all ills.

panache \puh-NASH\ *n.* **1.** A bunch of feathers. **2.** A dashing style sense.

pancake \PAN-kayk\ *n.* A thin cake of batter fried in a pan.

pancreas \PANG-kree-us\ *n.* (Md) A crescent-shaped gland that secretes digestive fluids. pancreatic *adj.*

panda \PAN-duh\ *n.* **1.** A black and white bearlike mammal of the Far East. **2.** Raccoonlike carnivore.

pandemonium \pan-duh-MOH-nee-um\ *n.* A noisy and disorderly assembly.

pander \PAN-dur\ *v.* pandered; pandering. **1.** To arrange sexual affairs. **2.** To profit from the lust of others. pander *n.*

pane \payn\ *n.* A square plate of glass.

panel \PAN-l\ *n.* **1.** A square piece of a door, etc. **2.** A group of selected specialists. paneling *n.*; panelist *n.*

pang *n.* A sudden feeling of extreme pain.

panic \PAN-ik\ *v.* panicked; panicking. To be overcome by terror or anxiety. panic-stricken *adj.*; panicky *adj.*; panic *n.*

panorama \pan-uh-RAM-uh\ *n.* **1.**

A wide view from a singular point. **2.** Comprehensive view. panoramic *adj.*

pant *v.* panted; panting. **1.** To breathe hard. **2.** To long.

pantheism \PAN-thee-iz-um\ *n.* **1.** The doctrine that identifies nature with God. **2.** The worship of several gods. pantheistic *adj.*; pantheist *n.*

pantheon \PAN-thee-on\ *n.* (Fo) **1.** A temple dedicated to all the gods. **2.** A building serving as a memorial.

panther \PAN-thur\ *n.* A spotted wild feline beast.

pantomine \PAN-tuh-mime\ *n.* **1.** A representation in gesture and dumb show. **2.** A mimic. pantomine *v.*

pants *pl. n.* Trousers.

pantsuit \PANT-soot\ *n.* An article of clothing consisting of a pair of trousers and a tailored jacket.

papal \PAY-pul\ *adj.* Relating to the pope. papacy *n.*

paparazzi \pah-pah-RAH-zee\ *pl. n.* [It] Those in the media who sensationalize the private existence of celebrities.

papaya \puh-PAH-yuh or puh-PIE-yuh\ *n.* An oblong, yellow, sweet, juicy fruit.

paper \PAY-pur\ *n.* **1.** A substance on which to write. **2.** A newspaper. **3.** An essay. paper *adj.*

paper \PAY-pur\ *v.* papered; papering. To cover a wall with a decorative paper.

papier-mache \pay-pur-muh-SHAY\ *n.* (Fr) A substance made of paper pulp and paste that can be molded when wet.

papoose \pa-POOS\ *n.* A Native American word for a child.

paprika \pa-PREE-kuh\ *n.* A mildly spicy red pepper.

Pap smear *n.* (Md) A pelvic exam for cancer using a sample of tissue cells and cervical mucus.

papyrus \puh-PIE-rus\ *n. pl.* papyruses or papyri. **1.** A plant resembling grass. **2.** A paper once derived from this plant.

par \pahr\ *n.* The state of equality. parity *n.*

parade \puh-RAYD\ *n.* A showy public procession to celebrate a ceremonial event.

parade \puh-RAYD\ *v.* paraded; parading. **1.** To participate in a showy public procession. **2.** To show off.

paradigm \PAR-uh-diem\ *n.* **1.** An example. **2.** A model. paradigmatic *adj.*

paradise \PAR-uh-dies\ *n.* **1.** A blissful place. **2.** Heaven.

paradox \PAR-uh-doks\ *n.* An opinion that appears absurd, but may be true. paradoxical *adj.*; paradoxically *adv.*

paragon \PAR-uh-gon\ *n.* A perfect model.

paralegal \par-uh-LEE-gul\ *n.* (Le) A trained legal assistant.

parallel \PAR-uh-lel\ *adj.* **1.** Being a uniform distance away, apart. **2.** Not meeting. **3.** Closely resembling. parallel *n.*; parallel *v.*

paralyze \PAR-uh-liez\ *v.* paralyzed; paralyzing. To lose motion or feeling in a body part. paralytic *adj.*; paralytic *n.*; paralysis *n.*

paramedic \par-uh-MED-ik\ *n.* (Md) A trained assistant to a physician. paramedical *adj.*

parameter \puh-RAM-i-tur\ *n.* A characteristic factor. parametric *adj.*

paramilitary \par-uh-MIL-i-ter-ee\ *adj.* Based on a military pattern.

paramount \PAR-uh-mownt\ *adj.* Above all others. paramount *n.*

paramour \PAR-uh-muur\ *n.* An illicit lover.

paranoia \par-uh-NOI-uh\ *n.* A mental disorder characterized by delusions of grandeur and persecution. paranoid *adj.*; paranoid *n.*

paraphernalia \par-uh-fur-NAYL-yuh\ *pl. n.* **1.** One's personal belongings. **2.** Equipment.

paraphrase \PAR-uh-frayz\ *v.* paraphrased; paraphrasing. To restate. paraphrase *n.*

parasite \PAR-uh-siet\ *n.* **1.** Animal or plant living on or in another. **2.** Someone taking from others. parasitic *adj.*; parasitical *adj.*

parasol \PAR-uh-sawl\ *n.* A lightweight umbrella to shelter from the sun.

parcel \PAHR-sul\ *n.* **1.** A small bundle. **2.** A piece of land.

parcel \PAHR-sul\ *v.* parcelled; parcelling. To divide into portions.

parched \pahrchd\ *adj.* **1.** Dried by the heat. **2.** Thirsty. parch *v.*

pardon \PAHR-dn\ *v.* pardoned; pardoning. **1.** To forgive. **2.** To excuse. pardonable *adj.*; pardonably *adv.*; pardon *n.*

parent \PAR-unt\ *n.* One's father or mother. parental *adj.*; parentage *n.*; parenthood *n.*; parenting *n.*; parent *v.*

parenthesis \puh-REN-thuh-sis\ *n. pl.* parentheses. **1.** A clause included in a sentence. **2.** Curved punctuation to enclose a clause. parenthetic *adj.*; parenthetical *adj.*; parenthetically *adv.*

par excellence \par-EX-suh-lawns\ *adj.* (Fr) Being above all others.

parfait \pahr-FAY\ *n.* (Fr) **1.** A frozen dessert having whipped cream and eggs. **2.** An ice cream sundae.

pariah \puh-RIE-uh\ *n.* (Fo) An outcast.

parietal \par-ee-ET-ul\ *adj.* (Md) Pertaining to the inner walls of the body.

pari-mutuel \par-i-MYOO-choo-ul\ *n.* A method of dividing up winnings among all the bettors and the management.

parish \PAR-ish\ *n.* An ecclesiastical district. parishioner *n.*

park \pahrk\ *n.* **1.** Recreational play area. **2.** Industrial work area. **3.** Land around an estate.

park \pahrk\ *v.* parked; parking. To leave a vehicle in a temporary location.

parka \PAHR-kuh\ *n.* A hooded jacket.

Parkinson's disease \PAHR-kin-sunz\ *n.* (Md) A form of paralysis with rigid muscles, weakness, and shaking.

parlay \PAHR-lay\ *n.* A bet in which an earlier stake and its winnings are risked. parlay *v.*

Parliament \PAHR-luh-munt\ *n.* A legislative assembly, especially of England. parliamentary *adj.*

parlor \PAHR-lur\ *n.* A room for sitting and conversation.

parochial \puh-ROH-kee-ul\ *adj.* **1.** Belonging to a church parish. **2.** Narrow-minded. parochialism *n.*

parody \PAR-uh-dee\ *n. pl.* parodies. A caricature of another's words or performance. parody *v.*

parole \puh-ROHL\ *n.* An early release of a prisoner based on the promise of good behavior. parolee *n.*; parole *v.*

parquet \pahr-KAY\ *n.* (Fr) **1.** Floor of fine patterned woodwork. **2.** The main floor of a theatre.

parrot \PAR-ut\ *n.* Tropical bird of brilliant plumage and capable of repeating speech. parrot *v.*

parsimonious \PAHR-suh-moh-nee-us\ *adj.* Very sparing in expenditure. parsimoniously *adv.*; parsimony *n.*

parsnip \PAHR-snip\ *n.* A garden plant with a white, edible root.

part \pahrt\ *n.* **1.** A portion of a whole. **2.** Region. **3.** One's share or contribution. **4.** Role.

part \pahrt\ *v.* parted; parting. **1.** To go away from someone. **2.** To divide. **3.** To let go of. **4.** To cease.

partake \pahr-TAYK\ *v.* partook; partaken; partaking. **1.** To take part of. **2.** To have some food. partaker *n.*

parterre \pahr-TAIR\ *n.* (Fr) **1.** A decorative arrangement of flower beds. **2.** Theatre floor parquet circle.

partial \PAHR-shul\ *adj.* **1.** Biased. **2.** Not total. partially *adv.*; partiality *n.*

participate \pahr-TIS-uh-payt\ *v.* participated; participating. To take part in an activity. participatory *adj.*; participant *n.*; participation *n.*; participator *n.*

participle \PAHR-tuh-sip-ul\ *n.* A verb form that can also act as an adjective. participial *adj.*

particle \PAHR-ti-kul\ *n.* **1.** A minute part. **2.** The least possible amount. **3.** Minor part of speech; article

particleboard *n.* A length of wood consisting of several smaller bits of wood bonded together.

particular \pur-TIK-yuh-lur\ *adj.* **1.** Exact. **2.** Unique. **3.** Demanding. particularly *adv.*; particularity *n.*; particularize *v.*

particular \pur-TIK-yuh-lur\ *n.* A single instance or point.

parting \PAHR-ting\ *n.* **1.** A division. **2.** The action of going away from another. parting *adj.*

partisan \PAHR-tuh-zun\ *adj.* Being loyal to a party. partisan *n.* partisanship *n.*

partition \pahr-TISH-un\ *n.* **1.** A division. **2.** An act of dividing. **3.** A part. partition. *v.*

partly \PAHRT-lee\ *adv.* **1.** In some measure. **2.** In part.

partner \PAHRT-nur\ *n.* **1.** One who takes part with another in a common venture. **2.** A business associate.

partridge \PAHR-trij\ *n.* A small round-bodied game bird.

party \PAHR-tee\ *n. pl.* parties. **1.** Social gathering. **2.** Political group. **3.** Group with a mission.

parvenu \PAHR-vuh-noo\ *n.* (Fr) One who has recently come into notice or wealth.

Pascal \pas-KAL\ *n.* (Cm) A high-level programming language.

pass \pas\ *n.* **1.** Narrow entrance or passage. **2.** A permit. **3.** A flirtatious proposition.

pass \pas\ *v.* passed; passing. **1.** To proceed. **2.** To change. **3.** To die. **4.** To elapse. **5.** To be enacted.

passable \PAS-uh-bul\ *adj.* **1.** Acceptable. **2.** Able to be traveled. passably *adv.*

passage \PAS-ij\ *n.* **1.** The act of traveling. **2.** An access. **3.** A part of a book.

passé \pa-SAY\ *adj.* Out of use.

passenger \PAS-un-jur\ *n.* A traveller in a vehicle operated by another.

passing \PAS-ing\ *n.* A death.

passion \PASH-un\ *n.* 1. An unreasonable emotion. 2. A lust. 3. An object of lust. 4. An anger. passionate *adj.*; passionately *adv.*

passive \PAS-iv\ *adj.* 1. Not active. 2. Unresisting. 3. Expressing inaction by subject. passively *adv.*; passive *n.*; passivity *n.*

passive aggressive *n.* One who irrationally fluctuates between being assertive and weak. passive aggressive *adj.*

passive smoking *n.* The act of receiving second-hand tobacco smoke.

password \PAS-wurd\ *n.* 1. Secret word for entry. 2. Anything that gains access.

past *adj.* 1. Gone by. 2. Former. past *n.*

past *adv.* Gone by. past *prep.*

pasta \PAH-stuh\ *n.* (It) A dough of flour and water formed into various shapes; dish made from this.

paste \payst\ *n.* 1. A mixture used as adhesive. 2. Soft food mixture. 3. Gem-making mixure.

paste \payst\ *v.* pasted; pasting. To glue together.

pastel \pa-STEL\ *n.* 1. A light, muted color. 2. A paste or crayon of colored ground pigment. pastel *adj.*

pasteurize \PAS-chuh-rize\ *v.* pasteurized; pasteurizing. To partially sterilize a liquid through heating or radiating it. pasteurization *n.*; pasteurizer *n.*

pastime \PAS-time\ *n.* A hobby occupying one's leisure time.

pastor \PAS-tur\ *n.* A minister or priest who runs church services.

pastoral \PAS-tor-ul or PAS-tur-ul\ *adj.* 1. Relating to rural existence. 2. Relating to a minister or priest.

pastrami *also* **pastromi** \puh-STRAH-mee\ *n.* (Yd) A highly seasoned smoked beef.

pastry \PAY-stree\ *n. pl.* pastries. A pie, tart, or other baked sweet good having a crust.

pasture \PAS-chur\ *n.* An area of land set aside for grazing. pasture *v.*

pasty \PAY-stee\ *adj.* pastier; pastiest. 1. Sticky and doughy like paste. 2. Appearing pale and sickly.

pat *adj.* Aptly suited. pat *adv.*

pat *n.* 1. A gentle hit. 2. A small shaped portion of something, such as butter. pat *v.*

patch \pach\ *n.* 1. A piece of fabric to mend a torn area. 2. A piece of material worn.

patch \pach\ *v.* patched; patching. 1. To mend a torn area with fabric. 2. To repair quickly.

patch up *v.* To resolve differences.

patchwork \PACH-wurk\ *n.* A quilt, dress, etc. made of sewn together fragments of different fabrics.

pâté \pah-TAY\ *n.* (Fr) **1.** A meat or fish pastry. **2.** A paste of highly spiced and mashed meat.

patent \PAT-nt\ *adj.* **1.** Blatant. **2.** Protected from duplication.

patent \PAT-nt\ *n.* A document guaranteeing the inventor the sole rights to their invention.

path *n. pl.* paths. **1.** A route for passing. **2.** A means of behavior.

pathetic \puh-THET-ik\ *adj.* Pitiful. pathetically *adv.*

pathogen \PATH-uh-jun\ *n.* (Md) A bacterium, fungus, virus, or other agent responsible for causing illness. pathogenic *adj.*; pathogenetic *adj.*; pathogenesis *n.*; pathogeny *n.*

pathology \puh-THOL-uh-jee\ *n.* (Md) **1.** The study of illnesses. **2.** The conditions, etc. of a disease. pathological *adj.*; pathologist *n.*

pathos \PAY-thos\ *n.* A characteristic in something or someone that evokes sad emotions.

patient \PAY-shunt\ *adj.* Able to withstand discomfort without discontentment. patiently *adv.*; patience *n.*

patient \PAY-shunt\ *n.* One under medical attention.

patisserie \puh-TI-suh-ree\ *n.* (Fr) A pastry shop.

patriarch \PAY-tree-ahrk\ *n.* **1.** Male head of a family, tribe. **2.** Revered elder. **3.** Bishop of Orthodox church. patriarchal *adj.*; partriarchate *n.*; patriarchy *n.*

patrician \puh-TRISH-un\ *n.* An aristocrat.

patricide \PA-truh-side\ *n.* **1.** The act of killing one's own father. **2.** One who kills one's own father.

patriotic \pay-tree-OT-ik\ *adj.* Being loyal to one's country. patriotically *adv.*; patriot *n.*; patriotism *n.*

patrol \puh-TROHL\ *v.* patrolled; patrolling. To walk about a designated area for security purposes. patrol *n.*

patron \PAY-trun\ *n.* **1.** A regular customer. **2.** A financial supporter. patronage *n.*

patronize \PAY-truh-nize\ *v.* patronized; patronizing. **1.** To be a regular customer. **2.** To treat as inferior.

pattern \PAT-urn\ *n.* **1.** A model on which to base construction. **2.** A decorative marking. pattern *v.*

paunch \pawnch\ *n.* A fat tummy.

pauper \PAW-pur\ *n.* One who is poor. pauperism *n.*; pauperize *v.*

pause \pawz\ *n.* A short delay. pause *v.*

pave \payv\ *v.* paved; paving. To cover or surface with bricks, asphalt, concrete, etc.

pavilion \puh-VIL-yun\ *n.* **1.** A spacious tent. **2.** A temporary structure for entertainment.

paw *n.* An animal's clawed foot.

paw *v.* pawed; pawing. To scratch, grab, or brush with the hand or paw.

pawn *n.* Valuables given as collateral for a loan. pawn *v.*

pay *n.* A salary for work.

pay *v.* paid; paying. **1.** To give what is due for goods or services. **2.** To resolve. **3.** To visit.

payload \PAY-lohd\ *n.* The additional weight a vehicle transports in freight or passengers.

payroll \PAY-rohl\ *n.* A directory of those to receive wages, or the wages provided.

pea \pee\ *n. pl.* peas. A leguminous vine bearing round edible green seeds in pods.

peace \pees\ *n.* **1.** A relaxing state. **2.** The lack of war and other conflicts. peaceable *adj.*; peaceful *adj.*; peaceably *adv.*; peacefully *adv.*

peacekeeper \PEES-kee-pur\ *n.* One who maintains a state of har-mony. peacekeeping *adj.*; peacekeeping *n.*

peacemaker \PEES-may-kur\ *n.* One who works to resolve a war or settle a conflict. peacemaking *adj.*; peacemaking *n.*

peach \peech\ *n.* A sweet, succulent fruit having a thin yellow and red skin.

peak \peek\ *n.* **1.** A sharp or projecting area. **2.** The uppermost point of a hill or mountain. peak *v.*

peaked \PEE-kid\ *adj.* Appearing pale and ill.

peal \peel\ *n.* The clanging of bells. peal *v.*

pear \pair\ *n.* A bell-shaped apple-like edible juicy fruit.

pearl \purl\ *n.* **1.** A smooth, spherical, precious gem derived from the oyster. **2.** Bluish gray. pearly *adj.*

peasant \PEZ-unt\ *n.* Any of a class of rural laborers and small farm-owners. peasantry *n.*

pecan \pee-KAN\ *n.* An edible nut having a thin, smooth oval shell.

peck \pek\ *n.* Dry weight equal to eight quarts.

peck \pek\ *v.* Striking with a beak.

peculiar \pi-KYOOL-yur\ *adj.* **1.** Deviating from the norm. **2.** Distinctive. **3.** Belonging to one person. peculiarly *adv.*; peculiarity *n.*

pedal \PED-l\ *n.* A lever operated by the foot.

pedal \PED-l\ *v.* pedaled; pedaling or pedalled; pedalling. **1.** To operate a lever using the foot. **2.** To cycle.

pedantic \puh-DAN-tik\ *adj.* **1.** Parading one's knowledge. **2.** Educated, but in a narrow and stodgy way. pedantically *adv.*; pedant *n.*; pedantry *n.*

peddle \PED-l\ *v.* peddled; peddling. To sell one's goods from place to place. peddler or pedlar *n.*

pedestrian \puh-DES-tree-un\ *adj.* **1.** Progressing on foot. **2.** Everyday.

pedestrian \puh-DES-tree-un\ *n.* One who progresses on foot.

pedigree \PED-i-gree\ *adj.* Purebred. pedigreed *adj.*

pedigree \PED-i-gree\ *n.* An ancestral lineage.

pee *v.* (Sl). To urinate. pee *n.*

peek *v.* peeked; peeking. **1.** To look quickly. **2.** To observe from a concealed point. peek *n.*

peel *n.* A fruit's skin or rind.

peel *v.* peeled; peeling. **1.** To take off the outer skin, clothing, etc. **2.** To flake off.

peep *v.* peeped; peeping. **1.** To look quickly. **2.** To glance from a concealed point. **3.** To chirp. peep *n.*; peeper *n.*

peer *n. pl.* peers. **1.** One's equal. **2.** A member of nobility. peerage *n.*

peer *v.* peered; peering. To stare.

peeve \peev\ *n.* **1.** An annoyance. **2.** An irritable mood. peevish *adj.*; peevishly *adv.*; peeve *n.*; peevishness *n.*

peg *n.* **1.** A pin of wood, etc. for fastening. **2.** A pin on which things are hung.

peg *v.* pegged; pegging. **1.** To secure with a pin. **2.** To get exactly right.

pejorative \pi-JOR-uh-tiv\ *adj.* Derogatory.

pekoe \PEE-koh\ *n.* A black tea made from tiny leaves.

pelican \PEL-i-kun\ *n.* An aquatic bird characterized by webbed feet and a pouched lower bill.

pelt *n.* An animal hide.

pelt *v.* pelted; pelting. To bombard repeatedly.

pelvis \PEL-vis\ *n. pl.* pelvises or pelves. (Md) The body's bony girdle directly over the lower and hind limbs.

pen *n.* **1.** An enclosed area. **2.** An ink-flowing writing device.

pen *v.* penned; penning. **1.** To place in an enclosed area. **2.** To write.

penal \PEEN-l\ *adj.* Punishing.

penalty \PEN-l-tee\ *n. pl.* penalties. **1.** Punishment for wrongdoing. **2.** Sum paid as punishment. **3.** Loss or handicap. penalize *v.*

penance \PEN-uns\ *n.* **1.** Sacramental rite for admitting sin. **2.** Atonement for sin.

penchant \PEN-chunt\ *n.* A partiality to.

pencil \PEN-sul\ *n.* A writing device made of a soft graphite lead encased in a cylinder of wood. pencil *v.*

pendant *also* **pendent** \PEN-dunt\ *n.* A dangling piece of jewelry. pendant or pendent *adj.*

pending \PEN-ding\ *adj.* **1.** Forthcoming. **2.** Still undecided.

penetrate \PEN-i-trayt\ *v.* penetrated; penetrating. **1.** To enter or break into. **2.** To pass through. **3.** To comprehend. penetrable *adj.*; penetrative *adj.*; penetratingly *adv.*; penetration *n.*

penguin \PENG-gwin\ *n.* A web-footed flightless aquatic bird of southern hemisphere.

penicillin \pen-uh-SIL-in\ *n.* (Md) A disease- and infection-fighting antibiotic derived from fungus.

peninsula \puh-NIN-suh-luh\ *n.* A length of land surrounded on three sides by water. peninsular *adj.*

penis \PEE-nis\ *n. pl.* penes or penises. (Md) The external male reproductive organ.

penitence \PEN-i-tuns\ *n.* An emotion of grief for acts of sin or wrongdoing. penitent *adj.*; penitential *adj.*; penitent *n.*

penitentiary \pen-i-TEN-shuh-ree\ *n. pl.* penitentiaries. A prison. penitentiary *adj.*

penny \PEN-ee\ *n. pl.* pennies. A copper unit of American currency equal to 1/100th of a dollar.

pension \PEN-shun\ *n.* An amount of money regularly paid to a retired person. pensioner *n.*; pension *v.*

pensive \PEN-siv\ *adj.* Immersed in thought. pensively *adv.*; pensiveness *n.*

pentagon \PEN-tuh-gon\ *n.* **1.** A form having five angles and five sides. **2.** [Cap] U.S. government building. pentagonal *adj.*

penultimate \pi-NUL-tuh-mit\ *n.* The one preceeding the last. penultimate *adj.*; penult *n.*

peon \PEE-un\ *n. pl.* peons or peones. **1.** [Sp] A menial laborer. **2.** One who is enslaved to work for payment of a debt. peonage *n.*

peony \PEE-uh-nee\ *n. pl.* peonies. An ornamental garden plant bearing spherical red, pink, or white flowers.

people \PEE-pul\ *pl. n.* **1.** The human beings composing a unified group. **2.** The population.

people \PEE-pul\ *v.* peopled; peopling. To populate.

pep *n.* A vigor and motivation. peppy *adj.*; pep *v.*

pepper \PEP-ur\ *n.* **1.** A zestful spice. **2.** An edible bell-shaped fruit also used as a condiment. peppery *adj.*; pepper *v.*

per capita \PUR-KAP-i-tuh\ *adj.* Pertaining to each person. per capita *adv.*

perceive \pur-SEEV\ *v.* perceived; perceiving. **1.** To become knowledgeable of through the senses. **2.** To comprehend. perceivable *adj.*; perceptible *adj.*; perceptive *adj.*; perceptual *adj.*; perceptible *adj.*

percent \pur-SENT\ *adv.* For or part of each 100th. percent *n.*; percentage *n.*

percentile \pur-SEN-tile\ *n.* Any of 100 points at equal intervals used to denote place in a series.

perch \purch\ *n.* **1.** A place where birds rest. **2.** An elevated lookout point. **3.** An edible fish.

percolate \PUR-kuh-layt\ *v.* percolated; percolating. To extract the flavor by filtering through hot water. percolator *n.*

perennial \puh-REN-ee-ul\ *adj.* **1.** Existing throughout the year. **2.** Eternal. perennially *adv.*

perennial \puh-REN-ee-ul\ *n.* A plant that lives throughout the year.

perestroika \pair-uh-STROY-kuh\ *n.* (Fo) Changeover from a communist form to a democratic form of government, as Russia.

perfect \PUR-fikt\ *adj.* **1.** Flawless. **2.** Whole. **3.** Accurate. **4.** Verb tense of action in the past. perfectible *adj.*; perfectly *adv.*; perfectibility *n.*; perfection *n.*; perfectness *n.*

perform \pur-FORM\ *v.* performed; performing. **1.** To carry out. **2.** To work. **3.** To entertain publicly. performance *n.*; performer *n.*

performance art *n.* Medium of expression revolving around bodily movement and theatrics.

perfunctory \pur-FUNGK-tuh-ree\ *adj.* Mechanically. perfunctorily *adv.*; perfunctoriness *n.*

perhaps \pur-HAPS\ *adv.* Possibly.

peril \PER-ul\ *n.* A hazard. perilous *adj.*; perilously *adv.*

perimeter \pur-RIM-i-tur\ *n.* **1.** Boundary enclosing an area. **2.** Measurement of exterior boundary.

period \PEER-ee-ud\ *n.* **1.** Punctuation ending a sentence. **2.** Portion of time. **3.** Menstrual cycle.

periodical \peer-ee-OD-i-kul\ *adj.* Happening at fixed intervals. periodic *adj.*; periodically *adv.*; periodical *n.*

peripatetic \per-uh-puh-TET-ik\ *adj.* Constantly mobile.

periphery \puh-RIF-uh-ree\ *n. pl.* peripheries. **1.** The outer edge. **2.** The area past a boundary. peripheral *adj.*; peripherally *adv.*

perish \PER-ish\ *v.* perished; perishing. **1.** To become or cause to become ruined. **2.** To die.

perishable \PER-i-shuh-bul\ *adj.* Prone to spoiling.

perjury \PUR-juh-ree\ *n.* (Le) A lie stated while under oath. perjurer *n.*; perjure *v.*

perk \purk\ *n.* A benefit.

perk \purk\ *v.* **1.** To pop one's head up. **2.** To percolate. **3.** To regain energy. **4.** To refreshen.

perky \PUR-kee\ *adj.* perkier; perkiest. Energetic and spirited.

perm \purm\ *v.* permed; perming. To either straighten or make wavy one's hair by giving a permanent. perm *n.*

permanent \PUR-muh-nunt\ *adj.* Enduring. permanently *adv.*; permanence *n.*; permanency *n.*

permanent \PUR-muh-nunt\ *n.* A chemical process of either straightening or making wavy the hair.

permeable \PUR-mee-uh-bul\ *adj.* Having pores able to allow liquid or gas to filter through. permeability *n.*

permeate \PUR-mee-ayt\ *v.* permeated; permeating. **1.** To filter through the pores of. **2.** To spread throughout. permeation *n.*

permission \pur-MISH-un\ *n.* An authorization. permissible *adj.*; permissive *adj.*; permissibly *adv.*; permissiveness *n.*

permit \PUR-mit\ *n.* A document providing authorization.

permit \pur-MIT\ *v.* permitted; permitting. **1.** To authorize. **2.** To enable.

permutation \pur-myuu-TAY-shun\ *n.* **1.** A metamorphosis. **2.** Rearrangement. **3.** Change in order of sequence.

perpendicular \pur-pun-DIK-yuh-lur\ *adj.* **1.** At right angles. **2.** Standing upright. perpendicularly *adv.*; perpendicular *n.*; perpendicularity *n.*

perpetrate \PUR-pi-trayt\ *v.* perpetrated; perpetrating. To be guilty of. perpetration *n.*; perpetrator *n.*

perpetual \pur-PECH-oo-ul\ *adj.* **1.** Enduring. **2.** Always occurring.

perpetually *adv.*; **perpetuation** *n.*; **perpetuate** *v.*

perplex \pur-PLEKS\ *v.* perplexed; perplexing. To confuse. perpexedly *adv.*; perplexity *n.*

persecute \PUR-si-kyoot\ *v.* persecuted; persecuting. To bother persistently, especially on the basis of difference. persecution *n.*; persecutor *n.*

persevere \pur-suh-VEER\ *v.* persevered; persevering. To continue on despite hardship. perseverance *n.*

persist \pur-SIST\ *v.* persisted; persisting. **1.** To continue on despite hardship. **2.** To endure. persistent *adj.*; persistently *adv.*; persistence *n.*; persistency *n.*

person \PUR-sun\ *n.* A human body, personality, or being.

persona \pur-SOH-nuh\ *n. pl.* personae. **1.** An individual. **2.** A mask. **3.** [Pl] The characters in a story.

personal \PUR-suh-nl\ *adj.* **1.** Relating to the individual self. **2.** Private. **3.** Done before one's self. personally *adv.*

personality \pur-suh-NAL-i-tee\ *n. pl.* personalities. The distinctive characteristics of an individual.

personify \pur-SON-uh-fie\ *v.* personified; personifying. **1.** To con-ceptualize or show as a person. **2.** To exemplify. personification *n.*

personnel \pur-suh-NEL\ *n.* The group of individuals working for an institution.

perspective \pur-SPEK-tiv\ *n.* **1.** The art of representing dimensions on a flat surface. **2.** A viewpoint.

perspicuous \pur-SPIK-yoo-us\ *adj.* Easily understood. perspicuity *n.*

perspire \pur-SPIER\ *v.* perspired; perspiring. To sweat. perspiration *n.*

persuade \pur-SWAYD\ *v.* persuaded; persuading. To convince through reasoning. persuasive *adj.*; persuasively *adv.*; persuasion *n.*; persuasiveness *n.*

pert \purt\ *adj.* **1.** Forward. **2.** Energetic. **3.** Animated.

pertain \pur-TAYN\ *v.* pertained; pertaining. **1.** To be part of a whole. **2.** To apply to.

pertinent \PUR-tn-unt\ *adj.* Applying to. pertinently *adv.*; pertinence *n.*

perturb \pur-TURB\ *v.* perturbed; perturbing. To irritate greatly. perturbation *n.*

peruse \puh-ROOZ\ *v.* perused; perusing. To examine carefully. perusal *n.*; peruser *n.*

pervade \pur-VAYD\ *v.* pervaded;

pervading. To spread throughout. pervasive *adj.*

perverse \pur-VURS\ *adj.* **1.** Against what is morally proper. **2.** Unreasonable. perversely *adv.*; perverseness *n.*; perversion *n.*; perversity *n.*

pervert \pur-VURT\ *v.* perverted; perverting. **1.** To cause to deviate from morally proper conduct. **2.** To put to the wrong use. pervert *n.*

pessimism \PES-uh-miz-um\ *n.* A tendency to expect a negative outcome. pessimistic *adj.*; pessimist *n.*

pest *n.* An irritating person or thing. pester *v.*

pet *n.* **1.** An animal living in the domestic environment as a companion. **2.** A favorite. pet *adj.*

pet *v.* petted; petting. **1.** To have an animal stay in one's home. **2.** To stroke caringly.

pet peeve *n.* The most irritating annoyance.

petal \PET-l\ *n.* A colorful leaf of a flower. petalled *adj.*

petite \puh-TEET\ *adj.* (Fr) Having a shorter and thinner figure than other women.

petite bourgeoisie *n.* (Fr) The lower middle class. petit bourgeois *adj.*; petit bourgeois *n.*

petit four \PET-ee-FOR\ *n. pl.* petits fours or petit fours. A small cut of frosted sponge or pound cake.

petition \puh-TISH-un\ *n.* A written plea to one in power. petitioner *n.*; petition *v.*

petri dish \PEE-tree-DISH\ *n.* (Sc) A slightly concave glass used to study bacteria cultures.

petrochemical \pe-troh-KEM-i-kul\ *n.* A chemical extracted from petroleum or natural gas.

petroleum \puh-TROH-lee-um\ *n.* Flammable fluid extracted from wells drilled in the earth and processed.

petty \PET-ee\ *adj.* pettier; pettiest. **1.** Of minor significance. **2.** Small-minded. pettily *adv.*; pettiness *n.*

petty cash *n.* Money carried with one's self in order to pay for everyday minor needs.

petulant \PECH-uh-lunt\ *adj.* Moody. petulantly *adv.*; petulance *n.*

pewter \PYOO-tur\ *n.* An alloy of tin and some lead that is similar to silver. pewter *adj.*

phantasm \fan-TAZ-um\ *n.* The result of illusion.

phantom \FAN-tum\ *n.* **1.** A ghost. **2.** A product of the imagination.

pharaoh \FAIR-oh\ *n.* (Fo) **1.** An ancient Egyptian ruler. **2.** A tyrannical ruler. pharaonic *adj.*

pharmacologist \fahr-muh-KOL-uh-jist\ *n.* One who studies drugs. pharmacology *n.*

pharmacopoeia *also* **pharmacopeia** \fahr-muh-kuh-PEE-uh\ *n.* **1.** A text on drugs and other healing preparations. **2.** A supply of drugs.

pharmacy \FAHR-muh-see\ *n. pl.* pharmacies. **1.** The science or practice of mixing and dispensing drugs. **2.** A drugstore. pharmacist *n.*

pharynx \FAIR-ingks\ *n. pl.* pharynges or pharynxes. (Md) The food and air canal between the palate and esophagus.

phase \fayz\ *n.* A period in life of something.

pheasant \FEZ-unt\ *n.* A lavishly colored, long-tailed game bird.

phenomenon \fi-NOM-uh-non\ *n. pl.* phenomena or phenomenons. A rare occurrence. phenomenal *adj.*

phenotype \FEE-nuh-tipe\ *n.* Aggregate of genetic characteristics obvious in an organism.

philanderer \fi-LAN-dur-ur\ *n.* A person who has many love affairs. philander *v.*

philanthropic \fil-un-THROP-ik\ *adj.* Charitable. philanthropist *n.*; philanthropy *n.*

philatelist \fi-LAT-uh-list\ *n.* A collector and enthusiast of postage and imprinted stamps. philately *n.*

Philistine \FIL-uh-steen\ *n.* One more concerned with material than intellectual or artistic wealth. Philistine *adj.*

philology \fi-LOL-uh-jee\ *n.* The study of linguistics. philological *adj.*; philologist *n.*

philosophical *also* **philosophic** \fil-uh-SOF-i-kul\ *adj.* **1.** Thinking deeply. **2.** Calm. philosophically *adv.*

philosophy \fi-LOS-uh-fee\ *n.* **1.** Discussion and study of the principles of reality. **2.** System of wisdom. philosophically *adv.*

phlegm \flem\ *n.* Mucus from the nose and throat.

phobia \FOH-bee-uh\ *n.* A fear. phobic *adj.*

phone \fohn\ *v.* phoned; phoning. To call someone using a telephone.

phonic \FON-ik\ *adj.* Pertaining to sound. phonically *adv.*

phonics \FON-iks\ *n.* **1.** Phonetic skills taught for reading and pronunciation. **2.** Acoustics.

phosphorus \FOS-fur-us\ *n.* Non-metallic chemical element important in the manufacturing of glass, steel. phosphoric *adj.*; phosphorous *adj.*

photocopy \FOH-tuh-kop-ee\ *n.* The mechanical image produced from a copier. photocopier *n.*; photocopy *v.*

photo-essay \FOH-toh-ES-say\ *n.* An account communicated through a layout of several photographs.

photogenic \foh-tuh-JEN-ik\ *adj.* Aesthetically pleasing to the photographic eye.

photograph *also* **photo** \FOH-tuh-graf\ *n.* A still picture taken with a camera. photograph *v.*

photographic \foh-tuh-GRAF-ik\ *adj.* Exact in detail. photographically *adv.*

photography \fuh-TOG-ruh-fee\ *n.* Chemical processing of forming and fixing an image on printed paper. photographer *n.*

phrase \frayz\ *n.* A group of words.

phrase \frayz\ *v.* phrased; phrasing. To express in words carefully.

phylum \FIE-lum\ *n. pl.* phyla. (Sc) A category of animal and plant classification.

physical \FIZ-i-kul\ *adj.* **1.** Material. **2.** Concerning the body.

physiology \fiz-ee-OL-uh-jee\ *n.* (Md) The study of the functional processes of an organism. physiologic *adj.*; physiological *adj.*; physiologically *adv.*; physiologist *n.*

physique \fi-ZEEK\ *n.* The build of the human body.

pi \pie\ *n. pl.* pis. A symbol expressing the ratio of a circle's circumference to its diameter.

piano \pee-AN-oh\ *n. pl.* pianos. Musical instrument of felt covered hammers worked by a keyboard. pianist *n.*

piazza \pee-AZ-uh\ *n. pl.* piazzas or piazze. (It) **1.** A town square. **2.** An arched roof walkway.

pica \PIE-kuh\ *n.* A type in which 10 characters exist in one inch.

piccolo \PIK-uh-loh\ *n. pl.* piccolos. A small, high-pitched flute.

pick \pik\ *v.* picked; picking. **1.** To choose. **2.** To gather. **3.** To break into something closed.

picket \PIK-it\ *n.* **1.** A post of structure. **2.** A person who demonstrates for a cause.

picket \PIK-it\ *v.* picketed; picketing. To protest against. picketer *n.*

pickle \PIK-ul\ *n.* **1.** Cucumber, other food that has been preserved in vinegar. **2.** Sticky situation.

pickle \PIK-ul\ *v.* pickled; pickling. To preserve fruit or vegetable by storing in vinegar.

pick on *v.* To provoke.

pickpocket \PIK-pok-it\ *n.* One who takes from other's pockets. pickpocket *v.*

pick up *v.* **1.** To lift. **2.** To obtain. **3.** To improve. **4.** To call for socially.

picky \PIK-ee\ *adj.* Choosy.

picnic \PIK-nik\ *n.* **1.** An outdoor meal. **2.** A very easy undertaking. picnicker *n.*; picnic *v.*

picture \PIK-chur\ *n.* **1.** Representation of something. **2.** A perfect example. **3.** An entertainment film.

picture \PIK-chur\ *v.* pictured; picturing. **1.** To depict. **2.** To form a vision in one's mind.

picturesque \pik-chuh-RESK\ *adj.* Very attractive, especially scenery.

pie *n.* A pastry crust filled with fruit or meat and baked.

piece \pees\ *n.* **1.** A part of something. **2.** A work of art, music, or writing.

piece \pees\ *v.* pieced; piecing. To put together.

piece de resistance \pee-ES-duh-ri-zee-STAHNS\ *n. pl.* pieces de resistance. (Fr) **1.** The main course. **2.** An exceptional item.

piecemeal \PEES-meel\ *adv.* Bit by bit. piecemeal *adj.*

pier \peer\ *n.* A support, especially for boats.

pierce \peers\ *v.* pierced; piercing. To penetrate.

pietà \pee-ET-uh\ *n.* [It] A depiction of the Virgin Mary lamenting over the dead body of Christ.

pig *n.* **1.** A chubby animal with hooves, curly tail, and short snout. **2.** A big eater. piggish *adj.*

pigeon \PIJ-un\ *n.* A bird having a round body, thick coat of feathers, and short legs.

pigeonhole \PIJ-un-hohl\ *v.* pigeonholed; pigeonholing. **1.** To file in a compartment set aside for letters or documents. **2.** To set aside.

pigment \PIG-munt\ *n.* A coloring matter. pigmentation *n.*

pilaf *also* **pilaff** \PEE-lahf\ *n.* A seasoned rice.

pilaster \pi-LAS-tur\ *n.* A raised column that decorates or buttresses a wall.

pile \piel\ *n.* **1.** A heap of something. **2.** A wealth. pile *v.*

pilgrim \PIL-grum\ *n.* **1.** Traveler, esp. to holy lands. **2.** [Cap] An English colonizer of Plymouth.

pilgrimage \PIL-gruh-mij\ *n.* A long journey, especially to a holy land.

pill \pil\ *n. pl.* pills. **1.** A capsule of medicine. **2.** [Sl] A person who is very annoying.

pillage \PIL-ij\ *v.* pillaged; pillaging. To plunder. pillage *n.*; pillager *n.*

pillar \PIL-ur\ *n.* **1.** A column of a building. **2.** A source of strength.

pilot \PIE-lut\ *n.* One who guides an aircraft, ship, or other vehicle. pilot *v.*

pimiento *also* **pimento** \pi-MYEN-toh\ *n. pl.* pimientos or pimentos. A red sweet pepper.

pimp *n.* A person who arranges clients for prostitutes. pimp *v.*

pimple \PIM-pul\ *n.* A small swelling on the skin.

pin *n.* **1.** Length of wire used for fastening. **2.** Ornamental jewelry.

pin *v.* pinned; pinning. To hold in place.

pina colada \PEE-nuh-koh-lah-duh\ *n.* (Sp) A mixed drink of rum, coconut, pineapple juice, and ice.

pincers *also* **pinchers** \PIN-surs\ *pl. n.* An instrument used to grip.

pinch *v.* pinched; pinching. **1.** To press tightly. **2.** To be stingy. **3.** To steal. **4.** To arrest.

pinch *n.* **1.** A tight pressing. **2.** A very small amount. **3.** A predicament.

pin down *v.* To force someone to make a commitment.

pine \pien\ *n.* A cone-bearing evergreen tree having needlelike leaves.

pine \pien\ *v.* pined; pining. To long for.

pineal \PIN-ee-ul\ *adj.* Shaped like a pinecone.

pineapple \PIE-nap-ul\ *n.* A tropical plant having sweet edible fruit enclosed by a tough skin.

pinecone \PIEN-COHN\ *n.* The oval-shaped grouping of pollen-bearing scales of a pine tree.

pink \pingk\ *n.* **1.** A rose color. **2.** The best condition.

pink \pingk\ *v.* pinked; pinking. To cut in zigzag.

pinnacle \PIN-uh-kul\ *n.* A top.

pinochle *also* **pinocle, penuchle, or penuckle** \PEE-nok-ul\ *n.* A two-four person game played with a forty-eight-card deck.

pinpoint \PIN-point\ *v.* pinpointed; pinpointing. To define.

pinto \PIN-toh\ *n. pl.* pintos or pintoes. A spotted horse.

pioneer \pie-uh-NEER\ *n.* **1.** One who finds a new place. **2.** One who founds something. pioneer *adj.*; pioneer *v.*

pious \PIE-us\ *adj.* **1.** Religious. **2.** Dedicated. piously *adv.*; piousness *n.*

pipe \piep\ *n.* **1.** A tubular passage. **2.** [Mu] Flutelike wind instrument. **3.** [Mu] Organ tubes.

pipe \piep\ *v.* piped; piping. **1.** Conduct through a tube. **2.** To make a peeping sound. **3.** [Mu]. To sound a flute. piper *n.*

piquant \PEE-kant\ *adj.* Flavorful.

pique \peek\ *n.* An anger. pique *v.*

piranha \pi-RAHN-uh\ *n.* A carnivorous freshwater fish native to South America.

pirate \PIE-rut\ *n.* A person who robs ships at sea. piratical *adj.*; piracy *n.*; pirate *v.*

pirouette \pir-oo-ET\ *n.* (Fr) A full spin on one foot or toe. pirouette *v.*

pistachio \pi-STASH-ee-oh\ *n. pl.* pistachios. A tree bearing a small edible green nut.

pistol \PIS-tl\ *n.* A small handgun.

piston \PIS-tun\ *n.* A sliding cylinder that moves up and down in a tube.

pit *n.* **1.** A cavity. **2.** A game ring. **3.** [Mu] A sunken area before a theatre stage.

pit *v.* pitted; pitting. To put in opposition.

pita \PEE-tuh\ *n.* (Fo) A flat, hollow bread that can be filled.

pitch \pich\ *n.* **1.** A tilt. **2.** A tone of sound. **3.** [Cl] A talk to convince.

pitch \pich\ *v.* pitched; pitching. **1.** To throw. **2.** To put up. **3.** To dive.

pitch in *v.* To help.

pitcher \PICH-ur\ *n.* **1.** Pouring container for liquids. **2.** In baseball, the deliverer of the ball.

pitfall \PIT-fawl\ *n.* A hazard.

pituitary \pi-TOO-i-ter-ee\ *n.* (Md) Small gland located at the base of the brain that controls the body's hormones. pituitary *adj.*

pity \PIT-ee\ *n.* **1.** A feeling of mercy toward another. **2.** A sad situation. pitiful *adj.*; pitifully *adv.*; pityingly *adv.*

pity \PIT-ee\ *v.* pitied; pitying. **1.** To feel sorry for. **2.** To spare.

pivot \PIV-ut\ *n.* A center point about which something revolves. pivot *v.*

pivotal \PIV-uh-tl\ *adj.* Very important.

pixie *also* **pixy** \PIK-see\ *n. pl.* pixies. A mischievous fairylike being.

pizza \PEET-suh\ *n.* (It) A baked dough pie with tomato sauce, cheese, and other toppings.

placard \PLAK-urd\ *n.* A large notice or sign. placard *v.*

placate \PLAY-kayt\ *v.* placated; placating. To pacify. placatory *adj.*: placative *adj.*; placation *n.*

place \plays\ *n.* **1.** A location with a

purpose. **2.** A rank. **3.** An appointment. **4.** A duty.

place \plays\ *v.* placed; placing. **1.** To situate. **2.** To put in order. **3.** To recognize.

placebo \pluh-SEE-boh\ *n. pl.* placebos or placeboes. (Md) An inactive medicine administered as if it were a real drug.

placebo effect *n.* (Md) A reaction to taking a placebo.

placecard \PLAYS-KARD\ *n.* A folded note that marks something's location.

placid \PLAS-id\ *adj.* Calm. placidly *adv.*

plagiarism \PLAY-juh-riz-um\ *n.* A copying of another's written work. plagiarist *n.*; plagiarize *v.*

plague \playg\ *n.* **1.** A disease that is widespread. **2.** An annoyance. plague *v.*

plaid \plad\ *adj.* A pattern or fabric of uneven, varicolored checks.

plain \playn\ *adj.* **1.** Obvious. **2.** Straightforward in speech. **3.** Normal. **4.** Unembellished. **5.** Ugly.

plain \playn\ *n.* An open, level land.

plaintiff \PLAYN-tif\ *n.* (Le) A person filing a lawsuit in court.

plaintive \PLAYN-tiv\ *adj.* Pathetic. plaintively *adv.*

plan *n.* **1.** A scheme, design, or way of doing things. **2.** A written description.

plan *v.* planned; planning. **1.** To prepare in advance. **2.** To intend. planner *n.*

plane \playn\ *n.* **1.** A flat surface. **2.** An aircraft. **3.** A tool for leveling wood.

planet \PLAN-it\ *n.* A celestial body orbiting a star.

planetarium \plan-i-TAIR-ee-um\ *n. pl.* planetariums or planetaria. A building or room where stars and planets may be viewed through a device.

planetary \PLAN-i-tair-ee\ *adj.* Of or pertaining to the planets.

plant *n.* **1.** Multicellular organisms that make their own food. **2.** An industrial workplace.

plant *v.* planted; planting. **1.** To put in the ground for growing. **2.** To establish. planter *n.*

plantain \plan-TAYN\ *n.* A tree native to tropical regions bearing edible green bananalike fruit.

plaque \plak\ *n.* **1.** A commemorative tablet. **2.** A coating of bacteria on the teeth.

plasma \PLAZ-muh\ *n.* **1.** [Md] Blood and lymph fluid. **2.** [Sc] A gas of ionized particles. plasmatic *adj.*; plasmic *adj.*

plaster \PLAS-tur\ *n.* A thick,

gooey material that hardens. plaster *v.*

plastic \PLAS-tik\ *adj.* **1.** Flexible. **2.** Made of manufactured, treated compounds. **3.** Easily influenced. plastic *n.*; plasticity *n.*

plastic surgery *n.* (Md) The repair or reconstruction of body parts for improvement.

plate \playt\ *n.* **1.** A flat serving dish. **2.** A dish or meal served. **3.** A thin coating of metal.

plate \playt\ *v.* plated; plating. To coat, especially with a metallic material.

plate tectonics *n.* (Sc) The study of the moving plates in the Earth's surface.

plateau \pla-TOH\ *n. pl.* plateaus or plateaux. A flat, often high, land. plateau *v.*

platform \PLAT-form\ *n.* **1.** A stand or stage. **2.** A political stance or promise.

platinum \PLAT-n-um\ *n.* A white heavy precious metallic element.

platitude \PLAT-i-tood\ *n.* A dull, overused saying. platitudinal *adj.*; platitudinous *adj.*; platitudinously *adv.*

platonic \pluh-TON-ik\ *adj.* Expressing nonphysical love.

platoon \pluh-TOON\ *n.* A group of military people.

platter \PLAT-ur\ *n.* **1.** A large flat dish. **2.** A phonograph.

platypus \PLAT-i-pus\ *n. pl.* platypuses. A small, aquatic, egg-laying Australian mammal with a ducklike bill.

plausible \PLAW-zuh-bul\ *adj.* Believable.

play *n.* **1.** A theater piece. **2.** A form of amusement. **3.** A range.

play *v.* played; playing. **1.** Have fun. **2.** Compete in sport. **3.** To take part of. **4.** Gamble. **5.** Make music.

playful \PLAY-ful\ *adj.* Fun-loving.

play up *v.* To emphasize.

playwright \PLAY-riet\ *n.* A person who writes for theater.

plaza \PLAH-zuh\ *n.* A central location.

plea \plee\ *n.* **1.** A begging request. **2.** An excuse.

plea-bargain \PLEE-bar-gin\ *v.* (Le). To plead guilty to a lesser crime. plea bargain *n.*

plead \pleed\ *v.* pleaded; pleading. **1.** To beg. **2.** To present a defense.

pleasant \PLEZ-unt\ *adj.* Acceptable. pleasantly *adv.*; pleasantness *n.*

please \pleez\ *v.* pleased; pleasing. **1.** To delight. **2.** To elect to do. pleasing *adj.*; pleasingly *adv.*

pleasure \PLEZH-ur\ *n.* **1.** A delight. **2.** A will. pleasurable *adj.*; pleasurably *adv.*

plebeian \pli-BEE-un\ *n.* A person of lower class. plebeian *adj.*

plebiscite \PLEB-uh-site\ *n.* A vote on a proposal made by the citizens.

pledge \plej\ *n.* **1.** A word of honor. **2.** A sign of good faith. pledge *v.*

plenitude \PLEN-i-tood\ *n.* A large quantity of something. plenitudinous *adj.*

plenty \PLEN-tee\ *n.* An abundance. plentiful *adj.*; plentifully *adv.*

plenum \PLE-num\ *n. pl.* plenums or plena. **1.** A full assembly of a legislature or group. **2.** A filled space.

plethora \PLETH-ur-uh\ *n.* An excess.

plexus \PLEK-sus\ *n. pl.* plexus or plexuses. **1.** [Md] Interconnected nerves, blood vessels, or lymph vessels. **2.** A network.

plié \plee-AY\ *n.* A ballet move with the knees bent and the back straight.

pliers \PLIE-urs\ *pl. n.* A tool having adjustable jaws used for holding or bending something.

plod *v.* plodded; plodding. **1.** To walk heavily. **2.** To work slowly and under duress. ploddingly *adv.*; plodder *n.*

plot *n.* **1.** A plan. **2.** A story line. **3.** A tract of land.

plot *v.* plotted; plotting. **1.** To plan. **2.** To map out.

plow *n.* A vehicle equipped for breaking up soil and snow.

plow *v.* plowed; plowing. **1.** To dig up ground for cultivation. **2.** To remove snow. **3.** To work slowly.

ploy \ploi\ *n.* A game.

plug *n.* **1.** A stopper. **2.** A metal-pronged end of a cord that goes into an electrical outlet.

plum *n.* **1.** Fruit of any of various rose family trees. **2.** Something desirable.

plumber \PLUM-ur\ *n.* A person who repairs or assembles a water-supply system. plumbing *n.*

plummet \PLUM-it\ *v.* plummeted; plummeting. To fall hard and fast.

plump *adj.* Chubby.

plunder \PLUN-dur\ *v.* plundered; plundering. To steal. plunder *n.*; plunderer *n.*

plunge \plunj\ *v.* plunged; plunging. To dive or fall fast. plunge *n.*

plural \PLUUR-ul\ *adj.* More than one in number. plural *n.*

pluralism \PLUUR-uh-liz-um\ *n.* **1.** Being plural. **2.** Social community mixed religiously, racially, and ethnically.

plus *adj.* **1.** Positive. **2.** Added.

plus *n.* **1.** A sign indicating addition. **2.** A positive amount. **3.** A helpful factor.

plush *adj.* Luxurious.

Pluto \PLOO-toh\ *n.* The planet farthest from the Sun.

ply \plie\ *v.* plied; plying. **1.** To work at. **2.** To travel across a route regularly. **3.** To mold or twist.

pneumonia \nuu-MOHN-yuh\ *n.* (Md) A disease in which one or both of the lungs are inflamed.

pocket \POK-it\ *adj.* Portable.

pocket \POK-it\ *n.* **1.** A pouch. **2.** Region different from surrounding area.

pocket \POK-it\ *v.* To steal.

pockmarked \POK-mahrkt\ *adj.* Inscribed with holes or dents.

pod *n.* **1.** An encasement of vegetable seeds. **2.** A school of marine mammals.

podium \POH-dee-um\ *n.* A structure from which speakers orate.

poem \POH-um\ *n.* A highly expressive, rhythmical literary piece. poetry *n.*

poet \POH-it\ *n.* One who writes expressive, rhythmic verse. poetic *adj.*; poetical *adj.*; poetically *adv.*

pogrom \puh-GRUM\ *n.* An organized massacre, especially of the Jews. pogrom *v.*

poignant \POIN-yunt\ *adj.* **1.** Painful. **2.** Bitter. poignantly *adv.*; poignance *n.*; poignancy *n.*

poinsettia \poin-SET-ee-uh\ *n.* A shrub bearing showy scarlet leaves and yellow-green flowers.

point *n.* **1.** A speck. **2.** A sharp end. **3.** An area of land projecting into a body of water.

point *v.* pointed; pointing. **1.** To show as probable. **2.** To direct.

pointed \POIN-tid\ *adj.* **1.** Having a sharp end or part. **2.** Penetrating. **3.** Biting. pointedly *adv.*; pointedness *n.*

pointillism \POIN-til-iz-um\ *n.* Painting using tiny dots of color that blend together when viewed from afar. pointillist *adj.*; pointillist *n.*

poise \poiz\ *n.* **1.** A state of balance. **2.** A peaceful state of mind. **3.** Carriage of the head. poised *adj.*; poise *v.*

poison \POI-zun\ *n.* A harmful or fatal substance. poison *adj.*; poisonous *adj.*; poison *v.*

poke \pohk\ *n.* **1.** A thrust. **2.** A dawdler. **3.** The brim of a bonnet. **4.** A bag.

poke \pohk\ *v.* poked; poking. **1.** To push at, especially with a finger. **2.** To force one's way through a crowd.

polar \POH-lur\ *adj.* **1.** Opposite. **2.** Relating to the North or South Pole.

polarize \POH-luh-riez\ *v.* polarized; polarizing. **1.** To divide into two. **2.** To cause light rays to oscillate in a certain plane.

polemic \puh-LEM-ik\ *n.* **1.** Controversial opinion, esp. one opposing another. **2.** Controversial person. polemic or polemical *adj.*

polenta \poh-LEN-tuh\ *n.* A dish of boiled cornmeal.

police \puh-LEES\ *pl. n.* A governmental division charged with upholding law and order. police *v.*

police action *n.* A local military movement without formal declaration of war.

police state *n.* Government rule by suppressive police control.

policy \POL-uh-see\ *n. pl.* policies. A procedure.

polish \POL-ish\ *n.* **1.** A shine. **2.** Something used to shine a surface. **3.** Cultivated look, style. polish *v.*

polish off *v.* To consume.

polite \puh-LIET\ *adj.* politer; politest. Mannerly. politely *adv.*; politeness *n.*

political \puh-LIT-i-kul\ *adj.* **1.** Concerning governmental admin-istration. **2.** Concerning issues and policies. political *adj.*; politi-cally *adv.*

politically correct *adj.* Adhering to orthodox social beliefs.

politics \POL-i-tiks\ *n.* An art and science of administration of government. politician *n.*

polka \POHL-kuh\ *n.* **1.** Bohemian dance of three quick steps and a hop. **2.** [Mu] Music for this dance. polka *v.*

polka dot \POH-kuh-dot\ *n.* **1.** A pattern involving one or more rounded spots. **2.** One such rounded spot. polka-dot *adj.*; polka-dotted *adj.*

poll \pohl\ *n.* **1.** The casting of votes in an election. **2.** [Pl] A place where votes are cast. poll *v.*

pollute \puh-LOOT\ *v.* polluted; polluting. **1.** To make dirty. **2.** To corrupt. pollutant *n.*; pollution *n.*

polychrome \pol-ee-KROME\ *adj.* Having or in many colors. poly-chrome *n.*

polyester \POL-ee-es-tur\ *n.* A synthetic fiber or polymer. polyester *adj.*

polygamy \puh-LIG-uh-mee\ *n.* The practice of having more than one spouse at a time. polygamous *adj.*; polygamist *n.*

polyglot \POL-ee-glot\ *adj.* Knowing or using several languages. polyglot *n.*; polyglotism *n.*

polytheism \POL-ee-thee-iz-um\ *n.* A belief in or worship of more than one god. polytheistic *adj.*; polytheist *n.*

polyunsaturated \pol-ee-un-SACH-uh-ray-tid\ *adj.* Having unsaturated double chemical bonds, as in an oil or fat.

pomp *n.* A showy display.

pompadour \POM-puh-dor\ *n.* A hairstyle in which the hair is raised high up and back off the forehead.

pompous \POM-pus\ *adj.* **1.** Arrogant. **2.** Characterized by excessive display. pompously *adv.*; pompousness *n.*

poncho \PON-choh\ *n. pl.* ponchos. A blanketlike cloak having a slit in the middle for placing it over the head.

pond *n.* A small body of water.

ponder \PON-dur\ *v.* pondered; pondering. To think about seriously.

ponderous \PON-dur-us\ *adj.* Characterized by excessive weight.

pontiff \PON-tif\ *n.* **1.** The pope. **2.** A bishop.

pontificate \pon-TIF-i-kayt\ *n.* A pontiff's term.

pontificate \pon-TIF-i-kayt\ *v.* pontificated; pontificating. **1.** To speak dogmatically. **2.** To manage a pontiff's office. pontification *n.*; pontificator *n.*

pooch *n.* A dog.

poodle \POO-dl\ *n.* A breed of dog having a curly coat.

pool *n.* **1.** Collection of water, especially for swimming. **2.** A supply of money or goods.

pool *v.* pooled; pooling. To combine.

poor \puur\ *adj.* poorer; poorest. **1.** Lacking sufficient money. **2.** Inadequate. **3.** Weak. **4.** Unfortunate. poorly *adv.*

pop *n.* **1.** A bang. **2.** [Sl] A soda.

pop *v.* popped; popping. **1.** To emit an explosive sound. **2.** To cause to explode. **3.** To expand suddenly.

pop art *n.* A modern art style appropriating everyday objects and images. pop artist *n.*

poplar \POP-lur\ *n.* A slender, fast-growing tree of the willow family.

poplin \POP-lin\ *n.* A plain, woven, corded fabric.

populace \POP-yuh-lus\ *n.* **1.** The common people. **2.** The population.

popular \POP-yuh-lur\ *adj.* **1.** Well-known. **2.** Favored. **3.** Common. **popularly** *adv.*; **popularity** *n.*; **popularize** *v.*

population \pop-yuh-LAY-shun\ *n.* The inhabitants of a place. **populous** *adj.*; **populace** *n.*; **populate** *v.*

population explosion A rapid increase in the number of inhabitants of a place.

populism \POP-yuh-liz-um\ *n.* A political philosophy promoting the common people. **populist** *adj.*; **populist** *n.*

pop-up *adj.* Having parts that become visible when activated; three-dimensional. **pop-up** *n.*

porcupine \POR-kyuh-pine\ *n.* A chubby rodent covered with stiff, sharp spines.

pore \por\ *n.* **1.** A small opening in skin. **2.** A space in rock or soil. **porous** *adj.*; **porousness** *n.*

pore \por\ *v.* pored; poring. To go over carefully.

pornography \por-NOG-ruh-fee\ *n.* Explicit sexual activity in pictures or literature. **pornographic** *adj.*; **pornographically** *adv.*; **pornographer** *n.*

porpoise \POR-pus\ *n.* A blunt-nosed sea mammal of the whale family.

port *n.* **1.** Place for boat docking and storage. **2.** A city with a harbor.

port *v.* ported; porting. **1.** To turn a boat or vehicle to the left. **2.** To transport or transmit.

portable \POR-tuh-bul\ *adj.* Easily transported.

portend \por-TEND\ *v.* portended; portending. To foreshadow.

portent \POR-tent\ *n.* **1.** A forewarning. **2.** A miracle. **portentous** *adj.*; **portentously** *adv.*; **portentousness** *n.*

portico \POR-ti-koh\ *n. pl.* porticos or porticoes. An entranceway preceded by a column-supported roof.

portion \POR-shun\ *n.* **1.** A share of something. **2.** A destiny. **portion** *v.*

portly \PORT-lee\ *adj.* portlier; portliest. Bulky. **portliness** *n.*

portrait \POR-trit\ *n.* **1.** A representation, esp. of the human face. **2.** Vivid description. **portraitist** *n.*; **portraiture** *n.*

portray \por-TRAY\ *v.* portrayed; portraying. To represent. **portrayal** *n.*

pose \pohz\ *v.* posed; posing. **1.** To sit or stand in place. **2.** To assume a fake position. **3.** To ask. **pose** *n.*

posh *adj.* **1.** Luxurious. **2.** Exclusive. **poshly** *adv.*; **poshness** *n.*

position \puh-ZISH-un\ *n.* **1.** Physical place. **2.** Posture. **3.** A point of view. **4.** A stature. **5.** Response. **position** *v.*

positive \POZ-i-tiv\ *adj.* **1.** Definite. **2.** Beneficial. **3.** Pertaining to an amount greater than zero.

posse \POS-ee\ *n.* **1.** A body of people organized to assist lawmen. **2.** [Sl] One's friends.

possess \puh-ZES\ *v.* possessed; possessing. **1.** To own. **2.** To obtain. **3.** To place under a spell.

possession \puh-ZESH-un\ *n.* **1.** An ownership. **2.** A property.

possible \POS-uh-bul\ *adj.* Likely. possibly *adv.*; possibility *n.*

post \pohst\ *n.* **1.** An upright support. **2.** A job. **3.** A lookout. **4.** The mail service.

post \pohst\ *v.* posted; posting. **1.** To situate. **2.** To advise.

postal \POHS-tl\ *adj.* Of or concerning the post office or mail.

poster \POH-stur\ *n.* A large paper advertisement.

posterior \po-STEER-ee-ur\ *adj.* **1.** Rear. **2.** Subsequent. posterior *n.*

posterity \po-STER-i-tee\ *n.* The future generations.

postfeminist \POHST\ *adj.* Of or concerning the period after the 1970s' feminist movement.

postmodern *also* **post-modern** \POHST\ *adj.* Relating to a rebellion against modernism. postmodernist *adj.*; postmodernism *n.*; postmodernist *n.*

postmortem \pohst-MOR-tum\ *adj.* Following death. postmortem *n.*

post office *n.* **1.** A system for the handling of mail services. **2.** Buildings for this system.

postulate \POS-chuh-layt\ *v.* postulated; postulating. To suppose. postulate *n.*; postulation *n.*

posture \POS-chur\ *n.* **1.** A way of carrying the body. **2.** An attitude.

posture \POS-chur\ *v.* postured; posturing. **1.** To adopt a pose. **2.** To display an attitude.

pot *n.* **1.** A container. **2.** A game fund. **3.** [Sl] Marijuana. **4.** [Sl] A toilet.

pot *v.* potted; potting. To plant in a container.

potato \puh-TAY-toh\ *n. pl.* potatoes. A starchy tuber plant and its vegetable.

potent \POHT-nt\ *adj.* **1.** Effective. **2.** Powerful. **3.** Sexually able, as used to describe a male. potency *n.*

potential \puh-TEN-shul\ *n.* A possibility for achievement. potential *adj.*; potentially *adv.*; potentiality *n.*

potion \POH-shun\ *n.* A concoction prepared for mental or physical effect.

potpourri \poh-puu-REE\ *n.* A miscellaneous assortment.

pottery \POT-uh-ree\ *n. pl.* potter-ies. Containers made from moist-ened clay and hardened with heat. potter *n.*

pouch \powch\ *n.* **1.** A soft con-tainer, esp. cloth or skin. **2.** A pocketlike space in a marsupial.

poultice \POHL-tis\ *n.* A med-icated, heated mass applied to a wound or sore spot. poultice *v.*

poultry \POHL-tree\ *n.* Domestic birds raised for food.

pounce \powns\ *v.* pounced; pounc-ing. **1.** To leap at. **2.** To take by surprise. pounce *n.*

pound \pownd\ *n.* **1.** A weight mea-surement equal to 16 ounces or .454 kilograms. **2.** A heavy hit.

pound \pownd\ *v.* pounded; pound-ing. **1.** To beat; palpitate. **2.** To make someone listen. **3.** To move along noisily.

pour \por\ *v.* poured; pouring. To be or make flowing. pour *n.*

pout \powt\ *v.* pouted; pouting. To make a sad face. pouty *adj.*; pout *n.*

poverty \POV-ur-tee\ *n.* The state of being deficient, especially in money. poverty-stricken *adj.*

powder \POW-dur\ *n.* Fine, loose grains made by crushing a solid. powdery *adj.*

powder \POW-dur\ *v.* powdered;

powdering. **1.** To crush into fine, loose grains. **2.** To dust with a fine substance. powdery *adj.*

power \POW-ur\ *n.* **1.** An ability. **2.** A control. **3.** A physical capacity. powerful *adj.*; powerfully *adv.*

power-hungry *adj.* Excessively greedy about attaining power.

powerless \POW-ur-lis\ *adj.* **1.** Lacking control. **2.** Absent of mental or physical capabilities.

power structure *n.* The system of authority within an organization.

powwow \POW-wow\ *n.* A discus-sion. powwow *v.*

practical \PRAK-ti-kul\ *adj.* **1.** Use-ful. **2.** Experienced. **3.** Rational. practically *adv.*; practicality *n.*

practice \PRAK-tis\ *n.* **1.** A routine. **2.** An exercise. **3.** A business. practice *v.*

pragmatic \prag-MAT-ik\ *adj.* Sen-sible. pragmatical *adj.*; pragmati-cally *adv.*; pragmatism *n.*; pragmatist *n.*

prairie \PRAIR-ee\ *n.* A large area of treeless grassland.

praise \prayz\ *v.* praised; praising. To congratulate. praise *n.*

praiseworthy \PRAYZ-wur-thee\ *adj.* Deserving congratulations.

praline \pruh-LEEN\ *n.* A confec-tion made of carmelized nuts and sugar.

prank \prangk\ *n.* A playful trick or joke.

pray *v.* prayed; praying. To ask earnestly for, especially of God.

prayer \prair\ *n.* **1.** Earnest request, esp. of God. **2.** A religious service.

preach \preech\ *v.* preached; preaching. **1.** To give a sermon. **2.** To give moral advice insistently. preacher *n.*

precarious \pri-KAIR-ee-us\ *adj.* Uncertain or insecure. precariously *adv.*; precariousness *n.*

precaution \pri-KAW-shun\ *n.* An act done to prevent harm or seek a good result. precautionary *adj.*

precede \pri-SEED\ *v.* preceded; preceding. To come or go before in time, order, or importance.

precedence \PRE-i-duns\ *n.* A priority in time, order, or importance.

precedent \PRES-i-dunt\ *n.* **1.** [Le] A judicial decision used as a guide for subsequent cases. **2.** A custom. precedent *adj.*; precedential *adj.*

precinct \PREE-singkt\ *n.* A district, especially one delineated for purposes of police protection.

precious \PRESH-us\ *adj.* **1.** Very special or of great worth. **2.** Considerable. preciousness *n.*

precipitate \pri-SIP-i-tayt\ *v.* precipitated; precipitating. **1.** To cause to start abruptly. **2.** To cause to rain, snow, sleet, or hail. precipitation *n.*

precise \pri-SIES\ *adj.* **1.** Clearly defined. **2.** Accurate. **3.** Exact. precisely *adv.*; preciseness *n.*; precision *n.*

preclude \pri-KLOOD\ *v.* precluded; precluding. To make impossible. preclusive *adj.*; preclusively *adv.*; preclusion *n.*

preconceive \pree-kun-SEEV\ *v.* preconceived; preconceiving. To form an opinion or idea beforehand. preconception *n.*

precursor \pri-KUR-sur\ *n.* A forerunner of something to come. precursory *adj.*

predator \PRED-uh-tur\ *n.* An animal that hunts other animals. predatory *adj.*; predatoriness *n.*

predecessor \PRED-uh-ses-ur\ *n.* **1.** Something that has been replaced by another. **2.** A former holder of office.

predicament \pri-DIK-uh-munt\ *n.* A difficult or unpleasant situation.

predict \pri-DIKT\ *v.* predicted; predicting. To foretell. predictable *adj.*; prediction *n.*

predominant \pri-DOM-uh-nunt\ *adj.* Being the strongest or most important. predominantly *adv.*; predominance *n.*

preeminent \pree-EM-uh-nunt\ *adj.* Being superior to all others. preeminently *adv.*; preeminence *n.*

preempt \pree-EMPT\ *v.* preempted; preempting. **1.** To take the place of. **2.** To seize first. preemptory *adj.*; preemption *n.*

preface \PREF-is\ *n.* An introduction. prefatory *adj.*; preface *v.*

prefect \PREE-fekt\ *n.* A chief administrative officer or person of authority.

prefer \pri-FUR\ *v.* preferred; preferring. To favor. preferable *adj.*; preference *n.*

prefix \PREE-fiks\ *n.* A group of letters at the beginning of a word that contributes to the meaning. prefix *v.*

pregnant \PREG-nunt\ *adj.* **1.** Containing a maturing baby. **2.** Full. **3.** Creative. pregnancy *n.*

prejudice \PREJ-uh-dis\ *n.* **1.** A judgment formed before knowing the facts. **2.** Dislike for a group. prejudiced *adj.*; prejudicious *adj.*; prejudicially *adv.*; prejudiciously *adv.*

preliminary \pri-LIM-uh-nar-ee\ *adj.* Introductory. preliminary *n.*

prelude \PREL-yood\ *n.* **1.** An in-troduction. **2.** [Mu] A short, freestyle composition played on the piano. prelude *v.*

premarital \pree-MAR-i-tul\ *adj.* Occurring before marriage.

premature \pree-muh-CHUUR\ *adj.* Occurring before the proper time. prematurely *adv.*; prematureness *n.*

premeditated \pri-MED-i-tay-tud\ *adj.* Planned in advance. premeditative *adj.*; premeditatedly *adv.*; premeditation *n.*

premier \pri-MEER\ *adj.* **1.** First in rank. **2.** Occurring earliest.

premier \pri-MEER\ *n.* A prime minister or other head of government. premiership *n.*

premiere \pri-MEER\ *n.* A first performance or showing. premiere *v.*

premise \PREM-is\ *n.* **1.** Grounds for an argument. **2.** Land with property.

premium \PREE-mee-um\ *n.* **1.** A sum paid for insurance. **2.** Something paid over the value. **3.** A reward.

premonition \pree-muh-NISH-un\ *n.* A forewarning. premonitory *adj.*

preoccupied \pree-OK-yuh-pied\ *adj.* **1.** Mentally or physically distracted. **2.** Already in use. preoccupation *n.*; preoccupy *v.*

prepare \pri-PAIR\ *v.* prepared;

preparing. **1.** To get ready. **2.** To assemble, esp. in cooking. **3.** To equip. preparedly *adv.*; preparation *n.*; preparedness *n.*

preposterous \pri-POS-tur-us\ *adj.* Utterly absurd. preposterously *adv.*; preposterousness *n.*

preppy *also* **preppie** \PREP-ee\ *n. pl.* preppies. (Sl) **1.** Attendee of preparatory school. **2.** One who dresses or acts like such. preppily *adv.*; preppiness *n.*

prep school *n.* A private school.

prerequisite \pri-REK-wuh-zit\ *n.* Something required beforehand. prerequisite *adj.*

prerogative \pri-ROG-uh-tiv\ *n.* An exclusive right or privilege.

prescribe \pri-SKRIEB\ *v.* prescribed; prescribing. **1.** To advise the use of a medicine, etc. **2.** To lay down as a rule.

prescription \pri-SKRIP-shun\ *n.* **1.** A written instruction for use, as for medicine. **2.** The medicine prescribed.

presence \PREZ-uns\ *n.* **1.** The state of being present. **2.** A person's demeanor. **3.** One's state of mind.

present \PREZ-unt\ *adj.* **1.** Being at hand. **2.** Existing now. **3.** Expressing a current action, in grammar. presently *adv.*

present \PREZ-unt\ *n.* **1.** A gift. **2.** The current time. **3.** A verb expressing a current action.

present \pri-ZENT\ *v.* presented; presenting. **1.** To introduce. **2.** To give or offer as a gift. **3.** To offer for display. presentation *n.*; presenter *n.*

preserve \pri-ZURV\ *v.* preserved; preserving. **1.** To keep safe. **2.** To maintain a condition. **3.** To prepare to prevent spoilage. preservation *n.*

preserves \pri-ZURVZ\ *pl. n.* **1.** Fruit prepared for canning. **2.** Protected wildlife area.

preset \PREE-set\ *v.* preset; presetting. To set in advance.

preside \pri-ZIED\ *v.* presided; presiding. **1.** To be the leader of a meeting. **2.** To exercise control or authority. presider *n.*

president \PREZ-i-dunt\ *n.* **1.** A person appointed chief of state. **2.** An organization's chief officer. presidential *adj.*; presidency *n.*

presidio \pri-SID-ee-oh\ *n. pl.* presidios. (Sp) A military post.

press \pres\ *n.* **1.** Machine that squeezes or applies force. **2.** A printing machine. **3.** The media.

press \pres\ *v.* pressed; pressing. **1.** To push on with force. **2.** To iron. **3.** To squeeze. **4.** To pressure. **5.** To hug.

pressing \PRES-ing\ *adj.* Urgent. pressingly *adv.*

pressure \PRESH-ur\ *n.* **1.** A force upon something. **2.** Physical or mental stress. **3.** An urgency. pressure *v.*

prestige \pre-STEEZH\ *n.* Respect or good reputation. prestigious *adj.*; prestigiously *adv.*; prestigiousness *n.*

presto \PRES-toh\ *adv.* **1.** Immediately. **2.** [Mu] In a fast tempo. presto *adj.*

presume \pri-ZOOM\ *v.* presumed; presuming. **1.** To take for granted. **2.** To take the liberty of. presumable *adj.*; presumedly *adv.*; presumingly *adv.*

pretend \pri-TEND\ *v.* pretended; pretending. **1.** To deceive. **2.** To make believe. **3.** To fake. pretender *n.*

pretense \pri-TENS\ *n.* **1.** A false claim. **2.** A false show. **3.** Something created. **4.** Pretending act.

pretentious \pri-TEN-shus\ *adj.* **1.** Making a false claim. **2.** Being ostentatious. pretentiously *adv.*; pretentiousness *n.*

pretzel \PRET-sul\ *n.* A baked good that is often brittle, salted, and in a twisted shape.

prevail \pri-VAYL\ *v.* prevailed; prevailing. **1.** To be triumphant. **2.**

To be predominant. **3.** To exist in general use. prevailingly *adv.*

prevalent \PREV-uh-lunt\ *adj.* Generally existing or practiced. prevalently *adv.*; prevalence *n.*

prevent \pri-VENT\ *v.* prevented; preventing. **1.** To stop from happening. **2.** To make impossible. preventable *adj.*; preventative *adj.*; preventible *adj.*; preventive *adj.*; preventer *n.*

preview *also* **prevue** \PREE-vyoo\ *n.* An advance showing of a performance, movie, or exhibition. preview or prevue *v.*

prey \pray\ *n.* An animal hunted or killed by another for food. prey *v.*

price \pries\ *n.* **1.** Money for which something is bought or sold. **2.** Cost of obtaining. **3.** Value.

price \pries\ *v.* priced; pricing. **1.** To ask as to cost. **2.** To shop for the lowest cost.

priceless \PRIES-lis\ *adj.* **1.** Invaluable. **2.** Very funny. pricelessly *adv.*; pricelessness *n.*

prick \prik\ *v.* pricked; pricking. **1.** To pierce slightly. **2.** To bother. **3.** To tingle. prick *n.*

pride \pried\ *n.* **1.** Self-respect. **2.** Satisfaction with one's achievements, qualities, etc. prick *n.*

priest \preest\ *n.* An ordained minister in a Catholic or Orthodox church. priestly *adj.*

prim *adj.* primmer; primmest. **1.** Excessively proper. **2.** Very neat. **3.** Prudish. primly *adv.*; primness *n.*

prima ballerina \PREE-muh\ *n.* A ballet company's principal female dancer.

prima donna \PREE-muh-DON-uh\ *n.* **1.** An extremely fussy person. **2.** [Mu] The principal female singer in a musical.

primal \PRIE-mul\ *adj.* **1.** Primitive. **2.** Fundamental.

primal scream therapy *n.* A form of psychotherapy in which the patient is encouraged to scream.

primary \PRIE-mer-ee\ *adj.* **1.** Most important. **2.** Earliest. **3.** First in rank or order. **4.** Fundamental.

primary \PRIE-mer-ee\ *n.* **1.** Preliminary election within a political party. **2.** Three basic colors.

primate \PRIE-mayt\ *n.* **1.** Order of mammals including man, apes, etc. **2.** Highest prelate in rank.

prime \priem\ *adj.* **1.** Most important. **2.** Fundamental. **3.** Divisable only by itself.

prime \priem\ *n.* **1.** Earliest part. **2.** Age of physical, mental perfection. **3.** Indivisible number.

prime \priem\ *v.* primed; priming. To prepare or equip for use.

primeval *also* **primaeval** \prie-MEE-vul\ *adj.* Relating to the ancient ages. primevally *adv.*

primitive \PRIM-i-tiv\ *adj.* **1.** Relating an early stage of progress. **2.** Lacking sophistication. primitively *adv.*; primitive *n.*; primitiveness *n.*; primitivity *n.*

prince \prins\ *n.* **1.** Royal family male who is not king. **2.** Male monarch. **3.** One of highest rank. princely *adj.*

princess \PRIN-sis\ *n.* **1.** A female of a royal family who is not queen. **2.** The wife of a prince.

principal \PRIN-suh-pul\ *adj.* Most important. principally *adv.*

principal \PRIN-suh-pul\ *n.* **1.** Head of an institution, esp. a school. **2.** A central actor in a piece.

principality \prin-suh-PAL-i-tee\ *n. pl.* principalities. A territory ruled by a prince.

principle \PRIN-suh-pul\ *n.* **1.** A fundamental truth. **2.** A personal code of conduct. **3.** A source.

print *n.* **1.** Mark made by pressure. **2.** Written material. **3.** Photograph or image.

print *v.* printed; printing. **1.** To put words or pictures on paper. **2.** To publish. **3.** To make photographs.

printing press *n.* A machine for reproducing writing and photos.

prior \PRIE-ur\ *adj.* Earlier in order or importance.

prior \PRIE-ur\ *n.* A superior in a religious order.

prison \PRIZ-un\ *n.* A place of captivity.

prissy \PRIS-ee\ *adj.* prissier; prissiest. Overly neat and proper. prissily *adv.*; prissiness *n.*

private \PRIE-vit\ *adj.* **1.** Belonging to an individual. **2.** Confidential. **3.** Not open to the public. privately *adv.*; privacy *n.*

private \PRIE-vit\ *n.* An enlisted man of the lowest rank.

privilege \PRIV-uh-lij\ *n.* A right granted to one or more people. privileged *adj.*; privilege *v.*

privy \PRIV-ee\ *adj.* **1.** Being in on something secret. **2.** Secret.

prize \priez\ *n.* **1.** Something won in a competition. **2.** Something very desirable.

prize \priez\ *v.* prized; prizing. To cherish highly.

pro \proh\ *adv.* In favor.

pro \proh\ *n. pl.* pros. **1.** Professional. **2.** An argument favoring something. **3.** Expert.

pro-abortion *adj.* Supporting the legal right to an abortion. proabortionist *n.*

probable \PROB-uh-bul\ *adj.* **1.** Expected to happen. **2.** Likely to be true. probably *adv.*; probability *n.*

probe \prohb\ *n.* **1.** Instrument for an intensive examination. **2.** An exploratory spacecraft. probingly *adv.*; probe *v.*

problem \PROB-lum\ *adj.* **1.** Irritating. **2.** Confronting a moral or social dilemma. problematic *adj;* problematically *adv.*

problem \PROB-lum\ *n.* **1.** A question needing a solution. **2.** A source of irritation or puzzlement.

procedure \pruh-SEE-jur\ *n.* **1.** Particular way of doing something. **2.** Method of doing business, etc. procedural *adj.*

proceed \pruh-SEED\ *v.* proceeded; proceeding. **1.** To go forward. **2.** To continue on. **3.** To issue forth. **4.** [Le] File a lawsuit.

proceeding \pruh-SEE-ding\ *n.* **1.** A mode of action. **2.** [Pl] Record of discussions. **3.** [Pl] Court action.

proceeds \PROH-seedz\ *pl. n.* The profit or return from a sale or fundraiser.

process \PROS-es\ *n. pl.* processes. **1.** A course of action. **2.** Forward movement. **3.** [Le] Judicial writ.

process \PROS-es\ *v.* **1.** To go through a procedure. **2.** [Le]. To serve with a court summons. **3.** Prepare.

procession \pruh-SESH-un\ *n.* A group advancing in an orderly manner.

pro-choice *adj.* Supporting a woman's legal right to choose whether or not to have an abortion.

proclaim \proh-KLAYM\ *v.* proclaimed; proclaiming. **1.** To announce publicly. **2.** To commend. proclamatory *adj.*; proclaimer *n.*; proclamation *n.*

procrastinate \proh-KRAS-tuh-nayt\ *v.* procrastinated; procrastinating. To defer action. procrastination *n.*; procrastinator *n.*

procreate \PROH-kree-ayt\ *v.* procreated; procreating. To produce offspring naturally. procreative *adj.*; procreation *n.*; procreator *n.*

proctology \prok-TOL-uh-jee\ *n.* (Md) The branch of medicine caring for the colon, rectum, and anus. proctologist *n.*

procure \proh-KYUUR\ *v.* procured; procuring. **1.** To acquire through effort. **2.** To bring about. **3.** To get for another. procurement *n.*

prod *v.* prodded; prodding. **1.** To poke with something. **2.** To incite. prod *n.*; prodder *n.*

prodigious \pruh-DIJ-us\ *adj.* **1.** Amazing. **2.** Enormous. prodigiously *adv.*; prodigiousness *n.*

prodigy \PROD-i-jee\ *n. pl.* prodigies. **1.** Exceptionally gifted person, especially a child. **2.** An extraordinary thing.

produce \PROD-oos\ *n.* **1.** Goods yielded. **2.** Fresh fruit and vegetables.

produce \pruh-DOOS\ *v.* produced; producing. **1.** To bring about. **2.** To create. **3.** To present to an audience.

product \PROD-ukt\ *n.* **1.** Something made for use. **2.** A result.

production \pruh-DUK-shun\ *n.* **1.** The preparing of goods. **2.** The goods prepared. **3.** A supervised performance.

productive \pruh-DUK-tiv\ *adj.* **1.** Bringing forth or capable of bringing forth. **2.** Producing abundantly. productively *adv.*; productiveness *n.*; productivity *n.*

profane \proh-FAYN\ *adj.* **1.** Irreverent. **2.** Obscene. profanely *adv.*; profaneness *n.*; profanity *n.*; profane *v.*

profess \pruh-FES\ *v.* professed; professing. **1.** To claim openly. **2.** To pretend. **3.** To affirm belief in. professedly *adv.*

profession \pruh-FESH-un\ *n.* **1.** A vocation. **2.** The people working at a certain occupation. **3.** A declaration.

professional \pruh-FESH-uh-nl\ *adj.* **1.** Relating to a vocation. **2.** Done by paid experts. **3.** Skillful and competent. professionally *adv.*; professional *n.*; professionalism *n.*

professor \pruh-FES-ur\ *n.* A university or college teacher. professorial *adj.*; professorship *n.*

proficient \pruh-FISH-unt\ *adj.* Marked by advanced expertise. proficiently *adv.*; proficiency *n.*; proficient *n.*

profile \PROH-fiel\ *n.* **1.** An outline, as of the face. **2.** A short biography. profile *v.*

profit \PROF-it\ *n.* **1.** A beneficial gain. **2.** The financial yield of a business venture. profitable *adj.*; profitably *adv.*; profitability *n.*; profitableness *n.*; profit *v.*

profound \pruh-FOWND\ *adj.* profounder; profoundest. **1.** Having or requiring great knowledge. **2.** Intense and thorough. **3.** Deep. profoundly *adv.*; profoundness *n.*; profundity *n.*

profuse \pruh-FYOOS\ *adj.* **1.** Abundant. **2.** Generous. profusely *adv.*; profuseness *n.*; profusion *n.*

progeny \PROJ-uh-nee\ *n. pl.* progenies. **1.** A child. **2.** One's offspring. **3.** A product yielded through creative effort.

prognosis \prog-NOH-sis\ *n. pl.* prognoses. **1.** A forecast. **2.** [Md] The likely outcome of an illness.

program \PROH-gram\ *n.* **1.** A list of events or performers. **2.** A radio or TV broadcast. **3.** An agenda.

program \PROH-gram\ *v.* programmed; programming. **1.** To include in an event or procedure. **2.** To plan the activities of.

progress \PROG-res\ *n.* **1.** A forward movement. **2.** A gradual improvement.

progress \pruh-GRES\ *v.* progressed; progressing. **1.** To move forward. **2.** To improve gradually.

progressive \pruh-GRES-iv\ *adj.* **1.** Moving forward. **2.** Improving gradually. **3.** Favoring rapid change.

prohibit \proh-HIB-it\ *v.* prohibited; prohibiting. **1.** To forbid. **2.** To prevent. prohibitive *adj.*; prohibitory *adj.*; prohibitively *adv.*; prohibitiveness *n.*

project \PROJ-ekt\ *n.* **1.** A plan. **2.** An undertaking needing organized effort. **3.** A housing development.

project \pruh-JEKT\ *v.* projected; projecting. **1.** To jut out. **2.** To cast forward. **3.** To show on a surface. **4.** To propose.

projectile \pruh-JEK-tile\ *n.* Something fired, as a missile or bullet. projectile *adj.*

projection \pruh-JEK-shun\ *n.* **1.** Something over a line or surface. **2.** Something cast forward. **3.** An image. projectile *adj.*

prolapse *also* **prolapsus** \proh-LAPS\ *n.* (Md) A part or organ that is displaced. prolapse *v.*

proletarian \proh-li-TAIR-ee-un\ *n.* A member of the working class. proletarian *adj.*; proletariat *n.*

pro-life \proh-lief\ *adj.* Supporting the legal protection of unborn children, esp. by opposing abortion.

proliferate \pruh-LIF-uh-rayt\ *v.* proliferated; proliferating. **1.** To expand or reproduce. **2.** To increase.

prolong \proh-LAWNG\ *v.* prolonged; prolonging. To extend. prolonged *adj.*; prolongation *n.*

promenade \prom-uh-NAYD\ *n.* **1.** A public walkway. **2.** A stroll. **3.** A grand march at the opening of a ball. promenade *v.*

prominent \PROM-uh-nunt\ *adj.* **1.** Jutting out. **2.** Obvious. **3.** Famous. prominently *adv.*; prominence *n.*

promiscuous \pruh-MIS-kyoo-us\ *adj.* **1.** Having frequent casual sexual relations. **2.** Not restricted.

promiscuously *adv.*; promiscuity *n.*; promiscuousness *n.*

promise \PROM-is\ *n.* **1.** A pledge. **2.** Something pledged. **3.** A sign of good results.

promise \PROM-is\ *v.* promised; promising. **1.** To pledge. **2.** To give grounds for expectation.

promising \PROM-uh-sing\ *adj.* Hopeful. promisingly *adv.*

promote \pruh-MOHT\ *v.* promoted; promoting. **1.** To raise to a higher office or rank. **2.** To encourage progress or growth. promisingly *adv.*

prompt *adj.* prompter; promptest. **1.** On time. **2.** Carried out immediately. promptly *adv.*; promptness *n.*

prompt *n.* **1.** The process of reminding. **2.** [Cm] Computer reminder of place.

prompt *v.* prompted; prompting. **1.** To urge to action. **2.** To remind. **3.** To assist. prompter *n.*

prone \prohn\ *adj.* **1.** Lying face down. **2.** Likely or liable. pronely *adv.*; proneness *n.*

pronounce \pruh-NOWNS\ *v.* pronounced; pronouncing. **1.** To say in an approved way. **2.** State phonetically. **3.** To proclaim officially. pronounceable *adj.*; pronunciation *n.*

pronto \PRON-toh\ *adv.* (Sl) Immediately.

pronunciation \pruh-nun-see-AY-shun\ *n.* **1.** Saying of a word; approved way of saying it. **2.** The phonetic respelling.

proof *n.* **1.** Evidence establishing proof. **2.** Methodical solving of a problem.

prop *n.* **1.** A rigid support. **2.** Property, as in a theatrical production. prop *v.*

propaganda \prop-uh-GAN-duh\ *n.* Publicity of selected information for a cause. propagandistic *adj.*; propagandistically *adv.*; propagandist *n.*; propagandize *v.*

propagate \PROP-uh-gayt\ *v.* propagated; propagating. **1.** To breed from a parent. **2.** To reproduce itself. **3.** To cause to spread. propagation *n.*

propel \pruh-PEL\ *v.* propelled; propelling. To push forward.

propeller *also* **propellor** \pruh-PEL-ur\ *n.* A revolving, bladed shaft for moving a vehicle.

proper \PROP-ur\ *adj.* **1.** Appropriate. **2.** Correct. **3.** Adhering to rules, conventions. **4.** Belonging to. properly *adv.*; properness *n.*

property \PROP-ur-tee\ *n. pl.* properties. **1.** A thing or things owned. **2.** A characteristic trait.

prophecy \PROF-uh-see\ *n. pl.* prophecies. A foretelling. prophesy *v.*

prophet \PROF-it\ *n.* **1.** A person who foretells. **2.** An advocate. prophetic *adj.*

prophylaxis \proh-fuh-LAK-sis\ *n. pl.* prophylaxes. (Md) A preventive or protective treatment against disease.

proponent \pruh-POH-nunt\ *n.* An advocate.

proportion \pruh-POR-shun\ *n.* **1.** A portion. **2.** A ratio of a part to the whole. **3.** A symmetry. proportional *adj.*; proportionate *adj.*; proportionally *adv.*; proportion *v.*

propose \pruh-POHZ\ *v.* proposed; proposing. **1.** To suggest. **2.** To plan. **3.** To offer oneself in marriage. **4.** To nominate. proposal *n.*; proposer *n.*

proposition \prop-uh-ZISH-un\ *n.* **1.** Something offered for consideration. **2.** An undertaking. **3.** Indecent request. propositional *adj.*; proposition *v.*

proprietor \pruh-PRIE-i-tur\ *n.* An owner. proprietorial *adj.*; proprietorially *adv.*; proprietorship *n.*

prosciutto \prosh-YUU-toh\ *n. pl.* prosciutti or prosciuttos. (It) A thinly sliced, salted ham.

prose \prohz\ *n.* Unmetered writing.

prosecute \PROS-i-kyoot\ *v.* prosecuted; prosecuting. **1.** [Le]. To start legal proceedings against. **2.** To follow through. prosecution *n.*; prosecutor *n.*

prospect \PROS-pekt\ *n.* **1.** An expectation. **2.** A potential customer. **3.** An extensive view. **4.** Looking.

prospect \PROS-pekt\ *v.* prospected; prospecting. To search for gold. prospector *n.*

prospective \pruh-SPEK-tiv\ *adj.* Expected to be. prospectively *adv.*

prospectus \pruh-SPEK-tus\ *n. pl.* prospectuses. A document describing an institution or enterprise.

prosper \PROS-pur\ *v.* prospered; prospering. To attain success. prosperous *adj.*; prosperously *adv.*; prosperity *n.*

prostate gland \PROS-tayt\ *n.* A gland in the bladder of male mammals important for the production of semen.

prostitute \PROS-ti-toot\ *n.* **1.** A person who engages in sex for payment. **2.** Ingratiating person. prostitution *n.*; prostitute *v.*

prostrate \PROS-trayt\ *adj.* **1.** Lying face down. **2.** Physically or emotionally rendered unable. prostration *n.*; prostrate *v.*

protagonist \proh-TAG-uh-nist\ *n.* **1.** The main dramatic character. **2.** An advocate.

protect \proh-TEKT\ *v.* protected; protecting. To keep from harm. protective *adj.*; protectively *adv.*; protection *n.*; protector *n.*

protégé \PROH-tuh-zhay\ *n.* A person under the protection or guidance of another. protégée *n.*

protein \PROH-teen\ *n.* A complex organic compound made of amino acid chains.

protest \PROH-test\ *v.* protested; protesting. To oppose strongly. protest *n.*; protestation *n.*; protester *n.*

protocol \PROH-tuh-kawl\ *n.* **1.** Official moral conduct. **2.** An original draft. **3.** Procedure to be followed.

prototype \PROH-tuh-tipe\ *n.* **1.** An original that stands as a model. **2.** A primitive example. prototypal *adj.*; prototypic *adj.*; prototypical *adj.*

protract \proh-TRAKT\ *v.* protracted; protracting. To prolong. protractive *adj.*; protractedly *adv.*; protraction *n.*

protrude \proh-TROOD\ *v.* protruded; protruding. To jut out. protrusive *adj.*; protrusion *n.*

proud \prowd\ *adj.* prouder; proudest. **1.** Feeling greatly pleased. **2.** Having or showing self-respect. **3.** Arrogant. proudly *adv.*; proudness *n.*

prove \proov\ *v.* proved or proven; proving. **1.** To demonstrate the truth. **2.** To emerge as. **3.** To test. provable *adj.*

proverb \PROV-urb\ *n.* A short, popular saying expressing a truth. proverbial *adj.*; proverbially *adv.*

provide \pruh-VIED\ *v.* provided; providing. **1.** To supply. **2.** To take precautionary measures. **3.** To stipulate in a document. provider *n.*; provision *n.*

province \PROV-ins\ *n.* **1.** An administrative division of a country. **2.** A sphere of interest. provincial *adj.*; provincialism *n.*

provision \pruh-VIZH-un\ *n.* **1.** The act of equipping. **2.** Something furnished. **3.** A precautionary act. provincial *adj.*; provincialism *n.*

proviso \pruh-VIE-zoh\ *n. pl.* provisos or provisoes. A qualifying or restricting clause within a document.

provocative \pruh-VOK-uh-tiv\ *adj.* Tending to incite. provocatively *adv.*; provocation *n.*; provocativeness *n.*

provoke \pruh-VOHK\ *v.* provoked; provoking. To incite.

prowess \PROW-is\ *n.* **1.** An expertise. **2.** A bravery.

prowl *v.* prowled; prowling. To roam secretly, especially in search of prey or loot. prowl *n.*; prowler *n.*

proximity \prok-SIM-i-tee\ *n.* A state of nearness.

prude \prood\ *n.* An excessively moral person. prudish *adj.*; prudishly *adv.*; prudishness *n.*

prudent \PROOD-unt\ *adj.* **1.** Having common sense. **2.** Cautious. prudent *adj.*; prudential *adj.*; prudentially *adv.*; prudently *adv.*

prune \proon\ *n.* **1.** A dried plum. **2.** A person who has held a pampered position for a long time.

prune \proon\ *v.* pruned; pruning. **1.** To trim a bush or tree. **2.** To lessen.

pry \prie\ *v.* pried; prying. **1.** To ask impertinently. **2.** To pull apart with effort. pryingly *adv.*

psalm \sahm\ *n.* **1.** A sacred song. **2.** [Pl] A book of the Old Testament.

pseudonym \SOOD-n-im\ *n.* A fictitious name.

psoriasis \suh-RIE-uh-sis\ *n.* (Md) A skin disease characterized by red scaly patches.

psyche \SIE-kee\ *n.* **1.** The spirit. **2.** The mind.

psychedelic \sie-kuh-DEL-ik\ *adj.* **1.** Hallucinatory. **2.** Bright and abstract in pattern or color.

psychiatry \si-KIE-uh-tree\ *n.* (Md) The study and treatment of mental and emotional illness. psychiatric *adj.*; psychiatrist *n.*

psychic \SIE-kik\ *adj.* **1.** Having supernatural powers. **2.** Concerning the soul or mind. psychically *adv.*

psychic \SIE-kik\ *n.* One sensitive to extrasensory phenomena. psychically *adv.*

psychoanalysis \sie-koh-uh-NAL-uh-sis\ *n.* (Md) Psychotherapy that analyzes unconscious factors revealed in dreams, etc. psychoanalytic *adj.*; psychoanalyst *n.*; psychoanalyze *v.*

psychobabble \sie-koh-BA-bul\ *n.* (Md) Casual talk using the jargon of psychiatry or psychotherapy.

psychology \sie-KOL-uh-jee\ *n.* **1.** Study of the human mind and its operations. **2.** Behavior of an entity.

psychosexual \sie-koh-SEKS-yoo-ul\ *adj.* Relating to the mental aspects of sexual development.

psychosis \sie-KOH-sis\ *n. pl.* psychoses. (Md) A mental illness characterized by a loss of touch with reality.

psychotherapy \sie-koh-THER-uh-pee\ *n.* (Md) The treatment of mental illness by psychology. psychotherapist *n.*

psychotic \sie-KOT-ik\ *adj.* Of or afflicted with psychosis. psychotic *n.*

pterodactyl \ter-uh-DAK-til\ *n.* An extinct flying reptile.

pub *n.* An establishment where alcoholic beverages are sold and consumed.

puberty \PYOO-bur-tee\ *n.* The period of sexual maturation.

public \PUB-lik\ *adj.* **1.** Of the people as a whole. **2.** Open to all. **3.** Of or concerning government. publicly *adv.*

public \PUB-lik\ *n.* A community or section of it.

publication \pub-li-KAY-shun\ *n.* **1.** The act of publishing printed material. **2.** A book, magazine, newspaper, etc.

publicity \puh-BLIS-i-tee\ *n.* **1.** Information offered to the public. **2.** Something of public interest.

public television *n.* Educational broadcasting made possible by donations.

puck \puk\ *n.* The rubber disk used in hockey.

pucker \PUK-ur\ *v.* puckered; puckering. To draw up into wrinkles or folds. pucker *n.*

puddle \PUD-l\ *n.* A small pool of liquid.

pudgy \PUJ-ee\ *adj.* pudgier; pudgiest. Plump. pudginess *n.*

puerile \PYOO-ur-il\ *adj.* Childish. puerility *n.*

puff \puf\ *n.* **1.** A quick blast of breath. **2.** A quantity of material blasted. **3.** A soft lump.

puff \puf\ *v.* puffed; puffing. **1.** To breathe out a quick blast of air. **2.** To smoke. **3.** To swell. **4.** To brag. puffy *adj.*; puffiness *n.*

puffin \PUF-in\ *n.* A sea bird with large head and triangular bill.

pugnacious \pug-NAY-shus\ *adj.* Quarrelsome. pugnaciously *adv.*; pugnacity *n.*

pull \puul\ *n.* **1.** The act of pulling. **2.** Something to pull. **3.** Long swallow. **4.** Power.

pull \puul\ *v.* pulled; pulling. **1.** Drag; tug. **2.** Move from fixed place. **3.** Rip; tear. **4.** Deliver light punch.

pulley \PUUL-ee\ *n. pl.* pulleys. A grooved wheel upon which a cord is pulled to change the direction of a force.

pull off *v.* To manage successfully in spite of difficulties.

pull through *v.* To recover from an illness or injury.

pulp *n.* **1.** Soft fleshy part of fruit or vegetable. **2.** Soft, wet ground wood.

pulsar \PUL-sahr\ *n.* A celestial source of pulses of radiation.

pulsate \PUL-sayt\ *v.* pulsated; pulsating. **1.** To throb. **2.** To quiver. pulsatory *adj.*; pulsation *n.*

pulse \puls\ *n.* **1.** A regular throbbing. **2.** A single beat. **3.** [Md] Regular beat of the heart. pulse *v.*

pulverize \PUL-vuh-riez\ *v.* pulverized; pulverizing. **1.** To crumble into fine particles. **2.** To ruin. pulverization *n.*; pulverizer *n.*

puma \POO-muh\ *n.* A cougar.

pumice \PUM-is\ *n.* A light, porous, volcanic rock, often used as an abrasive.

pummel \PUM-ul\ *v.* pummeled; pummeling or pummelled; pummelling. To strike repeatedly with the fists. pummel *n.*

pump *n.* A device for raising or moving liquids.

pump *v.* pumped; pumping. **1.** Raise or move liquid with a device. **2.** Fill with air. **3.** Ask repeatedly. pumper *n.*

pun *n.* A use of a word that gives it more than one meaning. pun *v.*

punch *n.* **1.** Poke or strike. **2.** A tool for piercing. **3.** Energy. **4.** Fruit beverage.

punch *v.* punched; punching. **1.** To poke or strike. **2.** [Cl]. To herd cattle. punch *n.*

punchy \PUN-chee\ *adj.* punchier; punchiest. **1.** Energized. **2.** Dazed and befuddled. punchiness *n.*

punctual \PUNGK-choo-ul\ *adj.* Prompt. punctually *adv.*; punctuality *n.*

punctuation \pungk-choo-AY-shun\ *n.* A system of marks used in writing. punctuate *v.*

puncture \PUNGK-chur\ *n.* **1.** The act of piercing. **2.** A hole made by piercing. **3.** To let the air out of. puncture *v.*

pungent \PUN-junt\ *adj.* **1.** Strong in taste or smell. **2.** Caustic. pungently *adv.*; pungency *n.*

punish \PUN-ish\ *v.* punished; punishing. **1.** To impose a penalty for a wrongdoing. **2.** To injure. punishable *adj.*; punishment *n.*

punitive \PYOO-ni-tiv\ *adj.* Imposing punishment, especially one that is severe.

punk \pungk\ *n.* **1.** A hoodlum. **2.** A petty criminal. **3.** Radical teenage dress, behavior.

punk rock *n.* (Mu) Deliberately brash rock music. punk rocker *n.*

punt *n.* **1.** Square, flat-bottomed boat. **2.** A long football kick. punt *v.*

puny \PYOO-nee\ *adj.* punier; puniest. Undersized.

pupil \PYOO-pul\ *n.* **1.** A student. **2.** The dark center of the eye.

puppet \PUP-it\ *n.* **1.** Toy figure moved by hand, strings, or wire. **2.** Someone controlled by others. puppeteer *n.*; puppetry *n.*

purchase \PUR-chus\ *v.* purchased; purchasing. To buy with money. purchase *n.*

pure \pyuur\ *adj.* purer; purest. **1.** Unmixed. **2.** Lacking flaws. **3.** Whole. **4.** Moral. **5.** Theoretical. purely *adv.*; pureness *n.*

puree \pyuu-RAY\ *n.* A food made by grinding or straining. puree *v.*

purgatory \PUR-guh-tor-ee\ *n.* **1.** A place of punishment after death. **2.** A place of suffering. purgatory *adj.*; purgatorial *adj.*

purge \purj\ *v.* purged; purging. **1.** To cleanse by removing flaws. **2.**

To rid oneself of guilt. **3.** To vomit. purge *n.*; purgative *n.*

purify \PYUUR-i-fie\ *v.* purified; purifying. **1.** To cleanse by removing flaws **2.** To free oneself from sin. purification *n.*; purifier *n.*

purity \PYUUR-i-tee\ *n.* **1.** A cleanliness. **2.** A homogeneity. **3.** A lack of sin.

purl *n.* **1.** A stitch in knitting. **2.** A ripple. purl *v.*

purloin \pur-LOIN\ *v.* purloined; purloining. To steal.

purple \PUR-pul\ *n.* The color produced when red and blue are mixed. purple *adj.*; purplish *adj.*; purple *v.*

purpose \PUR-pus\ *n.* **1.** An aim. **2.** A determination. purposeful *adj.*; purposeless *adj.*; purposely *adv.*; purposefully *adv.*; purpose *v.*

purr \pur\ *n.* A low murmur, especially one made by a cat. purr *v.*

purse \purs\ *n.* **1.** Bag for carrying money and personal items. **2.** Funds; treasury. **3.** Prize.

purse \purs\ *v.* pursed; pursing. To pucker.

pursue \pur-SOO\ *v.* pursued; pursuing. **1.** To chase. **2.** To strive for. **3.** To go further. **4.** To follow an interest.

purvey \pur-VAY\ *v.* purveyed; purveying. To supply. purveyor *n.*

push \puush\ *v.* pushed; pushing. **1.** Drive with force. **2.** Urge on. **3.** Advertise. **4.** Sell drugs illegally. push *n.*; pusher *n.*

push around *v.* To bully.

pushover \PUUSH-oh-vur\ *n.* **1.** Someone easily defeated. **2.** Something easily accomplished.

push up \PUUSH-up\ *n.* Exercise done prone pushing the body up with the arms.

pushy \PUUSH-ee\ *adj.* pushier; pushiest. Aggressive. pushily *adv.*; pushiness *n.*

put \puut\ *v.* put; putting. **1.** To position in a location. **2.** To bring to a certain state. **3.** To explain. put *n.*

put away *v.* **1.** To keep in reserve. **2.** To jail. **3.** To consume. **4.** To kill.

put down *also* **put-down** *n.* A critical remark.

put down *v.* **1.** To remark critically. **2.** To euthanize. **3.** To list.

put off *v.* To delay.

put on *v.* **1.** To pretend. **2.** To stage a performance.

put out *v.* **1.** To inconvenience. **2.** To extinguish.

putrid \PYOO-trid\ *adj.* **1.** Rotting. **2.** Immoral. putridity *n.*

putt \put\ *v.* putted; putting. To strike a golf ball gently. putt *n.*

putter \PUT-ur\ *v.* puttered; puttering. To dawdle. putterer *n.*

put upon *v.* To inconvenience.

puzzle \PUZ-ul\ *v.* puzzled; puzzling. **1.** To perplex. **2.** To be perplexed. **3.** To solve by mental effort.

puzzle \PUZ-ul\ *n.* **1.** A confusing problem. **2.** Test of knowledge. **3.** Toy with fitted pieces.

pygmy \PIG-mee\ *n. pl.* pygmies. A very small person or animal. pygmy *adj.*

pylon \PIE-lon\ *n.* **1.** A massive gateway. **2.** A tall tower.

pyramid \PIR-uh-mid\ *n.* Large structure with square base, triangular sides, often used as a tomb. pyramidal *adj.*

pyre \pier\ *n.* A mound of inflammable material, often used in a funeral to burn a dead body.

pyrogenic *also* **pyrogenous** \pie-ROH-jen-ik\ *adj.* Making or made by heat.

pyromania \pie-ruh-MAY-nee-uh\ *n.* An obsessive desire to start fires. pyromaniac *adj.*, pyromaniacal *adj.*; pyromaniac *n.*

python \PIE-thon\ *n.* A large tropical snake that suffocates its prey.

Q

q \kyoo\ *n. pl.* q's or qs. The 17th letter of the alphabet.

qua \kway or kwah\ *prep.* In the capacity of.

Quaalude \KWAY-lood\ *n.* A sedative drug.

quack \kwak\ *n.* **1.** A duck's cry. **2.** [Sl] A fake or unqualified doctor. quackery *n.*

quack \kwak\ *v.* quacked; quacking. To make the cry of a duck.

quadrangle \KWOD-rang-gul\ *n.* **1.** Math configuration having four sides and four angles. **2.** A yard enclosed.

quadraphonic *also* **quadriphonic** \kwod-ruh-FON-ik\ *adj.* Relating to a four-speaker stereo system.

quadrilateral \kwod-ruh-LAT-ur-ul\ *adj.* Having four sides. quadrilaterally *adv.*; quadrilateral *n.*

quadriplegia \kwod-ruh-PLEEZH-uh\ *n.* (Md) A paralysis of all limbs and part of the body from a spinal cord injury. quadriplegic *adj.*; quadriplegic *n.*

quaff \kwof\ *v.* quaffed; quaffing. To guzzle. quaffable *adj.*; quaff *n.*; quaffer *n.*

quagmire \KWAG-mire\ *n.* **1.** A muddy bog. **2.** A dilemma.

quail \kwayl\ *n.* A game bird having spotted brown feathers and a short tail.

quail \kwayl\ *v.* quailed; quailing. To show fear.

quaint \kwaynt\ *adj.* quainter; quaintest. Unique, especially in an antiquated way. quaintly *adv.*; quaintness *n.*

quake \kwayk\ *n.* An earthquake.

quake \kwayk\ *v.* quaked; quaking. To tremble.

qualification \kwol-uh-fi-KAY-shun\ *n.* **1.** Act of ascribing characteristics to. **2.** Appropriate ability. **3.** Restriction.

qualify \KWOL-uh-fie\ *v.* qualified; qualifying. **1.** To ascribe characteristics to. **2.** To be or be made fit for a purpose.

quality \KWOL-i-tee\ *n.* **1.** An attribute. **2.** A degree of excellence. qualitative *adj.*; qualitatively *adv.*

qualm \kwahm\ *n.* **1.** A sudden doubt. **2.** A sudden ill feeling. qualmish *adj.*

quandary \KWON-duh-ree\ *n. pl.* quandaries. A predicament.

quantitative \KWON-ti-tay-tiv\ *adj.* Of or concerning an amount. quantitatively *adv.*; quantitativeness *n.*

quantity \KWON-ti-tee\ *n. pl.* quantities. **1.** An amount. **2.** A considerable portion.

quantum \KWON-tum\ *n. pl.* quanta. **1.** An amount. **2.** [Sc] The tiniest unit of radiation energy.

quark \kwahrk\ *n.* (Sc) An elementary particle.

quarrel \KWOR-ul\ *n.* A disagreement. quarrelsome *adj.*; quarrel *v.*

quarry \KWOR-ee\ *n. pl.* quarries. **1.** A site from which stone is obtained. **2.** Hunted game. quarry *v.*

quart \kwort\ *n.* **1.** Liquid 32 ounces or two pints. **2.** Container with this capacity.

quarter \KWOR-tur\ *n.* **1.** One of four equal parts. **2.** A US coin equal to one-fourth of the dollar.

quartz \kworts\ *n.* A crystalline silica mineral.

quartz heater *n.* Portable electric heater.

quasar \KWAY-zahr\ *n.* A celestial object that emits radiation.

quasi \KWAY-zie or KWAH-zie\ *adv.* **1.** Almost. **2.** Seemingly. quasi *adj.*

quaver \KWAY-vur\ *v.* quavered; quavering. **1.** To shake. **2.** To utter in a trembling voice. quavery *adj.*; quaver *n.*

quay \kee\ *n.* A loading dock.

queasy *also* **queazy** \KWEE-zee\ *adj.* queasier; queasiest or queazier; queaziest. **1.** Nauseous. **2.** Easily made ill. queasily *adv.*; queasiness *n.*

queen \kween\ *n.* **1.** A female ruler. **2.** The wife or widow of a king. **3.**

The highest chess piece. queenly *adj.*; queenliness *n.*

queer \kweer\ *adj.* queerer; queerest. **1.** Strange. **2.** Eccentric. **3.** Feeling ill. **4.** Fake. queerly *adv.*; queer *n.*; queerness *n.*

quell \kwel\ *v.* quelled; quelling. **1.** To suppress. **2.** To calm.

quench \kwench\ *v.* quenched; quenching. **1.** To satisfy a desire. **2.** To extinguish with water. **3.** To demolish.

querulous \KWER-uh-lus\ *adj.* Complaining. querulously *adv.*; querulousness *n.*

query \KWEER-ee\ *n. pl.* queries. A question. query *v.*

quest \kwest\ *n.* A search. quest *v.*

question \KWES-chun\ *n.* **1.** An expression seeking an answer. **2.** A disputable subject. **3.** A dilemma. questioner *n.*; questioning *n.*; question *v.*

questionable \KWES-chuh-nuh-bul\ *adj.* Doubtful. questionably *adv.*

queue \kyoo\ *n.* **1.** A waiting line. **2.** [Cm] Stored data in line for processing. queue *v.*

quibble \KWIB-ul\ *v.* quibbled; quibbling. To argue, especially by using petty objections. quibble *n.*

quick \kwik\ *adj.* quicker; quickest. **1.** Taking a short time. **2.** Prompt. **3.** Able to learn in a short time. quick *adv.*; quickly *adv.*; quickness *n.*

quick \kwik\ *n.* **1.** Soft sensitive flesh. **2.** The heart of emotions.

quick fix *n.* (Sl) An expedient solution.

quick-tempered \KWIK-tem-purd\ *adj.* Easily angered.

quick-witted \KWIK-WIT-id\ *adj.* Mentally astute. quick-wittedness *n.*

quiet \KWIE-it\ *adj.* quieter; quietest. **1.** Not loud. **2.** Peaceful. **3.** Not showy. **4.** Relaxing. quietly *adv.*; quietness *n.*; quiet *v.*

quietude \KWIE-i-tood\ *n.* The state of peacefulness.

quilt \kwilt\ *n.* A padded blanket. quilter *n.*; quilting *n.*; quilt *v.*

quinine \KWIE-nien\ *n.* (Md) A bitter drug derived from tree bark.

quintessential \kwin-tuh-SEN-shul\ *adj.* Having the utmost essence of something. quintessentially *adv.*; quintessence *n.*

quintet \kwin-TET\ *n.* **1.** A group of five. **2.** [Mu] Music for five performers.

quintuplet \kwin-TUP-lit\ *n.* One of five children born in a single birth.

quip \kwip\ *n.* A clever saying. quip *v.*

quirk \kwurk\ *n.* **1.** A peculiar feature. **2.** A prompt twist. quirky *adj.*; quirkiness *n.*

quit \kwit\ *v.* quit or quitted; quitting. **1.** To abandon. **2.** To stop doing something. quitter *n.*

quite \kwiet\ *adv.* **1.** Completely. **2.** Very.

quiver \KWIV-ur\ *v.* quivered; quivering. To vibrate rapidly. quiver *n.*

quiz \kwiz\ *n. pl.* quizzes. A short test of knowledge. quiz *v.*

quizzical \KWIZ-i-kul\ *adj.* **1.** Expressing mild confusion. **2.** Unique. quizzically *adv.*

quorum \KWOR-um\ *n.* A minimum number of members required for a meeting.

quota \KWOH-tuh\ *n.* **1.** An equal share of goods. **2.** The highest quantity to be admitted.

quotation \kwoh-TAY-shun\ *n.* **1.** Something said that is expressed by another. **2.** The act of citing something.

quote \kwoht\ *v.* quoted; quoting. **1.** To cite something expressed by another. **2.** To state a bid, offer, or price. quote *n.*

quotient \KWOH-shunt\ *n.* The number produced when one number is divided by another.

R

r \ahr\ *n. pl.* r's or rs. The 18th letter of the English alphabet.

rabbit \RAB-it\ *n.* A small plant-eating rodent.

rabble \RAB-ul\ *n.* **1.** A disorderly crowd. **2.** The lower class.

rabble-rouser \RAB-ul-row-zur\ *n.* A troublemaker.

rabid \RAB-id\ *adj.* **1.** Affected with rabies. **2.** Violent. **3.** Obsessive. rabidly *adv.*

rabies \RAY-beez\ *n.* Deadly virus transmitted through the bite of an infected animal.

raccoon *also* **racoon** \ra-KOON\ *n.* A North American mammal with a masklike face and a bushy tail.

race \rays\ *n.* **1.** Contest of speed. **2.** Any contest. **3.** Subdivision of mankind; tribe; stock.

racism \RAY-siz-um\ *n.* **1.** Irrational belief in the superiority of a race. **2.** Any action based on that. racist *adj.*; racist *n.*

rack \rak\ *n.* **1.** A framework for holding things. **2.** A toothed rod meshing with a gear.

rack \rak\ *v.* racked; racking. **1.** To secure in a framework. **2.** To move quickly. **3.** To strain in thinking.

racket \RAK-it\ *n.* **1.** Tennis frame for hitting the ball. **2.** Scheme. **3.** Business; occupation.

racket \RAK-it\ *v.* racketed; racketing. To make an uproar.

racy \RAY-see\ *adj.* racier; raciest. **1.** Lively. **2.** Indecent. raciness *n.*

radar \RAY-dahr\ *n.* Electronic device that locates objects with radio-frequency impulses.

radial \RAY-dee-ul\ *adj.* **1.** Radiating from or meeting in a central point. **2.** Resembling a ray. raciness *n.*

radial keratotomy *n.* (Md) A surgery to correct nearsightedness.

radiant \RAY-dee-unt\ *adj.* **1.** Giving off light. **2.** Happy in appearance. radiantly *adv.*; radiance *n.*; radiant *n.*

radiate \RAY-dee-ayt\ *v.* radiated; radiating. **1.** To come from and extend in rays from a point. **2.** To scatter from a center. radiate *adj.*

radiation \ray-dee-AY-shun\ *n.* **1.** Radiating from a center. **2.** Emission of radioactive energy. radiate *adj.*

radical \RAD-i-kul\ *adj.* **1.** Essential. **2.** Deviating from the typical. **3.** Advocating extreme change. radically *adv.*; radical *n.*; radicalism *n.*

radicchio \ruh-DEE-kee-oh\ *n. pl.* radicchios. A bitter red and white lettuce having a compact head.

radio \RAY-dee-oh\ *n. pl.* radios. **1.** Wireless transmission, reception of sound. **2.** An apparatus for this.

radioactive \ray-dee-oh-AK-tiv\ *adj.* Relating to the emission of radiation from the disintegration of atomic nuclei. radioactivity *n.*

radiology \ray-dee-OL-uh-jee\ *n.* (Md) Study of radiant energy and its applications. radiologist *n.*

radish \RA-dish\ *n. pl.* radishes. A plant that yields an edible pungent root.

radius \RAY-dee-us\ *n. pl.* radii or radiuses. **1.** Straight line from the center of a circle. **2.** Forearm bone.

radon \RAY-don\ *n.* A gaseous radioactive chemical element.

raffish \RAF-ish\ *adj.* Unmindful of social conventions. raffishly *adv.*; raffishness *n.*

raffle \RAF-ul\ *n.* A lottery for a prize. raffle *v.*

raft *n.* A flat floating structure.

rag *n.* **1.** A worn cloth. **2.** [Sl] A sensationalist newspaper. **3.** [Pl] Worn clothing. ragged *adj.*; raggedy *adj.*

rag *v.* ragged; ragging. To tease.

ragamuffin \RAG-uh-muf-in\ *n.* A dirty child wearing worn clothing.

rage \rayj\ *n.* **1.** An extreme anger. **2.** An intense growth. **3.** Something in vogue. raging *adj.*; rage *v.*

raid \rayd\ *n.* A sneak attack. raid *v.*

rail \rayl\ *n.* **1.** A bar or series of bars supported by vertical posts. **2.** The railway.

rail \rayl\ *v.* railed; railing. To complain strongly.

rain \rayn\ *n.* **1.** Moisture falling from the sky. **2.** Anything falling abundantly. rain *v.*

rainbow \RAYN-boh\ *n.* Prismatic colors in the sky from dispersion of light through raindrops. rainbow *adj.*

raise \rays\ *v.* raised; raising. **1.** To lift higher. **2.** To place upright. **3.** To build. **4.** To make appear. raised.

raisin \RAY-zin\ *n.* A dried grape.

rake \rayk\ *n.* **1.** Lawn and garden tool having a long handle and a row of teeth. **2.** A womanizer.

rake \rayk\ *v.* raked; raking. **1.** Scrape together with a rake. **2.** Direct gunfire along an area.

rally \RAL-ee\ *v.* rallied; rallying. **1.** To bring together for a purpose. **2.** To bring together again. **3.** To increase.

ram *n.* **1.** A castrated male sheep. **2.** Any machine applying force to push or destroy. ram *v.*

ramble \RAM-bul\ *v.* rambled; rambling. **1.** To travel aimlessly. **2.** To babble. **3.** To progress down an erratic path. rambling *adj.*; ramble *n.*; rambler *n.*

rambunctious \ram-BUNGK-shus\ *adj.* Unruly. rambunctiously *adv.*; rambunctiousness *n.*

ramification \ram-uh-fi-KAY-shun\ *n.* A consequence.

ramp *n.* A slope.

rampage \RAM-payj\ *v.* rampaged; rampaging. To rush violently. rampage *n.*

rampant \RAM-punt\ *adj.* Uncontrolled. rampantly *adv.*; rampancy *n.*

rampart \RAM-pahrt\ *n.* A protective wall.

ramshackle \RAM-shak-ul\ *adj.* Flimsy.

ranch *n.* A sprawling farm on which livestock is raised. rancher *n.*; ranch *v.*

rancid \RAN-sid\ *adj.* **1.** Bad smelling or tasting. **2.** Rotten. rancidity *n.*; rancidness *n.*

rancor \RANG-kur\ *n.* A deep hatred. rancorous *adj.*; rancorously *adv.*

random \RAN-dum\ *adj.* Made or done without conscious choice. randomly *adv.*; randomness *n.*; randomize *v.*

range \raynj\ *n.* **1.** Sphere of sight, intelligence, or ability. **2.** Possible variations.

range \raynj\ *v.* ranged; ranging. **1.** To set in order. **2.** To wander. **3.** To extend a certain distance. **4.** To differ.

rank *adj.* ranker; rankest. **1.** Growing abundantly. **2.** Stinking. **3.** Utter.

rank *n.* **1.** A position in a hierarchy. **2.** A row, array, or order.

rank \rangk\ *v.* ranked; ranking. **1.** To have a place in an order. **2.** To arrange, classify, or grade.

ransack \RAN-sak\ *v.* ransacked; ransacking. To search thoroughly.

ransom \RAN-sum\ *n.* A sum demanded for a captive. ransom *v.*

rant *v.* ranted; ranting. To make a violent speech. rantingly *adv.*; rant *n.*

rap *v.* rapped; rapping. **1.** Knock sharply and quickly. **2.** To speak abruptly. **3.** To criticize. rap *n.*

rape \rayp\ *v.* raped; raping. To force someone to have sexual intercourse. rape *n.*; rapist *n.*

rapid \RAP-id\ *adj.* rapider; rapidest. Very fast. rapidly *adv.*; rapidity *n.*; rapidness *n.*

rapid eye movement *also* **REM** *n.* Shifting movements of the eyes during dreaming.

rapier \RAY-pee-ur\ *n.* A thin, double-edged sword having a cuplike handle.

rapport \ra-POR\ *n.* A harmonious relationship.

rapprochement \rap-rohsh-MAHN\ *n.* (Fr) An establishment of friendly relations.

rapt *adj.* Absorbed. raptly *adv.*

rapture \RAP-chur\ *n.* A great delight. rapturous *adj.*; rapturously *adv.*

raquetball \RA-ket-bal\ *n.* Inside racket sport played on enclosed court with small rubber ball.

rare \rair\ *adj.* rarer; rarest. **1.** Cooked lightly. **2.** Very uncommon. **3.** Precious. rarely *adv.*; rareness *n.*; rarity *n.*

rarefy *also* **rarify** \RAIR-uh-fie\ *v.* rarefied; rarefying or rarified; rarifying. To make or become less dense. rarefiable *adj.*; rarefier *n.*

rarely \RAIR-lee\ *adv.* **1.** Hardly ever. **2.** Unusually.

rascal \RAS-kul\ *n.* A mischievous person. rascal *adj.*

rash *adj.* rasher; rashest. Reckless. rashly *adv.*; rashness *n.*

rash *n. pl.* rashes. **1.** [Md] An eruption of red patches on the skin. **2.** An epidemic.

raspberry \RAZ-ber-ee\ *n.* A plant bearing edible, many-seeded, soft, red or black fruits.

raspy \RASP-ee\ *adj.* raspier; raspiest. Scratchy and harsh.

Rasta \RAH-stuh\ *n.* A religion native to Jamaica whose followers see Africa as the Promised Land. Rastafarian *adj.*; Rastafarian *n.*; Rastafarianism *n.*

rat *n.* **1.** A rodent slightly larger than a mouse. **2.** [Sl] A scoundrel. rat *v.*

ratatouille \rat-uh-TWEE\ *n.* A vegetable stew.

rate \rayt\ *n.* **1.** A proportionate quantity. **2.** Money charged. **3.** Speed of occurrence.

rate \rayt\ *v.* rated; rating. **1.** To judge. **2.** To yell at. **3.** To be entitled to.

rather \RATH-ur\ *adv.* **1.** Preferably. **2.** More exactly. **3.** Moderately.

ratify \RAT-uh-fie\ *v.* ratified; ratifying. To confirm formally. ratification *n.*

ratio \RAY-shoh\ *n. pl.* ratios. A relationship between two numbers or quantities.

ration \RASH-un\ *n.* An amount allowed to a person during a shortage. ration *v.*

rational \RASH-uh-nul\ *adj.* Reasonable. rationally *adv.*

rationale \rash-uh-NAL\ *n.* A logic for belief or action.

rationalize \RASH-uh-nl-ize\ *v.* rationalized; rationalizing. **1.** To justify. **2.** To think logically. rationalization *n.*

raucous \RAW-kus\ *adj.* **1.** Noisy. **2.** Rowdy. raucously *adv.*; raucousness *n.*

raunch \rawnch\ *n.* (Sl) **1.** An obscenity. **2.** Erotic material. raunchy *adj.*; raunchiness *n.*

ravage \RAV-ij\ *v.* ravaged; ravaging. To do great damage. ravage *n.*

rave \rayv\ *v.* raved; raving. To talk enthusiastically. rave *n.*

raven \RAY-vun\ *n.* A large black bird like a crow.

ravenous \RAV-uh-nus\ *adj.* Very hungry. ravenously *adv.*

ravine \ruh-VEEN\ *n.* A deep valley through which a stream runs.

ravioli \rav-ee-OH-lee\ *n. pl.* ravioli or raviolis. (It) A pasta case filled with cheese, meat, or vegetables.

ravish \RAV-ish\ *v.* ravished; ravishing. **1.** To enchant. **2.** To rape. **3.** To kidnap. ravisher *n.*; ravishment *n.*

raw *adj.* rawer; rawest. **1.** Not cooked. **2.** Natural and unprepared. **3.** Inexperienced. **4.** Damp and cold. rawly *adv.*; rawness *n.*

ray *n. pl.* rays. **1.** Narrow line of a form of energy. **2.** A slim chance. **3.** Radiating part. **4.** Fish.

rayon \RAY-on\ *n.* An artificial silky fabric.

raze *also* **rase** \rayz\ *v.* razed; razing or rased; rasing. To destroy by knocking down.

razor \RAY-zur\ *n.* A sharp instrument used for shaving.

razzle-dazzle \RAZ-ul-DAZ-ul\ *n.* Showy effect. razzle-dazzle *v.*

reach \reech\ *v.* reached; reaching. **1.** Stretch out the hand. **2.** To arrive at. **3.** To communicate with. **4.** To attain. razzle-dazzle *v.*

react \ree-AKT\ *v.* reacted; reacting. To act or have a feeling caused by something. reactive *adj.*

reaction \ree-AK-shun\ *n.* **1.** Action caused by something. **2.** A response. **3.** [Sc] A chemical response.

reactionary \ree-AK-shuh-ner-ee\ *adj.* Opposed to progress and change. reactionary *n.*

reactivate \ree-AK-tuh-vayt\ *v.* reactivated; reactivating. To start again. reactive *adj.*; reactivation *n.*; reactivity *n.*

read \reed\ *v.* read; reading. **1.** To apprehend the meaning of writing. **2.** To utter writing aloud. **3.** Discover. readable *adj.*; read *n.*; readability *n.*; reader *n.*

readership \REE-dur-ship\ *n.* The readers of a periodical.

readily \RED-i-lee\ *adv.* **1.** Quickly. **2.** Cooperatively. **3.** Simply.

readiness \RED-ee-nus\ *n.* Eagerness.

reading \REE-ding\ *n.* **1.** Practice of one who reads. **2.** Formal recital of writing. **3.** Meter marking.

readout *also* **read-out** \REED-owt\ *n.* (Cm) A computer's output.

ready \RED-ee\ *adj.* readier; readiest. **1.** Prepared. **2.** Willing. **3.** Probably or about to do something. readily *adv.*; readiness *n.*

ready-made *also* **readymade** \RED-ee-MAYD\ *adj.* Already prepared.

real \REE-ul\ *adj.* **1.** Existing. **2.** True. reality *n.*; realness *n.*

realign \REE-uh-line\ *v.* realigned; realigning. To put back into position. realignment *n.*

realistic \ree-AL-is-tik\ *adj.* Relating to a seeing of things as they truly are.

reality \ree-AL-i-tee\ *n.* **1.** The facts of existence. **2.** That which is present in truth.

realize \REE-uh-liez\ *v.* realized; realizing. **1.** To come to understand something. **2.** To accomplish. realizable *adj.*; realization *n.*

really \REE-uh-lee\ *adv.* **1.** Truly. **2.** Thoroughly.

realm \relm\ *n.* **1.** An area of rule. **2.** A field of activity or interest.

realpolitik \ray-AHL-poh-li-TEEK\ *n.* (Po) A political policy based on power rather than ideals.

Realtor *also* **realtor** \REE-ul-tur\ *n.* A person qualified to sell property and buildings.

realty *also* **real estate** \REE-ul-tee\ *n.* Property or buildings to be sold.

reap \reep\ *v.* reaped; reaping. **1.** To cut and gather crops. **2.** To achieve through work. reaper *n.*

reappear \ree-uh-PEER\ *v.* reappeared; reappearing. To appear again. reappearance *n.*

rear \reer\ *n.* The back of something. rear *adj.*

rear \reer\ *v.* reared; rearing. **1.** To bring up young children or animals. **2.** To elevate.

rear-end \reer-END\ *v.* rear-ended; rear-ending. (Sl) To hit from the rear, as one vehicle may do to another. rear-ender *n.*

reason \REE-zun\ *n.* **1.** An excuse for action. **2.** An intention. **3.** Sound judgment.

reason \REE-zun\ *v.* reasoned; reasoning. **1.** Exercise sound judgement. **2.** To discuss rationally. **3.** To change one's mind.

reasonable \REE-zuh-nuh-bul\ *adj.* **1.** Sensible. **2.** Moderate. reasonably *adv.*; reasonability *n.*; reasonableness *n.*

reassure \ree-uh-SHUUR\ *v.* reassured; reassuring. To remove doubts and fears. reassurance *n.*

rebate \REE-bayt\ *n.* A partial refund. rebate *v.*

rebel \ri-BEL\ *v.* rebelled; rebelling. To refuse to obey authority. rebellious *adj.*; rebelliously *adv.*; rebel *n.*

rebellion \ri-BEL-yun\ *n.* An act of disobeying authority.

rebound \ri-BOWND\ *v.* rebounded; rebounding. **1.** To bounce back. **2.** To overcome a mental setback. rebound *n.*; rebounder *n.*

rebuff \ri-BUF\ *v.* rebuffed; rebuffing. Snub. rebuff *n.*

rebuke \ri-BYOOK\ *v.* rebuked; rebuking. To speak severely to a wrongdoer. rebuke *n.*

rebuttal \ri-BUT-l\ *n.* An argument opposing something. rebut *v.*

recall \ri-KAWL\ *v.* recalled; recalling. **1.** To request for return. **2.** To remember. **3.** To revoke.

recant \ri-KANT\ *v.* recanted; recanting. To take back something said. recantation *n.*

recapitulate \ree-kuh-PICH-uh-layt\ *v.* recapitulated; recapitulating. To go over the main points again. recapitulatory *adj.*; recapitulation *n.*

recede \ri-SEED\ *v.* receded; receding. To go back. recession *n.*

receipt \ri-SEET\ *n.* **1.** The act of receiving something. **2.** A written proof of payment. receipt *v.*

receivable \ri-SEEV-uh-bul\ *n.* Money owed by customers.

receive \ri-SEEV\ *v.* received; receiving. **1.** To take something sent. **2.** To welcome someone. **3.** To endure. **4.** To accept.

recent \REE-sunt\ *adj.* Made or done a short time ago. recently *adv.*

receptacle \ri-SEP-tuh-kul\ *n.* **1.** A container. **2.** An electrical outlet.

reception \ri-SEP-shun\ *n.* **1.** A welcome. **2.** A party of welcome or celebration. **3.** Welcoming area.

receptive \ri-SEP-tiv\ *adj.* **1.** Friendly when welcoming. **2.** Open to new ideas. receptively *adv.*; receptiveness *n.*; receptivity *n.*

recess \ri-SES\ *n.* **1.** A part set back from the whole. **2.** Break or recreation time. recess *v.*

recession \ri-SESH-un\ *n.* **1.** The reversal of action. **2.** A period of economic decline.

recherché \ruh-SHAIR-shay\ *adj.* (Fr) **1.** Rare. **2.** Excessively showy.

recipe \RES-uh-pee\ *n.* **1.** Directions for cooking food. **2.** A plan for attaining a goal. **3.** Prescription.

reciprocal \ri-SIP-ruh-kul\ *adj.* Exchanged. reciprocally *adv.*; reciprocal *n.*; reciprocity *n.*

reciprocate \ri-SIP-ruh-kayt\ *v.* reciprocated; reciprocating. **1.** To exchange. **2.** To move forward and backward alternately. reciprocally *adv.*; reciprocal *n.*; reciprocity *n.*; reciprocation *n.*; reciprocator

recital \ri-SIET-l\ *n.* **1.** Reading aloud in public. **2.** A long account of events. **3.** A dance or musical. recitalist *n.*

recite \ri-SIET\ *v.* recited; reciting. To speak aloud from memory. recitation *n.*

reckless \REK-lis\ *adj.* Not thinking about consequences. recklessly *adv.*; recklessness *n.*

reckon \REK-un\ *v.* reckoned; reckoning. **1.** To calculate. **2.** To see as. **3.** [Sl] To think or suppose. reckoning *n.*

reclaim \ri-KLAYM\ *v.* reclaimed; reclaiming. To recover and make usable. reclamation *n.*

recline \ri-KLIEN\ *v.* reclined; reclining. To lean or lie back. recliner *n.*

recluse \REK-loos\ *n.* A person who avoids social life. reclusive *adj.*; reclusively *adv.*; reclusion *n.*; reclusiveness *n.*

recognition \rek-ug-NISH-un\ *n.* 1. An acknowledgment of identification. 2. An appreciation granted.

recognize \REK-ug-niez\ *v.* recognized; recognizing. 1. To acknowledge identification. 2. To express as valid. recognizable *adj.*; recognizably *adv.*

recoil \ri-KOIL\ *v.* recoiled; recoiling. 1. To pull back. 2. To shrink away.

recollect \rek-uh-LEKT\ *v.* recollected; recollecting. To remember. recollection *n.*

recombinant DNA *n.* (Md) A DNA that has been altered to make a new combination.

recommend \rek-uh-MEND\ *v.* recommended; recommending. 1. To suggest to another. 2. To endear. 3. To give advice. recommendable *adj.*; recommendation *n.*

recompense \REK-um-pens\ *v.* recompensed; recompensing. To repay somebody for something.

recompensation *n.*; recompense *n.*

reconcile \REK-un-siel\ *v.* reconciled; reconciling. 1. To settle a difference. 2. To overcome intolerance. reconciliatory *adj.*; reconcilement *n.*; reconciliation *n.*

reconsider \ree-kun-SID-ur\ *v.* reconsidered; reconsidered. To think about again. reconsideration *n.*

reconstruct \ree-kun-STRUKT\ *v.* reconstructed; reconstructing. To rebuild. reconstructible *adj.*; reconstruction *n.*

record \REK-urd\ *n.* 1. A written account for reference. 2. A magnetic media of sound, images, etc.

record \ri-KORD\ *v.* recorded; recording. 1. To write down for reference. 2. To store sounds or images on magnetic media. recorder *n.*; recording *n.*

recount \ri-KOWNT\ *v.* recounted; recounting. To tell in detail.

recoup \ri-KOOP\ *v.* recouped; recouping. To compensate.

recourse \REE-kors\ *n.* A source of help.

recover \ri-KUV-ur\ *v.* recovered; recovering. 1. Return to normal health. 2. To get back something that was lost. recoverable *adj.*; recovery *n.*

recreate \REK-ree-ayt\ *v.* recre-ated; recreating. To relax.

recreation \rek-ree-AY-shun\ *n.* Games or hobbies done in leisure time.

recruit \ri-KROOT\ *n.* A person who just joined the armed forces or an organization.

recruit \ri-KROOT\ *v.* recruited; recruiting. To gather new resources or members. recruiter *n.*; recruitment *n.*

rectify \REK-tuh-fie\ *v.* rectified; rectifying. To make something right. rectifiable *adj.*; rectification *n.*

rectum \REK-tum\ *n. pl.* rectums or recta. The last section of the intestine joining the colon and anus. rectal *adj.*

recumbent \ri-KUM-bunt\ *adj.* **1.** Reclining. **2.** Out of action.

recuperate \ri-KOO-puh-rayt\ *v.* recuperated; recuperating. **1.** To become healthy again. **2.** To regain financial strength. recuperative *adj.*; recuperation *n.*

recur \ri-KUR\ *v.* recurred; recurring. **1.** To happen again. **2.** To repeat in one's mind. recurrent *adj.*; recurrently *adv.*; recurrence *n.*

recycle \ree-SIE-kul\ *v.* recycled; recycling. To treate waste material so it can be used again. recyclable *adj.*

red *adj.* redder; reddest. Colored like blood. reddish *adj.*; red *n.*; redden *v.*

redeem \ri-DEEM\ *v.* redeemed; redeeming. **1.** To get something back by making a payment. **2.** To atone for sin. redeeming *adj.*; redemption *n.*

red eye \red-ie\ *n. pl.* red eyes. A long-distance flight leaving late at night. red-eye *adj.*

redolent \RED-l-unt\ *adj.* **1.** Smelling strongly. **2.** Suggestive. redolently *adv.*; redolence *n.*

reduce \ri-DOOS\ *v.* reduced; reducing. **1.** To make something smaller. **2.** To make lower in rank. **3.** To humble. reducible *adj.*; reduction *n.*

redundant \ri-DUN-dunt\ *adj.* More than is needed. redundantly *adv.*; redundancy *n.*

reed *n.* **1.** A plant growing in or near the water. **2.** [Mu] Thin plate on an instrument. reedy *adj.*

reef *n. pl.* reefs. A ridge of rock or coral around the edge of a sea.

reek *v.* reeked; reeking. To give off an unpleasant odor. reek *n.*

reel *n.* **1.** A stagger. **2.** A cylinder or device on which something can be wound.

reel *v.* reeled; reeling. To stagger.

refectory \ri-FEK-tuh-ree\ *n. pl.* refectories. A dining room of a college or monastery.

refer \ri-FER\ *v.* referred; referring. **1.** To guide as a source. **2.** To submit to someone else's attention. referable *adj.*; referral *n.*; reference *n.*

referee \ref-uh-REE\ *n.* A person who upholds the rules in a sport or game. referee *v.*

reference \REF-ur-uns\ *n.* **1.** Words mentioning something. **2.** A book of information. **3.** Recommendation. referential *adj.*; referentially *adv.*

referendum \ref-uh-REN-dum\ *n.* *pl.* referendums or referenda. A question given to a general vote by the people.

refine \ri-FIEN\ *v.* refined; refining. **1.** To cleanse. **2.** To attain a sophistication.

refined \re-FIEND\ *adj.* **1.** Cleansed. **2.** Sophisticated. refinement *n.*; refinery *n.*

reflect \ri-FLEKT\ *v.* reflected; reflecting. **1.** To throw back light. **2.** To show an image in a mirror. **3.** To think deeply. reflective *adj.*; reflection *n.*; reflector *n.*

reflection \ri-FLEK-shun\ *n.* **1.** Light thrown back at something. **2.** An image in a mirror. **3.** Deep thought.

reflex \REE-fleks\ *n.* *pl.* reflexes. An action done without conscious thought. reflex *adj.*

reflexive \ri-FLEK-siv\ *adj.* Showing that the action of the verb is done on its subject.

reflux \REE-fluks\ *n.* A flowing back.

reform \ri-FORM\ *v.* reformed; reforming. To make better by removing faults. reform *adj.*; reform *n.*; reformer *n.*; reformist *n.*

reformation \ref-ur-MAY-shun\ *n.* A time or movement of reform. reformative *adj.*

reformatory school \ri-FOR-muh-tor-ee\ *n.* A school for those with criminal behavior.

refrain \ri-FRAYN\ *n.* (Mu) The chorus of a song.

refrain \ri-FRAYN\ *v.* refrained; refraining. To hold back from doing something.

refresh \ri-FRESH\ *v.* refreshed; refreshing. To make like new. refreshing *adj.*; refreshingly *adv.*; refreshen *v.*

refreshment \ri-FRESH-munt\ *n.* **1.** The act of making like new. **2.** Something to eat or drink that refreshes.

refrigerate \ri-FRIJ-uh-rayt\ *v.* refrigerated; refrigerating. To cool. refrigeration *n.*; refrigerator *n.*

refuge \REF-yooj\ *n.* A place of shelter.

refugee \ref-yuu-JEE\ *n.* A person who flees his home or country for safety.

refund \ri-FUND\ *v.* refunded; refunding. To pay back money. refundable *adj.*; refund *n.*

refurbish \ree-FUR-bish\ *v.* refurbished; refurbishing. To renovate. refurbishment *n.*

refusal \ri-FYOOZ-ul\ *n.* An unwillingness.

refuse \REF-yoos\ *n.* Rubbish.

refuse \ri-FYOOZ\ *v.* refused; refusing. To express an unwillingness to something asked or required. refusal *n.*

refusenik \ri-FYOOS-nik\ *n.* A Soviet citizen not allowed to exit the country.

refutable \ri-FYOOT-uh-bul\ *adj.* Able to be proven wrong. refutability *n.*

refute \ri-FYOOT\ *v.* refuted; refuting. **1.** To prove wrong by argument. **2.** To claim false. refutation *n.*; refuter *n.*

regain \ree-GAYN\ *v.* regained; regaining. **1.** To get something back. **2.** To reach somewhere again.

regal \REE-gul\ *adj.* **1.** Relating to a king or queen. **2.** Fit for royalty. regally *adv.*; regality *n.*

regale \ri-GAYL\ *v.* regaled; regaling. To throw a party. regale *n.*

regalia \ri-GAYL-yuh\ *pl. n.* Emblems of royalty or rank.

regard \ri-GAHRD\ *v.* regarded; regarding. **1.** Look closely at something. **2.** To have an attitude toward. **3.** To be relevant.

regardless \ri-GAHRD-lis\ *adv.* Despite everything. regardless *adj.*

regards \ri-GAHRDZ\ *pl. n.* Kind wishes.

regatta \ri-GAT-uh\ *n. pl.* regattas. An organized yacht race.

regenerate \ri-JEN-uh-rayt\ *v.* regenerated; regenerating. To give new life. regenerable *adj.*; regenerate *adj.*; regenerate *n.*; regeneration *n.*

reggae \REG-ay\ *n.* (Mu) A style of music native to Jamaica characterized by a calypso rhythm.

regime \ruh-ZHEEM\ *n.* **1.** A system of administration. **2.** A period of rule. **3.** A system of behavior.

regimen \REJ-uh-mun\ *n.* A system of behavior.

regiment \REJ-uh-munt\ *n.* A permanent unit in the army.

regiment \REJ-uh-munt\ *v.* regimented; regimenting. **1.** To devise a system of behavior. **2.** To follow strictly. regimental *adj.*; regimentation *n.*

region \REE-jun\ *n.* **1.** An area set off by a distinctive quality. **2.** A domain of interest. regional *adj.*; regionally *adv.*; regionalize *v.*

register \REJ-uh-stur\ *n.* **1.** A book in which information is recorded. **2.** A mechanical device that records.

register \REJ-uh-stur\ *v.* registered; registering. **1.** To record information officially. **2.** To show. **3.** To have an effect.

regress \REE-gres\ *v.* regressed; regressing. To return to an earlier way or place. regressive *adj.*; regressively *adv.*; regression *n.*; regressor *n.*.

regret \ri-GRET\ *v.* regretted; regretting. To be sad or sorry about something. regretful *adj.*; regrettable *adj.*; regretfully *adv.*; regrettably *adv.*; regret *n.*

regular \REG-yuh-lur\ *adj.* **1.** Evenly spaced. **2.** Conforming to rule or habit. **3.** Fixed. regularly *adv.*; regularity *n.*; regularize *v.*

regulate \REG-yuh-layt\ *v.* regulated; regulating. **1.** Govern according to rules. **2.** To organize. **3.**

To adjust to a proper setting. regulative *adj.*; regulatory *adj.*; regulation *n.*; regulator *n.*

regurgitate \ri-GUR-ji-tayt\ *v.* regurgitated; regurgitating. To spit up or throw back out, esp. of the mouth. regurgitation *n.*

rehabilitate \ree-huh-BIL-i-tayt\ *v.* rehabilitated; rehabilitating. To restore to a good condition. rehabilitative *adj.*; rehabilitation *n.*

rehash \ree-HASH\ *v.* rehashed; rehashing. **1.** To put old material into a new form with little change. **2.** To go over again. rehash *n.*

rehearse \ri-HURS\ *v.* rehearsed; rehearsing. To practice something that is to be performed. rehearsal *n.*

reign \rayn\ *n.* **1.** The period during which a leader governs. **2.** Sovereignty. reign *v.*

reimburse \ree-im-BURS\ *v.* reimbursed; reimbursing. To pay back. reimbursement *n.*

rein \rayn\ *n.* A strap used to guide a horse or other animal. rein *v.*

reindeer \RAYN-deer\ *n.* A deer native to cold regions that has branched antlers.

reinforce \ree-in-FORS\ *v.* reinforced; reinforcing. To make something stronger. reinforcement *n.*

reinstate \ree-in-STAYT\ *v.* reinstated; reinstating. To give back responsibility. reinstatement *n.*

reiterate \ree-IT-uh-rayt\ *v.* reiterated; reiterating. To say or do repeatedly. reiteration *n.*; reiterator *n.*

reject \ri-JEKT\ *v.* rejected; rejecting. **1.** To refuse to. **2.** To refuse to allow. **3.** To throw out. reject *n.*; rejection *n.*

rejoice \ri-JOIS\ *v.* rejoiced; rejoicing. To feel or show great happiness.

rejuvenate \ri-JOO-vuh-nayt\ *v.* rejuvenated; rejuvenating. To restore youthful appearance or vigor to. rejuvenation *n.*; rejuvenator *n.*

relapse \ri-LAPS\ *v.* relapsed; relapsing. To fall back into a former condition. relapse *n.*

relate \ri-LAYT\ *v.* related; relating. **1.** To give an account of. **2.** To connect in some way. relation *n.*

related \ri-LAYTD\ *adj.* Being connected in some way.

relation \ri-LAY-shun\ *n.* **1.** A relative. **2.** A connection. **3.** [Pl] Sexual intercourse.

relationship \ri-LAY-shun-ship\ *n.*

A connection between people or things.

relative \REL-uh-tiv\ *adj.* **1.** Thought of in reference to something else. **2.** Relying on another. relatively *adv.*; relativity *n.*

relative \REL-uh-tiv\ *n.* A person related to another by descent or marriage.

relax \ri-LAKS\ *v.* relaxed; relaxing. To become less stiff, tense, or strict. relaxation *n.*

relay \REE-lay\ *n.* **1.** An act of receiving and passing on. **2.** A race between teams.

relay \REE-lay\ *v.* relayed; relaying. To receive and pass on.

release \ri-LEES\ *v.* released; releasing. **1.** To free. **2.** To issue to the public. release *n.*

relegate \REL-i-gayt\ *v.* relegated; relegating. **1.** To put down to a lower rank. **2.** To consign for action. relegation *n.*

relent \ri-LENT\ *v.* relented; relenting. To show mercy. relentless *adj.*; relentlessly *adv.*; relentlessness *n.*

relevant \REL-uh-vunt\ *adj.* Related to the matter at hand. relevantly *adv.*; relevance *n.*

reliable \ri-LIE-uh-bul\ *adj.* Trustworthy. reliably *adv.*; reliability *n.*

reliance \ri-LIE-uns\ *n.* The act of trusting or being trusted.

relic \REL-ik\ *n.* Something that has survived time..

relief \ri-LEEF\ *n.* **1.** The end of pain, worry, or trouble. **2.** Help or assistance.

relieve \ri-LEEV\ *v.* relieved; relieving. **1.** To end pain, worry, or trouble. **2.** To help or assist.

religion \ri-LIJ-un\ *n.* **1.** An organized system of worship. **2.** A set of beliefs. religious *adj.*; religiously *adv.*

relinquish \ri-LING-kwish\ *v.* relinquished; relinquishing. To give up or stop doing. relinquishment *n.*

relish \REL-ish\ *n. pl.* relishes. **1.** An enjoyment. **2.** A condiment for food.

relish \REL-ish\ *v.* relished; relishing. To enjoy.

relive \ree-LIV\ *v.* relived; reliving. To experience again.

reluctant \ri-LUK-tunt\ *adj.* Not wanting to do something. reluctantly *adv.*; reluctance *n.*

rely \ri-LIE\ *v.* relied; relying. **1.** To depend on. **2.** To place confidence in.

remain \ri-MAYN\ *v.* remained; remaining. **1.** To be left over. **2.** To stay in a similar state.

remainder \ri-MAYN-dur\ *n.* Something left over. remainder *v.*

remains \ri-MAYNZ\ *pl. n.* **1.** Everything left over. **2.** Ruins. **3.** A dead body.

remark \ri-MAHRK\ *n.* **1.** Something said about something or somebody. **2.** A notice of something. remark *v.*

remarkable \ri-MAHR-kuh-bul\ *adj.* Worth noticing. remarkably *adv.*

remedy \REM-i-dee\ *n. pl.* remedies. A cure. remedial *adj.*; remedy *v.*

remember \ri-MEM-bur\ *v.* remembered; remembering. **1.** To keep in the mind and be able to recall it at will. **2.** To bestow a gift. rememberable *adj.*; remembrance *n.*

remind \ri-MIEND\ *v.* reminded; reminding. To help someone think of something. reminder *n.*

reminisce \rem-uh-NIS\ *v.* reminisced; reminiscing. To think or talk about past events. reminiscent *adj.*; reminiscently *adv.*; reminiscence *n.*

remission \ri-MISH-un\ *n.* A reduction of intensity.

remnant \REM-nunt\ *n.* A small piece left over.

remorse \ri-MORS\ *n.* A deep regret for a wrongdoing. remorseful *adj.*; remorsefully *adv.*

remote \ri-MOHT\ *adj.* remoter; remotest. Far away. remotely *adv.*; remoteness *n.*

remote \ri-MOHT\ *n.* **1.** A broadcast done on location. **2.** A device for controlling machinery. remotely *adv.*; remoteness *n.*

remove \ri-MOOV\ *v.* removed; removing. **1.** To move something from one place to another. **2.** To get rid of something. removable *adj.*; removal *n.*; remove *n.*; remover *n.*

renaissance \ren-uh-SAHNS\ *n.* **1.** A rebirth. **2.** [Cap] Period of revival of the arts etc. in medieval Europe.

rend *v.* rended; rending. To tear violently into pieces.

render \REN-dur\ *v.* rendered; rendering. **1.** To give something. **2.** To portray. **3.** To force to become. renderable *adj.*; render *n.*; renderer *n.*; rendering *n.*

rendezvous \RAHN-day-voo\ *n. pl.* rendevous. **1.** An appointment to meet. **2.** A meeting place. rendezvous *v.*

rendition \ren-DISH-un\ *n.* The way something is performed or given.

renegade \REN-i-gayd\ *n.* **1.** A traitor. **2.** A rebel.

renege \ri-NIG\ *v.* reneged; reneging. To break a promise. reneger *n.*

renew \ri-NOO\ *v.* renewed; renewing. **1.** To make new again. **2.** To replace. **3.** To resume. renewable *adj.*; renewal *n.*

renounce \ri-NOWNS\ *v.* renounced; renouncing. To give up by formal declaration. renouncement *n.*; renunciation *n.*

renovate \REN-uh-vayt\ *v.* renovated; renovating. To restore to good condition. renovation *n.*; renovator *n.*

renowned \ri-NOWND\ *adj.* Famous. renown *n.*

rent *n.* A regular payment for the use of a place or thing. rental *n.*; rent *v.*

repair \ri-PAIR\ *v.* repaired; repairing. To fix. reparable *adj.*; reparably *adv.*; repair *n.*

reparation \rep-uh-RAY-shun\ *n.* **1.** The act of fixing. **2.** An offering of compensation.

repatriate \ri-PAY-tree-ayt\ *v.* repatriated; repatriating. To send or bring a person back to their country of origin. repatriate *n.*; repatriation *n.*

repay \ri-PAY\ *v.* repaid; repaying. **1.** To pay back. **2.** To do in return. repayable *adj.*; repayment *n.*

repeal \ri-PEEL\ *v.* repealed; repealing. To withdraw a law officially. repeal *n.*

repeat \ri-PEET\ *v.* repeated; repeating. **1.** To say again. **2.** To do again. **3.** To happen again. repeat *adj.*; repeatable *adj.*; repeatedly *adv.*; repeat *n.*

repel \ri-PEL\ *v.* repelled; repelling. **1.** To force to go away. **2.** To cause a feeling of dislike.

repellent *also* **repellant** \ri-PEL-unt\ *n.* **1.** Something that drives away. **2.** Something that causes a feeling of dislike.

repent \ri-PENT\ *v.* repented; repenting. To be sorry for something. repentant *adj.*

repentance \ri-PEN-tuns\ *n.* A sorrow for something done.

repercussion \ree-pur-KUSH-un\ *n.* **1.** An effect or reaction to something done. **2.** An echo.

repertoire \REP-ur-twahr\ *n.* The songs, plays, etc. that a person or group is able to perform.

repertory \REP-ur-tor-ee\ *n. pl.* repertories. **1.** A repertoire. **2.** A performance space. **3.** A storage space.

repetition \rep-i-TISH-un\ *n.* **1.** Doing, saying, making something again. **2.** Something repeated.

replace \ri-PLAYS\ *v.* replaced; replacing. **1.** Put something back in its place. **2.** Take the place of. **3.** Refund.

replenish \ri-PLEN-ish\ *v.* replenished; replenishing. To refill or renew. replenishment *n.*

replete \ri-PLEET\ *adj.* Stocked. repletion *n.*

replica \REP-li-kuh\ *n.* An exact reproduction.

reply \ri-PLIE\ *n.* An answer. reply *v.*

report \ri-PORT\ *v.* reported; reporting. **1.** To give information. **2.** To tattle on. **3.** To gather news. report *n.*

reporter \ri-POR-tur\ *n.* A person employed to collect and tell news for publication or broadcasting.

repose \ri-POHZ\ *v.* reposed; reposing. **1.** To lay down. **2.** To relax. **3.** To rely.

repose \ri-POHZ\ *n.* A relaxation. repose *v.*

reprehensible \rep-ri-HEN-suh-bul\ *adj.* Deserving disapproval. reprehensibly *adv.*; reprehensibility *n.*

represent \rep-ri-ZENT\ *v.* represented; representing. **1.** To be an example of. **2.** To act on someone else's behalf. **3.** To depict.

representation \rep-ri-zen-TAY-shun\ *n.* **1.** Example of something. **2.** Someone acting on another's behalf. **3.** Description.

representative \rep-ri-ZEN-tuh-tiv\ *adj.* Typical of a group or class.

representative \rep-ri-ZEN-tuh-tiv\ *n.* **1.** Example. **2.** Person who acts on another's behalf. **3.** [Po] Legislator.

repress \ri-PRES\ *v.* repressed; repressing. To suppress. repressive *adj.*; repression *n.*

reprieve \ri-PREEV\ *n.* **1.** A delay or cancellation of punishment. **2.** A temporary relief. reprieve *v.*

reprimand \REP-ruh-mand\ *v.* reprimanded; reprimanding. To speak severely to someone for a wrongdoing. reprimand *n.*

reprint \ree-PRINT\ *v.* reprinted; reprinting. To print again. reprint *n.*

reprisal \ri-PRIE-zul\ *n.* An act of revenge.

reproach \ri-PROHCH\ *v.* reproached; reproaches. **1.** To find fault with someone. **2.** To dishonor. reproach *n.*

reproduce \ree-pruh-DOOS\ *v.* reproduced; reproducing. **1.** To cause something be made again. **2.** To produce offspring. reproductive *adj.*; reproduction *n.*

repudiate \ri-PYOO-dee-ayt\ *v.* repudiated; repudiating. **1.** To deny the truth of. **2.** To turn one's back on. repudiation *n.*

repugnant \ri-PUG-nunt\ *adj.* Distasteful. repugnantly *adv.*

repulse \ri-PULS\ *v.* repulsed; repulsing. **1.** To push away. **2.** To disgust. repulsive *adj.*; repulsively *adv.*

reputation \rep-yuh-TAY-shun\ *n.* A widely held opinion of a person's character.

reputed \ri-PYOO-tid\ *adj.* Thought to be such. reputedly *adv.*

request \ri-KWEST\ *v.* requested; requesting. To ask for something politely. request *n.*

requiem \REK-wee-um\ *n.* A church service or music for the dead.

require \ri-KWIER\ *v.* required; requiring. **1.** To need. **2.** To order something done.

requirement \re-KWIER-munt\ *n.* **1.** Something needed. **2.** Something ordered to be done.

requisition \rek-wuh-ZISH-un\ *n.* **1.** A formal written demand. **2.** A need. requisition *v.*

rerun \REE-run\ *n.* A reshowing of a broadcast. rerun *v.*

reschedule \ree-SKED-yool\ *v.* rescheduled; rescheduling. To schedule for another or later time.

rescind \ri-SIND\ *v.* rescinded; rescinding. To cancel. recission *n.*

rescue \RES-kyoo\ *v.* rescued; rescuing. To save or bring away from danger or capture. rescue *n.*; rescuer *n.*

research \ri-SURCH\ *n.* A careful study and investigation of the facts. researcher *n.*; research *v.*

resemble \ri-ZEM-bul\ *v.* resembled; resembling. To look or be like. resemblance *n.*

resent \ri-ZENT\ *v.* resented; resenting. To feel angry about something. resentful *adj.*; resentfully *adv.*; resentment *n.*

reservation \rez-ur-VAY-shun\ *n.* 1. Act of setting aside for future use. 2. Something set aside for future use.

reserve \ri-ZURV\ *n.* 1. Something set aside for future use. 2. Area reserved for a special purpose.

reserve \ri-ZURV\ *v.* reserved; reserving. 1. To set aside for future use. 2. To hold back.

reservoir \REZ-ur-vwahr\ *n.* An artificial storage lake.

reside \ri-ZIED\ *v.* resided; residing. 1. To live in for an extended time. 2. To exist within.

residence \REZ-i-dens\ *n.* 1. A living place. 2. The time during which one lives in a place.

resident \REZ-i-dunt\ *n.* 1. Permanent inhabitant. 2. Physician in clinical training. resident *adj.*; residency *n.*

residual \ri-ZIJ-oo-ul\ *adj.* Left over. residually *adv.*

residue \REZ-i-doo\ *n.* Leftover material.

resign \ri-ZIEN\ *v.* resigned; resigning. 1. To give up a job or position. 2. To decide to endure something. resignedly *adv.*; resignation *n.*

resilient \ri-ZIL-yunt\ *adj.* Springing back quickly. resiliently *adv.*; resilience *n.*

resin \REZ-in\ *n.* A sticky plant substance that is also made synthetically. resinous *adj.*

resist \ri-ZIST\ *v.* resisted; resisting. 1. To use force to oppose. 2. To refuse to give in. resistant *adj.*; resistance *n.*

resolute \REZ-uh-loot\ *adj.* Bold and dedicated. resolutely *adv.*; resolution *n.*

resolution \rez-uh-LOO-shun\ *n.* 1. Boldness and dedication. 2. Decision to do something. 3. A formal statement. resolutely *adv.*; resolution *n.*

resolve \ri-ZOLV\ *n.* A great determination to do something.

resolve \ri-ZOLV\ *v.* resolved; resolving. **1.** To decide. **2.** To divide into parts. **3.** To rid of doubt. **4.** Decide by vote. resolvability *n.*; resolvableness *n.*

resonant \REZ-uh-nunt\ *adj.* Vibrant in sound. resonantly *adv.*; resonance *n.*

resort \ri-ZORT\ *n.* **1.** A luxurious vacation place. **2.** One turned to for help.

resort \ri-ZORT\ *v.* resorted; resorting. **1.** To make use of. **2.** To turn to for help.

resource \ri-ZORS\ *n.* **1.** A useful thing. **2.** [Pl] Available assets.

resourceful \ri-ZORS-ful\ *adj.* Clever at finding ways of doing things. resourcefully *adv.*; resourcefulness *n.*

respect \ri-SPEKT\ *n.* **1.** An admiration given by others. **2.** An eagerness to express admiration. respectable *adj.*; respectful *adj.*; respectfully *adv.*; respect *v.*

respective \ri-SPEK-tiv\ *adj.* Belonging to each individual. respectively *adv.*

respiration \res-puh-RAY-shun\ *n.* Breathing.

respirator \RES-puh-ray-tur\ *n.* A device to artificially assist breathing.

respire \ri-SPIER\ *v.* respired; respiring. To breathe.

respite \RES-pit\ *n.* A suspension in activity.

resplendent \ri-SPLEN-dunt\ *adj.* Radiant. resplendently *adv.*; resplendence *n.*

respond \ri-SPOND\ *v.* responded; responding. To act in answer to something. respondent *adj.*

response \ri-SPONS\ *n.* The act of answering or reacting to something.

responsible \ri-SPON-suh-bul\ *adj.* **1.** Accountable. **2.** Involving important duties. **3.** Trustworty. responsibly *adv.*; responsibility *n.*

rest *n.* **1.** A suspension of activity. **2.** Sleep. **3.** Death. **4.** [Mu] A pause; silence.

rest *v.* rested; resting. **1.** To suspend activity. **2.** To sleep. **3.** To support or be supported by something.

restaurant \RES-tur-unt or RES-tur-awnt\ *n.* A business establishment serving food and drink. restaurateur or restauranteer *n.*

restitution \res-ti-TOO-shun\ *n.* The bringing back of something to its owner or original state.

restless \REST-lis\ *adj.* Unable to rest or be still. restlessly *adv.*; restlessness *n.*

restore \ri-STOR\ *v.* restored; restoring. **1.** Make exist again. **2.** To put back to an original condition. **3.** To bring back. **restorative** *adj.*; restoration *n;* restorative *n.*; restorer *n.*

restrain \ri-STRAYN\ *v.* restrained; restraining. **1.** To place restrictions on. **2.** To control.

restraint \ri-STRAYNT\ *n.* **1.** Act of restricting or being restricted. **2.** A controlling of one's emotions.

restrict \ri-STRIKT\ *v.* restricted; restricting. To keep within certain limits. restricted *adj.*; restriction *n.*

result \ri-ZULT\ *n.* **1.** Outcome of action, process, etc. **2.** Calculated value or quantity.

result \ri-ZULT\ *v.* resulted; resulting. To happen because of certain actions or events. resultant *adj.*

résumé \REZ-uu-may\ *n.* A summary of one's work and school experience.

resume \ri-ZOOM\ *v.* resumed; resuming. To begin again after stopping for a time. resumption *n.*

resurgence \ri-SURJ-uns\ *n.* Revival after destruction or disappearance. resurgent *adj.*

retain \ri-TAYN\ *v.* retained; retaining. **1.** To keep or hold something in place. **2.** To hire. retainable *adj.*; retainability *n.*; retention *n.*

retake \ri-TAYK\ *v.* retook; re-

taken; retaking. **1.** To take again. **2.** To capture again. **3.** To photograph again. retake *n.*

retaliate \ri-TAL-ee-ayt\ *v.* retaliated; retaliating. To pay back for an unkind action. retaliative *adj.*; retaliatory *adj.*; retaliation *n.*

retard \ri-TAHRD\ *v.* retarded; retarding. To cause delay. retardant *adj.*; retardant *n.*; retardation *n.*

retch \rech\ *v.* retched; retching. To strain the throat as if vomiting.

reticent \RET-uh-sunt\ *adj.* Not revealing one's feelings or thoughts. reticently *adv.*; reticence *n.*

reticular \ri-TIK-yoo-lur\ *adj.* **1.** Weblike. **2.** Complex. reticulate *adj.*; reticulate *v.*

retina \RET-n-uh\ *n. pl.* retinas or retinae. Light-sensitive inner membrane at the back of the eyeball.

retire \ri-TIER\ *v.* retired; retiring. **1.** To withdraw. **2.** To leave a place of responsibility. **3.** To go to sleep.

retired \ri-TIERD\ *adj.* **1.** Withdrawn. **2.** Withdrawn from a place of responsibility. retirement *n.*

retiring \ri-TIER-ing\ *adj.* Avoiding social life.

retort \ri-TORT\ *v.* retorted; retorting. To respond in a witty or angry way. retort *n.*

retread \ri-TRED\ *v.* retreaded; re-treading. **1.** To put a new tread on. **2.** To revive without much change. retread *n.*

retreat \ri-TREET\ *n.* **1.** A moving away when in danger. **2.** A place or time of seclusion. retreat *v.*

retribution \re-truh-BYOO-shun\ *n.* A deserved punishment.

retrieve \ri-TREEV\ *v.* retrieved; retrieving. To bring or get back. retrievable *adj.*; retrievability *n.*; retriever *n.*

retro \re-TROH\ *adj.* **1.** Retroactive. **2.** Of or concerning an earlier time.

retroactive \re-troh-AK-tiv\ *adj.* Operating or effective from an earlier time. retroactively *adv.*; retroactivity *n.*

retrograde \RE-truh-grayd\ *adj.* **1.** Going backward. **2.** Against the typical order. **3.** Becoming inferior. retrogradation *n.*; retrograde *v.*

retrospect \RE-truh-spekt\ *n.* A recollection of the past. retrospective *adj.*; retrospectively *adv.*; retrospection *n.*

retrovirus \re-truh-VIE-rus\ *n. pl.* retroviruses (Md) An RNA virus forming DNA during replication. retroviral *adj.*

return \ri-TURN\ *n.* **1.** Act,

process, etc. of coming back. **2.** That which is returned. **3.** Profit. return *adj.*

return \ri-TURN\ *v.* returned; returning. **1.** Come or go back. **2.** Give back. **3.** To yield. returnable *adj.*

reveal \ri-VEEL\ *v.* revealed; revealing. **1.** To allow something to be seen. **2.** To make known. revealment *n.*

revel \REV-ul\ *v.* reveled; reveling or revelled; revelling. To take pleasure in. reveler or reveller *n.*; revelry *n.*

revelation \rev-uh-LAY-shun\ *n.* **1.** An act of allowing to be seen or known. **2.** Something made seen or known.

revelry \REV-ul-ree\ *n. pl.* revelries. A time of merrymaking. revelrous *adj.*

revenge \ri-VENJ\ *n.* A retaliation for wrongdoing. revengeful *adj.*; revengefully *adv.*; revengefulness *n.*; revenge *v.*

revenue \REV-un-yoo\ *n.* Income, especially that of a state or country.

reverberate \ri-VUR-buh-rayt\ *v.* reverberated; reverberating. To vibrate in sound. reverberant *adj.*; reverberation *n.*

revere \ri-VEER\ *v.* revered; revering. To respect deeply. reverent *adj.*; reverently *adv.*; reverence *n.*

reverend \REV-ur-und\ *n.* A person of the clergy.

reverie \REV-uh-ree\ *n.* A daydream.

reverse \ri-VURS\ *n.* 1. The opposite of something. 2. The back of something. 3. Switch to opposite.

revert \ri-VURT\ *v.* reverted; reverting. To return to an earlier condition. revertible *adj.*; reversion *n.*

review \ri-VYOO\ *n.* 1. Another look at. 2. Critique of something read or seen. 3. Consideration. reviewer *n.*; review *v.*

revise \ri-VIEZ\ *v.* revised; revising. 1. To read and edit something written. 2. To rethink and alter. revision *n.*

revive \ri-VIEV\ *v.* revived; reviving. 1. To bring back to life. 2. To make active again. revivable *adj.*; revival *n.*; revivification *n.*; revivify *v.*

revoke \ri-VOHK\ *v.* revoked; revoking. To take back and cancel. revocable or revokable *adj.*; revocation *n.*

revolt \ri-VOHLT\ *v.* revolted; revolting. 1. To rebel. 2. To nauseate. revolt *n.*

revolting \ri-VOHL-ting\ *adj.* Ex-

tremely disgusting. revoltingly *adv.*

revolution \rev-uh-LOO-shun\ *n.* 1. Overthrow and replacement. 2. A full turn of a wheel, part. 3. Full cycle. revoltingly *adv.*

revolve \ri-VOLV\ *v.* revolved; revolving. 1. To turn around a central part. 2. To occur cyclically.

reward \ri-WORD\ *n.* Something promised or received for good behavior. reward *v.*

rewarding \ri-WORD-ing\ *adj.* Giving satisfaction or gain. rewardingly *adv.*

rhapsody \RAP-suh-dee\ *n. pl.* rhapsodies. 1. Emotional enthusiasm in talk or writing. 2. [Mu] Irregular instrumental. rhapsodize *v.*

rhetoric \RET-ur-ik\ *n.* 1. Verbal conversation. 2. Intellectually pretentious language. rhetorical *adj.*; rhetorically *adv.*

rheumatic fever *n.* (Md) A complication of a strep infection causing arthritis and heart problems.

rheumatism \ROO-muh-tiz-um\ *n.* (Md) Any of several illnesses causing pain and swollen joints.

rhinestone \RIEN-stohn\ *n.* An imitation diamond.

rhinoceros \rie-NOS-ur-us\ *n.* Large herbivorous mammal of

Africa and Asia with one or two horns on snout.

rhinoplasty \rie-noh-PLAS-tee\ *n. pl.* rhinoplasties. Plastic surgery on the nose.

rhododendron \roh-duh-DEN-drun\ *n.* A flowering evergreen shrub.

rhubarb \ROO-bahrb\ *n.* A plant bearing acidic edible stalks.

rhyme \riem\ *n.* Correspondence of sounds in two or more words, as in poetry.

rhythm \RITH-um\ *n.* **1.** Regular pattern of movement. **2.** Regular pattern of sound. **3.** Harmony in art. rhythmic *adj.*; rhythmical *adj.*; rhythmically *adv.*

rhythm and blues *also* **R & B** *pl. n.* (Mu) A form of popular music combining the blues and jazz.

rib *n.* **1.** One of the curved bones of the chest. **2.** Something resembling this.

riboflavin \RIE-boh-flay-vun\ *n.* A property of vitamin B found in milk, leafy vegetables, and egg yolks.

rice \ries\ *n.* A starcy edible grain.

rich *adj.* richer; richest. **1.** Having much money or property. **2.** Splendid. **3.** Deep and strong.

Richter scale \RIK-tur-scayl\ *n.* (Sc) A scale for measuring the intensity of an earthquake.

rickets \RIK-uts\ *pl. n.* (Md) A disease of the bones caused by lack of Vitamin D.

rickety \RIK-i-tee\ *adj.* ricketier; ricketiest. Frail. ricketiness *n.*

rickshaw *also* **ricksha** \RIK-shaw\ *n.* A two-wheeled hooded Eastern vehicle that is pulled.

ricochet \rik-uh-SHAY\ *v.* ricocheted; ricocheting. To bounce off something. ricochet *n.*

rid *v.* rid or ridded; ridding. **1.** To free yourself of something. **2.** To remove or throw away. riddance *n.*

riddle \RID-l\ *n.* A puzzling question. riddler *n.*

riddle \RID-l\ *v.* riddled; riddling. To puncture with many holes.

ride \ried\ *v.* rode; ridden. **1.** To sit in or on and be transported. **2.** To be supported on. **3.** To depend upon.

ridge \rij\ *n.* A narrow, raised strip or region. ridged *adj.*

ridicule \RED-i-kyool\ *v.* ridiculed; ridiculing. To make fun of. ridicule *n.*

ridiculous \ri-DIK-yuh-lus\ *adj.* Absurd. ridiculously *adv.*; ridiculousness *n.*

rife \rief\ *adj.* rifer; rifest. **1.** Widespread. **2.** Occurring frequently.

rifle \RIEF-ul\ *n.* A gun with a long barrel.

rifle \RIEF-ul\ *v.* rifled; rifling. To rummage through with intent to steal.

rift *n.* **1.** A crack in a rock. **2.** A dispute between friends.

rig *n.* **1.** Equipment. **2.** Framework of sails and masts on a ship. **3.** A tractor-trailer.

rig *v.* rigged; rigging. **1.** Equip. **2.** Put sails and supports on a ship. **3.** Put something together.

rigamarole *also* **rigmarole** \RIG-muh-rohl\ *n.* **1.** An elaborate procedure. **2.** Meaningless talk.

right \riet\ *adj.* **1.** Morally proper. **2.** True. **3.** Appropriate. **4.** Healthy. **5.** Opposite the left.

right \riet\ *adv.* **1.** Toward the side opposing the left. **2.** Directly. **3.** Immediately. **4.** Exactly.

right \riet\ *n.* **1.** That which is morally proper. **2.** That which is true. **3.** Opposite of left.

right \riet\ *v.* righted; righting. **1.** To put back to a correct position. **2.** To order. **3.** To correct.

righteous \RYCH-us\ *adj.* Morally proper. righteously *adv.*; righteousness *n.*

right-on \riet-ON\ *adj.* (Sl) **1.** Precise. **2.** Current.

right-to-life \riet-to-lief\ *adj.* Advocating laws making abortion illegal.

rigid \RIJ-id\ *adj.* **1.** Unbendable. **2.** Immobile. **3.** Strictly maintained. rigidly *adv.*; rigidity *n.*; rigidness *n.*

rigor \RIG-ur\ *n.* A strictness.

rigor mortis \RIG-ur-MOR-tis\ *n.* (Md) A stiffening of the body after death.

rigorous \RIG-ur-us\ *adj.* **1.** Strict. **2.** Severe. **3.** Precise. rigorously *adv.*; rigorousness *n.*

rim *n.* The outer edge of an object.

rind \riend\ *n.* The hard outer skin, such as the one covering fruit or cheese.

ring *n.* **1.** A circular object. **2.** A band worn on the finger. **3.** A circular progression.

ring *v.* **1.** To cause a bell to emit sound. **2.** To fill up with noise. **3.** To announce.

rinse \rins\ *v.* rinsed; rinsing. To wash clean with water. rinse *n.*

riot \RIE-ut\ *n.* **1.** Noisy and violent behavior by a crowd. **2.** An uncontrollable explosion. riotous *adj.*; riotously *adv.*; rioter *n.*; riot *v.*

rip *v.* ripped; ripping. **1.** To pull or be pulled apart roughly. **2.** [Sl] To proceed with speed. rip *n.*

rip off *v.* To steal. rip-off *n.*

ripe \riep\ *adj.* riper; ripest. **1.** Ready for harvesting and eating. **2.** Matured. **3.** Appropriate. ripened *adj.*; ripely *adv.*; ripeness *n.*; ripen *v.*

ripple \RIP-ul\ *v.* rippled; rippling. To make tiny waves.

ripple effect *n.* A widespread consequence from a single event.

rise \riez\ *n.* **1.** An upward slope. **2.** An increase.

rise \riez\ *v.* rose; risen; rising. **1.** To get or go upwards. **2.** To become bigger. **3.** To become apparent. **4.** To rebel.

risk *n.* The chance of danger, injury, or loss. risky *adj.*; risk *v.*

risotto \ri-OT-toh\ *n. pl.* risottos. (It) An Italian rice dish prepared with broth and saffron.

risqué \ri-SKAY\ *adj.* Slightly indecent.

rite \riet\ *n.* A ceremony.

ritual \RICH-oo-ul\ *n.* A ceremony that is regularly repeated. ritualistic *adj.*; ritualistically *adv.*; ritually *adv.*; ritualism *n.*

river \RIV-ur\ *n.* **1.** A stream of water flowing into a sea, lake, or river. **2.** A flowing liquid.

RNA *n.* Ribonucleic acid.

road \rohd\ *n.* A path upon which travel occurs.

roam \rohm\ *v.* roamed; roaming. To wander. roamer *n.*

roar \ror\ *v.* roared; roaring. **1.** To make a loud deep sound. **2.** To laugh loudly. roar *n.*

rob *v.* robbed; robbing. **1.** To steal. **2.** To deprive of something due. robber *n.*; robbery *n.*

robe \rohb\ *n.* A loose, casual garment. robed *adj.*; robe *v.*

robot \ROH-bot\ *n.* **1.** A machine made to act like a person. **2.** One who functions mechanically. robotic *adj.*

robotics \roh-BOT-iks\ *pl. n.* The study of robots and their operation.

robust \roh-BUST\ *adj.* Strong and healthy. robustly *adv.*; robustness *n.*

rock \rok\ *n.* **1.** A large stone. **2.** [Mu] A type of popular music. **3.** [Sl] A sizable diamond.

rock \rok\ *v.* rocked; rocking. **1.** To sway back and forth. **2.** [Mu] To listen to rock music. **3.** To upset.

rocket \ROK-it\ *n.* **1.** A device used to launch a missile or spacecraft. **2.** A propelled spacecraft.

rock 'n' roll *also* **rock-and-roll** \ROK-un-ROHL\ *n.* (Mu) Form of popular music with repetitious melody and insistent beat.

rocky \ROK-ee\ *adj.* rockier; rockiest. **1.** Full of rocks. **2.** Unyielding. **3.** Characterized by barriers. **4.** Unstable. rockiness *n.*

rococo \ruh-KOH-koh\ *n.* **1.** Decorative in style. **2.** [Cap] Ornate style of decoration from 18th c Europe. rococo *adj.*

rod *n.* **1.** A straight stick or bar. **2.** A measure of length.

rode \rohd\ *v.* The past participle of ride.

rodent \ROHD-nt\ *n.* An animal that gnaws, as a rat or mouse.

rodeo \ROH-dee-oh\ *n. pl.* rodeos. A display of horse riding and cattle roundups.

roentgenology \RENT-gun-ol-oh-jee\ *n.* (Md) Diagnosis and therapy using X Rays. roentgenologist *n.*

rogue \rohg\ *n.* A rascal. roguish *adj.*; roguishly *adv.*; roguery *n.*; roguishness *n.*

role \rohl\ *n.* **1.** An actor's part in a performance. **2.** A person's function in a group.

Rolfing \ROL-fing\ *n.* A type of massage therapy.

roll \rohl\ *n.* **1.** Act of turning over. **2.** Spherical shape. **3.** Actor's part. **4.** Register.

roll \rohl\ *v.* rolled; rolling. **1.** To turn or make turn over and over, as a ball. **2.** To gather into a sphere.

roller skating *n.* A sport of moving on rolling shoes.

rollicking \ROL-ik-ing\ *adj.* Frolicsome.

rollover \rohl-OH-vur\ *n.* An investment moved from one form to another.

romaine \roh-MAYN\ *n.* A bitter, loose-leafed variety of lettuce.

roman à clef \ROH-man-uh-klef\ *n. pl.* romans à clef. (Fr) A historical novel made to seem like fiction.

romance \roh-MANS\ *n.* **1.** A love affair. **2.** Any artistic work whose main theme is idealized love.

romance \roh-MANS\ *v.* romanced; romancing. **1.** To be involved in a love affair. **2.** To seduce. **3.** Tell or write romances.

romp *v.* romped; romping. **1.** To play roughly. **2.** To jog in a carefree manner. romp *n.*

rookery \RUUK-uh-ree\ *n. pl.* rookeries. A nest or colony of penguins or seals.

rookie \RUUK-ee\ *n.* (Sl) A inexperienced recruit.

room *n.* **1.** Space used for a purpose. **2.** Space enclosed on all sides.

room *v.* roomed; rooming. To live with others.

roomy \ROO-mee\ *adj.* Able to contain much. roominess *n.*

root *n.* **1.** The underground part of a plant. **2.** Cause; origin. **3.** Root-like part.

root *v.* rooted; rooting. **1.** To grow underground, as a plant does. **2.** To dig up or cut off.

rope \rohp\ *n.* **1.** Cord made with twisted strands. **2.** Collection in a line.

rope \rohp\ *v.* roped; roping. **1.** To bind with a thick cord made with twisted strands. **2.** To partition off.

Rorschach \ROR-shahk\ *n.* (Md) Personality test using interpretation of inkblot patterns.

rose \rohz\ *n.* A thorny-stemmed plant bearing fragrant flowers.

rose \rohz\ *v.* The past participle of rise.

roster \ROS-tur\ *n.* A list of names or items.

rosy \ROH-zee\ *adj.* rosier; rosiest. **1.** Pink, like roses. **2.** Cheerful. rosily *adv.*; rosiness *n.*

rot *n.* Decay. rot *v.*

rotary \ROH-tuh-ree\ *n.* *pl.* rotaries. **1.** A mechanism that spins around a central rod. **2.** A traffic circle. rotary *adj.*

rotate \ROH-tayt\ *v.* rotated; rotating. **1.** To spin around a center. **2.** To come around again and again. rotational *adj.*; rotation *n.*

rotisserie \roh-TIS-uh-ree\ *n.* **1.** A revolving device for roasting food. **2.** Restaurant serving this food.

rotten \ROT-n\ *adj.* Decayed.

rouge \roozh\ *n.* A cosmetic for adding color to the cheeks. rouge *v.*

rough \ruf\ *adj.* rougher; roughest. **1.** Bumpy. **2.** Stormy and violent. **3.** Rude. **4.** Done quickly. roughly *adv.*; roughness *n.*; roughen *v.*

roughage \RUF-ij\ *n.* The fiber eaten in one's diet.

roulette \roo-LET\ *n.* A gambling game played with a ball and wheel.

round \rownd\ *n.* **1.** Something ball-shaped. **2.** A stage in a contest. **3.** A unit of ammunition. roundness *n.*

round \rownd\ *adj.* rounder; roundest. **1.** Ball-shaped. **2.** Complete. **3.** Full-bodied. **4.** Rich in sound. **5.** Honest. roundness *n.*

round \rownd\ *v.* rounded; rounding. **1.** To make spherical or curved. **2.** To go around something. **3.** To complete. roundness *n.*

roundabout \rownd-uh-BOWT\ *adj.* Not going the shortest way.

roundabout \rownd-uh-BOWT\ *n.* (Fo) A road with a circular junction.

roundup \ROWND-up\ *n.* A grouping together for shipping or examination. round up *v.*

rouse \rowz\ *v.* roused; rousing. **1.** To wake up. **2.** To stimulate. rousingly *adv.*; rouse *n.*

rout \rowt\ *v.* routed; routing. To defeat overwhelmingly. rout *n.*

route \root\ *n.* **1.** A way between two places. **2.** An assigned course. route *v.*

routine \roo-TEEN\ *n.* **1.** A habitual way of doing things. **2.** A practiced performance. routine *adj.*; routinely *adv.*

row \roh\ *n.* **1.** A number of things arranged in a line. **2.** A continuous occurrence. **3.** Fight.

row \roh\ *v.* rowed; rowing. To move a boat with oars. rower *n.*

rowdy \ROW-dee\ *adj.* rowdier; rowdiest. Rough and noisy. rowdily *adv.*; rowdiness *n.*; rowdy *n.*

royal \ROI-ul\ *adj.* **1.** Relating to the king, queen, or their family. **2.** Of superior quality. royally *adv.*; royal *n.*

royalty \ROI-ul-tee\ *n. pl.* royalties. **1.** King, queen, and their family.

2. A payment to an author for books sold.

rub *v.* rubbed; rubbing. **1.** To move or pass over the surface with pressure. **2.** To clean, shine.

rub out *n.* (Sl) A murder.

rubbish \RUB-ish\ *n.* **1.** Waste material. **2.** Nonsense.

rubble \RUB-ul\ *n.* **1.** Broken rock or stone. **2.** Garbage.

rubella \roo-BEL-uh\ *n.* A contagious disease, also called the German measles.

ruble *also* **rouble** \ROO-bl\ *n.* A unit of money in Russia.

ruckus \RUK-us\ *n. pl.* ruckuses. A disturbance.

ruddy \RUD-ee\ *adj.* ruddier; ruddiest. Glowing and healthy. ruddiness *n.*

rude \rood\ *adj.* ruder; rudest. **1.** Impolite. **2.** Vulgar. **3.** Roughly made. rudely *adv.*; rudeness *n.*

rudimentary \roo-duh-MEN-tuh-ree\ *adj.* **1.** Incomplete. **2.** Basic. rudiment *n.*

rue \roo\ *v.* rued; rueing. To sympathize with.

ruffian \RUF-ee-un\ *n.* A troublemaker.

ruffle \RUF-ul\ *n.* **1.** A gather in material. **2.** A prolonged quiet beating of a drum.

ruffle \RUF-ul\ *v.* ruffled; ruffling.

1. To gather material into a ruffle. **2.** To upset. **3.** To fluff the feathers.

rugged \RUG-id\ *adj.* **1.** Rough. **2.** Displaying strength. ruggedly *adv.*; ruggedness *n.*

ruin \ROO-in\ *n.* **1.** A situation of devastation. **2.** Remains of something. **3.** Loss of honor, etc.

ruin \ROO-in\ *v.* ruined; ruining. **1.** To devastate. **2.** To make immoral.

rule \rool\ *n.* **1.** A period of governing power. **2.** A law, regulation, or custom.

rule \rool\ *v.* ruled; ruling. **1.** To govern. **2.** To make a decision. **3.** To draw parallel lines.

rule out *v.* To exclude from consideration.

ruler \ROO-lur\ *n.* **1.** One who governs. **2.** A tool for measuring and drawing straight lines.

ruling \ROO-ling\ *adj.* **1.** Governing. **2.** Omnipotent.

ruling \ROO-ling\ *n.* A decision.

rumble \RUM-bul\ *v.* rumbled; rumbling. To emit a low thunderous sound. rumble *n.*

ruminate \ROO-muh-nayt\ *v.* ruminated; ruminating. **1.** To chew the cud, as would a cow. **2.** To think about seriously. ruminative *adj.*; rumination *n.*

rummage \RUM-ij\ *v.* rummaged; rummaging. To make a mess when looking for something. rummage *n.*

rumor \ROO-mur\ *n.* A bit of information spread that may not be true. rumored *adj.*; rumor *v.*

rump *n.* **1.** The tail end of an animal. **2.** The buttocks.

rumple \RUM-pul\ *v.* rumpled; rumpling. To crease.

run *n.* **1.** A period of moving with quick steps. **2.** A political campaign. **3.** A pathway.

run *v.* ran; run; running. **1.** To move with quick steps. **2.** To seek political office. **3.** To manage.

run around *n.* An evasive response.

runaway \RUN-uh-way\ *n.* An escapee. runaway *adj.*

run down *n.* A summary.

rundown *also* **run-down** \RUN-DOWN\ *adj.* **1.** Dilapidated. **2.** Tired.

rung *n.* A crossbar on a ladder.

run-in *n.* **1.** An argument. **2.** Extra text to be added.

run-through \run-throo\ *n.* A quick practice.

rupture \RUP-chur\ *n.* **1.** A break. **2.** A disagreement. rupture *v.*

rural \RUUR-ul\ *adj.* Relating to the countryside.

ruse \rooz\ *n.* A deceptive plan.

rush *n.* **1.** A powerful move forward. **2.** A hurried act. **3.** A period of frenzied activity.

rush *v.* rushed; rushing. **1.** To move ahead with force. **2.** To force to hurry. **3.** To seek to join.

rust *n.* A reddish-brown substance that forms on iron exposed to moisture. rusty *adj.*; rust *v.*

rustic \RUS-tik\ *adj.* Countrylike. rustically *adv.*; rustic *n.*; rusticity *n.*

rustle \RUS-ul\ *v.* rustled; rustling. **1.** To make a gentle brushing sound. **2.** To steal animals. rustler *n.*

rusty \RUS-tee\ *adj.* rustier; rustiest. **1.** Covered with rust. **2.** Out of practice. rustiness *n.*

rut *n.* **1.** A groove made by wheels on the ground. **2.** A routine of daily life.

rutabaga \roo-tuh-BAY-guh\ *n.* A plant bearing an edible fleshy turniplike vegetable.

ruthless \ROOTH-lis\ *adj.* Lacking mercy. ruthlessly *adv.*; ruthlessness *n.*

rye \rie\ *n.* A type of cereal plant bearing seeds found in breads and processed into whiskey.

S

s \es\ *n. pl.* s's or ss. The 19th letter of the English alphabet.

sabbath \SAB-uth\ *n.* A day of rest and worship for some Jews and Christians.

sabbatical \suh-BAT-i-kul\ *n.* A leave granted for study or travel. sabbatical *adj.*

saber \SAY-bur\ *n.* A sword with a curved blade. saber *v.*

sable \SAY-bul\ *n.* A small arctic mammal with dark fur. sable *adj.*

sabotage \SAB-uh-tahzh\ *v.* sabotaged; sabotaging. To deliberately destroy or undermine. sabotage *n.*

sac \sak\ *n.* A baglike part in an animal or plant.

saccharin \SAK-ur-in\ *n.* A sugar substitute.

saccharine \SAK-ur-in\ *adj.* **1.** Sugary. **2.** Sappy.

sachet \sa-SHAY\ *n.* A small bag filled with sweet-smelling material.

sack \sak\ *n.* **1.** A bag constructed out of durable material. **2.** [Sl] Dismissal from one's job. sack *v.*

sacrament \SAK-ru-munt\ *n.* A Christian rite or symbol. sacramental *adj.*

sacred \SAY-krid\ *adj.* Holy. sacredness *n.*

sacrifice \SAK-ruh-fies\ *n.* **1.** Killing as a gift to a deity. **2.** The giving up of something valuable. sacredness *n.*

sacrilege \SAK-ruh-lij\ *n.* A disrespectful treatment of something sacred. sacrilegious *adj.*; sacrilegiously *adv.*; sacrilegiousness *n.*

sad *adj.* sadder; saddest. **1.** Unhappy. **2.** Inciting unhappiness. **3.** Regrettable. sadly *adv.*; sadness *n.*

safari \suh-FAHR-ee\ *n. pl.* safaris. An expedition to see or hunt wild animals.

safari park *n.* A wild animal reservation open to the public.

safe \sayf\ *adj.* safer; safest. **1.** Lacking danger. **2.** Lacking risk. **3.** Cautious. safely *adv.*; safety *n.*

safe \sayf\ *n.* **1.** An impenetrable box locked to secure items. **2.** [Sl] A condom.

safeguard \SAYF-gahrd\ *v.* safeguarded; safeguarding. To protect. safeguard *n.*

safe sex *n.* Sexual relations using protection from disease and pregnancy.

safety \SAYF-tee\ *n.* **1.** Freedom from danger. **2.** Any mechanism employed to protect from harm.

safety net *n.* Something that offers protection and security.

safflower \SAF-flow-ur\ *n.* A thistlelike plant bearing seeds containing an oil used in cooking, medicines.

sag *v.* sagged; sagging. To hang down because of weight or pressure. sag *n.*

saga \SAH-guh\ *n.* **1.** A long story **2.** A 12th to 15th century legend about heroes.

sagacious \suh-GAY-shus\ *adj.* Showing wisdom. sagaciously *adv.*; sagacity *n.*

said \sed\ *v.* The past tense and past participle of say.

sail \sayl\ *n.* **1.** Canvas that catches the wind and drives a boat. **2.** A trip on a boat.

sail \sayl\ *v.* sailed; sailing. **1.** To travel on water, esp. a boat driven by sails. **2.** Control a boat. **3.** Glide.

sailboat \SAYL-boht\ *n.* A ship or boat propelled by the use of sails.

sailor \SAY-lur\ *n.* A member of a ship's crew.

saint \saynt\ *n.* **1.** A holy person. **2.** A moral person. saintly *adv.*; sainthood *n.*; saintliness *n.*

sake \sayk\ *n.* **1.** A reason. **2.** Purpose.

salaam \suh-LAHM\ *n.* (Fo) A bow or salutation, especially practiced in Islamic countries.

salad \SAL-ud\ *n.* A dish usually made of cut-up raw vegetables or fruit.

salami \suh-LAH-mee\ *n. pl.* salamis. A spicy Italian sausage.

salary \SAL-uh-ree\ *n. pl.* salaries. Regular payment to an employee. salaried *adj.*

sale \sayl\ *n.* **1.** Transfer, exchange for money. **2.** A time of reduced prices on goods. sale *adj.*

salient \SAYL-yunt\ *adj.* **1.** Projecting. **2.** Noticeable. saliently *adv.*; salient *n.*

saline \SAY-leen\ *adj.* Salty. saline *n.*

saliva \suh-LIE-vuh\ *n.* Fluid secreted by glands of the mouth.

salivary \SAL-uh-vair-ee\ *adj.* Secreting saliva. salivation *n.*; salivate *v.*

sallow \SAL-oh\ *adj.* sallower; sallowest. Having a yellow complexion often unhealthy in appearance. sallowness *n.*; sallow *v.*

salmagundi \sal-muh-GUN-dee\ *n. pl.* salmagundis. **1.** A mixture. **2.** A salad containing lettuce, meat, eggs, anchovies, and onions.

salmon \SAM-un\ *n.* A large pink-fleshed edible fish. salmon *adj.*

salon \suh-LAHN\ *n.* **1.** A room for receiving guests. **2.** A hairdresser's shop. **3.** A regular meeting.

saloon \suh-LOON\ *n.* An establishment for the consumption of alcoholic beverages.

salsa \SAWL-suh\ *n. pl.* salsas. **1.** A spicy tomato sauce. **2.** A type of Latin American music and dance.

salt \sawlt\ *n.* A substance from mines or sea water used to season and preserve food. salty *adj.*; saltiness *n.*; salt *v.*

salute \suh-LOOT\ *n.* A gesture of respect or greeting. salute *v.*

salvage \SAL-vij\ *v.* salvaged; salvaging. **1.** To save from ruin. **2.** To recycle. salvageable *adj.*; salvage *n.*; salvager *n.*

salvation \sal-VAY-shun\ *n.* A redemption from disaster or sin.

salve \sav\ *n.* A soothing ointment. salve *v.*

samba \SAHM-buh\ *n. pl.* sambas. A Brazilian dance or its music. samba *v.*

same \saym\ *adj.* **1.** Being of one kind, value, or size. **2.** Unchanged. same *adv.*; sameness *n.*; same *pron.*

sample \SAM-pul\ *n.* A fragment typical of the whole. sample *adj.*; sampling *n.*; sample *v.*

sampler \SAM-plur\ *n.* **1.** A piece of embroidery work. **2.** A mixture.

samurai \SAM-uu-rie\ *n. pl.* samurai or samurais. (Fo) A Japanese warrior or soldier.

sanatorium *also* **sanatarium** \san-uh-TOR-ee-um\ *n. pl.* sanatoriums or sanatoria; sanatariums or sanataria. An establishment for caring for sick persons.

sanctify \SANGK-tuh-fie\ *v.* sanctified; sanctifying. To make sacred. sanctification *n.*; sanctifier *n.*

sanctimonious \sangk-tuh-MOH-nee-us\ *adj.* Overtly righteous. sanctimoniously *adv.*; sanctimoniousness *n.*; sanctimony *n.*

sanction \SANGK-shun\ *n.* **1.** Authorization. **2.** A penalty. sanction *v.*

sanctuary \SANGK-choo-er-ee\ *n. pl.* sanctuaries. **1.** A holy place. **2.** A place of escape. **3.** A protected environment for wildlife.

sanctum \SANGK-tum\ *n. pl.* sanctums or sancta. A holy or private place.

sand *n.* Fine loose fragments of crushed rock. sandy *adj.*

S and L *also* **savings and loan association.** A government-regulated savings bank.

sandwich \SAND-wich\ *n. pl.* sandwiches. Two slices of bread enclosing some filling. sandwich *v.*

sane \sayn\ *adj.* saner; sanest. Having a healthy, sound mind. sanely *adv.*

sangria \sang-GREE-uh\ *n.* (Sp) A drink consisting of wine, fruit juice, and soda water.

sanguine \SANG-gwin\ *adj.* **1.** Having a healthy red complexion. **2.** Optimistic. sanguinely *adv.*; sanguineness *n.*

sanitary \SAN-i-ter-ee\ *adj.* Free from germs.

sanity \SAN-i-tee\ *n.* The condition of having a healthy, sound mind. saneness *n.*

sank \sangk\ *v.* The past tense of sink.

sans \sanz\ *prep.* (Fr) Without.

sap *n.* **1.** The juices of plants that transport growth materials. **2.** [Sl] Foolish person.

sap *v.* sapped; sapping. To drain one's energy.

sapient \SAY-pee-unt\ *adj.* Wise. sapiently *adv.*; sapience *n.*

sapphire \SAF-ier\ *n.* A transparent blue gem. sapphire *adj.*

sarcasm \SAHR-kaz-um\ *n.* **1.** A mocking remark. **2.** A sense of humor intended to mock its subject. sarcastic *adj.*; sarcastically *adv.*

sarcophagus \sahr-KOF-uh-gus\ *n. pl.* sarcophagi or sarcophaguses. A stone coffin.

sardonic \sahr-DON-ik\ *adj.* Having a sarcastic or grim sense of humor. sardonically *adv.*

sari \SAHR-ee\ *n. pl.* saris. (Fo) A

length of cloth draped around the body, especially worn by Indian women.

sarong \suh-RONG\ *n.* A skirt wrapped about the waist.

sash *n. pl.* sashes. **1.** Cloth worn around the waist or over one shoulder. **2.** A window frame.

sashay \sah-SHAY\ *v.* sashayed; sashaying. To walk gracefully.

sassafras \SAS-uh-fras\ *n.* A North American tree and its aromatic bark.

sassy \SAS-ee\ *adj.* sassier; sassiest. **1.** Lacking respect. **2.** Energetic. **3.** Fashionable. sassily *adv.*; sassiness *n.*

Satan \SAYT-n\ *n.* The devil. satanic *adj.*; satanical *adj.*; satanically *adv.*; Satanism *n.*; Satanist *n.*

satchel \SACH-ul\ *n.* A large bag swung over the shoulder for carrying.

satellite \SAT-l-ite\ *n.* **1.** A body that orbits a planet. **2.** A man-made object that orbits a planet.

satiate \SAY-shee-ayt\ *v.* satiated; satiating. To satisfy completely. satiable *adj.*; satiation *n.*

satin \SAT-n\ *n.* A silky material. satin *adj.*; satiny *adj.*

satire \SAT-ier\ *n.* A performance or piece of writing that ridicules

something. satirical *adj.*; satirically *adv.*; satirist *n.*; satirize *v.*

satisfaction \sat-is-FAK-shun\ *n.* A gratification of one's needs.

satisfactory \sat-is-FAK-tuh-ree\ *adj.* Sufficient. satisfactorily *adv.*

satisfy \SAT-is-fie\ *v.* satisfied; satisfying. **1.** To fulfill one's needs **2.** To give what is required. **3.** To provide proof.

saturate \SACH-uh-rayt\ *v.* saturated; saturating. **1.** To soak thoroughly. **2.** To fill up. saturation *n.*

Saturday \SAT-ur-day\ *n. pl.* Saturdays. The seventh day of the week.

Saturn \SAT-urn\ *n.* The sixth planet from the Sun.

sauce \saws\ *n.* A liquid or semiliquid preparation used to flavor food.

saucy \SAW-see\ *adj.* saucier; sauciest. Disrespectful. saucily *adv.*; sauciness *n.*

sauerkraut \SOW-ur-krowt\ *n.* Pickled chopped cabbage.

sauna \SAW-nuh\ *n.* A dry-heat bath.

saunter \SAWN-tur\ *v.* sauntered; sauntering. To walk in a relaxed manner. saunter *n.*; saunterer *n.*

sauté \soh-TAY\ *v.* sautéed; sautéeing. To fry quickly in a little fat or oil. sauté *n.*

savage \SAV-ij\ *adj.* **1.** Wild. **2.** Uncivilized. **3.** Fierce. savagely *adv.*; savage *n.*; savageness *n.*; savagery *n.*

savanna *also* **savannah** \suh-VAN-uh\ *n.* A grassy plain located in hot regions.

savant \sa-VAHNT\ *n.* An learned person.

save \sayv\ *v.* saved; saving. **1.** To make safe. **2.** To prevent harm to. **3.** To keep for later use. **4.** To avoid.

savings \SAY-vings\ *pl. n.* Money set aside for later use.

savior \SAYV-yur\ *n.* A person who aids in times of difficulty.

savoir-faire \SAV-wahr-FAIR\ *n.* (Fr) Social know-how.

savor \SAY-vur\ *v.* savored; savoring. **1.** To smell or taste. **2.** To delight in thoroughly. savor *n.*

savory \SAY-vuh-ree\ *adj.* **1.** Agreeable to one's taste or smell. **2.** Morally proper. savoriness *n.*

savvy \SAV-ee\ *adj.* savvier; savviest. Knowledgeable, especially in a practical way. savvy *v.*

saxophone \SAK-suh-fohn\ *n.* (Mu) A brass woodwind instrument played with finger keys.

say *n.* **1.** A power to decide. **2.** An opportunity to speak.

say *v.* said; saying. **1.** To state in words. **2.** Declare. **3.** State positively.

saying \SAY-ing\ *n.* A well-known remark.

scabies \SKAY-beez\ *pl. n.* A contagious itchy skin disease.

scaffold \SKAF-uld\ *n.* An elevated wooden framework. scaffolding *n.*; scaffold *v.*

scalawag *also* **scallywag** \SKAL-uh-wag\ *n.* **1.** A troublemaker. **2.** Worthless person.

scald \skawld\ *v.* scalded; scalding. **1.** To burn with hot liquid or steam. **2.** To clean with hot liquid or steam. scald *n.*

scale \skayl\ *n.* **1.** Thin, horny membrae on most fish. **2.** Similar formation or part. **3.** Coating.

scale \skayl\ *n.* **1.** Instrument of measurement. **2.** System of measurement. **3.** [Mu] Musical tones.

scale \skayl\ *v.* scaled; scaling. **1.** To become dried, cracked, and flaky. **2.** To climb. **3.** To adjust by gradation.

scallion \SKAL-yun\ *n.* A type of green onion.

scallop \SKAL-up\ *n.* **1.** Bivalve mollusk of with ridged shell. **2.** Semicircular curves. scalloped *adj.*; scalloper *n.*; scallop *v.*

scalp \skalp\ *n.* Skin on the skull, usually covered with hair. scalp *v.*

scalpel \SKAL-pul\ *n.* (Md) A sharp straight knife used in surgery.

scaly \SKAY-lee\ *adj.* Of or covered with flakes or structures resembling flakes.

scam \skam\ *n.* A fraudulent scheme. scam *v.*

scamper \SKAM-pur\ *v.* scampered; scampering. To run hastily. scamper *n.*

scan \skan\ *v.* scanned; scanning. **1.** To glance at quickly. **2.** To pass an electronic beam over to read.

scandal \SKAN-dl\ *n.* **1.** A public disgrace. **2.** Gossip about a wrongdoing. scandalous *adj.*; scandalously *adv.*; scandouslesness *n.*

scant *also* **scanty** \skant\ *adj.* Insufficient. scantily *adv.*

scapegoat \SKAYP-goht\ *n.* One held responsible for the mistakes of others.

scar \skahr\ *n.* **1.** Blemish from a previous injury. **2.** A prolonged mental hurt. scarred *adj.*; scar *v.*

scarab \SKAR-ub\ *n.* **1.** A beetle. **2.** A representation of a beetle, esp. in ancient Egypt.

scarce \skairs\ *adj.* scarcer; scarcest. **1.** In short supply. **2.** Difficult to locate. scarcely *adv.*; scarceness *n.*; scarcity *n.*

scare \skair\ *v.* scared; scaring. To frighten. scare *adj.*; scare *n.*

scathe \skayth\ *v.* scathed; scathing. **1.** To criticize harshly. scathing *adj.*; scathingly *adv.*

scatter \SKAT-ur\ *v.* scattered; scattering. To throw or move things in various directions. scatter *n.*

scatterbrained \SKAT-ur-braynd\ *adj.* Not thinking clearly. scatterbrain *n.*

scavenge \SKAV-inj\ *v.* scavenged; scavenging. To search through waste for useful items. scavenger *n.*

scenario \si-NAIR-ee-oh\ *n.* *pl.* scenarios. **1.** A plot summary. **2.** An imagined sequence of events.

scene \seen\ *n.* **1.** Setting of a performance or event. **2.** Part of a performance. **3.** Display.

scenery \SEE-nuh-ree\ *n.* **1.** The general appearance of the landscape. **2.** Props used on a theater stage.

scenic \SEE-nik\ *adj.* Picturesque. scenically *adv.*

scent \sent\ *n.* **1.** An aroma. **2.** A fragrance. **3.** The smell of something left as a trail.

scent \sent\ *v.* scented; scenting. **1.** To smell or find by smell. **2.** To give a pleasant smell.

scepter *also* **sceptre** \SEP-tur\ *n.* An ornamental rod carried by a ruler.

schedule \SKEJ-uul\ *n.* **1.** List of details or items. **2.** Timetable. **3.** Detailed, timed plan. schedule *v.*

schematic \ski-MAT-ik\ *adj.* In the form of a diagram. schematically *adv.*; schematic *n.*

scheme \skeem\ *n.* A plan, often manipulative in nature. scheming *adj.*; scheme *v.*

schism \SIZ-um\ *n.* A division.

schizophrenia \skit-suh-FREE-nee-uh\ *n.* A serious mental disorder marked by delusions and irrationality. schizophrenic *adj.*, schizophrenically *adv.*; schizophrenic *n.*

schlemiel *also* **shlemiel** \shluh-MEEL\ *n.* (Yd) A bungler.

schlock *also* **shlock** \shlok\ *n.* (Sl) Something cheap and inferior. schlocky *adj.*

schmaltz *also* **schmalz** \shmahlts\ *n.* (Sl) Exaggerated sentimentality. schmaltzy *adj.*; schmalzy *adj.*; schmaltziness *n.*

schnitzel \SHNIT-zul\ *n.* (Gr) A cutlet, especially of veal.

schnook \shnook\ *n.* (Yd) A gullible person.

scholar \SKOL-ur\ *n.* A person who is very involved in education and learning. scholarly *adv.*; scholarliness *n.*

scholastic \skuh-LAS-tik\ *adj.* Relating to schools and education. scholastically *adv.*

school \skool\ *n.* **1.** An educational institution. **2.** Students and teachers. **3.** Part of university.

school \skool\ *v.* schooled; schooling. To teach.

schooner \SKOO-nur\ *n.* **1.** A type of sailing ship. **2.** A tall beer glass.

schtick *also* **shtick** \shtik\ *n.* (Sl) One's special interest, talent, or routine.

schwa \shwah\ *n.* A neutral vowel sound, as a in alone, and the symbol that represents it.

sciatica \sie-AT-i-kuh\ *n.* (Md) A pain that originates in the buttocks and descends the back of the thigh. sciatic *adj.*

science \SIE-uns\ *n.* **1.** Any branch of knowledge using experimentation. **2.** Skill. scientific *adj.*; scientifically *adv.*; scientist *n.*

scintillating \SIN-tl-ay-ting\ *adj.* Sparkling. scintillation *n.*; scintillate *v.*

scion \SIE-un\ *n.* **1.** A plant shoot cut for grafting. **2.** A descendant.

scissors \SIZ-urz\ *pl. n.* A cutting

instrument with two hinged blades. scissor *v.*

sclerosis \skli-ROH-sis\ *n. pl.* scleroses. (Md) An abnormal hardening of body tissue. sclerotic *adj.*

scold \skohld\ *v.* scolded; scolding. To speak crossly to a wrongdoer. scolding *n.*

scone \skohn\ *n.* A sweetened biscuit.

scoop \skoop\ *n.* **1.** A ladlelike device. **2.** Picking up with ladle. **3.** A scoopful.

scope \skohp\ *n.* **1.** The range of a subject or work. **2.** An opportunity or ability to do something.

scorch \skorch\ *v.* scorched; scorching. To burn or become burnt on the surface. scorch *n.*

score \skor\ *n.* **1.** Number of points made in a game. **2.** Debt one seeks to settle. **3.** Twenty years

score \skor\ *v.* scored; scoring. **1.** To make points in a game. **2.** To tally the points in a game. **3.** To mark.

scorn \skorn\ *n.* A strong contempt. scornful *adj.*; scornfully *adv.*; scorn *v.*

scorpion \SKOR-pee-un\ *n.* A spiderlike animal with a long tail ending in a poisonous stinger.

scoundrel \SKOWN-drul\ *n.* A wicked person.

scour \SKOW-ur\ *v.* scoured; scouring. **1.** To scrub clean. **2.** To search thoroughly.

scourge \skurj\ *n.* **1.** A heavy whip. **2.** Any cause of great suffering. scourge *v.*

scout \skowt\ *n.* **1.** A member of the Boy or Girl Scouts. **2.** A person sent to gather information. scouting *n.*; scout *v.*

scowl \skowl\ *v.* scowled; scowling. To make an angry frown. scowl *n.*

scrabble \SKRAB-ul\ *v.* scrabbled; scrabbling. **1.** To search with one's hands or feet. **2.** To struggle with another. scrabble *n.*

scraggly \SKRAG-lee\ *adj.* scragglier; scraggliest. **1.** Uneven. **2.** Unkempt.

scram \skram\ *v.* scrammed; scramming. (Sl) To leave immediately.

scramble \SKRAM-bul\ *v.* scrambled; scrambling. **1.** To move hastily. **2.** To struggle awkwardly. **3.** To beat and cook eggs.

scrap \skrap\ *n.* **1.** A fragment. **2.** Waste material. **3.** [Sl] A fight. **4.** [Pl] Leftover bits of food

scrap \skrap\ *v.* scrapped; scrapping. **1.** To throw away something useless. **2.** [Sl] To fight.

scrape \skrayp\ *n.* **1.** Mark or sound

made by scraping. **2.** Difficult situation.

scrape \skrayp\ *v.* scraped; scraping. **1.** To rub, damage, or smooth with something hard or sharp. **2.** To manage.

scratch \skrach\ *n.* **1.** A cut or mark from something sharp. **2.** Sound of scratching. **3.** Erasing.

scratch \skrach\ *v.* scratched; scratching. **1.** To cut or mark with something sharp. **2.** To scrape with the fingernails.

scrawl \skrawl\ *v.* scrawled; scrawling. To write hurriedly and illegibly. scrawl *n.*

scrawny \SKRAW-nee\ *adj.* scrawnier; scrawniest. Very thin. scrawniness *n.*

scream \skreem\ *v.* screamed; screaming. To cry out loudly and shrilly. scream *n.*

screen \skreen\ *n.* **1.** Partition, etc. to separate, conceal. **2.** Wire mesh on window. **3.** TV surface.

screen \skreen\ *v.* screened; screening. **1.** To shield. **2.** To show on a screen.

screenwriter \SKREEN-rite-ur\ *n.* A scriptwriter for motion pictures. screenwriting *n.*

screw \skroo\ *n.* A metal pin with a spiral groove cut into it.

screw \skroo\ *v.* screwed; screwing. **1.** To twist a metal pin in or out of a surface. **2.** To twist something.

screwdriver \SKROO-drie-vur\ *n.* A tool for turning screws.

screw over *v.* To cheat.

screw up *v.* To bungle.

scribble \SKRIB-ul\ *v.* scribbled; scribbling. To write sloppily. scribble *n.*

scribe \skrieb\ *n.* **1.** A person who makes handwritten copies of writings. **2.** A religious scholar. scribal *adj.*

scrimmage \SKRIM-ij\ *n.* **1.** A confused struggle. **2.** In football, the action of a complete play. scrimmage *v.*

script \skript\ *n.* **1.** The text of a performance. **2.** Handwriting. script *v.*

scripture \SKRIP-chur\ *n.* Any sacred writing. scriptural *adj.*

scrounge \skrownj\ *v.* scrounged; scrounging. To collect by foraging. scrounger *n.*

scrub \skrub\ *v.* scrubbed; scrubbing. To clean by rubbing with something coarse. scrub *n.*; scrubber *n.*

scruffy \SKRUF-ee\ *adj.* scruffier; scruffiest. Sloppy. scruffiness *n.*

scrumptious \SKRUMP-shus\ *adj.*

Delicious. scrumptiously *adv.*; scrumptiousness *n.*

scruple \SKROO-pul\ *n.* A doubt arising from a moral dilemma. scruple *v.*

scrupulous \SKROO-pyuh-lus\ *adj.* Morally careful. scrupulously *adv.*; scrupulousness *n.*

scrutiny \SKROOT-n-ee\ *n.* A careful examination. scrutinization *n.*; scrutinize *v.*

scuba \SKOO-buh\ *n.* A self-contained underwater breathing apparatus.

scuba diver *n.* A person who explores underwater wearing a self-contained breathing apparatus. scuba diving *n.*

scuffle \SKUF-ul\ *v.* scuffled; scuffling. **1.** To struggle confusedly. **2.** To drag one's feet while walking. scuffle *n.*

sculpture \SKULP-chur\ *n.* **1.** Art of three-dimensional figures. **2.** Figure or design carved or molded. sculptural *adj.*; sculptor *n.*; sculpture *v.*

scum \skum\ *n.* **1.** A layer of dirt. **2.** A dirty froth on top of a liquid. **3.** Despicable person. scummy *adj.*

scurrilous \SKUR-uh-lus\ *adj.* Rudely abusive. scurrilously *adv.*; scurrility *n.*

scurry \SKUR-ee\ *v.* scurried; scurrying. To run hurriedly. scurry *n.*

scuzzy \SKUZ-ee\ *adj.* scuzzier; scuzziest. (Sl) Repulsively unkempt. scuzziness *n.*

scythe \sieth\ *n. pl.* scythes. A tool with a long, curved blade for cutting.

sea \see\ *n.* **1.** Salt water covering the Earth's surface. **2.** A particular area of salt water.

seal \seel\ *n.* **1.** Sea mammal with thick fur, four flippers. **2.** Wax or design impression.

seam \seem\ *n.* **1.** Line where two pieces of material are sewn together. **2.** Stratum of rock.

seamy \SEE-mee\ *adj.* seamier; seamiest. Disreputable. seaminess *n.*

seance \SAY-ahns\ *n.* A session in which the participants try to speak with spirits.

sear \seer\ *v.* seared; searing. To scorch.

search \surch\ *v.* searched; searching. To look for in hopes of finding. search *n.*

seashore \SEE-shor\ *n.* The land bordering the sea.

season \SEE-zun\ *n.* **1.** One of four divisions of a year. **2.** A time when something is done, played, etc. seasonal *adj.*; seasonably *adv.*

season \SEE-zun\ *v.* seasoned; seasoning. To give flavor to food by treating it with additives. seasoning *n.*

seasonable \SEE-zuh-nuh-bul\ *adj.* 1. Suitable for the time of year. 2. Appropriate.

seat \seet\ *n.* 1. A thing made or used for sitting on. 2. The buttocks. 3. A position.

seat \seet\ *v.* seated; seating. 1. To sit or cause to sit. 2. To be based in.

sebaceous \si-BAY-shus\ *adj.* Secreting fat or oil.

secede \si-SEED\ *v.* seceded; seceding. To withdraw from membership. secession *n.*; secessionist *n.*

seclude \si-KLOOD\ *v.* secluded; secluding. To keep apart from others. seclusion *n.*

second \SEK-und\ *adj.* 1. Next after the first. 2. Another.

second \SEK-und\ *v.* seconded; seconding. To offer a vote of support.

second \SEK-und\ *n.* 1. The next after the first. 2. One-sixtieth of a minute. 3. Moment.

secondary \SEK-un-der-ee\ *adj.* Coming after what is primary. secondarily *adv.*

second-rate \SEK-und-RAYT\ *adj.* Of lesser quality.

secret \SEE-krit\ *adj.* 1. Not to be made known. 2. Not generally known. secretive *adj.*; secretly *adv.*; secrecy *n.*; secret *n.*

secretary \SEK-ri-ter-ee\ *n. pl.* secretaries. 1. Office helper. 2. Department head in government. 3. Writing desk. secretarial *adj.*

secrete \si-KREET\ *v.* secreted; secreting. 1. To put in a place of concealment. 2. To produce and emit. secretion *n.*

secretive \si-KREE-tiv or SEE-kri-tiv\ *adj.* Making a secret of things. secretively *adv.*; secretiveness *n.*

sect \sekt\ *n.* A group organized around common beliefs, often religious in nature. sectarian *adj.*; sectarianism *n.*

section \SEK-shun\ *n.* A division of something. sectional *adj.*; section *v.*

sector \SEK-tur\ *n.* 1. Part of an area. 2. A branch of activity. 3. The part of a circle.

secular \SEK-yuh-lur\ *adj.* Relating to worldly, not religious, matters. secularism *n.*; secularization *n.*; secularize *v.*

secure \si-KYUUR\ *adj.* securer;

securest. **1.** Safe from danger. **2.** Firmly fixed. securely *adv.*; secure *v.*

security \si-KYUUR-i-tee\ *n.* **1.** Safety. **2.** Freedom from worry. **3.** Guarantee of full payment.

sedate \si-DAYT\ *adj.* Calm and dignified. sedately *adv.*; sedateness *n.*

sedate \si-DAYT\ *v.* sedated; sedating. To make calm by treating with drugs or some other influence. sedation *n.*

sedative \SED-uh-tiv\ *n.* A drug or influence with a calming effect. sedative *adj.*

sedentary \SED-n-ter-ee\ *adj.* Characterized or requiring much sitting. sedentarily *adv.*

Seder \SAY-dur\ *n. pl.* [He] Seders or Sedarim. A ceremonial Jewish dinner at the beginning of Passover.

sediment \SED-uh-munt\ *n.* Solid matter settling at the bottom of a liquid. sedimentary *adj.*

seduce \si-DOOS\ *v.* seduced; seducing. **1.** To persuade to commit immoral acts. **2.** To tempt into sexual relations. seductive *adj.*; seducer *n.*; seduction *n.*; seductress *n.*

see *v.* saw; seen. **1.** Use the eyes to perceive. **2.** To understand. **3.** To imagine. **4.** To experience.

seed *n. pl.* seed or seeds. **1.** A small part of a plant from which new plants are produced. **2.** An origin.

seedy \SEE-dee\ *adj.* seedier; seediest. **1.** Full of seeds. **2.** Shabby and disreputable. seediness *n.*

seek *v.* sought; seeking. **1.** To look for. **2.** To try to do something. seeker *n.*

seem *v.* seemed; seeming. **1.** To appear to exist. **2.** To give the impression.

seen *v.* The past participle of see.

seep *v.* seeped; seeping. To ooze.

seer \SEE-ur\ *n.* One who has visions of the future.

seersucker \SEER-suk-ur\ *n.* A puckered fabric.

seethe \seeth\ *v.* seethed; seething. **1.** To bubble. **2.** To be very agitated.

see-through *adj.* Transparent.

segment \SEG-munt\ *n.* A separate section of something. segmented *adj.*; segmentation *n.*; segment *v.*

segregation \seg-ri-GAY-shun\ *n.* The practice or condition of putting something apart from others. segregationist *n.*; segregate *v.*

seismic \SIEZ-mik\ *adj.* Of or caused by an earthquake. seismically *adv.*

seismography \siez-MOG-ruh-fee\ *n.* (Sc) The measuring and recording of earthquakes. seismograph *n.*; seismographer *n.*; seismology *n.*

seize \seez\ *v.* seized; seizing. **1.** Take hold of forcibly. **2.** [Le] To take by legal right. **3.** To affect suddenly.

seizure \SEE-zhur\ *n.* **1.** Taking hold forcibly. **2.** [Le] Taking by legal right. **3.** [Md] A sudden attack.

seldom \SEL-dum\ *adj.* Not often. seldomly *adv.*

select \si-LEKT\ *adj.* Carefully chosen, especially for excellence. selective *adj.*; selectively *adv.*; selectivity *n.*

select \si-LEKT\ *v.* selected; selecting. To choose. selection *n.*; selector *n.*

self *n. pl.* selves. An individual's personality or identity. self *adj.*

self-centered \SELF-SEN-turd\ *adj.* Thinking mainly of oneself and one's own interests. self-centeredness *n.*

self-confident \self-KON-fi-dens\ *adj.* Being sure of one's own abilities. self-confidence *n.*

self-conscious \SELF-KON-shus\ *adj.* Being embarrassed or worried about what others think. self-consciously *adv.*; self-consciousness *n.*

self-control \SELF-kun-TROHL\ *n.* A dominance over one's behavior and emotions. self-controlled *adj.*

self-explanatory \SELF-ik-PLAN-uh-tor-ee\ *adj.* Needing no explanation.

self-interest \self-IN-tur-ist\ *n.* One's own benefit. self-interested *adj.*

selfish \SEL-fish\ *adj.* Acting or done for one's own interests without regard for others. selfishly *adv.*; selfishness *n.*

self-respect \SELF-ri-SPEKT\ *n.* Proper regard or esteem for oneself. self-respecting *adj.*

self-righteous \self-RIE-chus\ *adj.* Smugly sure of one's own goodness. self-righteously *adv.*; self-righteousness *n.*

self-satisfaction \SELF-sat-is-FAK-shun\ *n.* Pleasure with oneself and one's achievements. self-satisfied *adj.*

self-starter *n.* **1.** A person who shows initiative. **2.** Engine mechanism. self-starting *adj.*

self-sufficient \self-suh-FISH-unt\ *adj.* Able to cope without outside assistance. self-sufficiency *n.*

sell \sel\ *v.* sold; selling. **1.** Transfer property for money. **2.** Offer for sale. **3.** Deliver. **4.** Promote. seller *n.*

sellout \SEL-owt\ *n.* (Sl) **1.** Performance for which all the seats are sold. **2.** Compromiser.

seltzer \SETL-sur\ *n.* Carbonated water.

semantics \si-MAN-tiks\ *pl. n.* **1.** The study of meaning in language. **2.** Meaning or connotation. semantic *adj.*; semantically *adv.*

semblance \SEM-bluns\ *n.* **1.** An external appearance. **2.** A likeness. **3.** A reproduction.

semen \SEE-mun\ *n.* The sperm-bearing fluid of male animals.

semester \si-MES-tur\ *n.* An academic session, usually consisting of four to six months.

semiannual \sem-ee-AN-yoo-ul\ *adj.* **1.** Occurring twice a year. **2.** Lasting half a year. semiannually *adv.*

semicolon \SEM-i-koh-lun\ *n.* The punctuation mark (;) with more separation than a comma.

seminar \SEM-uh-nahr\ *n.* A course of study or session for advanced discussion or research.

seminary \SEM-uh-ner-ee\ *n.* An educational institution for priests, ministers, rabbis, etc.

semiotics \SEM-ee-ot-iks\ *pl. n.* The study of signs, symbols, and language. semiotic *adj.*; semiotician *n.*

Semitic \suh-MIT-ik\ *adj.* Of or concerning the Jewish and Arabic peoples. Semite *n.*; Semitic *n.*; Semitics *n.*; Semiticist *n.*; Semitism *n.*

semolina \sem-oh-LEE-nuh\ *n.* Coarse particles from wheat grinding used to make pasta.

senate \SEN-it\ *n.* The highest legislative group in some governments, as in the U.S.

senator \SEN-uh-tur\ *n.* A member of the highest legislative group in some governments. senatorial *adj.*; senatorship *n.*

send *v.* sent; sending. **1.** To cause to go or order to a destination. **2.** To produce. **3.** To convey.

senile \SEE-nile\ *adj.* **1.** Showing signs of old age. **2.** Infirm; weak. senility *n.*

senior \SEEN-yur\ *adj.* **1.** Older. **2.** Having more authority. **3.** Relating to the uppermost level in school senior *n.*

seniority \seen-YOR-i-tee\ *n. pl.* seniorities. Precedence in authority.

sensation \sen-SAY-shun\ *n.* **1.** A

feeling. **2.** An exciting happening or person. sensational *adj.*; sensationally *adv.*; sensationalism *n.*

sense \sens\ *n. pl.* senses. **1.** Perception by sight, hearing, touch, taste, smell, sight. **2.** Understanding. sensory

sense \sens\ *v.* sensed; sensing. To perceive something through sight, hearing, taste, smell, or touch.

senseless \SENS-lis\ *adj.* **1.** Lacking the power to think and make wise decisions. **2.** Lacking meaning. senselessly *n.*; senselessness *n.*

sensibility \sen-suh-BIL-i-tee\ *n. pl.* sensibilities. The capacity for feeling and discrimination.

sensible \SEN-suh-bul\ *adj.* **1.** Having or showing wiseness and awareness. **2.** Easily understood. sensibly *adv.*

sensitive \SEN-si-tiv\ *adj.* **1.** Impressionable. **2.** Easily hurt. **3.** Quickly offended. sensitively *adv.*; sensitiveness *n.*; sensitivity *n.*

sensitize \SEN-si-tize\ *v.* sensitized; sentitizing. To make or become impressionable. sensitization *n.*

sensory \SN-suh-ree\ *adj.* Of or concerning the senses or sensation.

sensual \SEN-shoo-ul\ *adj.* Gratifying or indulging the body with physical pleasure. sensually *adv.*; sensuality *n.*

sensuous \SEN-shoo-us\ *adj.* Affecting the senses pleasantly. sensuously *adv.*; sensuousness *n.*

sent *v.* The past tense and past participle of send.

sentence \SEN-tns\ *n.* **1.** Words that makes a complete statement or question. **2.** [Le] A punishment.

sentence \SEN-tns\ *v.* [Le] To announce a punishment given to a criminal.

sentiment \SEN-tuh-munt\ *n.* **1.** A thought or feeling. **2.** An appeal to one's feeling. **3.** Excessive emotion.

sentimental \sen-tuh-MEN-tl\ *adj.* **1.** Catering to emotions. **2.** Excessively sensitive or reminiscent. sentimentally *adv.*; sentimentalism *n.*; sentimentality *n.*

separable \SEP-ur-uh-bul\ *adj.* Able to be set apart. separably *adv.*; separability *n.*

separate \SEP-ur-it\ *adj.* Divided from others. separately *adv.*

separate \SEP-uh-rayt\ *v.* separated; separating. To make or become divided. separation *n.*

sepia \SEE-pee-uh\ *n.* A reddish-brown coloring.

September \sep-TEM-bur\ *n.* The ninth month of the year.

septic \SEP-tik\ *adj.* Infected with harmful microorganisms.

sequel \SEE-kwul\ *n.* Something that follows, as another book or performance.

sequence \SEE-kwuns\ *n.* A number of things or events that follow each other in an order.

sequential \si-KWEN-shul\ *adj.* Forming or occurring in a successive order. sequentially *adv.*

sequester \si-KWES-tur\ *v.* sequestered; sequestering. To remove or withdraw into solitude.

sequin \SEE-kwin\ *n.* A small, shiny decorative disk. sequined *adj.*

sequoia \si-KWOI-uh\ *n. pl.* sequoias. A very large coniferous tree of North America.

serape *also* **sarape** \suh-RAH-pee\ *n.* (Sp) A brightly colored wool shawl of Mexico.

serenade \ser-uh-NAYD\ *n.* (Mu) A song played by a lover to show affections. serenade *v.*

serene \suh-REEN\ *adj.* Calm and undisturbed. serenely *adv.*; sereness *n.*; serenity *n.*

serf \surf\ *n.* A medieval laborer bound to the land and owned by the lord. serfdom *n.*

sergeant \SAHR-junt\ *n.* **1.** A non-commissioned military officer above a corporal. **2.** High-ranking police.

serial \SEER-ee-ul\ *n.* A story told or presented in episodes. serially *adv.*; serialization *n.*; serialize *v.*

series \SEER-eez\ *n. pl.* series. A number of related things that occur or are arranged in a sequence.

serious \SEER-ee-us\ *adj.* **1.** Lacking humor. **2.** Solemn. **3.** Important. **4.** Risky. seriously *adv.*; seriousness *n.*

sermon \SUR-mun\ *n.* **1.** A talk given during a religious service. **2.** A tedious, righteous lecture. sermonize *v.*

seroconversion \SER-oh-kun-vur-zhun\ *n.* (Md) The production of antibodies in blood in response to infection or immunization.

serology \ser-ol-OH-jee\ *n.* (Md) **1.** The study of serum. **2.** The properties of an infection. serologist *n.*

serpent \SUR-punt\ *n.* A large snake.

serrated \SER-ay-tud\ *adj.* Having

a notched edge, especially for cutting. serrate *adj.*; serration *n.*

serum \SEER-um\ *n. pl.* serums or sera. (Md) **1.** Fluid that remains when blood has clotted. **2.** Watery fluid of animal tissue.

servant \SUR-vunt\ *n.* **1.** A domestic worker. **2.** One who demonstrates obedience or respect to another.

serve \surv\ *v.* served; serving. **1.** Do a particular job or duty. **2.** To give food or drink at a meal. **3.** Help. server *n.*

service \SUR-vis\ *n.* **1.** The doing of a job or duty. **2.** The armed forces. **3.** The act of giving food. service *v.*

servile \SUR-vil\ *adj.* Excessively submissive. servilely *adv.*; servility *n.*

servitude \SUR-vi-tood\ *n.* Compulsory service or slavery.

sesame \SES-uh-mee\ *n.* A plant with seeds used for oil or food.

session \SESH-un\ *n.* **1.** A meeting or period for business dealings. **2.** A period of any activity. sessional *adj.*

set *adj.* **1.** Positioned. **2.** Hardened. **3.** Intentional. **4.** Stubborn. **5.** Prepared.

set *n.* **1.** A group of related things or people. **2.** A device for receiving communication.

set *v.* set; setting. **1.** Put, arrange, place, or fix in position. **2.** To become hard. **3.** To go below.

setback \SET-bak\ *n.* Something that stops or hinders progress. set back *v.*

set off *v.* **1.** To separate so as to enhance. **2.** To begin a trip. **3.** To cause to explode.

settee \suh-TEE\ *n.* A type of small sofa.

setting \SET-ing\ *n.* **1.** Way or place in which something is positioned. **2.** Utensils or dishes for one.

settle \SET-l\ *v.* settled; settling. **1.** To make a home somewhere. **2.** To put in a position. **3.** To make steady. settler *n.*

settlement \SET-l-munt\ *n.* **1.** A business or financial arrangement. **2.** A community.

set up *v.* set up; setting up. **1.** To construct. **2.** To establish. **3.** To lure into a bad situation.

sever \SEV-ur\ *v.* severed; severing. **1.** To cut apart. **2.** To dissociate. severance *n.*

several \SEV-ur-ul\ *adj.* Existing in a small quantity. several pron.

severe \suh-VEER\ *adj.* severer; severest. **1.** Strict. **2.** Stern. **3.** Demanding. **4.** Intense. **5.** Violent. severely *adv.*; severity *n.*

sew \soh\ *v.* sewed; sewn; sewing. To make or fasten with a thread and needle. sewing *n.*

sewage \SOO-ij\ *n.* Waste drained from homes and buildings for disposal.

sewer \SOO-ur\ *n.* A drainage system for carrying away waste.

sex \seks\ *n. pl.* sexes. **1.** State of being male or female. **2.** A physical attraction between organisms. sexual *adj.*

sex symbol *n.* A person or celebrity with great appeal.

sexual harassment *n.* Unwelcome sexual advances.

sexuality \sik-shoo-AL-i-tee\ *n.* A person's sexual character.

sexually transmitted disease *also* **STD** *n.* (Md) Any disease transmitted by sexual contact.

sexy \SEK-see\ *adj.* sexier; sexiest. Attractive or stimulating to others. sexily *adv.*; sexiness *n.*

shabby \SHAB-ee\ *adj.* shabbier; shabbiest. **1.** Worn and in poor condition. **2.** Unfair. shabbily *adv.*; shabbiness *n.*

shade \shayd\ *n.* **1.** A place of relative darkness. **2.** Object blocking light. **3.** Color variation.

shade \shayd\ *v.* shaded; shading. **1.** To block from bright light. **2.** To darken. **3.** To grade light and dark.

shadow \SHAD-oh\ *n.* **1.** An area of shade. **2.** A dark image. **3.** Ghost. shadowy *adj.*; shadow *v.*

shady \SHAY-dee\ *adj.* shadier; shadiest. **1.** Giving or situated in the shade. **2.** [Sl] Not to be trusted. shadiness *n.*

shag \SHAG\ *n.* **1.** A rough, wooly mass. **2.** A thick, bumpy rug. **3.** Shredded coarse tobacco.

shake \shayk\ *v.* shook; shaken; shaking. **1.** To move quickly up and down or to and fro. **2.** To tremble. shaker *n.*

shaky \SHAY-kee\ *adj.* shakier; shakiest. **1.** Trembling. **2.** Unreliable. shakily *adv.*; shakiness *n.*

shallot \SHAL-ut\ *n.* An onionlike plant.

shallow \SHAL-oh\ *adj.* shallower; shallowest. **1.** Not deep. **2.** Superficial. shallowness *n.*

shalom \shah-LOHM\ *interj.* (He) Used as a greeting or goodbye.

sham \sham\ *n.* A hoax. sham *v.*

shaman \SHAH-mun\ *n.* One who communicates between the physical and the spiritual world. shamanic *adj.*; shamanism *n.*; shamanist *n.*

shambles \SHAM-bulz\ *pl. n.* A mess or scene of destruction.

shame \shaym\ *n.* **1.** Painful guilt. **2.** State if dishonor, disgrace. shameful *adj.*; shamefully *adv.*; shamefulness *n.*

shameless \SHAYM-lis\ *adj.* Lacking any sense of guilt or regret. shamelessly *adv.*; shamelessness *n.*

shanty \SHAN-tee\ *n. pl.* shanties. **1.** A shack. **2.** A sailors' song.

shape \shayp\ *n.* **1.** The outline of something. **2.** The condition of something. shapely *adj.*

shape \shayp\ *v.* shaped; shaping. **1.** To give form to. **2.** To adapt.

shape up *v.* **1.** To arrange into a satisfactory form. **2.** To become disciplined.

share \shair\ *n.* **1.** One's portion of a whole. **2.** One of the parts forming a company's capital.

share \shair\ *v.* shared; sharing. **1.** To divide up or give part of a whole. **2.** To use along with others.

shareholder \SHAIR-hohl-dur\ *n.* A person who owns stock in a company.

shark \shahrk\ *n.* **1.** A large, fierce sea fish. **2.** [Cl] A swindler.

sharp \shahrp\ *adj.* sharper; sharpest. **1.** Having a fine cutting edge. **2.** Pointy. **3.** Abrupt and severe. **4.** Well-defined. sharp *adv.*;

sharply *adv.*; sharpness *n.*; sharpen *v.*

shatter \SHAT-ur\ *v.* shattered; shattering. **1.** To burst. **2.** To utterly destroy.

shave \shayv\ *v.* shaved; shaving. **1.** To cut or scrape hair growing out of the skin. **2.** To cut thin slices off. shave *n.*; shaver *n.*; shaving *n.*

sheathe \sheeth\ *v.* sheathed; sheathing. To put into a case or covering. sheath *n.*; sheathing *n.*

shed *n.* A small storage building.

shed *v.* shed; shedding. **1.** To lose by a natural falling off. **2.** To take off. **3.** To flow out.

sheen *n.* A gloss.

sheep *n. pl.* sheep. **1.** A grass-eating animal bred for wool and meat. **2.** [Sl] A shy person.

sheepish \SHEE-pish\ *adj.* Shy. sheepishly *adv.*; sheepishness *n.*

sheer *adj.* **1.** Complete. **2.** Very steep. **3.** Transparent. sheerly *adv.*; sheerness *n.*

sheet *n.* **1.** A large piece of fabric for covering a mattress. **2.** A piece of paper.

sheik *also* **sheikh** \sheek\ *n.* (Ar) An Arab leader. sheikhdom *n.*

shelf *n. pl.* shelves. **1.** A board positioned horizontally for storage. **2.** A ledge.

shell \shel\ *n.* **1.** Hard encasement, as for mollusk. **2.** Covering of fruit, nut, e.g. **3.** Outline. shell *v.*

shell-shocked *also* **shellshocked** *adj.* Being nervous after a traumatic incident. shellshock *n.*

shelter \SHEL-tur\ *n.* **1.** Protection. **2.** A structure that gives protection. shelter *v.*

shelve \shelv\ *v.* shelved; shelving. **1.** To set up shelves. **2.** To arrange on a shelf. **3.** To set aside.

shepherd \SHEP-urd\ *n.* A person who looks after sheep.

sheriff \SHER-if\ *n.* A county law enforcement officer.

shiatsu \shee-AT-soo\ *n.* (Fo) Therapeutic massage technique in which pressure is applied to particular points.

shibboleth \SHIB-uh-lith\ *n.* (He) **1.** A password. **2.** A saying or intonation peculiar to a group.

shield \sheeld\ *n.* Something that protects one from harm, such as armor. shield *v.*

shift *n.* **1.** A change of position. **2.** Group of workers assigned to a certain time.

shift *v.* shifted; shifting. To move or change position.

shifty \SHIF-tee\ *adj.* shiftier; shiftiest. Tricky or deceitful. shiftily *adv.*; shiftiness *n.*

shilling \SHIL-ing\ *n.* The basic monetary unit of Austria.

shimmer \SHIM-ur\ *n.* A shine produced by a soft, quivering light. shimmer *v.*

shine \shien\ *v.* shone; shining. **1.** To reflect light. **2.** To rub until a glossiness appears. **3.** To excel. shine *n.*

shingle \SHING-gul\ *n.* **1.** A roof tile. **2.** A small business sign. **3.** Small pebbles on the beach.

Shintoism \SHIN-to-iz-um\ *n.* (Fo) A Japanese religion based on nature and ancestor worship. Shinto *adj.*; Shintoist *adj.*; Shinto *n.*; Shintoist *n.*

ship *n.* A large sea-going vessel.

ship *v.* shipped; shipping. **1.** To send by ship. **2.** To transport on any vehicle. shipment *n.*; shipper *n.*; shipping *n.*

shirk \shurk\ *v.* shirked; shirking. To avoid duty. shirker *n.*

shish kebab *also* **shish kebob or shish kabob** \SHISH-kuh-bob\ *n.* [Fo] Meat and vegetables cooked and served on skewers.

shiver \SHIV-ur\ *v.* shivered; shivering. To tremble with cold or fear. shivery *adj.*; shiver *n.*

shoal \shohl\ *n.* **1.** A large number of fish swimming together. **2.** A shallow place.

shock \shok\ *n.* **1.** A sudden, forceful blow. **2.** An electric jolt. **3.** [Md] A dangerous collapse.

shoddy \SHOD-ee\ *adj.* shoddier; shoddiest. Of poor quality. shoddily *adv.*; shoddiness *n.*

shoot *n.* **1.** New branch or growth from a plant. **2.** Hunting expedition. **3.** Photo session.

shoot *v.* shot; shooting. **1.** To send a projectile through the air. **2.** To wound or kill with a projectile.

shop *n.* **1.** A place where goods and services are sold. **2.** A place set aside for work.

shop *v.* shopped; shopping. To look for goods or services to buy. shopper *n.*; shopping *n.*

shopping mall *n.* A group of shops enclosed within one large building.

shore \shor\ *n.* The land at the edge of an ocean, sea, or lake.

short *adj.* shorter; shortest. **1.** Measuring little in space or time. **2.** Not tall. **3.** Abrupt. shortly *adv.*; shortness *n.*

shortage \SHOR-tij\ *n.* An insufficient amount for what is needed.

shortcoming \SHORT-kum-ing\ *n.* A fault or deficiency.

short fuse *n.* (Sl) A quick, bad temper.

short-lived \SHORT-LIVD\ *adj.* Not lasting.

shortsighted \SHORT-SIE-tid\ *adj.* **1.** Unable to see far. **2.** Lacking foresight. shortsightedly *adv.*; shortsightedness *n.*

should \shuud\ *v.* Ought to.

shot *n.* **1.** The firing of a weapon. **2.** Something fired. **3.** Ball in track and field.

shot *v.* The past tense and past participle of shoot.

shoulder \SHOHL-dur\ *n.* **1.** [Md] Body part where the arm joins the trunk. **2.** Edges of roadway.

shoulder \SHOHL-dur\ *v.* shouldered; shouldering. To take on a responsibility.

shout \showt\ *v.* shouted; shouting. To speak or cry out loudly. shout *n.*; shouter *n.*

shove \shuv\ *v.* shoved; shoving. To push. shove *n.*

show \shoh\ *n.* **1.** A spectacle. **2.** An entertaining event. **3.** A false front.

show \shoh\ *v.* showed; shown or showing. **1.** To allow something to be seen. **2.** To be visible. **3.** To prove.

showdown \SHOH-down\ *n.* A final confrontation.

showoff \SHOH-awf\ *n.* **1.** A pretentious display. **2.** A person trying to impress others. show off *v.*

showy \SHOH-ee\ *adj.* showier;

showiest. Brilliant and gaudy. showily *adv.*; showiness *n.*

shrapnel \SHRAP-nl\ *n.* Pieces of metal scattered from an exploding shell.

shred *v.* shredded; shredding. To cut or tear into thin strips. shred *n.*; shredder *n.*

shrewd \shroo\ *adj.* shrewder; shrewdest. Clever, especially in a practical way. shrewdly *adv.*; shrewdness *n.*

shriek \shreek\ *v.* shrieked; shrieking. To scream. shriek *n.*

shrill \shril\ *adj.* shriller; shrillest. Making a high, piercing sound. shrilly *adv.*; shrillness *n.*

shrine \shrien\ *n.* **1.** A sacred place. **2.** A place of worship. **3.** Container enclosing sacred relics.

shrink \shringk\ *v.* shrank or shrunk; shrunken or shrinking. **1.** To make or become smaller. **2.** To move back in fear or embarrassment. shrinkable *adj.*; shrinkage *n.*

shrink-wrap *also* **shrinkwrap** \SHRINGK-rap\ *n.* A plastic wrap that seals a product. shrink-wrap *v.*

shrivel \SHRIV-ul\ *v.* shriveled; shriveling. To become or make dry and wrinkled.

shrub *n.* A small treelike plant.

shuck \shuk\ *n.* A husk or pod as an outer covering. shuck *v.*

shuck \shuk\ *v.* shucked; shucking. To remove or get rid of.

shudder \SHUD-ur\ *v.* shuddered; shuddering. To shake, especially from horror.

shuffle \SHUF-ul\ *v.* shuffled; shuffling. **1.** To drag the feet while walking. **2.** To mix up playing cards before dealing. shuffle *n.*

shun *v.* shunned; shunning. To avoid.

shut *v.* shut; shutting. **1.** To close and fasten. **2.** To forbid entrance, exit. **3.** To bring together.

shut down \SHUT-down\ *v.* To stop operations. shutdown *n.*

shutter \SHUT-ur\ *n.* **1.** Something that excludes, as a screen. **2.** Light control in camera. shutter *v.*

shuttle \SHUT-l\ *n.* **1.** A device that moves to and fro. **2.** Transport between two points. shuttle *v.*

shuttle diplomacy *n.* Mediation by traveling between two negotiating parties.

shut up \SHUT-up\ *v.* shut up; shutting up. To stop talking.

shy \shie\ *adj.* shyer; shyest or shier; shiest. **1.** Reluctant to be around others. **2.** Easily frightened. shyly *adv.*; shyness *n.*

shyster \SHIE-stur\ *n.* (Sl) An unscrupulous lawyer or other pro-fessional.

sibling \SIB-ling\ *n.* A brother or sister.

sick \sik\ *adj.* sicker; sickest. **1.** Not feeling well. **2.** Vomiting. **3.** Distressed. **4.** [Sl] Sadistic and perverted. sickness *n.*; sicken *v.*

sickening \SIK-uh-ning\ *adj.* Causing sickness, distress, or disgust.

sickle cell anemia \SIK-ul-SEL\ *n.* (Md) A chronic hereditary blood disease resulting in joint pain, fever, and weakness.

sickly \SIK-lee\ *adj.* sicklier; sickliest. **1.** Unhealthy. **2.** Caused by an unhealthiness. **3.** Pale. **4.** Weak. sickliness *n.*

side \sied\ *n.* **1.** Surface of an object. **2.** Edge. **3.** One of two or more contrasts. side *adj.*; sided *adj.*

side effect *n.* A secondary, often bad, result.

sideshow \SIED-shoh\ *n.* A small performance apart from a larger one.

sideways \SIED-wayz\ *adv.* **1.** To or from one side. **2.** With one side forward. sideways *adj.*

siege \seej\ *n.* A surrounding and blockading of a place.

sienna \see-EN-uh\ *n.* A reddish-brown clay or color.

sierra \see-ER-uh\ *n.* A chain of mountains with jagged peaks.

siesta \see-ES-tuh\ *n.* (Sp) An afternoon rest.

sift *v.* sifted; sifting. To separate and make finer by putting through a sieve.

sight \siet\ *n.* **1.** The ability to see. **2.** An unsightly thing. **3.** Something noticed. sight *v.*

sightsee \SIET-see\ *v.* To visit places of interest. sightseeing *n.*; sightseer *n.*

sign \sien\ *n.* **1.** Action of indication. **2.** Board, placard, etc. **3.** Mark or symbol. **4.** Omen.

sign \sien\ *v.* signed; signing. **1.** To write one's name on a document. **2.** To communicate using gestures.

signal \SIG-nul\ *n.* **1.** A sign or gesture giving information or a command. **2.** Electrical impulses. signaller *n.*; signal *v.*

signature \SIG-nuh-chur\ *n.* **1.** A person's name or initials on a document. **2.** A distinctive characteristic. signature *adj.*

significant \sig-NIF-i-kunt\ *adj.* **1.** Abounding with meaning. **2.** Important and special. significantly *adv.*; significance *n.*

silent \SIE-lunt\ *adj.* **1.** Not talking or making sound. **2.** Not active. silently *adv.*; silence *n.*; silence *v.*

silhouette \sil-oo-ET\ *n.* **1.** The outline or general shape of something. **2.** A dark outline against light. silhouette *v.*

silicon \SIL-i-kun\ *n.* Nonmetallic element from the Earth's crust, widely distributed.

silk *n.* A fine thread used to make a soft, delicate fabric. silken *adj.*; silky *adj.*

silly \SIL-ee\ *adj.* sillier; silliest. **1.** Foolish. **2.** Not serious. silliness *n.*

silo \SIE-loh\ *n. pl.* silos. A storage structure.

silver \SIL-vur\ *n.* **1.** A shiny, white, precious metal. **2.** Coins. **3.** Utensils made from such a metal. silvery *adj.*

similar \SIM-uh-lur\ *adj.* Like or alike, but not the same. similarly *adv.*; similarity *n.*

simile \SIM-uh-lee\ *n.* A figure of speech comparing one thing to another.

simmer \SIM-ur\ *v.* simmered; simmering. **1.** To heat near or just below the boiling point. **2.** To be about to erupt. simmer *n.*

simple \SIM-pul\ *adj.* simpler; simplest. **1.** Not complex. **2.** Easily understood. **3.** Plain. **4.** Lacking a sophistication. simpleness *n.*; simplicity *n.*

simplify \SIM-pluh-fie\ *v.* simplified; simplifying. **1.** To make less complex. **2.** To make easier to understand. **3.** To reduce. simplification *n.*

simply \SIM-plee\ *adv.* **1.** In an uncomplicated manner. **2.** Merely. **3.** Totally.

simulate \SIM-yuh-layt\ *v.* simulated; simulating. **1.** To imitate. **2.** To pretend. simulation *n.*; simulator *n.*

simultaneous \sie-mul-TAY-nee-us\ *adj.* Occurring or operating at the same time. simultaneously *adv.*

sin *n.* A serious wrongdoing that violates a religious or moral law. sinful *adj.*; sinner *n.*; sin *v.*

since \sins\ *conj.* **1.** From a past time and now. **2.** Before now; ago.

since \sins\ *prep.* **1.** During or within the time after. **2.** Continuously throughout the time after. since *adv.*

sincere \sin-SEER\ *adj.* sincerer; sincerest. **1.** Genuine. **2.** Honest. sincerely *adv.*; sincerity *n.*

sinew \SIN-yoo\ *n.* **1.** A tough, fibrous tissue, like a tendon. **2.** A physical strength. sinewy *adj.*

sinful \SIN-ful\ *adj.* Evil. sinfully *adv.*; sinfulness *n.*

sing *v.* sang or sung; singing. **1.** [Mu] To make music with the voice. **2.** To make a continuous sound. singer *n.*

sing-along *n.* (Mu) **1.** An outbreak of singing. **2.** An informal gathering in which people sing.

singe \sinj\ *v.* singed; singeing. To burn slightly.

single \SING-gul\ *adj.* **1.** Separate and different. **2.** Alone. **3.** Not married. **4.** For the use of one.

single \SING-gul\ *n.* **1.** One person, thing. **2.** A thing for use by one person. **3.** An unmarried person.

single \SING-gul\ *v.* singled; singling. To choose as distinct from others.

singular \SING-gyuh-lur\ *adj.* **1.** Referring to one person or thing. **2.** Extraordinary. singularly *adv.*; singularness *n.*

sinister \SIN-uh-stur\ *adj.* **1.** Suggesting wickedness. **2.** Foreboding. **3.** With or causing misfortune. sinisterly *adv.*; sinisterness *n.*

sink \singk\ *n.* A water basin with a drainage pipe.

sink \singk\ *v.* sank or sunk; sinking. **1.** To go down, esp. into something. **2.** To cause to go down. **3.** To weaken.

sinus \SIE-nus\ *n. pl.* sinuses. A cavity, esp. the open space inside the nose active in smelling and breathing.

sip *v.* sipped; sipping. To drink in small mouthfuls. sip *n.*

siphon \SIE-fun\ *n.* **1.** A bent of flexible tube for liquid transfer. **2.** A siphon bottle. siphon *v.*

sir \sur\ *n.* A polite form of address for a man, knight, or baronet.

sire \sier\ *n.* **1.** A polite form of address for a king. **2.** The male parent of an animal.

sire \sier\ *v.* sired; siring. To father an animal.

siren \SIE-run\ *n.* **1.** A device that lets out a long, loud sound as a signal. **2.** A seductress.

sirloin \SUR-loin\ *n.* A cut of beef from the uppermost portion of the loin.

sissy \SIS-ee\ *n. pl.* sissies. **1.** A coward. **2.** An effeminate male. sissy *adj.*

sister \SIS-tur\ *adj.* Related.

sister \SIS-tur\ *n.* **1.** A daughter of the same parents as another person. **2.** A nun. **3.** Lady friend. sisterly *adv.*

sisterhood \SIS-tur-huud\ *n.* **1.** Condition of being sisters. **2.** Sisterly relationship. **3.** Female camaraderie.

sit *v.* sat; sitting. **1.** Rest on buttocks. **2.** Be passive. **3.** Pose. **4.** Occupy seat. **5.** Babysit.

sitar \si-TAHR\ *n.* (Mu) An Indian musical instrument resembling a guitar.

sitcom *also* **situation comedy** \sit-KOM\ *n.* A series of broadcasts about a fixed group of characters.

site \siet\ *n.* **1.** Place where something stands. **2.** Place where an event happens.

situation \sich-oo-AY-shun\ *n.* **1.** Position of something. **2.** Status of something. **3.** Condition, circumstances.

six \siks\ *n. pl.* sixes. One more than five. sixth *adj.*, sixth *n.*

six-pack \SIKS-PAK\ *n.* A package containing six identical items, as soda or beer.

sizable *also* **sizeable** \SIE-auh-bul\ *adj.* Fairly large.

size \siez\ *n.* **1.** The largeness or smallness of something. **2.** A particular measurement.

size \siez\ *v.* sized; sizing. To differentiate or distribute according to size. sizing *n.*

sizzle \SIZ-ul\ *v.* sizzled; sizzling. **1.** To make a hissing sound, as in frying. **2.** To be very hot. sizzle *n.*

skate \skayt\ *n.* **1.** Boot with metal runner underneath. **2.** Ice skate or roller skate. skater *n.*; skate *v.*

skateboard \SKAYT-bord\ *n.* A short, narrow board with wheels underneath, for riding. skateboarder *n.*; skateboarding *n.*

skeleton \SKEL-i-tn\ *n.* **1.** The framework of bones within an animal's body. **2.** Any structure's framework.

skeptic *also* **sceptic** \SKEP-tik\ *n.* A person who doubts that which is generally accepted as valid. skeptical *adj.*; skeptically *adv.*

skepticism \SKEP-ti-siz-um\ *n.* A belief that the validity of all knowledge must be questioned.

sketch \skech\ *n. pl.* sketches. **1.** A rough drawing. **2.** A brief account. **3.** A short skit. sketch *v.*

sketchy \SKECH-ee\ *adj.* sketchier; sketchiest. Roughly done. sketchily *adv.*; sketchiness *n.*

ski \skee\ *n. pl.* skis. One of pair of runners attached to the feet for gliding over snow or water. skier *n.*; skiing *n.*; ski *v.*

skid *v.* skidded; skidding. To slide uncontrollably. skid *n.*

skill \skil\ *n.* An ability to do something well. skilled *adj.*

skillet \SKIL-it\ *n.* A frying pan.

skim *adj.* Having the cream removed.

skim *v.* skimmed; skimming. **1.** To remove something from surface of a liquid. **2.** To look, read quickly.

skimp *v.* skimped; skimping. To give or use much less than necessary.

skin *n.* **1.** Outer layer of animal body. **2.** Outer layer of fruit. **3.** Animal pelt.

skin *v.* skinned; skinning. **1.** To remove the skin from something. **2.** To wound by scraping.

skinhead \SKIN-hed\ *n.* (Sl) **1.** One who is bald. **2.** White-supremacist youth with a shaved head.

skinny \SKIN-ee\ *adj.* skinnier; skinniest. Very thin. skinniness *n.*

skinny-dip \SKIN-ee-dip\ *v.* skinny-dipped; skinny-dipping. (Sl) To swim in the nude. skinny-dip *n.*

skip *v.* skipped; skipping. **1.** To move by hopping on alternate feet. **2.** To jump a rope. skip *n.*

skirmish \SKUR-mish\ *n.* A minor fight. skirmish *v.*

skirt \skurt\ *n.* A woman's garment that hangs from the waist.

skirt \skurt\ *v.* skirted; skirting. To go or be on the edge of.

skit *n.* A short theatrical act.

skittish \SKIT-ish\ *adj.* Shy, restless, and uncertain. skittishly *adv.*; skittishness *n.*

skoal \skohl\ *interj.* A drinking toast. skoal *n.*

skull \skul\ *n.* The bony framework of a head.

sky \skie\ *n. pl.* skies. The atmosphere and region just above the Earth.

skydive \SKIE-diev\ *v.* skydived; skydiving. To jump from an airplane and fall freely, parachuting at the last moment. skydiver *n.*; skydiving *n.*

skyjack \SKIE-jak\ *v.* skyjacked; skyjacking. To hijack an aircraft. skyjacker *n.*

skyscraper \SKIE-skray-pur\ *n.* A very tall building.

slab *n.* A thick, flat piece of something.

slack \slak\ *adj.* slacker; slackest. **1.** Not tight or tense. **2.** Lazy. **3.** Negligent. **4.** Not active. slack *n.*; slackness *n.*; slack *v.*; slacken *v.*

slalom \SLAH-lum\ *n.* (Fo) Skiing in a zigzag course down a hill or on water. slalom *v.*

slam *n.* **1.** A shutting or hitting forcefully and noisily. **2.** [Sl] A severe criticism.

slam *v.* slammed; slamming. **1.** To shut or hit forcefully and noisily. **2.** [Sl] To criticize severely. slam *n.*

slander \SLAN-dur\ *n.* A false statement that damages a person's reputation. slanderous *adj.*; slanderer *n.*; slander *v.*

slang *n.* An informal expression used in speech but rarely in writing.

slant *v.* slanted; slanting. **1.** To slope. **2.** To express with a bias.

slap *v.* slapped; slapping. **1.** To strike with an open hand or something flat. **2.** To insult. slap *n.*

slash *v.* slashed; slashing. **1.** To slit open with sweeping cuts. **2.** To reduce dramatically. slash *n.*; slasher *n.*

slate \slayt\ *n.* **1.** A type of rock that splits easily into smooth, flat pieces. **2.** A bluish-gray. slate *v.*

slaughter \SLAW-tur\ *v.* slaughtered; slaughtering. **1.** To kill for food. **2.** To murder ruthlessly. slaughter *n.*

slavery \SLAY-vuh-ree\ *n.* **1.** The practice of owning human beings. **2.** The condition of servitude, bondage. slavish *adj.*; slavishly *adv.*; slave *n.*; slave *v.*

slay *v.* slew; slain. To kill. slayer *n.*

sleazy \SLEE-zee\ *adj.* (Sl) **1.** Disreputable. **2.** Flimsy. **3.** Constructed with inferior materials. sleazily *adv.*; sleaze *n.*; sleaziness *n.*

sleek *adj.* sleeker; sleekest. **1.** Smooth and glossy. **2.** Appearing well-groomed. sleekly *adv.*; sleekness *n.*

sleep *n.* The state of complete rest and unconsciousness. sleepy *adj.*; sleepily *adv.*; sleepiness *n.*; sleep *v.*

sleigh \slay\ *n.* A vehicle on blades used for snow travel.

slender \SLEN-dur\ *adj.* slenderer; slenderest. Thin. slenderness *n.*

slice \slies\ *n.* **1.** A thin, broad piece cut from a whole. **2.** A share.

slice \slies\ *v.* sliced; slicing. **1.** Cut into thin, broad pieces. **2.** Cut away from whole.

slick \slik\ *adj.* slicker; slickest. **1.** Clever. **2.** Slippery.

slick \slik\ *n.* A patch of oil floating on water.

slide \slied\ *n.* **1.** Act of slipping on a smooth surface. **2.** An inclined slippery surface.

slide \slied\ *v.* slid; sliding. To slip smoothly over a surface.

slight \sliet\ *adj.* slighter; slightest. **1.** Not much. **2.** Not important. **3.** Slender. slightly *adv.*; slightness *n.*

slight \sliet\ *v.* slighted; slighting. **1.** To ignore. **2.** To disrespect.

slim *adj.* slimmer; slimmest. **1.** Thin. **2.** Insufficient. slimness *n.*; slim *v.*

slime \sliem\ *n.* A thick, unpleasant, oily liquid. slimy *adj.*

slimnastics \slim-NAS-tiks\ *pl. n.* A type of weight-reducing exercise involving gymnastics.

sling *n.* **1.** A device for throwing stones. **2.** Support for hurt arm.

sling *v.* slung; slinging. **1.** To throw. **2.** To hang something up.

slingshot \SLING-shot\ *n.* A Y-shaped shooting weapon.

slink \slingk\ *v.* slunk; slinking. To sneak around. slinky *adj.*

slip *n.* **1.** An accidental sliding. **2.** A mistake. **3.** A woman's undergarment for a skirt.

slip *v.* slipped; slipping. **1.** To slide accidentally. **2.** To escape one's memory. **3.** To escape. **4.** To err.

slippery \SLIP-uh-ree\ *adj.* **1.** Smooth enough to cause an accidental sliding. **2.** Tricky. **3.** Elusive. slipperiness *n.*

slipshod \SLIP-shod\ *adj.* Careless or untidy.

slit *n.* A long, narrow opening or cut. slit *v.*

slither \SLITH-ur\ *v.* slithered; slithering. To slide around as a snake.

sliver \SLIV-ur\ *n.* A small, thin strip of material.

slob *n.* (Sl) A sloppy, rude person.

slobber \SLOB-ur\ *v.* slobbered; slobbering. **1.** To drool. **2.** To state incoherently. slobbery *adj.*

slogan \SLOH-gun\ *n.* A word or phrase used as a motto.

slop *v.* slopped; slopping. To spill carelessly. slop *n.*

slope \slohp\ *n.* A line or surface that goes gradually up or down. sloping *adj.*; slope *v.*

sloppy \SLOP-ee\ *adj.* sloppier; sloppiest. **1.** Wet and runny. **2.** Careless. **3.** Sentimental. sloppily *adv.*; sloppiness *n.*

slot *n.* A narrow opening into which something fits. slot *v.*

sloth \slawth\ *n. pl.* sloths. **1.** Slow-moving South American animal that hangs from tree branches. **2.** Laziness. slothful *adj.*; slothfulness *n.*

slouch \slowch\ *v.* slouched; slouching. To sit, stand, or walk with one's shoulders lazily drooped forward. slouch *n.*

slovenly \SLOV-un-lee\ *adj.* Careless and untidy. sloven *n.*; slovenliness *n.*

slow \sloh\ *adj.* slower; slowest. **1.** Not fast. **2.** Taking a very long time. **3.** Behind the correct time. **4.** Late. slowly *adv.*; slowness *n.*

slowdown \SLOH-down\ *n.* A delay in progress. slow down *v.*

sluggish \SLUG-ish\ *adj.* **1.** Lazy. **2.** Slow. sluggishly *adv.*; sluggishness *n.*

slum *n.* An area of poor, squalid housing. slummy *adj.*; slumminess *n.*

slumber \SLUM-bur\ *v.* slumbered; slumbering. To sleep. slumber *n.*

slumlord \SLUM-lord\ *n.* (Sl) An absentee owner of poor, squalid housing.

slump *n.* A sudden great fall, as in price, demand, or activity. slump *v.*

slur *v.* slurred; slurring. **1.** To say with sounds running together. **2.** [Mu] To run successive notes together slur *n.*

slush *n.* Parly melted snow or ice. slushy *adj.*

sly \slie\ *adj.* slyer; slyest or slier; sliest. Cunning and deceitful. slyly or slily *adv.*; slyness *n.*

smack \smak\ *v.* smacked; smacking. **1.** To hit with the palm of the hand. **2.** To kiss so as to make a loud noise. smack *n.*

small \smawl\ *adj.* smaller; smallest. **1.** Not large. **2.** Of minor importance. smallness *n.*

smart \smahrt\ *adj.* smarter; smartest. **1.** Intelligent. **2.** Neat. **3.** Fashionable. **4.** Energetic. **5.** Painful. smartly *adv.*; smart *n.*; smartness *n.*; smart *v.*; smarten *v.*

smash *n.* **1.** A violent hit. **2.** A violent breaking. **3.** An overwhelming success.

smash *v.* smashed; smashing. To break into pieces, esp. violently.

smear \smeer\ *v.* smeared; smearing. **1.** To spread with dirt or grease. **2.** To try to damage a reputation. smear *n.*

smell \smel\ *n.* **1.** The ability to perceive odors with the nose. **2.** The odor of something. smelly *adj.*

smell \smel\ *v.* smelled; smelling. **1.** To use the nose to perceive odors. **2.** To give out an odor. **3.** To perceive.

smile \smiel\ *n.* A pleased, happy facial expression. smile *v.*

smirk \smurk\ *n.* A smug smile. smirk *v.*

smog \smawg\ *n.* A dense, smoky fog. smoggy *adj.*

smoke \smohk\ *n.* **1.** The gas given off from a burning material. **2.** The act of smoking. smoky *adj.*; smoker *n.*; smoke *v.*

smoke detector *n.* A device that signals upon the detection of smoke or fire.

smokestack \SMOHK-stak\ *n.* A pipe through which smoke is discharged.

smolder *also* **smoulder** \SMOHL-dur\ *v.* smoldered; smoldering. **1.** To burn and smoke in the absence of. **2.** To live in a suppressed manner.

smooth *adj.* smoother; smoothest. **1.** Having an even, unmarred surface. **2.** Not bumpy in movement. **3.** Not lumpy. smoothly *adv.*; smoothness *n.*; smooth *v.*

smorgasbord \SMOR-gus-bord\ *n.* (Fo) A wide variety of choices, especially of food.

smother \SMUTH-ur\ *v.* smothered; smothering. **1.** To suffocate. **2.** To suppress. smother *n.*

smudge \smuj\ *n.* A blurred, dirty mark. smudge *v.*

smug *adj.* smugger; smuggest. Condescendingly self-satisfied. smugly *adj.*; smugness *n.*

smuggle \SMUG-ul\ *v.* smuggled; smuggling. To transport secretly, especially illegal goods to be sold. smuggler *n.*

smut *n.* **1.** Dirt. **2.** Indecent literature or conversation.

snack \snak\ *n.* A small meal. snack *v.*

snag *n.* **1.** Jagged projection. **2.** A rip caused by a jagged thing. **3.** Unexpected problem. snag *v.*

snake \snayk\ *n.* **1.** A long, tubular, scaly reptile. **2.** [Sl] One who is deceitful. snakelike *adj.*; snaky *adj.*

snake \snayk\ *v.* snaked; snaking. To proceed or wind as would a snake.

snap *n.* **1.** A quick bite. **2.** A fastener that clicks shut. **3.** Spell of cold weather.

snap *v.* snapped; snapping. **1.** To bite quickly. **2.** To speak angrily at. **3.** [Sl] To lose mental control.

snappy \SNAP-ee\ *adj.* snappier; snappiest. **1.** Quick. **2.** Easily angered. **3.** [Sl] Stylish.

snare \snair\ *n.* **1.** A trap. **2.** [Mu] A length of wire or gut stretched across a drum's bottom. snare *v.*

snarl \snahrl\ *v.* snarled; snarling. **1.** To growl with the teeth bared, as would a dog. **2.** To speak angrily at. snarly *adj.*; snarlingly *adv.*; snarl *n.*

snatch \snach\ *v.* snatched; snatching. To seize unexpectedly. snatch *n.*

sneak \sneek\ *v.* sneaked; sneaking. To move secretly. sneak *adj.*; sneaky *adj.*; sneakily *adv.*; sneak *n.*; sneakiness *n.*

sneer *n.* A scornful expression marked by a curled upper lip. sneer *v.*

snicker \SNIK-ur\ *v.* snickered; snickering. To giggle slyly. snicker *n.*

snide \snied\ *adj.* Mean or disparaging. snidely *adv.*

sniff \snif\ *v.* sniffed; sniffing. **1.** To draw air into the nose. **2.** To perceive smell by drawing in air. sniff *n.*

snip *v.* snipped; snipping. To cut in a quick stroke, as with scissors. snip *n.*; snippers *n.*

sniper \SNIE-pur\ *n.* A person who shoots a weapon from a concealed position. snipe *v.*

snippet \SNIP-it\ *n.* A small piece.

snob *n.* A person with exaggeraged respect for wealth, social position, and possessions. snobbish *adj.*; snobbery *n.*; snobbishness *n.*

snoop *v.* snooped; snooping. To pry into other people's affairs. snoop *n.*

snooze \snooz\ *v.* snoozed; snoozing. To have a short sleep. snooze *n.*

snore \snor\ *v.* snored; snoring. To breathe noisily while sleeping. snorer *n.*

snow \snoh\ *n.* Frozen drops of water that fall to the ground as white flakes. snowy *adj.*; snow *v.*

snow blower *n.* A machine for removing snow from driveways and sidewalks.

snowmobile \SNOH-muh-beel\ *n.* A motor vehicle with skis for riding on snow. snowmobiler *n.*; snowmobiling *n.*

snub *v.* snubbed; snubbing. To re-ject someone unkindly. snub *adj.*; snub *n.*

snuff \snuf\ *n.* Powdered tobacco.

snuff \snuf\ *v.* snuffed; snuffing. **1.** To sniff. **2.** To put out a candle. **3.** To stop the continuation of. snuffer *n.*

snug *adj.* snugger; snuggest. **1.** Comfortable and warm. **2.** Fitting tightly. snugly *adv.*

snuggle \SNUG-ul\ *v.* snuggled; snuggling. To nestle.

so \soh\ *adv.* **1.** To such a degree. **2.** As indicated. **3.** More or less. **4.** For that reason.

soak \sohk\ *v.* soaked; soaking. **1.** To make very wet. **2.** To absorb. **3.** [Sl] To extort money from. soak *n.*

soar \sor\ *v.* soared; soaring. To rise in the air and fly.

sob *v.* sobbed; sobbing. To gasp while crying. sob *n.*

so-called \SOH-KAWLD\ *adj.* Designated thus, often incorrectly.

soccer \SOK-ur\ *n.* A field sport played with a round ball.

sociable \SOH-shuh-bul\ *adj.* **1.** Friendly. **2.** Fond of companionship. sociably *adv.*; sociability *n.*; sociable *n.*

social \SOH-shul\ *adj.* **1.** Relating to human interaction. **2.** Of or concerning society. **3.** In community. socially *adv.*

social \SOH-shul\ *n.* A casual gathering.

socialism \SOH-shuh-liz-um\ *n.* Political system of public collective ownership and equitable share of goods. socialistic *adj.*; socialist *n.*

society \suh-SIE-i-tee\ *n. pl.* societies. **1.** An organized community. **2.** All people. **3.** Companionship. **4.** Highest class. societal *adj.*

socioeconomic \soh-see-oh-ek-uh-NOM-ik\ *adj.* Of or concerning a combination of social and economic factors. socioeconomically *adv.*; socioeconomics *n.*

sociology \soh-see-OL-uh-jee\ *n.* The study of human society. sociological *adj.*; sociologically *adv.*; sociologist *n.*

sock \sok\ *n.* A knitted covering for the foot and ankle.

sock \sok\ *v.* socked; socking. To hit hard. sock *n.*

sod *n.* Grass-covered earth.

sodden \SOD-n\ *adj.* **1.** Soaked. **2.** Dull and foolish, as from drink. soddenly *adv.*; soddenness *n.*

soft \sawft\ *adj.* softer; softest. **1.** Not hard. **2.** Easily reformed. **3.** Smooth and pleasant. **4.** Nonalco-

holic. softly *adv.*; softness *n.*; soften *v.*

soft rock \SAWFT-ROK\ *n.* (Mu) A type of rock and roll that has a softer beat and a melodic style.

software \SAWFT-wair\ *n.* (Cm) Computer programs.

soggy \SOG-ee\ *adj.* soggier; soggiest. Soaked. soggily *adv.*; sogginess *n.*

soil *n.* The uppermost layer of earth in which plant life thrives.

soil *v.* soiled; soiling. **1.** To make filthy. **2.** To demoralize.

soiree \swah-RAY\ *n.* (Fr) An evening party.

sojourn \SOH-jurn\ *n.* A temporary stay in a place. sojourner *n.*; sojourn *v.*

solace \SOL-is\ *n.* Comfort in a time of distress. solace *v.*

solar \SOH-lur\ *adj.* Of or concerning the sun.

solarium \suh-LAIR-ee-um\ *n. pl.* solaria or solariums. A room exposed to the sun.

solar panel *n.* A bank of solar cells that convert sunlight into electricity.

soldier \SOHL-jur\ *n.* A member of an army. soldierly *adv.*; soldier *v.*

sole \sohl\ *adj.* Single. solely *adv.*

sole \sohl\ *n.* **1.** The bottom of a foot

or foot covering. **2.** An edible flat-fish.

solemn \SOL-um\ *adj.* **1.** Not cheerful. **2.** Serious. **3.** Holy. solemnly *adv.*; solemnity *n.*

solicit \suh-LIS-it\ *v.* solicited; soliciting. **1.** To seek to obtain by request or plea. **2.** To tempt. solicitation *n.*; solicitor *n.*

solicitude \suh-LIS-i-tood\ *n.* Concern.

solid \SOL-id\ *adj.* **1.** Firm. **2.** Not liquid or gas. **3.** Three-dimensional. **4.** Continuous. solidly *adv.*; solid *n.*; solidity *n.*; solidness *n.*; solidify *v.*

solidarity \sol-i-DAR-i-tee\ *n.* Unity for a purpose.

solid-state \SOL-id-STAYT\ *adj.* **1.** Pertaining to solids at molecular, atomic level. **2.** Made of solid components.

soliloquy \suh-LIL-uh-kwee\ *n. pl.* soliloquies. A speech made aloud to oneself or as if to oneself. soliloquize *v.*

solitary \SOL-i-ter-ee\ *adj.* **1.** Existing alone. **2.** Only one. solitude *n.*

solitude \SOL-i-tood\ *n.* Being alone or on your own.

solstice \SOL-stis\ *n.* The times of the year when the sun is furthest from the equator.

solution \suh-LOO-shun\ *n.* **1.** An answer to a problem. **2.** Dissolving in liquid. **3.** Something dissolved.

solve \solv\ *v.* solved; solving. To find the answer to a problem. solvable *adj.*; solver *n.*

solvent \SOL-vunt\ *n.* A liquid used for dissolving something. solvent *adj.*; solvency *n.*

somatotherapy \soh-mah-tuh-THER-uh-pee\ *n.* (Md) Treating mentally ill through physical means, including drugs, shock therapy.

somber \SOM-bur\ *adj.* Dark and gloomy. somberly *adv.*; somberness *n.*

sombrero \som-BRAIR-oh\ *n. pl.* sombreros. A broad-brimmed tall hat worn in Mexico.

some \sum\ *adj.* **1.** Not named or known. **2.** An unspecified amount. **3.** Approximately. some *adv.*; some pron.

somebody \SUM-bod-ee\ *pron.* An unspecified person.

someday \SUM-day\ *adv.* At some future time.

somehow \SUM-how\ *adv.* By some means or in some way.

something \SUM-thing\ *n.* An unspecified thing. something pron.

sometime \SUM-tiem\ *adv.* At an unspecified moment.

sometimes \SUM-tiemz\ *adv.* Occasionally.

somewhat \SUM-hwut\ *adv.* To some extent.

somewhere \SUM-hwair\ *adv.* At, in, or to an unspecified place.

sonar *also* **sound navigation and ranging** \SOH-nahr\ *n.* Device using underwater waves for navigation, detection, etc. sonar *adj.*

sonata \suh-NAH-tuh\ *n.* (Mu) A musical piece with several related movements for one or two instruments.

song \sawng\ *n.* (Mu) **1.** Singing. **2.** Music for singing. **3.** Ballad; poetry.

sonnet \SON-it\ *n.* A poem with 14 lines in any rhyme scheme.

sonogram \SON-uh-gram\ *n.* (Md) Visual image, as of a fetus, produced by reflected sound waves.

soon *adv.* sooner; soonest. **1.** In a short time. **2.** Early. **3.** Readily. **4.** Quickly.

soot \suut\ *n.* A black powdery substance made by something burning. sooty *adj.*

soothe \sooth\ *v.* soothed; soothing. **1.** To make relaxed. **2.** To save from pain.

sophistication \suh-FIS-ti-kay-shun\ *n.* **1.** The living of a knowl-edgeable and cultured life. **2.** Complexity. sophisticated *adj.*; sophisticate *n.*; sophisticate *v.*

sophomore \SOF-uh-mor\ *n.* A second-year student in a high school or university.

sophomoric \sof-uh-MOR-ik\ *adj.* Immature. sophomorically *adv.*

soprano \suh-PRAN-oh\ *n. pl.* sopranos. (Mu) **1.** The highest singing voice. **2.** A singer with this voice. **3.** Music for this. soprano *adj.*

sorcery \SOR-suh-ree\ *n. pl.* sorceries. The practice of magic. sorcerer *n.*; sorceress *n.*

sordid \SOR-did\ *adj.* Dirty and vile. sordidly *adv.*; sordidness *n.*

sore \sor\ *adj.* sorer; sorest. **1.** Painful. **2.** Annoying. **3.** [Sl] Distressed. soreness *n.*

sore \sor\ *n.* An infected spot on the body.

sorely \SOR-lee\ *adv.* **1.** Painfully. **2.** Very much.

sorrow \SAHR-oh\ *n.* A sadness due to disappointment. sorrowful *adj.*; sorrowfully *adv.*

sorry \SAHR-ree or SOR-ee\ *adj.* sorrier; sorriest. **1.** Feeling pity or regret. **2.** Inferior. **3.** Causing sorrow.

sort *n.* A particular kind or type.

sort *v.* sorted; sorting. To arrange

things into groups by type. sorter *n.*

sortie \SOR-tee\ *n.* **1.** A rapid movement of troops. **2.** A flying combat mission. sortie *v.*

so-so \SOH-SOH\ *adj.* Neither very good or very bad. so-so *adv.*

soufflé \soo-FLAY\ *n.* (Fr) A light and fluffy baked dish made with beaten egg whites.

sought \sawt\ *v.* The past tense and past participle of seek.

soul \sohl\ *n.* **1.** A person's spirit. **2.** One's moral and emotional nature. **3.** An essential part.

soul food *n.* Traditional southern African-American cuisine.

sound \sownd\ *adj.* sounder; soundest. **1.** Healthy and fit. **2.** Reliable. **3.** Reasonable. **4.** Thorough. soundly *adv.*; soundness *n.*

sound \sownd\ *n.* **1.** Waves caused by vibrations. **2.** Something heard. **3.** Significance.

sound bite *n.* (Sl) A brief striking remark made to the media.

soup \soop\ *n.* A liquid food mixture made from vegetables or meat.

sour \sowr\ *adj.* sourer; sourest. **1.** Having a sharp taste. **2.** Not fresh. **3.** Bad-tempered. sourly *adv.*; sourness *n.*; sour *v.*

source \sors\ *n.* The place from which something starts.

sourdough \SOWR-doh\ *n.* Fermented dough for making bread.

souse \sows\ *v.* soused; sousing. To drench. souse *n.*

south \sowth\ *n.* The direction or point to the right of a person facing east. south *adj.*; south *adv.*

South America *n.* The continent directly south of North America. South American *adj.*

souvenir \soo-vuh-NEER\ *n.* A keepsake serving as a reminder of a place or event.

sovereign \SOV-rin\ *n.* A reigning king or queen. sovereign *adj.*; sovereignty *n.*

sow \soh\ *n.* A female pig.

sow \soh\ *v.* sowed; sown or sowing. To plant seeds.

soybean \SOI-been\ *n.* A plant whose seeds are used for oil, flour, and food.

space \spays\ *n.* **1.** A boundless area. **2.** Infinite expanse. **3.** Interval. **4.** Area for purpose.

space \spays\ *v.* spaced; spacing. To arrange with gaps inbetween.

space-age \SPAYS-ayj\ *adj.* Of or concerning the period of space exploration. space age *n.*

spaced-out \SPAYST-owt\ *adj.* (Sl) Dazed and confused.

spaceship \SPAYS-ship\ *n.* A vehicle for travelling in outer space.

space shuttle *n.* A reusable space-craft or orbiter.

space walk \SPAYS-wawk\ *n.* An astronaut's walk in space outside of the vehicle. space walker *n.*; space walk *v.*

spacious \SPAY-shus\ *adj.* With plenty of room. spaciously *adv.*; spaciousness *n.*

spacy *also* **spacey** \SPAY-see\ *adj.* spacier; spaciest. (Sl) **1.** Dazed and confused. **2.** Eccentric. spaciness *n.*

spaghetti \spuh-GET-ee\ *n.* **1.** Long, thin strings of pasta. **2.** A dish made with such pasta.

spaghetti Western *n.* (Ja) A low-budget Western movie made in Italy.

span *n.* **1.** A part of a bridge between supports. **2.** A length of time. **3.** A length across.

span *v.* spanned; spanning. To stretch from one side to the other.

spank \spangk\ *v.* spanked; spanking. To smack, usually on the buttocks, as a punishment. spank *n.*; spanking *n.*

spare \spair\ *n.* **1.** An additional thing. **2.** In bowling, knocking down all the pins in two turns.

spare \spair\ *v.* spared; sparing. **1.** To allow someone or something to go unharmed. **2.** To use economically. spare *adj.*

sparing \SPAIR-ing\ *adj.* Economical. sparingly *adv.*

spark \spahrk\ *n.* **1.** A fiery particle. **2.** A small bit capable of being developed.

spark \spahrk\ *v.* sparked; sparking. **1.** To ignite. **2.** To give off sparks.

sparkle \SPAHR-kul\ *v.* sparkled; sparkling. **1.** To shine with flashes of light. **2.** To be brilliant. sparkle *n.*; sparkler *n.*

sparse \spahrs\ *adj.* Thinly scattered. sparsely *adv.*; sparseness *n.*; sparsity *n.*

spasm \SPAZ-um\ *n.* **1.** A strong, sudden jerk or contraction of a muscle. **2.** Burst of activity.

spasmodic \spaz-MOD-ik\ *adj.* Occurring irregularly. spasmodically *adv.*

spat *n.* **1.** A short, petty fight. **2.** A socklike covering for the instep and ankle.

spatter \SPAT-ur\ *v.* spattered; spattering. To scatter and fall in small drops. spatter *n.*

spatula \SPACH-uh-luh\ *n.* A blunt-bladed knifelike tool.

spawn *n.* The eggs of fish, frogs, or shellfish. spawn *v.*

speak \speek\ *v.* spoke; spoken. **1.** To use the voice to make words. **2.** To converse. **3.** To know a language. speaker *n.*

special \SPESH-ul\ *adj.* **1.** Of a rare or unusual kind. **2.** Of a particular kind or for a certain purpose. specially *adv.*

specialist \SPESH-uh-list\ *n.* An expert in a certain field.

specialize \SPESH-uh-liez\ *v.* specialized; specializing. **1.** Be or become an expert in a certain field. **2.** To adapt for a special purpose. specialization *n.*

specialty *also* **speciality** \SPESH-ul-tee\ *n. pl.* specialties. **1.** Peculiar characteristic. **2.** Special skill. **3.** Unique product.

species \SPEE-sheez or SPEE-seez\ *n. pl.* species. A group of animals or plants that are alike in certain ways.

specific \spi-SIF-ik\ *adj.* **1.** Detailed and definite. **2.** Particular to something. specifically *adv.*

specify \SPES-uh-fie\ *v.* specified; specifying. To mention definitely. specification *n.*

specimen \SPES-uh-mun\ *n.* An example of something.

speck \spek\ *n.* A small particle or mark.

spectacle \SPEK-tuh-bul\ *n.* **1.** An exciting sight. **2.** A public show. **3.** [Pl] A pair of eyeglasses.

spectacular \spek-TAK-yuh-lur\ *adj.* Impressive. spectacularly *adv.*; spectacular *n.*

spectator \SPEK-tay-tur\ *n.* A person watching an event.

spectrum \SPEK-trum\ *n. pl.* spectra or spectrums. **1.** Prism's colors when white light passes through. **2.** Range or extent. spectral *adj.*

speculate \SPEK-yuh-layt\ *v.* speculated; speculating. To form an opinion by guessing. speculative *adj.*; speculation *n.*; speculator *n.*

speech *n. pl.* speeches. **1.** Speaking. **2.** The ability to vocalize words. **3.** That which is vocalized.

speechless \SPEECH-lis\ *adj.* **1.** Unable to vocalize words. **2.** Made silent, as from surprise. speechlessness *n.*

speed *n.* **1.** Quickness. **2.** The measurement of the rate at which something moves.

speed *v.* sped; speeding. To move excessively fast. speed *v.*

speedometer \spee-DOM-i-tur\ *n.* A device for measuring a vehicle's speed.

speed-read *v.* speed-read; speed-reading. To rapidly assimilate text through skimming it or focusing in on key words. speed-reader *n.*

spell \spel\ *n.* **1.** A length of time. **2.**

A saying that has supposed magical power.

spell \spel\ *v.* spelled; spelling. **1.** To put letters in the right order to make a word. **2.** To indicate. speller *n.*

spellbound \SPEL-bownd\ *adj.* Enchanted. spellbind *v.*

spend *v.* spent; spending. **1.** To pay out money for goods or services. **2.** To use up. **3.** To pass time. spender *n.*

spendthrift \SPEND-thrift\ *n.* A wasteful spender.

spent *adj.* **1.** Fatigued. **2.** Used up. **3.** Expended.

sperm \spurm\ *n.* The male reproductive cell.

sperm bank *n.* A facility for storing sperm for future use.

spew \spyoo\ *v.* spewed; spewing. To throw or cast out. spew *n.*

sphere \sfeer\ *n.* **1.** A perfectly round three-dimensional object. **2.** Range; scope; extent. spherical *adj.*

spice \spies\ *n.* A plant substance used to flavor food and drink. spicy *adj.*; spice *v.*

spiel \speel\ *n.* (Sl) A persuasive speech. spieler *n.*; spiel *v.*

spike \spiek\ *n.* **1.** A sharp point. **2.** A type of long nail. spiky *adj.*

spike \spiek\ *v.* spiked; spiking. **1.** To secure with a long nail. **2.** To pierce with a long nail. **3.** Add alcohol. spiky *adj.*

spill \spil\ *v.* spilled or spilt; spilling. **1.** To cause or allow to run over a container's edge. **2.** To shed, as blood. spill *n.*

spin *n.* **1.** The act of rotating. **2.** A trip in an automobile.

spin *v.* spun; spinning. **1.** To twirl around and around. **2.** To twist into a thread. **3.** To construct. spinner *n.*

spine \spien\ *n.* **1.** Series of bones in middle of the back. **2.** A sharp spike. **3.** Toughness. spinal *adj.*; spiny *adj.*

spineless \SPIEN-lis\ *adj.* **1.** Having no backbone. **2.** Lacking determination. spinelessness *n.*

spirit \SPIR-it\ *n.* **1.** The soul. **2.** A person's nature or state of mind. **3.** An individual. **4.** Ghost.

spirited \SPIR-i-tid\ *adj.* Lively and bold.

spiritual \SPIR-i-choo-ul\ *adj.* **1.** Of or concerning the human soul. **2.** Of or concerning religion. spiritually *adv.*; spirituality *n.*

spit *n.* **1.** Saliva in the mouth, sometimes ejected. **2.** A rod for roasting meat.

spit *v.* spit or spat; spitting. To eject saliva from the mouth.

spite \spiet\ *n.* A malicious desire to hurt someone. spiteful *adj.*; spitefully *adv.*; spitefulness *n.*; spite *v.*

splash *v.* splashed; splashing. **1.** To cause liquid to fly about in drops. **2.** To move through the air in drops. splash *n.*

splashdown \SPLASH-down\ *n.* A spacecraft's landing on water.

splat *n.* A sound made by splashing and scattering.

spleen *n.* Vascular organ above the abdominal cavity, which modifies the blood.

splendid \SPLEN-did\ *adj.* **1.** Glowing. **2.** Magnificent. **3.** Showy. **4.** [Sl] Great. splendidly *adv.*

splendor \SPLEN-dur\ *n.* Magnificence.

splice \splies\ *v.* spliced; splicing. To join by interweaving or overlapping. splice *n.*

splint *n.* **1.** Flexible wood for basketweaving. **2.** [Md] Rigid material for healing fracture.

splinter \SPLIN-tur\ *n.* A thin, sharp piece of wood or other material. splinter *v.*

split *n.* **1.** A crack or separation. **2.** An acrobatic position in which the legs are spread.

split *v.* split; splitting. **1.** To crack or separate something. **2.** To come apart and form separate pieces.

splurge \splurj\ *n.* An ostentatious display of wealth by spending. splurge *v.*

spoil *v.* spoilt or spoiled; spoiling. **1.** To damage and make useless. **2.** To decay and become unfit for consumption. spoilage *n.*; spoiler *n.*

spoke \spohk\ *n.* A bar connecting the hub to the rim of a wheel.

spoke \spohk\ *v.* The past tense of speak.

spokesperson \SPOHKS-pur-sun\ *n.* A person who speaks on behalf of another or for a group.

sponge \spunj\ *n.* **1.** Underwater animal with a porous structure. **2.** This used for household acts. spongy *adj.*

sponge \spunj\ *v.* sponged; sponging. **1.** To clean with a sponge. **2.** [Sl] To live greedily off the goodness of others.

sponsor \SPON-sur\ *n.* A person who supports another individual or an organization, especially monetarily. sponsorship *n.*; sponsor *v.*

spontaneous \spon-TAY-nee-us\ *adj.* Happening or done naturally. spontaneously *adv.*; spontaneity *n.*

spoof *n.* (Sl) A hoax or parody. spoof *v.*

spook *n.* (Sl) A ghost. spooky *adj.*; spookily *adv.*; spookiness *n.*; spook *v.*

spoon *n.* A long-handled eating utensil ending in a shallow bowl. spoonful *n.*; spoon *v.*

sporadic \spuh-RAD-ik\ *adj.* Occurring now and then. sporadically *adv.*

spore \spor\ *n.* Reproductive cells of fungi, ferns, etc. spore *v.*

sport *n.* **1.** A recreational activity requiring athletic ability. **2.** Harmless humor. sport *adj.*; sporting *adj.*; sportive *adj.*; sports *adj.*; sporty *adj.*

sport *v.* sported; sporting. **1.** To play athletically. **2.** To joke. **3.** To wear or display.

sports medicine *n.* (Md) A branch of medicine specializing in athletic injuries.

spot *n.* **1.** A small round mark or stain. **2.** A small drop of something. **3.** A place.

spot *v.* spotted; spotting. **1.** To mark or become marked with spots. **2.** To see and recognize. **3.** To protect. spotter *n.*

spotless \SPOT-lis\ *adj.* Free from stain or blemish. spotlessly *adv.*; spotlessness *n.*

spotlight \SPOT-liet\ *n.* **1.** Bright beam on an area. **2.** Intense attention. **3.** Public recognition.

spouse \spows\ *n.* One's husband or wife.

sprawl *v.* sprawled; sprawling. To spread out loosely. sprawl *n.*

spread \spred\ *n.* **1.** Open area or expanse. **2.** Act of spreading. **3.** Meal. **4.** Ranch.

spread \spred\ *v.* spread; spreading. **1.** To open, unfold. **2.** To distribute over surface. **3.** To force apart. **4.** Extend.

spree *n.* **1.** A boisterous frolic. **2.** A bout of drinking. **3.** A period of overindulgence.

spring *n.* **1.** A sudden leaping. **2.** Device that recoils. **3.** Season of new vegetation. spring *adj.*

spring *v.* sprang or sprung; sprung. **1.** To leap suddenly, esp.. **2.** To show up suddenly. **3.** To issue from. spring *n.*

spring roll *n.* An Oriental fried or steamed stuffed shell.

sprinkle \SPRING-kul\ *v.* sprinkled; sprinkling. **1.** To scatter drops or small pieces. **2.** To rain lightly. sprinkle *n.*; sprinkler *n.*

sprint *v.* sprinted; sprinting. To run or swim at full speed. sprint *n.*; sprinter *n.*

sprout \sprowt\ *n.* A new or young growth on a plant.

sprout \sprowt\ *v.* sprouted; sprouting. To begin to grow or appear.

spruce \sproos\ *adj.* sprucer; sprucest. Neat and stylish. sprucely *adv.*; spruceness *n.*

spruce \sproos\ *n.* An evergreen tree with long, slender needles, cones, and soft wood.

spruce up \sproos-up\ *v.* spruced up; sprucing up. To make neat and stylish.

spry \sprie\ *adj.* spryer; spryest or sprier; spriest. Active and lively. spryly *adv.*; spryness *n.*

spunk \spungk\ *n.* Gumption. spunky *adj.*

spur *n.* **1.** A pricking device worn on a boot to urge on a horse. **2.** Any stimulus. spur *v.*

spurn *v.* spurned; spurning. To turn away scornfully.

sputnik \SPUUT-nik\ *n.* (Fo) A Soviet space satellite.

sputter \SPUT-ur\ *v.* sputtered; sputtering. **1.** To eject bits sporadically and explosively. **2.** To speak confusedly.

spy \spie\ *n. pl.* spies. A person who tries to discover secret information. spy *v.*

squabble \SKWOB-ul\ *v.* squabbled; squabbling. To quarrel in a petty manner. squabble *n.*

squad \skwod\ *n.* A small group working or training together.

squalid \SKWOL-id\ *adj.* **1.** Dirty and unpleasant. **2.** Degraded or sordid.

squalor \SKWOL-ur\ *n.* A dirty and unpleasant condition.

squander \SKWON-dur\ *v.* squandered; squandering. To spend wastefully.

square \skwair\ *adj.* **1.** Having four equal sides joined at right angles. **2.** Forming a right angle. squarely *adv.*; squareness *n.*

square \skwair\ *n.* **1.** Figure with four equal sides. **2.** Area in city. **3.** Measuring instrument. square *v.*

squash \skwosh\ *n.* **1.** A racquet game played on a closed court. **2.** A type of edible gourd.

squash \skwosh\ *v.* squashed; squashing. **1.** To crush or squeeze. **2.** To suppress or silence. squashy *adj.*

squat \skwot\ *adj.* squatter; squattest. Short and thick. squatty *adj.*; squatness *n.*

squat \skwot\ *v.* squatted; squatting. **1.** To rest on one's heels with the knees bent. **2.** To live on without permission. squatter *n.*

squawk \skwawk\ *n.* **1.** A loud, harsh cry. **2.** [Sl] To complain. squawk *v.*

squeak \skweek\ *n.* A short, high-pitched cry or sound. squeaky *adj.*; squeak *v.*

squeal \skweel\ *v.* **1.** To utter a long, shrill cry. **2.** [Sl] To let a secret be known. squeal *n.*; squealer *n.*

squeamish \SKWEE-mish\ *adj.* **1.** Easily disgusted. **2.** Overly fussy. squeamishly *adv.*; squeamishness *n.*

squeeze \skweez\ *v.* squeezed; squeezing. **1.** To exert pressure on. **2.** To press and extract liquid. **3.** To get out of. squeeze *n.*; squeezer *n.*

squelch \skwelch\ *v.* squelched; squelching. To suppress completely. squelch *n.*

squint \skwint\ *v.* squinted; squinting. **1.** To look through half-shut eyes. **2.** To look at something stealthily. squint *n.*

squire \skwier\ *n.* **1.** A country gentleman who owns a large estate. **2.** A female's escort.

squirm \skwurm\ *v.* squirmed; squirming. To wriggle and twist, especially in a show of discomfort or disgust. squirmy *adj.*; squirm *n.*

squirrel \SKWUR-ul\ *n.* A small, tree-climbing rodent with a bushy tail.

squirt \skwurt\ *n.* **1.** A jet of liquid sent out. **2.** [Cl] A small, unimportant person.

squirt \skwurt\ *v.* squirted; squirting. To sent out a liquid in a jet.

stab *n.* **1.** Thurst with pointed weapon. **2.** An attempt. stab *v.*

stable \STAY-bul\ *adj.* stabler; stablest. **1.** Steady. **2.** Likely to stay on the same course. stably *adv.*; stability *n.*; stabilization *n.*; stabilizer *n.*; stableness *n.*

stable \STAY-bul\ *n.* A place where horses are kept.

staccato \stuh-KAH-toh\ *adv.* (Mu) In a sharp, disconnected manner. staccato *adj.*; staccato *n.*

stack \stak\ *n.* **1.** A pile or heap. **2.** The part of a chimney above the roof. **3.** [Pl] Bookshelves. stack *v.*

stadium \STAY-dee-um\ *n.* A sports arena.

staff \staf\ *n.* **1.** Pole or stick as support, measure, or weapon. **2.** A managed working group.

staff \staf\ *v.* staffed; staffing. To supply with a group of workers. staffer *n.*

stage \stayj\ *n.* **1.** A raised floor for performances. **2.** Theatrical profession. **3.** Stagecoach.

stage \stayj\ *v.* staged; staging. **1.** To present on a stage. **2.** To arrange and carry out.

stagflation \stag-FLAY-shun\ *n.* A time when unemployment and inflation go up and business decreases.

stagger \STAG-ur\ *v.* staggered; staggering. **1.** To walk unsteadily. **2.** To overwhelm with grief. **3.** To alternate. staggering *adj.*; stagger *n.*

stagnate \STAG-nayt\ *v.* stagnated; stagnating. To be or become inactive or stale. stagnant *adj.*; stagnation *n.*

staid \stayd\ *adj.* Steady and serious.

stain \stayn\ *v.* stained; staining. **1.** To color or discolor something. **2.** To spoil or blemish. stain *n.*

stair *n. pl.* stairs. **1.** Step or one of a series of steps. **2.** [Pl] Flight of steps. staircase *n.*; stairway *n.*; stairwell *n.*

stake \stayk\ *n.* **1.** A pointed post for driving into the ground. **2.** Money wagered. **3.** Share. stake *v.*

stale \stayl\ *adj.* staler; stalest. **1.** Not fresh. **2.** Overused. staleness *n.*; stale *v.*

stalemate \STAYL-mayt\ *n.* **1.** A situation when no chess move is possible. **2.** Any deadlock. stalemate *v.*

stalk \stawk\ *n.* **1.** A plant's stem. **2.** Any supporting part.

stalk \stawk\ *v.* stalked; stalking. To hunt secretively. stalker *n.*

stall \stawl\ *n.* **1.** A storage compartment. **2.** An open-air booth. **3.** A cessation of activity.

stall \stawl\ *v.* stalled; stalling. **1.** To stop suddenly, especially due to malfunction. **2.** To hold off an action.

stallion \STAL-yun\ *n.* An uncastrated male horse.

stalwart \STAWL-wurt\ *adj.* Strong and brave. stalwart *n.*; stalwartness *n.*

stamen \STAY-mun\ *n.* The pollen-bearing part of a flower.

stamina \STAM-uh-nuh\ *n.* The ability to withstand physical or mental strain.

stammer \STAM-ur\ *v.* stammered; stammering. To hesitate and repeat sounds while talking. stammer *n.*

stamp *n.* **1.** Act of stamping. **2.** Device for printing symbols. **3.** Postage sticker.

stamp *v.* stamped; stamping. **1.** To bring the foot down heavily on the ground. **2.** To press or print firmly.

stampede \stam-PEED\ *n.* A sudden rush of animals or people. stampede *v.*

stance \stans\ *n.* **1.** One's manner of standing. **2.** Attitude.

stand *n.* **1.** An upright position. **2.** Resistance to an attack. **3.** Rack or upright thing.

stand *v.* stood; standing. **1.** To be upright on the feet. **2.** To reach a certain height. **3.** Be vertical.

standard \STAN-durd\ *adj.* **1.** Of a usual quality. **2.** Accepted as a reliable source. **3.** Following a rule.

standard \STAN-durd\ *n.* **1.** A flag or banner. **2.** A degree of skill or success. **3.** Criterion.

standardize \STAN-dur-dize\ *v.* standardized; standardizing. To cause to conform to a usual or normal quality. standardization *n.*

standoffish \STAND-AW-fish\ *adj.* Aloof. standoffishness *n.*

stand out *v.* **1.** To be easily seen. **2.** To stick out.

standstill \STAND-stil\ *n.* An inability to proceed.

stand up *v.* **1.** To rise to an upright position. **2.** To be as true or sturdy.

standup *also* **stand-up** \STAND-up\ *adj.* **1.** In an upright position. **2.** Done or used while standing.

stanza \STAN-zuh\ *n.* A verse in a poem or song.

staple \STAY-pul\ *n.* **1.** Main commodity. **2.** A basic dietary need. **3.** A small, U-shaped, metal piece. staple *adj.*; stapler *n.*; staple *v.*

star \stahr\ *n.* **1.** Celestial body of light. **2.** Figure with five or more radiating points. starry *adj.*

star \stahr\ *v.* starred; starring. **1.** To have a main part in a performance. **2.** To mark with a star or asterisk.

stardom \STAHR-dum\ *n.* The status of a famous entertainer.

stare \stair\ *v.* stared; staring. To gaze fixedly. stare *n.*

stark \stahrk\ *adj.* starker; starkest. **1.** Desolate and bare. **2.** Evident. starkly *adv.*; starkness *n.*

starlet \STAHR-lit\ *n.* A woman entertainer who is being promoted as the next famous actor.

starlight \STAHR-liet\ *n.* The light given off by the stars.

start \stahrt\ *v.* started; starting. **1.** To begin or set something going. **2.** To move suddenly. start *n.*; starter *n.*

start-up \STAHRT-up\ *adj.* Of or concerning a new project or venture. start-up or startup *n.*

starve \stahrv\ *v.* starved; starving. **1.** To suffer or die from lack of food. **2.** To deprive another of food. starvation *n.*

stash *v.* stashed; stashing. To stow away. stash *n.*

state \stayt\ *n.* **1.** A group of circumstances defining a person or thing. **2.** The way something is. state *adj.*

state \stayt\ *v.* stated; stating. To express in words.

state of the art *n.* The latest and most sophisticated stage of an art, science, or technology. state-of-the-art *adj.*

statement \STAYT-munt\ *n.* **1.** Something expressed in words. **2.** An account or report.

static \STAT-ik\ *adj.* **1.** Not moving. **2.** Electricity within a body, but not a current. statically *adv.*; static *n.*

station \STAY-shun\ *n.* **1.** Headquarters or depot. **2.** Assigned place. **3.** Broadcast studio. station *v.*

stationary \STAY-shuh-ner-ee\ *adj.* **1.** Not moving or movable. **2.** Not changing.

stationery \STAY-shuh-ner-ee\ *n.* Materials for writing, like paper and envelopes.

statistics \stuh-TIS-tiks\ *n.* **1.** Numerical data gathered and tabulated. **2.** The science of this. satistical *adj.*; statistically *adv.*

statue \STACH-oo\ *n.* A figure made of stone, metal, or other materials.

statuesque \stach-oo-ESK\ *adj.* Stately, graceful, and dignified.

stature \STACH-ur\ *n.* **1.** Bodily height. **2.** A great achievement or ability.

status \STAT-us or STAY-tus\ *n. pl.* statuses. **1.** One's rank in relation to others. **2.** A high rank.

statute \STACH-oot\ *n.* **1.** One of the rules of an institution. **2.** A law passed by a legislature.

statutory \STACH-uu-tor-ee\ *adj.* **1.** Required by statute. **2.** Punishable by statute.

staunch \stawnch\ *adj.* stauncher; staunchest. Firm and loyal. staunchly *adv.*

stay *v.* stayed; staying. **1.** To continue in the same place or state. **2.** To dwell. **3.** To postpone or pause. stay *n.*

steadfast \STED-fast\ *adj.* Firm and unyielding. steadfastly *adv.*; steadfastness *n.*

steady \STED-ee\ *adj.* steadier; steadiest. **1.** Not shaky or unbalanced. **2.** Regular and uniform. **3.** Calm and in control. steadily *adv.*; steadiness *n.*; steady *v.*

steak \stayk\ *n.* A thick slice of meat or fish for eating.

steal \steel\ *v.* stole; stolen. **1.** To take property without permission. **2.** To take secretly or deceptively. steal *n.*

stealth \stelth\ *n.* Moving quietly to

avoid notice. stealthy *adj.*; stealthily *adv.*; stealthiness *n.*

steam \steem\ *n.* **1.** Vapor produced by boiling water. **2.** [Sl] Energy. steamer *n.*; steam *v.*

steel *n.* **1.** A very strong alloy of iron and carbon. **2.** Immense strength. steel *adj.*; steely *adj.*

steel *v.* steeled; steeling. To make resolute.

steep *adj.* steeper; steepest. **1.** Rising or falling sharply. **2.** Extreme. steeply *adv.*; steepness *n.*

steep *v.* steeped; steeping. To soak.

steer *n.* A young bull raised for beef.

steer *v.* steered; steering. To control the direction in which something is to move. steerable *adj.*

stellar \STEL-ur\ *adj.* **1.** Of or concerning a star or stars. **2.** Amazing.

stellar wind *n.* An outflow of gas from a star.

stem *n.* **1.** Part of a plant growing up from the ground. **2.** Base part. **3.** Watch winder. stem *v.*

stench *n.* A bad smell.

stencil \STEN-sul\ *n.* **1.** Sheet in which a pattern is cut for tracing. **2.** Decoration made this way. stencil *v.*

stenography \stuh-NOG-ruh-fee\ *n.* Shorthand writing. stenographic *adj.*; stenographer *n.*

step *n.* **1.** Lifting and then lowering the foot when walking. **2.** The sound of walking. step *v.*

stepfamily \STEP-fam-uh-lee\ *n. pl.* stepfamilies. A family formed by remarriage.

stepfather \STEP-fah-thur\ *n.* A father due to remarriage.

stepmother \SETP-muth-ur\ *n.* A mother due to remarriage.

steppe \step\ *n.* A grassy plain, especially in Europe or Asia.

stereo \STAIR-ee-oh\ *n. pl.* stereos. A device that plays sounds from two or more channels. stereo *adj.*; stereophonic *adj.*

stereotype \STAIR-ee-oh-tipe\ *n.* **1.** A printing plate made from a mold. **2.** Conventional expression. stereotypical *adj.*; stereotypically *adv.*; stereotype *v.*

sterile \STAIR-il\ *adj.* **1.** Free from microorganisms. **2.** Unproductive or barren. sterility *n.*; sterilization *n.*; sterilizer *n.*; sterilize *v.*

stern \sturn\ *adj.* sterner; sternest. **1.** Strict. **2.** Unkind and grim. sternly *adv.*; sternness *n.*

stern \sturn\ *n.* The back end of a ship.

stet *v.* stetted; stetting. To let a piece of writing or printing stand as is, thus overriding deletion.

stew \stoo\ *n.* **1.** A cooked meat and

vegetable mixture. **2.** A state of anxiety.

stew \stoo\ *v.* stewed; stewing. **1.** To cook by simmering. **2.** To become very anxious.

steward \STOO-urd\ *n.* **1.** Attendant on an aircraft, ship, or train. **2.** Manager of property or servants.

stick \stik\ *n.* **1.** A thin length of wood or tree branch. **2.** A rod-shaped piece of material.

stick \stik\ *v.* sticked; sticking. **1.** To thrust a thing into something. **2.** To put, fasten, or fix. **3.** To remain.

sticky \STIK-ee\ *adj.* stickier; stickiest. **1.** Covered with glue or other sticking substance. **2.** Hot and humid. stickily *adv.*; stickiness *n.*

stiff \stif\ *adj.* stiffer; stiffest. **1.** Not easily bent or moved. **2.** Difficult. **3.** Formal in manner. **4.** Strong. stiffly *adv.*; stiffness *n.*; stiffen *v.*

stifle \STIE-ful\ *v.* stifled; stifling. **1.** To suffocate or feel unable to breathe. **2.** To suppress.

stigma \STIG-muh\ *n. pl.* stigmas or stigmata. **1.** A mark of shame. **2.** A part of a flower's pistil that receives pollen. stigmatic *adj.*; stigmatize *v.*

stiletto \sti-LET-oh\ *n. pl.* stilettos or stilettoes. **1.** A slender dagger. **2.** A daggerlike heel on women's shoes.

still \stil\ *adj.* **1.** Without movement. **2.** Quiet. **3.** Calm. **4.** Dead; inanimate. still *n.*; stillness *n.*; still *v.*

still \stil\ *adv.* **1.** At or up to an indicated time. **2.** Even. **3.** Nevertheless. **4.** Greater.

stilted \STIL-tid\ *adj.* Stiffly formal.

stimulate \STIM-yuh-layt\ *v.* stimulated; stimulating. To make more active or excited. stimulation *n.*

stimulus \STIM-yuh-lus\ *n. pl.* stimuli. Something that causes activity or excitement.

sting *n.* **1.** The act of inflicting a wound. **2.** An animal body part used for attacks. stinger *n.*

sting *v.* stung; stinging. **1.** To inflict a wound by pricking. **2.** To feel sharp mental or physical pain.

stink \stingk\ *v.* stank or stunk; stunk. To smell bad. stink *n.*

stint *n.* A time spent doing a certain amount of work.

stipend \STIE-pend or STI-pend\ *n.* A salary.

stipulate \STIP-yuh-layt\ *v.* stipulated; stipulating. **1.** To demand or insist on as part of an agreement. **2.** To organize definitively. stipulation *n.*

stir \stur\ *n.* Commotion or excitement.

stir \stur\ *v.* stirred; stirring. **1.** To move a liquid or soft substance around to mix. **2.** To excite or stimulate.

stir-fry \STUR-FRIE\ *v.* stir-fried; stir-frying. To cook quickly in oil over high heat. stir-fry *n.*

stirrup \STIR-up\ *n.* A loop for a horse-rider's foot.

stock \stok\ *n.* **1.** A supply waiting to be sold. **2.** Animals kept. **3.** Food broth. stock *adj.*; stock *v.*

stockade \sto-KAYD\ *n.* A protective wall.

stockbroker \STOK-broh-kur\ *n.* One who sells stocks and bonds.

stock market *n.* A place where stocks and bonds are sold.

stocky \STOK-ee\ *adj.* stockier; stockiest. Solidly built and short. stockily *adv.*; stockiness *n.*

stodgy \STOJ-ee\ *adj.* stodgier; stodgiest. Dull and boring. stodginess *n.*

stoic \STOH-ik\ *adj.* Calm and uncomplaining. stoical *adj.*; stoic *n.*; stoically *adv.*; stoicism *n.*

stoke \stohk\ *v.* stoked; stoking. To tend and put fuel on. stoker *n.*

stole \stohl\ *v.* The past tense of steal.

stolid \STOL-id\ *adj.* Impassive. stolidness *n.*

stomach \STUM-uk\ *n.* **1.** The first digestive organ of the body. **2.** The abdomen.

stomach \STUM-uk\ *v.* stomached; stomaching. To endure.

stone \stohn\ *n.* **1.** A rock or mineral that is not metal. **2.** A piece of rock. **3.** A jewel. stone *adj.*

stone \stohn\ *v.* stoned; stoning. **1.** To hit with stones. **2.** To remove a stone from a fruit.

stoned \stohnd\ *adj.* (Sl) Intoxicated.

stonewall \STOHN-wawl\ *v.* stonewalled; stonewalling. To be evasive or uncooperative.

stoop *n.* A small porch.

stoop *v.* stooped; stooping. To bend forward and downward.

stop *v.* stopped; stopping. **1.** To come to an end. **2.** To bring something to an end. **3.** To prevent or hinder. stop *n.*

stoppage \STOP-ij\ *n.* **1.** The cessation of something. **2.** An obstructed state.

store \stor\ *n.* **1.** A collection of

things kept for future use. **2.** Storage place.

store \stor\ *v.* stored; storing. To put something away for future use. storage *n.*

storm *n.* **1.** Period of violent weather. **2.** A sudden violent attack. **3.** Emotional outburst. storm *v.*

stormy \STOR-mee\ *adj.* stormier; stormiest. **1.** Experiencing violent weather. **2.** Enraged. stormily *adv.*

story \STOR-ee\ *n. pl.* stories. **1.** Words that explain real or imagined happenings. **2.** Lie. **3.** One floor.

stout \stowt\ *adj.* stouter; stoutest. **1.** Thick and strong. **2.** Brave. stoutly *adv.*; stoutness *n.*

stow \stoh\ *v.* stowed; stowing. To place in storage. stowaway *n.*

strafe \strayf\ *v.* strafed; strafing. To bombard with gunfire. strafe *n.*

straggle \STRAG-ul\ *v.* straggled; straggling. **1.** To grow or spread untidily. **2.** To lag behind. straggly *adv.*; straggler *n.*

straight \strayt\ *adj.* straighter; straightest. **1.** Not curved or bent. **2.** Correctly placed and tidy. **3.** Honest and direct. straight *adv.*; straightness *n.*; straighten *v.*

straightforward *also* **straightforwards** \strayt-FOR-wurd\ *adj.* **1.** Honest. **2.** Without complications. straightforwardly *adv.*

strain \strayn\ *v.* strained; straining. **1.** Stretch and pull hard. **2.** To make a great effort at something. **3.** To injure. strain *n.*; strainer *n.*

strait \strayt\ *n.* A narrow body of water joining two larger ones.

strand *n.* **1.** A thread or fiber, especially one twisted to make rope. **2.** A shore.

stranded \STRAN-dud\ *adj.* Left in a helpless position.

strange \straynj\ *adj.* stranger; strangest. **1.** Not familiar. **2.** Unusual. strangely *adv.*; strangeness *n.*

stranger \STRAYN-jur\ *n.* **1.** One who is new to you. **2.** A newcomer.

strangle \STRANG-gul\ *v.* strangled; strangling. **1.** To kill or be killed by squeezing the throat. **2.** To restrict. strangler *n.*; strangulation *n.*

strap *n.* A strip of leather or other material. strap *v.*

strapped \STRAPT\ *adj.* (Sl) Needy or broke.

strapping \STRAP-ping\ *adj.* Tall and healthy.

strategy \STRAT-i-jee\ *n. pl.* strategies. A plan for doing something. strategic *adj.*; strategist *n.*

stratosphere *n.* A region of the upper atmosphere.

stratum *n. pl.* strata. One of a series of layers or levels.

straw *n.* **1.** A piece or bunch of dried grain. **2.** A plastic tube for drinking liquid.

strawberry \STRAW-ber-ee\ *n. pl.* strawberries. A small, soft, juicy, red fruit.

stray *v.* strayed; straying. To wander or become lost. stray *adj.*, stray *n.*

streak \streek\ *n.* **1.** A thin line or band of color. **2.** A trait or spell.

streak \streek\ *v.* streaked; streaking. **1.** To mark with streaks. **2.** To run fast. **3.** To run fast while naked. streaky *adj.*; streaker *n.*

stream \streem\ *n.* **1.** Water that flows in one direction. **2.** Any liquid or group that has a current. stream *v.*

stream of consciousness *n.* A series of thoughts or images that come to mind. stream-of-consciousness *adj.*

street *n.* A road in a town with houses along it.

street-smart \STREET-smahrt\ *adj.* Shrewdly aware. street smarts *n.*

streetwise \STREET-wiez\ *adj.* Shrewdly aware.

strength \strengkth\ *n.* **1.** Being strong. **2.** Endurance. **3.** The power or resistance. strengthen *v.*

strenuous \STREN-yoo-us\ *adj.* Requiring great effort. strenuously *adv.*

streptococcus \strep-tuh-KOK-us\ *n.* (Md) A bacteria that causes disease.

stress \stres\ *n. pl.* stresses. **1.** A strain. **2.** Great anxiety. **3.** Emphasis. **4.** An accent given to a syllable. stress *v.*

stretch \strech\ *n. pl.* stretches. **1.** Making something wider, longer, or tighter. **2.** A strain from extending.

stretch \strech\ *v.* stretched; stretching. **1.** To make something wider, longer, or tighter. **2.** To extend. **3.** To strain. stretchy *adj.*

stretch mark *n.* A streak in the skin due to rapid weight gain and loss.

strict \strikt\ *adj.* stricter; strictest. **1.** Requiring obedience. **2.** Precisely defined. strictly *adv.*; strictness *n.*

stride \stried\ *v.* strode; stridden. To walk with long steps. stride *n.*

strident \STRIED-nt\ *adj.* Loud and harsh. stridently *adv.*

strife \strief\ *n.* A conflict or fight.

strike \striek\ *v.* struck; struck or stricken. **1.** To hit. **2.** To attack suddenly. **3.** To permeate suddenly, as a disease. strike *n.*

striking \STRIE-king\ *adj.* Attractive and noticeable. strikingly *adv.*

string *n.* **1.** A thin cord used to tie things. **2.** [Mu] Length of wire, catgut on instrument. stringy *adj.*; string *v.*

string along *v.* strung along; stringing along. **1.** To deceive. **2.** To go along with. **3.** To keep uncertain.

stringent \STRIN-junt\ *adj.* Strict and restricted. stringently *adv.*; stringency *n.*

strip *n.* A long, narrow piece of something.

strip *v.* stripped; stripping. **1.** To undress. **2.** To take the covering off. **3.** To deprive of something. stripper *n.*

stripe \striep\ *n.* **1.** A long, narrow, unique mark or band. **2.** A cloth badge showing rank, etc. striped *adj.*; stripe *v.*

strive \striev\ *v.* strove; striven or strived. **1.** To make a great effort. **2.** To struggle for.

stroke \strohk\ *n.* **1.** A striking movement. **2.** A spontaneous attack. **3.** A sequence of movements.

stroke \strohk\ *v.* stroked; stroking. To rub one's hand gently over a surface.

stroll \strohl\ *v.* strolled; strolling. To walk leisurely. stroll *n.*; stroller *n.*

strong \strawng\ *adj.* stronger; strongest. **1.** Having great power. **2.** Not easily broken or damaged. **3.** Able to resist. strongly *adv.*

stronghold \STRAWNG-hohld\ *n.* A fortified place.

structure \STRUK-chur\ *n.* **1.** A thing that has been built or put together. **2.** Building. **3.** Organization. structural *adj.*; structurally *adv.*; structure *v.*

strut *n.* **1.** A bar of wood or metal for support. **2.** A jaunty walk.

strut *v.* strutted; strutting. To walk quickly and pompously.

stub *n.* A short piece of something, especially when part has been used.

stub *v.* stubbed; stubbing. **1.** To hit something against another thing. **2.** To extinguish by rubbing out.

stubble \STUB-ul\ *n.* **1.** Short hairs

that grow after shaving. **2.** Stalks left behind after a harvest.

stubborn \STUB-urn\ *adj.* Obstinate. stubbornly *adv.*; stubbornness *n.*

stubby \STUB-ee\ *adj.* stubbier; stubbiest. Short and thick. stubbiness *n.*

stucco \STUK-oh\ *n. pl.* stuccoes or stuccos. A plaster or cement used for coating or molding a building. stucco *v.*

student \STOOD-nt\ *n.* A person engaged in studying something.

studied \STUD-eed\ *adj.* **1.** Delivered after careful investigation. **2.** Deliberate and artificial.

studious \STOO-dee-us\ *adj.* Keenly involved in study. studiously *adv.*; studiousness *n.*

study \STUD-ee\ *n. pl.* studies. **1.** Gaining of knowledge. **2.** Work requiring careful research. **3.** Room for study.

study \STUD-ee\ *v.* studied; studying. **1.** To learn by reading, research, etc. **2.** To research closely. **3.** To examine.

stuff \stuf\ *n.* **1.** The material out of which anything is constructed. **2.** The basic elements.

stuff \stuf\ *v.* stuffed; stuffing. To fill or pack tightly.

stuffy \STUF-ee\ *adj.* stuffier; stuffiest. **1.** Lacking ventilation. **2.** [Sl] Boring and incapable of having fun. stuffiness *n.*

stumble \STUM-bul\ *v.* stumbled; stumbling. **1.** Miss a step in walking; trip. **2.** Speak falteringly. **3.** Find by chance. stumble *n.*; stumbler *n.*

stump *n.* **1.** The part of a tree that remains after it is cut down. **2.** A similar remnant. stumpy *adj.*

stump *v.* stumped; stumping. **1.** To make too difficult for someone. **2.** To campaign for political office.

stun *v.* stunned; stunning. **1.** To cause to lose consciousness, as by a blow. **2.** To amaze or daze.

stunning \STUN-ing\ *adj.* Amazingly beautiful. stunningly *adv.*

stunt *n.* A difficult or dangerous feat.

stunt *v.* stunted; stunting. To hinder growth or development.

stupefy \STOO-puh-fie\ *v.* stupefied; stupefying. **1.** To stun. **2.** To confuse. stupefaction *n.*

stupendous \stoo-PEN-dus\ *adj.* Amazingly great. stupendously *adv.*

stupid \STOO-pid\ *adj.* **1.** Not clever. **2.** Slow at learning or understanding. **3.** Silly. stupidly *adv.*; stupidity *n.*

stupor \STOO-pur\ *n.* A dazed, almost unconscious condition.

sturdy \STUR-dee\ *adj.* sturdier; sturdiest. Strongly built and hardy. sturdily *adv.*; sturdiness *n.*

stutter \STUT-ur\ *v.* stuttered; stuttering. To speak with involuntary interruptions. stutter *n.*

style \stiel\ *n.* **1.** The way or manner in which something is done. **2.** Elegance. style *v.*

stylish \STIE-lish\ *adj.* Fashionable. stylishly *adv.*; stylishness *n.*

stymie *also* **stymy** \STIE-mee\ *v.* stymied; stymieing or stymying. To hinder.

Styrofoam \STIE-roh-fohm\ *n.* A light plastic made from polystyrene.

suave \swahv\ *adj.* Smooth in manner. suavely *adv.*; suaveness *n.*; suavity *n.*

sub *n.* **1.** A submarine. **2.** A substitute. **3.** A deli sandwich.

subcompact \sub-KOM-pakt\ *n.* A very small automobile.

subconscious \sub-KON-shus\ *n.* The mental activities of which one is not aware. subconscious *adj.*; subconsciously *adv.*

subdivision \SUB-di-vizh-un\ *n.* **1.** A division of land into several

lots. **2.** Division into several parts. subdivide *v.*

subdue \sub-DOO\ *v.* subdued; subduing. **1.** To bring under control. **2.** To diminish the intensity of.

subject \SUB-jikt\ *adj.* **1.** Under the control of another. **2.** Tending to. **3.** Exposed. **4.** Depending on.

subject \SUB-jikt\ *n.* **1.** A controlled being. **2.** A topic; branch of learning. **3.** Person to be treated.

subject \sub-JEKT\ *v.* subjected; subjecting. To cause to undergo. subjection *n.*

subjective \sub-JEK-tiv\ *adj.* Dependent on personal opinion or taste. subjectively *adv.*; subjectiveness *n.*; subjectivity *n.*

sublimate \SUB-luh-mayt\ *v.* sublimated; sublimating. To refine or purify. sublimation *n.*

sublime \suh-BLIEM\ *adj.* Most impressive. sublimely *adv.*; sublimity *n.*

subliminal \sub-LIM-uh-nul\ *adj.* Below the level of conscious awareness. subliminally *adv.*

submarine \sub-muh-REEN\ *n.* A vessel that can operate under water. submarine *adj.*

submerge \sub-MURJ\ *v.* submerged; submerging. **1.** To put or go below the surface of a liquid. **2.** To flood. submergence *n.*; submersion *n.*; submerse *v.*

submission \sub-MISH-un\ *n.* **1.** Showing to others for consideration. **2.** Consideration. **3.** Presentation.

submissive \sub-MIS-iv\ *adj.* Surrendering to authority. submissively *adv.*; submissiveness *n.*

submit \sub-MIT\ *v.* submitted; submitting. **1.** To show to others for consideration. **2.** To surrender to an authority.

subordinate \suh-BOR-dn-it\ *adj.* **1.** Lower in rank and importance. **2.** Of a clause dependent upon another. subordinate *n.*; subordination *n.*; subordinate *v.*

subpoena \suh-PEE-nuh\ *n.* (Le) A document demanding an appearance in court. subpoena *v.*

subscribe \sub-SKRIEB\ *v.* subscribed; subscribing. **1.** To request and pay for an order. **2.** To give consent. subscriber *n.*; subscription *n.*

subservient \sub-SUR-vee-unt\ *adj.* Servile and subordinate. subservience *n.*

subside \sub-SIED\ *v.* subsided; subsiding. **1.** To sink or recede to a lower level. **2.** To become quiet. subsidence *n.*

subsidiary \sub-SID-ee-er-ee\ *adj.* **1.** Assisting. **2.** Being subordinate to.

subsidiary \sub-SID-ee-er-ee\ *n. pl.* subsidiaries. A company owned by another company.

subsidize \SUB-si-diez\ *v.* subsidized; subsidizing. To provide money to keep a price low or support. subsidization *n.*; subsidy *n.*

subsist \sub-SIST\ *v.* subsisted; subsisting. To exist and keep alive. subsistence *n.*

substance \SUB-stuns\ *n.* **1.** Basic matter. **2.** Density. **3.** Solidity.

substantial \sub-STAN-shul\ *adj.* **1.** Consisting of physical matter. **2.** Real. **3.** Hardy. **4.** Weighty. **5.** Wealthy. substantially *adv.*

substantiate \sub-STAN-shee-ayt\ *v.* substantiated; substantiating. To provide evidence. substantiation *n.*

substitute \SUB-sti-toot\ *n.* A person or thing that takes the place of another. substitute *adj.*; substitution *n.*; substitute *v.*

subterranean \sub-tuh-RAY-nee-un\ *adj.* Underground.

subtext \sub-TEKST\ *n.* The underlying or implicit meaning of a work. subtextual *adj.*

subtle \SUT-l\ *adj.* subtler; subtlest.

1. Slight and difficult to detect. **2.** Ingenious. subtly *adv.*; subtlety *n.*

subtraction \sub-TRAK-shun\ *n.* Taking away one number or amount from another. subtract *v.*

suburb \SUB-urb\ *n.* An area of homes on the edge of a town or city. suburban *adj.*; suburbanite *n.*; suburbia *n.*

subversive \sub-VUR-siv\ *adj.* Causing or attempting to cause the downfall or ruin of something. subversion *n.*; subvert *v.*

succeed \suk-SEED\ *v.* succeeded; succeeding. **1.** To do what you intended. **2.** To do something well. **3.** To come after. succession *n.*

success \suk-SES\ *n. pl.* successes. **1.** Reaching a goal. **2.** Doing something well. **3.** Person, etc. that does well. successful *adj.*; successfully *adv.*

succinct \suk-SINGKT\ *adj.* Concise and clear. succinctly *adv.*

succulent \SUK-yuh-lunt\ *adj.* **1.** Juicy. **2.** Having thick, fleshy leaves or stems. succulently *adv.*; succulence *n.*; succulency *n.*; succulent *n.*

succumb \suh-KUM\ *v.* succumbed; succumbing. To give in to a stronger power.

such *adj.* **1.** Of this, that, or the same kind. **2.** Of a degree or quality mentioned.

sudden \SUD-n\ *adj.* Happening or done quickly and unexpectedly. suddenly *adv.*; suddenness *n.*

sudden infant death syndrome SIDS *n.* (Md) Unexpected death of a seemingly healthy infant; crib death.

sue \soo\ *v.* sued; suing. (Le) To claim compensation from somebody in a court of law.

suede \swayd\ *n.* A type of leather having one side rubbed to a velvety texture.

suffer \SUF-ur\ *v.* suffered; suffering. **1.** To feel pain, loss, or disappointment. **2.** To endure. sufferer *n.*; suffering *n.*

suffice \suh-FIES\ *v.* sufficed; sufficing. To be enough.

sufficient \suh-FISH-unt\ *adj.* Enough. sufficiently *adv.*; sufficiency *n.*

suffix \SUF-iks\ *n. pl.* suffixes. Letters added to the end of a word to change its meaning or use.

suffocation \suf-uh-KAY-shun\ *n.* **1.** Cutting off breath. **2.** Smothering. suffocate *v.*

suffrage \SUF-rij\ *n.* The right to vote in political elections.

suggest \sug-JEST\ *v.* suggested;

suggesting. **1.** To put forward an idea. **2.** To give an impression of something. suggestion *n.*

suggestive \sug-JES-tiv\ *adj.* **1.** Putting forward an idea. **2.** Conveying an idea, especially an indecent one. suggestively *adv.*

suit \soot\ *n.* **1.** Clothes set of the same material and color. **2.** One of four playing card types

suit \soot\ *v.* suited; suiting. **1.** To be appropriate. **2.** To satisfy.

suitable \SOO-tuh-bul\ *adj.* Appropriate. suitably *adv.*; suitability *n.*

suite \sweet\ *n.* **1.** A set of rooms. **2.** A set of furniture.

suitor \SOO-tur\ *n.* A man who is courting a woman.

sulfuric acid *n.* An oily, colorless, corrosive chemical compound.

sulk *v.* sulked; sulking. To be silent and bad-tempered. sulky *adj.*; sulkily *adv.*; sulkiness *n.*

sullen \SUL-un\ *adj.* **1.** Exhibiting sadness and resentment. **2.** Dark and threatening. sullenly *adv.*; sullenness *n.*

sultry \SUL-tree\ *adj.* sultrier; sultriest. **1.** Hot and humid. **2.** Steamy, as with passion.

sum *n.* **1.** The total when numbers are added. **2.** An amount of money. **3.** Gist. sum *v.*

summary \SUM-uh-ree\ *n. pl.* summaries. A statement of the main points of something. summary *adj.*; summarily *adv.*

summer \SUM-ur\ *n.* The season after spring and before fall. summery *adj.*

summit \SUM-it\ *n.* **1.** The highest point. **2.** A conference between heads of states.

summon \SUM-un\ *v.* summoned; summoning. **1.** To call for a meeting. **2.** To command someone to appear and do something.

sumptuous \SUMP-choo-us\ *adj.* Splendid and magnificent. sumptuously *adv.*

sun *n.* **1.** The celestial body around which the Earth orbits. **2.** Warmth or light from it. sunny *adj.*

Sunbelt *n.* The southern United States.

sun block *n.* A liquid preparation that stops sun rays from harming the skin.

Sunday \SUN-day\ *n.* The day after Saturday and before Monday.

sunrise \SUN-ries\ *n.* The time during the day when the sun appears above the eastern horizon.

sunroof \SUN-roof\ *n. pl.* sunroofs. A section in the top of an automobile that can be opened.

sunset \SUN-set\ *n.* The time during the day when the sun disappears below the western horizon.

sunshine \SUN-shien\ *n.* Light coming from the sun.

super \SOO-pur\ *adj.* Excellent.

superb \suh-PURB\ *adj.* Magnificent. suberbly *adv.*

supercomputer \soo-pur-kom-PYOO-tur\ *n.* (Cm) A very fast and powerful mainframe computer.

superego \soo-pur-EE-goh\ *n.* A person's conscience.

superficial \soo-pur-FISH-ul\ *adj.* Not deep or penetrating. superficially *adv.*; superficiality *n.*

superfluous \suu-PUR-floo-us\ *adj.* Extra, more than is required. superfluously *adv.*; superfluity *n.*

superintendent \soo-pur-in-TEN-dunt\ *n.* A supervisor or director of an organization or place. superintendence *n.*

superior \suh-PEER-ee-ur\ *adj.* **1.** Higher in rank. **2.** Better in quality. **3.** Being proud of oneself. superiority *n.*

superior \suh-PEER-ee-ur\ *n.* **1.** A person higher in rank than others. **2.** A religious leader.

superiority complex *n.* An exaggerated feeling of one's own worth.

superlative \suh-PUR-luh-tiv\ *adj.* **1.** Of the highest degree or quality. **2.** The grammatical form expressing "most." superlatively *adv.*

supernatural \soo-pur-NACH-ur-ul\ *adj.* Of or concerning a power outside of nature. supernaturally *adv.*; supernatural *n.*

supersede \soo-pur-SEED\ *v.* superseded; superseding. To take the place of. supersession *n.*

superstition \soo-pur-STISH-un\ *n.* A belief that goes against fact and rationality, especially a belief in magic. superstitious *adj.*; superstitiously *adv.*

supertanker \soo-pur-TANG-kur\ *n.* A very large cargo or oil ship.

supervise \SOO-pur-viez\ *v.* supervised; supervising. To direct and inspect work. supervisory *adj.*; supervision *n.*; supervisor *n.*

supple \SUP-ul\ *adj.* suppler; supplest. **1.** Easily bent. **2.** Submitting easily. supply *adv.*; suppleness *n.*

supplement \SUP-luh-munt\ *n.* An extra part or amount meant to improve. supplemental *adj.*; supplementary *adj.*; supplement *v.*

supply \suh-PLIE\ *n. pl.* supplies. **1.** The act of making something available for use. **2.** A stock of something.

supply \suh-PLIE\ *v.* supplied; supplying. To make something available for use. supplier *n.*

support \suh-PORT\ *v.* supported; supporting. **1.** To hold something up, keep it going or in place. **2.** To help. **3.** To encourage. supportive *adj.*; support *n.*; supporter *n.*

support hose *n.* A specially made nylon stocking that offers leg support.

suppose \suh-POHZ\ *v.* supposed; supposing. **1.** To guess or think. **2.** To consider as true, as in an argument. **3.** To expect. supposedly *adv.*; supposition *n.*

suppository \suh-POZ-i-tor-ee\ *n. pl.* suppositories. (Md) A dose of medicine that is absorbed when it melts in a body cavity.

suppress \suh-PRES\ *v.* suppressed; suppressing. **1.** To put down forcefully. **2.** To censor. **3.** To hold back. suppression *n.*; suppressor *n.*

supreme \suh-PREEM\ *adj.* Highest in rank, importance, or quality. supremely *adv.*; supremacist *n.*; supremacy *n.*

sure \shuur\ *adj.* surer; surest. **1.** Certain. **2.** Reliable. **3.** Not easily

questioned. **4.** Bound to occur. surely *adv.*; sureness *n.*

surf *n.* The white, foamy waves of a sea.

surf *v.* surfed; surfing. To ride toward shore on the crest of a wave. surfer *n.*; surfing *n.*

surface \SUR-fis\ *n.* **1.** Outside of something. **2.** Top, outside of something. **3.** Outward aspect. none.

surface \SUR-fis\ *v.* surfaced; surfacing. **1.** To come to the outermost layer. **2.** To add a layer to the top of a thing.

surfeit \SUR-fit\ *n.* An overabundance, especially of food and drink. surfeit *v.*

surge \surj\ *v.* surged; surging. **1.** To move forward in or like waves. **2.** To increase in intensity. surge *n.*

surgery \SUR-juh-ree\ *n. pl.* surgeries. (Md) A medical operation. surgical *adj.*; surgically *adv.*; surgeon *n.*

surly \SUR-lee\ *adj.* surlier; surliest. Rude and bad-tempered. surliness *n.*

surmise \sur-MIZE\ *v.* surmised; surmising. To guess. surmise *n.*

surmount \sur-MOWNT\ *v.* surmounted; surmounting. **1.** To overcome. **2.** To be at the highest level. **3.** To ascend. surmountable *adj.*

surpass \sur-PAS\ *v.* surpassed; surpassing. **1.** To do better or be better than others at something. **2.** To move beyond.

surplus \SUR-plus\ *n.* An amount left over after the needed amount has been used. surplus *adj.*

surrealism \suh-REE-uh-liz-um\ *n.* Movement in art and literature of 20th century, stressing nonrational. surrealist *adj.*; surrealistic *adj.*; surrealist *n.*

surrender \suh-REN-dur\ *v.* surrendered; surrendering. **1.** To hand over ownership of. **2.** To abandon. **3.** To give oneself up to an enemy. surrender *n.*

surreptitious \sur-up-TISH-us\ *adj.* Acting or done stealthily. surreptitiously *adv.*

surrogate \SUR-uh-gut\ *n.* **1.** A substitute. **2.** [Le] A probate judge. surrogate *adj.*; surrogacy *n.*; surrogate *v.*

surround \suh-ROWND\ *v.* surrounded; surrounding. To encircle.

surroundings \suh-ROWN-dingz\ *pl. n.* The environment, especially around a person.

surveillance \sur-VAY-luns\ *n.* A close watch over a person, place, or thing.

survey \sur-VAY\ *n.* **1.** A detailed examination. **2.** An overall view. **3.** Inspection. **4.** Map surveyor *n.*; survey *v.*

survive \sur-VIEV\ *v.* survived; surviving. To continue to live, especially after another has died or after serious danger. survival *n.*; survivor *n.*

susceptible \suh-SEP-tuh-bul\ *adj.* Easily affected. susceptibility *n.*

suspect \suh-SPEKT\ *v.* suspected; suspecting. **1.** To have a suspicion. **2.** To have a feeling that someone is guilty. suspect *adj.*; suspect *n.*

suspend \suh-SPEND\ *v.* suspended; suspending. **1.** To bar from privilege, work, for a time. **2.** Withhold temporarily. **3.** Hang. suspension *n.*

suspense \suh-SPENS\ *n.* **1.** Anxious uncertainty. **2.** Building excitement. suspenseful *adj.*

suspension \suh-SPEN-shun\ *n.* **1.** Act or state of suspending. **2.** Mechanical system of springs, bars, etc.

suspicion \suh-SPISH-un\ *n.* **1.** Suspecting or being suspected of wrongdoing. **2.** A state of doubt.

3. A hint. suspicious *adj.*; suspiciously *adv.*; suspiciousness *n.*

sustain \suh-STAYN\ *v.* sustained; sustaining. **1.** To keep alive or going continuously. **2.** To support. **3.** To uphold validity of.

sustenance \SUS-tuh-nuns\ *n.* **1.** The process of sustaining life by nourishment. **2.** Food that sustains life.

svelte \sfelt\ *adj.* Slender and graceful.

swagger \SWAG-ur\ *v.* swaggered; swaggering. To walk or behave with aggressive pride. swagger *n.*

swallow \SWOL-oh\ *n.* **1.** Act of swallowing. **2.** Amount swallowed.

swallow \SWOL-oh\ *v.* swallowed; swallowing. **1.** To allow food and drink to pass down the throat. **2.** To take something in.

swami \SWAH-mee\ *n. pl.* swamis. (Fo) A title of honor for a Hindu religious teacher.

swamp \swomp\ *n.* A marsh. swampy *adj.*

swamp \swomp\ *v.* swamped; swamping. **1.** To overwhelm. **2.** To flood. **3.** To sink by flooding with water.

swanky \SWANG-kee\ *adj.* swankier; swankiest. Showy and stylish. swankily *adv.*; swank *n.*; swankiness *n.*

swap \swop\ *v.* swapped; swapping. To exchange. swap *n.*

swarm \sworm\ *n.* **1.** A large group of insects, especially bees. **2.** A mobile crowd. swarm *v.*

swarthy \SWOR-thee\ *adj.* swarthier; swarthiest. Having a dark complexion. swarthiness *n.*

swat \swot\ *v.* swatted; swatting. To hit hard with something flat. swat *n.*; swatter *n.*

SWAT team \swot-teem\ *n.* Law enforcement group trained to deal with terrorism, violence, etc.

sway *v.* swayed; swaying. **1.** To move from side to side. **2.** To change or cause to change an opinion. sway *n.*

swear \swair\ *v.* swore; sworn; swearing. **1.** To promise on oath. **2.** To state emphatically. **3.** To utter profane language. swearer *n.*; swearing *n.*

sweat \swet\ *n.* **1.** Moisture given off by the body through the pores. **2.** Droplets on surface. sweaty *adj.*; sweat *v.*

sweep *v.* swept; sweeping. **1.** To clear or clean with a broom or brush. **2.** To move or remove by pushing. sweep *n.*; sweeper *n.*

sweet *adj.* sweeter; sweetest. **1.** Tasting of sugar. **2.** Not bitter, salty, or sour. **3.** Fragrant. **4.** Melodious. sweetness *n.*

sweet *n.* **1.** A food tasting of sugar. **2.** A candy. **3.** A beloved person.

sweetheart \SWEET-hahrt\ *n.* A lover.

swell \swel\ *adj.* (Sl) Fine.

swell \swel\ *v.* swelled; swollen; swelling. To make or become larger or more intense. swell *n.*

sweltering \SWEL-tur-ing\ *adj.* Extremely hot. swelter *v.*

swerve \swurv\ *v.* swerved; swerving. To veer off of a straight line while moving. swerve *n.*

swift *adj.* swifter; swiftest. Very fast. swiftly *adv.*; swiftness *n.*

swim *v.* swam; swum; swimming. **1.** To move oneself through the water. **2.** To proceed smoothly. **3.** To float on. swim *n.*; swimmer *n.*

swimmingly \SWIM-ing-lee\ *adv.* With easy progress.

swindle \SWIN-dl\ *v.* swindled; swindling. **1.** To cheat in a business transaction. **2.** To obtain by fraud. swindle *n.*; swindler *n.*

swing *n.* **1.** Movement to and fro. **2.** The act of doing this. **3.** A sweeping motion.

swing *v.* swung; swinging. **1.** To move to and fro, as would a pen-dulum. **2.** To turn suddenly. **3.** To hang. swinger *n.*

swipe \swiep\ *v.* swiped; swiping. **1.** To hit with a swinging blow. **2.** To steal. swipe *n.*

swirl \swurl\ *v.* swirled; swirling. To whirl. swirly *adj.*; swirl *n.*

switch \swich\ *n. pl.* switches. **1.** A device for turning an electric current on and off. **2.** A transfer or change.

switch \swich\ *v.* switched; switching. **1.** To turn an electric current on, off. **2.** To transfer or change. **3.** To divert.

swivel \SWIV-ul\ *v.* swivelled; swivelling. To pivot or revolve. swivel *n.*

swollen \SWOH-lun\ *v.* The past participle of swell.

swoop *v.* swooped; swooping. To rush downward suddenly and attack. swoop *n.*

sword \sord\ *n.* A weapon with a long, sharp blade.

sycamore \SIK-uh-mor\ *n.* A large tree of the maple family.

sycophant \SIK-uh-fant\ *n.* A person who flatters others to gain favors. sycophantic *adj.*; sycophantically *adv.*

syllable \SIL-uh-bul\ *n.* A unit of sound in a word. syllabic *adj.*; syllabically *adv.*

symbiosis \sim-bee-OH-sis\ *n. pl.* symbioses. (Sc) Different organisms living in close association and in harmony. symbiotic *adj.*

symbol \SIM-bul\ *n.* A sign, object, mark, etc., that represents something. symbolic *adj.*; symbolical *adj.*; symbolically *adv.*; symbolism *n.*; symbolize *v.*

symmetry \SIM-i-tree\ *n.* The state of having parts that correspond in size, shape, and position. symmetrical *adj.*; symmetrically *adv.*

sympathy \SIM-puh-thee\ *n. pl.* sympathies. **1.** Tenderness toward another. **2.** Sharing of another's emotions. sympathetic *adj.*; sympathetically *adv.*; synpathizer *n.*; sympathize *v.*

symposium \sim-POH-zee-um\ *n. pl.* symposiums or symposia. **1.** Meeting for discussing a subject in detail. **2.** A published account of this.

symptom \SIMP-tum\ *n.* A sign of the existence of a condition. symptomatic *adj.*

synagogue \SIN-uh-gog\ *n.* A place for Jewish worship.

syncopation \sing-kuh-PAY-shun\ *n.* (Mu) Rhythmic tone and a weak beat. syncopate *v.*

syndicate \SIN-di-kit\ *n.* **1.** Business group seeking capital. **2.** Agency selling to several periodicals. syndicate *v.*

syndicate \SIN-di-kayt\ *v.* syndicated; syndicating. **1.** To function as or combine into a syndicate. **2.** To publish through an agency. syndication *n.*

syndrome \SIN-drohm\ *n.* A group of signs, symptoms, and behavior that indicate a condition.

synergism \SIN-ur-jiz-um\ *n.* Joint action to produce a greater effect that individuals would have. synergistic *adj.*; synergistically *adv.*; synergy *n.*

synonym \SIN-uh-nim\ *n.* A word having the same or almost the same meaning as another. synonymic *adj.*; synonymical *adj.*; synonymist *n.*; synonymity *n.* synonymize *v.*

synonymous \si-NON-uh-mus\ *adj.* Equivalent in meaning. synonymously *adv.*

synopsis \si-NOP-sis\ *n. pl.* synopses. A summary or brief survey.

syntax \SIN-taks\ *n.* The way words are arranged to form phrases and sentences. syntactic *adj.*; syntactical *adj.*; syntactically *adv.*

synthesize \SIN-thuh-size\ *v.* synthesized; synthesizing. To make by combining artificially. synthesis *n.*

synthesizer \SIN-thuh-siez-ur\ *n.* (Mu) An electronic musical instrument that can make a variety of sounds.

synthetic \sin-THET-ik\ *adj.* Artificially produced. synthetic *n.*; synthetically *adv.*

syringe \si-RINJ\ *n.* A device for drawing in liquid and forcing it out and into a fine stream.

system \SIS-tum\ *n.* **1.** A series of things that form a whole. **2.** A set of rules or practices.

systematic \sis-tuh-MAT-ik\ *adj.* **1.** Based on a series of things that form a whole. **2.** Organized. systematically *adv.*; systematize *v.*

systemic \si-STEM-ik\ *adj.* Of or concerning a system, like that of a whole body.

systems analysis *n.* Study of methods to find the most productive way to obtain the desired results. systems analyst *n.*

T

t \tee\ *n. pl.* t's or ts. The 20th letter of the English alphabet.

tab *n.* **1.** A loop for fastening. **2.** A small projecting piece or addition. **3.** A bill.

table \TAY-bul\ *n.* **1.** A piece of furniture with a top rested on legs. **2.** Facts or figures arranged.

table \TAY-bul\ *v.* tabled; tabling. **1.** To put on an agenda. **2.** To set aside from consideration temporarily.

tablet \TAB-lit\ *n.* **1.** Slab with an inscription. **2.** A medicine pill. **3.** A sheath of paper bound.

tabloid \TAB-loid\ *n.* A smaller-sized newspaper containing sensational journalism.

taboo \ta-BOO\ *n.* A ban or prohibition made for social or religious reasons. taboo *adj.*; taboo *v.*

tabulate \TAB-yuh-layt\ *v.* tabulated; tabulating. To arrange in a table or list. tabulation *n.*; tabulator *n.*

taciturn \TAS-i-turn\ *adj.* Saying little. taciturnity *n.*

tack \tak\ *n.* **1.** A small nail with a broad head. **2.** A loose stitch to temporarily hold. taciturnity *n.*

tackle \TAK-ul\ *n.* **1.** Equipment. **2.** System of ropes and pulleys. **3.** Football linemen.

tackle \TAK-ul\ *v.* tackled; tackling. **1.** To grab hold of. **2.** To try to deal with. **3.** In football, seize and stop. tackler *n.*

tacky \TAK-ee\ *adj.* tackier; tackiest. **1.** Having poor taste. **2.** Sticky.

tact \takt\ *n.* A skill in not hurting others' feelings. tactful *adj.*; tactfully *adv.*

tactics \TAK-tiks\ *pl. n.* The art of organizing an attack or plan of action. tactical *adj.*; tactician *n.*

tactile \TAK-til\ *adj.* Of or concerning touch.

tae kwon do \TIE-kwawn-doh\ *n.* (Fo) A Korean martial art like karate.

tag *n.* **1.** A label. **2.** The tip at the end of a shoelace. **3.** A chasing game.

tag *v.* tagged; tagging. **1.** To label. **2.** To choose. **3.** To touch in a game. **4.** To follow closely. tagger *n.*

tag sale *n.* A garage or yard sale.

tai chi t'ai chi \TIE-CHEE\ *n.* (Fo) A Chinese system of meditation involving slow, calculated movements.

tail \tayl\ *adj.* From the rear.

tail \tayl\ *n.* **1.** Hindmost part of animal. **2.** Flexible member on back of animal.

tail \tayl\ *v.* tailed; tailing. To follow closely.

tailor \TAY-lur\ *n.* A person who makes and alters clothing. tailor *v.*

taint \taynt\ *v.* tainted; tainting. To corrupt or contaminate. taint *n.*

take \tayk\ *v.* took; taken; taking. **1.** To get hold of something. **2.** To capture. **3.** To carry. **4.** To remove.

take back *v.* To retract something mentioned.

take down *v.* To record.

take in *v.* **1.** To include. **2.** To make a garment smaller. **3.** To understand. **4.** To fool.

taken \TAYK-un\ *v.* The past participle of take.

takeoff \TAYK-awf\ *n.* **1.** The process of beginning a flight. **2.** A humorous mimicry. take off *v.*

take-out \TAYK-owt\ *n.* Food prepared to be bought and eaten elsewhere. take-out or takeout *adj.*

takeover *also* **take-over** \TAYK-oh-vur\ *n.* The act or process of assuming management of something. takeover *adj.*; take over *v.*

talcum *also* **talc** or **talcum powder** \TAL-kum\ *n.* A soft powder for the skin.

tale \tayl\ *n.* **1.** A story. **2.** An invented excuse.

talent \TAL-unt\ *n.* A special ability. talented *adj.*

talk \tawk\ *v.* talked; talking. To convey ideas by words. talk *n.*

talkative \TAW-kuh-tiv\ *adj.* Fond

of chatting. talkativeness **n.**; talker **n.**

talk show \tawk shoh\ **n.** A TV broadcast featuring interviews.

tall \tawl\ **adj.** taller; tallest. **1.** Of more than average height. **2.** Of a specific height. **3.** Exaggerated. tallness **n.**

tally \TAL-ee\ **n. pl.** tallies. A total or cumulative score. tally **v.**

tamale \tuh-MAH-lee\ **n. pl.** tamales. (Sp) A Mexican dish of meat and fillings wrapped in dough and corn husks and steamed.

tambourine \tam-buh-REEN\ **n.** A small percussion instrument with jingling metal disks.

tame \taym\ **adj.** tamer; tamest. **1.** Domesticated. **2.** Gentle and docile. **3.** Not exciting. tameness **n.**; tamer **n.**; tame **v.**

tamper \TAM-pur\ **v.** tampered; tampering. To meddle, fiddle, or interfere with.

tan **adj.** tanner; tannest. Warm yellow-brown in color.

tan **v.** tanned; tanning. **1.** To make into leather by treating. **2.** To turn brown. **3.** To whip. tan **n.**

tandem \TAN-dum\ **adv.** One behind another. tandem **adj.**; tandem **n.**

tandoori \tan-DOOR-ee\ **adj.**. (Fo) Cooked in an Indian clay oven.

tang **n.** **1.** A strong taste, flavor, or smell. **2.** The part of a knife inside the handle. tangy **adj.**

tangent \TAN-junt\ **n.** **1.** Line, surface that touches but does not intersect another. **2.** Digression. tangent **adj.**; tangential **adj.**

tangerine \tan-jur-EEN\ **n.** A tree bearing a type of small orange. tangerine **adj.**

tangible \TAN-juh-bul\ **adj.** **1.** Clear and definite. **2.** Perceptible by touch. tangibly **adv.**; tangibility **n.**; tangible **n.**; tangibleness **n.**

tangle \TANG-gul\ **v.** tangled; tangling. **1.** To twist or become twisted into a confused mass. **2.** To become involved with. tangly **adj.**; tangle **n.**

tango \TANG-goh\ **n. pl.** tangos. **1.** A ballroom dance with gliding steps. **2.** [Mu] The music for this dance. tango **v.**

tank \tangk\ **n.** **1.** A container for liquid or gas. **2.** Armored combat vehicle on treads.

tantalize \TAN-tl-iez\ **v.** tantalized; tantalizing. To torment with a desired thing. tantalization **n.**

tantamount \TAN-tuh-mownt\ **adj.** Equivalent.

tantrum \TAN-trum\ *n.* An outburst of anger.

Taoism \DOW-iz-um\ *n.* (Fo) A Chinese philosophy and religion based on simplicity and selflessness. Taoist *adj.*; Taoist *n.*

tap *n.* **1.** A quick, light hit. **2.** A device for controlling the flow of liquid or gas.

tap *v.* tapped; tapping. **1.** To hit lightly and quickly. **2.** To draw off a liquid, gas. **3.** To listen in on.

tape \tayp\ *n.* Narrow piece of material used for binding, tying, recording, etc. tape *v.*

taper \TAY-pur\ *n.* **1.** A thin candle. **2.** A gradual narrowing.

taper \TAY-pur\ *v.* tapered; tapering. To become gradually narrower on one end.

tapestry \TAP-uh-stree\ *n. pl.* tapestries. A textile ornamentally woven or embroidered.

tapioca \tap-ee-OH-kuh\ *n.* A starchy grain from cassava used in making a pudding.

tarantula \tuh-RAN-chuh-luh\ *n. pl.* tarantulas or tarantulae. A large, hairy, menacing spider native to tropical regions.

tardy \TAHR-dee\ *adj.* tardier; tardiest. Late or slow to act, move, or happen. tardily *adv.*; tardiness *n.*

target \TAHR-git\ *n.* Something aimed at, especially a board marked with concentric circles; goal. target *v.*

tariff \TA-rif\ *n.* **1.** A list of fixed charges on imported goods. **2.** A tax.

tarnish \TAHR-nish\ *v.* tarnished; tarnishing. **1.** To lose shininess of and become dull or discolored. **2.** To hurt reputation. tarnish *n.*

tarot \TA-roh\ *n.* A set of 22 cards used for fortunetelling.

tart \tahrt\ *adj.* tarter; tartest. Acid in taste or manner. tartly *adv.*; tartness *n.*

tart \tahrt\ *n.* **1.** A small pie with fruit or sweet filling. **2.** [Sl] A prostitute.

task *n.* **1.** A piece of work to be done. **2.** An overwhelming undertaking.

task *v.* tasked; tasking. To make great demands on.

tassel \TAS-ul\ *n.* An ornamental group of hanging threads. tasselled *adj.*

taste \tayst\ *n.* **1.** Sensation of salt, sweet, etc. **2.** Small quantity tasted. **3.** Experience.

taste \tayst\ *v.* tasted; tasting. **1.** To use the tongue and mouth to sense. **2.** To experience or consume slightly.

tasteful \TAYST-ful\ *adj.* Exhibiting good taste. tastefully *adv.*; tastefulness *n.*

tasteless \TAYST-lis\ *adj.* **1.** Exhibiting poor taste. **2.** Having little or no flavor. tastelessly *adv.*; tastelessness *n.*

tasty \TAY-stee\ *adj.* tastier; tastiest. Pleasingly flavored.

tattle \TAT-l\ *v.* tattled; tattling. To reveal secrets or inform on another. tattler *n.*; tattletale *n.*

tattoo \ta-TOO\ *n. pl.* tattoos. **1.** A pigment mark drawn on the skin with a needle. **2.** A call to go to quarters. tattoo *v.*

taught \tawt\ *v.* The past tense and past participle of teach.

taunt \tawnt\ *v.* taunted; taunting. To mock in a hurtful way. taunt *n.*

taut \tawt\ *adj.* Stretched tightly. tautly *adv.*; tautness *n.*

tavern \TAV-urn\ *n.* **1.** A bar. **2.** An inn.

tawdry \TAW-dree\ *adj.* tawdrier; tawdriest. Cheap and showy. tawdriness *n.*

tax \taks\ *n. pl.* taxes. **1.** Obligation paid to government. **2.** Heavy demand. **3.** Assessment made. taxable *adj.*; taxation *n.*; tax *v.*

taxing \TAK-sing\ *adj.* Demanding.

teach \teech\ *v.* taught; teaching. **1.** To pass on knowledge. **2.** To give instruction in a subject. **3.** To show. teachable *adj.*; teacher *n.*

team \teem\ *n.* **1.** People working together. **2.** Sports group playing together. team *adj.*; teammate *n.*; team *v.*

tear \tair\ *n.* **1.** A rip. **2.** A drop of salty water from the eye. tear *v.*

tear \tair\ *v.* tore; torn; tearing. **1.** To pull apart into pieces. **2.** To pull away forcibly. **3.** To disrupt. tear *n.*

tear gas \teer\ *n.* A gas that causes one's eyes to water painfully. tear-gas *v.*

tease \teez\ *v.* teased; teasing. **1.** To try to provoke or make fun of in an unkind way. **2.** To tempt. tease *n.*

teat \teet\ *n.* A nipple or nipplelike thing that secretes milk.

techie *also* **tekkie** \TEK-ee\ *n.* (Sl) A technical expert.

technical \TEK-ni-kul\ *adj.* **1.** Concerning machinery or the way things work. **2.** Expert in technology. technically *adv.*; technicality *n.*; technician *n.*

technique \tek-NEEK\ *n.* A skilled method of doing or performing something.

technology \tek-NOL-uh-jee\ *n. pl.* technologies. The science of machines and their applications.

technological *adj.*; technologically *adv.*; technologist *n.*

technophobia \tek-noh-foh-BEE-uh\ *n.* A fear of high technology.

tectonics \tek-TON-iks\ *n.* [Sc] The branch of geology that studies changes in the Earth's structure.

tedious \TEE-dee-us\ *adj.* Tiresome because of length or dullness. tediously *adv.*; tediousness *n.*; tedium *n.*

teem *v.* teemed; teeming. **1.** To be full of or present in large numbers. **2.** To pour.

teenager *also* **teen or teen-ager** \TEEN-ay-jur\ *n.* A person aged 13 to 19. teenaged *adj.*

teeny \TEE-nee\ *adj.* teenier; teeniest. Very small.

teenybopper \TEE-nee-BOP-ur\ *n.* (Sl) A trendy teenager.

teeter \TEE-tur\ *v.* teetered; teetering. To stand or move unsteadily.

teeth *n.* The plural form of tooth.

teethe \teeth\ *v.* teethed; teething. To have the first teeth appear through the gums.

telecast \TELi-kast\ *n.* A TV broadcast. telecaster *n.*; telecast *v.*

teleconference \TEL-i-kon-fur-uns\ *n.* A business meeting held via telecommunications equipment.

telegraph \TEL-i-graf\ *n.* A device that sends messages over wires through electrical impulses. telegram *n.*; telegraph *v.*

telekinesis \TEL-i-kin-ee-sus\ *n.* The ability to move or re-form inaminate objects with the mind. telekinetic *adj.*; telekinetically *adv.*

telemarketing \TEL-uh-MAR-kuh-ting\ *n.* Selling or advertising by telephone.

telepathy \tuh-LEP-uh-thee\ *n.* Communication between minds without other senses. telepathic *adj.*

telephone \TEL-uh-fohn\ *n.* Device or system for transmitting sound and data over wire or other channel. telephone *v.*

telescope \TEL-uh-skohp\ *n.* An optical instrument that makes distant objects visible. telescopic *adj.*

telethon \TEL-uh-thon\ *n.* A long TV broadcast to raise money.

televangelist \tel-uh-VAN-jul-ist\ *n.* A preacher who performs services on TV. televangelism *n.*

television *also* **TV** \TEL-uh-vizh-un\ *n.* **1.** Transmission of visual images to cathode ray tubes (CRT). **2.** A receiving CRT.

telex \TEL-eks\ *n. pl.* telexes. A two-way typewriter communications service for subscribers; messages sent. telex *v.*

tell \tel\ *v.* told; telling. **1.** To make known by speech or writing. **2.** To give information. **3.** To reveal.

tell off *v.* (Sl) To reprimand.

temper \TEM-pur\ *n.* **1.** A tendency to become angry. **2.** A state of mind. **3.** Calmness of mind.

temper \TEM-pur\ *v.* tempered; tempering. **1.** To make a metal be the correct hardness or consistency. **2.** To moderate.

tempera \TEM-pur-uh\ *n.* A method of painting using powdered color and egg.

temperament \TEM-pruh-munt\ *n.* **1.** A person's character. **2.** A tendency to become easily irritated.

temperamental \tem-pruh-MEN-tl\ *adj.* Easily irritated. temperamentally *adv.*

temperance \TEM-pur-uns\ *n.* **1.** Self-restraint. **2.** Abstinence, especially from liquor.

temperate \TEM-pur-it\ *adj.* **1.** Observing moderation, esp. with liquor. **2.** Moderate in temperature.

temperature \TEM-pur-uh-chur\ *n.* The amount or measurement of the hotness or coldness of something.

tempest \TEM-pist\ *n.* A violent storm. tempestuous *adj.*

template \TEM-plit\ *n.* A pattern.

temple \TEM-pul\ *n.* **1.** A building used for worship. **2.** The forehead.

tempo \TEM-poh\ *n.* The speed, rhythm, or pace of something, as music.

temporal \TEM-pur-ul\ *adj.* **1.** Of or concerning time. **2.** Relating to the material world. temporally *adv.*

temporary \TEM-puh-rer-ee\ *adj.* Lasting for a limited time. temporarily *adv.*; temporary *n.*

tempt *v.* tempted; tempting. **1.** To persuade or try to persuade with a pleasurable thing. **2.** To be inviting. temptation *n.*; tempter *n.*; temptress *n.*

tempura \TEM-puh-ruh\ *n.* (Fo) A deep-fried Japanese seafood or vegetable dish.

tenacious \tuh-NAY-shus\ *adj.* **1.** Holding firmly. **2.** Persistent. tenaciously *adv.*; tenacity *n.*

tenant \TEN-unt\ *n.* A person who rents a place to live or work.

tend *v.* tended; tending. **1.** To take care of something. **2.** To have an inclination.

tendency \TEN-dun-see\ *n. pl.* tendencies. An inclination.

tender \TEN-dur\ *adj.* tenderer; tenderest. **1.** Delicate. **2.** Painful to the touch. **3.** Emotionally sensitive. **4.** Easily cut. tenderly *adv.*; tenderness *n.*

tendon \TEN-dun\ *n.* A strip of strong tissue connecting a muscle to a bone.

tendonitis \ten-dun-IE-tis\ *n.* (Md) A painful inflammation of a tendon from overuse or misuse.

tenement \TEN-uh-munt\ *n.* A large house with rooms for rent, esp. rundown.

tenet \TEN-it\ *n.* A firm belief.

tenor \TEN-ur\ *n.* **1.** General inclination or meaning. **2.** [Mu] The highest adult male voice. tenor *adj.*

tense \tens\ *adj.* tenser; tensest. **1.** Stretched tightly. **2.** Stressed or strained. tensely *adv.*; tenseness *n.*; tense *v.*

tense \tens\ *n.* Any verb form that indicates the time of action.

tent *n.* A portable shelter made of fabric.

tentacle \TEN-tuh-kul\ *n.* A slender, flexible part of invertebrates used for feeling or locomotion.

tentative \TEN-tuh-tiv\ *adj.* **1.** Existing on trial basis. **2.** Hesitant. tentatively *adv.*; tentativeness *n.*

tenuous \TEN-yoo-us\ *adj.* Very thin or slight. tenuously *adv.*; tenuity *n.*; tenuousness *n.*

tenure \TEN-yur\ *n.* **1.** Holding right to a property. **2.** Permanent employment status. tenured *adj.*

tepid \TEP-id\ *adj.* **1.** Lukewarm. **2.** Lacking excitement. tepidly *adv.*; tepidity *n.*; tepidness *n.*

tequila \tuh-KEE-luh\ *n.* A strong Mexican liquor made from agave.

tergiversate \tur-JI-vur-sayt\ *v.* tergiversated; tergiverating. **1.** To be evasive. **2.** To change sides. tergiversation *n.*

teriyaki \ter-ee-YAH-kee\ *n.* (Fo) A Japanese seasoning sauce used on meat and vegetable dishes. teriyaki *adj.*

term \turm\ *n.* **1.** Period of time. **2.** Closing point. **3.** Word for a definite thing. **4.** Conditions. term *v.*

terminal \TUR-muh-nl\ *adj.* **1.** Of or concerning an ending. **2.** Of or concerning a fatal disease.

terminal \TUR-muh-nul\ *n.* **1.** An end. **2.** Electrical connection point. **3.** Transportation station.

terminate \TUR-muh-nayt\ *v.* terminated; terminating. To end or stop. termination *n.*

terminology \tur-muh-NOL-uh-jee\ *n.* The technical or specialized terms of a subject. terminological *adj.*; terminologically *adv.*

terra cotta \TER-uh-KOT-uh\ *n.* A reddish brown clay used for making pottery and sculpture. terra-cotta *adj.*

terrain \tuh-RAYN\ *n.* Land and its natural features.

terrarium \tuh-RAIR-ee-um\ *n. pl.* terrariums or terraria. A small enclosed container for growing plants.

terrestrial \tuh-RES-tree-ul\ *adj.* **1.** Of or concerning the earth. **2.** Consisting only of land. **3.** Living on land.

terrible \TER-uh-bul\ *adj.* **1.** Frightening. **2.** Intense. **3.** Very bad. terribly *adv.*

terrific \tuh-RIF-ik\ *adj.* **1.** Frightening. **2.** Very bad. **3.** Very great. **4.** Excellent. terrifically *adv.*

terrify \TER-uh-fie\ *v.* terrified; terrifying. To fill someone with fear.

terrine \tuh-REEN\ *n.* **1.** An earthenware dish for casseroles. **2.** A food cooked in such a dish.

territory \TER-i-tor-ee\ *n. pl.* territories. **1.** An area of land. **2.** An area of land belonging to an individual or nation. territorial *adj.*

terror \TER-ur\ *n.* **1.** Extreme fear. **2.** Something or someone that causes extreme fear. terrorize *v.*

terse \turs\ *adj.* terser; tersest. Concise and curt. tersely *adv.*; terseness *n.*

tertiary \TUR-shee-er-ee\ *adj.* Third in rank or importance.

test *n.* **1.** An examination or trial. **2.** A set of problems for evaluating knowledge. test *v.*

testament \TES-tuh-munt\ *n.* **1.** [Le] A will. **2.** Statement of beliefs. **3.** [Cap] Two sections of the Bible. testamentary *adj.*

test-drive \test driev\ *v.* test-drove; test-driven; test-driving. To evaluate a motor vehicle's performance on the road.

testify \TES-tuh-fie\ *v.* testified; testifying. (Le) To bear witness to or give evidence.

testimonial \tes-tuh-MOH-nee-ul\ *n.* **1.** Formal recommendation. **2.** Something given or done to show appreciation.

testimony \TES-tuh-moh-nee\ *n.* (Le) A declaration supporting evidence, especially under oath.

testis \TES-tis\ *n. pl.* testes. Either of the two sperm-bearing male sex glands.

test-tube baby *n.* (Md) An infant developed from an egg fertilized by a sperm in a test tube.

testy \TES-tee\ *adj.* testier; testiest. Irritable.

tetanus \TET-nus\ *n.* (Md) A potentially fatal infection caused by poisonous bacteria.

tête-a-tête \TAYT-uh-TAYT\ *n.* (Fr) A private conversation, usually between two people.

tether \TETH-ur\ *n.* **1.** A leash. **2.** The extent of one's abilities, resources, etc. tether *v.*

Teutonic \TOO-tahn-ik\ *adj.* Of or concerning the Germanic peoples or their languages.

Tex-Mex *adj.* Of or concerning the combined cultures of Texas and Mexico, as in cooking.

text \tekst\ *n.* **1.** The words of a book or other collection of writing. **2.** Any theme or topic. textual *adj.*

textbook \TEKST-buuk\ *n.* A book intended to teach the basic facts of a subject.

textile \TEKS-tiel\ *n.* Fabric. textile *adj.*

textual \TEKS-choo-ul\ *adj.* Of or concerning a text. textually *adv.*

texture \TEKS-chur\ *n.* **1.** A fabric character. **2.** The organization of the parts of a complex whole. textural *adj.*; texturally *adv.*; texturize *v.*

thalamus \THAL-uh-mus\ *n.* Organ of the brain that that transmits sensory impulses to the cerebral cortex.

thalidomide \thuh-LID-uh-mied\ *n.* A sedative drug.

than *conj.* Used to introduce the second element of a comparison.

thank \thangk\ *v.* thanked; thanking. To express gratitude. thanks *n.*

thankful \THANGK-ful\ *adj.* Feeling or expressing much gratitude. thankfully *adv.*; thankfulness *n.*

thankless \THANGK-lis\ *adj.* **1.** Unappreciating. **2.** Not likely to be rewarded. thanklessly *adv.*; thanklessness *n.*

that *pron.* **1.** The person or thing spoken of. **2.** The second one. **3.** Who, whom, or which. that *adj.*

thaw *v.* thawed; thawing. **1.** To unfreeze. **2.** To become more friendly. thaw *n.*

theater *also* **theatre** \THEE-uh-tur\ *n.* **1.** Building or room for entertainment. **2.** Theatrical world. **3.** Scene of events. theatrical *adj.*; theatrically *adv.*; theatricality *n.*; theatricalness *n.*

theft *n.* Stealing.

their \thair\ *adj.* Belonging to them.

theirs \thairz\ *pron.* The one or ones belonging to them.

theme \theem\ *n.* **1.** Subject being discussed, used. **2.** A short essay. **3.** [Mu] A brief melody. thematic *adj.*

theme park \theem-pahrk\ *n.* An amusement park based on one or several notions.

then *adv.* **1.** At that time. **2.** At another time. **3.** Next. **4.** In that case.

theology \thee-OL-uh-jee\ *n.* The study of religion. theological *adj.*

theorem \THEE-ur-um\ *n.* **1.** A mathematical statement to be proved by reasoning. **2.** A fact.

theory \THEE-uh-ree\ *n. pl.* theories. **1.** Conjecture. **2.** Formulated ideas that explain, prove something. theoretical *adj.*; theoretically *adv.*; theoretician *n.*; theorist *n.*; theorize *v.*

therapeutic \ther-uh-PYOO-tik\ *adj.* Helping to cure or beneficial. therapeutically *adv.*

therapy \THER-uh-pee\ *n. pl.* therapies. A curative or beneficial treatment. therapist *n.*

there \thair\ *adv.* **1.** In, at, or to that place. **2.** In that matter. **3.** Then. there *n.*

thereafter \thair-AF-tur\ *adv.* After that.

therefore \thair-FOR\ *adv.* For that reason.

thermometer \thur-MOM-i-tur\ *n.* An instrument for measuring heat.

thesaurus \thi-SOR-us\ *n. pl.* the-sauri or thesauruses. A reference book of synonyms and antonyms.

thesis \THEE-sis\ *n. pl.* theses. **1.** A theory put forward and supported by reasoning. **2.** A long written essay.

thespian \THES-pee-un\ *adj.* Of or concerning drama or dramatic performances. thespian *n.*

thick \thik\ *adj.* thicker; thickest. **1.** Not thin. **2.** Broad. **3.** Crowded and dense. **4.** Stiff in consistency. thickish *adj.*; thickly *adv.*; thickness *n.*; thicken *v.*

thief \theef\ *n. pl.* thieves. One who steals. thievish *adj.*; thievery *n.*

thigh \thie\ *n.* The upper part of a leg between the hip and knee.

thimble \THIM-bul\ *n.* A metal cap used to protect a finger in sewing.

thin *adj.* thinner; thinnest. **1.** Not fat. **2.** Not thick or broad. **3.** Lacking substance. **4.** See-through. thinly *adv.*; thinness *n.*; thin *v.*

thing *n.* **1.** Any object that can be touched or seen. **2.** A creature or person. **3.** Deed. thinly *adv.*; thinness *n.*; thin *v.*

think \thingk\ *v.* thought; thinking. **1.** To use the mind. **2.** To believe. thinker *n.*

thinkable \THINGK-uh-bul\ *adj.* Conceivable.

think tank *n.* (Ja) A research organization employed to analyze problems and issues.

third \thurd\ *adj.* Next after second. thirdly *adv.*; third *n.*

third \thurd\ *n.* One of three equal parts of something.

Third World *also* **third world** *n.* Underdeveloped or developing countries.

thirst \thurst\ *n.* A strong desire for something, especially a drink. thirsty *adj.*; thirstily *adv.*; thirstiness *n.*; thirst *v.*

thistle \THIS-ul\ *n.* A prickly plant. thistly *adv.*

thong *n.* **1.** A narrow strip for holding something in place. **2.** A sandal with one strap.

Thorazine \thor-uh-ZEEN\ *n.* An antipsychotic drug.

thorn *n.* **1.** A sharp, pointed growth on a plant stem. **2.** A cause of constant irritation. thorny *adj.*

thorny \THOR-nee\ *adj.* thornier; thorniest. Painful or controversial.

thorough \THUR-oh\ *adj.* **1.** Complete in every way. **2.** Detailed. **3.** Absolute. thoroughly *adv.*; thoroughness *n.*

thoroughbred \THUR-oh-bred\ *adj.* Bred from pure or pedigree stock. thoroughbred *n.*

thou \thow\ *pron.* You.

though \thoh\ *adv.* However.

though \thoh\ *conj.* **1.** In spite of the fact that. **2.** However. though *adv.*

thought \thawt\ *n.* **1.** Thinking. **2.** An idea or opinion. **3.** Caring.

thoughtful \THAWT-ful\ *adj.* **1.** Involved in thought. **2.** Caring toward others. thoughtful *adj.*; thoughtfully *adv.*; thoughtfulness *n.*

thoughtless \THAWT-lis\ *adj.* **1.** Done withouth consideration. **2.** Inconsiderate. thoughtlessly *adv.*; thoughtlessness *n.*

thousand \THOW-zund\ *n.* Ten hundred. thousand *adj.*; thousandth *adj.*; thousandth *n.*

thrall \thrawl\ *n.* Slavery or bondage. thralldom or thraldom *n.*

thrash *v.* thrashed; thrashing. **1.** To whip. **2.** To defeat thoroughly. **3.** To make flailing movements. thrasher *n.*

thread \thred\ *n.* **1.** Length of a substance used to sewing or binding. **2.** Any long, thin piece. thready *adj.*; thread *v.*

threadbare \THRED-bair\ *adj.* Extremely worn and shabby.

threat \thret\ *n.* **1.** Statement of intention to harm. **2.** A warning or sign of danger. **3.** Danger. threaten *v.*

threshold \THRESH-ohld\ *n.* **1.** Door plank. **2.** A point of entry. **3.** Time when stimulus gets a response.

threw \throo\ *v.* The past tense of throw.

thrift *n.* Carefulness with money or resources. thrifty *adj.*; thriftily *adv.*; thriftiness *n.*

thrill \thril\ *n.* **1.** A feeling of great excitement. **2.** Something that causes great excitement. thrilling *adj.*; thriller *n.*; thrill *v.*

thrive \thriev\ *v.* thrived or throve; thrived or thriven; thriving. **1.** To prosper. **2.** To develop well.

throb *v.* throbbed; throbbing. **1.** To beat steadily. **2.** To experience excitement. throb *n.*

throne \throhn\ *n.* **1.** A seat for a ruler or official. **2.** The rank of a ruler or official.

throng *n.* A crowd. throng *v.*

throttle \THROT-l\ *n.* A device controlling the flow of gas to an engine.

throttle \THROT-l\ *v.* throttled; throttling. **1.** To strangle. **2.** To suppress. **3.** To lessen the flow of gas using the throttle.

through \throo\ *adv.* **1.** Into something and out the other end or side. **2.** From beginning to end.

through \throo\ *adj.* **1.** Going from one location to another. **2.** Reaching a destination without stops.

through \throo\ *prep.* **1.** Into something and out the other end or side. **2.** Among. **3.** By means of.

throughout \throo-OWT\ *adv.* Everywhere.

throughout \throo-OWT\ *prep.* Right through from beginning to end.

throw \throh\ *n.* **1.** Launch through the air; fling. **2.** Distance of fling. **3.** Cast of dice.

throw \throh\ *v.* threw; thrown; throwing. **1.** To launch through the air; fling. **2.** To direct. **3.** To cause to fall. thrower *n.*; throw *n.*

throw away *v.* **1.** To discard as useless. **2.** To fail to take advantage of.

throwaway \THROH-uh-way\ *adj.* Made or intended to be discarded after use. throwaway *n.*

throw pillow *n.* A small, decorative cushion.

throw up *v.* **1.** To vomit. **2.** To build haphazardly. **3.** To project, as on a screen.

thrust *v.* thrust; thrusting. To push forcibly. thrust *n.*

thud *n.* The sound of something hard hitting something softer. thud *v.*

thunder \THUN-dur\ *n.* The loud

noise that accompanies lightning. thunderous *adj.*; thunder *v.*

Thursday \THURZ-day\ *n.* The day after Wednesday and before Friday.

thus *adv.* **1.** In this way. **2.** Therefore.

thwart \thwort\ *v.* To prevent from doing or accomplishing.

thy \thie\ *adj.* Your.

thyme \tiem\ *n.* An herb with fragrant leaves used for seasoning.

tiara \tee-AR-uh\ *n.* A woman's jeweled crown.

tibia \TIB-ee-uh\ *n. pl.* tibiae or tibias. The thick, inner bone of the lower leg.

tic \tik\ *n.* An involuntary muscle twitch.

tick \tik\ *n.* **1.** A regular clicking sound. **2.** A checkmark. **3.** Blood-sucking insect. tick *v.*

ticket \TIK-it\ *n.* **1.** Card of admission or permission. **2.** A label. **3.** Sales tag. **4.** Summons. ticket *v.*

tickle \TIK-ul\ *v.* tickled; tickling. **1.** To touch, causing a tingling sensation. **2.** To amuse. tickle *n.*

tidbit \TID-bit\ *n.* A small amount of food or information.

tide \tied\ *n.* **1.** The sea's rising and falling twice a day. **2.** A trend. **3.** A period of time. tidal *adj.*

tide \tide\ *v.* tided; tiding. To help temporarily.

tidings \TIE-dingz\ *pl. n.* News.

tidy \TIE-dee\ *adj.* tidier; tidiest. Neat and orderly. tidily *adv.*; tidiness *n.*

tie \tie\ *n.* **1.** Strip of material worn from the neck of a shirt. **2.** Binding cord, string.

tie \tie\ *v.* tied; tying. **1.** Make a knot. **2.** To fasten with cord or string. **3.** To unite. **4.** To restrict. tie *n.*

tie-dye \TIE-die\ *v.* tie-dyed; tie-dyeing. To die by tying parts together so they won't absorb dye. tie-dye *n.*

tier \teer\ *n.* Any of a series of rows or ranks of a structure placed one above the other. tiered *adj.*

tiff \tif\ *n.* **1.** A petty argument. **2.** A slight fit of anger.

tiger \TIE-gur\ *n.* A large, striped animal of the cat family.

tight \tiet\ *adj.* tighter; tightest. **1.** Firmly fastened. **2.** Closely fitting. **3.** Completely stretched. **4.** Crowded. tightly *adv.*; tightness *n.*; tighten *v.*

till \til\ *n.* A receptacle for holding money at a sales counter.

till \til\ *prep.* Up to a specified time. till *conj.*

till \til\ *v.* tilled; tilling. To prepare

and use land for growing crops.
tillage *n.*; tiller *n.*

tilt *v.* tilted; tilting. To lean or cause to lean. tilt *n.*

timber \TIM-bur\ *n.* Wood for building.

time \tiem\ *n.* **1.** Continuous existence. **2.** Measurement of duration. **3.** Specific duration.

time \tiem\ *v.* timed; timing. **1.** To measure duration. **2.** To correspond in time. **3.** To arrange the time for.

time frame *n.* A period during which something takes place.

timely \TIEM-lee\ *adj.* timelier; timeliest. Occurring at an opportune moment. timeliness *n.*

time-release *also* **timed-release** *adj.* Gradually releasing so as to prolong the effect.

time-share *v.* time-shared; time-sharing. To use or occupy by sharing according to a schedule. time-share *n.*

timid \TIM-id\ *adj.* Shy and easily alarmed. timidly *adv.*; timidity *n.*; timidness *n.*

tin *n.* **1.** A soft, silvery-white metal. **2.** A container made of such a metal. tin *v.*

tincture \TINGK-chur\ *n.* **1.** A dye. **2.** A trace. **3.** A solution of medicine in alcohol. tincture *v.*

tinder \TIN-dur\ *n.* Any dry substance that catches fire easily.

tinge \tinj\ *n.* A slight trace, especially of color.

tingle \TING-gul\ *v.* tingled; tingling. To have or give a slight pricking sensation. tingle *n.*

tinker \TING-kur\ *v.* tinkered; tinkering. To work casually at trying to repair or improve something. tinker *n.*; tinkerer *n.*

tinkle \TING-kul\ *n.* A series of short, light ringing sounds. tinkle *v.*

tinny \TIN-ee\ *adj.* tinnier; tinniest. **1.** Of or containing tin. **2.** Flimsy. tinnily *adv.*; tinniness *n.*

tinsel \TIN-sul\ *n.* Glittering, decorative metallic strips.

tint *n.* A variety or shade of color. tint *v.*

tiny \TIE-nee\ *adj.* tinier; tiniest. Very small. tininess *n.*

tip *n.* **1.** Thin end of thing. **2.** A cap or point. **3.** Small gift of money. tip *v.*; tipper *n.*

tip *v.* tipped; tipping. **1.** To overturn. **2.** To put a point or cap on. **3.** To give extra money for service. tip *n.*

tipsy \TIP-see\ *adj.* **1.** Capable of being overturned easily. **2.** Slightly drunk.

tirade \TIE-rayd\ *n.* A long, angry outburst.

tire \tier\ *n.* A ring or band of rubber covering a wheel on a vehicle.

tire *v.* tired; tiring. **1.** To reduce strength; fatigue. **2.** To reduce interest in. tired *adj.*; tiresome *adj.*

tissue \TISH-oo\ *n.* **1.** Aggregate of body cells with a function. **2.** Soft disposable paper.

titan \TIET-n\ *n.* A person or thing of great size, strength, or influence. titanic *adj.*

titillate \TIT-l-ayt\ *v.* titillated; titillating. To excite. titillation *n.*

title \TIET-l\ *n.* **1.** Name of something. **2.** Name of a position or office. **3.** [Le] Deed to property. titled *adj.*; title *v.*

titter \TIT-ur\ *n.* A reserved giggle. titter *v.*

to \too\ *prep.* **1.** In the direction of. **2.** As far as. **3.** Included in. **4.** In accordance with. **5.**

toad \tohd\ *n.* A froglike animal that lives mainly on land.

toast \tohst\ *n.* **1.** Bread browned under heat. **2.** Drinking testimonial.

toast \tohst\ *v.* toasted; toasting. **1.** To brown by heat. **2.** To propose praise when drinking.

toaster oven *n.* A small appliance that toasts bread and serves as an oven.

toasty \TOHST-ee\ *adj.* toastier; toastiest. Warm and cozy. toastiness *n.*

tobacco \tuh-BAK-oh\ *n.* A plant bearing leaves that are prepared for smoking or chewing.

toboggan \tuh-BOG-un\ *n.* A long sled for coasting down hills. toboggan *v.*

to-do \TOO-DOO\ *n.* (Sl) A fuss.

toe \toh\ *n.* **1.** Extensions of a foot. **2.** Footwear part covering toes. **3.** Lower end projection

tofu \TOH-foo\ *n.* A soft, cheeselike food made from soybeans.

together \tuh-GETH-ur\ *adv.* **1.** In conjunction with. **2.** Side by side. **3.** In contact. **4.** Simultaneously.

toggle \TOG-ul\ *n.* **1.** Pin, bead slipped into a loop. **2.** A projecting lever for an on/off switch. toggle *v.*

toil *v.* toiled; toiling. To work laboriously. toilsome *adj.*; toil *n.*

toilet \TOI-lit\ *n.* **1.** Bathroom. **2.** Bathroom fixture for human waste.

toiletry \TOI-li-tree\ *n.* *pl.* toiletries. A personal article used for cleaning or grooming.

token \TOH-kun\ *n.* **1.** A sign or symbol. **2.** A keepsake. **3.** A voucher or coin that replaces money.

tolerance \TOL-ur-uns\ *n.* **1.** A

willingness to put up with something. **2.** An ability to endure something. tolerable *adj.*; tolerant *adj.*; tolerantly *adv.*; toleration *n.*; tolerate *v.*

toll \tohl\ *n.* **1.** Payment made for use. **2.** Loss or damage from a disaster. **3.** A bell's ring.

toll \tohl\ *v.* tolled; tolling. To ring with slow strokes. toll *n.*

tomato \tuh-MAY-toh\ *n. pl.* tomatoes. Plant with edible red or yellow fruit, often thought of as vegetable.

tomb \toom\ *n.* A grave or burial site.

tomboy \TOM-boi\ *n.* A girl who enjoys boyish recreation.

ton \tun\ *n.* A unit of weight equal to 2,000 pounds (short ton) or 2,240 pounds (long ton).

tone \tohn\ *n.* **1.** [Mu] A musical sound. **2.** A quality indicating mood. **3.** A shade of a color. tone *v.*

tongs \tongz\ *pl. n.* A tool for picking things up that has two arms connected at the top by a hinge.

tongue \tung\ *n.* **1.** Muscular organ of the mouth. **2.** A language or dialect.

tonic \TON-ik\ *n.* **1.** An invigorating medicine. **2.** Quinine water. **3.** Animated thing. tonic *adj.*

too *adv.* **1.** In addition. **2.** To a greater extent than desirable. **3.** [Cl] Very.

tool *n.* **1.** Instrument for a certain job. **2.** Anything useful for a trade, profession.

tool *v.* tooled; tooling. **1.** To shape using a specified instrument. **2.** [Sl] To drive around leisurely.

toot *n.* A short horn or whistle sound. toot *v.*

tooth *n. pl.* teeth. **1.** Hard structures of the mouth. **2.** Something resembling a tooth. toothed *adj.*

toothpick \TOOTH-pik\ *n.* A small, pointed stick for removing food from between the teeth.

top *n.* **1.** Highest part, end of a thing. **2.** Extremity. **3.** Lid, cover. **4.** Highest rank.

top *v.* topped; topping. **1.** To give or be a cover to. **2.** To be the best; surmount. **3.** To remove the top.

topiary \toh-pee-AIR-ee\ *adj.* Of a plant or tree, clipped or trimmed into an ornamental shape. topiary *n.*

topic \TOP-ik\ *n.* A subject for discussion or study.

topical \TOP-i-kul\ *adj.* Referring to current events or news.

topography \tuh-POG-ruh-fee\ *n.* **1.** Landforms of an area. **2.** The study of these features. topographic *adj.*; topographical *adj.*

topple \TOP-ul\ *v.* toppled; toppling. To fall over, especially from being top-heavy. topple *n.*

topsy-turvy \TOP-see-TUR-vee\ *adv.* **1.** Upside down. **2.** Greatly disordered.

tore \tor\ *v.* The past tense of tear.

toreador \TOR-ee-uh-dor\ *n.* A bullfighter.

torment \TOR-ment\ *n.* **1.** Severe suffering or torture. **2.** Something that causes suffering or torture. tormenter *n.*; tormentor *n.*; torment *v.*

torn *v.* The past participle of tear.

torpedo \tor-PEE-doh\ *n. pl.* torpedoes. An explosive, underwater missile. torpedo *v.*

torpid \TOR-pid\ *adj.* Inactive or sluggish. torpidly *adv.*; torpidity *n.*

torrent \TOR-unt\ *n.* **1.** A rushing stream. **2.** Any similar flow. torrential *adj.*

torrid \TOR-id\ *adj.* torrider; torridest. **1.** Excessively hot. **2.** Full of passion. **3.** Quick. torridly *adv.*; torridity *n.*; torridness *n.*

tortilla \tor-TEE-yuh\ *n.* (Sp) A round, unleavened bread of corn or wheat flour used for Mexican dishes.

tortoise \TOR-tus\ *n.* A slow-moving land reptile that is protected by a large, hard shell.

tortuous \TOR-choo-us\ *adj.* **1.** Full of twists and turns. **2.** Deceitful. **3.** Complicated. tortuously *adv.*; tortuosity *n.*; tortuousness *n.*

torture \TOR-chur\ *n.* **1.** A severe pain. **2.** A painful punishment or cruel treatment. torturer *n.*; torture *v.*

toss \taws\ *v.* tossed; tossing. **1.** To throw lightly. **2.** To move from side to side. **3.** To jerk up. **4.** To flip. toss *n.*

tot *n.* A small child.

total \TOHT-l\ *adj.* Complete and inclusive. totally *adv.*

total \TOHT-l\ *n.* The entire amount. totality *n.*; total *v.*

totalitarian \toh-tal-i-TAIR-ee-un\ *adj.* Of or concerning rule in which no rival parties or philosophies are allowed. totalitarian *n.*; totalitarianism *n.*

totem \TOH-tum\ *n.* An animal, plant, or object emblematic of a clan or family among some peoples.

toucan \TOO-kan\ *n.* A tropical, brightly colored bird with a large beak.

touch \tuch\ *v.* touched; touching. **1.** To use the hand or fingers to feel. **2.** To handle. **3.** To contact. touch *n.*

touch-and-go *adj.* Precarious and risky. touch and go *n.*

touchdown \TUCH-down\ *n.* In football, a scoring play worth six points. touch down *v.*

touché \too-SHAY\ *interj.* (Fr) Acknowledgement of a hit in fencing or valid criticism in discussion.

touch up *v.* To improve with small changes. touchup *n.*

touchy \TUCH-ee\ *adj.* touchier; touchiest. **1.** Easily offended. **2.** Risky. touchiness *n.*

tough \tuf\ *adj.* tougher; toughest. **1.** Strong. **2.** Flexible. **3.** Hard to cut or chew. **4.** Rough. **5.** Persistent. tough *n.*; toughness *n.*; toughen *v.*

toupee \too-PAY\ *n.* A wig or piece of artificial hair.

tour \tuur\ *n.* A journey through a series of places. tour *v.*

tour de force \tuur-duh-FORS\ *n.* *pl.* tours de force. (Fr) A feat of strength or skill.

tourism \TUUR-iz-um\ *n.* **1.** Organized journeys to places. **2.** Business of entertaining travelers. tourist *n.*

tournament \TUUR-nuh-munt\ *n.* A series of contests or games.

tourniquet \TUR-ni-kit\ *n.* (Md) A first-aid device that compresses a blood vessel to stop bleeding.

tousle \TOW-zul\ *v.* tousled; tousling. To untidy by ruffling.

tout \towt\ *v.* touted; touting. To solicit business by advertising boastfully.

tow *v.* towed; towing. To pull behind something by a rope, chain, etc. towable *adj.*; tow *n.*; tower *n.*

toward *also* **towards** \tord\ *prep.* **1.** In the direction of something. **2.** Facing. **3.** As a contribution to.

towboat \TOH-boht\ *n.* A boat that pulls others behind it.

towel \TOW-ul\ *n.* A piece of absorbent cloth for drying. towel *v.*

tower \TOW-ur\ *n.* A tall building or building part.

tower \TOW-ur\ *v.* towered; towering. To be of great height.

town *n.* A place to live that is smaller than a city.

townhouse *also* **town house** \TOWN-hows\ *n.* A city dwelling within a row of similar dwellings joined by common side walls.

toxic \TOK-sik\ *adj.* Poisonous or caused by poison. toxicity *n.*

toxicology \tok-si-KOL-uh-jee\ *n.* The study of poisons. toxicological *adj.*; toxicologist *n.*

toxic shock syndrome *n.* (Md) A disease caused by bacteria that often attack menstruating women.

toxin \TOK-sin\ *n.* A poisonous substance produced by an organism.

toy \toi\ *n.* Something to play with. toy *adj.*; toy *v.*

trace \trays\ *n.* **1.** A path or clue left by something or someone. **2.** A barely noticeable quantity.

trace \trays\ *v.* traced; tracing. **1.** To copy something by drawing on paper covering it. **2.** To follow a path. traceable *adj.*; tracer *n.*

trachea \TRAY-kee-uh\ *n. pl.* tracheae or tracheas. The windpipe.

tracheotomy \tray-kee-OT-uh-mee\ *n.* (Md) An operation cutting into the trachea to aid breathing in an emergency.

track \trak\ *n.* **1.** A path made by regular use. **2.** Mark left by a moving thing. **3.** Rails.

track \trak\ *v.* tracked; tracking. **1.** To follow, find the path of something. **2.** To discover by clues. tracker *n.*

tract \trakt\ *n.* **1.** A piece of land. **2.** System of connected parts. **3.** A pamphlet on a subject.

traction \TRAK-shun\ *n.* Adhesive friction or pulling.

trade \trayd\ *n.* **1.** A business. **2.** Commerce. **3.** Barter, buying, or selling. **4.** Customers. trader *n.*

trade \trayd\ *v.* traded; trading. To buy, sell, or exchange goods.

trademark \TRAYD-mahrk\ *n.* A manufacturer's registered emblem or name used to identify a product.

tradeoff *also* **trade-off** \TRAYD-awf\ *n.* An exchange in which one advantage is sacrificed for a better one. trade off *v.*

tradition \truh-DISH-un\ *n.* A belief or custom handed down from one generation to another. traditional *adj.*; traditionally *adv.*

traffic \TRAF-ik\ *n.* **1.** Moving vehicles, pedestrians, etc. **2.** Trading. trafficker *n.*; traffic *v.*

tragedy \TRAJ-i-dee\ *n. pl.* tragedies. **1.** A very sad event. **2.** A story having a sad ending. tragic *adj.*; tragically *adv.*

trail \trayl\ *n.* **1.** Something that follows behind. **2.** A clue left. **3.** Path in a forest.

trail \trayl\ *v.* trailed; trailing. **1.** To drag something along behind. **2.** To follow.

train \trayn\ *n.* **1.** Line of coupled railway cars. **2.** Connected things. **3.** Trailing dress skirt.

train \trayn\ *v.* trained; training. **1.** To instruct and prepare. **2.** To make obedient. **3.** To fix the shape of. **trainable** *adj.*; **trainee** *n.*; **trainer** *n.*

traipse \trayps\ *v.* traipsed; traipsing. To walk, wander, or tramp around.

trait \trayt\ *n.* A unique characteristic.

traitor \TRAY-tur\ *n.* A person who behaves disloyally. **traitorous** *adj.*

tramp *n.* **1.** A heavy-footed walk; walking journey. **2.** A vagrant. **3.** [Sl] Immoral woman.

tramp *v.* tramped; tramping. **1.** To walk with heavy footsteps. **2.** To walk a long distance. **tramp** *n.*

trample \TRAM-pul\ *v.* trampled; trampling. To crush or tread heavily on.

trance \trans\ *n.* **1.** A sleeplike condition. **2.** A daze. **trancelike** *adj.*; **trance** *v.*

tranquil \TRANG-kwil\ *adj.* Calm and peaceful. **tranquilly** *adv.*; **tranquility** *n.*; **tranquilization** *n.*; **tranquilizer** *n.*

transaction \tran-ZAK-shun\ *n.* **1.** A business dealing. **2.** An interaction. **transact** *v.*

transcend \tran-SEND\ *v.* transcended; transcending. To surpass or go beyond the normal range. **transcendent** *adj.*; **transcendence** *n.*

transcendentalism \tran-sen-DEN-tl-iz-um\ *n.* A philosophy advocating spiritual intuition as a means of finding reality. **transcendental** *adj.*; **transcendentalist** *n.*

transcribe \tran-SKRIEB\ *v.* transcribed; transcribing. **1.** To copy into writing or a recording. **2.** To represent in another language.

transcript \TRAN-skript\ *n.* A written or recorded copy. **transcription** *n.*

transfer \trans-FUR\ *v.* transferred; transferring. To convey or move from one place, person, or situation to another. **transferable** or **transferrable** *adj.*; **transfer** *n.*; **transferability** *n.*; **transferal** *n.*

transfiguration \trans-FIG-yur-ay-shun\ *n.* **1.** A change in form or appearance. **2.** A glorification of. **transfigure** *v.*

transfix \trans-FIKS\ *v.* transfixed; transfixing. **1.** To impale. **2.** To make motionless through fear or surprise.

transform \trans-FORM\ *v.* transformed; transforming. **1.** To change greatly in appearance or character. **2.** To change electric voltage. **transformation** *n.*; **transformer** *n.*

transgression \trans-GRESH-un\

n. **1.** Breaking a rule or law. **2.** Going beyond a limit. transgressor *n.*; transgress *v.*

transient \TRAN-shunt or TRANS-ee-unt\ *adj.* Passing quickly. transcience *n.*; transciency *n.*; transient *n.*

transit \TRANS-sit\ *n.* The process of traveling across, over, or through. transit *v.*

transition \tran-ZISH-un\ *n.* Changing from one stage to another. transitional *adj.*

translate \trans-LAYT\ *v.* translated; translating. **1.** To express in another language. **2.** To change from one condition to another. translatable *adj.*; translation *n.*; translator *n.*

transmission \trans-MISH-un\ *n.* **1.** A passing or sending along. **2.** A broadcast. **3.** A geared device giving power.

transmit \trans-MIT\ *v.* transmitted; transmitting. **1.** To send or pass along. **2.** To send out a signal, as in broadcast. transmittable or transmittible *adj.*; transmittal *n.*; transmittance n

transparent \trans-PAR-unt\ *adj.* **1.** Clear enough to see through. **2.** Easily comprehended. transparently *adv.*; transparency n.

transpire \tran-SPIER\ *v.* tran-spired; transpiring. **1.** To occur or happen. **2.** To become known. **3.** To give off water vapor.

transplant \trans-PLANT\ *v.* transplanted; transplanting. **1.** To remove and plant elsewhere. **2.** [Md] To replace a body organ. transplantable *adj.*; transplant *n.*; transplantation *n.*

transport \trans-PORT\ *n.* **1.** Conveying from one place to another. **2.** Any means or system of conveyance. transportable *adj.*; transportive *adj.*; transportability *n.*; transport *v.*

transportation \trans-pur-TAY-shun\ *n.* Any means or system of moving from one place to another.

trap *n.* **1.** A device for catching something. **2.** Pipe bend that prevents return flow. trapper *n.*; trap *v.*

trash *n.* Rubbish. trashy *adj.*

trash *v.* trashed; trashing. **1.** To destroy. **2.** [Sl] To criticize harshly.

trattoria \truh-tor-EE-uh\ *n. pl.* trattorias or trattorie. (It) A cafe serving simple Italian meals.

trauma \TROW-muh\ *n. pl.* traumas or traumata. A serious wound, injury, or shock, especially one that has prolonged effects. traumatic *adj.*; traumatize *v.*

travail \truh-VAYL\ *n.* **1.** Labor. **2.** Agony. travail *v.*

travel \TRAV-ul\ *v.* traveled; traveling or travelled; travelling. To go or journey from one place to another. travel *n.*; traveler *n.*; travels *n.*

travelogue *also* **travelog** \TRAV-uh-lawg\ *n.* A slide show, film, or lecture about someone's travels.

traverse \truh-VURS\ *v.* traversed; traversing. To travel, lie, or extend across. traversable *adj.*; traversal *n.*; traverse *n.*

travesty \TRAV-uh-stee\ *n.* **1.** An exaggerated parody. **2.** A perverse similarity. travesty *v.*

tray *n.* A board with raised edges, used for carrying things.

treachery \TRECH-uh-ree\ *n.* A breach of trust. treacherous *adj.*; treacherously *adv.*; treacherousness *n.*

tread \tred\ *n.* **1.** Walking. **2.** The horizontal portion of a step. **3.** The mark of a tire.

tread \tred\ *v.* trod, trodden or trod; treading. To walk or put one's foot on the ground.

treason \TREE-zun\ *n.* A betrayal of one's country to aid an enemy. treasonable *adj.*; treasonous *adj.*; treasonably *adv.*; treasonously *adv.*

treasure \TREZH-ur\ *n.* **1.** A store of valuable things. **2.** Something highly valued. treasure *v.*

treasurer \TREZH-ur-ur\ *n.* The person in charge of the finances of an institution.

treasury \TREZH-uh-ee\ *n. pl.* treasuries. **1.** A storage place for treasure or money. **2.** The funds available.

treat \treet\ *n.* **1.** Pleasurable thing. **2.** Edible confection.

treat \treet\ *v.* treated; treating. **1.** To behave a certain way toward others. **2.** To chemically alter. **3.** To offer.

treatise \TREE-tis\ *n.* A formal written work on one subject.

treatment \TREET-munt\ *n.* **1.** Way of dealing with something. **2.** Medical care for a problem.

treaty \TREE-tee\ *n. pl.* treaties. (Po) A formal agreement made between countries.

tree *n.* **1.** Large woody plant with trunk and branches. **2.** Hierarchy.

tremble \TREM-bul\ *v.* trembled; trembling. **1.** To quiver involuntarily. **2.** To experience fear. trembly *adj.*; tremblingly *adv.*; tremble *n.*

tremendous \tri-MEN-dus\ *adj.* **1.** Enormous. **2.** Horrifying. **3.** [Sl] Great. tremendously *adv.*; tremendousness *n.*

tremor \TREM-ur\ *n.* A slight trembling or shaking.

trench *n. pl.* trenches. A long, deep, narrow ditch used for cover in a battle. trench *v.*

trend *n.* **1.** A continuing tendency. **2.** A current fashion. trend *v.*

trendsetter \TREND-set-ur\ *n.* A person or group that establishes a continuing tendency.

trendy \TREN-dee\ *adj.* trendier; trendiest. Following the latest fad. trendiness *n.*

trepidation \trep-i-DAY-shun\ *n.* Nervousness.

trespass \TRES-pus\ *v.* trespassed; trespassing. To enter or intrude on property unlawfully. trespasser *n.*

trestle \TRES-ul\ *n.* **1.** A supportive beam supported by four legs. **2.** Open framework of bridge.

triad \TRIE-ad\ *n.* A group of three.

triage \TREE-ahzh\ *n.* A process of separating injured people into groups for efficient treatment.

trial \TRIEL\ *n.* **1.** [Le] A session conducted in a court of law. **2.** Attempt; try. trial *adj.*

triangle \TRIE-ang-gul\ *n.* A shape, object with three straight sides, three angles. triangular *adj.*

triathlon \trie-ATH-lon\ *n.* A competition including swimming, biking, and distance running. triathlete *n.*

tribe \trieb\ *n.* A group or race of people living as a community under one or more chiefs. tribal *adj.*

tribulation \trib-yuh-LAY-shun\ *n.* A great problem or the cause of it.

tributary \TRIB-yuh-ter-ee\ *adj.* **1.** Flowing into a larger stream or lake. **2.** Contributory. tributary *n.*

tribute \TRIB-yoot\ *n.* Something said, done, or given out of respect and admiration.

trichinosis \trik-i-NOH-sus\ *n.* (Md) A disease contracted from eating infected or undercooked meat.

trick \trik\ *n.* **1.** Something to deceive or outwit someone. **2.** A prank. **3.** A skillful feat. trick *adj.*; tricky *adj.*; trickery *n.*; trickster *n.*; trick *v.*

trickle \TRIK-ul\ *v.* trickled; trickling. To flow slowly or thinly. trickle *n.*

tricot \TREE-koh\ *n.* A fine, knitted fabric.

tried \tried\ *adj.* Completely tested and proven.

tried \tried\ *v.* The past tense and past participle of try.

trifle \TRIE-ful\ *n.* **1.** Something of

almost no importance. **2.** A small quantity. trifler *n.*; trifle *v.*

trigger \TRIG-ur\ *n.* A small lever for releasing a spring, as on a gun.

trigger \TRIG-ur\ *v.* triggered; triggering. **1.** To pull a small lever and release a spring, as on a gun. **2.** Start something.

trim *adj.* trimmer; trimmest. **1.** Neat. **2.** Lean. trimly *adv.*

trim *v.* trimmed; trimming. **1.** Cut away anything unwanted. **2.** To decorate. **3.** Make a boat evenly balanced. trim *n.*; trimness *n.*

trimester \TRIE-mes-tur\ *n.* A period of three months.

Trinity \TRIN-i-tee\ *n.* The father, son, and holy ghost.

trinket \TRING-kit\ *n.* **1.** A small piece of jewelry. **2.** A toy, especially one of little importance.

trio \TREE-oh\ *n. pl.* trios. **1.** A group or set of three. **2.** [Mu] Music for three instruments or voices.

triple \TRIP-ul\ *adj.* **1.** Having three parts. **2.** Three times as much or as many. triply *adv.*

triple \TRIP-ul\ *n.* **1.** Three times as much or as many. **2.** In baseball, a hit getting one to third base. triple *v.*

triptych \TRIP-tik\ *n.* A picture having three panels.

trite \triet\ *adj.* Hackneyed and ineffective. triteness *n.*

triumph \TRIE-umf\ *n.* **1.** A victory or success. **2.** A celebration of a victory or success. triumphal *adj.*; triumph *v.*

triumvirate \trie-UM-vur-it\ *n.* A group of three, especially a government run by a group of three.

trivia \TRIV-ee-uh\ *pl. n.* Unimportant facts and details. trivial *adj.*; triviality *n.*

Trojan horse \TROH-jun-HORS\ *n.* A person or thing intended to undermine or destroy from within.

troll \trohl\ *n.* In folklore, a supernatural being that lives in caves or underground.

trombone \trom-BOHN\ *n.* A large, brass, wind instrument sounded by the movement of a sliding piece.

troop *n.* A group of animals or people, soldiers, or scouts.

troop *v.* trooped; trooping. To move along in large numbers.

trophy \TROH-fee\ *n. pl.* trophies. A prize or souvenir of victory or success.

tropical \TROP-ik-ul\ *adj.* **1.** Hot and humid. **2.** Relating to equatorial regions.

tropics *also* **Tropics** \TROP-iks\ *pl. n.* Extremely hot regions near the equator.

trot *v.* trotted; trotting. To move at a pace between a walk and a gallop. trot *n.*; trotter *n.*

troubadour \TROO-buh-dor\ *n.* A wandering singer or poet, esp. from Europe's 12th-13th centuries.

trouble \TRUB-ul\ *n.* **1.** State of anxiety, risk, or need. **2.** Source of anxiety, difficulty.

trouble \TRUB-ul\ *v.* troubled; troubling. **1.** To disturb. **2.** To cause to hurt, be uncomfortable. **3.** To cause to be anxious.

trough \trawf\ *n.* **1.** A long, narrow feeding or drinking bin. **2.** A gutter for directing rain.

troupe \troop\ *n.* A company of actors or performers. trouper *n.*; troupe *v.*

trousseau \TROO-soh\ *n. pl.* trousseaux or trousseaus. A bride's collection of clothing for her married life.

truce \troos\ *n.* An agreement to temporarily stop hostilities.

truck \truk\ *n.* **1.** A large vehicle for carrying goods. **2.** An open railway wagon. trucker *n.*; truckload *n.*; truck *v.*

trudge \truj\ *v.* trudged; trudging. To walk laboriously. trudge *n.*

true \troo\ *adj.* truer; truest. **1.** Correct and in agreement with the facts. **2.** Faithful. **3.** Accurately fitted. true *adv.*; truly *adv.*; trueness *n.*

truffle \TRUF-ul\ *n.* A rich-flavored, underground fungus valued as a delicacy.

trumpet \TRUM-pit\ *n.* A brass, wind instrument with a flared tube. trumpeter *n.*; trumpet *v.*

truncate \TRUNG-kayt\ *v.* truncated; truncating. To shorten. truncate *adj.*; truncately *adv.*; truncation *n.*

trunk \trungk\ *n.* **1.** Main woody stem of a tree. **2.** Main part of a human body. **3.** Car storage. truncate *adj.*; truncately *adv.*; truncation *n.*

trust *n.* **1.** A belief in the goodness or truth. **2.** Responsibility. **3.** Property held. trusty *adj.*; trustful *adj.*; trustfully *adv.*

trust *v.* trusted; trusting. **1.** To believe in the goodness or truth of something or someone. **2.** To hope.

trust fund *n.* Money, stock, securities, etc., held in trust.

trustworthy \TRUST-wur-thee\

adj. Deserving of trust. trustworthiness *n.*

truth \trooth\ *n.* **1.** A fact. **2.** A proven statement. **3.** Reality. **4.** Honesty. **5.** Loyalty. truthful *adj.*; truthfully *adv.*; truthfulness *n.*

try \trie\ *v.* tried; trying. **1.** Make an effort. **2.** To test something. **3.** [Le] To examine a case in a court. try *n.*

trying \TRIE-ing\ *adj.* Challenging to one's patience.

tryst \trist\ *n.* An appointed meeting of lovers.

tsar *also* **tzar or czar** \zahr\ *n.* (Fo) A title for emperors of Russia.

tsetse fly \TSET-see-FLIE\ *n.* An African fly whose bite is often infectious.

tsunami \tsuu-NAH-mee\ *n.* Unusually large sea wave of a seaquake or underwater volcanic eruption.

tuba \TOO-buh\ *n.* A large, deep-sounding brass wind instrument.

tube \toob\ *n.* **1.** Hollow length of material used to convey a liquid. **2.** Cylindrical container.

tuberculosis \tuu-bur-kyuh-LOH-sis\ *n.* (Md) A long-term bacterial disease, mainly of the lungs.

tuck \tuk\ *v.* tucked; tucking. **1.** To push a loose end into a secure po-sition. **2.** To fold or sew into folds. tuck *n.*

Tuesday \TOOZ-day\ *n.* The day after Monday and before Wednesday.

tuft *n.* **1.** A bunch of threads or threadlike items growing together. **2.** A thick clump. tufted *adj.*; tuft *v.*

tug *v.* tugged; tugging. To pull suddenly. tug *n.*

tuition \too-ISH-un\ *n.* Money paid for education.

tulip \TOO-lip\ *n.* A bulb plant bearing a colorful cup-shaped flower.

tumble \TUM-bul\ *v.* tumbled; tumbling. **1.** To fall clumsily. **2.** To do gymnastics. tumble *n.*; tumbler *n.*

tumor \TOO-mur\ *n.* (Md) An abnormal growth of tissue in or on the body.

tumult \TOO-mult\ *n.* **1.** An uproar. **2.** A disruption. tumultuous *adj.*

tundra \TUN-druh\ *n.* A vast, level region of frozen subsoil.

tune \toon\ *n.* **1.** [Mu] A melody. **2.** [Mu] The proper musical pitch. **3.** An accordance. tuneful *adj.*

tune \toon\ *v.* tuned; tuning. **1.** [Mu] To bring an instrument into the correct pitch. **2.** To adjust a dial. tuner *n.*

tunnel \TUN-ul\ *n.* An underground passage. tunnel *v.*

turban \TUR-bun\ *n.* A long cloth wrapped around the head as a covering.

turbine \TUR-bin\ *n.* An engine operated by a jet of gas, steam, or water. turbine *adj.*

turbo \TUR-boh\ *adj.* Propelled by an engine operated by a jet of gas, steam, or water.

turbulence \TUR-byuh-luns\ *n.* A movement in the atmosphere that disrupts the flow of wind; disturbance. turbulent *adj.*; turbulently *adv.*

tureen \tuu-REEN\ *n.* A deep, covered dish for soup.

turf *n.* Short grass and its topsoil.

turgid \TUR-jid\ *adj.* **1.** Swollen and inflexible. **2.** Pompous. turgidly *adv.*; turgidity *n.*

turkey \TUR-kee\ *n.* A large bird native to North America that is raised for food.

turmoil \TUR-moil\ *n.* Commotion.

turn *n.* **1.** The act of rotating. **2.** A singular rotation. **3.** A reversal of direction, etc.

turn *v.* turned; turning. **1.** To move around a point or axis. **2.** To reverse, change position. **3.** Bend.

turnaround *n.* **1.** A rotary. **2.** A complete change. **3.** A move in the opposite direction. turn around *v.*

turn down *v.* **1.** To decrease the volume, speed, or intensity. **2.** To reject. **3.** To fold over.

turn in *v.* **1.** To submit. **2.** To yield. **3.** To tell on. **4.** [Cl] To go to bed.

turning point *n.* A stage at which a decisive change takes place.

turnip \TUR-nip\ *n.* A plant with a white root used as a vegetable.

turn off *v.* **1.** To switch off or stop. **2.** To cause to lose interest.

turn on *v.* **1.** To switch on or begin. **2.** To cause to be interested or aroused.

turn over *v.* **1.** To flip or move into the opposite position. **2.** To give back.

tutelage \TOOT-lij\ *n.* **1.** Guardianship. **2.** Instruction.

tutor \TOO-tur\ *n.* A private instructor. tutor *v.*

tutu \TOO-too\ *n.* A dancer's short, frilly skirt.

TV \tee-vee\ *abbr.* Television.

TV dinner *n.* A frozen, precooked dinner that is heated and served in its own tray.

twilight \TWIE-liet\ *n.* **1.** The period when the sun is just below the horizon. **2.** A slow decline.

twill \twil\ *n.* A heavy, woven fabric.

twin *adj.* Being made up of, or being one of a pair of, two alike things. twin *n.*

twine *n.* A strong thread consisting of many strands twisted together. twine *v.*

twinge \twinj\ *n.* A short, sudden, sharp pain. twinge *v.*

twinkle \TWING-kul\ *v.* twinkled; twinkling. To give off a flickering light. twinkle *n.*

twirl \twurl\ *v.* twirled; twirling. **1.** To spin rapidly. **2.** To move in a circle. **3.** To maneuver a baton. twirl *n.*; twirler *n.*

twist *v.* twisted; twisting. **1.** To turn or cause to turn around. **2.** To turn things around each other. twist *n.*

twitch \twich\ *v.* twitched; twitching. To pull or move with a light jerk every few moments. twitch *n.*

two \too\ *adj.* One more than one. two *n.*

twosome \TOO-sum\ *n.* A pair.

two-way mirror *n.* A piece of glass reflective on one side and transparent on the other.

tycoon \tie-KOON\ *n.* A rich and powerful industrialist.

type \tiep\ *n.* **1.** An example of a group. **2.** A set, class, or kind. **3.** Printed letters, symbols.

type \tiep\ *v.* typed; typing. **1.** To classify according to kind. **2.** To write with a keyboard.

typewriter \TIEP-rite-ur\ *n.* A machine for producing printlike characters on paper.

typhoid \TIE-foid\ *n.* (Md) A bacterial infection transmitted through tainted milk, water, or food.

typhoon \tie-FOON\ *n.* A violent hurricane.

typical \TIP-i-kul\ *adj.* **1.** Serving as an example. **2.** Usual in quality. typically *adv.*

typify \TIP-uh-fie\ *v.* typified; typifying. To represent the normal or usual qualities.

typography \tie-POG-ruh-fee\ *n.* The art of printing with type. typographic *adj.*; typographical *adj.*; typographically *adv.*; typographer *n.*

tyranny \TIR-uh-nee\ *n. pl.* tyrannies. An oppressive and cruel power or rule. tyrannic *adj.*; tyrannical *adj.*; tyrannically *adv.*; tyrant *n.*; tyrannize *v.*

U

u \yoo\ *n. pl.* The 21st letter of the English alphabet.

ubiquitous \yoo-BIK-wi-tus\ *adj.* Found everywhere. ubiquity *n.*

udder \UD-ur\ *n.* A baglike milk gland of a cow, goat, etc.

ugly \UG-lee\ *adj.* uglier; ugliest. **1.** Not pleasant to look at. **2.** Hostile or threatening. ugliness *n.*

ukulele \yoo-kuh-LAY-lee\ *n.* (Mu) A small, four-stringed guitar.

ulcer \UL-sur\ *n.* [Md] An open sore or mucous membrane lesion caused by inflammation, infection. ulcerous *adj.*; ulceration *n.*; ulcerate *v.*

ulterior \ul-TEER-ee-ur\ *adj.* Beyond the obvious or admitted. ulteriorly *adv.*

ultimate \UL-tuh-mit\ *adj.* **1.** Last. **2.** Essential. **3.** Being the most removed. **4.** Being the greatest possible. ultimately *adv.*; ultimate *n.*

ultimatum \ul-tuh-MAY-tum\ *n. pl.* ultimatums or ultimata. A final, threatening demand.

ultra- \UL-truh\ *prefix* **1.** Beyond. **2.** Extremely.

ultrasonic \ul-truh-SON-ik\ *adj.* Beyond the range of normal human hearing.

ultrasound \ul-truh-SOWND\ *n.* (Md) Therapeutic or diagnostic method using high frequency sound waves.

ultraviolet \ul-truh-VIE-uh-lit\ *adj.* Concerning radiation having shorter wavelengths than those visible to the eye.

ululate \YOOL-yuh-layt\ *v.* ululated; ululating. To howl or wail. ululation *n.*

umbilical cord \um-BIL-i-kul\ *n.* A tubular structure connecting the fetus with the placenta.

umbrella \um-BREL-uh\ *n.* A folding frame covered with fabric and used as protection from rain.

umlaut \UUM-lowt\ *n.* A diacritical mark used over a vowel in certain languages.

umpire \UM-pire\ *n.* A referee in certain games. umpire *v.*

un- *prefix* **1.** Not. **2.** Opposite of. **3.** Reversal of.

unable \un-AY-bul\ *adj.* Not able.

unabridged \un-uh-BRIJD\ *adj.* Not shortened.

unaccustomed \un-uh-KUS-tumd\ *adj.* **1.** Not used to. **2.** Not typical.

unaffected \un-uh-FEK-tid\ *adj.* **1.** Not altered. **2.** Not pretentious. unaffectedly *adv.*

unanimous \yoo-NAN-uh-mus\ *adj.* Lacking dissent. unanimously *adv.*; unanimity *n.*

unassuming \un-uh-SOO-ming\ *adj.* Not pretentious.

unauthorized \un-AW-thor-izd\ *adj.* Not approved.

unavoidable \un-uh-VOI-duh-bul\ *adj.* Impossible to escape from.

unaware \un-uh-WAIR\ *adj.* Not knowledgeable of.

unawares \un-uh-WAIRZ\ *adv.* **1.** Not deliberately. **2.** Unexpectedly.

unbalanced \un-BAL-unst\ *adj.* **1.** Not in a state of equilibrium. **2.** Not symmetrical. **3.** Not sane.

unbearable \un-BAIR-uh-bul\ *adj.* Not able to be endured. unbearably *adv.*

unbecoming \un-bi-KUM-ing\ *adj.* Not attractive.

unbelievable \un-bi-LEE-vuh-bul\ *adj.* Not credible.

unbiased \un-BIE-ust\ *adj.* Lacking prejudice.

uncanny \un-KAN-ee\ *adj.* Strange and extraordinary.

uncertain \un-SUR-tn\ *adj.* **1.** Not known for sure. **2.** Changeable. uncertainly *adv.*; uncertainness *n.*; uncertainty *n.*

uncivilized \un-SIV-ul-iezd\ *adj.* **1.** Savage. **2.** Lacking manners.

uncomfortable \un-KUMF-tuh-bul\ *adj.* Not at ease. uncomfortably *adv.*

uncommon \un-KOM-un\ *adj.* **1.** Rare. **2.** Odd. uncommonly *adv.*; uncommonness *n.*

unconditional \un-kun-DISH-un-ul\ *adj.* Not subject to limitations. unconditionally *adv.*

unconscionable \un-KON-shuh-nuh-bul\ *adj.* Contrary to what one's conscience sees as right. unconscionably *adv.*

unconscious \un-KON-shus\ *adj.* **1.** Lacking awareness. **2.** Not deliberate. unconsciously *adv.*; unconsciousness *n.*

unconscious \un-KON-shus\ *n.* In psychoanalysis, the totality of all thoughts, experiences, desires, etc. unconsciously *adv.*; unconsciousness *n.*

unconventional \un-kun-VEN-shuh-nl\ *adj.* Not traditional. unconventionally *adv.*

uncouth \un-KOOTH\ *adj.* **1.** Bad-mannered. **2.** Clumsy.

uncover \un-KUV-ur\ *v.* uncovered; uncovering. **1.** To reveal. **2.** To take the top off from.

undecided \un-dee-SIED-ud\ *adj.* Not yet certain.

undeniable \un-di-NIE-uh-bul\ *adj.* Impossible to challenge the truth of. undeniably *adv.*

under \UN-dur\ *prep.* **1.** Beneath or lower than. **2.** Covered by. **3.** Less than. **4.** During. under *adj.*; under *adv.*

underachiever \un-dur-u-CHEEV-ur\ *n.* A person who does not reach their potential. underachieve *v.*

underage \un-dur-AYJ\ *adj.* Being below the legal or required age.

underclass \un-dur-KLAS\ *n.* A low social class.

undercover \un-dur-KUV-ur\ *adj.* Acting or carried out in secret.

undercurrent \UN-dur-kur-unt\ *n.* **1.** A current flowing beneath the surface. **2.** An underlying feeling or influence.

underdog \UN-dur-dawg\ *n.* A person in an inferior position.

underestimate \un-dur-ES-tuh-mayt\ *v.* underestimated; underestimating. To set too low a value on. underestimation *n.*

underground \UN-dur-grownd\ *adj.* **1.** Below the Earth's surface. **2.** Secret. **3.** Alternative. underground *adv.*; underground *n.*

underlying \UN-dur-lie-ing\ *adj.* Existing as the basis or support of something.

undermine \un-dur-MIEN\ *v.* undermined; undermining. **1.** To weaken gradually. **2.** To make a tunnel beneath.

underneath \un-dur-NEETH\ *prep.* Below. underneath *adv.*

underprivileged \UN-dur-PRIVlijd\ *adj.* Deprived of fundamental rights and security. underprivileged *n.*

understanding \un-dur-STAN-ding\ *n.* **1.** Comprehension. **2.** The ability to think clearly. **3.** An agreement. **4.** Sympathy.

understand \un-dur-STAND\ *v.* understood; understanding. **1.** To comprehend the meaning of something. **2.** To know the character of someone. understandable *adj.*; understandably *adv.*

undertake \un-dur-TAYK\ *v.* undertook; undertaken; undertaking. **1.** To take responsibility for. **2.** To promise to do.

undertone \UN-dur-tohn\ *n.* An underlying quality or feeling.

underwear \UN-dur-wair\ *n.* Garments worn beneath clothes.

underworld \UN-dur-wurld\ *n.* **1.** Hell. **2.** Those involved in the world of crime.

underwrite \un-dur-RIET\ *v.* underwrote; underwritten; underwriting. **1.** To accept liability through signing one's name. **2.** To finance something. underwriter *n.*

undesirable \un-di-ZIER-uh-bul\ *adj.* **1.** Not wished for. **2.** Unacceptable. **3.** Offensive. undesirably *adv.*

undeveloped \UN-di-vel-opt\ *adj.* Not fully matured.

undo \un-DOO\ *v.* undid; undone; undoing. **1.** To unfasten or unwrap. **2.** To cancel the effect of. **3.** To bring to ruin.

undoubtedly \un-DOW-tid-lee\ *adv.* Certainly. undoubted *adj.*

undress \un-DRES\ *v.* undressed; undressing. To take clothes off. undress *n.*

undulate \UN-juh-layt\ *v.* undulated; undulating. To move in a wavy way. undulation *n.*

unearth \un-URTH\ *v.* unearthed; unearthing. **1.** To dig up something buried. **2.** To discover something.

uneasy \un-EE-zee\ *adj.* uneasier; uneasiest. Anxious and uncomfortable. uneasily *adv.*; uneasiness *n.*

unequivocal \un-i-KWIV-uh-kul\ *adj.* Clear and lacking ambiguity. unequivocally *adv.*

unethical \un-ETH-i-kul\ *adj.* Lacking morals. unethically *adv.*

uneven \un-EE-vun\ *adj.* Unbalanced. unevenly *adv.*

uneventful \un-i-VENT-ful\ *adj.* Absent of important or interesting incidents. uneventfully *adv.*

unexpected \un-ik-SPEK-tid\ *adj.*

Surprising. unexpectedly *adv.*; unexpectedness *n.*

unfair \un-FAIR\ *adj.* Not just. unfairly *adv.*; unfairness *n.*

unfaithful \un-FAYTH-ful\ *adj.* **1.** Not loyal. **2.** Inaccurate. unfaithfully *adv.*; unfaithfulness *n.*

unfamiliar \un-fuh-MIL-yur\ *adj.* **1.** Strange. **2.** Not having knowledge of something.

unfavorable \un-FAY-vuh-ruh-bul\ *adj.* Disadvantageous. unfavorably *adv.*

unfit \un-FIT\ *adj.* Physically or mentally not suitable.

unfold \un-FOHLD\ *v.* unfolded; unfolding. **1.** To open or spread out. **2.** To become known.

unforeseen \un-fohr-SEEN\ *adj.* Unexpected.

unfortunate \un-FOR-chuh-nit\ *adj.* **1.** Having bad luck. **2.** Regrettable. **3.** Unfit. unfortunately *adv.*; unfortunate *n.*

unfriendly \un-FREND-lee\ *adj.* Not nice. unfriendliness *n.*

ungrateful \un-GRAYT-ful\ *adj.* Not thankful. ungratefully *adv.*; ungratefulness *n.*

unhappy \un-HAP-ee\ *adj.* unhappier; unhappiest. **1.** Sad. **2.** Unsuitable. **3.** Unfortunate. unhappily *adv.*; unhappiness *n.*

unhealthy \un-HEL-thee\ *adj.* **1.** Sickly. **2.** Not beneficial to one's mind or body. unhealthily *adv.*; unhealthiness *n.*

unheard-of \un-HERD-uv\ *adj.* **1.** Not known previously. **2.** Outlandish.

unicameral \yoo-ni-KAM-ur-ul\ *adj.* (Po) Of a legislature, having a single chamber or house.

unidentified \un-i-DEN-tuh-fied\ *adj.* Not recognized.

uniform \YOO-nuh-form\ *adj.* Remaining the same. uniformly *adv.*; uniformity *n.*

uniform \YOO-nuh-form\ *n.* Distinctive clothing for an organization or profession. uniform *v.*

unify \YOO-nuh-fie\ *v.* unified; unifying. To bring or come together. unification *n.*

unimaginable \un-i-MAH-jun-uh-bul\ *adj.* Not conceivable in the mind.

unimportant \un-im-POR-tunt\ *adj.* Lacking significance, value, or authority.

uninhibited \un-in-HIB-i-tud\ *adj.* Free from mental and emotional restraints. uninhibitedly *adv.*

unintentional \un-in-TEN-shun-ul\ *adj.* Not deliberate. unintentionally *adv.*

uninterrupted \un-in-tur-UP-tud\ *adj.* Continuous.

union \YOON-yun\ *n.* **1.** Bringing together. **2.** A group organized for a specific purpose. unionization *n.*; unionize *v.*

unique \yoo-NEEK\ *adj.* **1.** Being the only one of its kind. **2.** Unequaled. **3.** Odd. uniquely *adv.*; uniqueness *n.*

unisex \YOO-nuh-seks\ *adj.* Designed for use by both males and females.

unison \YOO-nuh-sun\ *n.* Togetherness.

unit \YOO-nit\ *n.* **1.** A single thing. **2.** A quantity or amount in a system of measurement.

unite \yoo-NIET\ *v.* united; uniting. To join or act together.

unity \YOO-ni-tee\ *n.* **1.** Being joined together. **2.** A complex whole. **3.** An agreement.

universal \yoo-nuh-VUR-sul\ *adj.* **1.** Existing everywhere. **2.** Including everything. **3.** Designed for all. universally *adv.*; universality *n.*; universalize *v.*

universe \YOO-nuh-vurs\ *n.* The totality of existing matter and space.

unjust \un-JUST\ *adj.* Not fair. unjustly *adv.*

unkempt \un-KEMPT\ *adj.* **1.** Not groomed. **2.** Untidy.

unkind \un-KIEND\ *adj.* **1.** Inconsiderate. **2.** Mean. unkindly *adv.*; unkindness *n.*

unknown \un-NOHN\ *adj.* **1.** Not acquainted with. **2.** Not previously identified. unknown *n.*

unlike \un-LIEK\ *adj.* Different. unlikeness *n.*; unlike *prep.*

unlikely \un-LIEK-lee\ *adj.* **1.** Not bound to happen. **2.** Not apt to be true. unlikelihood *n.*

unload \un-LOHD\ *v.* unloaded; unloading. **1.** To remove a burden from something. **2.** To relieve of anxiety.

unlucky \un-LUK-ee\ *adj.* unluckier; unluckiest. Unfortunate. unluckily *adv.*

unmitigated \un-MIT-uh-gay-tid\ *adj.* Absolute and not modified.

unnatural \un-NACH-ur-ul\ *adj.* **1.** Going against one's innate character. **2.** Artificial. unnaturally *adv.*; unnaturalness *n.*

unnecessary \un-NES-uh-ser-ee\ *adj.* Not needed. unnecessarily *adv.*

unnerve \un-NURV\ *v.* unnerved; unnerving. To cause to lose courage or determination.

unobtrusive \un-ob-TROO-siv\ *adj.* Hardly noticed or unnoticed. unobtrusively *adv.*

unorthodox \un-or-THOH-doks\ *adj.* Unconventional.

unparalleled \un-PAR-uh-leld\ *adj.* Not yet equaled.

unprecedented \un-PRES-i-den-tid\ *adj.* Unheard of.

unpredictable \un-pre-DIK-tuh-bul\ *adj.* Not easily foreseen. unpredictably *adv.*

unpretentious \un-pre-TEN-shus\ *adj.* Not pompous or showy. unpretentiousness *n.*

unprincipled \un-PRIN-suh-puld\ *adj.* Without good morals or ethics.

unprofessional \un-pruh-FESH-uh-nul\ *adj.* Not abiding by the moral codes of a work environment. unprofessionally *adv.*

unquestionable \un-KWES-chuh-nuh-bul\ *adj.* Beyond doubt. unquestionably *adv.*

unreal \un-REEL\ *adj.* Imaginary.

unreasonable \un-REE-zuh-nuh-bul\ *adj.* **1.** Irrational. **2.** Excessive. unreasonably *adv.*

unrelated \un-re-LAYT-ud\ *adj.* Not connected, as by origin or relationship.

unrelenting \un-ri-LEN-ting\ *adj.* **1.** Stubborn. **2.** Not lessening in vigor or speed. unrelentingly *adv.*

unreliable \un-ri-LIE-uh-bul\ *adj.* Not dependable.

unresolved \un-ri-SOLVD\ *adj.* Wavering in determination of purpose.

unrest \un-REST\ *n.* An agitated or disturbed state.

unruly \un-ROO-lee\ *adj.* Badly behaved and out of control. unruliness *n.*

unsafe \un-SAYF\ *adj.* Dangerous.

unsavory \un-SAY-vuh-ree\ *adj.* **1.** Disagreeable in taste or smell. **2.** Immoral.

unscathed \un-SKAYTHD\ *adj.* Not injured or suffering.

unselfish \un-SEL-fish\ *adj.* Considerate and helpful. unselfishly *adv.*; unselfishness *n.*

unsophisticated \un-suh-FIS-ti-kay-tid\ *adj.* **1.** Simple. **2.** Not worldly.

unspeakable \un-SPEE-kuh-bul\ *adj.* **1.** Not able to be described in words. **2.** Horrible.

unstable \un-STAY-bul\ *adj.* **1.** Unbalanced. **2.** Lacking emotional control. **3.** [Sc] Tending to decompose.

unsuitable \un-SOO-tuh-bul\ *adj.* Not appropriate.

unsure \un-SHOOR\ *adj.* Not confident.

unthinkable \un-THING-kuh-bul\ *adj.* Too bad or unlikely to be thought about.

until \un-TIL\ *prep.*, *conj.* Up to the time when.

untimely \un-TIEM-lee\ *adj.* Premature or inopportune.

untold \un-TOHLD\ *adj.* **1.** Not told. **2.** Too much to be counted.

unusual \un-YOO-zhoo-ul\ *adj.* Rare and remarkable. unusually *adv.*; unusualness *n.*

unwanted \un-WAN-tud\ *adj.* Not wanted.

unwarranted \un-WAR-un-tud\ *adj.* Not justified or authorized.

unwilling \un-WIL-ing\ *adj.* Not willing. unwillingness *n.*; unwillingly *adv.*

unwind \un-WIEND\ *v.* unwound; unwinding. **1.** To unroll. **2.** To relax.

unwise \un-WIEZ\ *adj.* Foolish. unwisely *adv.*

unworthy \un-WUR-thee\ *adj.* Not deserving or worthy.

unwritten \un-RIT-un\ *adj.* Not written down.

unyielding \un-YEE-ul-ding\ *adj.* Not allowing change.

upbeat \UP-beet\ *adj.* Optimistic and cheerful.

update \UP-dayt\ *v.* updated; updating. To bring up to the present time. update *n.*

upgrade \UP-grayd\ *v.* upgraded; upgrading. To bring up in grade, level, or quality. upgrade *n.*

upheaval \up-HEE-vul\ *n.* A sudden violent disturbance or change.

uphill \UP-HIL\ *adj.*, *adv.* Going or sloping upward.

uphold \up-HOHLD\ *v.* upheld; upholding. To support.

upkeep \UP-keep\ *n.* **1.** Keeping something in good shape. **2.** Cost of keeping something in shape.

upper \UP-ur\ *adj.* Higher in place, position, or rank.

uppermost \UP-ur-mohst\ *adj.*, *adv.* In, on, or to the top position.

upright \UP-riet\ *adj.* **1.** In a vertical position. **2.** Honest or honorable.

uprising \UP-rie-zing\ *n.* Rebellion.

uproar \UP-ror\ *n.* Outburst of excitement or anger.

uproot \up-ROOT\ *v.* uprooted; uprooting. To pull out of the ground or a place with force.

upscale \UP-SKAYL\ *adj.* Of or concerning things that are for the top economic and social classes.

upset \up-SET\ *v.* upset; upsetting. **1.** To overturn or tip over. **2.** To disturb or bother.

upside-down \UP-sied-DOWN\

adj. **1.** With the bottom at the top. **2.** Disordered.

upstairs \UP-STAIRZ\ *adv.*, *adj.* To or on a higher floor. upstairs *n.*

upstanding \up-STAN-ding\ *adj.* Honorable and upright.

upstream \UP-STREEM\ *adj.*, *adv.* Against the current.

uptight \UP-TIET\ *adj.* Tense and annoyed.

up-to-date \UP-too-DAYT\ *adj.* Modern.

upward *also* **upwards** \UP-wurd\ *adj.* Toward a higher position.

upwardly mobile *adj.* Moving toward a higher social level. upward mobility *n.*

uranium \yuu-RAY-nee-um\ *n.* A valuable metal used as a source of nuclear energy.

Uranus \YUUR-uh-nus or YUUR-ay-nus\ *n.* The seventh planet from the sun.

urban \UR-bun\ *adj.* Of or concerning a city or large town.

urbane \ur-BAYN\ *adj.* Smooth in manner. urbanely *adv.*; urbanity *n.*

urchin \UR-chin\ *n.* A mischievous and poor boy.

uremia \yuu-REE-mee-uh\ *n.* The presence of urine products in the blood.

urethra \yuu-REE-thruh\ *n. pl.* urethrae; urethras. The duct that con-

veys urine, and semen in males, outside the body.

urge \urj\ *v.* urged; urging. **1.** To drive onward or to do something. **2.** To persuade or recommend strongly. urge *n.*

urgent \UR-junt\ *adj.* Needing immediate attention or action. urgently *adv.*; urgency *n.*

urinalysis \YUUR-uh-nal-uh-sis\ *n.* A diagnostic analysis of the urine.

urine \YUUR-in\ *n.* The liquid waste of mammals.

urn *n.* A metal container or vase.

urology \yuu-ROL-uh-jee\ *n.* The scientific study of the urinary tract. urologist *n.*

use \yooz\ *v.* used; using. **1.** To employ for a purpose. **2.** To consume. **3.** To know and experience regularly. use *n.*; used *adj.*; useful *adj.*; usefulness *n.*; user *n.*

useless \YOOS-lis\ *adj.* Not usable or useful. uselessly *adv.*; uselessness *n.*

user-friendly \YOO-zur-FREND-lee\ *adj.* Easily understood and operated.

usher \USH-ur\ *n.* A person who takes people to their seats in a theater or public place.

usual \YOO-zhoo-ul\ *adj.* Normal and customary. usually *adv.*

usurp \yoo-SURP\ *v.* usurped; usurping. To take power wrongfully or by force. usurpation *n.*; usurper *n.*

utensil \yoo-TEN-sul\ *n.* An instrument, tool, or container.

utilitarian \yoo-til-i-TAIR-ee-un\ *adj.* Designed to be useful and practical. utilitarian *n.*; utilitarianism *n.*

utility \yoo-TIL-i-tee\ *n.* **1.** Usefulness. **2.** A useful thing. **3.** Purveyor of power or energy. utility *adj.*

utilize \YOOT-l-ize\ *v.* utilized; utilizing. To use or find a use for. utilization *n.*

utmost \UT-mohst\ *adj.*, *n.* Greatest, furthest, or most extreme.

utopia \yoo-TOH-pee-uh\ *n.* A perfect imaginary place or state. utopian *adj.*

utter \UT-ur\ *adj.* Complete, total, or absolute. utterly *adv.*

utter \UT-ur\ *v.* uttered; uttering. To speak. utterance *n.*

uvula \YOO-vyuh-luh\ *n.* (Md) *pl.* uvulas; uvulae. The small fleshy piece hanging at the back of the throat. uvular *adj.*

V

v \vee\ **n. pl.** v's or vs. The 22nd letter of the alphabet.

vacant \VAY-kunt\ **adj.** Empty or unoccupied. vacantly **adv.**; vacancy **n.**

vacate \VAY-kayt\ **v.** vacated; vacating. To leave a place unoccupied.

vacation \vay-KAY-shun\ **n.** **1.** A holiday from work or home. **2.** Time between school terms.

vaccinate \VAK-suh-nayt\ **v.** vaccinated; vaccinating. To inoculate against disease. vaccination **n.**

vacuous \VAK-yoo-us\ **adj.** Inane and expressionless. vacuously **adv.**; vacuousness **n.**; vacuity **n.**

vacuum \VAK-yoom\ **n.** **1.** An empty space with no air in it. **2.** A machine that sucks up dirt and dust. vacuum **adj.**

vagabond \VAG-uh-bond\ **n.** A tramp or homeless person.

vagary \VAY-guh-ree\ **n. pl.** vagaries. An unpredictable or wild action or idea.

vagina \vuh-JIE-nuh\ **n.** The passage from the vulva to the uterus in female mammals. vaginal **adj.**

vagrant \VAY-grunt\ **n.** A tramp or wanderer. vagrancy **n.**

vague \vayg\ **adj.** vaguer; vaguest. Not clear or certain. vaguely **adv.**; vagueness **n.**

vain \vayn\ **adj.** vainer; vainest. **1.** Proud and conceited. **2.** Unsuccessful or useless. vainly **adv.**

valediction \val-i-DIK-shun\ *n.* Farewell. valedictory *adj.*

valet \va-LAY\ *n.* A personal attendant. valet *v.*

valiant \VAL-yunt\ *adj.* Very brave. valiantly *adv.*

validate \VAL-i-dayt\ *v.* validated; validating. To approve or confirm. validation *n.*

validity \vuh-LID-i-tee\ *n.* Soundness and authority. valid *adj.*

valise \vuh-LEES\ *n.* A suitcase.

valley \VAL-ee\ *n.* A low area or region between hills.

valor \VAL-ur\ *n.* Bravery.

value \VAL-yoo\ *n.* **1.** Amount of money equivalent to something. **2.** Importance or worth of something. value *v.*; valueless *adj.*

value \VAL-yoo\ *v.* valued; valuing. **1.** To regard highly. **2.** To estimate the value of.

value-added tax or VAT *n.* A tax on the marginal value each processor puts into a product or process.

valve \valv\ *n.* **1.** Device to control the flow of a liquid or gas. **2.** A hinged lid or part. valvular *adj.*

vandal \VAN-dl\ *n.* A person who deliberately destroys or damages. vandalism *n.*

vanilla \vuh-NIL-uh\ *n.* A flavoring from the pods of a tropical orchid.

vanish \VAN-ish\ *v.* vanished; vanishing. To disappear.

vanity \VAN-i-tee\ *n.* Conceit or excessive pride.

vanquish \VANG-kwish\ *v.* vanquished; vanquishing. To defeat or overcome. vanquishment *n.*

vapid \VAP-id\ *adj.* Dull and uninteresting. vapidity *n.*; vapidly *adv.*

vapor \VAY-pur\ *n.* Steam, mist or gaslike substance made by heat changing a liquid or solid. vaporous *adj.*

variable \VAIR-ee-uh-bul\ *adj.* Changeable or varying. variable *n.*; variability *n.*

variation \vair-ee-AY-shun\ *n.* **1.** Varying or changing. **2.** Something that has been changed.

varietal \vuh-RIE-uh-tul\ *adj.* Of or concerning a variety.

variety \vuh-RIE-uh-tee\ *n.* **1.** Change or diversity. **2.** A number of different things. **3.** Limited class.

various \VAIR-ee-us\ *adj.* **1.** Different. **2.** Several. variously *adv.*

varnish \VAHR-nish\ *n.* A liquid that dries to a shiny coating. varnish *v.*

vary \VAIR-ee\ *v.* varied; varying. To make or become different or changed.

vase \vays or vayz\ *n.* A jar or vessel used to hold something or be ornamental.

vassal \VAS-ul\ *n.* A subordinate or slave.

vast *adj.* Very large or great. vastly *adv.*; vastness *n.*

vaudeville \VAWD-vil\ *n.* Variety entertainment.

vault \vawlt\ *n.* **1.** An arched roof. **2.** An underground room or cellar. **3.** A burial chamber.

vault \vawlt\ *v.* vaulted; vaulting. To jump over something with the help of the hands or a pole. vaulter *n.*

VCR \vee-see-ar\ *n.* An abbreviation for videocassette recorder.

veal \veel\ *n.* The meat of a calf.

vegetable \VEJ-tuh-bul\ *n.* A plant, esp. one that is used as a food. vegetable *adj.*

vegetate \VEJ-i-tayt\ *v.* vegetated; vegetating. **1.** To live uneventfully and inactively. **2.** To grow as or like a plant. vegetation *n.*

vehement \VEE-uh-munt or vi-HEE-munt\ *adj.* Showing strong feeling. vehemently *adv.*; vehemence *n.*

vehicle \VEE-i-kul\ *n.* A device for carrying people or things on land or through space. vehicular *adj.*

veil \vayl\ *n.* A thin cloth used to cover something. veil *v.*

vein \vayn\ *n.* **1.** Tubes that convey blood to the heart. **2.** Distinctive trait. **3.** Mood. veined *adj.*

vellum \VEL-um\ *n.* Fine parchment or smooth writing paper. vellum *adj.*

velour \vuh-LUUR\ *n.* A plush velvety fabric.

velvet \VEL-vit\ *n.* A plush, thick material with a short pile on one side. velvety *adj.*

vend *v.* vended; vending. To offer for sale. vendor *n.*

vendetta \ven-DET-uh\ *n.* A feud or quarrel.

veneer \vuh-NEER\ *n.* A thin layer of fine wood over inexpensive wood or material. veneer *v.*

venerable \VEN-ur-uh-bul\ *adj.* Worthy of respect due to age, experience, or status. venerability *n.*

venereal \vuh-NEER-ee-ul\ *adj.* Of or concerning infections contracted by sexual relations.

vengeance \VEN-juns\ *n.* Retaliation. vengeful *adj.*

venom \VEN-um\ *n.* Poison from a

snake or other animal. venomous *adj.*

vent *n.* A slit or hole in something. vent *v.*

ventilate \VEN-tl-ayt\ *v.* ventilated; ventilating. **1.** To cause air to circulate freely. **2.** To express publicly. ventilation *n.*

venture \VEN-chur\ *n.* An undertaking that involves some risk.

venture \VEN-chur\ *v.* ventured; venturing. To dare or risk.

venue \VEN-yoo\ *n.* The scene or locale of an event.

Venus \VEE-nus\ *n.* The second planet from the sun.

veracity \vuh-RAS-i-tee\ *n.* Truthfulness and correctness.

veranda *also* **verandah** \vuh-RAN-duh\ *n.* A roofed terrace or porch.

verb \vurb\ *n.* A word indicating action or something experienced. verbal *adj.*

verbal \VUR-bul\ *adj.* **1.** Spoken or in words. **2.** Of a verb. verbally *adv.*

verbatim \vur-BAY-tim\ *adv.*, *adj.* In exactly the same words.

verbose \vur-BOHS\ *adj.* Using more words than necessary. verbosely *adv.*; verbosity *n.*

verdict \VUR-dikt\ *n.* A decision or opinion reached by a jury or judge.

verge \vurj\ *n.* A border, limit, or edge. verge *v.*

verify \VER-uh-fie\ *v.* verified; verifying. To show the truth of something. verification *n.*

veritable \VER-i-tuh-bul\ *adj.* Real or genuine. veritably *adv.*

vermicelli \vur-mi-CHEL-ee\ *n.* Pasta in long, very fine threads.

vernacular \vur-NAK-yuh-lur\ *n.* Ordinary language of a people or area. vernacular *adj.*

versatile \VUR-suh-tl\ *adj.* Flexible and able to do different things. versatility *n.*

verse \vurs\ *n.* **1.** A piece of rhymed writing, as poetry. **2.** A group of rhymed lines from a song.

versed \vurst\ *adj.* Experienced in.

version \VUR-zhun\ *n.* **1.** A particular account of a matter. **2.** Translation or variant form.

verso \VUR-soh\ *n. pl.* versos. The lefthand page of an open book or the back of a page.

versus \VUR-sus\ *prep.* Against.

vertebra \VUR-tuh-bruh\ *n. pl.* vertebrae. A segment of the backbone. vertebral *adj.*; vertebrate *n.*

vertex \VUR-teks\ *n. pl.* vertices. The highest point or apex.

vertical \VUR-ti-kul\ *adj.* Up and down or upright. vertical *n.*; vertically *adv.*

vertigo \VUR-ti-goh\ *n.* Dizziness. vertiginous *adj.*

very \VAIR-ee\ *adv.* **1.** In a high degree. **2.** Extremely. **3.** Exactly.

vesper *also* **vespers** \VES-pur\ *n.* A church service held in the evening.

vessel \VES-ul\ *n.* **1.** A receptacle or container. **2.** A ship or boat. **3.** A tubelike container.

vest *n.* A sleeveless garment for the trunk of the body.

vestibule \VES-tuh-byool\ *n.* An entrance hall or porch.

vestige \VES-tij\ *n.* A trace or very small amount.

veteran \VET-ur-un\ *n.* **1.** Person with much experience. **2.** Former member of the armed forces.

veto \VEE-toh\ *n. pl.* vetoes. A statement forbidding something. veto *v.*

vex \veks\ *v.* vexed; vexing. To annoy or bother. vexation *n.*

via \VEE-uh or VIE-uh\ *prep.* By way of or through.

viable \VIE-uh-bul\ *adj.* Practicable and likely; capable of living. viability *n.*

vial \VIE-ul\ *n.* A small, narrow bottle or tube.

vibe \vieb\ *also* **vibes** *n.* Vibrations.

vibrant \VIE-brunt\ *adj.* Vibrating or filled with energy.

vibrate \VIE-brayt\ *v.* vibrated; vibrating. To move rapidly and continuously to and fro. vibration *n.*

vicarious \vie-KAIR-ee-us\ *adj.* Felt or shared in the imagination. vicariously *adv.*

vice \vies\ *n.* **1.** Wickedness; bad habit. **2.** A gripping instrument. **3.** A police department.

vice- \vies\ *pref.* Substitute or deputy.

vice versa \VIES-VUR-suh\ *adv.* In reverse order.

vicinity \vi-SIN-i-tee\ *n.* The surrounding area or neighborhood.

vicious \VISH-us\ *adj.* Evil or spiteful. viciously *adv.*; viciousness *n.*

victim \VIK-tim\ *n.* A person suffering, injured, or killed. victimize *v.*

victory \VIK-tuh-ree\ *n.* Success in battle or competition. victorious *adj.*; victoriously *adv.*

victuals \VIT-uls\ *pl. n.* Food.

video \VID-ee-oh\ *n.* **1.** A device for recording TV pictures and sound. **2.** A TV recording or videotape. video *adj.*

videocassette *n.* A magnetic tape in a box for recording and viewing TV pictures and sound.

videodisc *n.* An optical disc on

which a film or TV program is recorded for playback on a TV.

video recorder *n.* An electronic device for recording video signals on magnetic tape or videodisc.

videotape \VID-ee-oh-tayp\ *n.* A magnetic tape on which a TV program, film, etc., can be recorded. videotape *v.*

vie \vie\ *v.* vied; vying. To compete or be rivals.

view \vyoo\ *n.* **1.** Scene or scenery. **2.** A sight or look. **3.** Visual or mental survey. view *v.*

viewpoint \VYOO-point\ *n.* An opinion or point of view.

vigil \VIJ-ul\ *n.* A period of wakefulness for watching or prayer.

vigilance \VIJ-uh-luns\ *n.* Watchfulness. vigilant *adj.*

vigilante \vij-uh-LAN-tee\ *n.* A self-appointed authority of the law who intends to avenge crime.

vignette \vin-YET\ *n.* **1.** A short description or episode. **2.** A decorative design or illustration.

vigor \VIG-ur\ *n.* Active physical or mental strength. vigorous *adj.*; vigorously *adv.*; vigorousness *n.*

vile \viel\ *adj.* Extremely disgusting or despicable. vilely *adv.*; vileness *n.*

village \VIL-ij\ *n.* A small town or collection of houses. villager *n.*

villain \VIL-un\ *n.* A wicked person or scoundrel. villainous *adj.*; villainy *n.*

vinaigrette \vin-uh-GRET\ *n.* An oil-based salad dressing with vinegar and spices.

vindicate \VIN-duh-kayt\ *v.* vindicated; vindicating. To clear of blame. vindication *n.*; vindicatory *adj.*

vindictive \vin-DIK-tiv\ *adj.* Seeking revenge. vindictively *adv.*; vindictiveness *n.*

vine \vien\ *n.* A climbing or trailing woody-stemmed plant.

vineyard \VIN-yurd\ *n.* A field or plantation for growing vines and grapes.

vintage \VIN-tij\ *n.* **1.** Wine from a particular harvest or crop. **2.** A particular grape-growing season. vintage *adj.*

violate \VIE-uh-layt\ *v.* violated; violating. **1.** To break a promise or law. **2.** To treat irreverently. **3.** To rape. violation *n.*; violator *n.*

violence \VIE-uh-luns\ *n.* Extreme, intense physical force. violent *adj.*; violently *adv.*

violin \vie-uh-LIN\ *n.* A stringed instrument played with a bow. violinist *n.*

virgin \VUR-jin\ *adj.* Pure and untouched.

virgin \VUR-jin\ *n.* A person who has not engaged in sexual relations. virgin *adj.*; virginal *adj.*

virile \VIR-ul\ *adj.* Manly and powerful. virility *n.*

virtual \VUR-choo-ul\ *adj.* In effect but not in name. virtually *adv.*; virtuality *n.*

virtually \VUR-choo-uh-lee\ *adv.* For the most part.

virtual reality *n.* Realistic interactive simulation of an environment by a computer.

virtue \VUR-choo\ *n.* **1.** Goodness. **2.** A particular type or characteristic of goodness. virtuous *adj.*

virtuoso \vur-choo-OH-soh\ *n. pl.* virtuosi. An expert performer. virtuosity *n.*

virulent \VIR-yuh-lunt\ *adj.* **1.** Of a disease or poison, extremely strong. **2.** Very hostile. virulently *adv.*; virulence *n.*

virus \VIE-rus\ *n. pl.* viruses. **1.** Tiny organism capable of causing disease. **2.** Destructive code in a computer. viral *adj.*

visa \VEE-zuh\ *n.* A temporary permit to enter a country.

visage \VIZ-ij\ *n.* A person's face.

visceral \VIS-uh-rul\ *adj.* Of or concerning the internal organs of the body. viscera *n. pl.*

viscose \vi-SKOS\ *n.* A thick cellulose or a fabric made from it.

viscous \VIS-kus\ *adj.* Thick and sticky. viscosity *n.*

visible \VIZ-uh-bul\ *adj.* Able to be seen. visibly *adv.*; visibility *n.*

vision \VIZH-un\ *n.* **1.** Sight. **2.** Imagination and understanding. **3.** A dream.

visionary \VIZH-uh-ner-ee\ *n. pl.* visionaries. A person with fanciful, impractical ideas. visionary *adj.*

visit \VIZ-it\ *v.* visited; visiting. **1.** To go to see someone or someplace. **2.** To stay somewhere temporarily. visit *n.*

visual \VIZH-oo-ul\ *adj.* Of or concerning sight.

visualize \VIZH-oo-uh-lize\ *v.* visualized; visualizing. To imagine. visualization *n.*

vital \VITE-l\ *adj.* Essential to life or extremely important. vitally *adv.*

vitriolic \vi-tree-OL-ik\ *adj.* Very hostile or mean. vitriol *n.*

vivacious \vi-VAY-shus\ *adj.* Lively and high-spirited. vivaciously *adv.*; vivacity *n.*

vivid \VIV-id\ *adj.* Bright, clear, and strong. vividly *adv.*; vividness *n.*

vixen \VIK-sun\ *n.* A female fox.

vocabulary \voh-KAB-yuh-ler-ee\ *n. pl.* vocabularies. **1.** List of words, meanings. **2.** The words known or used by a person or group.

vocal \VOH-kul\ *adj.* Of or concerning the voice. vocal *n.*

vocalize \VOH-kuh-lize\ *v.* vocalized; vocalizing. To utter or say. vocalization *n.*

vocation \voh-KAY-shun\ *n.* A trade or profession. vocational *adj.*

vogue \vohg\ *n.* A current fashion or style. vogue *adj.*

voice \vois\ *n.* **1.** The sound of speaking or singing. **2.** The power to speak or sing. voice *v.*

voice mail \vois-mayl\ *n.* An electronic communications system that records oral messages.

voice-over *n.* The voice of a narrator on a TV program or film. voice-over *v.*

voiceprint *n.* A graphic representation of a person's voice.

void *n.* Empty space.

void *adj.* **1.** Empty. **2.** Not valid.

void *v.* voided; voiding. To invalidate or make empty.

volatile \VOL-uh-tl\ *adj.* Changing very quickly. volatility *n.*

volcano \vol-KAY-noh\ *n. pl.* volcanoes. A mountain with an opening through which molten lava, gases, etc. are emitted. volcanic *adj.*

volley \VOL-ee\ *n. pl.* volleys. **1.** A shower of missiles. **2.** Hitting of a ball before it bounces. volley *v.*

volume \VOL-yum\ *n.* **1.** A book. **2.** Quantity of a three-dimensional space. **3.** Loudness. **4.** Large quantity.

voluminous \vuh-LOO-muh-nus\ *adj.* Having great volume.

voluntary \VOL-un-ter-ee\ *adj.* **1.** Done of one's own free will. **2.** Done without expecting payment. voluntarily *adv.*

volunteer \vol-un-TEER\ *n.* A person who offers to do something. volunteer *adj.*

voluptuous \vuh-LUP-choo-us\ *adj.* **1.** Having a full figure. **2.** Full or fond of pleasure and luxury. voluptuously *adv.*; voluptuousness *n.*

vomit \VOM-it\ *v.* vomited; vomiting. To eject matter from the stomach through the mouth. vomit *n.*

voracious \vuh-RAY-shus\ *adj.* Very hungry or desirous. voracity *n.*

vortex \VOR-teks\ *n. pl.* vortexes; vortices. A whirlpool or whirlwind.

vote \voht\ *n.* **1.** A formal expression of preference. **2.** A choice. vote *v.*

vouch \vowch\ *v.* vouched; vouching. To guarantee accuracy or reliability.

voucher \VOW-chur\ *n.* A document issued as a receipt or useable for goods or services.

vow *n.* A promise or oath. vow *v.*

vowel \VOW-ul\ *n.* A speech sound or letter made without audible stopping of the breath.

voyage \VOI-ij\ *n.* A journey made on water or in space. voyage *v.*

voyeur \vwah-YUR\ *n.* A person who gets gratification from watching sexual relations of others. voyeurism *n.*

vulgar \VUL-gur\ *adj.* Obscene or rude. vulgarly *adv.*; vulgarity *n.*

vulnerable \VUL-nur-uh-bul\ *adj.* Easily attacked or damaged. vulnerability *n.*

W

w \DUB-ul-yoo\ *n. pl.* The 23rd letter of the alphabet.

wacky \WAK-ee\ *adj.* wackier; wackiest. Being zany.

wad \wod\ *n.* **1.** A small clump. **2.** Wad of dough [Id]: A ball of money.

wad \wod\ *v.* wadded; wadding. **1.** To mold into a little ball. **2.** To stuff.

wade \wayd\ *v.* waded; wading. **1.** To walk through a dense substance, esp. water. **2.** To work through.

wafer \WAY-fur\ *n.* A thin, dry cracker.

waft *v.* wafted; wafting. To blow past as if carried by a breeze.

wag *n.* **1.** The act of waving back and forth. **2.** (Sl) One who is funny or witty.

wag *v.* wagged; wagging. To wave back and forth.

wage \wayj\ *n.* A fee for work done.

wage \wayj\ *v.* waged; waging. To carry on, especially in a war or campaign.

wager \WAY-jur\ *n.* **1.** Money bet on a gamble. **2.** Something on which money is bet. wagerer *n.*; wager *v.*

wagon \WAG-un\ *n.* **1.** Four-wheeled horse-drawn vehicle. **2.** Toy cart or wagon. **3.** Station wagon.

waif \wayf\ *n.* **1.** An orphaned child or animal. **2.** Very thin person.

wail \wayl\ *v.* wailed; wailing. **1.** To cry. **2.** To whine. wail *n.*

waist \wayst\ *n.* **1.** Human body between the chest and the hips. **2.** Garment area around waist.

wait \wayt\ *n.* A period of standing by in anticipation.

wait \wayt\ *v.* waited; waiting. **1.** To stand by in anticipation. **2.** To hold something up in anticipation. waiter *n.*; waitress *n.*

waive \wayv\ *v.* waived; waiving. **1.** To let go of a right to. **2.** To put off. waiver *n.*

wake \wayk\ *n.* **1.** The act of not sleeping. **2.** A funeral service. waken *v.*

wake \wayk\ *v.* woke or waked; woken or waked or woke; waking. **1.** To stop sleeping. **2.** To activate. waken *v.*

walk \wawk\ *n.* **1.** Traveling on foot. **2.** A pathway for walking. **3.** The way someone walks.

walk \wawk\ *v.* walked; walking. To travel on foot.

wall \wawl\ *n.* **1.** Enclosing, separating structure. **2.** The interior surface of a structure.

wall \wawl\ *v.* To use a structure to enclose, separate, or fortify. walled *adj.*

wallaby \WAWL-uh-bee\ *n.* *pl.* wallaby or wallabies. A small Australian kangaroo.

wallet billfold \WAWL-it\ *n.* Small pocketbook for paper money, credit cards, etc.

wallop \WOL-up\ *n.* A blow.

wallop \WOL-up\ *v.* walloped; walloping. To severely beat.

wallow \WOL-oh\ *v.* wallowed; wallowing. **1.** To lounge while immersed in something. **2.** To indulge.

wallpaper \WAWL-pay-pur\ *n.* A decorative wall covering.

waltz \wawlts\ *n.* **1.** Music having three beats to a measure. **2.** A dance done to such music.

waltz \wawlts\ *v.* waltzed; waltzing. **1.** To dance a waltz. **2.** To move lightly and freely. waltzer *n.*

wan \wahn\ *adj.* wanner; wannest. Appearing haggard. wanly *adv.*; wanness *n.*

wand \wond\ *n.* **1.** A staff having magical or divine powers. **2.** A processional staff.

wander \WON-dur\ *v.* wandered; wandering. **1.** To proceed without aim. **2.** To babble. wanderer *n.*

wanderlust \WON-dur-lust\ *n.* A strong desire to proceed without aim.

wane \wayn\ *v.* waned; waning. **1.** To become smaller. **2.** To lose superiority. **3.** To come to a conclusion. wane *n.*

wannabe \WON-uh-bee\ *n.* (Sl) A term used to put down a person who copies another person's style, etc.

want \wont\ *n.* **1.** A need of something that is lacking. **2.** A yearning for.

want \wont\ *v.* wanted; wanting. **1.** To need something that is lacking. **2.** To yearn for. wanting *adj.*

wanton \WON-tn\ *adj.* **1.** Promiscuous. **2.** Unfair. **3.** Being without reason. wantonly *adv.*; wanton *n.*; wantonness *n.*

war \wor\ *n.* **1.** A conflict involving weapons. **2.** An ongoing hostility. **3.** A fight.

war \wor\ *v.* warred; warring. To be involved in a conflict.

ward \word\ *n.* warded; warding. **1.** A wing of a hospital or prison. **2.** Division of city government. **3.** Trustee.

ward \word\ *v.* To avert.

warden \WOR-dn\ *n.* **1.** A guardian. **2.** One in charge of supervising a town, game, or prison.

ward off *v.* To deflect.

wardrobe \WOR-drohb\ *n.* **1.** Cabinet for clothing. **2.** All the garments of one person.

warehouse \WAIR-hows\ *n.* A storage place.

warfare \WOR-fair\ A conflict involving weapons.

warlike \WOR-like\ *adj.* **1.** Aggressive **2.** Related to an armed conflict.

warlock \WOR-lok\ *n.* A male witch.

warm \worm\ *adj.* **1.** Being hot. **2.** Having or giving heat. **3.** Excited. **4.** Affectionate. warmly *adv.*; warmth *n.*

warm \worm\ *v.* warmed; warming. **1.** To give heat to. **2.** To reheat leftover food.

warmonger \WOR-mung-gur\ *n.* One who incites war.

warm up \WORM-up\ *v.* The act of one or that which warms up. warm-up *n.*

warn \worn\ *v.* warned; warning. **1.** To inform of something before it happens. **2.** To caution of future danger.

warning \WOR-ning\ *n.* **1.** Act of revealing future events. **2.** Act of cautioning against future. warning *adj.*

warp \worp\ *v.* warped; warping. **1.** To misshape. **2.** To make or become dishonest. warped *adj.*

warrant \WOR-unt\ *n.* **1.** Authorization. **2.** Reason for an action. **3.** [Le] Judicial authorization.

warrant \WOR-unt\ *v.* **1.** To promise protection. **2.** To definitely assert. **3.** To authorize.

warranty \WOR-un-tee\ *n. pl.* warranties. **1.** Assurance regarding property, risks, etc. **2.** Guarantee.

warrior \WOR-ee-ur\ *n.* One skilled in armed combat.

warship \WOR-ship\ *n.* A ship outfitted for armed conflict.

wary \WAIR-ee\ *adj.* warier; wariest. Cautious. warily *adv.*; wariness *n.*

wash \wosh\ *n.* **1.** Cleaning or being cleaned. **2.** Clothes to be washed. **3.** Breaking waves.

wash \wosh\ *v.* washed; washing. **1.** To get rid of dirt. **2.** To wet or cover with liquid. **3.** To purify. washable *adj.*

WASP \wosp\ *n.* An American whose ancestors were British Protestants. waspish *adj.*

wasp \wosp\ *n.* A stinging insect.

waste \wayst\ *adj.* **1.** Uncultivated. **2.** Reduced to rubble. **3.** Being thrown away after use.

waste \wayst\ *v.* wasted; wasting. **1.** To use without care. **2.** To ruin. **3.** To lose strength, weight, or health. wastefully adv; wastefulness *n.*

wastebasket \WAYST-bas-kit\ *n.* A bin for storing refuse.

watch \woch\ *n.* **1.** Personal timepiece. **2.** Scrutiny. **3.** Guard duty or period of guarding.

watch \woch\ *v.* watched; watching. **1.** To observe. **2.** To be on guard. watchful *n.*

waterbed \WAW-tur-BED\ *n.* A water-filled mattress.

wave \wayv\ *n.* **1.** Ridge on surface of a liquid. **2.** Curve. **3.** Vibratory impulse in a medium. wavy *adj.*

wave \wayv\ *v.* waved; waving. **1.** To move back and forth or up and down. **2.** To undulate. **3.** To signal.

wax \waks\ *n.* **1.** Material bees secrete. **2.** A substance similar to beeswax. **3.** Earwax.

wax \waks\ *v.* waxed; waxing. **1.** To shine with a polishing agent. **2.** To grow bigger.

way *n.* **1.** A route for passage. **2.** A course of action. **3.** A technique. **4.** A distance.

way-out *adj.* (Sl) Unusual or odd.

wayward \WAY-wurd\ *adj.* **1.** Unmanageable. **2.** Unpredictable. **3.** Being against what one anticipated. waywardly *adv.*; waywardness *n.*

weak \week\ *adj.* weaker; weakest. **1.** Lacking strength. **2.** Unable to support. **3.** Lacking ability, influence. weakly *adv.*; weakness *n.*; weaken *v.*

wealth \welth\ *n.* **1.** Having an abundance of material objects and money. **2.** Having an abundance. wealthy *adj.*

wean \ween\ *v.* weaned; weaning. **1.** To take off mother's milk as food. **2.** To remove from a habit.

weapon \WEP-un\ *n.* **1.** Instrument of injury, fighting. **2.** Any means used in a struggle.

wear \wair\ *n.* **1.** The act of being adorned. **2.** Clothing style. **3.** Destructive effect.

wear \wair\ *v.* wore; worn; wearing. **1.** To clothe or adorn oneself. **2.** To carry on the body. **3.** To erode, decrease. wearable *adj.*; wearer *n.*

weary \WEER-ee\ *adj.* wearier; weariest. **1.** Lacking in energy. **2.** Expressing a lack of energy. **3.** Discontented. wearisome *adj.*; wearily *adv.*; weariness *n.*; wear *v.*

weasel \WEE-zul\ *n.* **1.** A mammal that lives on fish. **2.** [Sl] A troublemaker.

weather \WETH-ur\ *n.* Atmospheric conditions, esp. the temperature, humidity, storms, etc.

weather \WETH-ur\ *v.* weathered; weathering. **1.** To undergo changes from exposure to weather. **2.** To resist being worn down.

weave \weev\ *n.* The texture or way of weaving.

weave \weev\ *v.* wove or weaved; woven or weaved; weaving. **1.** To make fabric by interlacing thread, yarn, etc. **2.** To make up. weaver *n.*

web *adj.* Having toes joined by tissue.

web *n.* **1.** Structure made by spiders to trap their prey. **2.** Entanglement. **3.** A tissue. web *v.*

wed *v.* wedded or wed; wedding. **1.** To become married. **2.** To combine.

wedding \WED-ing\ *n.* A marriage rite and celebration.

wedge \wej\ *n.* **1.** A triangular object. **2.** A pointed object or tool. **3.** Anything shaped this way.

Wednesday \WENZ-day\ *n.* The fourth day of the week.

weep *v.* wept; weeping. **1.** To sob. **2.** To drip. weepy *adj.*; weeping *adj.*; weeper *n.*

weevil \WEE-vul\ *n.* Any beetle with a curved, long head.

weigh \way\ *v.* weighed; weighing. **1.** To calculate heaviness. **2.** To have a degree of heaviness. **3.** To think about.

weigh down *v.* To burden.

weigh in *v.* To have one's heaviness calculated in order to qualify for a sports competition.

weight \wayt\ *n.* **1.** A degree of heaviness. **2.** A unit for measuring heaviness. **3.** Share; portion. weighty *adj.*; weight *v.*

weightlifting \wayt-lif-ting\ *n.* Exercise or competition using objects of varying heaviness. weightlifter *n.*; weightlift *v.*

weird \weerd\ *adj.* Unusual. weirdly *adv.*; weirdness *n.*

welcome \WEL-kum\ *adj.* **1.** Being cordially greeted. **2.** Pleasurable. **3.** Allowed to.

welcome \WEL-kum\ *n.* A friendly reception.

welcome \WEL-kum\ *v.* welcomed; welcoming. **1.** To receive kindly. **2.** To willingly accept.

welfare \WEL-fair\ *n.* **1.** Prosperity and good health. **2.** Government assistance for the downtrodden.

well \wel\ *adj.* **1.** Being comfortable. **2.** Healthy. **3.** Successful.

well \wel\ *adv.* better; best. **1.** In a correct way. **2.** In a pleasant way. **3.** Easily. **4.** Plentifully.

well \wel\ *n.* **1.** Underground source of water or oil. **2.** Something that provides.

well \wel\ *v.* To overflow.

well-behaved \WEL-BEE-hayvd\ *adj.* Obeying proper conduct.

well-being \WEL-BEE-ing\ *n.* A mental and physical state of prosperity.

well-bred \WEL-BRED\ *adj.* Coming from a cultivated family.

well-known \WEL-NOHN\ *adj.* Widely recognized.

well-off \WEL-AWF\ *adj.* In a fortunate situation, especially financially.

were \wur\ *v.* The past singular, past plural, or past subjunctive of be.

weren't \wurnt\ *v.* The contraction of were not.

werewolf \WAIR-wuulf\ *n.* *pl.* werewolves. One who transforms into a wolf when the moon is full.

west *n.* **1.** The direction in which the sun sets. **2.** [Cap] Any place near that of sunset. west *adj.*; westerly *adj.*; western *adj.*; westward *adj.*; westerly *adv.*

western \WES-turn\ *n.* A book or film about life in the West. westernize *v.*

wet *adj.* wetter; wettest. **1.** Saturated with moisture. **2.** Not dry. **3.** Rainy. wet *n.*; wetness *n.*; wet *v.*

wet bar *n.* **1.** A liquor counter equipped with plumbing. **2.** A poolside liquor counter.

wet look *n.* A style of appearing as if one has just stepped out of the shower.

wet nurse *n.* One who provides human milk to another's newborn.

whack \hwak\ *n.* **1.** A slap. **2.** A part of. **3.** A condition. **4.** A single attempt.

whack \hwak\ *v.* whacked; whacking. **1.** To slap. **2.** To kill.

whale \hwayl\ *n.* **1.** A large aquatic mammal. **2.** [Sl] A huge person.

wharf \hworf\ *n. pl.* wharves or wharfs. A shoreside structure for loading and docking boats.

what \hwot or hwut\ *adj.* **1.** Being which one or type of. **2.** Extraordinary.

what \hwot or hwut\ *adv.* **1.** In which manner. **2.** What for: Why. **3.** What with: Because of.

what \hwot or hwut\ *pron.* **1.** Which being, object, or situation. **2.** That which. **3.** Anything,

whatever \hwut-EV-ur\ *adj.* Of any sort.

whatever \hwut-EV-ur\ *pron.* **1.** Anything. **2.** No matter what.

whatnot \HWOT-not\ *n.* A knicknack shelf.

whatnot \HWOT-not\ *pron.* Anything that could also be mentioned.

wheel \hweel\ *n.* **1.** A disk that spins around a central rod. **2.** Something similar to a disk.

wheel \hweel\ *v.* wheeled; wheeling. **1.** To rotate. **2.** To carry in something supported by one or more spinning disks.

wheelbarrow \HWEEL-bar-oh\ *n.* A tub supported by one central wheel used for transporting small loads.

wheeler-dealer \HWEE-lur-DEE-lur\ *n.* A deceitful businessperson or politician.

wheeze \hweez\ *n.* **1.** A murmur caused by obstructed breathing. **2.** A cliche.

wheeze \hweez\ *v.* wheezed; wheezing. **1.** To experience breathing difficulties. **2.** To murmur from obstructed breathing. wheezy *adj.*

when \hwen\ *adv.* At or during which time. when *n.*; when *pron.*

when \hwen\ *conj.* **1.** At the same time. **2.** Though.

whence \hwens\ *adv.* From where. whence *conj.*

where \hwair\ *adv.* **1.** In, to, or at what place. **2.** Any which place. where *conj.*

where \hwair\ *n.* A location.

whereabouts \HWAIR-uh-bowts\ *n.* The location of something.

whereas \hwair-AZ\ *conj.* **1.** When indeed. **2.** Because.

wherewithal \HWAIR-with-awl\ *n.* An asset, especially financial.

whet \hwet\ *v.* whetted, whetting. **1.** To sharpen. **2.** To arouse.

whether \HWETH-ur\ *conj.* **1.** If it is or was indeed. **2.** If it be the case that. **3.** Either.

whey \hway\ *n.* The watery residue remaining after milk is processed into cheese.

which \hwich\ *adj.* **1.** Being what member of a group. **2.** Whichever or whatever. which *pron.*

whiff \hwif\ *n.* **1.** A subtle odor. **2.** A light breeze. whiff *v.*

while \hwiel\ *conj.* **1.** Throughout the time. **2.** As long as. **3.** Even though.

while \hwiel\ *n.* A period of time.

while \hwiel\ *v.* whiled; whiling. To pass time in a relaxing manner.

whim \hwim\ *n.* A spontaneous fantasy.

whimper \HWIM-pur\ *v.* whimpered; whimpering. To weep quietly. whimper *n.*

whimsical \HWIM-zi-kul\ *adj.* Fanciful. whimsically *adv.*; whimsicality *n.*

whimsy *also* **whimsey** \HWIM-zee\ *n. pl.* whimsies or whimseys.

1. Playfulness. **2.** Something unusual and charming.

whine \hwine\ *v.* whined; whining. **1.** To plaintively cry. **2.** To complain, especially using a high-pitched voice. whiny *adj.*; whine *n.*; whiner *n.*

whinny \HWIN-ee\ *v.* whinnied; whinnying. **1.** To quietly neigh like a horse.

whisk \hwisk\ *n.* **1.** A wire tool for mixing ingredients. **2.** A short-handled clothes brush.

whisk \hwisk\ *v.* whisked; whisking. **1.** To move quickly. **2.** To brush lightly. **3.** To gently mix food ingredients.

whisper \HWIS-pur\ *n.* **1.** Quiet speech. **2.** A secret. **3.** A trace.

whisper \HWIS-pur\ *v.* whispered; whispering. **1.** To speak quietly. **2.** To mention in confidence.

whistle \HWIS-ul\ *n.* **1.** A sharp sound. **2.** Something that produces a sharp sound.

whistle \HWIS-ul\ *v.* whistled; whistled. To make a sharp sound by forcing air through pursed lips. whistler *n.*

white \hwiet\ *adj.* whiter; whitest. **1.** Having no color. **2.** Of the color of alabaster. **3.** Having pale skin.

white \hwiet\ *n.* **1.** The absence of

color. **2.** The lightest part of something, such as an egg.

whitewash \HWIET-wosh\ *v.* whitewashed; whitewashing. **1.** To make very light using a bleaching liquid. **2.** To conceal wrongdoing. whitewash *n.*

whittle \HWIT-l\ *v.* whittled; whittling. **1.** To carve away at a piece of wood. **2.** To gradually wear away. whittler *n.*

whiz \hwiz\ *n.* **1.** A whooshing noise. **2.** [Sl] A genius.

whiz *also* **whizz** \hwiz\ *v.* whizzed; whizzing. To speed by.

who \hoo\ *pron.* **1.** Which person or persons. **2.** The person or persons that.

whoa \woh\ *interj.* Slow down or stop, especially said to an animal.

whodunit *also* **whodunnit** \hoo-DUN-it\ *n.* A mystery drama.

whole \hohl\ *adj.* **1.** Complete. **2.** Focused. **3.** In good health. **4.** An integral mathematic number.

whole \hohl\ *n.* **1.** Something in its entirety. **2.** On the whole: In light of events.

wholehearted \HOHL-hahr-tid\ *adj.* Dedicated. wholeheartedness *n.*

wholesale \HOHL-sayl\ *adj.* **1.** All-inclusive. **2.** Pertaining to the sale of a quantity of goods to retailers. wholesale *adv.*

wholesale \HOHL-sayl\ *n.* A sale of a quantity of goods to retailers. wholesaler *n.*; wholesale *v.*

wholesome \HOHL-sum\ *adj.* **1.** Healthy. **2.** Having proper morals. wholesomely *adv.*; wholesomeness *n.*

who'll \hool\ *v.* The contraction of who will.

whoosh \hwoosh\ *n.* A whistling sound produced from something speeding by. whoosh *v.*

whopping \HWOP-ing\ *adj.* Of tremendous size.

whore \hor\ *n.* One who exchanges sex for money. whorish *adj.*

why \hwie\ *adv.* For what purpose. why *conj.*

why \hwie\ *interj.* **1.** Approval granted. **2.** Impatience expressed.

wick \wik\ *n.* Joined fibers that draw up wax or oil to maintain a candle or lamp flame.

widespread \WIED-SPRED\ *adj.* Scattered about an extensive area.

width *n.* The amount of something from side to side.

wield \weeld\ *v.* wielded; wielding. **1.** To operate. **2.** To command. wielder *n.*

wife \wief\ *n. pl.* wives. A female

spouse. wifeless *adj.*; wifely *adj.*; wifehood *n.*

wig *n.* Something of natural or synthetic hair.

wiggle \WIG-ul\ *v.* wiggled; wiggling. To shake back and forth. wiggle *n.*

wild \wield\ *adj.* **1.** Undomesticated. **2.** Growing or existing without human contact. **3.** Unmanageable wild *adv.*; wildly *adv.*; wildness *n.*

wild \wield\ *n.* An uncultivated area. wilderness *n.*

wild card *n.* (Sl) Something that could not have been foreseen.

wildlife \WIELD-lief\ *n.* Animals living in their natural state.

wile \wiel\ *n.* A crafty seduction. wile *v.*

will \wil\ *n.* **1.** Ambition. **2.** A wish. **3.** A manner of acting toward others. **4.** Death wishes.

will \wil\ *v.* willed; willing. **1.** To wish. **2.** To order. **3.** To leave for another after death.

willful *also* **wilful** \WIL-ful\ *adj.* **1.** Stubborn. **2.** Intended. willfully *adv.*; willfullness *n.*

willing \WIL-ing\ *adj.* **1.** Wanting. **2.** Quick to react. **3.** Intended. **4.** Pertaining to choice. willingly *adv.*; willingness *n.*

willow \WIL-oh\ *n.* Rapidly growing tree or shrub with flexible branches; its wood.

willowy \WIL-oh-wee\ *adj.* **1.** Flexible. **2.** Being tall and thin.

willpower \WIL-pow-ur\ *n.* Personal discipline.

wilt \wilt\ *v.* wilted; wilting. **1.** To lose water and shrivel. **2.** To weaken.

wily \WIE-lee\ *adj.* wilier; wiliest. Deceptive. wiliness *n.*

win \win\ *n.* A triumph.

win \win\ *v.* won; winning. **1.** To triumph. **2.** To attain through work. **3.** To charm. winner *n.*

wind \wind\ *n.* **1.** A flow of air. **2.** Respiratory breath. **3.** [Sl] A notfication of. **4.** [Cl] Stomach gas.

wind \wiend\ *v.* wound or winded; winding. **1.** Bend along the way. **2.** To encircle around something. **3.** To continually turn.

windchill \WIND-chil\ *n.* The cooling effects of wind.

window \WIN-doh\ *n.* An opening in a wall to let in light.

windowpane \WIN-doh-payn\ *n.* A piece of glass spanning an opening in a wall.

windsurfer \WIND-Surf-ur\ *n.* **1.** A surfboard having an attached sail. **2.** One who operates such a vehicle. windsurf *v.*

windward \WIND-wurd\ *adj.*

Moving against the air current. windward *n.*

windy \WIN-dee\ *adj.* windier; windiest. **1.** Very breezy. **2.** (Sl) Afflicted with abundant stomach gas. **3.** (Sl) Chatty.

wine \wien\ *n.* A alcoholic beverage or cooking ingredient of fermented grape juice.

wine \wien\ *v.* wined; wining. To celebrate or drink wine.

wing *n.* **1.** An organ of flight. **2.** Something like a bird wing. **3.** Political faction.

wing *v.* winged; winging. **1.** To allow to fly. **2.** To fly. **3.** To disable. winged *adj.*

wink \wingk\ *n.* **1.** The act of signalling by quickly closing and opening one eye. **2.** A nap.

wink \wingk\ *v.* winked; winking. **1.** To signal by quickly closing and opening one eye. **2.** To blink. winker *n.*

winner \WIN-ur\ *n.* One who triumphs.

winter \WIN-tur\ *n.* **1.** The coldest months of the year. **2.** A period of little activity or growth. winter *adj.*; wintry or wintery *adj.*; winter *v.*

wipe \wiep\ *v.* wiped; wiping. **1.** To use a cloth to clean or dry. **2.** To take away. **3.** To pass over a surface. wipe *n.*; wiper *n.*

wire \wier\ *n.* **1.** A metal thread for electric current passage. **2.** A telegraph message.

wire \wier\ *v.* wired; wiring. **1.** Fit so that electricity can pass through. **2.** [Le] To hook up to a microphone.

wired \wierd\ *adj.* **1.** [Sl] Overanxious. **2.** [Sl] Socially connected. **3.** Hooked up via wire.

wiry \WIRE-ee\ *adj.* wirier; wiriest. Thin and muscular. wiriness *n.*

wisdom \WIZ-dum\ *n.* **1.** An outstanding knowledge. **2.** A keen sense.

wise \wiez\ *adj.* wiser; wisest. **1.** Having an outstanding knowledge. **2.** Having a keen sense. **3.** Well-informed. wisely *adv.*

wish *n.* **1.** A desire. **2.** Something yearned for.

wish *v.* wished; wishing. **1.** To desire. **2.** To express a desire for. wishful *adj.*; wishfully *adv.*

wishy-washy \WISH-ee-WOSH-ee\ *adj.* **1.** Indecisive. **2.** Bland.

wisp *n.* **1.** A bit of something. **2.** A strand. **3.** Something dainty. wispy *adj.*

wisteria \wi-STEER-ee-uh\ *n.* An Asian woody vine that has ornate blue, white, purple, or red flowers.

wistful \WIST-ful\ *adj.* Hopelessly longing. wistfully *adv.*; wistfulness *n.*

wit *n.* **1.** A clever sense of humor. **2.** A humorous person.

witch \wich\ *n.* **1.** Woman who practices sorcery. **2.** Hag. **3.** Bewitching woman. witchery *n.*; witch *v.*

with *prep.* **1.** In the company of. **2.** Close to. **3.** Full of. **4.** In support of. **5.** By the way.

withdraw \with-DRAW\ *v.* withdrew; withdrawn; withdrawing. **1.** To take back. **2.** To go back.

withdrawal \with-DRAWL\ *n.* **1.** The act of taking or going back. **2.** The process and effects of quitting.

withdrawn \with-DRAWN\ *adj.* **1.** Isolated. **2.** Unsociable.

wither \WITH-ur\ *v.* withered; withering. **1.** To shrivel from a lack of moisture. **2.** To become less lively.

withhold \with-HOHLD\ *v.* withheld; withholding. To keep back.

within \with-IN\ *adv.* **1.** Inside. **2.** Inwardly. within *n.*; within *prep.*

with-it *adj.* (Sl) Knowledgeable of current social and cultural events.

without \with-OWT\ *adv.* **1.** Externally. **2.** Lacking. without *prep.*

withstand \with-STAND\ *v.* withstood; withstanding. **1.** To face bravely. **2.** To oppose.

witness \WIT-nis\ *n.* **1.** A spectator to an event. **2.** [Le] Person summoned to appear in court. witness *v.*

witty \WIT-ee\ *adj.* wittier; wittiest. Having a clever sense of humor. wittily *adv.*; wittiness *n.*

wizard \WIZ-urd\ *n.* **1.** A sorcerer. **2.** A genius. wizardry *n.*

wizened \WIZ-und\ *adj.* Having lost water and appearing shriveled or wrinkled.

wobble \WOB-ul\ *v.* wobbled; wobbling. **1.** To move from one side to the other. **2.** To be unstable. wobbly *adj.*; wobble *n.*

wolf \wuulf\ *n. pl.* wolves. A meat-eating mammal related to the dog that hunts in packs.

wolf \wuulf\ *v.* To gobble down food. wolfish *adj.*

woman \WUUM-un\ *n. pl.* women. **1.** An adult female human. **2.** The females in the human race. womanlike *adj.*; womanly *adj.*; womanhood *n.*; womankind *n.*

womb \woom\ *n.* The female organ capable of reproduction that is also known as the uterus.

wombat \WOM-bat\ *n.* An Australian bearlike burrowing marsupial.

wonder \WUN-dur\ *n.* **1.** A spectacle. **2.** A phenomenon. **3.** Something that confuses. wonderful *adj.*; wondrous *adj.*; wonder *v.*

won't \wohnt\ *v.* The contraction of will not.

won ton \WON-TAHN\ *n. pl.* won tons. (Fo) Filled dough pockets boiled and served in soup.

woo *v.* **1.** To charm in the hopes of marrying. **2.** To please in hopes of gaining favor.

wood \wuud\ *n.* **1.** Durable material located beneath the bark of trees and shrubs. **2.** Forest. wood *adj.*; wooded *adj.*; wooden *adj.*; wood-edness *n.*; wood *v.*

woof \wuuf\ *n.* **1.** The crosswise threads in a woven fabric. **2.** The bark of a dog.

word \wurd\ *n.* **1.** Unit of letters and sounds that communicates a meaning. **2.** [Sl] A discussion.

word processing *n.* (Cm) Producing a document using a computer for typing, editing, etc. word processor *n.*

wore \wor\ *v.* The past tense of wear.

work \wurk\ *n.* **1.** Labor. **2.** A means of earning wages. **3.** Something received through effort.

work \wurk\ *v.* worked; working. **1.** To labor. **2.** To earn wages for labor. **3.** To produce a desired effect. work *adj.*; workable *adj.*; worker *n.*

workaholic \wurk-uh-HAW-lik\ *n.* One who obsessively works.

work ethic *n.* A belief that doing one's job well is morally responsible.

work on *v.* **1.** To have an influence on. **2.** To seek to persuade.

work out *v.* worked out; working out. **1.** To exercise. **2.** To resolve a conflict. **3.** To be effective. **4.** To formulate.

work up *v.* To arouse.

workout \WURK-owt\ *n.* **1.** A exercise session. **2.** A session that measures one's ability.

world \wurld\ *n.* **1.** The earth. **2.** The universe. **3.** Humankind. **4.** The happenings of humankind.

worldly \WURLD-lee.\ *adj.* worldlier; worldliest. **1.** Physical rather than the spiritual realm. **2.** Well-traveled. **3.** Sophisticated. worldliness *n.*

worldwide \WURLD-WIED\ *adj.* Being present internationally.

worn *v.* The past participle of wear.

worn-out \WORN-OWT\ *adj.* Tired or destroyed through use.

worrisome \WUR-ee-sum\ *adj.* **1.**

Full of emotional uneasiness. **2.** Causing emotional uneasiness.

worry \WUR-ee\ *v.* worried; worrying. **1.** To feel emotionally uneasy. **2.** To cause emotional uneasiness. worry *n.*; worrier *n.*

worrywart *n.* One who tends to experience emotional uneasiness unnecessarily.

worse \wurs\ *adj.* The comparative of bad and ill. worse *adv.*

worsen \WUR-sun\ *v.* worsened; worsening. **1.** To decline. **2.** To cause to decline.

worship \WUR-ship\ *n.* **1.** A glorification of an object or person. **2.** Devotion or admiration.

worship \WUR-ship\ *v.* worshiped or worshipped; worshiping or worshipping. **1.** To glorify an object or person. **2.** To be involved in religious ceremonies. worshipful *adj.*; worshiper or worshipper *n.*

worst-case *adj.* The least desirable.

worth \wurth\ *adj.* **1.** Deserving of. **2.** Having a certain value. **3.** Equal in value to. worthless *adj.*; worthy *adj.*; worthily *adv.*; worthiness *n.*; worthlessness *n.*

worth \wurth\ *n.* The expensiveness, usefulness, or emotional importance of an object or person.

worthwhile   \WURTH-HWIEL\

adj. Being deserving of the time and energy expended.

would \wuud\ *v.* The past tense of will.

wound \woond\ *v.* wounded; wounding. **1.** To cut the skin. **2.** To hurt one's feelings or reputation. wound *n.*

wound \wownd\ *v.* The past tense and past participle of wind.

wraith \rayth\ *n. pl.* wraiths. An apparition.

wrangle \RANG-gul\ *v.* wrangled; wrangling. **1.** To argue. **2.** To receive through an argument. **3.** To herd livestock. wrangle *n.*; wrangler *n.*

wrap \rap\ *n.* **1.** Something that surrounds. **2.** A shawl. **3.** [Pl] Confidence. wrapper *n.*; wrapping *n.*

wrap \rap\ *v.* wrapped; wrapping. **1.** To enclose with a covering. **2.** To get dressed. **3.** Under wraps (Pl): To keep in confidence.

wrap-up \RAP-up\ *n.* **1.** The close of a session. **2.** A summary. wrap up *v.*

wrath \rath\ *n.* **1.** A rage. **2.** A revenge. wrathful *adj.*; wrathfully *adv.*; wrathfulness *n.*

wreak \reek\ *v.* To bring about.

wreath \reeth\ *n. pl.* wreaths. An intertwined decorative circle of flowers, twigs, etc. wreathe *v.*

wreck \rek\ *n.* An object or person

damaged or in a state of devastation. wrecked *adj.*; wreckage *n.*; wreck *v.*

wrench \rench\ *n.* **1.** A forcible twist. **2.** A tool for grasping and twisting.

wrench \rench\ *v.* wrenched; wrenching. **1.** To injure through a forcible twist. **2.** To loosen or tighten through twisting.

wrestle \RES-ul\ *v.* wrestled; wrestling. **1.** To struggle on the ground in an attempt to pin the other down. **2.** To contend. wrestle *n.*; wrestler *n.*; wrestling *n.*

wretched \RECH-id\ *adj.* **1.** Sad. **2.** Mean. **3.** Being below standard in quality or ability. wretchedly *adv.*; wretch *n.*; wretchedness *n.*

wriggle \RIG-ul\ *v.* wriggled; wriggling. **1.** To move by twisting and turning. **2.** To free oneself from difficulties. wriggle *n.*; wriggler *n.*

wring \ring\ *v.* wrung; wringing. **1.** To squeeze dry. **2.** To draw out through force. **3.** To strangle. **4.** To twist. wringer *n.*

wrinkle \RING-kul\ *v.* wrinkled; wrinkling. To have or cause to have one or more tiny folds over the surface of. wrinkly *adj.*; wrinkle *n.*

wrist \rist\ *n.* The section between the hand and the arm.

wristband \RIST-band\ *n.* A strap or part around the part between the hand and arm.

writ \rit\ *n.* (Le) A written court order.

write \riet\ *v.* wrote; written; writing. **1.** To inscribe words or symbols on something. **2.** To author. writer *n.*

write-in \RIET-in\ *n.* **1.** A vote cast by adding a name to a ballot. **2.** A candidate who was written in. write in *v.*

write off \RIET-awf\ *v.* **1.** To forget about. **2.** To lower the value of.

writer's block *n.* A period in which an author's creativity suffers due to a lack of inspiration.

writhe \rieth\ *v.* writhed; writhing. To move back and forth in agony.

wrong \rawng\ *adj.* **1.** Incorrect. **2.** Against current standards of law and morals. **3.** Unsuitable. wrongful *adj.*; wrongfully *adv.*; wrongly *adv.*

wrong \rawng\ *n.* **1.** Harmful, unfair, immoral, or illegal act. **2.** The state of being such.

wrong \rawng\ *v.* wronged; wronging. **1.** To harm. **2.** To be unfair to. wrongdoer *n.*; wrongdoing *n.*; wrongfulness *n.*

wry \rie\ *adj.* wryer; wryest. **1.** Bent to one side, as in a facial feature. **2.** Sarcastic. wryly *adv.*; wryness *n.*

wurst \wuurst\ *n.* (Gr) A sausage.

X

x \eks\ *n. pl.* x's or xs. **1.** The 24th letter of the English alphabet. **2.** An unknown amount.

Xanadu \za-nuh-DOO\ *n.* A location of idyllic loveliness.

xanthous \zan-THUS\ *adj.* Yellow.

X chromosome *n.* (Sc) A cell chromosome that determines the female sex if paired.

xenophobia \zen-uh-FOH-bee-uh\ *n.* An irrational fear and hatred of that which is strange or foreign. xenophobic *adj.*; xenophobe *n.*

Xerox \ZEER-oks\ *n.* A photocopying process or a copy made by this process. xerox *v.*

Xmas *n.* An abbreviation for Christmas.

x-rated \eks-RAY-tud\ *adj.* (Sl) Containing daring or pornographic material suitable for mature audiences only.

X ray \EKS-ray\ *n.* (Md) Radiation having a short wavelength that is able to penetrate a solid surface. X-ray *adj.*; x-ray *v.*

X-ray astronomy *n.* (Sc) The study of celestial objects through the X rays they give off.

xylem \ZIE-lum\ *n.* A plant tissue responsible for carrying water and dissolved material upward.

xylophone \ZIE-luh-fohn\ *n.* (Mu) Percussion instrument of row of graduated wooden bars on a chromatic scale. xylophonist *n.*

Y

y \wie\ *n. pl.* y's or ys. The 25th letter of the English alphabet.

yacht \yot\ *n.* A sailing vehicle used for pleasure cruising or racing. yachting *n.*; yacht *v.*

yahoo \YAH-hoo\ *n. pl.* yahoos. An unintelligent and barbaric person.

Yahweh *also* **Yahveh** \YAH-we\ *n.* [He] The Hebrew God.

yank \yangk\ *n.* A quick and strong pull. yank *v.*

yap *v.* yapped; yapping. **1.** To bark shrilly. **2.** To babble. yap *n.*; yapper *n.*

yard \yahrd\ *n.* **1.** A measurement of three feet or 0.9144 meters. **2.** An area open to the sky.

yard sale *n.* A sale of donated or second-hand goods that is held outdoors.

yarn \yahrn\ *n.* **1.** A continuous strand of spun wool for knitting. **2.** A long, imaginative story.

yawn *v.* yawned; yawning. To spread open the mouth from exhaustion or boredom.

Y chromosome *n.* (Md) A cell chromosome that determines the male sex if paired with an X chromosome.

yea \yay\ *n.* **1.** An affirmative vote. **2.** One who casts an affirmative vote. yea *adv.*

yeah \yay\ *n.* (Sl) **1.** A reply. **2.** An affirmative response.

year \yeer\ *n.* A length of time from

January 1 to December 31 consisting of 365 days, 52 weeks.

year-end \YEER-END\ *adj.* Happening at the close of an annual period.

yearly \YEER-lee\ *adj.* Occurring annually.

yearn \yurn\ *v.* yearned; yearning. To experience an intense and lasting desire. yearning *n.*

yell \yel\ *v.* yelled; yelling. **1.** To shout. **2.** To communicate a team cheer. yell *n.*

yellow \YEL-oh\ *n.* Color lying between green and orange in the spectrum, as a lemon or banana. yellow *adj.*; yellow *v.*

yellow pages *n.* A telephone listing of businesses and services.

yelp *v.* yelped; yelping. To utter a short, high-pitched cry. yelp *n.*

yen *n.* A craving.

yes *n.* An affirmative reply, answer, or vote. yes *adv.*

yesterday \YES-tur-day\ *n.* **1.** The day prior to today. **2.** A time not long ago. yesterday *adv.*

yesteryear \YES-tur-yeer\ *n.* **1.** The past.

yet *adv.* **1.** Up until this moment. **2.** Even though. **3.** In addition. **4.** In a future time.

yet *conj.* However.

yield \yeeld\ *n.* **1.** An amount produced. **2.** A profit.

yield \yeeld\ *v.* yielded; yielding. **1.** To bring forth. **2.** To surrender. **3.** To agree.

yo \yoh\ *interj.* (Sl) **1.** Hello! **2.** Hey!

yoga \YOH-guh\ *n.* (Fo) **1.** [Cap] Hindu philosophy of spiritual insight. **2.** System of soft exercises.

yogi *also* **yogin** \YOH-gee\ *n.* (Fo) **1.** One who does yoga. **2.** One who practices Yoga.

yogurt *also* **yoghurt** \YOH-gurt\ *n.* A sour puddinglike food made of curdled milk.

yoke \yohk\ *n. pl.* yokes. **1.** Curved wood frame for coupling animals. **2.** Similar instrument; connector. yoke *v.*

yonder \YON-dur\ *adv.* In a faraway location. yonder *adj.*

you \yoo\ *pron.* The plural pronoun or second person singular in the subjective or objective case.

young \yung\ *adj.* younger; youngest. **1.** In an early stage of life. **2.** Experiencing something for the first time. youngish *adj.*

young \yung\ *n.* A person or animal that has recently come into life. youngster *n.*

your \yuur\ *adj..* Of or belonging to you.

you're \yor\ *v.* The contraction of you are.

yours \yuurs\ *pron.* One or the ones in your possession.

yourself \yor-SELF\ *pron. pl.* yourselves. The reflexive and emphatic form of you.

youth \yooth\ *n. pl.* youths. **1.** Life falling between childhood and adulthood. **2.** State of being young.

youth hostel *n.* A temporary lodging for young people.

youthful \YOOTH-ful\ *adj.* **1.** Being between childhood and adulthood. **2.** Young or new. youthfulness *n.*

yowl *v.* yowled; yowling. To release a long, loud cry. yowl *n.*

yo-yo \yoh-yoh\ *n. pl.* yo-yos. A toy that unwinds and rewinds on a string between two disks. yo-yo *v.*

yuck \yuk\ *interj.* (Sl) An expression of displeasure or offense.

yucky \YUK-ee\ *adj.* (Sl) Offensive.

Yule log *n.* Tree log placed on the hearth on Christmas Eve.

yuletide \YOOL-tied\ *n.* Christmas or the Christmas season.

yummy \YUM-ee\ *adj.* yummier; yummiest. (Sl) Pleasing to one's taste.

yuppie \YUP-ee\ *n.* (Sl) An often derogatory term for a young, upwardly mobile professional. yuppify *v.*

Z

z \zee\ *n. pl.* z's or zs. The 26th letter of the English alphabet.

zany \ZAY-nee\ *adj.* zanier; zaniest. **1.** Silly. **2.** Acting like a clown. zany *n.*

zeal \zeel\ *n.* A passionate devotion. zealous *adj.*; zealously *adv.*; zealousness *n.*

zebra \ZEE-bruh\ *n.* A striped horselike mammal native to Africa.

zed *n.* (Fo) The letter z.

zenith \ZEE-nith\ *n.* **1.** Point in sky directly above the observer. **2.** The uppermost point.

zephyr \ZEF-ur\ *n.* **1.** A wind from the west. **2.** A subtle breeze. **3.** Lightweight textile.

zero \ZEER-oh\ *n. pl.* zeros or zeroes. **1.** A word indicating the number zero. **2.** The lowest point. **3.** Nothing. zero *adj.*

zero hour *n.* The vital moment of a scheduled event, such as a military operation.

zero in *v.* zeroed in; zeroing in. **1.** To aim a weapon at. **2.** To surround. **3.** To focus.

zest *n.* **1.** Enthusiasm. **2.** A spicy flavor. **3.** A shredded lemon or orange peel. zestful *adj.*; zesty *adj.*; zestfully *adv.*; zestfulness *n.*

zigzag \ZIG-zag\ *n.* **1.** A jagged line. **2.** Any one of the several sharp turns in a jagged line. zigzag *adj.*; zigzag *adv.*; zigzag *v.*

zilch *adj.* Lacking everything under consideration. zilch *n.*

zing *n.* **1.** A shrill sound. **2.** Liveliness. zing *v.*

zip *n.* **1.** A short, hissing noise. **2.** Enthusiasm.

zip *v.* zipped; zipping. **1.** To open or close with a zipper. **2.** To proceed quickly. zippy *adj.*

zip code *n.* A five-digit identification code for a U.S. postal delivery area.

zipper \ZIP-ur\ *n.* A fastener having two rows of teeth that interlock, esp. on clothing. zipper *v.*

zodiac \ZOH-dee-ak\ *n.* **1.** Twelve ruling constellations or signs. **2.** These in fortunetelling. zodiacal *adj.*

zombie \ZOM-bee\ *n.* **1.** Dead body brought to life by voodoo. **2.** Person whose behavior is as if dead.

zone \zohn\ *n.* **1.** Area distinguished by a quality or purpose. **2.** Five climate regions of Earth. zonal *adj.*; zonally *adv.*

zone \zohn\ *v.* zoned; zoning. **1.** To separate into distinct areas. **2.** To encircle.

zonked \zongkt\ *adj.* (Sl) **1.** Being or acting as if one were intoxicated or high. **2.** Overwhelmed.

zoo *n. pl.* zoos. Collection of living animals on public display; the park itself.

zoology \zoh-OL-uh-jee\ *n.* (Sc) A branch of biology concerned with the study of animals and their environment. zoological *adj.*; zoologist *n.*

zoom *v.* zoomed; zooming. **1.** Quickly achieve a high altitude. **2.** To move with speed. **3.** To focus a lens. zoom *n.*

zoot suit \ZOOT-SOOT\ *n.* One-piece clothing that zips in front. zootsuiter *n.*

zucchini \zoo-KEE-nee\ *n. pl.* zucchini or zucchinis. A cylindrical, smooth-surfaced, green-skinned type of squash.

zygote \ZIE-goht\ *n.* (Md) The fertilized female egg.

Appendices

ABBREVIATIONS

A & M	Agricultural and Mechanical	alter	alteration
AD	anno Domini	Am, Amer	America, American
ab	about	AmerF	American French
abbr	abbreviation	AmerInd	American Indian
abl	ablative	AmerSp	American Spanish
absol	absolute, absolutely	AN	Anglo-Norman
Acad	Academy	anat	anatomy
acc	accusative	anc	ancient, anciently
act	active	angl	anglicized
adj	adjective	ant	antonym
adv	adverb	anthrop	anthropologist, anthropology
AF	Anglo-French	aor	aorist
AFB	Air Force Base	apos	apostrophe
Afr	Afrika	approx	approximate, approximately
Afrik	Afrikaans		
Agric	Agriculture	Ar	Arabic
Alb	Albanian, Albania	Arab	Arabian, Arabic
alt	altitude	Aram	Aramaic

arch	archaic
archaeol	archaeologist
archit	architecture
Argen	Argentine
Arm	Armenian
art	article
AS	Anglo-Saxon
assoc	association
Assyr	Assyrian
astron, astr	astronomer, astronomy
attrib	attributive, attributively
atty	attorney
aug	augmentative
Austral	Australian
av	average
AV	Authorized Version
Av	Avestan
b	born
BC	before Christ; British Columbia
Bab	Babylonian
bacteriol	bacteriologist
bef	before
Belg	Belgian, Belgium
Beng	Bengali
bet	between
bib	biblical
bibliog	bibliography
biochem	biochemist
biol	biologist
bot	botany

Braz	Brazilian
Bret	Breton
Brit	Britain, British
bro	brother
Bulg	Bulgarian, Bulgaria
C	centigrade; College
c	century
ca, c	circa
Canad, Can	Canadian, Canada
CanF	Canadian French
Cant	Cantonese
cap	capital, capitalized
Catal	Catalan
caus	causative
Celt	Celtic
cen	center, central
cent	century
Ch	Church
chem	chemistry, chemical
Chin	Chinese
Chron	Chronicles
class	classical
co(s)	county (counties)
Col	Columbia, Colossians
coll	college
collect	collective, collectively
colloq	colloquial, colloquially
comb	combining, combination
Comm	Community
compar	comparative

Confed	Confederate
conj	conjugation; conjunction
constr	construction
contr	contraction
cook	cookery
Copt	Coptic
Cor	Corinthians
Corn	Cornish
criminol	criminologist
Croat	Croatian
cu	cubic
d	died
D, Du	Dutch
Dan	Danish; Daniel
dat	dative
dau	daughter
def	definite
Den	Denmark
dept	department
deriv	derivative
derog	derogatory
Deut	Deuteronomy
dial	dialect
dim	diminutive
disc	discovered
dist	district
div	division
Dom Rep	Dominican Republic
Dor	Doric
dram	dramatist
DV	Douay Version
dyn	dynamics

e	eastern
e	estimate
E	east, eastern; English
e.g.	exempli gratia (for example)
eccl	ecclesiastical
econ	economist
Ed	Education
EE	Early English
EGmc	East Germanic
Egypt	Egyptian
elec	electrical
emp	emperor
Eng	England, English
equiv	equivalent
Esk	Eskimo
esp	especially
est	estimated, estimate
estab	established
et al	et alii (and others)
etc	et cetera (and so forth)
Eth	Ethiopic
ethnol	ethnologist
exc	except
excl	excludes, excluding, exclusive
exclam	exclamation
f	founded
F	French; Fahrenheit
Fahr	Fahrenheit
fam	family
fed	federation

fem, f	feminine
ff	following
fig	figurative, figuratively
Fin	Finland
Finn	Finnish
fl	flourished
Flem, Fl	Flemish
form	former, formerly
fr	from
Fr	France, French
fr	from
freq	frequentative
Fris	Frisian
ft	feet, foot
fut	future
G	German
Gael	Gaelic
gen	general; genitive
geog	geography
geol	geology
geom	geometry
Ger	German, Germany
Gk, Gr	Greek
Gmc	Germanic
Goth	Gothic
gov	governor
govt	government
Gr Brit	Great Britain
gram	grammar
Heb	Hebrew
her	heraldry
Hind	Hindustani
hist	historian, history
Hitt	Hittite
Hon	Honduras
hort	horticulture
Hung	Hungarian
Hung	Hungarian, Hungary
I	Indian
I	island
i.e.	id est (that is)
Icel	Icelandic
IE	Indo-European
imit	imitative
imper	imperative
in	inch
incho	inchoative
incl	included, includes, including
incorp	incorporated
Ind	India, Indian
indef	indefinite
indep	independent
indic	indicative
infin	infinitive
inst	institute, institution
instr	instrumental
intens	intensive
interj	interjection
interrog	interrogative
Ion	Ionic
Ir	Irish
Ire	Ireland
IrGael	Irish Gaelic
irreg	irregular

ISV	International Scientific Vocabulary
It, Ital	Italian, Italy
ital	italic
Jav	Javanese
joc	jocular, jocularly
Jp	Japanese, Japan
L	Latin
LaF	Louisiana French
lat	latitude
Lat	Latin
LG	Low German
LGk	Late Greek
LHeb	Late Hebrew
lit	literally; literary
Lith	Lithuanian, Lithuania
liturg	liturgical, liturgy
LL	Late Latin
long	longitude
m	meters; mile; masculine
manuf	manufacturer
masc	masculine
math	mathematician
max	maximum
MBret	Middle Breton
MD	Middle Dutch
ME	Middle English
Mech	Mechanical
mech	mechanics
Med	Medical
med	medicine
Medit	Mediterranean

met	metropolitan
meteor	meteorology
Mex	Mexican; Mexico
MexSp	Mexican Spanish
MF	Middle French
MFlem	Middle Flemish
mfr	manufacture
MGk	Middle Greek
MHG	Middle High German
mi	miles
mil	military
min	minister
MIr	Middle Irish
ML	Medieval Latin
MLG	Middle Low German
mod	modern
ModE	Modern English
modif	modification
Mongol	Mongolian
MPer	Middle Persian
MS	manuscript(s)
mt	mount, mountain
munic	municipal
mus	music
MW	Middle Welsh
myth	mythology
N	North, northern
n	northern; noun
n pl	noun plural
naut	nautical
NE	New England
Neth	Netherlands
neut, n	neuter

New Eng	New England
New Zeal	New Zealand
NGk	New Greek
NGmc	North Germanic
NHeb	New Hebrew
NL	New Latin
nom	nominative
nonstand	nonstandard
Norw	Norwegian, Norway
nov	novelist
nr	near
NT	New Testament
NZ	New Zealand
obs	obsolete
OCatal	Old Catalan
occas	occasionally, occasional
OE	Old English
OF	Old French
off	official
OFris	Old Frisian
OGael	Old Gaelic
OHG	Old High German
OIr	Old Irish
OIt	Old Italian
OL	Old Latin
ON	Old Norse
ONF	Old North French
Ont	Ontario
OPer	Old Persian
OPg	Old Portuguese
opp	opposite
OProv	Old Provençal

OPruss	Old Prussian
org	organized
orig	original, originally
ornith	ornithology
ORuss	Old Russian
OS	Old Saxon
OSlav	Old Slavic
OSp	Old Spanish
OT	Old Testament
OW	Old Welsh
p	page
PaG	Pennsylvania German
part, partic	participle
pass	passive
path	pathology
Pek	Pekingese
Per, Pers	Persian
perf	perfect
perh	perhaps
pers	person
Pg	Portuguese
Phil	Philippines
philos	philosopher
PhilSp	Philippine Spanish
photog	photography
phys	physics, physical
physiol	physiologist
pl	plural
poet	poetical
Pol	Polish, Poland
polit	political, politician
pop	population
Port	Portuguese, Portugal

pp	past participle; pages
PR	Puerto Rico
prec	preceding
predic	predictive, predicatively
prep	preposition
pres	present; president
prob	probably
pron	pronoun; pronunciation, pronounced
pronunc	pronunciation
propr	proprietary
Prov	Provençal
prp	present participle
Pruss	Prussian
pseud	pseudonym
psychol	psychologist
pub	published
qqv, qv	quod vide (which see)
R.C. or RC	Roman Catholic
redupl	reduplication
refl	reflexive
rel	relative
relig	religion
resp	respectively
rev	revolution
rhet	rhetoric, rhetorical
riv	river
Rom	Roman; Romanian, Romania
RSV	Revised Standard Version

Rum	Rumanian
Russ	Russian
S	south, southern
S Afr	South Africa, South African
S Amer	South America, South American
Sc	Scotch, Scots
Scand, Scan	Scandinavian
ScGael	Scottish Gaelic
Sch	School
sci	science
Scot, Sc	Scotland, Scottish
Scrip	Scripture
secy	secretary
Sem	Seminary, Semitic
Serb	Serbian
Shak	Shakespeare
sig	signature
sing	singular
Skt	Sanskrit
Slav	Slavic
So Afr	South Africa, South African
sociol	sociologist
Sp, Span	Spanish
specif, spec	specifically
spp	species
St	Saint
Ste	Sainte
subj	subjunctive
substand	substandard
superl	superlative

Sw, Swed	Swedish
Switz	Switzerland
syn	synonym, synonymy
Syr	Syriac
Tag	Tagalog
Tasm	Tasmania
Tech	Technology
techn	technical
theat	theatre
theol	theologian, theology
Theol	Theological
Toch	Tocharian
trans	translation
treas	treasury
Turk	Turkish
U	University
UK	United Kingdom
Ukrain	Ukrainian
univ	university
US	United States, America, American
USA	United States of America
USSR	Union of Soviet Socialist Republic
usu	usually, usual
v, vb	verb
var	variant
Ven	Venezuela
vi	verb intransitive
VL	Vulgar Latin
voc	vocative
vt	verb transitive
W	Welsh; west, western
WGmc	West Germanic
zool	zoologist

AFFIXES (SUFFIXES, PREFIXES, AND COMBINING FORMS)

-able, -ible, -ile (form adjs) able to, fit to, worthy, capable; apt to; subject to being ~-ed

-ac characteristic of

-ac, -al, -ane, -ar, -ary, -ch, -ese, -ic, -ical, -id, -ile, -ine, -ish, -ory like, of, pertaining to; characterized by

-aceae families of plants

-aceous, -ous resemblance to a substance; full of

-acy, -age, -ance, -ancy, -asm, -dom, -ence, -ency, -hood, -ism, -ity, -ment, -mony, -ness, -ry, -ship, -th, -tude, -ty, -ure, -y (form nouns) state, condition, quality of being; result

-acy, -ate, -dom, -ric, -ship (form nouns) rank, office, jurisdiction, dominion

-ade product; action

-age place of; house

-age rate of; charge

-age, -ion, -sion, -tion, -ment, -ure (form nouns) act of; thing done, process

-age, -ry (form nouns) persons or things collectively; measure of; collection of

-al action or result of; process

-algia pain

-an, -ant, -ar, -ard, -art, -ary, -aster, -ate, -ean, -ee, -eer, -ent, -er, -ic, -iff, -ist, -ite, -ive, -or, -ster, -yte (form nouns) one who acts, one who is

-an, -ean, -ian adherent to; citizen of; language of; relating to, characteristic of

-ana, -iana collection

-ance, -ancy state, quality of being; action, process; degree

-androus man

-ant, -ent (form adjs) being, belonging to; performing

-archy government

-ary related, connected to

-ary, -ery, -ory, -ry (form nouns) place where, place which

-ary, -ice, -ment, -mony, -ory (form nouns) thing which

-ate salt, ester for acid (substitute for -ic)

-ate, -en, -fy, -ish, -ise, -ize (form verbs) to make; to put; to take; cause

-ate, -ful, -lent, -ose, -ous, -some, -y (form adjs) full of, abundant; having

-ation process, action; state of

-ative related, connected to; tending

-biosis life

-blast bud, germ, cell

-carpous fruit

-cele hollow, tumor

-celli, -cello little

-cephalic, -cephalous head

-chrome color, colored

-cide, -cidal kill, killing

-cle, -cule, -el, -en, -et, -ie, -kin, -le, -let, -ling, -ock, -ot, -ule, -y (form nouns) little, diminutive

-coccus berry-shaped

-coele, -coel cavity

-cracy/-ocracy, -crat/-ocrat government, rule; ruler

-dendron tree

-derm, -derma, -dermo skin, covering

-dom domain, office, jurisdiction

-drome large place; racing place

-dromous running

-eae names of sub-orders in botany

-ed (form adjs from nouns) having

-ed past tense, past participle of regular verbs

-ee one who is object of the verb

-ee small kind of ~; something suggestive of a ~

-eer one skilled, engaged in

-emia, -aemia, -hemia, -haemia blood

-en (form verbs) to cause to, to become, to make

-en (form adjs) made of; belonging to

-en plural form of some nouns

-en, -n, -ne past participle of some irregular verbs

-ene belonging to; carbon

-er a little; often

-er comparative form of adjective

-er having as characteristic

-er the thing contained; inhabitant of, native

-er, -or producer, agent; one that is

-erel little

-erly, -ward, -wards (form adverbs) direction

-ern (form adjs) direction

-ery, -ry condition or behavior of; location of; aggregate

-escent (adjs), -escence (nouns) growing, becoming; incipient state, beginning

-escent reflecting light

-ese member, native, style, language of

-ese originating in ~

-esque (form adjs) belonging to; like, having the properties, manner of

-ess noun of female sex

-est superlative form of adjective; second person singular present of some irregular verbs

-eth third person singular of some irregular verbs

-ette compact; imitation; feminine

-fid split

-fuge, fugal making flee, run away from

-ful holding all it can, full of; amount that fills

-ful providing ~; characterized by; tending to

-gamy marriage; possession

-gen, -genous, -geny, -gony bearing, producing, giving birth; producer

-gnomy, -gnosis knowledge

-gon angled

-gonium seed

-grade walking

-gram, -graph, -graphy writing; record

-hedral, -hedron side, many-sided

-hood period of a condition, state; membership

-ia things belonging to; territory

-ia, -iasis disease

-ia, -ious class, order or genus of plants and animals

-iatrics, -iatry medical treatment

-ic acid containing most oxygen

-ic having the properties of, related, in the manner of; using ~; affected with ~

-ic one having the nature of; producer

-ics, -ism, -ry, -ure thing relating to a system, practice, art, science; pecularity, characteristic(s)

-idae, -adae, -ides descendent

-ide, -ides (plural) chemical combination

-idean, -ides, -eides, -oides (preceded by 'o') resemblance, likeness to

-ify, -fy (form verbs) to make ~; make similar to

-ine chemical compound

-ine female

-ine made of

-ing imperative ending of regular verbs

-ing something made of such material; activity, process; noun referring to V

-ior more

-ique belonging to

-ish person of, language of

-ish, -like, -ly (form adjs) somewhat like, becoming; relating to

-isk little

-ism practice of; doctrine of, theory; act, process; state, condition

-ist skilled in, specialist; practicing ~, believer

-ite acid (-ous) combination

-ite body part

-ite one who; adherent, member, inhabitant; that which; product

-ite stone, mineral

-itious having the characteristic of

-itis inflammation of an organ, disease; excessive enthusiasm

-ity state, condition, quality of being; degree

-ive able to do, capable; doing, tending

-ix female

-ization action, result of making ~

-ize, -ise (form verbs) to make ~, to subject to ~; cause to be, be like; become, adopt manner

-kin little; son of

-kind kind; race

-kinesis division; movement

-le often (verb), little (noun)

-lepsy seizure, fit

-less without, deprived; unable

-let small, unimportant; thing worn on ~

-like like, resembling

-ling minor, offspring, one having quality of ~

-lite, -lith stone, mineral

-logy science of, study of, theory; list

-ly in a manner of, having the qualities of, like; to a degree

-ly recurring regularly

-lysis, -lyte dissolving; disintegration

-machy battle, fight

-mancy, -mantic foretelling

-mania, -maniac craving

-mere, -merous part

-meter, -metry measure; instrument

-morphic, -morphous shape

-most superlative form of adjective

-mycete fungus

-nomy science of, law of

-odont tooth of ~ nature

-odynia pain

-oecium, -oecious flowers' stamens and pistils in botany

-oid like, resembling

-oid likeness, resemblance

-oma tumor

-on unit, particle*

-on, -one, -oon (form nouns) large

-opia eye, sight condition

-opsia sight

-opsis appearance; thing resembling ~

-ous acid compound with less oxygen (than -ic)

-ous, -ious having the properties of; full of

-pathy suffering, disease; type of medical treatment

-pennale wing

-phage, -phagous, -phagia, -phagy eating, eater

-phany manifestation

-phobe one fearing ~

-phobia fear of ~

-phobic fearing; lacing affinity for

-phone, -phony sound, transmitting sound

-phonia speech disorder

-phyllous leafed, leaflike

-phyte plant; diseased growth

-plasia, -plasy, -plasis growth, formation

-plasm formed matter

-plast cell

-plegia paralysis

-plerous wing

-red state, condition; those who

-rrhagia, -rrhagic, -rrhea flow

-saur lizard

-scope, -scopy observation; observing instrument

-se to make

-sect, -section cut, divide; divided

-ship state or condition of; rank, position; skill; group participating in ~

-soma, -some body

-sophy wisdom, knowledge

-sperm, -spermous seed

-ster one who is involved in; one that is ~

-stichous row

-stome, -stomous mouth

-stress female

-taxis, -taxy order

-teen ten, to be added to

-th state, condition; act, process

-tomy cutting; section

-trophy feed, nutrition

-tropic changing; attracted to ~

-tropous, -tropy turning, turned, curving

-ty quality, degree; condition

-ty ten, to be multiplied by

-vorous eating

-ward, -wards in the direction of

-ways, -wise in the manner of, in the direction of; way of being or acting

-y somewhat like, rather, characterized by, tending

-y state, condition; activity; group

-y, -ey full of

a-, ab-, abs- from, away from

a-, an- at, in, on; in such a manner, state, or condition

a-, an- not, without, lacking

ac-, ad-, af-, ag-, al-, an-, ap-, as-, at- to, toward, near

acanth-, acantho- spiny, thorny

acous- hearing

acr-, acro- top; extremity, end

aden-, adeno- gland

adren-, adreno- adrenal gland

aer-, aero- air, gas

all-, allo- other, different

alti-, alto- high

am-, amb-, ambi-, amphi- both, both sides; round; about

amyl-, amylo- starch

ana- again; thorough, thoroughly

ana-, an- up, upward; back, backward

andr-, andro- man; male

anem-, anemo- wind

ant-, ante- before, prior, earlier; in front of

anthrop-, anthropo- man

anti-, ant-, anth- against, opposite; combating, defending

api- bee

apo-, ap- away; from; related

aqui-, aqua- water

arbor-, arbori- tree

arch-, archi- chief, principal, supreme; extreme

arche-, archeo-, archae-, archaeo- old, ancient

arteri-, arterio- artery

arthr-, arthro- joint

astr-, astro-, aster- star

atmo- vapor

audio- hearing, sound

auto- self-moving

avi- bird

az-, azo- nitrogenous

bacci- berry

bacteri-, bacterio- bacteria

bar-, baro- weight, pressure

bath-, batho-, bathy- deep, depth

be- to make, cause; to take from

be- on, over; against, across; thoroughly, excessively

bi-, bio- life, living

bi-, bis- twice, two, double, in two

biblio- book

blephar-, blepharo- eyelid, eyelash

bracchio- arm

brachy- short

brevi- short

bronch-, broncho-, bronchi-, bronchio- throat, lung

caco- evil

calci- lime

cardio- heart

carpo- fruit

cat-, cata-, cath-, cato- down, downward, under; against; completeness, thorough, thoroughly

cen-, ceno- new, recent

centi- hundred

cephal-, cephalo- head

cerebro- brain

cervic-, cervico-, cervici- neck

chiro- hand

chlor-, chloro- green

chol-, chole-, cholo- bile

chondr-, chondri-, chondro- cartilage

choreo- dance

choro- country

chrom-, chromo-, chromato- color, colored

chron-, chrono- time

chrys-, chryso- gold

circum-, circu- around, about

cirr-, cirri-, cirro- curl

cis- on this side; near

cleisto- closed

con-, co-, cog-, col-, com-, cor- together, with; thorough, thoroughly

contra- against, in opposition, contrasting, contrary

cosmo- universe

counter- against, in opposition; substitute

cranio- skull

cruci- cross

cry-, cryo- cold

crypt-, crypto- hidden

cupro- copper; bronze

cyst-, cysti-, cysto- bladder, sac

cyt-, cyto- cell

dactyl-, dactylo- finger, toe

de- down, from, separation; not; reverse; remove; get of; derived

deca-, deci-, dec-, deka-, dek- ten

demi- half, part of

dent-, denti-, dento- tooth

dentro- three

derm-, derma- dermo- skin

deut-, deuto-, deutero- second

dextr-, dextro- right side

di- two

dia-, di- through, across

digit-, digiti- finger

dipl-, diplo- double, twofold

dis- exclude, remove; do opposite

dis-, dif-, di- not, opposite; apart; two

dodeca-, dodec- twelve

dors-, dorsi-, dorso- back of body

dyna-, dynamo- force, power

dys-, dis- badly, difficult, hard; evil; abnormal

echin-, echino- spine

ect-, ecto- outside, external

ef-, e-, ec- out, not, absent

el-, em-, en- in, into, on, within

en-, em- cause to be, to make; to surround, cover

encephal-, encephalo- brain

end-, endo- inside, within

ennea- nine

ent-, ento- inside, within

enter-, entero- intestine

entomo- insect

eo- early, old

epi-, ep- on, upon, beside, above; out, on the outside; during

equi- equal, alike

erg-, ergo- work

erythr-, erythro- red

ethno- race, nation

eu- good, well; true

ex-, exo- from; out, out of, outside, external; without; former

extra- on the outside, external; beyond, in excess, additional, exceptionally

febri- fever

ferri-, ferro- iron

fibr-, fibro- threadlike, fibrous

fissi- split

fluvio- river

for- not; against, forth; away; prohibitive

fore- before, early; in front of, front part of

gain- against

galact-, galacto- milk

gam-, gamo- together; copulation

gastr-, gastro-, gastri- stomach, eating

ge-, geo- earth, land

gem-, gemmi- bud

geront-, geronto- old age

gloss-, glosso- tongue; language

gluc-, gluco-, glyc- sweet

glypto-, glyph- carving

gon-, gono- reproduction

grapho- writing

gymn-, gymno- naked

gynec-, gyneco-, gynaec-, gynaeco- woman

hagi-, hagio- holy

hal-, halo- salt, sea

hapl-, haplo- simple, single

hect-, hecto- hundred

heli-, helio- sun

helic-, helico- spiral

hem-, hemo-, haem-, haemo-, haemato-, hema- blood

hemi- half

hepat-, hepato- liver

hepta-, hept- seven

hetero-, heter- different, opposite, irregular, abnormal; another

hexa-, hex- six

hist-, histo- tissue

hodo- path, way

hol-, holo- whole, complete, total

hom-, homo-, homeo- similar, same, alike

hydr-, hydro- water, liquid

hyet-, hyeto- rain

hygr-, hygro- wet

hyl-, hylo- matter

hymeno- membrane

hyp-, hypo- under, beneath; deficient, less than

hyper- above, over, beyond, extreme; beyond three dimensions

hypn-, hypno- sleep

hypso- high

hyster-, hystero- womb; hysteria

iatro- medicine

ichthy-, ichthyo- fish

igni- fire

ile-, ileo- end of small intestine

ilio- upper hip bone, flank

in-, ig-, il-, im-, ir- (form adjs) not, opposite

in-, il-, im-, ir- (form nouns, verbs) in, into; on

infra- under, beneath; within

inter- between; among, in the midst

intra- within, interior, between; on the outside; during

intro- within; into, in

is-, iso- equal, uniform; equality, similarity

juxta- close to, near to, beside

kerat-, kerato- cornea

kinesi-, kineto- movement

labio- lip

lact-, lacti-, lacto- milk

laryng-, laryngo- larynx, voice box

lepto- slender

leuk-, leuko-, leuc- leuco- white

lign-, ligni-, ligno- wood

litho- stone

log-, logo- word, oral

luni- moon

lyo-, lysi- dissolving, dispersed

macr-, macro- large; long

magni- great

mal-, male- bad, badly; ill; evil; abnormal, inadequate

malac-, malaco- soft

mega-, megalo-, meg- great, large; million

melan-, melano- black, dark

mero- part

mes-, meso- middle, intermediate

meta-, met- beyond; after; over; changed/transferred/substituted

metr- measure

metr-, metro- uterus

micr-, micro- very small

mid- middle, mean

mini- very small, short

mis- degrading, less, lack of; ill

mis- divergence; defect; error, wrong, badly

mis-, miso- hatred

mon-, mono- one, alone, solitary, single

morph-, morpho- shape, form

multi-, mult- many, much

my-, myo- muscle

myc-, myco- fungus

myel-, myelo- spinal cord, marrow

naso- nose

nati- birth

ne-, n- no, not

ne-, neo- new, recent; revived

necr-, necro- dead body

nepho- cloud

nephr-, nephro- kidney

neur-, neuro- nerve

nocti- night

non- not; reverse; unimportant, lacking

noso- sickness

not-, noto- back of body

nycto- night

ob-, oc-, of-, o-, op- in the way of; against; out, inverse

octa-, octo-, oct- eight

ocul-, oculo- eye

odont-, odonto- tooth

of-, op- against

oleo- oil

olig-, oligo- few

ombro- rain

omni- all

oneiro- dream

ont-, onto- being, organism

oo-, o- egg

ophthalm-, ophthalmo- eye

ornith-, ornitho- bird

oro- mouth

orth-, ortho- straight

oste-, osteo-, ossi- bone

oto- ear

out- beyond, exceeding, surpassing; above

ov-, ovi-, ovo- egg

over- above, beyond, too much, excessive

oxy- sharp; oxygen

pachy- thick

pale-, paleo-, palae-, palaeo- ancient, old

pan-, panto- all, everything, group, whole; worldwide

para-, par- close, beside; like, alike

para-, par- unlike, contrary; abnormal, faulty

pari- equal

path-, patho- suffering, disease

ped-, pedo- child

penta-, pente-, pent- five

per-, pel- through; thoroughly; by; for

peri- round; about, enclosing

petr-, petri-, petro- stone; petroleum

phago- eating

phleb-, phlebo- vein

phon-, phono- sound, speech

phot-, photo- light; photograph

phren-, phreno- brain; diaphragm

phyll-, phyllo- leaf

phylo- species, organism

picr-, picro- bitter

piezo- pressure

pisci- fish

plan-, plano- flat; moving

pleur-, pleuro- side of body, lateral

pluto- wealth

pluvio- rain

pneum-, pneumo- respiration, lungs; air, gas

pneumat-, pneumato- breath, vapor

poly- many; excessive

post- after, afterwards; behind, following, later

pre-, prae- before, earlier, in advance, preparatory; priority

preter- beyond, more than

primi-, prim- first

pro- favoring; taking the place of

pro-, por-, pur- for, on the side of; front, forward, forth; before, earlier

pros- to, towards, near; in front of

prot-, proto- first, original; lowest

pseud-, pseudo- false, spurious

psycho-, psycho- mental; mind, spirit, soul

ptero- wing

pulmo- lung

pyo- pus

pyr-, pyro- fire, heat

quadri-, quadr-, quadru- four

quinque- five

re- again, back; anew, a second time

recti- straight

reni-, reno- kidney

retro- backward, back

rheo- flow

rhin-, rhino- nose

rhiz-, rhizo- root

sacchar-, sacchari-, sacchro- sugar

sacr-, sacro- pelvic; above tailbone

sangui- blood

sapr-, sapro- dead, rotten; decaying

sarc-, sarco- flesh, muscle

scelero- hard

schisto-, shiz-, schizo- split

se- aside, apart; separating

seba-, sebo- fatty

selen-, seleno- moon

semi- half; in part, incomplete

septi- seven

sero- serum, blood

sex-, sexi- six

sider-, sidero- star; iron

sine- without

somat-, somato- body

somn- sleep

sperm-, spermo-, sperma-, spermi-, spermat-, spermato- seed

spiro- breath

stato- resting position, equilibrium

stauro- cross

stell- star

sten-, steno- short, narrow, close

stere-, stereo- solid; multi-dimensional

stom-, stomo- mouth

styl-, styli-, stylo- style

styl-, stylo- pillar

sub-, suc-, suf-, sug-, sum-, sup-, sus- under; below, beneath; less, nearly, almost; secondary

subter- beneath; under

super-, supra-, sur- above, over, higher, in excess; very special, superior

syn-, sy-, syl-, sym-* with, together, at the same time

tachy- rapid

taut-, tauto- same

tele-, tel-, telo- distant; electronic communication

teleo- final, purpose

terra- land, earth

the-, theo- god

therm-, thermo- heat

thromb-, thrombo- blood clot

topo- place, point

tox-, toxi-, toxo- poison

trache-, tracheo- windpipe

trans-, tra- through; across, over, beyond, on the far side; from one place to another; change

tri-, tris- three

ultra- beyond; on the other side; extreme

un- do opposite, reverse; release, remove

un- not; the opposite of

undec- eleven

under- lower, beneath; too little

uni- one, single

up- aloft, on high, upwards

uter-, utero- uterus, womb

vari-, vario- different, diverse

vas-, vaso- blood vessel

ventr-, ventro- abdominal, belly

vice- assisting, substituting, deputy

with- from, opposing

xen-, xeno- foreign, strange

zo-, zoo- living, animal

zyg-, zygo- double, pair, union; egg yolk

zym-, zymo- enzyme, fermentation

AVOIDING SEXIST LANGUAGE

To avoid usage and grammar that minimizes or excludes women, scholars and linguists have developed language more appropriate to a non-sexist and multicultural society. The words he and his should be used with greater care when not knowing the sex or identity of the individual performing the action. For example, "The doctor saw his patient" is considered sexist, since, plainly, not all doctors are male.

Words endings to avoid

ess (waitress)
ette (sufragette)
ine (heroine)
trix (executrix)

In addition, words formed with the word "man" as a suffix should also be avoided wherever possible, as in the list below.

Outmoded	Preferred
Alderman	Aldermember, ward representative
Anchorman/ woman	Anchor, news anchor
Authoress	Author
Aviatrix	Aviator
Freshman	First-year student, newcomer

Gentlemen's agreement	Honorable agreement, informal agreement	Maintenance man	Maintenance worker
Goodwill to men	Goodwill to all, to people	Man and wife	Husband and wife, married couple, wife and husband, spouses
Governess	Child-care attendant, instructor	Male nurse	Nurse
Handyman	Odd-job worker	Manhole	Conduit, drain hole, sewer
Heiress	Heir	Man-hours	Work hours
Hostess	Host	Man in the street	Average person, ordinary person
Housewife	Homemaker		
Journeyman	Certified crafter, or specify: carpenter, metalworker, etc.	Mankind	Humanity, humankind
		Manmade	Artificial, manufactured, synthetic
Lady luck	Luck		
Landlord/ lady	Owner	Manned space flight	Piloted, staffed, with crew
Laundress	Laundry worker		
Layman	Layperson, nonprofessional	Manpower	Human resouces, staff, work force
Lineman	Line installer, line worker	Man's achieve- ment	Human achievement
Long- shoreman	Stevedore	Man-size	Big, large, sizable
Maid	Housekeeper, house worker	Man the phones	Operate, staff
Maiden name	Birth name	Master bedroom	Largest bedroom
Maiden voyage	First voyage, premier voyage	Master's degree	Graduate degree
Mailman	Mail carrier		

Meter maid	Traffic officer	Stewardess	Flight attendant
Modern man	Modern humanity	Tomboy	Active child
Newsboy	Newspaper carrier, newspaper vendor	TV cameraman	Camera operator
Newsman/ woman	Newscaster, reporter	Watchman	Guard
Old wives' tale	Superstitious folklore	Weatherman	Meteorologist, reporter, weathercaster
Penmanship	Script, handwriting	Woman's intuition	Hunch, intuition, premonition
Policeman/ woman	Police officer	Working man/ woman	Average wage earner, average worker
Proprietor/ proprietress	Owner	Workmanlike	Skillful, well executed
Repairman	Repairer	Workmen	Workers
Salesman/ woman	Sales representative, salesperson	Unmanned space flight	Mission controlled, unpiloted, unstaffed, without crew
Sculptress	Sculptor	Usherette	Usher
Seamstress	Sewer, tailor		
Spokesman/ woman	Speaker, spokesperson		
Sports- manship	Fair play, sportship		

FORMS OF ADDRESS

The forms of address listed below are for writing to officials in a letter or for a formal introduction.

Ambassador The Honorable ~; Dear M~. Ambassador; The American Ambassador

Associate Justice M~.; Justice ~; M~. Justice ~

baron/baroness The Right Honorable Lord/Lady ~; My Lord/Madam or Dear Lord/Lady ~; Lord/Lady ~

baronet Sir ~, Bt.; Dear Sir or Dear Sir ~; Sir ~

bishop/archbishop The Most Reverend ~, Bishop/Archbishop of ~; Your Excellency or Dear Bishop/Archbishop ~; His Excellency or Bishop/Archbishop ~

Brother Brother ~; Dear Brother ~ or Dear Brother; Brother ~

cabinet members The Honorable ~ or The Secretary of ~; Dear M~. Secretary; The Secretary of ~

cardinal His Eminence, ~, Archbishop of ~; Your Eminence or Dear Cardinal ~; His Eminence, Cardinal ~

Chief Justice The Chief Justice; Dear Mr. Justice or Dear Mr. Chief Justice; The Chief Justice

Consul-General The Honorable ~; Dear M~. ~; M~. ~

countess The Right Honorable the Countess of ~; Madam or Dear Lady ~; Lady ~

duke/duchess His/Her Grace, the D~ of ~; My Lord Duke/Madam or Dear D~ of; His/Her Grace, the D~ of ~

earl The Right Honorable the Earl of ~; My Lord or Dear Lord ~; Lord ~

Episcopal bishop The Right Reverend ~; Dear Bishop ~; The Right Reverend ~, Bishop of ~

foreign ambassador His/Her Excellency ~; Excellency or Dear M~. Ambassador; The Ambassador of ~

former President The Honorable ~; Dear Mr. ~; The Honorable ~

governor The Honorable ~; Dear M~. ~; M~. ~

judge The Honorable ~; Dear Judge ~; The Honorable ~ or M~. Justice ~ or Judge ~

king or queen His/Her Majesty King/Queen ~

knight Sir ~; Dear Sir or Dear Sir ~; Sir ~

marquess/marchioness The Most Honorable the M~ of ~; My Lord/Madam or Dear Lord/Lady ~; Lord/Lady ~

mayor The Honorable ~; Dear Mayor ~; Mayor ~ or The Mayor

military personnel 'full title'; Dear Admiral/Chief/Colonel/Commander/General/Lieutenant/Private/Sailor/Sergeant/Soldier~; 'full title'

monsignor The Right Reverend Monsignor ~; Right Reverend Monsignor or Dear Monsignor ~; Monsignor ~

Pope His Holiness, the Pope or His Holiness, Pope ~; Your Holiness or Most Holy Father; His Holiness or the Holy Father or the Pope or the Pontiff

President of the United States The President; Dear Mr. President; The President or The President of the United States

priest The Reverend ~; Reverend Father or Dear Father ~; Father ~

protestant minister The Reverend ~; Dear Dr./M~. ~; The Reverend/Dr. ~

rabbi Rabbi ~; Dear Rabbi/Dr. ~; Rabbi/Dr. ~

royalty in general His/Her Royal Highness, the ~/~ of ~; Your Royal Highness; His/Her Royal Highness, the ~/~ of ~

*Secretary-General of the United

Nations* His/Her Excellency ~;
Dear M~. Secretary-General; The
Secretary-General of the United
Nations

Sister Sister ~; Dear Sister ~ or
Dear Sister; Sister ~

Speaker of the House The Honorable ~; Dear M~. Speaker; The
Speaker of the House of Representatives

state legislator The Honorable ~;
Dear M~. ~; M~. ~

United Nations representative
The Honorable ~; Dear M~. Ambassador; The United States Representative to the United Nations

United States Representative The
Honorable ~; Dear M~. ~; Representative ~ of ~

United States Senator The Honorable ~; Dear Senator ~;
Senator ~ from ~

Vice President The Vice President; Dear Mr. Vice President;
The Vice President or the Vice
President of the United States

viscount/viscountess The Right
Honorable the V~ ~; My
Lord/Lady or Dear Lord/Lady ~;
Lord/Lady ~

wife of baronet Lady ~; Dear
Madam or Dear Lady ~; Lady ~

wife of knight Lady ~; Dear
Madam or Dear Lady ~; Lady ~

GEOGRAPHICAL INFORMATION

Listed below are nations of the world (capital, resident, chief of state legislative body).

Afghanistan, Kabul, Afghan, President, Revolutionary Council/ Council of Ministers

Albania, Tirana, Albanian, Chairman of the Presidium, People's Assembly

Algeria, Algiers/El Djazair, Algerian, President, National People's Assembly

Andorra, Andorra la Vella, Andorran, Bishop of Seo de Urgel/ President of France, General Council

Angola, Luanda, Angolan, President, National People's Assembly

Antigua and Barbuda, St. John's, Antiguan, Queen/Governor General, Parliament (House of Representatives, Senate)

Argentina, Buenos Aires, Argentine, President, National Congress (Senate, Chamber of Deputies)

Aruba, Oranjestad, Aruban, Acting Governor/Prime Minister

Australia, Canberra, Australian, Queen/Governor General, Federal Parliament (Senate, House of Representatives)

Austria, Vienna, Austrian, President, Federal Assembly (Federal Council/Bundesrat, National Council/Nationalrat)

Bahamas, Nassau, Bahamian, Queen/Governor General, Parliament (Senate, House of Assembly)

Bahrain, Manama, Bahraini, amir

Bangladesh, Dhaka, Bangladeshi, President, Constituent Assembly

Barbados, Bridgetown, Barbadian, Queen/Governor General, Parliament (Senate, House of Assembly)

Belgium, Brussels, Belgian, King, Parliament (Senate, Chamber of Representatives)

Belize, Belmopan, Belizean, Queen/ Governor General, National Assembly (Senate, House of Representatives)

Benin, Porto-Novo, Beninese, President, National Executive Council and Revolutionary National Assembly

Bhutan, Thimphu/Paro Dzong, Bhutanese, King, National Assembly

Bolivia, Sucre/La Paz, Bolivian, President, Congress (Senate, Chamber of Deputies)

Botswana, Gaborone, Motswana (singular)/Botswana (plural), President, National Assembly

Brazil, Brasilia, Brazilian, President, National Congress (Senate, Chamber of Deputies)

Brunei Darussalam, Bandar Seri Begawan, Bruneian, sultan and prime minister

Bulgaria, Sofia, Bulgarian, President of the Presidium, National Assembly

Burkina Faso, Ouagadougou, President

Burundi, Bujumbura, Burundian, President, National Assembly

Cambodia, Phnom Penh, Cambodian/Khmer, President, Council of Ministers

Cameroon, Yaounde, Cameroonian, President, National Assembly

Canada, Ottawa, Canadian/Canadien/Canuck (French Canadian), Queen/Governor General/Prime Minister, Parliament (Senate, House of Commons)

Cape Verde, Praia, Cape Verdean, President, National People's Assembly

Central African Republic, Bangui, Central African, Chief of State, Parliament (National Assembly, Social and Economic Council)

Chad, N'Djamena, Chadian, President, Council of Ministers and National Consultative Council

Chile, Santiago, Chilean, President

China, Beijing, Chinese, President, Standing Committee of National People's Congress

Colombia, Bogota, Colombian, President, Congress (Senate, House of Representatives)

Comoros, Moroni, Comoran, President, Federal Assembly

Congo, Brazzaville, Congolese, President, Council of State

Cook Islands, Avarua, Cook Islander, Prime Minister, Parliament

Costa Rica, San Jose, Costa Rican, President, Legislative Assembly

Cuba, Havanna, Cuban, President, National Assembly of the People's Power

Cyprus, Nicosia, Cypriot, President, Council of Ministers and House of Representatives

Czechoslovakia, Prague, Czechoslovak/Czech, President, Federal Assembly (Chamber of the People, Chamber of the Nations)

Denmark, Copenhagen, Dane, King, Parliament/Folketing

Djibouti, Djibouti, Afar/Issa, President, National Assembly

Dominica, Roseau, Dominican, President, House of Assembly

Dominican Republic, Santo Domingo, Dominican, President, National Congress (Senate, Chamber of Deputies)

East Germany/German Democratic Republic, East Berlin, East German, Chairman (Council of State), People's Chamber/Volkskammer

Ecuador, Quito, Ecuadorean, President, Chamber of Representatives

Egypt, Cairo, Egyptian, President, People's Assembly

El Salvador, San Salvador, Salvadoran, President, Legislative Assembly

Equatorial Guinea, Malabo, Equatorial Guinean, President, House of Representatives of the People

Ethiopia, Addis Ababa, Ethiopian, President, National Assembly

Faroe Islands, Torshavn, Faroese, Queen, Parliament

Fiji, Suva, Fijian, President/Prime Minister

Finland, Helsinki, Finn, President, Parliament/Eduskunta

France, Paris, Frenchman, President, Parliament (Senate, National Assembly)

French Guinea, Cayenne, French

Guianese, Commissioner of the Republic, General Council and Regional Council

French Polynesia, Papeete, French Polynesian, High Commissioner/ President, Territorial Assembly and Council of Government

Gabon, Libreville, Gabonese, President, National Assembly

Gambia, The, Banjul, Gambian, President, House of Representatives

Ghana, Accra, Ghanaian, Chairman (PNDC), Provisional National Defense Council (PNDC)

Greece, Athens, Greek, Prime Minister/President, Parliament/Vouli

Greenland/Kalaallit Nunaat, Gothab/ Nuuk, Greenlander, Queen, Parliament/Landsting

Grenada, St. George's, Grenadian, Queen/Governor General, House of Representatives and Senate

Guadeloupe, Basse-Terre, Guadeloupian, Prefect, General Council and Regional Council

Guatemala, Guatemala City, Guatemalan, President, Congress

Guinea, Conakry, Guinean, President, Military Committee of National Redressment (CMRN)

Guinea-Bissau, Bissau, Guinean, President, Council of State and National Popular Assembly

Guyana, Georgetown, Guyanese, President, National Assembly

Haiti, Port-au-Prince, Haitian, President, Consultative Council

Honduras, Tegucigalpa, Honduran, President, National Congress

Hungary, Budapest, Hungarian, President of the Presidential Council, National Assembly

Iceland, Reykjavik, Icelander, President, Parliament/Althing (Upper Chamber/Efi Deild, Lower Chamber/Neore Deild)

India, New Delhi, Indian, President, Parliament (Government Assembly/Rajya Sabha, People's Assembly/Lok Sabha)

Indonesia, Jakarta, Indonesian, President, Parliament (House of Representatives/DPR, People's Consultative Assembly/MPR)

Iran, Teheran, Iranian, President, Islamic Consultative Assembly

Iraq, Baghdad, Iraqi, President and Prime Minister, National Assembly

Ireland, Dublin, Irishman, Irishmen/Irish (plural), President, National Parliament/Oireachtas (Senate/Seaned Eireann, House of Representatives/Dail Eireann)

Israel, Jerusalem, Israeli, President, Parliament/Knesset

Italy, Rome, Italian, President, Parliament (Senate, Chamber of Deputies)

Ivory Coast/Côte d/Ivoire, Abidjan, Ivorian, President, National Assembly

Jamaica, Kingston, Jamaican, Queen/Governor General/Prime Minister, Parliament (Senate, House of Representatives)

Japan, Toyko, Japanese, Emperor, Diet (House of Councillors, House of Representatives)

Jordan, Amman, Jordanian, King, National Assembly (Senate, House of Representatives)

Kenya, Nairobi, Kenyan, President, National Assembly

Kiribati, Tarawa, Kiribatian, President, National Assembly

Kuwait, Kuwait, Kuwait, Amir, National Assembly

Laos, Vientiane, Lao/Laotian (singular)/Laotians (plural), President, Supreme People's Assembly

Lebanon, Beirut, Lebanese, (President), National Assembly

Lesotho, Maseru, Masotho (singular)/Basotho (plural), King, Military Council

Liberia, Monrovia, Liberian, President, Congress

Libya, Tripoli, Libyan, (Chief of State), General Peoples' Congress

Liechtenstein, Vaduz, Liechtensteiner, Prince, Diet

Luxembourg, Luxembourg, Luxembourger, Grand Duke, Parliament (Chamber of Deputies, Council of State)

Macau, Macau, Macanese, Governor, Legislative Assembly

Madagascar, Antananarivo, Malagasy, President, Popular National Assembly

Malawi, Lilongwe, Malawian, President, National Assembly

Malaysia, Kuala Lumpur, Malaysian, Paramount Ruler, Parliament (Senate, House of Representatives)

Maldives, Male, Maldivian, President, People's Council/Majlis

Mali, Bamako, Malian, President, National Council

Malta, Valletta, Maltese, President/Prime Minister, House of Representatives

Marshall Islands, Majuro, Marshall Islander, President, Parliament/Nitijela and Council of Chiefs/Iroj

Martinique, Fort-de-France, Martiniquais, Commissioner, Regional Council and General Council

Mauritania, Nouakchott, Mauritanian, President, Military Committee for National Salvation

Mauritius, Port Louis, Mauritian, Queen/Governor General, Legislative Assembly

Mexico, Mexico City, Mexican, President, National Congress (Senate, Federal Chamber of Deputies)

Monaco, Monaco-Ville, Monacan/Monegasque, Chief of State/Prince, National Council

Mongolia, Ulaanbaatar, Mongolian, Secretary-General, Great People's Hural

Morocco, Rabat, Moroccan, King, Chamber of Representatives

Mozambique, Maputo, Mozambican, President, People's Assembly

Myanmar, Yangon, Burmese, General, military government

Namibia, Windhoek, Namibian, Administrator-General, National Assembly

Nauru, Yaren, Nauruan, President, Parliament

Nepal, Kathmandu, Nepalese, King, National Assembly/Rastriya Panchayat

Netherlands, Amsterdam, Netherlander, Queen, States-General (First-Chamber, Second-Chamber)

Netherlands Antilles, Willemstad, Netherlands Antillean

New Caledonia, Noumea, New Caledonian, High Commissioner and President, Territorial Assembly

New Zealand, Wellington, New Zealander, Queen/Governor General, Parliament/House of Representatives

Nicaragua, Managua, Nicaraguan, President, National Assembly

Niger, Niamey, Nigerois, President, Supreme Military Council

Nigeria, Lagos, Nigerien, President, National Council of Ministers and National Council of States

Niue, Alofi, Niuean, Premier, Legislative Assembly

North Korea, P'yongyang, North Korean, President, Supreme People's Assembly

Norway, Oslo, Norwegian, King, Parliament (Storting-Lagting, Odelsting)

Oman, Muscat, Omani, Sultan and Prime Minister

Pakistan, Islamabad, Pakistani, President/ Prime Minister, Parliament

Panama, Panama, Panamanian, President, Legislative Assembly

Papua New Guinea, Port Moresby, Papua New Guinean, Queen/ Governor General, House of Assembly

Paraguay, Asuncion, Paraguayan, President, Congress (Senate, Chamber of Deputies)

Peru, Lima, Peruvian, President, Congress (Senate, Chamber of Deputies)

Phillippines, Quezon City/Manila, Filipino, President, National Assembly (Senate, House of Representatives)

Poland, Warsaw, Pole, President/ Prime Minister, Parliament/Sejm

Portugal, Lisbon, Portuguese, President/Prime Minister, Assembly of the Republic

Qatar, Doha, Qatari, Amir and Prime Minister, State Advisory Council

Reunion, Saint-Denis, Reunionese, Commissioner, General Council and Regional Assembly

Romania, Bucharest, Romanian, President of Socialist Republic, Grand National Assembly

Rwanda, Kigali, Rwandan, President, National Development Council

Saint Lucia, Castries, St. Lucian, Queen/Governor General, Parliament (Senate, House of Representatives)

Saint Vincent and the Grenadines, Kingstown, St. Vincentian/Vincentian, Queen/Governor General, House of Representatives and Senate

San Marino, San Marino, Sanmarinese, Secretary of Foreign and Political Affairs/Secretary for Internal Affairs and Justice, Grand and General Council

Sao Tome and Principe, Sao Tome, Sao Tomean, President, National People's Assembly

Saudi Arabia, Riyadh, Saudi, King and Prime Minister

Senegal, Dakar, Senegalese, President, National Assembly

Seychelles, Victoria, Setchellois, President, People's Assembly

Sierra Leone, Freetown, Sierra Leonean, President, House of Representatives

Singapore, Singapore, Singaporean, President/Prime Minister, Parliament

Solomon Islands, Honiara, Solomon

Islander, Queen/Governor General, National Parliament

Somalia, Mogadishu, Somali, President and Commander in Chief of the Army, National People's Assembly

South Africa, Pretoria/Cape Town/ Bloemfontein, South African, President, Parliament (House of Assembly, House of Representatives, House of Delegates)

South Korea, Seoul, South Korean, President, National Assembly

Soviet Union/Union of Soviet Socialist Republics, Moscow, Soviet, General Secretary of Central Committee of Communist Party/ Council of Ministers, Supreme Soviet

Spain, Madrid, Spaniard, King, Cortes Generales (Senate, Congress of Deputies)

Sri Lanka, Colombo, Sri Lankan, President

St. Kitts and Nevis, Basseterre, Kittsian/Nevisian, Queen/Governor General, House of Assembly and Nevis Island Legislature

Sudan, Khartoum, Sudanese, Prime Minister, Supreme Council and Civilian Cabinet

Suriname, Paramaribo, Surinamer, President

Swaziland, Mbabane, Swazi, King, Parliament (House of Assembly, Senate)

Sweden, Stockholm, Swede, King, Parliament/Riksdag

Switzerland, Bern, Swiss, President, Federal Assembly/Bundesversammlung (Council of States/Standerat, National Council/Nationrat)

Syria, Damascus, Syrian, President, People's Council

Taiwan, Taipei, Chinese, President, National Assembly

Tanzania, Dar-es-Salaam, Tanzanian, President, National Assembly

Thailand, Bangkok, Thai, King/ Prime Minister, National Assembly (Senate, House of Representatives)

Togo, Lomé, Togolese, President, National Assembly

Tonga, Nuku'alofa, Tongan, King, Legislative Assembly

Trinidad and Tobago, Port-of-Spain, Trinidadian/Tobagan, President, Parliament (Senate, House of Representatives)

Tunisia, Tunis, Tunisian, President, National Assembly

Turkey, Ankara, Turk, President, Grand National Assembly

Tuvalu, Funafuti, Tuvaluan, Queen/ Governor General, House of Parliament

Uganda, Kampala, Ugandan, President, National Resistance Council

United Arab Emirates, Abu Dhabi, Emirian, President, Federal National Council

United Kingdom of Great Britain and Northern Ireland, London, Briton (singular)/British (plural), Queen/Prime Minister, Parliament (House of Lords, House of Commons)

(contains Wales (Cardiff), Scotland (Edinburgh), Northern Ireland (Belfast), Guernsey (St. Peter Port), Jersey (Saint Helier), Gibraltar, Bermuda (Hamilton), Hong Kong (Victoria), Pitcairn Islands (Adamstown), Falkland Islands (Stanley), St. Helena (Jamestown), British Virgin Islands (Road Town), Montserrat (Plymouth), Anguilla (The Valley), Turks and Calicos Islands (Grand Turk), Cayman Islands (Georgetown), Isle of Man (Douglas).

United States, Washington, DC; American, President, Congress (Senate, House of Representatives)

Uruguay, Montevideo, Uruguayan, President, General Assembly (Senate, House of Deputies)

Vanuatu, Vila, Vanuatuan, President, Parliament

Vatican City, Vatican City, n/a, Supreme Pontiff (Pope)

Venezuela, Caracas, Venezuelan, President, National Congress (Senate, Chamber of Deputies)

Vietnam, Hanoi, Vietnamese, Chairman (President), National Assembly

Wallis and Futuna Islands, Mata-Utu, Wallisian/Futunan/Wallis and Futuna Islander, High Administrator, Territorial Assembly

West Germany/Federal Republic of Germany, Bonn, West German, Pressident/Chancellor, Parliament (Federal Council/Bundesrat, National Assembly/ Bundestag)

Western Samoa, Apia, Western Samoan, Head of State, Legislative Assembly

Yemen, Sana, Yemeni, President, People's Constituent Assembly

Yugoslavia, Belgrade, Yugoslav, President, Federal Assembly (Federal Chamber, Chamber of Republics and Provinces)

Zaire, Kinshasa, Zairian, President, National Legislative Council

Zambia, Lusaka, Zambian, President, National Assembly

Zimbabwe, Harare, Zimbabwean, President, Parliament (Senate, House of Assembly)

GEOGRAPHICAL INFORMATION

States' abbreviations: official and two-letter Postal Service (capital, resident)

Alabama . . . Ala. . . . AL Montgomery, Alabamian

Alaska . . . Alaska/Alas. . . . AK Juneau, Alaskan

American Samoa . . . Amer. Samoa . . . AS

Arizona . . . Ariz. . . . AZ Phoenix, Arizonan

Arkansas . . . Ark. . . . AR Little Rock, Arkansan

California . . . Calif/Cal. . . . CA Sacramento, Californian

Canal Zone . . . CZ

Colorado. . . . Colo. . . . CO Denver, Coloradan

Connecticut . . . Conn. . . . CT Hartford, Connecticuter

Delaware . . . Del. . . . DE Dover, Delawarean

District of Columbia . . . D.C. . . . DC Washington

Florida . . . Fla. . . . FL Tallahassee, Floridian

Georgia . . . Ga. . . . GA Atlanta, Georgian

Guam . . . GU

Hawaii . . . HI Honolulu, Hawaiian

Idaho . . . Idaho/Id. . . . ID Boise, Idahoan

Illinois . . . Ill. . . . IL Springfield, Illinoisan

Indiana . . . Ind. . . . IN Indianapolis, Indianian

Iowa . . . Iowa/Ia. . . . IA   Des Moines, Iowan

Kansas . . . Kans/Kan. . . . KS Topeka, Kansan

Kentucky . . . Ky. . . . KY   Frankfort, Kentuckian

Louisiana . . . La. . . . LA   Baton Rouge, Louisianian

Maine . . . Maine/Me. . . . ME Augusta, Mainer

Maryland . . . Md. . . . MD   Annapolis, Marylander

Massachusetts . . . Mass. . . . MA Boston, Massachusettsan

Michigan . . . Mich. . . . MI   Lansing, Michiganite

Minnesota . . . Minn. . . . MN   St. Paul, Minnesotan

Mississippi . . . Miss. . . . MS Jackson, Mississippian

Missouri . . . Mo. . . . MO   Jefferson City, Missourian

Montana . . . Mont. . . . MT   Helena, Montanan

Nebraska . . . Nebr/Neb. . . . NE Lincoln, Nebraskan

Nevada . . . Nev. . . . NV   Carson City, Nevadan

New Hampshire . . . N.H. . . . NH Concord, New Hampshirite

New Jersey . . . N.J. . . . NJ   Trenton, New Jerseyite

New Mexico . . . N.Mex/N.M. . . . NM   Santa Fe, New Mexican

New York . . . N.Y. . . . NY   Albany, New Yorker

North Carolina . . . N.C. . . . NC Raleigh, North Carolinian

North Dakota . . . N.Dak/N.D. . . . ND   Bismarck, North Dakotan

Northern Mariana Is . . . CM

Ohio . . . OH . . . Columbus, Ohioan

Oklahoma . . . Okla. . . . OK   Oklahoma City, Oklahoman

Oregon . . . Oreg/Ore. . . . OR Salem, Oregonian

Pennsylvania . . . Pa/Penn/Penna. . . . PA   Harrisburg, Pennsylvanian

Puerto Rico . . . PR   Puerto Rican

Rhode Island . . . R.I. . . . RI   Providence, Rhode Islander

South Carolina . . . S.C. . . . SC   Columbia, South Carolinian

South Dakota . . . S.Dak/S.D. . . . SD   Pierre, South Dakotan

Tennessee . . . Tenn. . . . TN Nashville, Tennessean

Texas . . . Tex. . . . TX   Austin, Texan

Trust Territories . . . TT

Utah . . . UT.   Salt Lake City, Utahn

Vermont . . . Vt. . . . VT   Montpelier, Vermonter

Virginia . . . Va. . . . VA Richmond, Virginian

Virgin Islands . . . VI

Washington . . . Wash. . . . WA Olympia, Washingtonian

West Virginia . . . W.Va. . . . WV Charleston, West Virginian

Wisconsin . . . Wis/Wisc. . . . WI Madison, Wisconsinite

Wyoming . . . Wyo. . . . WY Cheyenne, Wyomingite

Province and Territory Abbreviations (two-letter)

Alberta . . . AB

British Columbia . . . BC

Labrador . . . LB

Manitoba . . . MB

New Brunswick . . . NB

Newfoundland . . . NF

Nova Scotia . . . NS

Northwest Territories . . . NT

Ontario . . . ON

Prince Edward Island . . . PE

Quebec . . . PQ

Saskatchewan . . . SK

Yukon Territory . . . YT

MATHEMATICAL SIGNS AND SYMBOLS

+	Addition / Plus		π	Pi (3.1416)
–	Subtraction / Minus		□	Square
×	Multiplication / Times		▭	Rectangle
÷	Division / Divided by		△	Triangle
±	Plus or minus		°	Degree
√	Square root		∠	Angle
=	Equal to		∟	Right Angle
≈	Approximately equal to		⊥	Perpendicular to
≡	Identical to		( )	Parentheses
≅	Congruent to		[ ]	brackets
≠	Not equal to		{ }	braces
>	Greater than		‖	Parallel to
<	Less than		∪	Union with or two sets
≥	Greater than or equal to		∩	Intersection with
≤	Less than or equal to		⊂	Contained in / subset of
:	Is to		⊃	Contains as a subset
∴	Therefore	o or ∧		Empty set / null set
∞	Infinity		ε	Is an element of
o	Circle		'	foot
∩	Arc of circle		"	inch

PROOFREADING SIGNS AND SYMBOLS

|| align
≡ all capitals
bf boldface
][center
✕ check type
◡ close up
⌐ delete
⌐ delete and close up
—M̄— em dash
—N̄— en dash
fig figures
fl flush left
fr flush right
∨/∨ insert apostrophe
⧧ ⧧ insert brackets
⟨⟩ insert colon
∧ insert comma
! insert exclamation point
= insert hyphen

∧ insert letter
⧙( )⧘ insert parentheses
⊙ insert period
set ? insert question mark
∨∨ insert quotation marks
⌐ insert semicolon
insert space
ital italics
lc lowercase
⌐⌐ move up
⌐⌐ move down
⊏ move left
⊐ move right
¶ new paragraph
stet reinstate or let stand
rom roman type
sc a= small caps
sp spell out
tr a n transpose

PUNCTUATION AND STYLE

Apostrophe

- The apostrophe is not used in names of organizations unless actually part of the legal name. Apostrophe is used when leaving out a letter or number in a contraction.
- Plurals of letter abbreviations with periods and single letters use an ''s'. Plurals of letter combinations, numerals, and hyphenated nouns end in 's' with no apostrophe.
- The possessive of singular nouns end in ''s', including nouns ending in s, x, z, ch, or sh. The apostrophe follows the 's' of a word with two sibilant sounds, like Kansas' and Moses'. The apostrophe follows the 's' for the possessive of plural nouns except for plurals which do not end in 's'. No apostrophe is used for personal pronouns like hers, its, theirs; indefinite pronouns require one, e.g., one's lover. In compounds, the ''s' is added to the word nearest the object of possession. Joint possession is shown by putting the apostrophe on the last word of a series, e.g., Francis and Kucera's book.

Brace

Punctuation used to show the relationship of elements in a group.

Bracket

- Punctuation used to insert words in quoted matter, for explanatory, correctionary, or commentary reasons. Brackets are used to insert missing letters and to enclose insertions that take the place of or slightly alter the original text, e.g., [they] may replace a long list of names previously mentioned. Brackets are also used in unquoted matter for the same reasons.
- Brackets are used as parentheses within parentheses.
- Brackets are used in mathematical expressions (to show matter to be treated as a unit), chemical formulas, and for phonetic symbols.

Colon

- Punctuation used to introduce explanatory information, lists; for salutations, as 'Dear so-and-so'; and in clock time (e.g., 2:15), periodical reference (e.g., 4:3), and between book title and book subtitle (e.g., Dictionaries: The Art and Craft of Lexicography).
- A colon is used before a final clause that explains, amplifies something in that sentence, e.g., The dissertation needs work: it lacks flow.
- A colon introduces a series or summarizing statement, e.g., The following is on our list of places to go: grocery store, toy store, doughnut shop. She had one great love: him.
- A colon is used in proportions, e.g., 2:1, and as a ratio sign, e.g., 1:2::3:6.
- A colon may introduce a quotation, especially a long one.
- A colon is used in dialogue text, e.g., Kyle: Do you want to have lunch? Holly: Yes.
- A colon is used in correspondence for headings and introductory terms, e.g., To:, From:, Re: and to separate writer/typist and carbon-copy abbreviation from the recipients.

Comma

Punctuation most commonly used to separate or set off items as:

- Separate items that might otherwise be misunderstood.
- Separate members of a series used with 'and', 'or', or 'nor'.
- Separate main clauses or before the conjunction in a compound sentence.
- Separate two verb phrases in a sentence.
- Set off subordinate clauses/phrases within sentence.
- Set off an apposite (noun referring to previous noun, e.g., my sister, Nancy) or contrasting words/phrases (e.g., I need you, not anyone else.).
- Set off introductory items, e.g., "Sir, are you listening?".
- Set off interrupting or parenthetic items.
- Before quotation following an introductory phrase, e.g. "She said quietly, 'I love you.'"
- Inside a closing quotation mark, e.g., I said "wash," not "drawer."
- To show omission, e.g., The thing is, we need time.
- Between compound qualifiers, e.g., He has big, broad shoulders.
- Between name and title, title and organization, name and degree, surname and Junior/Jr./Senior/Sr.

In an inverted name, e.g., Kipfer, Barbara Ann.
- To separate thousands, millions, etc. in number of four or more digits, e.g., 2,000.
- To set off the day of the month, e.g., They got together on May 30, 1987, for the first time. To set off elements of an address, e.g., Write to him at The Language Centre, University of Exeter, Exeter, England EX4 4QH.
- After the salutation in informal correspondence, e.g., Dear T.B., and after the complimentary close in all correspondence, e.g., Respectfully,.

Dash

- Punctuation used to denote a sudden change or break in a sentence, e.g., 'He was gone—heaven forbid—for an hour and no one knew where he was.' No spaces are added before or after a dash and do not combine with a colon, comma, or semicolon. Other common uses:
- As a substitute for parentheses or commas in an attempt to clarify meaning or place emphasis, e.g.,

'She has this to accomplish today—work, study, cook, and household duties—as well as take care of her child.'

- Before an amplification, definition, explanation, or summary statement, e.g., 'To be or not to be—that is a question we each ask ourselves at night before we turn out the light.'
- At the end of an unfinished word or sentence, e.g., 'The story went on to say that—.'
- To precede an author's credit for a quotation.
- As a way of setting off something in page design, as for lists, outlines.
- The en dash is used in typeset material and is shorter than the em dash, which is represented in typewritten material by two hyphens. It is used as a replacement for a hyphen when the meaning intended is 'up to and including', e.g., 1987–91, Monday–Saturday.
- A two-em (four hyphens) dash is used to show missing letters in a word. A three-em (six hyphens) dash is used to show that a word is left out or that an unknown word or number is to be supplied.

Division of words

- Guidelines for dividing words at the end of lines are:
- Pay attention to the way the word is pronounced (syllables) and do not break the word so that it would be mispronounced or misunderstood.
- Divide between doubled consonants, except when it would divide a simple base form, e.g., re-com-men-da-tion, but sell-ing, buzz-er. When the doubled consonant comes before '-ing', the second consonant stays with the '-ing'.
- Do not divide a one-syllable word, even if there is an inflected ending like '-ed', e.g., spelled, bummed.
- Do not divide a word so that one or two letters is left either at the end of one line or the beginning of another. Division after a prefix, putting it at the end of a line, is permissible.
- Do not divide words of six letters or less.
- Divided hyphenated words at the hyphen.
- Do not divide before the follow-

ing suffixes; they should not be at the beginning of a line alone nor should they be divided themselves: -able, -ceous, -cial, -cion, -cious, -geous, -gion, -gious, -ible, -sial, -sion, -tial, -tion, -tious.

- When a vowel alone forms a syllable in the middle of a word, keep it with the previous syllable, e.g., physi-cal.
- A liquid or silent 'l' syllable at the end of a word or part of an inflected ending should not be put on the next line alone, e.g., read-able, twin-kling.
- Proper nouns, numerals, and abbreviations should not be divided.

Ellipsis points (or ellipses, points of ellipsis, suspension points)

Punctuation used when words are omitted: three periods in the middle of a sentence, four at the end of a sentence (unless the sentence ends with a question mark or exclamation point: then it is . . . ? or . . . !). They may also indicate a break or suspension in speech. Punctuation that normally falls before or after the ellipsis points can be retained for clarity. A space precedes and follows ellipses.

Exclamation point

Punctuation used to show surprise, incredulity, praise, a command—to show force in statement. An exclamation point may be used to replace a question mark when irony or an emphatic tone is meant, e.g., How could you! An exclamation point and question mark may be used together to show extreme force. If the exclamation point ends a sentence in a quotation, the comma or period is dropped.

Hyphen

Punctuation used:
- To connect the elements of some compound words, especially ones of three or more words
- To divide a word at the end of a line
- In fractions and compound numbers
- In measurements with numbers and unit
- In ages with number and unit

- In prefixed words when a vowel is doubled or consonant is tripled
- For certain prefixes as ex-
- To make a word clear from its homonym, as recover and re-cover
- Between a prefix and the second word if it is a proper noun and proper noun compounds
- For certain suffixes as -elect
- Compounds which begin with a single capital letter as H-bomb
- For compound adjectives, including those where the first adjective ends in -ly, as 'scholarly-written piece' (but not for compound modifiers of adverb-and-adjective as 'widely known author')
- For directions, as north-northwest
- For words spelled out letter-by-letter, as y-e-s
- To show stuttering speech.

Numerals / numbers

- The most common, Arabic numerals, are 0, 1, 2, etc. Roman numerals use the letters I (1), V (5), X (10), L (50), C (100), D (500), M (1000) and are used to number wars, for sequence in family and for rulers, vehicles, and major headings in documents. Cardinal numbers are 0, zero, 1, one, etc. Ordinal numbers are 1st, first, 2nd, second, etc.
- In general, write out the first nine cardinal (1–9) numbers (except for address numbers 2–9, dates, decimals, game scores, highways, latitude/longitude, mathematical expressions, measurement/weight, money/financial data, percentages, proportion, scientific expressions, statistics, technical expressions, temperature, time, unit modifiers, votes, and numbers not written out in a proper noun) and any number that begins a sentence; use figures for 10 and above.
- The first nine ordinal (1st–9th) numbers are usually written out, especially when describing order in time or location.
- Governmental, political, and military units numbered one hundred or less are usually written out. Labor unions and other organizations often use figures.
- Numbers of one million and above are easier to read if written as figures with the word 'million', 'billion', etc.

- Written-out numbers between 21 and 99 are hyphenated.
- Figures of four digits may be written with or without a comma.
- Numbers of checks, contracts, military hours, pages, policies, rooms/suites, streets, telephone numbers, and years are written without commas. Check, telephone, and serial numbers may contain hyphens.
- A fraction used as a modifier is hyphenated, e.g., three-quarter time.
- A fraction used with a whole number is written as a figure, e.g., 5½, as are measurements that are fractions, e.g., ¼ mile.
- A measurement as a modifier is hyphenated, e.g., nine-pound boy.
- Numbers in a series or set are written alike, e.g., '50 to 60 participants'.
- Street names that are numbers are written out, but may also be written as figures from 13 and over.
- Document divisions are usually written as figures, e.g., Psalm 100, page 7.
- Ordinal numbers are not used in full dates; commas are not used in between just a month and year.
- Money designations of one or two words are often written out, e.g., one dollar.
- Times are usually spelled out in text and may be when used with 'o'clock'. Figures are used for exact times, e.g., 8:13. Times may be used with a.m./A.M., p.m./P.M., 'o'clock', or 'in the ~' but those designations should not be combined.
- Year and page numbers may omit hundreds and replace with a dash, e.g., 1989–90, pp 140–50.
- If an abbreviation or symbol is used with a number, it should be written as a figure.
- Numbers should not be divided at the end of lines.
- Plurals of written-out numbers are formed by adding 's' or 'es.'
- Plurals of figures are formed by adding 's' or ''s.'
- The full sequence of Roman numerals are 1 = I, 2 = II, 3 = III, 4 = IV, 5 = V, 6 = VI, 7 = VII, 8 = VIII, 9 = IX, 10 = X, 11 = XI, 12 = XII, 13 = XIII, 14 = XIV, 15 = XV, 16 = XVI, 17 = XVII, 18 = XVIII, 19 = XIX, 20 = XX, 30 = XXX, 40 = XL, 50 = L, 60 = LX, 70 = LXX, 80 = LXXX, 90 = XC, 99 = IC, 100 = C, 150 = CL, 200 = CC, 300 = CCC, 400 = CD, 500

$= D$, $600 = DC$, $700 = DCC$, $800 = DCCC$, $900 = CM$, $1000 = M$, $1500 = MD$, $2000 = MM$, $4000 = M\overline{V}$, $5000 = \overline{V}$; $1,000,000 = \overline{M}$.

Parentheses

- Punctuation to enclose supplementary matter that is not intended to be part of the statement. At the end of a sentence, the period follows the closing parenthesis. A complete sentence within parentheses has its own punctuation. Parentheses may indicate something important, but their use is interruptive. Uses include:
- Numeric data, including Arabic numerals confirming a spelled-out number, and for other mathematical expressions.
- Explanation, definitions, translations, alternatives.
- Abbreviation of the spelled-out word or the spelled-out form of an abbreviation.
- Bibliographical data.
- Cross-references.
- Comments about a text.
- Numbers or letters indicating an item in a series are enclosed as, (1), (2), (3) and (a), (b), (c).

Period

Punctuation used:
- At the end of a declarative sentence and after a question that is a suggestion and is not requiring an answer.
- After a letter or number indicating an item in a series.
- As part of an ellipsis.
- In numbers with integers and decimals.
- In some abbreviations.
- After a person's initials.
- Centered, to indicate multiplication, as $2 \bullet 3 = 6$.

Possessives

- The possessive case of most nouns is formed by adding an apostrophe or an apostrophe and 's.'
- Possessive for singular and plurals nouns not ending in an 's' or 'z' sound are formed by adding ''s.'
- Possessive of singular nouns ending in an 's' or 'z' sound are usually formed by adding ''s', though some writers may prefer just an apostrophe. An exception is for multi-syllabic words if they

are followed by a word beginning with an 's' or 'z' sound.

- Possessive of plural nouns ending in an 's' or 'z' sound are formed by adding only an apostrophe. An exception is for one-syllable irregular plurals: add ''s.'

- In a phrase: individual possession is shown with a ''s' added to each noun, e.g., 'Barbara's and Kyle's bicycles'; joint possession is shown by adding an apostrophe or ''s' to the last noun in the series or by adding an apostrophe or ''s' to each noun, e.g., 'Barbara and Kyle's house.'

Question mark

Punctuation after a direct interrogatory statement and one expressing doubt. It is used after each element of an interrogative series when the series is not enumerated or lettered. Do not put a comma after a question mark that falls within quotation marks.

Quotation marks

- Punctuation that includes a period or comma which follows it in a sentence (but not a colon or

semicolon). The dash, question mark, and exclamation point fall inside quotation marks if they belong with the quoted matter but outside if they punctuate the sentence as a whole. For quotations which extend beyond one paragraph, a quotation mark begins each paragraph and the closing quotation mark is at the end of the last paragraph. Some writers now leave a preceding comma out before a quotation. Some writers leave periods and commas outside of quoted material if that punctuation belongs to the sentence as a whole. That convention is followed in this book. Quotation marks are used:

- For direct quotations. Each part of an interrupted quotation begins and ends with quotation marks, as "I am getting worried," she said, "that he has not called."

- For expressions following introductory terms as 'entitled', 'the word.' 'the term', 'marked', 'designated', 'classified', 'named', 'endorsed', 'cited as', 'referred to as', 'signed', which indicate a borrowing or special use. Quotations may be used around mottos, slang, misnomers, coined words, proverbs and maxims, ironical reference, and unspoken dialogue.

- Around words referred to as words, as "I said "tomato," not "potato.", and around sentences referred to as sentences, as An example of a question is, "Where the heck are they?"
- For translations of foreign terms.
- For single letters within a sentence, e.g., His name begins with a "K."
- Sometimes to enclose document titles and parts, and addresses within a sentence, e.g., Her book, "Roget's New American Thesaurus," is a bestseller.
- Single quotation marks are used to enclose a quotation within a quotation and may be used around words that are special terms or for words referred to as words.

Semi-colon

Punctuation sometimes regarded as a weak period or strong comma and is used in ways similar to periods and commas. A semicolon can mark the end of a clause and indicate that a clause following is closely related to it. A semicolon can also divide a sentence to make meaning clearer. A semicolon is placed outside quotation marks and parentheses. Uses in detail are:

- Separates independent clauses in place of a coordinating conjunction or ellipsis.
- Separates independent clauses when the second begins with a conjunctive adverb as: accordingly, all the same, also, as a result, besides, by the same token, consequently, furthermore, hence, however, indeed, in that case, likewise, moreover, nevertheless, on the other hand, otherwise, still, then, therefore, and thus. These usually explain or summarize preceding matter.
- Clarifies meaning in long sentences and in those with several commas. The indication of a strong pause by the semicolon helps the reader understand the meaning.
- May be used before explanation phrases and clauses as: e.g., for example, for instance, i.e., namely, that is.
- Separates lists or phrases in a series when the phrases themselves have commas.

Slash (also called virgule, diagonal, solidus, oblique, or slant)

- Punctuation used mainly used to show that a word is not written out.
- A slash represents 'or' or 'and/or' in alternatives as yours/mine.
- A slash may represent 'and', as 1990/91, Minneapolis/St. Paul.
- A slash may represent some prepositions—at, for, versus, with, as c/o addressee, w/dressing.

- A slash represents 'per' or 'to' in measures and ratios, as two ft./min., price/earnings ratio.
- A slash is used to separate numbers in dates, fractions, and telephone numbers. A slash used to separate parts of an address or divide lines of poetry when written as continuous text.
- A slash is used in pronunciations (phonemic transcriptions).

U.S. PRESIDENTS

1789-1797, George Washington

1797-1801, John Adams, Fed

1801-1809, Thomas Jefferson, Dem-Rep

1809-1817, James Madison, Dem-Rep

1817-1825, James Monroe, Dem-Rep

1825-1829, John Quincy Adams, Dem-Rep

1829-1837, Andrew Jackson, Dem

1837-1841, Martin Van Buren, Dem

1841, William Henry Harrison, Whig

1841-1845, John Tyler, Whig

1845-1849, James Knox Polk, Dem

1849-1850, Zachary Taylor, Whig

1850-1853, Millard Fillmore, Whig

1853-1857, Franklin Pierce, Dem

1857-1861, James Buchanan, Dem

1861-1865, Abraham Lincoln, Rep

1865-1869, Andrew Johnson, Dem-Nat

1869-1877, Ulysses Simpson Grant, Rep

1877-1881, Rutherford Birchard Hayes, Rep

1881, James Abram Garfield, Rep

1881-1885, Chester Alan Arthur, Rep

1885-1889, Stephen Grover Cleveland, Dem

1889-1893, Benjamin Harrison, Rep

1893-1897, Stephen Grover Cleveland, Dem

1897-1901, William McKinley, Rep

1901-1909, Theodore Roosevelt, Rep

1909-1913, William Howard Taft, Rep

1913-1921, Thomas Woodrow Wilson, Dem

1921-1923, Warren Gamaliel Harding, Rep

1923-1929, Calvin Coolidge, Rep

1929-1933, Herbert Clark Hoover, Rep

1933-1945, Franklin Delano Roosevelt, Dem

1945-1953, Harry S Truman, Dem

1953-1961, Dwight David Eisenhower, Rep

1961-1963, John Fitzgerald Kennedy, Dem

1963-1969, Lyndon Baines Johnson, Dem

1969-1974, Richard Milhous Nixon, Rep

1974-1977, Gerald Rudolph Ford, Rep

1977-1981, James Earl (Jimmy) Carter, Dem

1981-1989, Ronald Wilson Reagan, Rep

1989-1992, George Herbert Walker Bush, Rep

1992- , William Jefferson (Bill) Clinton, Dem

Dem=Democrat; Fed=Federalist; Nat=National Union; Rep=Republican

WEIGHTS AND MEASURES

Temperature conversion

Fahrenheit to Celsius: degrees F minus 32, divided by 1.8 = Celsius

Celsius to Fahrenheit: degrees C multiplied by 1.8, plus 32 = Fahrenheit

Linear Measure

10 angstroms = 1 nanometer
1000 nanometers = 1 micrometer
1000 micrometers = 1 millimeter
10 millimeters = 1 centimeter
10 centimeters = 1 decimeter = 100 millimeters
10 decimeters = 1 meter = 1,000 millimeters

10 meters = 1 dekameter
10 dekameters = 1 hectometer = 100 meters
10 hectometers = 1 kilometer = 1,000 meters

Area Measure

100 square millimeters = 1 square centimeter
10,000 square centimeters = 1 square meter = 1,000,000 square millimeters
100 square meters = 1 are
100 ares = 1 hectare = 10,000 square meters
100 hectares = 1 square kilometer = 1,000,000 square meters

Fluid Volume Measure

10 milliliters = 1 centiliter

10 centiliters = 1 deciliter = 100 milliliters

10 deciliters = 1 liter = 1,000 milliliters

10 liters = 1 dekaliter

10 dekaliters = 1 hectoliter = 100 liters

10 hectoliters = 1 kiloliter = 1,000 liters

1 kiloliter = 1 cubic meter

Cubic Measure

1,000 cubic millimeters = 1 cubic centimeter

1,000 cubic centimeters = 1 cubic decimeter = 1,000,000 cubic millimeters

1,000 cubic decimeters = 1 cubic meter = 1 stere = 1,000,000 cubic centimeters = 1,000,000,000 cubic millimeters

Weight

10 milligrams = 1 centigram

10 centigrams = 1 decigram = 100 milligrams

10 decigrams = 1 gram = 1,000 milligrams

10 grams = 1 dekagram

10 dekagrams = 1 hectogram = 100 grams

10 hectograms = 1 kilogram = 1,000 grams

1,000 kilograms = 1 metric ton

Tables of U.S. Customary Weights and Measures

Linear Measure

12 inches = 1 foot

3 feet = 1 yard

5 1/2 yards = 1 rod, pole, or perch (16 1/2 feet)

4 rods = 1 chain 40 rods = 1 furlong = 220 yards = 660 feet

8 furlongs = 1 statute mile = 1,760 yards = 5,280 feet

3 miles = 1 league = 5,280 yards = 15,840 feet

6076.11549 feet = 1 International Nautical Mile

Liquid Measure

4 gills = 1 pint = 28.875 cubic inches

2 pints = 1 quart = 57.75 cubic inches

4 quarts = 1 gallon = 231 cubic inches = 8 pints = 32 gills

Area Measure

144 square inches = 1 square foot

9 square feet = 1 square yard = 1,296 square inches

30 1/4 square yards = 1 square rod = 272 1/4 square feet

40 square rods = 1 rood

160 square rods = 1 acre = 4,840 square yards = 43,560 square feet

640 acres = 1 square mile

1 mile square = 1 section (of land)

6 miles square = 1 township = 36 sections = 36 square miles

Cubic Measure

1 cubic foot = 1,728 cubic inches

27 cubic feet = 1 cubic yard

Gunter's, or Surveyor's, Chain Measure

7.92 inches = 1 link

100 links = 1 chain = 4 rods = 66 feet

80 chains = 1 survey mile = 320 rods = 5,280 feet

Troy Weight

24 grains = 1 pennyweight

20 pennyweights = 1 ounce troy = 480 grains

12 ounces troy = 1 pound troy = 240 pennyweights = 5,760 grains

Dry Measure

2 pints = 1 quart = 67.2006 cubic inches

8 quarts = 1 peck = 537.605 cubic inches = 16 pints

4 pecks = 1 bushel = 2,150.42 cubic inches = 32 quarts

Avoirdupois Weight

27 11/32 grains = 1 dram

16 drams = 1 ounce = 437 1/2 grains

16 ounces = 1 pound = 256 drams = 7,000 grains

100 pounds = 1 hundredweight

20 hundredweights = 1 ton = 2,000 pounds

Tables of Equivalents

Lengths

1 angstrom = 0.1 nanometer = 0.0001 micrometer = 0.0000001 millimeter = .000000004 inch

1 cable's length = 120 fathoms = 720 feet = 219 meters

1 centimeter = 0.3937 inch

1 chain (Gunter's or surveyor's) = 66 feet = 20.1168 meters

1 chain (engineers) = 100 feet = 30.48 meters

1 decimeter = 3.937 inches

1 degree (geographical) = 364,566.929 feet = 69,047 miles = 111.123 kilometers

1 degree of latitude = 68.708 miles at equator = 69.403 miles at poles

1 degree of longitude = 69,171 miles at equator

1 dekameter = 32.808 feet

1 fathom = 6 feet = 1.8288 meters

100 fathoms = 1 cable length

1 foot = 0.3048 meters

1 furlong = 10 chains (surveyors) = 660 feet = 1/8 statute mile = 201.168 meters

1 hand = 4 inches

1 inch = 2.54 centimeters

1 kilometer = 0.621 mile = 3,281.5 feet

1 league = 3 survey miles = 4.828 kilometers

1 link (Gunter's or surveyor's) = 7.92 inches = 0.201 meter

1 link engineers = 1 foot = 0.305 meter

1 meter = 39.37 inches = 1.094 yards

1 micrometer = 0.001 millimeter = 0.00003937 inch

1 mil = 0.001 inch = 0.0254 millimeter

1 mile = 5,280 feet = 1.609 kilometers

1 international nautical mile = 1.852 kilometers = 1.150779 survey miles = 6,076.11549 feet

1 millimeter = 0.03937 inch

1 nanometer = 0.001 micrometer = 0.00000003937 inch

1 pica = 12 points

1 point = 0.013837 inch = 0.351 millimeter

1 rod, pole, or perch = 16 1/2 feet = 5.029 meters

1 yard = 0.9144 meter

Areas or Surfaces

1 acre = 43,560 square feet = 4,840 square yards = 0.405 hectare

1 are = 119.599 square yards = 0.025 acre

1 bolt length = 100 yards

1 bolt width = 45 or 60 inches

1 hectare = 2.471 acres

1 square (building) = 100 square feet

1 square centimeter = 0.155 square inch

1 square decimeter = 15.500 square inches

1 square foot = 929.030 square centimeters

1 square inch = 6.4516 square centimeters

1 square kilometer = 247.104 acres = 0.386 square mile

1 square meter = 1.196 square yards = 10.764 square feet

1 square mile = 258.999 hectares

1 square millimeter = 0.002 square inch

1 square rod, square pole, or square perch = 25.293 square meters

1 square yard = 0.836 square meter

Capacities or Volumes

1 barrel liquid = 31 to 42 gallons

1 barrel, standard, for fruits, vegetables, and other dry commodities except dry cranberries = 7,056 cubic inches = 105 dry quarts = 3.281 bushels, struck measure

1 barrel, standard, cranberry = 5,826 cubic inches = 86 45/64 dry quarts = 2.709 bushels, struck measure

1 board foot = a foot-square board 1 inch thick

1 bushel (U.S.) (struck measure) = 2,150.42 cubic inches = 35.239 liters

1 bushel, heaped (U.S.) = 2,747.715 cubic inches = 1.278 bushels, struck measure

1 bushel (British Imperial) (struck measure) = 1.032 U.S. bushels struck measure = 2,219.36 cubic inches

1 cord firewood = 128 cubic feet

1 cubic centimeter = 0.061 cubic inch

1 cubic decimeter = 61.024 cubic inches

1 cubic inch = 0.554 fluid ounce = 4.433 fluid drams = 16.387 cubic centimeters

1 cubic foot = 7.481 gallons = 28.317 cubic decimeters

1 cubic meter = 1.308 cubic yards

1 cubic yard = 0.765 cubic meter

1 cup, measuring = 8 fluid ounces = 1/2 liquid pint

1 dram, fluid (British) = 0.961 U.S. fluid dram = 0.217 cubic inch = 3.552 milliliters

1 dekaliter = 2.642 gallons = 1.135 pecks

1 gallon (U.S.) = 231 cubic inches = 3.785 liters = 0.833 British gallon = 128 U.S. fluid ounces

1 gallon (British Imperial) = 277.42 cubic inches = 1.201 U.S. gallons = 4.546 liters = 160 British fluid ounces

1 gill = 7.219 cubic inches = 4 fluid ounces = 0.118 liter

1 hectoliter = 26.418 gallons = 2.838 bushels

1 liter = 1.057 liquid quarts = 0.908 dry quart = 61.025 cubic inchs

1 milliliter = 0.271 fluid dram = 16.231 minims = 0.061 cubic inch

1 ounce liquid (U.S.) = 1.805 cubic inches = 29.573 milliliters = 1.041 British fluid ounces

1 ounce, fluid (British) = 0.961 U.S. fluid ounce = 1.734 cubic inches = 28.412 milliliters

1 peck = 8.810 liters

1 pint, dry = 33.600 cubic inches = 0.551 liter

1 pint, liquid = 28.875 cubic inches = 0.473 liter

1 quart dry (U.S.) = 67.201 cubic inches = 1.01 liters = 0.969 British quart

1 quart liquid (U.S.) = 57.75 cubic inches = 0.946 liter = 0.833 British quart

1 quart (British) = 69.354 cubic inches = 1.032 U.S. dry quarts = 1.201 U.S. liquid quarts

1 tablespoon = 3 teaspoons = 4 fluid drams = 1/2 fluid ounce

1 teaspoon = 1/3 tablespoon = 1 1/3 fluid drams

Weights or Masses

1 assay ton = 29.167 grams

1 bale = 500 pounds in U.S. = 750 pounds in Egypt

1 carat = 200 milligrams = 3.086 grains

1 dram avoirdupois = 27 11/32 or 27.344 grains = 1.772 grams

1 gamma = 1 microgram

1 grain = 64.799 milligrams

1 gram = 15.432 grains = 0.035 ounce, avoirdupois

1 hundredweight, gross or long = 112 pounds = 50.802 kilograms

1 hundredweight, net or short = 100 pounds = 45.359 kilograms

1 kilogram = 2.205 pounds

1 microgram = 0.000001 gram

1 milligram = 0.015 grain

1 ounce, avoirdupois = 437.5 grains = 0.911 troy ounce = 28.350 grams

1 ounce, troy = 480 grains = 1.097 avoirdupois ounces = 31.103 grams

1 pennyweight = 1.555 grams

1 pound, avoirdupois = 7,000 grains = 1.215 troy pounds = 453.59237 grams

1 pound, troy = 5,760 grains = 0.823 avoirdupois pound = 373.242 grams

1 ton, gross or long = 2,240 pounds = 1.12 net tons = 1.016 metric tons

1 ton, metric = 2,204.623 pounds = 0.984 gross ton = 1.102 net tons

1 ton, net or short = 2,000 pounds = 0.893 gross ton = 0.907 metric ton

ZODIAC SIGNS

Spring Signs

1. Aries: the Ram ♈
2. Taurus: the Bull ♉
3. Gemini: the Twins ♊, □, ♊

Summer Signs

4. Cancer: the Crab ♋ ♋
5. Leo: the Lion ♌
6. Virgo: the Virgin ♍

Autumnal Signs

7. Libra: the Balance ♎
8. Scorpio: the Scorpion ♏
9. Sagittarius: the Archer ♐

Winter Signs

10. Capricorn: the Goat ♄, ♑
11. Aquarius: the Water Bearer ♒
12. Pisces: the Fishes ♓